D1126613

Irish Nationalism

The reader should remember what is generally slurred over in narrating this part of Irish history, that when we are told that Ulster was planted by Scottish Presbyterians, it does not mean that the land was given to them. On the contrary, the vital fact was, and is, that the land was given to the English noblemen and to certain London companies of merchants who had lent money to the Crown, and that the Scottish planters were only introduced as tenants of these landlords. The condition of their tenancy virtually was that they should keep Ireland for the English Crown, and till the land of Ireland for the benefit of the English landlord.

That is in essence the demand of the Unionist Party leaders upon their followers today. In the past, as the landlords were generally English and Episcopalian, they all, during the eighteenth century, continually inserted clauses in all their leases, forbidding the erection of Presbyterian meeting houses. As the uprise of democracy has contributed to make this impossible today in Ireland, the landlord and capitalist class now seek an alliance with these Protestants they persecuted for so long in order to prevent a union of the democracy of all religious faiths against their lords and masters.

James Connolly, *Forward,*
12 July, 1913

IRISH NATIONALISM

A History of its Roots and Ideology

SEAN CRONIN

CONTINUUM · NEW YORK

1981
The Continuum Publishing Company
575 Lexington Avenue
New York, N.Y. 10022

Printed in the United States of America

Library of Congress Cataloging in Publication Data

Cronin, Sean.
Irish nationalism.

Bibliography: p. 365
Includes index.
1. Nationalism—Ireland. 2. Ireland—Politics and government. I. Title.
DA938.C76 320.5'4'09415 81-9773
ISBN 0-8264-0062-0 AACR2

CONTENTS

LIST OF APPENDICES

ACKNOWLEDGEMENTS

I wish to thank all who gave generously of their time, knowledge and views in discussing the subject of this study. Their names are listed in the sources, but I must mention particularly Eamon Timoney, Manus Canning and Seán O'Hegarty.

I have benefited from the teaching of Professor Hans J. Morgenthau on the relationship of power and politics. I have benefited from his advice on the organization of certain sections of the material. However, errors in interpretation are my own.

I should like to thank the staff of the libraries of the New School for Social Research, New York University, the City University, the British Library, London, and Kew Gardens, Manchester Library, and the National Library of Ireland, where I have worked during the course of this study.

This work is based on a thesis submitted to the Graduate Faculty of the New School for Social Research, New York, in partial fulfillment of the requirements for the degree of Doctor of Philosophy in political science.

Sean Cronin
New York, N.Y.

I
Introductory Survey

This study deals with the roots, history, growth and development of Irish nationalist ideology, particularly its revolutionary form, Irish republicanism. In Ireland a republican has come to mean one who maintains that England will not abdicate her role in Irish affairs unless forced to do so by superior power. From this it is argued that only violence will change the minds of England's rulers on the Irish question. At the very least, there must be the threat of violence, as with Daniel O'Connell's agitation for Catholic emancipation in the 1820s and Charles Stewart Parnell's agitation for tenant rights and Home Rule in the 1880s. Historically, peasant secret societies, really agrarian trade unions, employed violence to defend labourers and poor tenants from landlords, tithe proctors, bailiffs, police and military. The lesson of Irish history, this view holds, is that England never yields to right, reason or justice, only to force. Consequently, armed rebellion is an essential element in any attempt to win Irish independence.

The French Revolution gave Ireland its first republican movement, the Society of United Irishmen, which consisted of clubs like the Sons of Liberty in America and the Jacobins in France. These clubs corresponded among themselves and with similar movements abroad. The founders were mainly Protestants, Presbyterian in Belfast, Anglican with some Catholics in Dublin: for the most part descendants of English and Scottish colonists who had settled in Ulster in the early seventeenth century and in other parts of Ireland at various times. The native Gaelic Irish were tenant-at-will peasants who spoke their own language, practised Catholicism, which was proscribed by the state, and followed their priests in all things. The source of their oppression, as they saw it, was the landlord caste (the Ascendancy), which ruled and indeed owned the kingdom of Ireland. A few Catholic families had managed to hold on to their properties and were ultra loyal. Some Catholics had become rich merchants and vied with the Catholic aristocracy for leadership of the movement to abolish the penal laws.

—Republicanism of the United Irishmen kind was a product of the American and French revolutions and the era of the Enlightenment. The Irish peasantry at first were hostile to its ideas. They took their politics from their Church – insofar as they had any politics beyond their traditional hatred of English and Protestant rule. Irish republicanism is a product of the French Revolution because the only republicans in Ireland before that era were Cromwell's soldiers. However, the roots of Irish nationalism go deep into Irish history, and are a consequence of that history. Irish Republican ideology, too, in the narrow sense, stems from the French Revolution, but one must go much further back to uncover the ideological roots of Irish nationalism.

The United Irishmen, who hoped to use native hatred of England for republican ends, aroused a national feeling that was centuries old, forged by the tradition of resistance to the English conquest. The 'Declaration of the Rights of Man and the Citizen' stirred revolutionary fervour in Presbyterian Belfast, but the Irish Catholic masses, who had 'no more political rights than the serfs of Russia or of Poland' and 'were marked out by the law as a distinct nation, to be maintained in separation from the Protestants, and in permanent subjection to them,'[1] had no need of that stimulus. When England went to war with revolutionary France many Irish Catholics were willing, acting on their tradition, to seek the aid of their enemy's enemy – albeit reluctantly, because of the hostile attitude of their priests to the anti-clericalism of France. This ambivalence was evident up to the end of 1796, when the Directory sent an expedition under the brilliant General Lazare Hoche to Bantry Bay to help the United Irishmen launch an insurrection. Hoche's political adviser was the founder of the United Irishmen, Theobald Wolfe Tone.

The Meaning of Nationalism

Nationalism is a nineteenth-century term.[2] Nationalists seek to establish 'the nation' as a nation-state. Their criteria for nationhood may include common territory, language, descent, history, tradition, religion. The terms 'nation' and 'state' are of course distinct, except in American usage. The nation does not necessarily require a state to express its nationalism and a state may consist of several nations or part of a nation. The nation is a 'spiritual', the state a 'material' force. Hans Morgenthau's definition is worth quoting:

> Membership in a nation may be defined in terms of language, culture, common origin, race, or in the decision of the individual to belong to the nation. But no matter how it is defined, the membership always entails as its essence

> partaking in certain qualities, called the national character, which the members of a particular nation have in common and by which they are differentiated from the members of other nations. The preservation of the national character and, more particularly, the development of its creative faculties is the supreme task of the nation. In order to fulfil this task, the nation needs power that will protect it against other nations and will stimulate its own development. In other words, the nation needs a state. 'One nation – one state' is thus the political postulate of nationalism; the nation state is its ideal.[3]

Nation and state need each other: the nation needs the power of the state, the state needs the community of the nation. As Morgenthau notes,

> 'national sentiment and patriotism, are transformed by nationalism into a political mysticism in which the national community and the state become superhuman entities, apart from and superior to their individual members, entitled to absolute loyalty and, like the idols of old, deserving of the sacrifice of men and goods.'[4]

Strands of Irish Nationalism

One can identify five strands in Irish nationalism: *traditionalist* is Catholic and often Gaelic; *constitutional nationalism* is influenced, but not controlled by the Catholic Church, uses Henry Grattan's arguments on Ireland's right to nationhood as an independent kingdom, and opposes violence; *physical-force republicanism* refers to Tone and the United Irishmen for its justification, but is often socially conservative; *radical republicanism* argues that there can be no political change without social revolution and stresses the values of the secular state; *cultural nationalism* emphasizes the nation and its language rather than the state.

Movements display characteristics of the different strands. O'Connellism was traditionalist and constitutional. Young Ireland initially was a cultural and constitutional movement, but in the spring and summer of 1848 it adopted a policy of revolution and some of its leaders, notably John Mitchel, James Fintan Lalor, and Thomas Devin Reilly, were radical republicans. Fenianism was republic and revolutionary; its republicanism was American rather than French, and some of its leaders were socially conservative. Yet Fenianism, too, threw up radicals who later founded the Land League and linked up with the constitutional Home Rule party. Sinn Fein (founded in 1905) was non-republican, but attracted many republicans. The Gaelic League was cultural and non-political, but P.H. Pearse believed it prepared the ground for the 1916 Rising. The Irish Volunteers (founded 1913) demanded no more than Home Rule, but its leaders were physical-force nationalists. James Connolly's

Irish Socialist Republican Party (founded 1896) was Marxist Fenian.

The IRA of the late 1920s and early 1930s was radical, but by 1938 it was purely physical-force traditionalist. Republican Congress (founded 1934) was radical republican and played down physical force. Sinn Fein, in the post-Treaty years, was socially conservative, more so than Fianna Fail, which de Valera founded in 1926, before he entered the Free State Dail. Clann na Poblachta (founded 1946) was radical republican. The IRA in the 1950s was physical-force traditionalist. The IRA in the 1960s became radical socialist. The traditionalists, in 1969, broke away to form the Provisional IRA. A decade later it was under radical leadership. The strongest nationalist strand is the traditionalist, the weakest is radicalism.

Physical-force nationalism is traditionalist, sometimes radical, always romantic – after the rebel is in prison or dead. Gaelic poets praised the 'swordsmen' who harried the Ulster colonists, the 'Tories' who harassed the Cromwellians, the rapparees who waged guerrilla war on the Williamites. Radical republicanism is a legacy of the United Irishmen. It is represented in every phase of the struggle. Yet it must be concluded that Irish nationalism is usually socially conservative and Catholic, even the physical-force strand.

The Anglo-Norman Invasion

The war of Gael and Gall (Irish and Foreigner), as the native chroniclers called it, continued from the twelfth to the end of the seventeenth century, when Gaelic resistance finally was broken. It was a conflict of civilizations and of legal systems. Although religion played a major role from the start, it did not become a matter of national 'ideology' until the Reformation.

Adrian IV's Bull, *Laudabiliter,* gave Henry II of England 'the right' to invade Ireland in order 'to proclaim the truths of the Christian religion to a rude and ignorant people, and to root out the growths of vice from the field of the Lord'. For Henry's barons the conquest of Ireland meant large estates and revenues. For the Papacy it meant 'the annual tribute of one penny from every house' in Ireland.[5] Ireland, Christian for seven centuries, had converted Scotland, much of England and Western Europe, and was not in need of Henry's missionary efforts.[6]

The Anglo-Norman invaders met an Irish-speaking people with an ancient civilization. Ireland was a cultural but not a political unit, with about one hundred and fifty clan territories, or petty states, called *tuatha.* The Anglo-Norman conquest covered about two-thirds of Ireland after a century of warfare. The Normans brought central government to England and, had they succeeded in conquering all Ireland, might have assimilated the native population, as they did in England. They introduced the feudal system, as Marc Bloch describes it, where the military fief became a hereditary estate 'transmitted only from eldest son to eldest son'.[7] Manors were established with free and unfree tenants. The King of England assumed the title 'Lord of Ireland' not King of Ireland, in deference to the Pope's superior status, and a governor and council in Dublin acted for the Crown. In 1297 the English colony established a parliament which lasted until the Act of Union with Great Britain in 1801.

In the first centuries of the conquest two systems of law obtained in Ireland, feudal and Gaelic, the latter called the Brehon code,[8] from *breitheamh*, meaning judge. Ireland had never been part of the Roman Empire; it was uninfluenced by Roman law. Isolated on the edge of Christendom, it was free of the orthodoxy of Rome. The Celtic Church followed its own peculiar customs. It was a monastic rather than an episcopal Church; the abbot was the dominant clerical figure. Church and state were separated. Marriage was a secular matter and divorce was permitted. The Brehon code did not distinguish between legitimate and illegitimate children, unlike feudalism. The Gaelic chief was chosen by his peers of the *derbfine,* the ruling family, from 'the eldest and worthiest' of the candidates; his successor, the *tanist* (hence 'tanistry'), was elected during the chief's lifetime.

Some Norman families adopted tanistry and by the fifteenth century Ireland was Gaelic again, except for the colony in Dublin, the Pale, which was then thirty miles long by twenty miles broad. The Pale paid tribute to local Gaelic chiefs. The colonists petitioned the King to ask the Pope to declare a crusade against their Irish enemies and as late as 1572, four hundred years after Henry II's invasion, the King's Council in Dublin issued a general proclamation condemning the Brehon code. The language of Ireland was Irish except for the colony in Dublin, which spoke English. When Irish chiefs, that is to say the Gaelic aristocracy, first attended parliament in the reign of Henry VIII, in 1541, the proceedings had to be translated into Irish for their benefit. Land was the economic basis of Gaelic society. Wealth was judged by numbers of cattle owned. The chief tillage crops were oats and wheat. That the invaders were assimilated by the Gaels is evident from the colonial laws condemning assimilation, in particular the Statutes of Kilkenny of 1366.[9]

The Gaelic resurgence began early in the fourteenth century when Edward Bruce of Scotland — brother of King Robert — landed with an army, at the invitation of the Irish chiefs, to drive out the English.

The Gaelic princes told the Pope their reasons: 'More than 50,000 human beings of each nation' had died in the wars following Adrian IV's grant of Ireland to Henry II. English law sought 'the extermination of our race'. They would fight to defend 'the rights of our law and liberty against cruel tyrants and usurpers', and 'recover our native liberty, which for a time through them [the English] we lost. . .'. The English 'have striven with all their might and with every treacherous artifice in their power, to wipe our nation out entirely and utterly to extirpate it'.[10] The document was signed by Donal O'Neill, 'King of Ulster and by hereditary right true heir to the whole of Ireland' – an ancient claim of his family.

A Matter of Power Politics

It took five hundred years to complete the conquest of Gaelic Ireland, and its people were never completely assimilated. England faced a military problem on her western flank, the gateway to the Atlantic, long after the conquest was completed. This is the origin of the 'Irish question'. England controlled the seas from the 1650s at least, when Cromwell smashed the Dutch fleet; but a foreign landing in Ireland with Irish support in times of crisis posed a threat to this domination. When the Irish chiefs invited Edward Bruce to help them, they began a process that continued to the Second World War.

A papal force landed in Smerwick, County Kerry, in 1580. Philip II of Spain sent his Armada along the Irish coast. His son, in 1601, landed troops at Kinsale to aid Hugh O'Neill's rebellion. The Pope sent a legate in the 1640s to advise the Confederation of Kilkenny, then in arms against England; in the English Civil War the Irish opposed both Royalists and Puritans till conquered by Cromwell. Louis XIV dispatched 7000 troops to Ireland to help James II recover his throne in 1689-91. A century later the French Directory sent Hoche to Bantry Bay; several minor expeditions left France to help the United Irishmen defeat England. Robert Emmet had links with Napoleonic France when he planned his rebellion in 1803. Young Ireland sent delegates to France after the February Revolution in 1848, but the English warned Lamartine against linking his government with Irish rebels. John Mitchel, the Young Ireland leader, asked the Russians to help an Irish rebellion during the Crimean War; John Devoy, the exiled Fenian leader, made a similar approach to the Czar's minister at Washington in 1876. The Fenians tried to entangle America in Ireland's struggle in the late 1860s. They staged an invasion of Canada, with 750 Civil War veterans, to detach it from the British Empire. Sir Roger Casement, writing in March 1913, believed the Irish question could become 'a European, a world question' if Germany and England went to war and Irish rebels got help from their enemy's enemy. He wrote in the separatist *Irish Review*,[11]

> With the humbling of Great Britain and the destruction of her sea ownership, European civilization assumes a new stature, and Ireland, oldest and yet youngest of the European peoples, shall enter into free partnership with the civilization, culture, and prosperity that that act of liberation shall bring to mankind.

When war broke out in 1914, Devoy asked the German ambassador to the United States, Count von Bernstorff, for arms and men to be landed in Ireland. Casement went to Berlin to press the Irish case. The Germans sent an arms ship to Ireland at Easter 1916 and Casement returned home by U-boat. But the arms went to the bottom of the Atlantic and Casement was captured and hanged. Stalin offered to train IRA officers in the late 1920s, but changed his mind when the British got wind of it. Ribbentrop sent the IRA leader, Sean Russell, to Ireland by submarine in August 1940, to let him strike at England in his own way, but he died at sea. A US National Security Council staff review, in September 1950, noted Ireland's strategic location and suggested that air bases be built on the island for naval and anti-submarine operations. In this way the Irish could contribute to the defence of the West. But the Irish government saw partition as a greater evil than Communism and refused to join NATO.[12]

Through the centuries rebellions have been plotted in Ireland to take advantage of England's international difficulties. There were three major rebellions in the sixteenth century, three in the seventeenth, one in the eighteenth, three in the nineteenth, and four revolts — so far — in the twentieth century. These rebellions failed because of the power of England, not through Irish lack of determination. The Irish are old hands at terrorism: they were among the first to use dynamite as 'a weapon of the weak against the strong'. In the 1880s the Irish-American revolutionary organization Clan-na-Gael sent volunteers to blow up the House of Commons and London Bridge. In 1939–40, and again in the 1970s, Irish volunteers exploded bombs in English cities. They have assassinated English aristocrats and officials, the most notorious cases being the Cavendish-Burke killings of May 1882, the shooting of Field Marshal Sir Henry Wilson in June 1922, the death by explosives of Airey Neave in April 1979 and the murder of Lord Louis Mountbatten in August 1979.[13]

Winston Churchill wrote that the relations of England and Ireland 'were established during centuries when the independence of a hostile Ireland menaced the life of England'.[14] Sandwiched between her traditional enemy, France, and a hostile Ireland, England had to control one or the other. For a time she tried to control both and failed. The conquest of Ireland was always being undone and had to be undertaken several times. The Irish did not recognize that conquest gave any right other than the right of permanent resistance.

Confiscation and Colonization

Although the Irish sought foreign allies, none saved Ireland. England controlled the seas and Irish rebels found it difficult to persuade would-be allies to challenge the Royal Navy. When John Mitchel went to Washington in January 1854, to seek Russian help for his projected Irish rebellion, the Czar's minister, pointing to a map, remarked that the British navy stood between Russia and Ireland, and ended the interview. Defeated rebellions only strengthened the resolve of the Irish; in each generation the effort was repeated. The Bruce expedition lingered in folk memory for centuries, according to the chroniclers; its devastation was greater than the Black Death. The English massacred the Basques and Italians who landed at Smerwick in 1580 after they surrendered. The province of Munster was colonized and the colonists included Sir Walter Raleigh, his half-brother Humphrey Gilbert and the poet, Edmund Spenser. Raleigh formed a consortium of planters, bought out his partners and sold at a profit.[15] Spenser wrote *The Faerie Queen* in his new castle and a treatise on how England should deal with rebellion in Ireland: by seizing the food of the natives and letting them starve to death. When the inevitable rebellion broke out the Munster colony was swept away and Spenser with it: he fled to London where he died.

Spenser's main complaint had been that the English were not sufficiently bloody-minded; they should root out the Irish and establish strong military garrisons to protect the colonists, he maintained.[16] Intentionally or otherwise, Spenser's methods were adopted in the Ulster plantation following the defeat of Hugh O'Neill and his ally Hugh O'Donnell at Kinsale in 1601. A decade later English and Scots settled in the confiscated counties of Armagh, Cavan, Coleraine (now Londonderry), Donegal, Fermanagh and Tyrone. It was a capitalist enterprise in the age of mercantilism. The City of London had advanced money to Elizabeth for her Irish wars and was repaid in Irish land. The London companies financed the colony, and built two fortified towns (Londonderry and Coleraine) as sanctuaries for the colonists. Attempts to wipe out the colony failed. Colonial Ulster prospered.

The English settlers were Anglicans, the Scots Presbyterians: they were thrifty, industrious, skilled farmers. To the old national antagonism, religious hatred was added. There is no word for Presbyterian in the Irish language: the word used was *Albanach*, meaning 'Scotch'. An Anglican (Episcopal) was *Sassanach*, meaning 'English'. Gaelic and Catholic became synonymous terms in Ireland.[17]

The success of the Ulster colony sired plans to establish similar colonies in other parts of Ireland. There were two difficulties. First, the land-owning aristocracy in the other three provinces, who were English, preferred high rents from Gaelic tenants to yeoman farmers of English and Scots stock. Secondly, few settlers were attracted to Ireland. Prospective colonists preferred the wilderness of America to the wilds of Connacht or even the rich pastures of Tipperary.

Cromwell's conquest is folklore: 'The curse of Cromwell' is a malediction in the Irish-speaking West. The war of the 1640s and the plague that followed swept away half the population, according to Sir William Petty, Surgeon-General to the Cromwellian army in Ireland and adventurer extraordinary in the confiscations and settlement that followed. Petty, the first political economist, surveyed the lands of Ireland – and amassed thousands of acres for himself. One of Petty's solutions to the Irish problem was a proposal to deport most of Ireland's population to England to work as labourers, while turning the island into a cattle ranch. He would leave one-quarter of the Irish in Ireland as herdsmen and dairy maids. Although Petty's plan was not adopted, English policy in Ireland seemed to follow it in broad outline.[18] In the 1650s many Irish were shipped as slaves to the sugar plantations of the West Indies. Eric Williams, the West Indian economic historian, notes that they were replaced by black labour rather quickly for two reasons: first, the Africans worked better in the hot climate, and secondly many Irish escaped.[19] At home Catholics were expelled from the towns and forced to live outside the walls; to this day some Irish towns have sections called 'Irishtown' as their colonial legacy.

By the time of the Whig Revolution in 1688, eighty per cent of Irish land was owned by English and Scottish Protestants.[20] The Cromwellian settlement had established a landlord class that survived the Restoration and was to rule Ireland for England into the nineteenth century.

Seventeenth-Century National Wars

The three great wars, or conquests, of the seventeenth century were national as well as religious conflicts in Ireland. Hugh O'Neill announced twenty-two 'war aims' in 1599; the first half-dozen were concerned with freedom of religion, the rest with what might be loosely called 'the rights of Irishmen' – no doubt meaning the rights of Gaelic nobles.[21]

In 1644 the Catholic Confederation's demands to Charles I included the following, which had to do with Ireland as an independent kingdom – its ancient and recognized status:

> That an act shall be passed in the next parliament, declaratory that the parliament of Ireland is a free parliament of itself, independent of, and not subordinate to, the parliament of England, and that the subjects of Ireland are immediately subject to your majesty as in right of your crown, and that the members of the said parliament of Ireland, and all other subjects of Ireland are independent, and in no way to be ordered or concluded by the parliament of England, and are only to be ordered and governed within that kingdom by your majesty and such governors as are or shall be there appointed, and by the parliament of that kingdom according to the laws of the land.[22]

The third great conflict, 'the Glorious Revolution', was for Ireland a national and a religious war, and the parliament summoned by James II to meet in Dublin on 7 May, 1689, after his arrival, declared its independence of the English parliament. Its declaration is worth quoting in part:

> Whereas his majesty's realm of Ireland is, and hath been always a distinct kingdom from that of his majesty's realm of England, always governed by his majesty and his predecessors, according to the ancient customs, laws and statutes thereof, and as the people of this kingdom did never send members to any parliament ever held in England, but had their laws continually made and established by their own parliaments, so no acts passed in any parliament held in England were ever binding here, excepting such of them as by acts of parliament passed in this kingdom were made into laws here, yet of late times (especially in the times of distractions) some have pretended, that acts of parliament passed in England, mentioning Ireland were binding in Ireland; and as these late opinions are against justice and natural equity, and so they tend to the great oppression of the people here, and to the overthrow of the fundamental constitutions of this realm, and to the end, that by these modern and late opinions no person may be further deluded, be it therefore enacted. . . that no act of parliament passed, or to be passed in the parliament of England, though Ireland should be therein mentioned, can be, or shall be any way binding in Ireland; excepting such acts passed, or to be passed in England, as are or shall be made into law by the parliament of Ireland.[23]

Cultural Group or Nationality?

The Irish up to the Treaty of Limerick (1691) saw themselves as separate from, and independent of, England. Whether they saw their differences as cultural or religious, or both, need not delay us. In Ireland the Old Irish (the Gaels) and Old English (Anglo-Normans) retained their separate identities but both groups collaborated, on the basis of religion, in the 1640s and in 1689–91. Both lost and their leaders were exiled. These distinctions, however, were fading and the term 'Irish' took their place. The Treaty of Limerick was signed by the defeated *Irish* army officers on 'behalf of the *Irish* inhabitants in the city and county of Limerick, the counties of Clare, Kerry, Cork, Sligo, and Mayo'.[24] The Treaty spoke of 'the generals of the *Irish* army'; of garrisons 'now in the possession of the *Irish*'; of 'the *Irish* and their army'; it mentioned 'the kingdom of Ireland', as distinct from 'the kingdom of England', although sharing the same monarch, the victorious William III. It would seem that what is being spoken of here is a nationality, in our modern meaning. The 'Irish' consisted of Gaelic and Anglo-Norman residents of Ireland. How the peasantry saw themselves it is difficult to say, but in a traditionalist society, where clansman and chief shared a common heritage, one may assume that they shared cultural and national values too. In this society, little changed during the hundred years of the penal laws. The poets kept the sense of nationality alive, as the priests kept religion alive, and all waited 'for the ships of the brave, who come to join us with the sword', in the words of the Jacobite poet Pierce FitzGerald. Nationality, the literature reveals, was as important as religion, but the two buttressed each other. Both survived because they worked together.

England's First Colony

Friedrich Engels did some research for a proposed *History of Ireland,* going so far as to acquire a working knowledge of the Irish language to aid his studies. Remarking that the English knew how to reconcile the most diverse peoples under their rule, Engels observed:

> Only with the Irish the English could not cope. The reason for this is the enormous resilience of the Irish race. After the most savage suppression, after every attempt to exterminate them, the Irish, following a short respite, stood stronger than ever before: it seemed they drew their main strength from the very foreign garrison forced on them in order to oppress them. Within two generations, often within one, the foreigners became more Irish than the Irish, *Hiberniores ipsis Hibernis.* The more the Irish accepted the English language and forgot their own, the more Irish they became.[25]

Actually, what made the colonists more Irish than the native Gaels was the exploitation of Ireland in the interest of England.

Engels was not the first to comment on the assimilative powers of Ireland's traditionalist society, but his observation is important: as an historical materialist he did not arrive at his conclusion to encourage sentiment. Interested primarily in the economic structure of society, he may have been the first to note that Ireland was ruled as a colony after, as well as before, the Act of Union. He considered Ireland 'the first English colony'.[26] Viewed thus, Irish history takes on a different aspect. Since Engels, it has been examined in this light by James Connolly, *Labour in Irish History* (1910), Eric Strauss, *Irish Nationalism and British Democracy* (1951), Michael Hechter, *Internal Colonialism, the Celtic Fringe in British National Development, 1536–1966* (1975). Each conquest meant a new set of English land-owners who had raised money to finance the invasion, and were repaid in Irish lands. Some never bothered to live in Ireland but rented their estates, drew their incomes, and gave Ireland nothing in return.

In 1672 Petty estimated the annual rent paid absentee English owners of Irish estates amounted to £0.9 million out of a total national income of £4 million. By 1687, while the national income remained much as before, the rent to absentees had climbed to £1.2 million. In 1724 Jonathan Swift put Irish rents at £2 million, one-third of which went to England.[27] This capital flow from Ireland was an important factor in the industrial growth of England, while the Irish economy was starved of capital.

The various Cattle Acts, from the 1650s to the 1680s, kept Ireland's most important export, livestock, out of the English market. Sheep, pigs, beef, pork, mutton and dairy products, such as butter and cheese, were also denied entry. The prohibition was not lifted until 1759. Landlords, turning from tillage to grass, evicted their tenants and enclosed the commons on which the people grazed their milch cows, to make way for cattle. One result was the growth of an agrarian secret society, the Whiteboys, to protect tenants.

The Navigation Acts destroyed Ireland's thriving trade with the North American colonies and the West Indies. An Act of 1696 wiped out Irish shipping because, as Lecky notes, 'no goods of any kind could be imported directly from the colonies to Ireland'.[28] Three years later the English parliament prohibited the export of woollens from Ireland in order to protect England's premier industry. On the other hand, the linen industry was fostered in Ulster. From 1696 Irish linen and yarn were permitted into England duty free. The reason was that Ireland had a cheap labour force skilled in textiles. French Huguenots brought their technology to Ireland and between 1711, when a Linen Board was established, and 1734 Irish exports of linen quadrupled. The linen industry presented no threat to England and a manufacturing class developed among the Presbyterians of Ulster.

England's parliamentary enactments against Irish industry and trade were challenged by William Molyneux, philosopher and friend of John Locke. In *The Case of Ireland's Being Bound by Acts of Parliament in England Stated* (1698), Molyneux asserted that only laws made by the Irish parliament were binding in Ireland. The English Commons condemned his book and it was burned by the public hangman. Swift took up the argument twenty-two years later, going to the heart of the matter in his *Short View of Ireland* by saying that 'the superiority of mere power' prevented Ireland from exporting its own commodities and manufactures to wherever they could be sold. These English acts of parliament give force to Marx's charge that 'every time Ireland was about to develop industrially, she was crushed and reconverted into a purely agricultural land'; and to Engels's claim that 'all other countries were to become for England what Ireland already was – markets for her manufactured goods, supplying her in return with raw materials and food.'[29] One should add labour: Ireland supplied labour power to both England and America.

Anglo-Irish Nationalism

Those English laws which Molyneux criticized directly attacked the commercial interests of the Protestant settlers, who had created the woollen industry in the first place. It was their parliament that was declared subordinate to England. The constitutional position, as Molyneux explained, was that Ireland, an independent kingdom, shared with England a common sovereign. This was the point made by James II's Catholic parliament in 1689. A few years later, this independent kingdom of Ireland was a Protestant kingdom. English power had made it so. In time, as is true of most colonial societies, conflict developed with the mother country because the colonists resented interference in their affairs. It became clear, as Lecky remarks, that 'every form of Irish industry as soon as it became sufficiently prosperous to compete in any degree with her own manufactures' would be destroyed by England's commercial interests.[30]

Molyneux's constitutional arguments and Swift's Irish tracts, which he started to write in 1720, the year the English parliament declared that its laws bound the kingdom and people of Ireland,[31] developed a colonial nationalism, similar to what emerged in North America a half-century later, fuelled by the same commercial resentments. The result was a 'Patriot party' in the Irish House of Commons. The patriots represented the commercial middle class. They demanded the lifting of restrictions on Irish trade, one of the great themes of Dean Swift's tracts.

Swift called his first Irish pamphlet *A Proposal for the Universal Use of Irish Manufacture in Clothes and Furniture of Houses etc., utterly rejecting and renouncing everything wearable that comes from England.* The words that stand out on the title-page are *Proposal, Universal Use, Manufacture, Utterly* and *England.* Swift, an excellent journalist, knew the points that had to be made in order to arouse colonial indignation. He urged a campaign against English-manufactured goods and pressed the Irish parliament to retaliate against the English parliament. Swift asked 'whether a law to bind men without their own consent, be obligatory *in foro conscientiae*?' He remarked that ministers in England 'were apt, from their high elevation, to look down upon this kingdom, as if it had been one of their colonies of outcasts in America'. He attacked the landlords, Ireland's ruling class,

> who, by unmeasurable screwing and racking their tenants all over the kingdom, have already reduced the miserable people to a worse condition than the peasants in France, or the vassals in Germany and Poland; so that the whole species of what we call substantial farmers, will, in a very few years, be utterly at an end. . . . I have heard great divines affirm, that nothing is so likely to call down a universal judgment from heaven upon a nation, as universal oppression, and whether this be not already verified in part, their worships the landlords are now at full leisure to consider. Whoever travels this country, and observes the face of nature, or the faces, and habits, and dwellings of the natives, will hardly think himself in a land where either law, religion, or common humanity is professed.

Swift's indictment went far beyond the grievances of the colonists, who were not concerned with the evils of the land system. Here, the Dean of St Patrick's Cathedral spoke for the native Irish; he of course asserted he was an Englishman born in Ireland. Nevertheless, Swift's Irish tracts, particularly the 'Drapier's Letters', give him a claim to the title 'father of Irish nationalism'. His *proposal* drew little response, as he noted in the first 'Drapier's Letter' (1724), 'concerning the brass half-pence coined by one William Wood'. He addressed his letter, significantly, to 'the Shop-Keepers, Tradesmen, Farmers and Common-People of Ireland'. One wonders if this is the first time anyone had bothered to invoke the 'common people of Ireland'? At any rate Swift advised them all 'to wear the manufactures of this our own dear country'. There may be irony in this description of Ireland, but for the reader it was a call to patriotism, one not confined to the Protestant settlers. The problem of the settlers was that if they joined 'the common people', or, as the times had it, 'the common enemy' – the native Irish – against the English government they might be overwhelmed themselves later on. Swift did not address himself to this dilemma, but he did declare that by the laws of God, of nature, and of nations, the people of Ireland had the same right to freedom as the people of England.

> Were not the people of Ireland born as free as those of England? How have they forfeited their freedom? Is not their parliament as fair a representation of the people as that of England? Are they not subjects of the same King? Does not the same sun shine upon them? And have they not the same God for their protector? Am I a freeman in England, and do I become a slave in six hours by crossing the Channel?[32]

The fourth letter from the honest drapier, addressed to 'the whole people of Ireland', questioned England's claim to make laws for Ireland. 'For in reason, all government without the consent of the governed is the very definition of slavery. But in fact, eleven men well armed will certainly subdue one single man in his shirt'. An excellent definition of power.

> The remedy is wholly in your own hands, and therefore I have digressed a little in order to refresh and continue that spirit so seasonably raised among you, and to let you see that by the laws of God, of nature, of nations, and of your own country, you are and ought to be as free a people as your brethren in England.[33]

An Independent Irish Parliament

Swift's contribution to Irish national thinking is twofold: he saw English control of Ireland as 'the radical vice of our government', in the words of Wolfe Tone, 'and consequently that Ireland would never be either free, prosperous, or happy, until she was independent. . .',[34] and he examined the condition of the people, whose 'spirits are broken and made for slavery'. Swift's 'savage indignation' created that masterpiece of irony, *A Modest Proposal for Preventing the Children of Poor People from being a Burthen to their Parents and for Making them Beneficial to the Public* (1729), wherein he argued that 100,000 babies should be sold annually for eating, because everyone would feel happier as a result.

> I desire those politicians, who dislike my overture, and may perhaps be so bold to attempt an answer, that they will first ask the parents of these mortals, whether they would not, at this day, think it a great happiness to have been sold for food at a year old, in the manner I prescribe; and thereby have avoided such a perpetual scene of misfortunes, as they have since gone through; by the *oppression of the landlords;* the impossibility of paying rent, without money or trade; the want of common sustenance, with neither house nor clothes, to cover them from the inclemencies of the weather; and the most inevitable prospect of entailing the like, or greater miseries upon their breed forever.[35]

Swift hated the landlords because they were cruel, rapacious and beholden to English power, despite their control of the Irish parliament. (Tone was to level the same charges against them.) If parliament spoke for 'the whole people of Ireland', that is to say – although Swift did not say it – for Catholics as well as Protestants, it could assert its independence of England. Swift merely touched on the matter in passing: an appeal to Papists, in the 1720s, would be rank treason.

Parliament represented the Protestant oligarchy. The English government named the executive. Of the 300 members of the Irish Commons, only 64 were elected – on a severely restricted franchise. Of the rest, 124 were nominated by peers and 91 by commoners. Others were government placemen. Certain families passed on parliamentary seats, like property, from father to son. Powerful politicians, called 'undertakers', whipped members into line for Dublin Castle – the English executive in Ireland – and were rewarded with the patronage of the country.

From the middle of the eighteenth century the arguments of Molyneux and Swift were used by the so-called 'Patriot party' opposition to advance the interests of the commercial middle class, deeply concerned by restrictions on trade, manufactures and lack of legislative independence. The connection between England and Ireland 'soon became a subject of general inquiry and universal discussion among every rank and class of society', Sir Jonah Barrington assured us.[36] When the American colonists rebelled the patriots formed the Volunteers, ostensibly to defend the country from a French invasion while the British army was in America fighting the colonists. Backed by the Volunteers, the patriots under Henry Grattan won freedom of trade (1779) and legislative independence (1782). 'You are now beginning to have a country,' Edmund Burke told the Speaker of the Irish Commons.

The 'Revolution of 1782' had notable weaknesses: the English

Privy Council could veto Irish legislation and the executive continued to be named in London by the government of the day. But a reformed parliament would perhaps change that. Reform of parliament ran up against the Catholic question: the penal laws, property, civil rights. The Irish parliament could 'never be free till the Irish Catholic had ceased to be a slave', Grattan said. This raised the old spectre of 'the common enemy'. This ogre was sufficient to frighten even the patriots – the commercial middle class and its allies among the land-owners. Grattan, a child of his age, believed in the rule of property and the English connection as symbolized by the Crown. Under such conditions Ireland could not be independent.

The gains of 1782 satisfied the landlords, who needed English power to keep the Catholics in subjection. They opposed concessions to the Catholics, believing that when the majority ceased to be slaves the oligarchy would lose its lands, as John Fitzgibbon, Earl of Clare, put it in his blunt way during the debate on the Union. Clare, a native Irishman who had conformed in order to win a place in the system as Lord Chancellor of Ireland, reminded the landlords their properties were based on conquest and confiscation. He noted that much of the country had been confiscated twice or three times in the course of a century, because of the 'continued and persevering resistance of Ireland to the British crown', and in consequence English colonists held the power and property of Ireland. 'Confiscation is their common title, and from their first settlement they have been hemmed in on every side by the old inhabitants of the island, brooding over their discontents in sullen indignation.'[37]

The contradictions of Grattan's parliament[38] were not resolved. Its 'independence' it owed to the American Revolution and the Volunteers, but it remained a landlord parliament. The landlords, as Fitzgibbon remarked, depended on English power for their wealth and privileges. Without it they would lose everything. The commercial middle class wanted a parliament 'free from every tinge of English commercial or political influence', as Sir Jonah Barrington stated it, in order to advance its own interests. But the Irish parliament in fact was an instrument of English rule in Ireland and to change its character must mean the end of English rule. An English government could not tolerate that; therefore it could not tolerate a reformed parliament. And, as Barrington also noted, a reformed parliament would never have assented to its own destruction in 1800. The 'Revolution of 1782' set the stage for the United Irishmen.

Gaelic Ireland in the Eighteenth Century

Gaelic Ireland, traditionalist in politics, aristocratic in outlook, Celtic in language, Catholic in religion, had no need to stress its separate nationality: it was Irish and its English masters governed by force and the right of conquest. Each defeat of the Gaelic Irish had resulted in new confiscations and colonizations, and by the eighteenth century they had reached the nadir of their fortunes: their leaders banished, their religion and culture outlawed. To their rulers, the Catholic Irish (three-quarters of the island's population) were 'the common enemy'; a Lord Chancellor and a Chief Justice ruled 'that the law does not suppose any such person to exist as an Irish Roman Catholic'.[39] The Ascendancy held Ireland by penal laws and English power, which Lecky documents.[40] Burke said the penal laws were directed against

> no small sect or obscure party, but a very numerous body of men – a body which comprehends at least two-thirds of that whole nation. A law against the majority of the people is in substance a law against the people itself. Its extent determines its invalidity; it even changes its character as it enlarges its operation: it is not particular injustice, but general oppression; and can no longer be considered as a private hardship, which might be borne, but spreads and grows up into the unfortunate importance of a national calamity.[41]

The Gaelic Irish were a conquered people. They had to be oppressed lest they rise up and confound their conquerors.

As recited by its poets, however, the national identity of Gaelic Ireland had existed from before recorded history. 'The sentiment of nationality', in Lecky's phrase, remained. The Gaelic poetry of the century is rife with it. The poets looked to a restoration of Gaelic power, through the Stuarts. The *aisling* (vision) poetry preaches treason in the guise of love poems, although not all such verse looked to the Stuarts' return. The poet rests, falls asleep, dreams, sees a beautiful maiden weeping, asks her why? She is Ireland. She tells her sorrowful tale. The poet urges her to be of good cheer: the prince from over the water will rescue her in time. These Jacobite verses, recited at peasant gatherings, passed from generation to generation. The poets were wandering 'hedge school' teachers or labourers, often a combination of both – like Owen Roe O'Sullivan, the Irish Robert Burns. They mourned the old Gaelic aristocracy, whose descendants were serving France, Spain, Austria, even Russia. The greatest of the *aisling* poets was Aodhagán Ó Rathaille (Egan O'Rahilly) and his finest poem in this genre is *Gile na Gille* ('The Fairest of the Fair'). The last stanza sums up the whole:

Oh, my misery, my woe, my sorrow and my anguish,
My bitter source of dolour is evermore that she,
The loveliest of the Lovely, should thus be left to languish
Amid a ruffian horde till the Heroes cross the sea.[42]

Another example of Jacobite poetry is Pierce FitzGerald's 'The War Song of Munster'. It is not an *aisling* for it refuses to hide its political sentiments.

All ye whose hearts beat warm and fast
With Gaelic blood, the die is cast;
Rise up, rise out, like chiefs of old,
And smite the foe whose doom is told.
Oh! sweet in Munster, sweet abroad,
To the saddest race of each proud lord
Is the dash of the wave 'gainst the ships of the brave,
Who come to join us with the sword.[43]

The original is much more militant and the meter and Gaelic words when recited evoke the thunder of waves beating against the sides of a ship. FitzGerald is a lesser poet than O'Rahilly; but for the peasant listener the symbolism of his poem is much sharper than O'Rahilly's dreams: the Gael must be of good cheer and the 'sons of chiefs' must listen, for 'the ships of the brave' are drawing near.

Corkery observes that this Gaelic Ireland of poor peasants and hunted priests is a closed world to those ignorant of Irish, including a historian as fair-minded as Lecky. Hans Kohn, in writing that the war of Irish and English was 'a conflict of two different levels of civilization' which later became 'part of the great conflict of religions in England and in Europe' but was 'still no national conflict between Irish and English', fails to understand this hidden Ireland.

> When Irish nationhood was born in the later eighteenth century, it did not grow either from Gaelic or Catholic foundations. There was no revival of Irish language and literature or of Irish folk traditions and memories comparable to that of Wales. The period marked the lowest point in Gaelic literature, and the Gaelic language fell more and more into disuse except in parts of western Ireland.[44]

This is a misreading of Irish history and literature. The national idea is central to the vigorous literature of eighteenth-century *Gaelic* Ireland. Kohn is confusing 'Irish nationhood' with the colonial nationalism of the Protestant settlers, who resented English restrictions on their trade and commerce. Gaelic Ireland resented the entire system of English law and rule. Politically, colonial nationalism was a progressive force because it sought reform and renewal. Gaelic nationality was reactionary because it sought to restore an idealized Gaelic past. The Gaelic revival did not come until the last decade of the nineteenth century. In the eighteenth century Irish was the vernacular of Catholic Ireland. To study only English-speaking Ireland of the eighteenth century is to ignore the Catholic peasantry. Arthur Young, who travelled through Ireland between 1776 and 1778, found pure English (without mixture of Irish) spoken only in Dublin and the baronies of Forth and Bargie in Wexford. (Forth and Bargie were of Flemish origin and their people spoke a peculiar dialect of English.)

The decline of the Irish language had begun before the Great Famine (1845-48), but that catastrophic event, which mainly affected the western half of the island, gave Irish its death blow. Still, the 1861 census put the number of Irish speakers at 1,105,536, about one-fifth of the population: that is to say, nearly one hundred years after the time Kohn is describing! By the 1890s Irish was confined to isolated pockets along the Atlantic seaboard from Donegal in the north, to Kerry, Cork and Waterford in the south.[45]

The Ulster Presbyterians

Hans Kohn in *The Idea of Nationalism*, says 'nationality is formed by the decision to form a nationality.[46] This certainly applied to the Presbyterians of Ulster, the Scotch-Irish of American history, who formed an almost homogeneous bloc in the counties of Antrim and Down – the hinterland of Belfast – in north-east Ireland. They supported their kinsmen during the American Revolution and shared their political principles. Imbued with the Nonconformist drive, they helped to create the Industrial Revolution, whose technology they adapted to their own manufactures in Belfast. As Tone wrote, 'It was the Dissenters who composed the flower of the famous volunteer army of 1782, which extorted from the English minister the restoration of what is affected to be called the constitution of Ireland.[47]

They urged reform of the Irish Protestant parliament, espoused the principles of the French Revolution, proposed the emancipation of the Catholics: 'they determined to begin on a new system, and to raise the structure of the liberty and independence of their country, on the broad basis of equal rights to the whole people.'[48] In short, they wanted to form an Irish nation with their Catholic fellow-countrymen on the foundation of a secular state, universal suffrage and representative government. Some middle-class Catholics were willing to accept this alliance, but the bishops and their advisers, notably Edmund Burke, were hostile to any links with the Jacobin United Irishmen.[49]

In 1791 the commercial middle class of Dublin joined with the Presbyterian manufacturers of Belfast to form 'Societies of United Irishmen', with the goal of establishing a representative parliament. Influenced by the revolutions in America and France, they demanded 'a clear and radical reform of the representation of the people in parliament'.[50] They urged equal constituencies, universal (male) suffrage, payment of members of parliament, no property qualifications for members of parliament. They were not openly republican at first, they did not propose separation from England, although Wolfe Tone averred privately that 'such an event would be a regeneration for this country',[51] but their efforts if successful must have ended in an Ireland as independent of England as the United States of America.

The most avid reformers were the Presbyterians: 'the Scottish plantation in Ulster', Swift called them. He disliked them intensely. They were successful farmers and rising manufacturers. Their most important industry was linen. Although their economic progress was light years ahead of the rest of Ireland, they were trapped by the mercantilist economic policies of the Crown and thought an independent Ireland would serve their interests better than an Ireland bound to Britain. Republican in politics, like their brethren in America, they believed that a new social contract would benefit them personally and Ireland as a whole.

The Ulster Dissenters – as the Presbyterians were called – hated Popery, disliked the France of the old regime, its royal absolutism and established Catholic Church, and cheered the fall of the Bastille.

> It was the Dissenters who composed the flower of the famous volunteer army of 1782, which extorted from the English minister the restoration of what is affected to be called the constitution of Ireland; it was they who first promoted and continued the demand of a parliamentary reform, in which, however, they were baffled by the superior address and chicanery of the aristocracy; and it was they, finally, who were the first to stand forward, in the most decided and unqualified manner, in support of the principles of the French Revolution.[52]

Tom Paine's *Rights of Man* became the Koran of Belfast. Yet the anti-Papist Presbyterians embraced Catholic emancipation because, in Tone's words,

> They saw at a glance their true object, and the only means to obtain it; conscious that the force of the existing government was such as to require the united efforts of the whole Irish people to subvert it, and, long con-

> vinced . . . that to be free it was necessary to be just, they cast their eyes once more on the long neglected Catholic, and profiting of past errors. . . they determined to begin on a new system, and to raise the structure of the liberty and independence of their country, on the broad basis of equal rights to the whole people.[53]

For Ireland, this was a momentous decision because of Ulster's history of religious feuding. About half the population of the province was Catholic. The middle class of Belfast might be anxious for reconciliation and an alliance against the government, but in rural Ulster competition for land between Catholics and Protestants was fostered by landlords who charged higher rents when leases ran out. This is one reason for the high emigration rate to America of Ulster Protestants in the eighteenth century. Secret agrarian organizations, the Protestant 'Peep O' Day Boys' and the Catholic 'Defenders', fought pitched battles to resolve their differences. After one of these affrays in 1795, at the Diamond, County Armagh, the Orange Society was formed from the Peep O' Day Boys. It was destined to become very important in the politics of Ireland, particularly of Ulster. Exclusively Episcopalian at first, it included landlords as well as tenants. The members swore secret oaths of loyalty to the throne and 'the Protestant succession', and against Popery. In contrast, the Society of United Irishmen was open to all 'who know liberty, who love it, who wish to have it, and who will have it'. Its members toasted European liberty and the liberty of the world, swearing to maintain 'the right and prerogative of Ireland as an independent people'.[54]

Legacy of the United Irishmen

Despite the opposition of bishops and priests, the Catholic peasantry who supported the United Irishmen in the 1790s did so because they believed an independent Ireland would end their economic grievances: high rents, low wages, payment of tithes to the Established Church. According to Leonard McNally, the lawyer who became a government spy in the ranks of the United Irishmen, they scoffed at the sermons warning them against the principles of the French Revolution.[55] Previously the priests had acted as a kind of political police for the government.[56] McNally blamed the press and Paine, whose 'writings were printed at Belfast and Cork, and distributed gratis. . .'. If the French invaded, the peasantry would join them, McNally warned. 'Deism is daily superseding bigotry,' he reported, 'and every man who can read, or who can hear and understand what is read to him, begins in religion as in politics to think for himself.'[57]

The legacy of the United Irishmen to nationalism in Ireland is the contention that religion must be divorced from politics. In place of feuding sects, Wolfe Tone sought to substitute a secular religion. It did not succeed, but the ideal remained. Irish nationalism accepted and enshrined the sentiments of the first article of the constitution of the United Irishmen:

> This Society is constituted for the purpose of forwarding a brotherhood of affection, a communion of rights, and an Union of power among Irishmen of *every religious persuasion*; and thereby to obtain a complete reform in the Legislature, founded on the principles of civil, political, and religious liberty.[58]

This legacy, like nationalism itself, was confined to Catholic Ireland after the destruction of the United Irishmen in the rebellion of 1798. The legacy of the Presbyterian United Irishmen largely vanished in Ulster. In the nineteenth century Protestant Ulster adopted political Unionism, meaning union with Britain, denounced the principles of the United Irishmen, and made the Orange Order its most powerful institution. The result is political division along religious lines – what the United Irishmen tried so hard to prevent when the organization resolved:

> That the weight of English influence in the government of this country is so great, as to require a cordial union *among all the people of Ireland*, to maintain that balance which is essential to the preservation of our liberties and extension of our commerce.[59]

The United Irishmen created the ideology of the Irish nation-state as 'a cordial union' among its people to establish their individual and national freedom 'and extension of our commerce'. The Irish people would owe allegiance to neither king nor pope, but to their country. This concept was modified to meet the changed social relations of their times by Young Ireland, the Fenians and Sinn Fein, yet in essentials these movements remained true to the ideas of the United Irishmen concerning the need for a secular nation-state.

For the purpose of this study an Irish nationalist is one who wants Ireland ruled by the Irish people through a representative parliament, the end result of which must be a nation-state. An Irish republican, in theory, advocates the kind of republic envisaged by the United Irishmen, but in practice the term has come to mean one who seeks to separate Ireland from England by force. Some Irish republicans – John O'Leary, the Fenian, was one – were partial to monarchy. In Ireland, a republican is understood to be an instransigent nationalist.

The Nation-State in the Twentieth Century

Nationalism is defined by Hans Morgenthau as 'the aspiration for two freedoms, one collective, the other individual: the freedom of a nation from domination by another nation and the freedom of the individual to join the nation of his choice'.[60] This is the United Irishmen's aspiration noted above. Nationalism, in Morgenthau's view, grew out of the struggles of the territorial state against feudalism (internally) and the Holy Roman Empire (externally) in the sixteenth and seventeenth centuries. As 'the collective expression of a nation's political identity', nationalism is a product of the French Revolution. The 'Decree of Armed Propaganda' of November 1792, two months after the victory at Valmy, makes that clear:

> The National Convention declares in the name of the French nation that it shall accord fraternity and aid to all peoples who want to recover their liberty, and charges the executive power with giving to the generals the orders necessary to bring aid to those peoples and to defend the citizens who are or might be persecuted for the cause of liberty.[61]

In the nineteenth century national freedom also meant individual freedom, the liberty of the citizen who with his fellows, as part of Rousseau's 'general will', justified and legitimized popular sovereignty. Society would no longer be built upon servitude but upon the 'brotherhood of man'. The revolutions of 1848 were fought for such ideals. In Italy and Germany national unity became a goal of nationalism. In the First World War national self-determination was an issue on both sides: the Allies directed it against the multi-national Austro-Hungarian Empire, while the Germans raised it against Czarist Russia and indeed England in regard to Ireland. The inter-war years, 1919–39, were the hey-day of nationalism and the nation-state. When Hitler invoked the right of self-determination of the Sudeten Germans to carve up Czechoslovakia, he destroyed a myth.

'The justification of the nation-state, as of all political organization, is its ability to perform the functions for the sake of which political organization exists', Morgenthau writes in support of his theory that the nation-state has outlived its usefulness and is obsolete.[62] It was a product of the Industrial Revolution as well as the French Revolution; in the era of nuclear energy and super-powers it is an anachronism. It has ceased to be fully sovereign, it cannot protect its citizens and as a political organization cannot meet the challenge of the market. Economic logic is leading to the integration of nation-states, as in the European Economic Community.

Morgenthau also points out that the ideal of 'one nation, one state', which the principle of national self-determination implemented, 'postulated the primacy of individual choice over the political interests of government'. He adds: 'As a matter of principle, frontiers were to be determined by the will of the people not by considerations of political and military expediency'. After the Second World War the order was reversed and the interests of states took precedence over the interests of peoples.[63] Many new nation-states expelled 'unwanted foreigners' and adjusted frontiers to suit their 'strategic' needs.

It is clear then that the concept of the nation-state has changed a great deal. Whereas once it was necessary to have national sovereignty in order to industrialize the economy, and individual freedom in order to guard the citizen against authority and to develop commerce, these requirements are no longer considered necessary. While losing much of its external sovereign power, the modern nation-state has centralized its domestic power, especially its right to control the economy and the politics of citizens. The nation-states that developed out of the movement against colonialism in the 1950s and 1960s set little store on individual freedom. Many of them are one-party states, while others are military dictatorships. In many nation-states of the Third World, effective economic power is held by the giant multinational companies.[64]

Ideology as a Political Concept

If nationalism is the ideology of the nation-state how do we define ideology? For the purposes of this study ideology means 'the political ideas and outlook of Irish nationalism.' Karl Mannheim divides ideology in two: the first he calls 'total ideology', meaning 'the ideology of an age or of a concrete historico-social group'; the second, 'particular ideology' indicates that 'we are sceptical of the ideas and representations advanced by our opponent.' Ideology, total or particular, is 'a function of him who holds them, and of his position in the social milieu.'[65] In consequence ideology has an economic foundation and is firmly based in the social relations of production. 'The same men who establish social relations comformably with their material productivity, produce also the principles, the ideas, the categories, comformably with their social relations,' Mannheim states, quoting Marx's *The Poverty of Philosophy*.[66] The term ideology comes from the French Revolution. The ideologues were concerned with the science of ideas. They fell foul of Napoleon who was concerned with 'reality' rather than with 'ideas'. Are ideas then not a part of 'reality'? Marx and Engels in *The German Ideology* examined this and concluded: 'Life is not determined by consciousness, but consciousness by life.'[67]

For Marx, the class struggle is the motive force of history. All struggles within the state – for democracy, between aristocracy and monarchy, for the franchise – are class struggles. Every class struggling for mastery 'must first conquer for itself political power in order to represent its interest in turn as the general interest. . .'.[68] And again: 'The class making a revolution appears from the very start, if only because it is opposed to a *class*, not as a class but as the representative of the whole of society; it appears as the whole mass of society confronting the one ruling class.'[69] What counts is the economic structure – the foundation or infrastructure of society, in Marx's definition, with ideology as the superstructure erected on it. Ideology is a reflection of reality, often a distortion of it. Mannheim agrees. Ideology is 'false consciousness', he finds, 'when it fails to take account of the new realities applying to a situation, and when it fails to take account of the realities applying to new situation, and when it attempts to conceal them by thinking of them in categories which are inappropriate'. Avoiding such distortions is, 'in the last analysis, a quest for reality', Mannheim asserts. 'Every idea must be tested by its congruence with reality.'[70] Reality has to do with how we earn our daily bread.

The concept that our political thinking reflects our material interests is not peculiar to Marx. Machiavelli held it. Men change their opinions to correspond with their interests, he notes in the *Discourses*. Max Weber and Karl Mannheim agree. Mannheim's 'particular ideology' masks our real interests behind lies and self-deception.[71] This study deals with 'total ideology', meaning the whole outlook of Irish nationalism. It will examine the ideas of those who contributed to the nationalist ideology and will try to judge their thinking against 'the reality' of their times, meaning the economics of the society in which they wrote, spoke and struggled.

From Colony to Nation-State

The Irish struggle was national and agrarian. It sought control of the land of Ireland as well as the laws of Ireland. It may be seen as a class struggle of the peasantry, led by the Catholic middle class, against the landlords backed by English power. The thinkers – Tone, Davis, Davitt, Griffith, Pearse, Connolly – set goals that sometimes distorted 'the reality' of Irish life, but they were fashioning an ideology of struggle. How the common people who did the struggling felt is harder to determine. John Dillon once quoted words flung by Parnell across the floor of the British House of Commons that they sought to make Ireland a nation. That was 'the whole Irish question in a nutshell', Dillon argued. [72]

We will say it was a struggle for an Irish nation-state. It took many forms. Under O'Connell it was passive resistance, in theory at least. Under the Whiteboys and Ribbonmen it was 'agrarian outrages'. Under the Land League it was rent strikes and boycotts. Under Home Rule it was obstruction in the Commons and agitation at home. For Robert Emmet it was a demonstration in arms. For Smith O'Brien an armed protest in South Tipperary. The Fenians tried to bring about a rebellion. The Clan-na-Gael sent dynamiters into England from America. The Easter Week rebellion was another armed demonstration, almost a drama staged in the capital of Ireland. Out of it grew a popular resistance that created a nation-state in 1922.

Did that final struggle make Ireland a nation in the sense that Parnell and O'Brien meant? Except for partition, which was seen as a temporary expedient to get around the intransigence of Protestant Ulster and the determination of its people to oppose by force any attempt to detach them from the United Kingdom, the answer for many is 'Yes'. But while partition remained, the goal of a nation-state would also remain and nationalism would continue as a force in Irish life.

Nationalism in nineteenth century Ireland was a mass movement not a cult of intellectuals meeting in cafes talking revolution. At times of international crisis the Irish who believed in physical force plotted rebellion, often with the help of England's enemies. In December 1867 Marx began to understand the economic significance of the Irish question. It was not simply a nationality question, he wrote, 'but a question of land and existence.' [73] Fenianism had forced him to rethink the problem. 'Previously I thought Ireland's separation from England impossible. Now I think it inevitable, although after separation there may come *federation*.'[74] Ireland needed independence, an agrarian revolution and protective tariffs, he decided.

To understand the ideology one must understand the struggle. The Irish struggle moved in stages, the success of one establishing the goals of the next. In material terms Catholic emancipation meant little to the peasantry who won it, but it permitted Catholics to sit in parliament and without that a popular Irish party could not be built. The power of the Parliamentary Party, based on popular agitation against the landlord system, changed the balance in Ireland in the 1880s. The landlords lost their properties and their power base. After that Irish self-government became inevitable, although it took twenty-five years of constitutional bargaining and five years of violent conflict to win it. It also created the Unionism of the late 1880s and partition in 1921, two examples of 'particular ideology's' influence on Protestant Ulster.

The nationalist struggle for mastery of Ireland may be viewed as one long rebellion. Prime Minister W.E. Gladstone saw it so in his speech introducing the first Home Rule Bill in 1886. Gladstone noted that Ireland had been ruled 'normally' for only thirteen years of the nineteenth century. Irish nationalism, not British law, governed the behaviour of the Catholic peasantry. Why only the Catholics? The reason is economic, not religious. Ulster's Protestant farmers enjoyed tenant-right (Ulster custom),[75] the chief demand for nearly a century of the Catholic peasantry. Otherwise they too might have joined the struggle, as in the League of North and South in the late 1840s and early 1850s, which the Presbyterian Church supported, and which was sabotaged by Catholic prelates and politicians for sectarian ends.[76] Religious differences alone do not explain Irish politics.

The final phase in the independence struggle, from 1916 to 1921, had political, not social or economic goals. The land question was settled, the countryside prosperous – and in this respect at least Ireland resembled the France of 1789, as Alexis de Tocqueville described it in *The Ancien Regime and the French Revolution.* (The great estates had been broken up twenty years earlier and the centralization of government, which the Revolution completed, had begun.) In Ireland, local government was in the hands of nationalists by the early twentieth century; the Treaty of 1921 merely established a central native government. In fact from 1919 to 1921 a system of dual government of the kind described by Crane Brinton in *The Anatomy of Revolution*[77] existed. Nationalist county and urban councils recognized Sinn Fein's underground government as the legal government of Ireland. Nationalist Ireland gave its allegiance to the Dail (Assembly) established by Sinn Fein; Unionist Ireland maintained its allegiance to Britain. Two conflicting ideologies used all political means, including violence, to resolve the problem of sovereignty; the British government decided the issue by partitioning the country.

The stress here is on nationalist rather than on republican ideology. Irish republicanism, as an ideology, undoubtedly influenced the nationalist struggle, but after the United Irishmen it neither dominated it nor established a set of ideas, values, beliefs apart from it. The economic interpretation of the political struggle, advanced by Sinn Fein, was that Ireland needed native government to control its finances and rebuild its industries. The Treaty met these needs and was accepted despite the opposition of those in Sinn Fein who saw it as a betrayal of the Republic proclaimed in 1916. Again, practical struggle triumphed over ideology. Small farmers in the West and farm labourers generally had economic grievances that Sinn Fein said must wait until the independence struggle was won. (The grievances remained and helped to propel de Valera to power in 1932.)[78] But in 1919–21 land was a marginal issue.

In the new nation-state Sinn Fein had the opportunity to implement its ideology on the language (revival of Irish as a spoken tongue), economics (protection and industrialization) and national regeneration (the nationalist spirit). When Sinn Fein split over the Treaty, W.T. Cosgrave – after the deaths of Arthur Griffith and Michael Collins – led the majority, de Valera the minority wing. They adopted new names – Cumann na nGaedheal and Fianna Fail – but both wings tried to pursue the ideology of Sinn Fein on language, economics and nationalism generally. Apart from their attitude to the Treaty, their national values hardly differed. Cumann na nGaedheal saw in an Irish state governed by Irishmen Sinn Fein's apotheosis. Fianna Fail, the majority party after 1932, remained closer to the original Sinn Fein ideology. Yet it, too, was forced by the test of reality to abandon most of Sinn Fein's ideology in time.

First, the revival of the language. The Gaeltacht has virtually disappeared. The language performed its role as a nation-builder in the early years of the century,[79] in recognition of which Article 8 of the Constitution says 'the Irish language as the national language is the first official language'. Cultural nationalists, like Daniel Corkery, insisted that Ireland could not be a nation without its own language, but the people, despite some goodwill towards Irish, were unenthusiastic and the revival failed. Official help for the language, which the writer Máirtín Ó Cadhain insisted was insufficient and insincere, was not matched by public support. The explanation of Dr Eoin McKiernan, head of the Irish American Cultural Institute of St Paul, Minn., is probably correct: 'The Irish peasant identified the language with his peonage and could not, therefore, fly fast enough from it.'[80]

Economic self-sufficiency, Sinn Fein's chief plank, was expected to make the new Irish state relatively prosperous. It would also halt emigration. It was broadly supported yet failed to do either. In fact the people grew less prosperous and emigration increased. Economic self-sufficiency was part of nationalist ideology before Sinn Fein advanced it as their number one goal in 1905. Parnell had urged protective tariffs[81] and Marx, as we have seen, considered it the inevitable result of self-government. Arthur Griffith, who took his economics from Friedrich List, could have found the same concept in Alexander Hamilton.[82] All developing countries hope to bolster industry by bounties and tariffs.

A generation of post-Treaty Irish sacrificed themselves on the altar of Sinn Fein economics and one result of this dedication was a strong publicly-owned sector, for private enterprise would not do what was needed in the 1920s and 1930s. By the late 1950s, however, the ruling elite had decided to try another road. The first five-year programme for economic expansion, drafted in November 1958, offered tax and plant incentives to foreign manufacturers. Whether in consequence of this, or for some other reason, today the Republic of Ireland has the fastest-growing economy in Western Europe. Although it remains the poorest state in the wealthy EEC and suffers from high inflation and high unemployment, the standard of living of the people of the Republic is at the highest point in Irish history. The Irish currency is now independent of sterling and economic dependence on Britain has ended. Without Sinn Fein ideology this could not have been achieved. Even with Sinn Fein ideology it could not have been done without the multinational corporation as the means of change.[83] The only link with Sinn Fein ideology that remains is the policy of neutrality in international relations and there is some doubt about how long it will continue.[84]

The new Irish middle class responds, as one would expect, to its own interests and these are concerned with the Republic as a member of the EEC. In consequence, the Church's role in the state is less pronounced and nationalism of the traditional kind is not encouraged. Yet nationalism is still potent among the deprived, the dispossed and the oppressed Catholics of the North, who receive little encouragement from the Republic. Few in Dublin want a revival of the old Sinn Fein-style nationalism. An illustration is provided by a long-established Dublin publisher of books geared to national thinking. In 1918 the publishing house clashed with Dublin Castle censorship, which forbade publication of a collection of essays by James Fintan Lalor under the Defence of the Realm Act. 'The publication is intended to pander to the seditiously disposed,' the Chief Secretary's Office informed the Attorney General. That publishing house today offers a work calling separatist nationalism 'authoritarian and conservative'; in general it denounces nationalist ideology as backward.[85] There is no contradiction here. Publishers and writers generally reflect the material interests of the middle class. The ruling elite of the Republic does not want to get swamped in the Northern morass. 'Not ideas, but material and ideal interests directly govern man's conduct,' Max Weber remarked,[86] echoing Marx who insisted that the ruling ideas of a society are indeed the ideas of its ruling class.

The Republic meets all the tests of Samuel P. Huntington's modernizing societies. It enjoys legitimacy with its people, its institutions are stable, its party system works, there is high political participation (74.8 per cent of the electorate votes, on average); despite a powerful Catholic Church there is growing secularization. 'Constitutional stability has been shown to be a function of economic development and political participation,' according to Huntington.[87] The army follows the British model and stays out of politics.

Apart from the high cost of living and shortage of jobs, there are other flaws in this Irish Eden. The former peasantry who struggled for 'land and existence' in the past are in grave danger of losing both in the future. The peasant, who became a free farmer only in this century,[88] was the backbone of the national struggle. A study by the Economic and Social Research Institute of Dublin suggests that one-third of the country's small farms (under thirty acres) may disappear soon. When they go, nationalist Ireland and its traditional values are unlikely to survive.[89]

Utilizing foreign firms as the engine of industrialization and development has its own built-in dangers. Economic decisions, involving the livelihood of Irish citizens, are not made in Ireland and indeed may have nothing to do with Ireland. By pulling out or shutting down in time of recession, a few foreign companies could plunge the country into economic chaos. As the incentives cease, the foreign firms may go elsewhere. This happened in Puerto Rico in the early 1960s with dire results for that island's economy. Not until the 1970s did the Republic of Ireland succeed in breaking its economic dependency on Great Britain, by means of the EEC and foreign investment; but it remains a 'developing economy' – meaning that it is still part of the Third World and has not yet made the transition to the advanced industrialized First World.[90] Having abandoned, largely, the nationalist ideology that brought it to its present position, the Irish nation-state has found no substitute, apart from a vague liberalism built on a system of free enterprise and parliamentary party government modelled on Britain.

The Ideology of Unionism

As noted earlier, Irish Unionism is the politics of the *status quo*. Ulster Unionism is a reaction to Irish nationalism. It was the politics of those who wanted Ireland to remain in the United Kingdom. In the nineteenth century, Unionists consisted of the Protestant Ascendancy – landlords, big merchants, manufacturers, the professions – and, after 1886, the mass of Ulster Protestants: workers, small farmers, shopkeepers, could vote to retain the Union.

There were Catholic Unionists – lawyers who looked to Dublin Castle for advancement, old landed families, ambitious civil servants; and there were many Protestant nationalists. Yet by and large in Ireland, Protestants are Unionists, Catholics are nationalists.

The economic basis of Unionist politics, outside of Ulster, is simple enough to identify: the ownership of land and the privileges that came with British power. Most landlords derived their title deeds from the Cromwellian settlement. They were validated at the Restoration and reinforced by the Williamite conquest. They rested on force and British rule and were based on confiscation. (A few Gaelic and 'Old English' families managed to hold on to their properties through the upheavals of the centuries[91] and likewise were bound to English rule.) The landlords were England's garrison in Ireland in the view of Edmund Burke – later adopted by Fintan Lalor. They lost their ascendancy in religion with the disestablishment of the Church of Ireland in 1869; their ascendancy in land between 1882 and 1902; their ascendancy in politics, in the decade of the 1880s; they appeared to have lost political power in most of Ireland by 1922.

Protestants in the new nation-state made up only 6 per cent of the population – less than 4 per cent today – but controlled much of its wealth. Resentment against the Ascendancy which retained some of its privileges 'after the revolution' remained, as the power of the Catholic Church grew. Few Protestants, even nationalist Protestants, opposed this trend – with the exception of W. B. Yeats. In 1925, as a member of the Free State Senate, he denounced legislation banning divorce. Article 8 of the Free State Constitution guaranteed that no law would restrict the free exercise of religion, or impose 'any disability on account of religious belief or religious status. . .'. Yeats warned the government: '. . . you are to legislate on purely theological grounds and you are to force your theology upon persons who are not of your religion. . .'.[92] (Yeats, no Unionist, was proud of the Ascendancy heritage – though wrongly adding Burke to his list of Anglo-Irish notables in *The Seven Sages*: 'Goldsmith and Burke, Swift and the Bishop of Cloyne. . .'.

Irish nationalist ideology saw self-government in political terms only. Prelates like Cardinal Cullen of Dublin, who put Catholic claims before national rights, never established a political following. Parnell, according to his biographer F.S.L. Lyons, saw Home Rule as 'a healing and reconciling influence in Irish society', and had no fear of Catholic domination.[93] The bishops and many of the clergy probably had other views.[94] In general, Irish nationalists tried to keep religion and politics separate. The Irish Catholic experience was different from that of Catholicism on the Continent. There was no history of an Irish Catholic state Church. The clergy were recruited from the ordinary people. The folk memory of the penal laws made religious oppression an abomination. Nationalists were convinced, rightly, that England used the Vatican to condemn the Irish struggle, as witness Young Ireland, in the 1840s, the Fenians, in the 1860s, and the Plan of Campaign, in the 1880s. The most orthodox Catholic of the Irish leaders, O'Connell, said on one occasion he 'would as soon receive his politics from Constantinople as from Rome'.[95] Many Irish leaders, from Grattan to Parnell, were Protestants; they included Ireland's most heroic rebels, Wolfe Tone, Robert Emmet, John Mitchel. No physical-force nationalist at any rate equated religion with nationality although some constitutional nationalists during the Parnell crisis for opportunistic reasons and to obtain episcopal support enveloped themselves in the robes of religion.[96]

The new Irish Free State became, unofficially, a Catholic state. The old nationalist religious tolerance gave way to pettiness and narrow-mindedness. There was no outright discrimination because there were no poor Protestants to discriminate against and the former Ascendancy hardly bothered with Irish state institutions anyway. Ex-Unionists were labelled, in the public mind, 'British-Irish'. The anti-Free State Republicans were as much to blame for this attitude as their enemies. The former landlords supported the Treaty and some were appointed to the new Senate. In reprisal, Republicans burned their great houses; threatened with assassination, many of them left the country. No episcopal palace was burnt, no bishop was threatened with death for excommunicating Republicans in the Civil War. The Free State branded Erskine Childers 'a damned Englishman', although he was half-Irish and had grown up in Ireland; they meant to say Childers was 'a damned Protestant', a Protestant cleric suggested:

> Erskine Childers being the son of an English father and an Irish mother is a 'good Englishman' but Padraic Pearse from a similar union is Irish. The only fundamental difference seems to be in religion. In fact the only people who really believe the propaganda line about 'British-Irish' are the Roman Catholics![97]

When Dr Douglas Hyde, Protestant founder of the Gaelic League and first President of Ireland under the 1937 Constitution, died, his successor, as head of State, Sean T. O'Kelly, and members of the Irish government, remained 'ostentatiously outside' Christ Church Cathedral, Dublin. As Catholics they were forbidden to attend a Protestant service.[98]

The ecumenical pontificate of John XXIII introduced a new era in Ireland, as elsewhere. Tomás Cardinal O Fiaich, Archbishop of Armagh and Primate of all Ireland, supports separation of Church and state. 'It is good for the State and Church,' he says. 'I don't think churchmen should be in any way involved in trying to bring pressure on legislation'.[99] The attitude of the bishops in Ireland, like nationalism itself, was shaped by history: principally by the struggle for control of education. John Henry Newman (later Cardinal) was invited to Dublin to establish a Catholic university in the 1850s; after four frustrating years he returned to England with this comment:

> It seems to me that no small portion of the hierarchy and clergy of Ireland regard it as a mistake and a misfortune that they have any of the upper or middle classes among them – that they do but feel awkward when a gentleman is converted or shows himself a good Catholic – in fact, that they think that then only will Ireland become again the Isle of Saints when it has a population of peasants ruled over by patriotic priests patriarchally.[100]

Newman, an English Tory, was saying that the Catholic Church in Ireland was a peasant Church, staffed and led by peasants. It responded in large part to the political and social needs of its members, but did not always control them, as Emmet Larkin indicates in his history of the Irish Church in the Parnell era.

The *Rise of Ulster Unionism*

'A political ideology, in order to be effective, must reflect the life experiences of those whom it endeavours to reach'. Hans Morgenthau has written.[101] The heart of Ulster Unionism was Belfast. What united its socially diverse following was anti-Catholicism. From this one factor it is simple to construct the hypothesis that the Irish question is a religious question – easy and wrong. Unlike Irish nationalism, unionism is a negative concept – a defensive mechanism to maintain the *status quo*. It exists to defend the union with Britain and began as an anti-Home Rule movement organized by the Orange Order. 'Home Rule is Rome Rule', was the whole of its argument. The two ideologies, unionism and nationalism, are diametrically opposed, and nowhere are they more in conflict than in working-class Belfast, where communal and confessional strife among Protestants and Catholics has a long and far from noble history.[102]

Certainly this enmity has a religious character and its myths date from the seventeenth century wars of religion. But this explanation is too simple. After all, Protestants and Catholics have been in conflict in other countries; and still manage to live in the same political society. Examples, some of them flawed, are provided by Germany, Belgium, Holland, Switzerland, the United States. In these states, Catholics are the minority, as in Northern Ireland. What divides Protestants and Catholics in Northern Ireland is ideology: they disagree on who should govern them. Unionists reject and fear Irish nationalism, while Nationalists reject union with Britain, which for them has always taken the form of Protestant power. 'A better explanation for Protestant-Catholic conflict in Northern Ireland emphasizes its peculiar historical fate as a settler colony', Michael Hechter writes in *Internal Colonialism,* a study of 'the Celtic Fringe in British National Development, 1536-1966'.[103] Discussing Richard Rose's view that 'religion is the obstacle to the development of dual loyalties [to nation and United Kingdom state] there [in Ireland]', Hechter quotes the Irish socialist leader, James Connolly, to support his contention that Dr Rose and other writers may be overlooking equally important influences. In recent years Ulster Protestants have faced a national identity problem.[104] When all Ireland was British-ruled what bound them politically was their planter origin as a colony. Their settler background and consciousness, combined with force of character and determination to improve themselves economically, accounted for their superior economic and political status. Patrick Buckland, a historian of unionism, cites examples of social behaviour common to settler colonists elsewhere – in Algeria, Rhodesia, South Africa. Time does not erode such attitudes so long as there is a 'native' population to dominate. This was the 'consciousness' Lord Randolph Churchill appealed to in 1886 when, with an eye on the leadership of the Tory party, he decided to play 'the Orange card' and coined the anti-nationalist slogan, 'Ulster will fight and Ulster will be right'.[105] And it is the 'consciousness' James Connolly described in 1913, during another Tory-fomented anti-Home Rule crisis when he wrote:

> The religious affiliations of the population of Ulster determine their political leanings to a greater extent than is the case in any part of Europe outside the Balkans. But the manner in which this has developed is also unique. I believe that it is true to say that, politically speaking, the Protestantism

of the North of Ireland has no parallel outside this country, and that the Catholicism of the Irish Catholics is, likewise, peculiar in its political trend.

To explain – I mean that, whereas, Protestantism has in general made for political freedom and political Radicalism, it has been opposed to slavish worship of kings and aristocrats. Here, in Ireland, the word Protestant is almost a convertible term with Toryism, lickspittle loyalty, servile worship of aristocracy and hatred of all that savours of genuine political independence on the part of the 'lower classes'.

And in the same manner, Catholicism which in most parts of Europe is synonymous with Toryism, lickspittle loyalty, service worship of aristocracy and hatred of all that savours of genuine political independence on the part of the lower classes, in Ireland and is almost synonymous with rebellious tendencies, zeal for democracy, and intense feeling of solidarity with all strivings upward of those who toil.

Such a curious phenomenon is easily understood by those who know the history of Ireland. Unfortunately for their spiritual welfare – and I am using the word 'spiritual', not in its theological but in its better significance as controlling mental and moral development upward – the Protestant elements in Ireland were, in the main, a plantation of strangers upon the soil from which the owners had been dispossessed by force. The economic dispossession was, perforce, accompanied by a political and social outlawry. Hence every attempt of the dispossessed to attain citizenship, to emerge from their state of outlawry, was easily represented as a tentative step towards reversing the plantation and towards replanting the Catholic and dispossessing the Protestant.

Imagine this state of matters persisting for over 200 years and one realizes at once that the planted population – the Protestants – were bound to acquire insensibly a hatred of political reform, and to look upon every effort of the Catholic to achieve political recognition as an insidious move towards the expulsion of Protestants. Then the Protestant always saw that the kings and aristocrats of England and Ireland were opposed by the people whom he most feared and from recognizing that it was but an easy step to regard his cause as identical with theirs. They had a common enemy, and he began to teach his children that they had a common cause, and common ideals.

This is the reason – their unfortunate isolation as strangers holding a conquered country in fee for rulers alien to its people – that the so-called Scotch of Ulster have fallen away from and developed antagonism to political reform and mental freedom as rapidly as the Scots of Scotland have advanced in adhesion to these ideals.

The Catholics, for their part, and be it understood I am talking only of the Catholic workers, have been as fortunately placed for their political education as they were unfortunately placed for their political and social condition. . . . Every upward step of the Catholic has emancipated some one of the smaller Protestant sects; every successful revolt of the Catholic peasant has given some added security even to those Protestant farmers who were most zealously defending the landlord. And out of this struggle the Catholic has, perforce, learned toleration. He has learned that his struggle is, and has been, the struggle of all the lowly and dispossessed, and he has grown broad-minded with the broad-mindedness of the slave in revolt against slavery.[106]

Connolly's experience convinced him that socialist theories about the most developed industrially being also the most politically advanced (from a class point of view), did not hold true in Belfast. 'Here, the Orange working class are slaves in spirit because they have been reared up among a people whose conditions of servitude were more slavish than their own', he wrote. 'In Catholic Ireland the working class are rebels in spirit and democratic in feeling because for hundreds of years they have found no class as lowly paid or as hardly treated as themselves'.[107]

Connolly attributed responsibility for this situation to two factors: first, the ideology of Protestant, or colonial, supremacy; second, the Protestant privileged status *vis-a-vis* the Catholics. The two are perhaps one and the same. The ideology grew out of the Reformation, Irish rebellions, industrialization. The myths spring from the Ulster plantation, the Puritan Revolution, the war of William and James – the siege of Derry, the battles of the Boyne and Aughrim. It brings Ulster Protestants together every 12 July when the Orange Order stages mass marches to the beat of war drums.[108] It is an ideology of power; an ideology of colonial power.

The economic realities that kept Northern Ireland in the United Kingdom – British markets and raw materials – were associated with power: local power in Ulster and the world-wide power of the great British Empire. Unionist politics reflected this sense of power. The ideology of unionism is the ideology of colonialism: it uses religion, politics, culture and law to mirror its imperial view of the world. Industrial Belfast, with its great shipbuilding, engineering and textile industries, would suffer calamitously, cut off from the empire.[109]

The British Empire is part of history. Its markets vanished with its power. The ruling class of Ulster – landed gentry and Belfast industrialists – have also left the stage, banished by the troubles of the 1960s and 1970s. These changes are reflected in the call for an 'independent Northern Ireland' by the Ulster Defence Association, the umbrella organization of the Protestant paramilitary groups. An ideology, to be effective, must be linked with material interests, as Max Weber noted. Should Britain decide to quit Northern Ireland the Unionist role as defender of the *status quo* will end. Unionism must find a new role and a new ideology. It will make no accommodation with Irish nationalism, which it sees as the political arm of the Catholic Church. In a state dominated by Catholics, Protestants are convinced they would be second-class citizens. For that reason they are unlikely to assent to a united Ireland.

How far removed are nationalist and unionist ideologies from the realities of Northern Ireland? A good distance, one would surmise. If the ideologies are so distorted, surely the politics will be equally distorted, since they avoid dealing with reality. This has been the situation from the foundation of the state, in 1921, to its *de facto* abolition in 1972. The Nationalists did not believe the state would last. They held steadily to the axiom that partition was 'unnatural' and must fail. They did not participate in the politics of the state, except when it was necessary to safeguard Nationalist and/or Catholic interests. The Unionists would not permit any straying from the 'Protestant state for a Protestant people' principle. They created an atmosphere of permanent crisis about the security and the future of what they insisted on calling 'Ulster'. When the real crisis came the system collapsed. The British government insisted that the extra-constitutional features of Unionist rule – special police, gerrymandered local electoral districts – must be abolished. The building could not stand without these props. Unionist ideology had created the image of a 'laager' society, so its followers were prepared for the possibility of eventual catastrophe. The ruling 'oligarchy' abandoned Northern Ireland after 1970, realizing perhaps that its own leadership role was finished and that the state itself could not survive.

The exponent of colonial ideology, the Orange Order, appears to have lost some of its influence. It had transmitted the values, beliefs, visions of British colonial society to its mass following and ensured that the gulf between Protestants and Catholics would be as wide as that separating Boers and Zulus in South Africa.[110] The Orange Order remains, but today the influence of the Reverend Ian Paisley is stronger. His brand of religious and political fundamentalism has more appeal ideologically, perhaps because the colonial 'reality' has changed. The quest for a new reality is changing the ideology. The consequence is talk of an 'independent Northern Ireland' among other solutions. (Catholics might consider this last an example of 'particular ideology' – without using such a term – a mask to hide Protestant domination.)

A Post-Colonial Problem

Simply put, this nationalism implies some form of Irish self-government. The United Irishmen were the first to demand total separation from England in the manner of the American colonists, but this was a minority view among nationalists until 1918. 'We are now done with England', Cathal Brugha told the Sinn Féin deputies when they met as Dáil Éireann, the National Assembly of Ireland, in January 1919. Dáil Éireann's base was the Proclamation of the Irish Republic of 1916.

This faith inspired the young Jawharlal Nehru to commit himself to India's independence. 'Roger Casement's wonderful speech at his trial in 1916 seemed to point out exactly how a member of a subject nation should feel', he wrote. 'The Easter Week rising in Ireland by its very failure attracted, for was that not true courage which mocked at almost certain failure and proclaimed to the world that no physical might could crush the invincible spirit of a nation.' [111]

This 'invincible spirit' is the ideology of Irish nationalism, the theme of this study. Republicanism, the revolutionary expression of Irish nationalism, came to Ireland as a secular religion devised by Wolfe Tone for a country of conflicting, and intolerant, creeds and peoples. The phrases remain, their meaning forgotten, but the theory behind it – that the Irish people, regardless of religion or origin, should be citizens of one independent Irish state – lives on as a formula that could solve the 'Irish question'.

Viewed in this light, Irish history is a colonial conflict. The forms of struggle pioneered in Ireland were adopted later in India, Egypt, Palestine. Ireland's struggle was partly-successful, for it created a nation-state (the Irish Free State). It inflicted the first defeat, in the twentieth century, on the British Empire and began the break-up of the imperial system. For that reason alone, a study of the ideology of Irish nationalism is important.

The Irish settlement, however, accepted the partition of Ireland. This solution, too, was imposed later in India and Palestine, with as little success as in Ireland. Whatever the case for a Protestant-Unionist state within the United Kingdom, there was none for pressing the one-third Catholic-Nationalist population into an arrangement which they opposed.[112] In consequence the Northern Ireland conflict is really a post-colonial problem.

II
The United Irishmen and Secular Nationalism
Wolfe Tone versus Edmund Burke

The United Irishmen took their political ideas from many sources, none Gaelic. They accepted Henry Grattan's concept of the Irish nation, of the constitutional independence of the Irish parliament as set forth by William Molyneux, using the arguments of his friend, John Locke, and Swift's statement: 'For in reason, all government without the consent of the governed, is the very definition of slavery, but in fact, eleven men well armed will certainly subdue one single man in his shirt.'[1] Their intellectual stock, like that of their contemporaries in the English-speaking world, came from Locke's exposition of the social contract and popular rights – an original contract and deed of political association based on natural law and natural rights. Like the men who made a revolution in America, they had a colonial heritage. Indeed, their guide-lines included the American Revolution, 'the Glorious Revolution' of 1688 and the Anglo-Irish 'Revolution of 1782', as well as the Revolution in France. They could refer to Locke's 'right to revolution': that the king may be resisted if he puts himself in a state of war with his people.[2] The American Revolution had been won by force, the settlement of 1782 by the threat of force. Force was necessary for 'the public good'.

Edmund Burke declared that in 1782 'the Irish parliament and nation became independent'. It was Ireland's 'Glorious Revolution'.[3] In fact it was a victory for the English colony in Ireland. The natives, who made up almost four-fifths of the population, had no part in it. They continued to be excluded from the constitution. The Protestant Ascendancy, which Burke considered an English garrison 'to keep the natives in subjection', would not permit a broader constitution lest they lose their wealth and privileges. The English government continued to rule Ireland as a colony: the constitution of a colony could not be as independent as that of the mother country, the Cabinet noted in 1774.[4]

Grattan, who believed in the British connection and the empire, wanted a constitution for all men of property, Catholics as well as

Protestants. The great landlords who dominated the country would not permit it. The Dissenters of Belfast resented England's mercantilist policies of subordinating the Irish economy to English interests. The war in North America had ruined their linen exports. They wanted representative government and a reformed Irish parliament to complete 'the Revolution of 1782'. These Belfast merchants and manufacturers were concerned about markets and trade, about economic as well as political freedom. Too few in numbers to achieve a revolution by themselves, they looked about them for allies. Theobald Wolfe Tone, the best political mind of the day, urged them to link up with the Catholics in order to defeat the Ascendancy and the English government. The stage was set for the United Irishmen.

The Political Thought of Wolfe Tone

Wolfe Tone began political life as a Grattanite Whig. He soon realized that two powerful forces stood in the way of a reformed Irish parliament: the Ascendancy class and England. Tone's first pamphlet, *A Review of the Last Session of Parliament* (1790), praised Grattan's 'daring spirit' but doubted that he could win reform. Government, said Tone, rests on opinion. To change it one must change opinion. In the 1790s the opinion of the middle class as well as the Ascendancy had to be considered. The 300 members of parliament, who lorded it over four million, would discover that 'the power which elevated could abase'.[5] The 300 represented not four million, but the landlords. Dublin Castle (the seat of English government in Ireland) manipulated the landlords' representatives by trading votes for patronage. In his first pamphlet, Tone thought that Ireland's 'great grievance' was corruption.

Tone's second pamphlet, *An Enquiry How Far Ireland is Bound as of Right to Embark in the Impending Contest on the Side of Great Britain,* examined the Irish parliament's role in foreign relations. When England declared war, Ireland went to war. To defend the Asian trade monopoly of the East India Company, Britain prepared to wage war on Spain in 1790. The issue had nothing to do with Ireland. Tone thought the Irish Commons should examine Ireland's interest and establish a precedent regarding its obligations as an 'appendage' of Great Britain. 'We should spurn the idea of moving, an humble satellite round any power, however great, and claim at once, and enforce, our rank among the primary nations of the earth,' Tone wrote. 'Then should we have, what, under the present system, *we shall never see*, a national flag and spirit to maintain it.'[6] If government's role was to protect commerce and advance the prosperity of the country, 'the present system' should be re-examined and perhaps changed, Tone half-suggested in conclusion. He was feeling his way. The printer withdrew the pamphlet before it was distributed, after a member of the Commons said the author should be hanged.

Tone was attempting to change opinion because in 1782 an aroused Protestant public, backed by the Volunteers, had changed 'the present system' and Grattan proclaimed 'Ireland is now a nation'. But the 'independent Irish parliament' proved a bitter disappointment to Grattan and all reformers. Real power lay with England, even in parliament. The mass of the Irish people were not represented and Ireland remained, what it had been before the so-called Revolution of 1782, 'an oppressed, insulted, and plundered nation'.

The revolution in France turned the eyes of political liberals to the National Assembly in Paris where the middle class formed the third estate. Ireland's 'third estate' must similarly assert itself and claim the political power its economic status demanded, Tone decided. Thomas Russell, an army officer who listened to the debates in the gallery of the House of Commons with Tone, came to the same conclusion. Russell was posted to Belfast where he met kindred spirits among the Presbyterian manufacturers who on 14 July 1790 and 1791 celebrated the fall of the Bastille. When Tone went to Belfast, in October 1791, he discovered that 'the thermometer of Blefescu has risen, as to politics' and 'Paine's book [was] the Koran of Blefescu'.[7] The Presbyterian manufacturers denounced Edmund Burke's view of the French Revolution. They had set up a secret committee to organize a political club along radical lines based on the Volunteers and Tone was asked to write the resolutions and declaration of principles.

The French Revolution had 'become the test of every man's political creed', Tone wrote, 'and the nation was fairly divided into two great parties, the Aristocrats and the Democrats. . .'.[8] The Dissenters of Belfast were the leading democrats and Tone's declaration reflected their advanced opinions. It opened in fine revolutionary style:

> In the present great era of reform, when unjust governments are falling in every quarter of Europe; when religious persecution is compelled to abjure her tyranny over conscience; when the Rights of Men are ascertained in theory, and that theory substantiated by practice; when antiquity can no longer defend absurd and oppressive forms, against the common sense and common interests of mankind; when all governments are acknowledged to originate from the people, and to be so far only obligatory, as they protect their rights and promote their welfare: We think it our duty, as Irishmen,

> to come forward, and state what we feel to be our heavy grievance, and what we know to be its effectual remedy.
>
> We have no national government. We are ruled by Englishmen, and the servants of Englishmen, whose object is the interest of another country; whose instrument is corruption, and whose strength is the weakness of Ireland; and these men have the whole of the power and patronage of the country, as means to seduce and subdue the honesty of her representatives in the legislature. . . .

Wolfe Tone's remedy was 'an equal representation of all the people in parliament'.

Tone drafted three resolutions. The first declared 'that the weight of English influence in the government of this country is so great, as to require a cordial union among all the people of Ireland, to maintain that balance which is essential to the preservation of our liberties and extension of our commerce'. The second resolved 'that the sole constitutional mode by which this influence can be opposed, is by a complete and radical reform of the representation of the people in parliament'. The third asserted 'that no reform is practicable, efficacious, or just, which shall not include Irishmen of every religious persuasion'.

The association was called 'the Society of United Irishmen'. Divisions among Irishmen, the statement continued, encouraged the 'profligate, audacious, and corrupt administrations in measures, which, but for these divisions, they durst not have attempted'. It concluded: 'We submit our resolutions to the nation, as the basis of our political faith.'[9]

Appeal to Catholics

Commerce and politics were the chief concerns of the founding fathers of the United Irishmen. Indeed the unamended opening sentence of Tone's declaration ran: 'We are ruled by Englishmen and the servants of Englishmen, filled as to commerce and politics, with the short-sighted and ignorant prejudice of their country.' The declaration was a manifesto to the Protestant middle class of Belfast and Dublin.

Although the Catholic peasantry formed the tinder of revolution, there is nothing in these early United Irish statements about their grievances: payments of tithes to the Established Church, exorbitant rents to the Ascendancy class and middlemen, no legal rights. Mention of reform as applying to 'Irishmen of every religious persuasion' was a bid for the support of the Catholic middle class of Dublin.

There was some opposition among the Presbyterians in Belfast to full rights for Catholics. For the Presbyterians, France was the traditional fount of religious absolutism and they welcomed the revolution because it put an end to it. Yet they were fearful of Popery. Tone examined the role of religion in Ireland. The Established Church (Anglican), to which he belonged, was the Church of the Ascendancy. As in England at the time, the Presbyterian Dissenters represented enlightened opinion in politics and commerce. The Catholics had 'an inextirpable abhorrence of the English name and power' and would support any reform movement that improved their lot. The Protestants of the Established Church had a monopoly of economic and political power. The Dissenters had economic power but no political power. The Catholics had neither economic nor political power. Change in Ireland must follow an alliance of Dissenters and Catholics, Tone theorized:

> To subvert the tyranny of our execrable government, to break the connection with England, the never-failing source of all our political evils, and to assert the independence of my country – these were my objects. To unite the whole people of Ireland, to abolish the memory of all past dissensions, and to substitute the common name of Irishman in place of the denominations of Protestant, Catholic and Dissenter – these were my means.

To convince the Dissenters of the soundness of his propositions Tone wrote his third pamphlet, in August 1791, *An Argument on Behalf of the Catholics of Ireland.* It set out to prove that Dissenters and Catholics had the same 'common interest' and the same 'common enemy'. To guard their individual liberties and make Ireland independent they must forget old feuds and 'consolidate the entire strength of the whole nation, and to form for the future but one people'.[10]

The *Argument* is Tone's best pamphlet. The style is 'clear, masculine and smooth', in the manner of his model, Swift. (Tone's diary is very Swiftean, even to the styling of Belfast as *Blefescu.*) The case for Catholic rights is well organized and flows logically to the conclusion that Ireland could not enjoy liberty while the Catholics were unfree. There is no theology. Tone distrusted popes and priests as much as any Belfast Calvinist. Emancipation would weaken clerical influence, he maintained. (Burke thought the priests had little influence although Protestants blamed them for 'every disorder among the common people'.)[11] Tone claimed that 'one of the heavy misfortunes of Ireland [was] the consciences, the morals, and the religion of the bulk of the nation, are in the hands of men of low birth, low feelings, low habits, and no education'. In that enlightened age he felt no emancipated Catholic would pay attention to the 'extinguished thunderbolts of the Vatican', or the 'idle anathemas of the Pope'. Churches would have little say in an independent Ireland.

Tone asked: 'Does any man think that our rulers here recommend themselves to their creators in England, by promoting the interest of Ireland, when it can in the most remote degree interfere with the commerce of Great Britain?' (A footnote instances the Arigna Iron Works and the 'double loom' invention developed in Belfast for the linen industry; both were refused aid by the Irish parliament. In Belfast, two months later, Tone learned of the grievances of the linen manufacturers.) 'The people are utterly disregarded and defied: divided and distracted as they are, and distrustful of each other, they fall an easy prey to English rulers or their Irish subalterns.' And yet everywhere 'reform is going forward, and levelling ancient abuses in the dust'. Why not in Ireland? Because 'religious intolerance and political bigotry' divided the people. Tone castigated the 'Revolution of 1782'. It

> left three-fourths of our countrymen slaves as it found them, and the government of Ireland in the base and wicked and contemptible hands, who had spent their lives in degrading and plundering her: nay, some of whom had given their last vote decidedly, though hopelessly, against this our famous Revolution.

They must move on from 1782. No Irishman would agree that it was the final revolution. Much remained to be done. To counteract the influence of government, should it seek 'to thwart' Irish prosperity, there must be parliamentary reform; 'no reform is honourable, practicable, efficacious, or just, which does not include, as a fundamental principle, the extension of elective franchise to the Roman Catholics, under modifications hereafter to be mentioned.'[12]

Tone's *Argument* tackled hard questions of commerce and political justice. It was wrong 'to hold three millions of our fellow creatures and fellow subjects, in degradation and infamy and contempt, or, to sum up all in one word, in *slavery*'. No parliamentary reform was practicable that excluded the Catholics. The foreign government of the country had at its disposal 'the sword, the purse, and the honors [*sic*] of Ireland'.

The English government knew 'that the Catholics hold the balance between them and that fraction of the nation, which we choose to dignify with the name of *the People*'. In other words England could hold Ireland by professing itself the friend of the Catholics against 'the Protestant nation': those who had won the 'Revolution of 1782'. But the Catholics were not on the side of England.

> In a word, the alternative is, on the one hand, reform and the Catholics, justice and liberty; on the other, an unconditional submission to the present, and every future Administration. . . who may indulge with ease and safety their propensity to peculation and spoil and insult, while the people remain timid and divided.[13]
>
> If [Tone continued] the whole body of the people unite with cordial sincerity, and demand a general reform in parliament, which shall include restitution of the elective franchise to the Catholics, we shall then, and not otherwise, have an honest and independent representation of the people; we shall have a barrier of strength sufficient to defy the utmost efforts of the most profligate and powerful English Administration; we shall be enabled to avail ourselves of the infinite advantages with which Providence has endowed our country; corruption shall be annihilated, government shall become honest per force, and thereby recover at least some of that respectability which a long course of political depravity has exhausted. In a word, we shall recover our rank, and become a nation in something beside the name.
>
> If, on the other hand, we think reform too dear, when purchased by justice; if we are still illiberal and blind bigots, who deny that civil liberty can exist out of the pale of Protestantism, if we withhold the sacred cup of *Liberty* from our Catholic brother, and repel him from the communion of our natural rights, let us at least be consistent, and cease to murmur at the oppression of the government, which grinds us. . . let Administration proceed to play upon the terrors of the Protestants, the hopes of the Catholics, and balance the one party by the other, plunder and laugh at, and defy both; let English influence meet and check our rising commerce at every turn; let us remain obscure and wretched, and unknown in Europe; let the bulk of the people continue barbarians, in hopeless and incurable ignorance, and wretchedness and want. All is well, so long as we can prevent the Catholics from rising to a rank in society with ourselves. . . .[14]

The Birth of the United Irishmen

Tone's argument carried the Presbyterians, despite a 'furious battle' with an 'intolerant high priest' – a Presbyterian minister – who thought Catholic emancipation would mean an inquisition: that there was 'danger, generally, of throwing power into their hands, which would make this a Catholic government, incapable of enjoying or extending liberty'.[15] The first Society of United Irishmen was founded in Belfast on 18 October, 1791.

The movement was unique in Ireland: it had no predecessors and no successors, and it did not seek its title-deeds from history. It was a product of its times: the Enlightenment, the American and French revolutions, the Industrial Revolution. Its creators were Protestants: business and professional men who equated economic self-interest with the national interest. They hoped to create a socially progressive, tolerant and just society in Ireland. The descendants of settlers, they brought 'the Rights of Man' to Ireland and promised equality to all. Times were changing. In Paris the Pope was burned in effigy, Tone noted. In Ireland, the Pope had more power 'than he perhaps ought to have' because persecution had 'bound the Irish Papist to his priest, and the priest to the Pope. . .'. But 'relaxation will undo it'.[16]

Of the twenty-eight founders of the United Irishmen, twenty-six were Presbyterians; two, Wolfe Tone and Thomas Russell, were members of the Established Church; there were no Catholics. Their goal was a reformed parliament. They said nothing about a republic or separation from England. All would agree with Tone that 'the bane of Irish prosperity is in the influence of England'; most perhaps would accept his conclusion that separation 'would be a regeneration for this country'. Like the colonists in America, with whom they were linked by ties of trade, kinship, religion and politics, they must break with the King.[17]

The 'nationalism' of the United Irishmen was revolutionary: they were the first to develop the concept of one nation in Ireland, irrespective of national origin – Gaelic or settler; or sect – Catholic, Protestant or Presbyterian. They had little interest in the Gaelic past, its history or language. Modern men, they were concerned with modern issues: equal representation of all the people in a national parliament, abolition of religious discrimination, economic prosperity. These were not utopian goals in the Ireland of the 1790s. They could be realized, however, only in a democratic secular state. To establish such a state, the Ascendancy caste must be stripped of power. This required an alliance of Presbyterians and Catholics. The founders of the United Irishmen were as rational in politics as in economics.

'We are resolved to keep an established church, an established monarchy, an established aristocracy, and an established democracy, each in the degree it exists, and in no greater,' Burke said.[18] The only establishment the Presbyterians of Belfast would retain was 'democracy'. They were 'most obstinately attached to the principles of Locke, as put in practice at the revolution' (of 1688), one of them explained. 'If such principles are falsely, and for a purpose, said to originate from France, they will not, on that account, renounce them, as little as they did when the very same principles of Locke were illustrated in the plains of America.'[19] Locke's thesis that government exists for the community, not the community for government, was part of their political creed. 'For, when any number of men have, by the consent of every individual, made a community, they have thereby made that community one body, with a power to act as one body, which is only by the will and determination of the majority.' In Locke's representative assembly, 'the act of the majority passes for the act of the whole, and of course determines as having, by the law of nature and reason, the power of the whole'.[20]

The founders of the United Irishmen would establish a representative government with an independent legislature and executive, as in America. The only aspect of US government Wolfe Tone disliked was the presidency. 'What do people want with presidents?' he asked. One man, no matter how worthy and virtuous, should not be given too much power, he thought.[21]

Belfast's Economic Theories

The Belfast founders of the United Irishmen were merchants and manufacturers. After agriculture, linen was the chief industry of Ulster. The farmers produced the flax and were often the weavers; their wives and children spun it. This cottage industry made Ulster relatively prosperous – compared with the rest of the country. No wonder the merchants and manufacturers wanted a responsible, responsive, and representative parliament. The occupations of the founders tell us much about the United Irishmen. William Sinclair was the leading linen manufacturer of Belfast. Henry Joy McCracken was a cotton manufacturer. Samuel Neilson and Henry Haslett were woollen drapers. Gilbert McIlveen was a linen draper. William and Robert Simms were merchants. Thomas McCabe and Thomas Pearce had invented a double loom for the linen trade; Pearce took it to America when the Irish parliament refused to help them. These men believed that England, goaded by jealous competitors, was bent on destroying their manufacture and their commerce and they could get no help from the Irish parliament. The words 'our commerce' appear again and again in their declarations. To take control of parliament they must first break the power of the landed aristocracy. They were economic nationalists.

Tone kept a journal while in Belfast for the delectation of his wife in Dublin; it is full of insights into the thinking of the founding fathers of Irish republicanism. They complained that their industries were hurt by ancient laws enforced by the landlord-controlled Dublin parliament. English power curbed their commerce.[22] With free competition, Ireland could hold its own with Great Britain, Tone was told. Two days before the first open meeting of the United Irishmen, he wrote:

> Nothing to be done until the religious sects here are united and England engaged in a foreign war. If Ireland were free, and well governed, being

that she is unencumbered with debt, she would in arts, commerce and manufacture spring up like an air balloon, and leave England behind her at an immense distance. There is no computing the rapidity with which she would rise. . .[23]

There follows a reference to the matter of the 'double loom' invention of McCabe and Pearce. The Belfast men blamed John Foster, Speaker of the Irish House of Commons, for the treatment the two received in Dublin when they asked support from the Irish parliament.

The loom now in America, and a capital of 500,000 dollars subscribed to carry on the manufacture of linen; workmen the great want in America, which this loom goes precisely to obviate. America improving, silently and unnoticed, in manufactures. . . . Washington has adopted Pearce as his *protegé*, and declares him to be the first man in America. Great superiority of Ireland and John Foster, who can afford to fling away what America and Gen. Washington are glad to pick up. One and all of us damn the governmen. . . .[24]

Russell and Tone rode out to Sinclair's bleach-green and were astonished by the wide use of machinery. They learned that Sinclair was the first manufacturer of Belfast to introduce American potash to Ireland. Others followed. Tone describes a significant conversation:

Almost all the work now done by machinery; done thirty years ago by hand, and all improvements regularly resisted by the people. Mr. Sinclair, sen., often obliged to hire one and sometimes two companies of the garrison, to execute what is now done by one mill. Great command of water, which is omnipotent in the linen. . . . Sinclair a man of very superior understanding. Anecdotes of the linen trade. Nearly independent of England. Seven years ago application made to parliament for a bounty of 14d. per yard; resisted by England; carried at last. Before the bounty, not more than thirty or forty pieces shipped direct for the West Indies from Belfast; now, always fifty, sixty and seventy boxes in every ship. England threatened then to take off the duty in foreign linens, but did not venture it. Ireland able to beat any foreign linens for quality and cheapness, as appears by the American market, which gives no preference by duties, and is supplied entirely by Ireland. If England were disposed she might, for a time, check the trade of Ireland in linens; but she would soon give up that system for her own sake, because she could not be supplied elsewhere so good and so cheap.[25]

To illustrate his point about the superiority of Irish linen, Tone tells of Sinclair shipping some of his products to London as German linen; the royal house of Hanover preferred German products. Tone said Sinclair's shipment was 10 per cent cheaper and 20 per cent better than the German linen. 'Great orders for Irish German linen which he refused to execute. All but the royal family content to take it as mere Irish. *God save great George, our King.*'[26]

Tone's musings indicate that economic grievances were foremost in the minds of Belfast's Presbyterians in the autumn of 1791. If England was at war, as in the early 1780s, a better 'Revolution of 1782' could be won. Tone reports one discussion on the subject. (McTier was one of the most active and radical of the founders.)

> McTier asked what could we do against England. Sinclair hot. He and P.P. (Russell) agree that the army in Ireland would be annihilated, and could not be replaced. Sinclair defies the power of England as to our trade; admits that she could check it for a time, but that, after the revolution, it would spring up with inconceivable rapidity, Ireland being unencumbered with debt. . . . Sinclair bleaches annually 10,000 pieces of linen. P.P. of opinion that the weakness of England should be looked to, as well as that of Ireland; also Mr. Digges, who says, 'The first shot fired by England against this country, down go her stocks'.[27]

The phrase 'after the revolution' is significant.

Organizing Ulster

The movement spread through Ulster, among the Presbyterians, all radicalized by the American experience, according to James Hope, the linen weaver. He told Dr R.R. Madden, biographer of the United Irishmen:'The American struggle taught people that industry has its rights as well as aristocracy'.[28] Samuel Neilson's *Northern Star* carried the message of the brotherhood of man and Catholics and Protestants became 'sworn brothers'. The Catholic agrarian society, the Defenders, shortly became part of the movement in Ulster; but as Thomas Pakenham notes in his study of the rebellion of 1798, they were only 'partly assimilated'. When the Presbyterians of Antrim rose in June 1798 under Henry Joy McCracken, the Defenders did not join them, Pakenham says.[29]

That was in the future. In the early years, according to Hope:

> The influence of the union (United Irishmen) began to be felt at all public places, fairs, markets, and social meetings, extending to all counties of Ulster, for no man of an enlightened mind had intercourse with Belfast, who did not return home determined on disseminating the principles of the union among his neighbours. Strife and quarrelling ceased in all public places, and even intoxication.[30]

Hope's plain narrative tells of the extraordinary change the United Irishmen produced in the politics of Ulster; at any rate in areas where the Presbyterians were the majority. In south Ulster, where Catholics and Anglicans were evenly divided, the old feuding intensified. The issue was land and the landlords encouraged it. When the Protestant Peep O'Day Boys and the Catholic Defenders battled in

County Armagh, Tone and Neilson went to Rathfriland, nearby, to halt the sectarian feuding.

Tone blamed the government, 'who are notoriously spreading the vilest calumnies and falsehoods, to exasperate the two sects against each other, that they may with the greater ease and security plunder both'.[31] The local landlord was also 'much to blame in this business'. The Protestants said a Catholic priest had inflamed the situation; the bishop removed him and wrote a letter to be read in all chapels – as the illegal Catholic churches were called – urging calm. Tone was pleased and proposed at a meeting

> that the Catholics shall agree to desist from parading in bodies and firing, and the Dissenters shall declare that they will maintain the peace of the country against all who shall transgress, without *distinction* of party or religion. An amendment proposed by Neilson, that this declaration should be made by the Volunteers. The idea unanimously approved. . . . [32]

Tone sympathized with the Catholics, who were 'always ready to make peace and keep it'; although not with their priests, who he was glad to note, 'have almost totally lost their influence, since the people have got arms, so fatal to superstition and priestcraft is even the smallest degree of liberty'.[33] He had no patience with any kind of religious fanaticism, but felt the Catholics were the victims in County Armagh and had no choice but to defend themselves. Interestingly enough, Edmund Burke held the same view; indeed he expressed his feeling more vigorously than Tone. Burke believed the Ascendancy encouraged the feuding. 'The sufferers are accused of being the authors of the violence against them,' he wrote.[34] He was enraged when he read that the Catholic clergy had persuaded the Armagh Catholic tenants to surrender their arms. 'Dreadful it is, but it is now plain enough, that Catholic *defenderism* is the only restraint upon Protestant Ascendancy.'[35]

Dublin United Irishmen

The chief men of the Dublin Society of United Irishmen, which began a few weeks after the Belfast meeting, were James Napper Tandy, a radical democrat, and Dr William Drennan, a Belfast-born Presbyterian physician and doctrinaire republican, who wrote most of its declarations. William James McNevin, a Catholic physician educated on the Continent, and Richard McCormick, secretary of the Catholic Committee, were among others. Younger members of the gentry included Simon Butler, Lord Mountgarrett's brother; Alexander Hamilton Rowan, a landowner; and later, Lord Edward

Fitzgerald, brother of the Duke of Leinster. Arthur O'Connor, a Whig MP (like Fitzgerald) was also a member. There were lawyers like Thomas Addis Emmet, son of the state physician, and the brothers, Henry and John Sheares; manufacturers like Henry Jackson, who had three steam engines working his Dublin foundries; merchants like Oliver Bond. When the movement spread to Cork it consisted, according to a government report, of 'shopkeepers, merchants' clerks, one or two physicians, farmers . . . and very young men who attend for the pleasure of debate. . . . They were all Protestants.'[36]

The doctrines of the United Irishmen were widely disseminated. During the Wexford rebellion, in 1798, which was led by Catholic priests, the proclamations of the rebels promised protection to all religious denominations, spoke of the rights of man and the right 'of *all* Irish citizens to all the land'.[37]

In 1794 the Dublin United Irishmen proposed a plan of parliamentary reform, including universal (manhood) suffrage, equal electoral districts, annual parliaments, no property qualification for public representatives, payment of members of parliament. In only one particular did it differ from the six points of the People's Charter a half-century later: voice vote instead of a secret ballot.[38]

In a few years the political principles expounded by the Ulster Dissenters spread through Ireland; committees of correspondence, as in pre-revolution America, linked the various United Irish societies into a national movement. They were in advance of their brethren in Britain on the question of Catholic rights,[39] thanks to Tone's pamphlet. And they could assert, as Dr William Drennan did:

> I have made but poor claims for attention, in having, without scruple, professed myself an United Irishman, a Protestant Dissenter, and an advocate for Universal Suffrage: yet, a sense of superior obligation impels me to declare, before the face of man, as I do in the sight of God, that I believe in union among Irishmen, the only solid basis of national prosperity; a right of private judgment, the ground of true christianity; and an equalization of the elective franchise, the surest means of averting danger, and appeasing the spirit of the times.[40]

Burke and the United Irishmen

The Catholic peasantry did not join the United Irishmen until after 1796, when Dublin Castle and the Ascendancy forced them to weigh rebellion against their wretched condition. Middle-class Catholics joined the United Irishmen, not for love of the principles of the French Revolution, one must assume – for these were denounced by bishops and the exiled Irish nobility in the service of the *ancien regime* – but because the United Irishmen advocated equal rights and in Dublin some leading United Irishmen were Catholics.

Edmund Burke combined the impossible tasks of assuring England that for reasons of justice and tactics it should abolish the penal code to keep the Catholics from joining the United Irishmen, who in his view were Jacobins, while advising the Catholic leaders that the Ascendancy – 'a junto of robbers,' in his words – not the British government was responsible for their grievances. Unlike the founders of the United Irishmen, Burke was of native Irish Catholic stock. Educated in a hedge school by his mother's people, the Nagles of Ballyduff, near Castletown-Roche, County Cork, from the age of six to eleven, quite likely he knew Irish and spoke it. His teacher was a Master O'Halloran. Then he was sent to a boarding school at Ballitore, County Kildare, run by a Yorkshire Quaker, Abraham Shackleton, and to Trinity College, Dublin. Burke had a wide knowledge of his country's history and was clearly moved by the condition of his people; but after he went to England to study law he made his career there and his attachment to that country's institutions was genuine. He helped shape its policies. But his attachment to Ireland and his hatred of the Protestant Ascendancy hardly altered for all his years in England. Indeed, he entered English politics in the hope 'without injury to this country [England], to be somewhat useful to the place of my birth and education, which in many respects, internal and external, I thought ill and impolitically governed'.[41] He shared with Montesquieu the view that Ireland was a conquered country ruled by a foreign oligarchy. He supported all proposals to end curbs on Irish manufactures and trade.

'What was done, was not in the spirit of a contest between two religious factions; but between two adverse nations,' Burke wrote. 'The statutes of Kilkenny show that the spirit of the popery laws, and some even of their actual provisions, as applied between Englishry and Irishry, had existed in that harassed country before the words Protestant and Papist were heard of in the world.' Confiscations, inquisitions, 'the total extirpation of the natives in their own soil . . . kindled the flames of that rebellion which broke out in 1641.' Ireland was conquered again in 1691 and 'the ruin of the native Irish' accomplished. The victors used the penal laws to trample on a conquered people. When the English interest in Ireland became 'an independent Irish interest', the Revolution of 1782 occurred; parliament and nation became independent, Burke professed to believe.[42]

In naming Burke's son, Richard, political agent of the Catholic

Committee, in August 1790, the chief men of that organization affirmed that they knew the opinions of the father on the Catholic question, calling him 'our much admired countryman'. Edmund Burke tendered his advice through his son, which may be what the Committee wanted. More than any other public figure in England or Ireland, Edmund Burke understood the Irish question. He saw the need of Catholic emancipation because of the threat of revolutionary France.

The Catholic Relief Act of 1793[43] was a half-measure and Burke feared the Catholics would join the United Irishmen, he told Richard:

> The existence of quite another system of opinions and interests [than Protestant and Catholic] is now plain to the grossest sense. Are these the questions that raise a flame in the minds of men at this day? If ever the Church and the Constitution of England should fall in these islands (and they will fall together) it is not Presbyterian discipline nor Popish hierarchy that will rise upon their ruins. It will not be the Church of Rome nor the Church of Scotland, nor the Church of Calvin. On the contrary, all these churches are menaced, and menaced alike. It is the new fanatical religion, now in the heat of its first ferment, of the Rights of Man, which rejects all establishments, all discipline, all ecclesiastical, and in truth all civil order, which will triumph, and which will lay prostrate your Church, which will destroy your distinctions, and which will put all your properties to auction, and disperse you over the earth. If the present establishment should fall, it is this religion which will triumph in Ireland and in England, as it has triumphed in France. This religion, which laughs at creeds and dogmas and confessions of faith, may be fomented equally amongst all descriptions and all sects – amongst nominal Catholics, and amongst nominal Churchmen, and amongst those Dissenters who know little and care less about a presbytery, or any of its discipline, or any of its doctrine. Against this new, this growing, this exterminatory system, all these churches have a common concern to defend themselves. How the enthusiasts of this rising sect rejoice to see you of the old churches play their game, and stir and rake the cinders of animosities sunk in their ashes, in order to keep up the execution of their plan for your common ruin.[44]

Jacobin Danger to Ireland

Burke's fear of 'French principles' spreading among the Irish peasantry was based on economic reasoning. Like Marx later, Burke believed that Irish discontent was fundamentally economic. 'Alas! It is not about popes but about potatoes, that the mind of this unhappy people are agitated,' he told Richard in the letter quoted above. The solution for Ireland, he thought, was to give the remnants of the Catholic gentry full civil rights – he estimated there were a dozen to a score of such families left; establish seminaries for the education of Catholic priests; give the Catholic Church joint (established) status with the Anglican, as in Canada; make the Irish parliament truly representative of the property of Ireland by including Catholics; and bind Ireland to England in the unity of Empire. This was Grattan's programme too. Burke and Grattan remained political allies.

Burke believed his programme would ensure the loyalty of the Catholics of Ireland to the Crown of England and insulate them from the alien influence of the United Irishmen. Although Pitt was willing to listen, particularly after the Portland Whigs joined the coalition government, Burke's hopes of an independent kingdom of Ireland sharing the same sovereign with Great Britain was thwarted by the Ascendancy. Communities should be bound together by 'solid interest', not 'by coercion and force of arms', he told the Master of the Society of Merchants Adventurers of Bristol in April 1778, when he argued for Irish free trade, and appeared not to understand that the basis of conquest and empire is exploitation of the conquered in the interests of the conqueror. His one success was the College of St Patrick, established at Maynooth, in 1795, under the control of the Catholic bishops and bound to the Crown by statute oath.[45]

Ironically, Richard Burke's successor as political agent of the Catholic Committee was Wolfe Tone, who held the post during discussion of the 1793 Catholic Relief Bill. Tone travelled to London, via Belfast significantly, with a Catholic delegation; the Dissenters greeted them effusively and the gesture was not lost on the government. It riled the Ascendancy and hardly pleased Burke. Tone thought the Catholic leaders too timid for accepting half a loaf when they had so many advantages on their side. He had helped organize the Catholic Convention – the derisively named 'Back Lane Parliament' – in Dublin, early in December 1792. Backed by three million people, the Catholics 'had thundered out their demands,' said Tone, 'supported by all the spirit and intelligence of the Dissenters'.[46] But the Ascendancy insisted on excluding them from parliament – and carried the day.

The leaders of the Catholic Committee were Dublin merchants and Tone detected a 'sneaking spirit of compromise' in their counsels. 'As for merchants,' he wrote, 'I begin to see they are no great hands at revolutions.'[47]

If Tone saw the Dissenters as the saviours of the Catholics, Burke considered them a danger, not only to the Catholics but to Britain in the era of the French Revolution. In the letter to Langrishe, Burke wrote:

> Certain Protestant dissenters make seditious propositions to the Catholics, which it does not appear that they have yet accepted. It would be strange that the tempter should escape all punishment, and that he who, under circumstances full of seduction and full of provocation, has resisted the temptation, should incur the penalty. You know, that, in regard to the dissenters, who are *stated* to be the chief movers in this vile scheme of altering the principles of election to a right of voting by the head, you are not able to deprive them (if you ought even to wish such a thing) to deprive them of any part of the franchises and privileges which they hold on a footing of perfect equality with yourselves. *They* may do what they please with constitutional impunity; but the others cannot even listen with civility to an invitation from them to an ill-judged scheme of liberty, without forfeiting, for ever, all hopes of those liberties which we admit to be sober and rational.[48]

The 'others', of course, were the Catholics.

If the Catholics rejected political union with the Dissenters, would they win their rights? 'Oh, no, nothing at all like it!' The Dissenters offered the Catholics full constitutional rights; the Ascendancy refused them everything. 'The terms of alliance, from the dissenters, offer a representation of the commons, chosen out of the people by the head.' Burke did not like the electoral representation plan or its advocates, 'but if the question was to be put to you and me – *universal* popular representation, *or none at all for us and ours* – we should find ourselves in a very awkward position'.[49] Would it be safer for the establishment if the Catholics decided that their only way into the constitution was through the Dissenters? This 'bank of discontent' was every hour accumulating and seditious men could draw from it at pleasure.[50] 'On the other hand, they who wish for a democratic republic, will find a set of men who have no choice between civil servitude, and the entire ruin of a mixed constitution.'[51]

If the Ascendancy class – 'a handful of gentlemen, clergy and their dependents' – could not deal with this 'blind popular fury', rather than permitting such persons to a share in their franchises, 'they would throw up their independence and precipitate a union with Great Britain'. Burke's view of such union was 'it would not be for the mutual advantage of the two kingdoms'.[52]

The half-measure of 1793 did not conciliate the Catholics. Meagre as it was, the Ascendancy continued to ignore its provisions, as Burke learned a few days before Christmas 1793 from Bishop Francis Moylan of Cork. The Catholics thought 'that if the republicans in France were entirely suppressed, the favour granted would be retracted and their old chains riveted on them stronger than before',

Moylan wrote. The administration was as bigoted as ever. 'However, in such critical times, all friends of order, and the rulers, should rally about the throne, and speak aloud their sentiments and opinions,' he added. The Catholic bishops had drawn up an address of loyalty to the Crown and gratitude to George III personally 'for the concessions made to their body'. Bishop Moylan then assured Burke:

> This will serve to show to government, that the disaffection and republican opinion held by some weak Roman Catholics of the capital, are far from receiving any countenance from us, as has been most falsely and unjustly inculcated. It strikes me likewise, that such an address may also serve to prepare the way for application to be made at your side of the water, in favour of our clerical education.[53]

The fact that 'some weak Roman Catholics of the capital', meaning members of the Catholic Committee, held republican opinions, alarmed Burke. On 30 December, 1793 he wrote to Sylvester Douglas, Chief Secretary of Ireland, warning him that 'Ireland is in danger of being Jacobinized'. He blamed what he called 'the Click' – the Protestant Ascendancy – and his venom against the 'cabal' spilled over into his letter. 'They have a way of forcing people into disaffection,' he wrote, 'by acting towards them as if they were in Rebellion. This last part of the System is a trade carried on in Ireland for six hundred years and of course a long experience has made them perfect in it. . . .' He warned the newly-appointed Chief Secretary that the oligarchy 'represent themselves as the only persons true to the Monarchy, in order to prevail on the Monarchy to surrender its whole powers without a possibility of provocation into their hands'. Otherwise, he said, Ireland was a very pleasant country. He thought the best man in Ireland for a Chief Secretary to consult was Grattan, leader of the opposition in Dublin.[54]

There was speculation in the summer of 1794, when Pitt formed his coalition Cabinet with those Whigs who accepted Burke's opinions on the French Revolution, that Richard Burke would be named Chief Secretary of Ireland. Burke's influence with the new government was strong. (Burke over-estimated his son's abilities. When he retired from the House of Commons in June 1794, Richard took the seat, but died in August of consumption. Burke never recovered from the blow.) When Earl Fitzwilliam, nephew of Burke's patron the Marquis of Rockingham, became Lord Lieutenant of Ireland, the Catholics expected emancipation. Despite Burke's support and advice, Fitzwilliam failed to break the power of the Protestant Ascendancy 'cabal' in Dublin, who had made Ireland 'a back door for Jacobinism, to rush in expenses, and take us from the rear'. Ireland would be either 'a strong digue [dike] to keep out Jacobinism, or a broken bank to let it in', Burke cautioned. Jacobinism could be defeated in Ireland but power must be taken from the 'corrupt hands' of the 'cabal'.[55] Fitzwilliam tried and lost. Pitt would not support him.

The recall of Fitzwilliam put Ireland 'on the brink of civil war', Father Hussey, first president of Maynooth seminary, wrote to Burke.[56] Jacobinism was 'the channel in which all discontents will run', Burke told Fitzwilliam. Property could not stand against it alone.[57] But the threat of Jacobinism meant less to the Ascendancy than the threat to their privileges.

Burke lost the struggle against the United Irishmen when Fitzwilliam was recalled. As Burke would see it, the result was that the most staunchly Catholic people in Europe took the side of 'the armed doctrine' of the anti-clerical regicides in Paris. Burke did not seem to understand that justice for the Catholics of Ireland would mean the end of Protestant Ascendancy; and that would have weakened English rule in Ireland. When it came to a choice between justice and security, British governments – before and after Pitt – always chose security and the colonial interest in Ireland.

'The connection between England and Ireland rests absolutely on Protestant Ascendancy,' said Chief Secretary Hobart in 1792. If Ascendancy power was broken, the Catholics would take over. 'While you maintain the Protestant Ascendancy the ruling powers in Ireland look to England as the foundation of their authority,' Hobart continued. 'A Catholic government could maintain itself without the aid of England, and must inevitably produce a separation of the Executive which would speedily be followed by a separation between the countries.'[58] The Viceroy of the time, Lord Westmoreland, held a similar view and issued a similar warning. He told Pitt: 'Reflect what Ireland would be in opposition to England, and you will see the necessity of some very strong interior power or management that will render Ireland subservient to the general orders of the Empire.'[59] Pitt evidently accepted the advice of his officials in Ireland and rejected Burke's arguments.

Wolfe Tone in Exile

Wolfe Tone understood the matter perfectly. If power politics were to decide Ireland's future, then the Irish must play the same game by seeking the aid of England's enemy. If the alternative to Protestant Ascendancy was Catholic domination, then a revolutionary way had to be found to unite Catholics and Protestants against the

Ascendancy and England: an alliance of the middle class and the peasantry.

Three months after Fitzwilliam's recall, Tone went into exile – first in America, then in France – and did not return till the autumn of 1798, when he was captured, tried, and sentenced to death. Before leaving Belfast he took 'a solemn obligation', with other United Irish leaders, 'never to desist in our efforts, until we had subverted the authority of England over our country, and asserted her independence'.[60] The scene at Cave Hill, overlooking Belfast, has much symbolism for Irish republican ideology and sanctions later efforts by Irish revolutionaries to seek the aid of England's enemies for Ireland's freedom. It is Ireland's ultimate power-play against England. But it has never been applied with anything approaching Tone's skill.

The influence of priests was at least as strong among the Irish peasantry as that of French priests among the peasants of the *Vendée*, who opposed the revolution in arms. The Vendéan peasants were royalists because they were Catholics. The Irish Catholics were 'Jacobins' because they were Irish and France was the enemy of England, although republicanism was anathema to the Church. As Tone explained in a memorandum for the Committee of Public Safety, in the spring of 1794:

> In Ireland, a conquered and oppressed and insulted country, the name of England and her power is universally odious, save with those who have an interest in maintaining it, such as the Government and its connections, the Church and its dependencies, the great landed property, etc.; but the power of these people, being founded on property, the first convulsion would level it with the dust. On the contrary, the great bulk of the people would probably throw off the yoke, if they saw any force in the country sufficiently strong to resort to for defence.[61]

The Catholics had a 'hatred for the English name'. The Dissenters of the North were 'enemies to the English power, from reason and reflection', republicans by conviction, Tone said. William Drennan put the matter another way in his letter to Lord Fitzwilliam at the start of 1795. The Catholics had been 'always the devoted friends, and too often the devoted victims of, royalty'. But the Dissenters had made them republicans, and 'roused [them] from the sleep of ages, by the demon of democracy, by the satanic yell of John Calvin and John Knox'.

> The political pale is broken down, and the Papist and Presbyterian, after wondering at each other, like the visitors and natives of your new-discovered

islands, have concluded, from the resemblance of their faces and their hands, that their hearts, and what is more, their interests, must be the same; and are at this instant, beginning to form that nation into a family compact, formidable, as I think, to the sovereignty of your house, and to the integrity of the empire. . . .[62]

From this one might conclude that the principles of the United Irishmen were as much Protestant as Jacobin; they owed nothing to Catholicism. The 'cordial union' with the Catholics was based on political ideology; they maintained their suspicions of popes and priests. Their values were Protestant and revolutionary: the Reformation, the Commonwealth, 'the Glorious Revolution', the American Revolution, 'the Revolution of 1782', the Volunteers, the fall of the Bastille. Stories out of Wexford in the summer of 1798 rekindled some of the old animosities: Protestants were killed by Catholic adherents of United Irish principles. The Belfast papers wrote of priests leading mobs in a religious war of forcible conversions.[63] That was the end of the United Irish alliance and Orangeism became a force in Ulster.

The values of the Catholics remained traditionalist: land, altar, country. These were the values of the peasants of the *Vendée*, too. Burke denounced Jacobinism as a war against religion, a system that excited 'the lowest description of the people to range themselves under ambitious men for the pillage and destruction of the more eminent orders and classes of the community'.[64]

Popular fury against oppression does not depend on Jacobin doctrine, *pace* Burke. When a French force of a thousand men landed at Killala, in August 1798, too late to help either the Catholic rebels of the south, or Presbyterian rebels of the north, the peasantry of Mayo, Gaelic to a man, followed them into battle against the English.[65] Was this, too, the power of Jacobin doctrine? Or was it something much older, more traditionalist? Perhaps here is proof that Irish nationalism is a product, not of the French Revolution, though influenced by that event, but of English rule in Ireland, and of its agent, the Ascendancy.

The Doctrine of the United Irishmen

In the duel between Burke and Tone for the allegiance of the Irish people, Tone was victorious in the end, not because his arguments were better, but because he was condemned to death for his part in the rebellion and died in prison. His view that Ireland must break the connection with England has prevailed; Burke's contrary view is forgotten: as indeed is Burke himself among the common people.

The United Irishmen lost because the French lost. Although the United Irish movement represented only a minority of the population as far as its principles were concerned, it spoke for the mass of the people in demanding independence.

What type of Ireland would have emerged from a United Irish-French victory in 1798? A proclamation prepared for Hoche's expedition to Bantry Bay declared that the Irish would decide their own form of government. Some of the ideas echo Tone, but the style is not his. 'This is no longer the miserable strife between the house of Hanover and that of the Stuards [sic], the one to remain, the other to become again your despot,' it said. 'No. – True Republicans fight only to vindicate the Rights of Equality and detest even the name of a Master.'[66]

The manifestoes Tone prepared for the same landing were designed to appeal to the Catholic peasantry. They attacked the aristocracy, promised a representative government that would aid Irish commerce, protect Irish manufacture and promote Irish art, and enlighten the minds of the people. Church and state would be separated and tithes abolished. Men would win place and promotion according to merit and talents, rather than birth.

> Our commerce shall extend into the four quarters of the globe; our flag shall be seen on the ocean; our name shall be known among the nations; and we shall at length assume that station, for which God and nature have designed us. . . .[67]

A second manifesto may have been designed by Tone for the Ulster Dissenters. More ideological than the first, it attacked anti-French statements by the Catholic Church, whose 'aim is obvious'. It promised 'to promote your commercial interest, while confirming your independence'.[68]

As it happened, of course, no one in Ireland read these documents, because – as Burke put it – 'our best allies, the storms of heaven' protected Ireland that Christmas of 1796 from the 'old practiced assassin – Hoche'.[69] Burke's friend, Bishop Francis Moylan of Cork, denounced the French in a pastoral letter read at all masses. Germany, Italy, Holland and France itself could 'attest the irreparable ruin, desolation and destruction occasioned by French fraternity', he warned his flock. Other bishops wrote in similar vein.[70]

It is safe to assume that had the United Irishmen succeeded there would have been conflict with the the Catholic Church. The United Irishmen were anti-clerical in a way no successor republican organization could afford to be. Tone had scant patience with prelates who opposed him. In his last published letter Burke claimed the influence of the priests had kept Ireland from Jacobinism, while the repression of the Ascendancy 'junto' had helped to spread its doctrines. Hoche, 'a pure Protestant', led an army untainted by 'Popery', Burke wrote. If successful he would have destroyed Irish Catholicism in a month.[71]

It is idle speculation. Tone put that and other matters at rest when he told the court of military officers trying him for treason: 'In a cause like this success is everything. Success in the eyes of the vulgar, fixes its merits. Washington succeeded, Kosciusko failed.'[72]

Wolfe Tone was a political realist. His understanding of the play of economic and political interests was Madisonian – as in *The Federalist* No. 10 – and these interests shaped the ideas of the United Irishmen, not the other way around. Because of certain historical conditions an attempt was made to ally middle-class Presbyterians and Catholics, and the peasant masses. As conditions changed in the nineteenth century, after the Act of Union with Great Britain was rammed through the Irish parliament because of the rebellion of 1798,[73] some of the *ideas* and tactics of the United Irishmen were retained by the physical-force wing of Irish nationalism: separation from England, a secular republic, non-confessional politics, support for independence from England's enemies. But it lacked a Protestant base.

Tone's rational republicanism, with all its anti-clerical overtones, was rejected by Protestants and accepted by Catholics, who then purified it of its anti-Catholicism. In consequence the chief anti-cleric of Irish history, who in the spring of 1798, when the French captured Pius VI and Rome became a republic, wrote in his diary that here was 'an opportunity to destroy for ever the papal tyranny', adding 'He is now a prelate *in partibus,* his means are gone, his cardinals, his court, his wealth, all disappeared and nothing remains but his keys', is a hero to ardent Catholics. Tone could write after a visit to the cathedral of Rouen: 'Heard part of a sermon, this being Easter Sunday. Sad trash. . . . The church was full of women, but I did not see twenty men. I wonder how people can listen to such abominable nonsense.'[74] What matters is that Tone fought England and championed Catholic Ireland. He is 'the father of Irish Republicanism'. The descendants of the original United Irishmen, meanwhile, consider the doctrines of their ancestors, as interpreted today, an ideological mask for Catholic domination.

The change in ideology by the Protestants of Ulster must be seen as a change in the way they have perceived their economic interest.

In the nineteenth century the trade and manufactures of Protestant Ulster expanded with the empire. Belfast grew from a town of 20,000 people at the start of the century to more than 300,000 at the close. Britain supplied the raw materials and markets for Belfast's products. In the hey-day of capitalism Belfast was an outpost of British industry and profited accordingly. Linen, heavy engineering and shipbuilding prospered. Ulster's Presbyterians remained liberal in politics, but not republican.[75] Nationalism was seen, rightly perhaps, as the political movement of Irish Catholics, and Protestants opposed it.

When W.E. Gladstone introduced the first Home Rule for Ireland Bill, in 1886, the Presbyterians of Ulster joined other Protestants in opposing it; to maintain the union with Britain they joined the Orange Order.[76] Orangeism united Protestant capital and labour against a self-governing Ireland, which would impose tariffs and taxes on Ulster industry. From all this, the partition of Ireland seems an inevitable development. For fifty years – June 1921 to March 1972 – Northern Ireland was ruled by a Protestant Ascendancy not unlike the one Burke and Tone had denounced, and was opposed by a form of 'Catholic defenderism'.[77]

The Constitution of Ireland

The republican tradition of Tone and the United Irishmen was the ideal of the nationalist struggle for independence that culminated in 1921 when Catholic Ireland won Dominion status, like Canada, Australia, New Zealand, South Africa; the new state was rejected by Republicans because of partition and the link with the Crown.[78] In 1937 the Republican leader, Eamon de Valera, gave the Irish Free State a new name and Constitution.[79] The state claims its title deeds stem from the United Irishmen.[80] But the Constitution is a Catholic document, for a Catholic state, and has little connection with the secular republic of Tone's ideology.

De Valera, architect of the modern Irish state, would consider himself an heir of the United Irish tradition; yet his 1937 Constitution is based on 'Catholic principles', according to his authorized biographers.[81] He drafted it following a study of encyclicals and declarations by Popes Pius VII, Leo XIII, and Pius XI, the Constitutions of Poland (1921) and Austria (1934): the latter, the handiwork of Kurt von Schuschnigg, made Austria a corporate state. De Valera was under strong clerical pressure to produce a Catholic Constitution. The Catholic Church was given a 'special position', as the religion of the majority under Article 44, which was excised after a referendum in November 1972, with the consent of the Irish Catholic bishops.

Articles 2 and 3 claim that the 'national territory' consists of the whole island of Ireland; but effective jurisdiction, pending 're-integration of the national territory', is confined to the area of the Free State. The Catholic Church retains a strong influence over legislation and politics.[82]

This is far removed from the ideology of Wolfe Tone and the United Irishmen: the union in one nation of all persons who live in Ireland.

III
The Romantic Nationalism of Young Ireland

Irish nationalism created a mass movement before it developed an ideology. The usual order starts with an ideology; this is a matter for poets, scholars and journalists. They base the ideology on language, literature and history. Then they try to build a popular movement, small at first, the members drawn from the middle class.

In Ireland there was little need for ideology. The priests mobilized a great peasant army for O'Connell to lead and guide, a popular democracy, the first of its kind in Europe. Within a few years Ireland, in the words of Gustave de Beaumont, was 'a nation constitutionally in revolt'.[1] The movement was created out of the misery of the Irish poor and their religious, economic and national grievances. They really believed that Catholic emancipation meant *their* emancipation, for *they* won it. The Duke of Wellington proposed Catholic emancipation because the alternative was civil war, or so he feared. It did not touch peasant grievances – tithes, rack rents, insecurity of tenure. During his travels in Ireland in the mid-1830s, Alexis de Tocqueville learned of peasant disillusionment after emancipation:

> The law does nothing for us. We must save ourselves. We have a little land which we need for ourselves and our families to live on, and they drive us out of it. To whom should we address ourselves? Emancipation has done nothing for us. Mr O'Connell and the rich Catholics go to parliament. We die of starvation just the same.[2]

Emancipation meant that middle-class Catholics could sit in parliament, hold state offices, judgeships, commissions in the army and navy. Those who marched for it, in non-violent demonstrations, and voted openly against their landlords under threat of eviction, won nothing, it seemed. In the 1830s they used physical force, rather than O'Connell's 'moral force', against tithe collectors – proctors, police and soldiers – and won a partial victory in 1838 with the parliamentary support of O'Connell, who had become an ally of the 'base, brutal and bloody' Whigs.[3] In return, the Whigs gave O'Connell much of the patronage of Ireland. O'Connell traded grievances for favours. There was no principle involved, it seemed. It was good practical politics. It was for this reason, perhaps, that Giuseppe Mazzini decided that the Irish national movement was not 'nationalist' as he understood the term. It lacked high moral purpose.[4]

Mazzini's romantic nationalism had little appeal for O'Connell. He knew the Ossian cult that gave birth to European romanticism at first hand – from the source, as it were, rather than via Macpherson's fraudulent Gaelic 'translations'. (Macpherson's Ossian of course was the Irish *Oisin*[5], who went to the Land of Youth; he had nothing to do with the rise of Irish nationalism.) O'Connell was of minor Catholic gentry in Irish-speaking Kerry. An uncle was a colonel in the Irish Brigade of France, and Daniel was educated in Douai. He had no sympathy with the Revolution and his horror of bloodshed was popularly believed to stem from scenes he witnessed in France, but there appears to be little truth in this. His uncle, the colonel, fought against the Revolution, and it is fair to say that, despite his later liberalism, the young O'Connell, like his family, was a monarchist and his French Catholic schooling reinforced his conservatism.

O'Connell was a lawyer, a land-owner – a middleman who rented his estates – a brewer and a banker. He received a yearly 'tribute' from the Irish peasantry who idolized him as Ireland's champion against England.[6] The English establishment hated him: *The Times* and *Punch* portrayed him as the archetypal Irish rebel. He was in fact a nineteenth-century Whig, a Benthamite utilitarian, who believed in 'the greatest happiness of the greatest number', which O'Connell equated with 'justice' for the Catholics of Ireland. 'Justice' sometimes meant legal concessions but in the long term it meant restoration of the Irish parliament – representative of the Catholic middle class rather than the Protestant landlords, but by no means exclusively Catholic. When his allies, the Whigs, were in office, O'Connell said little about repealing the Union. But when the Tories came to power, in 1841, he made 'Repeal' the issue.

O'Connell advocated liberal causes. He supported civil rights for Jews (otherwise, he said, freedom of conscience was meaningless), the liberation of South America from Spain, the freedom of Poland and Belgium, and the unification of Italy. He believed in separation of Church and state, perhaps because in Ireland the 'Established Church' was Anglican and the 'Established state' English. He opposed slavery and told the Irish in America to do likewise, with little success. Early in his career he rejected a Catholic-controlled Ireland, in words that echoed Wolfe Tone:

> The Protestant alone could not expect to liberate his country, the Roman Catholic could not do it, neither could the Presbyterian – but amalgamate the three into the Irishman and the Union was repealed.[7]

Whatever his intention, O'Connell created a Catholic movement. His 1840s Repeal campaign was the 'Catholic Association' of the 1820s under a slightly-changed name, 'the Repeal Association'. There were some Protestant supporters but, as in the 1820s, the rank-and-file of the peasantry was clerical-dominated and the country priests were the officers of O'Connell's Repeal army.[8]

Thomas Davis and The Nation

Ireland in 1841 had 8,175,124 people, according to the census; it was the most densely populated country in Europe, Disraeli said. To win an Irish parliament, support of Protestants was essential; otherwise confessional politics would prevail. O'Connell never contemplated Catholic ascendancy, but Protestants distrusted him. Needing Protestant allies of national outlook, he discovered a way of reaching them through a weekly journal, *The Nation,* which began publication in October of 1842. The chief writer of the *Nation* was Thomas Davis, a Protestant barrister and graduate of Trinity College, Dublin, whose hobby was Irish history. With two Catholics, Charles Gavan Duffy and John Blake Dillon, he founded the *Nation* to make the Irish more conscious of their nationality and history. The *Nation* was 'racy of the soil'. Its writers received the name 'Young Ireland', although that was not of their doing. Young Ireland gave Irish nationalism an ideology, in part taken from the United Irishmen (non-sectarianism and the secular state), in part borrowed from European romantic nationalism. Young Ireland looked to France rather than to England for political ideas, and its nationalism embraced all Irishmen, as Davis explained:

> It must contain and represent all the races of Ireland. It must not be Celtic; it must not be Saxon; it must be Irish. The Brehon law, and the maxims of Westminster – the cloudy and lightning genius of the Gael, the placid strength of the Sacsanach, the marshalling insight of the Norman – a literature which shall exhibit in combination the passions and idioms of all, and which shall equally express our mind, in its romantic, its religious, its forensic, and its practical tendencies – finally, a native government, which shall know and rule by the might and right of all, yet yield to the arrogance of none – these are the components of such a nationality.[9]

Unlike Tone, who rarely spoke of Gaelic Ireland, the romantic Davis was forever tracing the roots of Irish culture. Yet he insisted that the new Irish nation could not be purely Gaelic. The English Pale, the Ulster settlement, 'and the filtered colonization of men and ideas', were also a part of Irish history. Swift and Grattan saw an anglicized Ireland of settlers. 'They mistook Ireland for a colony wronged, and great enough to be a nation.'[10] The Irish must 'sink the distinctions of blood as well as of sect', combine the descendants of Gaels, Normans, Welsh, Saxons and Scots, Catholics and Protestants in a union making 'for a tolerant and flexible character in literature, manners, religion, and life, of any nation on earth'.[11] Davis's nationalism was more cultural than political. The first step to nationality is the open and deliberate recognition of it by the people themselves. . . . Ireland must bid all whom it concerns to know that her interests are separate and her rights peculiar.'[12] This nationalism would create 'a race of men full of a more intensely Irish character and knowledge, and to that race it would give Ireland', he wrote. 'It would give them the seas of Ireland, to sweep with their nets and launch on with their navy; the harbours of Ireland, to receive a greater commerce than any island in the world; the soil of Ireland to live on, by more millions than starve here now; the fame of Ireland to enhance by their genius and valour; the Independence of Ireland to guard by laws and arms.'[13]

Young Ireland did not attempt to define the nation. They seemed to think that before their time there was no Irish nation. In explaining why they decided to found a weekly, Gavan Duffy, the editor, wrote: 'We desired to make Ireland a nation and the name would be a fitting prelude to the attempt.'[14] The weekly would preach 'self-reliance and self-respect which misgovernment had nearly extinguished in the mass of the people'.[15] Apart from the household names, Brian Boru, Patrick Sarsfield, Henry Grattan, Lord Edward Fitzgerald, the Irish people knew no history.[16] 'The leaders of '98 would doubtless have furnished other popular idols but that O'Connell continually disparaged them, and their names were seldom mentioned on the public platform.'[17] O'Connell's purpose was to remove the 'rebel' stigma from Irish Catholics, to prove they were as loyal as Protestants; he denounced physical force, because no cause was worth the shedding of human blood. Young Ireland felt that the use or non-use of force in Irish politics, was a matter of tactics, not a principle. They were willing to accept O'Connell's leadership, but reserved the right to criticize and disagree with him – a right 'the Liberator' rarely conceded to his followers.

Davis, a sensitive, studious man, was the opposite of the big, bluff, outgoing O'Connell. Like Tone, Davis began political life as a member of Trinity College's Historical Society, which Edmund

Burke had founded, going on to study law and then to pamphleteering as a radical Whig. He wrote for a monthly journal, *The Citizen*, on land tenure in Norway, a country he admired, British rule in India, and the Irish parliament of James II, which, he said, 'established liberty of conscience and equality of creeds. . .'. Davis seems to lean towards the Catholic-Gaelic side historically, unlike Tone who felt the Irish had no business supporting the Stuarts. But Davis proved that the Irish parliament of 1689 was not the bigoted body its enemies said it was; he was perhaps the first to note that 'the idea of 1782 is to be found full grown in 1689, the pedigree of our freedom is a century older than we thought, and Ireland has another parliament to be proud of'.[18]

Duffy and Davis agreed that the best way to teach history to a semi-literate people was through ballads. In this way they would foster national feeling and the hope of freedom. Sir Samuel Ferguson (1810–86) rather than Davis, is the father of this school of heroic poetry. He translated Gaelic poems for the *Dublin University Magazine* in 1834. Yeats linked him with Davis as a national writer. ('Davis, looking into the future, saw Ireland free and prospering', Yeats wrote. 'Ferguson saw her in the past before the curse had fallen.') Davis, a late beginner, turned out fifty ballads in three years, and they are still sung in Ireland. He studied Scott and Macaulay as models, and he was not a good poet, as Yeats points out.[19] But he was a good craftsman and his readers, who had gone to the new National Schools, learned his verse by rote.[20] There is more of Jacobitism than Jacobinism in his ballads and some, like 'Fontenoy', about the Irish Brigade turning defeat to victory, were considered seditious as late as 1920.[21]

The best poet of the *Nation* was James Clarence Mangan, the best prose writer John Mitchel, the best political analyst James Fintan Lalor – who wrote a few letters to the editor in 1847–48. Mitchel and Lalor, probably, were as influential as Davis; but much of what they wrote is dated because they dealt with contemporary affairs not the future, while Davis's essays are still worth reading. Yeats found them informative but dry.

A Secular Ideal

Davis urged the unity of Protestants and Catholics – they seem more disunited now than in the 1840s when he was writing – and pressed for undenominational education, which still does not exist below university level in Ireland. He feared Catholic ascendancy in an independent Ireland, which to some extent has come to pass.

He stressed the cultural side of nationalism and thought the state should be bilingual; that remains a dream in Ireland. He opposed censorship; Ireland is a country where censors abound, less so now than in the immediate past. He hoped to win the Protestants of Ulster to the United Irish ideal of an independent Ireland; that seems more remote now than in his day. For all that, Davis in a matter of three years moulded the ideology of nationalism, and although John Mitchel and Fintan Lalor built on his thought,[22] the credit for the original ideas must go to him. Yet before his premature death in 1845, at the age of thirty-one, Davis considered himself a political failure and had abandoned the Repeal movement and public life.

Davis could not master Irish, but he is the fount of bilingualism. The loss of one's native tongue, he wrote, is 'the worst badge of conquest – it is the chain on the soul'. 'A people without a language of its own is only half a nation. . . . A people should guard its language more than its territories.' He supplied the watchwords of the Gaelic League and the slogans of Arthur Griffith's Sinn Fein.[23] A bilingual Ireland would use English for commerce and Irish for history and song, he thought. His attitude to Irish contrasted with that of O'Connell, a native speaker, who held the utilitarian view that 'a diversity of tongues is no benefit' and 'the superior utility of the English tongue, as the medium of all modern communication, is so great, that I can witness without a sigh the gradual disuse of the Irish'.[24]

Davis seemed to think that small states could run their affairs well enough if left alone, and people of different origins and languages could live peacefully in a political community. He cited the United States, Switzerland, Hungary, Belgium as examples. It must be a secular society, he stressed, because in a country like Ireland it is dangerous to mix religion and politics. During the national resurgence of this century, Davis's ideas received a new birth, but only certain features were stressed. His statement on religion is as important as his remarks on industrialization, the Irish language, the ownership of the land. Here he links religious and economic interests, in a manner similar to a much-quoted passage by Wolfe Tone:

> Religion has for ages been so mixed with Irish quarrels that it is often hard to say whether patriotism or superstition was the animating principle of an Irish leader, and whether political rapacity or bigoted zeal against bigotry was the motive of an oppressor. Yet in no country was this more misplaced in our day than in Ireland. Our upper classes were mostly Episcopalians – masters not merely of the institutions, but the education and moral force of the

> country. The middle ranks and much of the peasantry of one of our greatest provinces were Presbyterians, obstinate in their simple creed – proud of their victories, yet apprehensive of oppression. The rest of the population were Catholics, remarkable for piety and tenderness, but equally noted for ignorance and want of self-reliance. To mingle politics and religion in such a country was to blind men to their common secular interests, to render political union impossible, and national independence hopeless.[25]

Because of this insistence on the religious issue, as the final sentence above makes clear, Davis was forced out of Irish politics. He clashed with O'Connell in 1845 over Peel's Universities Bill, because he thought the Irish leader was promoting *Catholic* rather than *national* interests. He would not be 'the conscious tool of bigots', or help set up 'a Catholic ascendancy', he told William Smith O'Brien.[26]

O'Connell did not fear Davis or Young Ireland as rivals, for he retained his great popular appeal till his death in May of 1847, but he resented their criticism, especially that of his surrender after Peel banned the Repeal mass meeting set for Clontarf, near Dublin, in October 1843. It marked the end of the Repeal agitation.[27] O'Connell suspected the *Nation* of spreading revolutionary ideas, because it condemned papal censorship, poked fun at talk of 'a miracle' when a prison sentence on O'Connell, for the Clontarf affair, was reversed by the House of Lords in London. There was a whispering campaign against the paper. Priests said its writers were free-thinkers. Circulation fell. The paper depended on O'Connell's Repeal Association for distribution outside Dublin, as Young Ireland had few links with the provinces.[28]

Writing in the *Nation*, Davis argued that 'united education' – which is to say 'undenominational education', but he had to be careful how he worded it – would counter sectarianism, and he accepted, with qualifications, Peel's scheme for middle-class university education, with colleges at Belfast, Cork and Galway, which some Catholic bishops, echoed by O'Connell, denounced as 'godless colleges'. During a Repeal Association debate Davis asked: 'Will you take the boys of Ireland in their earliest youth and deepen the differences between them?' O'Connell's answer was to attack Young Ireland. 'There is no such party as that styled Young Ireland', he said.

> There may be a few individuals who take that denomination on themselves. I am for Old Ireland. 'Tis time that this delusion should be put an end to. Young Ireland may play what pranks they please. I do not envy them the name they rejoice in. I shall stand by Old Ireland; and I have some slight notion that Old Ireland will stand by me.[29]

The Gulf Between Davis and O'Connell

The width and depth of the ideological gulf between O'Connell and Davis was revealed at that moment. Rational argument could not counter rhetoric. Davis could not match O'Connell's 'miracles'. O'Connell was talking for the hour, Davis for the future. O'Connell prevailed. But Davis has been a greater force in Irish history and politics than O'Connell, who spoke for seven million Irish at a time when Young Ireland could muster perhaps seventy.

O'Connell dominated the politics of Ireland for thirty-five years, but his mark has faded. Davis could not dominate a meeting hall, but his influence endures. The reason is ideology. O'Connell's ideology was practical politics. Davis's ideology, however he would have named it, was the expression of nationalist Ireland's discontents and hopes. Yet Davis did not know the Irish as well as O'Connell knew them. Still, he put into words certain ideas later nationalists thought important: the language, commerce, peasant proprietorship. Other of Davis's ideas they discarded, because in twentieth-century Catholic Ireland they were unacceptable. A function of ideology is to discard the unpalatable. A book on Davis, published under state auspices in 1945, ignores his views on education; because of course Irish education was denominational. There is passing reference to his anti-sectarianism, but it is not stressed.[30] Still, he is a hero in the Irish pantheon and a statue stands to him opposite Trinity College in Dublin near the old Irish parliament building, now the Bank of Ireland. He is not forgotten.

What Davis said about the Industrial Revolution and its inhumane factory system was lifted almost wholly by Mitchel during his radical period, 1847–48. Davis's ideas on industrialization were used by Arthur Griffith at the start of the century. The Gaelic League took Davis's bilingualism as its own, though not all of them agreed with him.[31] His ideas on peasant proprietorship were shaped by Lalor's compelling prose into battle cries; although nothing that Davis wrote about land approached Lalor's messianic fervour. While Davis talked theory Lalor sought a solution to the land question against a background of famine.

Davis was no radical. If Ireland had a decent aristocracy he would permit it to hold its estates. 'But what shall we say of an aristocracy . . . drawing from the producer an enormous rent, exacting a dishonourable submission, and giving nothing in exchange?' he asked.[32] He blamed utilitarianism and *laissez faire* for Irish poverty. He had read Sismondi's *Nouveau Principes d'Economie Politique,* which stressed distribution more than production of wealth. He thought a nation of peasant proprietors, as in Norway, could live happily in Ireland. He called for the emancipation of the peasantry from feudalism, which English law brought to Ireland; but he had no idea how this emancipation would take place. Lalor did: by expropriating the landlords and undoing 'the Conquest'.

This is Davis's weakness: he is never specific. He loathed the Manchester factory system and would roll back industrialization if he could. He wanted Ireland to protect its industries by tariffs. Ireland must industrialize and Irish entrepreneurs must do it, he said. Tariffs could only be imposed by a national government; so, Davis asks, 'Why not have a national government?'

From Davis, too, Arthur Griffith took his fierce dislike of Adam Smith. 'The equal distribution of comfort, education and happiness is the only true wealth of nations,' said Davis. 'What is it to the English father, with an emaciated body, that Manchester can sell cheap cottons, and Birmingham surpass the fame of Damascus?'[33] This was Sismondi's influence at work: wealth is not synonymous with production; production becomes wealth when it is 'proportionately distributed'. (Griffith objected to Adam Smith's ideas on free trade and his downgrading of the role of the nation 'with its special language and literature, with its peculiar origin and history'; List, by contrast, upgrades the role of the nation.[34] But unlike Davis, the production of wealth was more important to Griffith than its distribution.) 'If the economists could the world would be a factory, if the bigots could it would be a graveyard', Davis wrote. A conservative at heart, he looked back to a golden age and lamented the loss of cottage industry. 'We prefer the life of the old times, or of modern Norway' he wrote.[35] The peasant was free in Norway, which had an independent parliament under the Swedish Crown. Perhaps he felt such a system would suit Ireland. (It would not have suited Tone, whom he admired: he wrote a fine ballad about Tone's grave at Bodenstown and said once, 'a better ruler for Ireland than Theobald Wolfe Tone never lived'.[36] But his *beau ideal* was Grattan, whom he compared to Burke 'for grandeur and sublimity of thought, language and illustration'.)[37]

It is difficult to say what form of government Davis wanted for Ireland. He was not a republican. He was not a revolutionary. Yet he did not exclude physical force and always warned against 'English treachery'. His model, perhaps, was Grattan's Volunteers. He disliked mobs and uncontrolled violence. He condemned agrarian Ribbonism.[38] But he was a townsman with no understanding of the peasantry or their lives. He was a romantic without knowledge of the realities of the Irish land system. Emancipate the peasants, restore husbandry and cottage industry to a bilingual people who would learn the history of their country and of their locality and glory in the epic deeds of the past – this was his vision of an independent Ireland. With Davis, *restoration* was more important than revolution. He would not shrink from revolution if it was disciplined, as in 1782, and would save Ireland from English utilitarianism and industrialism. He had kind words for the early stages of the French Revolution; he praised 'Mirabeau and Danton, who treated primogeniture and landlordism as vulgar novelties, and restored the land to the people'.[39] In 1843, at the height of the Repeal agitation, when it seemed that all Ireland wanted the old Irish parliament restored, Davis wrote to a friend, Daniel Owen Maddyn:

> The machinery at present working for Repeal could never, under circumstances like the present, achieve it; but circumstances must change. Within ten or fifteen years England must be in peril. Assuming this much, I argue thus. Modern Anglicanism – *i.e.* Utilitarianism, the creed of Russell and Peel, as well as of the Radicals – this thing, call it Yankeeism or Englishism, which measures prosperity by exchangeable value, measures duty by gain, and limits desire to clothes, food, and respectability; this damned thing has come into Ireland under the Whigs, and is equally the favourite of the 'Peel' Tories. It is believed in the political assemblies in our cities, preached from our pulpits (always Utilitarian or persecuting); it is the very Apostles' Creed of the professions, and threatens to corrupt the lower classes, who are still faithful and romantic. To use every literary and political engine against this seems to me the first duty of an Irish patriot who can foresee consequences. Believe me, this is a greater though not so obvious a danger as Papal supremacy. So much worse do I think it, that, sooner than suffer the iron gates of that filthy dungeon to close on us, I would submit to the certainty of a Papal supremacy; knowing that the latter should end in some twenty years – leaving the people mad it might be, but not sensual and mean. Much more willingly would I take the chance of a Papal supremacy, which even a few of us laymen could check, shake, and prepare (if not effect) the ruin of. Still more willingly would I (if Anglicanism, *i.e.* Sensualism, were the alternative) take the hazard of open war, sure that if we succeeded the military leaders would compel the bigots down, establish a thoroughly national government, and one whose policy, somewhat arbitrary, would be anti-Anglican and anti-sensual; and if we failed it would be in our own power before dying to throw up huge barriers against English vices, and, dying, to leave example and a religion to the next age.[40]

The time was ripe, he continued. The Catholics were 'united, bold and orderly', and could be used for defence or attack, 'civil or military'. Lower-class Protestants, he thought, were neutral; educated Protestants were nationalists, but required 'a pledge against a Catholic ascendancy'. America offered 'men, money, and arms'. O'Connell could not retreat. 'I think we can beat Peel, if we can quietly get a Federal Government I shall for one agree to it and support it. If not, then anything but what we are.'[41] But O'Connell retreated. Davis's schemes came to nought. In a subsequent letter he told Maddyn that Irish landlords would support a federal solution, but did not want to repeal the Union. 'We Repealers hold peace and war in our hands,' Davis wrote. 'O'Connell could in three months take possession of Ireland, but he is adverse, wisely, humanely adverse, to fighting, save in the last extremity.'[42] Davis's estimate was unrealistic. There is no evidence that even a minority of landlords would opt for Federalism. O'Connell opposed physical force in all circumstances. Davis, it seems, was a man whose imagination sometimes ran away with him.

Irish Republicans claim Davis as one of their 'evangelists' – the word was used by Patrick Henry Pearse, leader of the Easter Rising.[43] Pearse was deeply influenced by Davis's concept of the Irish nation. He wrote a pamphlet on Davis's thought, titled *The Spiritual Nation,* two months before the 1916 rebellion.[44] Pearse does not specifically mention Davis's views on armed action; but his essay is a justification of the impending rebellion based on Davis's teaching. To rise against English rule, regardless of the outcome, is to succeed. Indeed Pearse rationalized the 1916 insurrection on the same grounds, and it is possible he got it from Davis. Pearse goes much further than Davis in linking language and nationality.

> Irish nationality is an ancient spiritual tradition, and the Irish nation could not die as long as that tradition lived in the heart of one faithful man or woman. But had the last repositor of the Gaelic tradition, the last unconquered Gael, died, the Irish nation was no more. Any free state that might thereafter be erected in Ireland, whatever it might call itself, would certainly not be the historic Irish nation.[45]

There is nothing in Davis to justify this statement. Pearse had difficulty with Davis's conception of the form of government a free Ireland should establish. This ambiguity in Davis's politics played some part in the negotiations between Lloyd George and Eamon de Valera in the autumn of 1921. In a letter to de Valera, Lloyd George cited Davis to prove that the British offer to Sinn Fein of Dominion status and the link of the Crown went further than anything Davis sought. Lloyd George wrote:

> The British Government have offered Ireland all that O'Connell and Thomas Davis asked and more, and we are met only by an unqualified demand that

> we should recognize Ireland as a foreign Power. It is playing with phrases to suggest that the principle of government by consent of the governed compels a recognition of that demand on our part, or that in repudiating it we are straining geographical and historical considerations to justify a claim to ascendancy over the Irish race.[46]

In his defence of the Treaty with Great Britain, which as head of the Irish delegation he had negotiated, Arthur Griffith summoned the ghost of Thomas Davis to his side when he told Dail Eireann:

> The prophet I followed throughout my life, the man whose words and teachings I tried to translate into practice in politics, the man whom I revered above all Irish patriots was Thomas Davis. In the hard way of fitting practical affairs into idealism I have made Thomas Davis my guide. I have never departed in my life one inch from the principles of Thomas Davis, and in signing this Treaty and bringing it here and asking Ireland to ratify it I am following Thomas Davis still.

Griffith went on to quote Davis: 'Peace with England, alliance with England and to some extent, and, under certain circumstances, confederation with England; but an Irish ambition, Irish hopes, strength, virtue, and rewards for the Irish.' In Griffith's view the Treaty permitted the Irish to carve out their own existence and to rebuild the Gaelic civilization defeated at the battle of Kinsale. 'I say we have translated Thomas Davis into the practical politics of the day,' he claimed.[47]

Davis could be quoted like Scripture because he expressed the purest Irish nationalism; like Scripture he is open to many interpretations. Was he a democrat, like Tone? Not really. He had a hankering after an ideal aristocracy, one

> attached by hereditary achievements to the glory of their country – conscious, from childhood, of a splendid responsibility – surrounded by the love of the many – invited by vistas of honourable distinction – refined by every gallant and every beautiful art – such an aristocracy would give the National army officers uniting proud honour, popularity, and instruction – to the Senate men (the best of all) having philosophical culture and ripening experience.[48]

This ideal hierarchical society owes more to Burke than to Tone, and is seldom mentioned by Davis's nationalist admirers. Many of his ballads praised the Gaelic aristocracy in the service of continental monarchs, 'from Almanza to Fontenoy, from Ramilles to Cremona', and Irish generals, like Marshal Brown of Austria, and Count Lacy of Russia.[49] This Cavalier romanticism, so alien to the Roundhead Tone, found a response in Catholic Ireland, where the aristocratic spirit was always strong. (Even in the General Post Office, headquarters of the Irish Republic during the 1916 rebellion, there was talk of naming a German prince 'King of Ireland'.)[50]

From Davis, Irish nationalist ideology received its cultural mission. He was not an original thinker. Much of his cultural nationalism came from Ferguson, his balladry from Scott, his history from Michelet and his economic theories from Sismondi. Yet Davis is Young Ireland and Young Ireland is Davis. His dedication and idealism influenced his colleagues and many, like Lalor, who did not know him at all. His writings converted the Fenian leader, John O'Leary, to nationalism and gave him the mental sustenance to face years in prison and exile. O'Leary introduced Yeats to Davis's writings. Yeats had harsh words for the Young Ireland school of 'intellectual nationalism', which he said subordinated art and literature to politics. 'Young Ireland had sought a nation unified by political doctrine alone, a subservient art and letters aiding and abetting. . . .'[51]

A writer should not try to popularize his work, Yeats said. Popularizing history, as Davis attempted to do, created a black-and-white perspective. 'All the past had been turned into a melodrama with Ireland for blameless hero and poet, novelist and historian had but one object, that we should hiss the villain, and only a minority doubted that the greater the talent the greater the hiss.'[52] If the romanticism of Young Ireland is seriously flawed, its strength is its moral sense: it is the conscience of Irish nationalist ideology. 'Davis showed this moral element not merely in his verse – I doubt if that could have had great effect alone – but in his action, in his defence, for instance, of the rights of his political opponents of the Royal Irish Academy,' Yeats wrote.[53] Yet Davis's vision of an Ireland where 'Orange and Green will carry the day' is no more than a platitude now. It would need a movement with his own broad religious and political tolerance to bring such an Ireland into being. All ideology is restrictive, and narrow men put Davis on their banner and made him over in their own image.

The Hatred of John Mitchel

Two figures of Young Ireland whose influence equals and at times surpasses Davis are John Mitchel, his successor as chief writer of the *Nation*, and James Fintan Lalor, the theorist of agrarian revolution.

Mitchel was one of 'a handful of Ulster Protestants'[54] who joined the Repeal Association in 1843. Like Davis, he was a graduate of Trinity College and a lawyer. Mitchel started out as a political conservative and when he came to Dublin after Davis's death, in

September 1845, Duffy said of him: 'He was silent and retiring, slow to speak and apt to deliver his opinion in a form which would be abrupt and dogmatic if it were not relieved by a pleasant smile'[55]

Mitchel did not remain 'silent and retiring' for long. After Young Ireland seceded from the Repeal Association, in the summer of 1846, over O'Connell's demand for a pledge, abjuring the use of all force except 'moral force' in the struggle for an Irish parliament, Mitchel grew more and more radical. In time he became the leader of the movement's left wing. When Young Ireland founded a new party, the Irish Confederation, in January 1847, in the hope of winning the landlords to nationalism, Mitchel doubted that the policy had any reality and said so. The country was in the throes of famine. James Fintan Lalor had written a letter to the *Nation* urging the movement to take up the land question.[56] Mitchel was a man who took the ideas of others and put them into elegant and angry prose. Once converted to the need for a peasant revolution, he tried to publicize his gospel in the *Nation*. Gavan Duffy, the editor, objected: after all the policy of the paper was the policy of the Irish Confederation, which was to convert the landlords to nationalism. At the end of 1847 Mitchel left the *Nation,* and in February 1848 took his followers out of the Irish Confederation and established the weekly *United Irishman* as 'an avowed organ of revolution'.

In the columns of the *United Irishman* Mitchel preached open rebellion, peasant insurrection and Red Republicanism. He welcomed the French 'February Revolution' and urged Young Ireland to emulate it. His wild ideas shocked his colleagues. There was a suggestion he might be a British agent. Mitchel was the first nationalist since the United Irishmen to demand an Irish Republic, 'one and indivisible'. Because of the famine and British repression, he wrote later, 'a kind of sacred wrath took possession of a few Irishmen. . . '.[57] The Whig government of Lord John Russell passed a special law to deport Mitchel, the Treason-Felony Act. Tried, convicted and transported 'over the seas' in record time, Mitchel escaped to America from Australia after about five years, took the side of the Confederate states in the Civil War, returned to Ireland at the end of his life in the 1870s to be elected a member of the British parliament for Tipperary, refused to sit and was denied his seat anyway as a convicted felon. For all these reasons the temperamental Mitchel, who could swing from conservatism to radicalism and back again with equal ease, who denounced Britain and imperialism in the most extravagant language, and defended slavery with similar extravagance, has become the quintessential Irish rebel because he never bent the knee to British rule in Ireland. A great stylist, he lives in his books. A hero to the workmen of Dublin in the spring of 1848 – Lord Clarendon, the Viceroy, was convinced he was an extreme socialist – when he learned of the June insurrection by workers in Paris, while aboard a British warship as a prisoner *en route* to Australia, he recorded his delight that they had been 'swept from the streets with grape and cannister – the only way of dealing with such unhappy creatures', in his *Jail Journal:*

> I cannot believe that all the party called Red Republicans are also Communists, though the English newspapers use the terms as synonymous – of course to cast odium on the thorough-going Republicans. I suspect that there is a numerous party of staunch Republicans who believe the Revolution is but half-accomplished, which, indeed may turn out to be the case. But then these ought to make no common cause with Socialists; Socialists are something worse than wild beasts.
>
> But I can see no French papers; I am in British darkness.[58]

James Connolly, the socialist revolutionary, excuses Mitchel for this judgment on the grounds that he was misinformed.[59] For one who reads the sixteen-issue file of Mitchel's *United Irishman* it is indeed an astonishing change. But Mitchel, fundamentally, was a radical conservative, like his hero, Carlyle. He hated British society and the 'cash nexus' that was part of it. He was a romantic.

More than any other revolutionary figure, not excluding Wolfe Tone, Mitchel contributed ideas that live on in the consciousness of physical-force nationalists. First, he believed that only through rebellion, indeed by the destruction of the British Empire itself, could Ireland gain freedom. Second, he maintained that 'every attempt [at rebellion] must fail while England is at peace with the world, and while no revolution has yet burst out within her own borders'.[60] (Friedrich Engels made the same observation.)[61] This principle of Mitchel's guided the 1916 rebellion, whose leaders held his memory in the highest esteem. Pearse spoke of 'his hymn of hate against the Empire';[62] Connolly of his 'holy hatred of tyranny'.[63] Yeats turned 'Mitchel's prayer' into verse:

> You that Mitchel's prayer have heard,
> 'Send war in our time, O Lord!'
> Know that when all words are said
> And a man is fighting mad.
> Something drops from eyes long blind. . . .

This simple creed of hatred and its corollary, to strike at England when she is at war and to seek the aid of her enemy, is Mitchel's chief legacy to Irish republicanism. He would have nothing to do with England's parliament, a policy later adopted by Sinn Fein. Griffith, the anti-socialist, like Connolly, the socialist, admired Mitchel greatly – perhaps for his powerful journalistic style as much as anything else. As a tribute to the short-lived 'organ of revolution' in 1848, Griffith called his own first newspaper, in 1899, the *United Irishman*. The republican paper in Dublin, the *United Irishman*, also took its title from Mitchel's weekly.

Apart from advocating rebellion only when Britain is at war, Mitchel borrowed most of his ideas from Davis and Lalor. He took over Lalor's land doctrines as 'readily as a man takes on a new religion', he said. He did not fully understand them, but if preaching them would create a rebellion he was content. Under the spell of Lalor, he addressed a series of letters to 'the tillers of the soil, farmers, cottiers and labourers', and to 'the Protestant democracy of Ulster' in an attempt to refire the embers of 1798.[64] But Ulster either did not read him, or ignored him, or the embers were truly dead.

Fintan Lalor's 'Reconquest of Ireland'

Lalor's first contribution to the *Nation*, the letter written in January 1847, was too extreme for Gavan Duffy to publish; it stirred debate in Young Ireland nevertheless. 'The right to the land and the right to legislation,' Lalor insisted, in a private letter to the Young Irelander, Thomas D'Arcy McGee, could be combined into one.[65] In April, at Gavan Duffy's bidding, he wrote a letter 'to the landowners of Ireland', in the course of which he urged them to

> Create what has never yet existed in Ireland – an active and affluent husbandry, a secure and independent agricultural peasantry, able to accumulate as well as to produce – do this and you raise a thriving and happy community, a solid social economy, a prosperous people, an effective nation. Create the husbandman, and you create the mechanic, the artisan, the manufacturer, the merchant.[66]

This may be the most important ideological statement made in nineteenth-century Ireland: out of it grew the Land League of 1879–82, which, under the leadership of Michael Davitt and Charles Stewart Parnell, defeated landlordism and won peasant proprietary. Lalor's contribution to Irish nationalism is that he linked the national struggle with the land struggle, because they were the same struggle.

The condition of the peasantry in the Ireland of the Great Famine was the question of the hour, rather than Repeal. A report in 1845, on the eve of the potato blight, by a commission of landlords set up by Sir Robert Peel, under the chairmanship of Lord Devon, found the conditions of life of the smallholders appalling. It said of the cottier population: 'We cannot forbear expressing our strong sense of the patient endurance which the labouring classes have generally exhibited under sufferings greater we believe than any other country in Europe have to sustain.'[67] They were 'badly housed, badly fed, badly clothed, and badly paid.' They lived on potatoes and water, their only property was 'their pig and manure heap'. When the potato crop failed, they starved. They had no money to buy food, yet the Whig government insisted that the market system must not be touched and Ireland continued to export food through three famine years.[68]

Lalor was the son of an O'Connellite member of parliament of the 1830s, Pat Lalor, a leader of the anti-tithe movement. Many of young Lalor's theories came from his knowledge of the resistance to tithes. He proposed a rent and harvest strike, which he called 'moral insurrection', to distinguish it from O'Connell's 'moral force'. He hated O'Connell with a passion and in 1843 offered his services to Peel against the Repeal movement, calling himself a Conservative 'in principle'.[69] Having decided that the land question was the root of the Irish question and the cause of Irish poverty and degradation, he built on Davis's concept of the origin of land ownership in Ireland, conquest and confiscation, and advocated repealing not merely the Act of Union but the entire English conquest of 700 years. He thought the right time for a rent and harvest strike was May of 1847; but Young Ireland, still panting after the landlords, would have none of it. He told Mitchel:

> I have nothing to do with the landlord-and-tenant question, as understood. The question of tenure by which the actual cultivator of the soil should hold his land is one for an Irish Parliament. My object is to repeal the conquest – not any part or portion of it but the whole and entire conquest of seven hundred years – a thing much more easily done than to repeal the Union. That the absolute (allodial) ownership of the land of Ireland is vested of right in the people of Ireland – that they, and none but they, are the first landowners and lord paramount as well as the lawmakers of this island – that all titles to land are invalid not conferred or confirmed by them – that no man has a right to hold one foot of Irish soil otherwise than by grant of tenancy and fee from them, and under such conditions as they may annex of suit and service, faith and fealty, etc., these are my principles. . . .
>
> The question of time is everything. I want a prepared, organized, and resistless revolution. *You* would only have an unprepared, disorderly and vile jacquerie. . . . You throw away the elections too, for no other argument

> than mine will you get a frieze coat to vote for you. Ireland was ready to strip for battle, and none flinched but the fire-eaters.[70]

Lalor's doctrines bothered Young Ireland. They believed in the rights of property: the landlords owned the land, the tenants rented the land, and this order could not be changed. But John Stuart Mill, in *Principles of Political Economy*, with the catastrophe of the Great Famine to guide him, said nothing less radical than Lalor. 'The land of Ireland, the land of every country, belongs to the people of that country,' he wrote, '. . .but justice requires that the actual cultivators should be enabled to become in Ireland what they will become in America – proprietors of the soil which they cultivate.'[71] However, it took the Irish peasantry more than half a century to achieve this 'justice'. The power of England maintained the landlord's right to his property against the tenant's right to subsistence.

The Rebellion of 1848

Young Ireland would not accept Lalor's thesis that the land question was the locomotive of national independence. Pure nationalists, of the John O'Leary and Charles J. Kickham[72] type, would not accept the thesis thirty years later, when John Devoy drafted his 'New Departure' programme.[73] So it was hardly surprising that a landlord like William Smith O'Brien rejected it in 1847–48, because he feared 'a war of property'.

Young Ireland rebelled in 1848 because Lord John Russell suspended *Habeas Corpus* in Ireland; O'Brien, Thomas Francis Meagher, John Blake Dillon, Thomas D'Arcy McGee and others thought this attack on personal liberty should be met with armed resistance. The Whig government had poured troops into Ireland through 1847 and 1848 to meet the crisis it saw coming. With Mitchel transported and his *United Irishman* suppressed, John Martin, another Ulster Protestant, established the *Irish Felon,* which he named in honour of 'the State prisoner' on his way to Australia. The chief writer of the *Felon* was Lalor. His incendiary articles calling for insurrection culminated on 22 July, 1848 with an editorial, 'Clearing Decks', urging that 'somewhere, somehow and by someone a beginning must be made'. Young Ireland decided to strike and the leaders fled to Tipperary to link up with the rebellious peasantry. Lalor, who still believed the moderate leaders of Young Ireland 'wished to preserve an aristocracy' and 'desired, not a democratic, but merely a national revolution',[74] also left Dublin for the countryside to stir up a social revolt. He went to Father John

Kenyon, one of the few Young Ireland priests, a friend of Mitchel and a fierce revolutionary – in debate. But Kenyon said his bishop forbade him to act. Lalor was unknown, no one would listen to him, and *he* was arrested within a few days.

The Young Irelanders with Smith O'Brien ran into a barrage of clerical criticism of their rebellion. Nevertheless the people of South Tipperary responded to O'Brien's call to arms. According to Michael Doheny, a local Repealer who had joined Young Ireland, the people turned out in great numbers and their enthusiasm was 'measureless'.[75] As he rode through the countryside, Doheny recalled,

> At every forge, pikes were manufactured. . . . We called at several villages, and were surrounded by the young men and the aged, by matron and maid, and from no lips did one sound of complaint, or discouragement, or fear fall. Everywhere hope, and resolution, and courage lit up the hearts and eyes of young and old. We rode at least a distance of twenty miles, and returned assured that there was not one man within that district who was not then prepared, and would not be armed ere night came.[76]

The priests tried to disperse the people. They told the peasantry not to heed Young Ireland. The miners in the Tipperary collieries joined the rebellion.

The revolt lasted three days. In the end the arguments of the priests prevailed, according to Smith O'Brien, who was embittered by his experiences. 'It is my sincere belief that it was through the instrumentality of the superior order of the Catholic clergy that the insurrection was suppressed' – rather than by the military or police – he wrote in the speech he prepared for his trial but did not deliver.[77] (However, O'Brien must bear some of the blame. He would not permit his followers to barricade the roads until they had received permission from the landlords to fell the trees.) Reports in *The Times* agree with O'Brien's charge. One said a well-known priest told his parishioners, 'that if they joined in a rebellion he would curse them from the altar by bell, book, and candle'. The *Times* continued: '. . . altogether there is no doubt that the Roman Catholic clergy here, as a body, have used their influence and most creditably for the preservation of the public peace by discountenancing rebellion'.[78]

The *Times* also denounced the 'Communist rebellion'. According to Smith O'Brien it was not even a republican rebellion. In the speech prepared for his trial he wrote: 'I have entertained no preference for republican institutions. I should myself have been perfectly satisfied with the ancient constitution of Ireland, a government of the Lords, Commons and Sovereign of Ireland. I cherished no no desire to change the dynasty.'[79] He wanted self-government for Ireland, 'the power to manage her own affairs. . . the power to make all the resources of this island subsidiary to the welfare and greatness not of another people but of the old Irish Nation'.[80]

The *Times* said the rebellion was 'not a conflict between the Queen and the people of Ireland', but 'between those who have something and those who have nothing',[81] the kind of conflict Smith O'Brien and his colleagues, except Lalor, rejected. No one paid any attention to Lalor, least of all the peasantry. He was not an inspiring figure by all accounts: he was sickly, he suffered from a disease of the spine that gave him the look of a hunchback, and he was a poor speaker. O'Brien had all the attributes of leadership: a well-spoken, handsome man, a landlord used to command, a descendant of King Brian Boru of Munster. But his rebellion was an act of despair. Everyone agreed, friend and foe, that he acted most honourably throughout the entire affair. The *Times* made fun of his absurd chivalry. He saved the children of a widow when police took refuge in her house, and in England the rising was called 'the Rebellion in the Widow McCormack's cabbage garden'.

The Whigs could afford to be magnanimous. They created no martyrs, as in '98. Most of the Young Ireland leaders escaped to France or America, bearing with them a grudge against the priests they felt had betrayed them. Yet anti-clericalism hardly surfaced in Irish republican ideology, except briefly among some Fenians in the 1860s. Archbishop Cullen of Dublin conducted a witch-hunt against Young Ireland professors in the new Catholic University when John Henry Newman was rector in the 1850s.[82] Cullen saw them all as Mazzinis and Garibaldis: he had been rector of the Irish College, Rome, when Pius IX was driven from the city. With Young Ireland in mind, Cullen warned a synod of Irish bishops at Thurles in 1850 against journals:

> in which loyalty is treated as a crime, a spirit of sedition is insinuated, and efforts are made to induce you to make common cause – to sympathize with, those apostles of socialism and infidelity, who, in other countries, under the pretence of promoting civil liberty, not only undermined the foundations of every government, but artfully assailed the rights of the Apostolic See and sought for the destruction of the Holy Catholic Church.[83]

In a time of famine people preferred to flee the country than to fight, O'Brien complained. But with the proper leadership they still might have fought; the Viceroy, Lord Clarendon, reporting to the Home Secretary at the start of 1849, said the 'treasonable movement' was still strong in Tipperary and there was no sign of repentance.

> The total absence of support of the authorities in their endeavours to suppress insurrection, the renewed attempt at rebellion in the vicinity of the town where the leaders of the movement were being brought to justice, and the disregard of proclamations requiring the surrender of arms, are facts which indicate that, however the failure of past attempts at insurrection may have weakened the confidence of the disaffected, the feeling which gave rise to and encouraged that movement still remains unchanged, and would again become active upon any occasion that appeared to offer even a distant prospect of success.[84]

The *Times* had 'a few grave facts and one grave question for the English people and government to ponder on', as a result of the rebellion. 'Is Ireland worth keeping?' the newspaper asked.[85] 'Shall we retain this diseased and feverish member of our common empire, or shall we fling it from us for ever?' Thirty years of O'Connell's agitation, it would be claimed, had never stirred such 'a grave question' in the establishment of England. The *Times* merely raised the question; it did not attempt to answer it. Put to a vote in Ireland, there could be no doubt of the answer. Nor would there be any doubt as to what prompted the question: rebellion. Perhaps that was Young Ireland's most important contribution to the ideology of Irish nationalism.

Still convinced the peasantry could be stirred into revolt, if 'somewhere, somehow and by someone' a beginning could be made, Fintan Lalor and his followers in September 1849 mobilized in the Cashel-Carrick-Clonmel region of Tipperary and Waterford one night between midnight and dawn. But the peasantry did not join them. Lalor died three months later.[86]

IV
The Struggle for an Irish Nation-State

Famine, eviction and emigration cleared the Irish countryside of its 'surplus population' between 1846 and 1866, when almost three million left the land, mostly for North America, and a new Irish nationalism was born under the generic name of Fenianism.[1] The landlords consolidated farm holdings by throwing the occupants off their farms, and the government enforced the decrees. Pasturage took the place of tillage after Irish grain lost its monopoly on the English market with the repeal of the corn laws (1846), and the price of meat and wool rose. Ireland exported cattle and sheep to England to feed and clothe its industrial population. Ireland imported English manufactures, having no industries of its own. This colonial relationship was seen by Irish nationalists as unjust and exploitative and a consequence of superior English power. Since it was based on force it would be ended only by force. This was the whole ideology of Fenianism.

The Fenian movement was a product of the Irish in America. It developed during the Civil War when the Irish joined the Union and, to a much lesser extent, the Confederate armies, in the belief that one day they could liberate their native country. Fenianism sought to establish an Irish Republic on the American model by armed rebellion. The United Irishmen and Young Ireland had looked to France for help and inspiration; the Fenians looked to America.[2] Unlike their predecessor movements they did not stress social aims, but those who joined did so because they believed an independent Ireland would solve the country's appalling poverty.

In November 1867 Marx informed Engels:

> What the English do not yet know is that since 1846 the economic content and therefore also the political aim of English domination in Ireland have entered into an entirely new phase, and that, precisely because of this, Fenianism is characterized by a socialistic tendency (in a negative sense, directed against the appropriation of the soil) and by being a lower orders movement.

Ireland needed 'self-government and independence from England,' 'an agrarian revolution' and 'protective tariffs against England'.[3] Fenianism changed Marx's mind on the right solution for the Irish question; the socialist revolution required an independent Ireland. This was the most important issue facing the British workers and he pressed the General Council of the International Workingmen's Association to support the Irish national struggle. He and Engels campaigned against death sentences on Fenians and the conditions of their imprisonment. Marx published several articles in continental socialist journals exposing British police tactics in Ireland.

'Previously I thought Ireland's separation from England impossible,' he wrote to Engels in November 1867, when Fenian fever was boiling over in England,

> Now I think it inevitable, although after separation there may come federation. . . . The Irish Viceroy, Lord Abicorn (that *seems* to be his name), 'cleared' his estate in the last few weeks by forcibly evicting thousands of people. Among them were prosperous tenants, whose improvements and investments were thus confiscated! In no other European country did foreign rule adopt this form of direct expropriation of the stock population. The Russians confiscate solely on political grounds; the Prussians in Western Prussia buy out.[4]

The English workers must make common cause with the Irish, Marx told his friend Ludwig Kugelmann, even take the initiative 'in dissolving the Union established in 1801 and replacing it by a free federal relationship'. He concluded: 'In fact, England never has and never *can* – so long as the present relations last – rule Ireland otherwise than by the most abominable reign of terror and the most reprehensible corruption.'[5] To a group of German *emigres* in London Marx gave this estimate of the situation:

> Ruin or revolution is the watchword; all the Irish are convinced that if anything is to happen at all it must happen quickly. . . . If that does not happen soon the Irish emigration will lead to a war with America. The domination over Ireland at present amounts to collecting rent for the English aristocracy.[6]

Hence Fenianism.

John Stuart Mill said the Irish had found their way out of poverty by emigrating to America.

> The census of 1851, compared with that of 1841, showed in round numbers a diminution of population of a million and a half. The subsequent census (of 1861) shows a further diminution of about half a million. The Irish having thus found the way to that flourishing continent which for generations will be capable of supporting in undiminished comfort the increase

> of the population of the whole world; the peasantry of Ireland having learnt to fix their eyes on a terrestrial paradise beyond the ocean, as a sure refuge both from oppression of the Saxon and from the tyranny of nature. . . .[7]

From these dispossessed emigrants and their offspring Fenianism became a force on two continents.

Cardinal Cullen and the Fenians

The Fenian leaders looked at Ireland from the outside – from America. They felt independence would solve Ireland's problems. They saw English rule as the source of evil, not the fact that 1 per cent of the population – the landlords – owned 88 per cent of the cultivated land. As a class, the landlords had undergone some changes following the Famine.[8] But the system itself could not be altered fundamentally because that would interfere with the rights of property. Even the Catholic Church acknowledged that the rights of landlords took precedence over the rights of tenants. Archbishop Cullen of Dublin, who became a Cardinal in 1865, declared that something should be done to improve the condition of the tillers of the soil. 'However, in every change the rights of property ought to be recognized,' he added.[9]

Cullen, an outspoken enemy of Fenianism, dominated the Irish Church for almost thirty years. He believed that Fenianism would destroy religion as well as English power in Ireland, given the chance. He considered the leaders socialists and agnostics. All Fenians, he declared, were excommunicated from the Church as members of a secret society, a view disputed in the *Irish People* by Charles Kickham, a devout Catholic.[10] Cullen insisted, in his public pronouncements, that if the Irish people were fairly treated by England 'revolutions and conspiracies, Whiteboys and Fenians, would no longer be heard of, the people would be happy and peaceable, and a source of strength to the empire at large'.[11] Cullen detected links between some Fenians and the First International. He denounced Mazzini and Garibaldi 'and their wicked associates'[12] and warned that revolutions, as in France, 'almost invariably terminate in massacres, anarchy and despotism'.[13] He accused the Fenian leaders of 'wearing the mask of patriotism', calling them 'needy and desperate adventurers', who would seize all property, public and private. They would 'destroy the faith of our people by circulating works like those of the impious Voltaire, to preach up socialism, to seize on the property of those who have any, and to exterminate both the gentry of the country and the Catholic clergy'.[14] He praised the government for suppressing the *Irish People*, because it circulated 'the most pernicious and poisonous maxims'.[15] He believed that Ireland's national objectives could be achieved in the manner of O'Connell: 'By peaceful means and by force of reason, without violating any law, he broke the chains which bound Ireland. . . .'[16]

This duel between the spokesman of the Catholic Church and an Irish revolutionary organization is significant because the two strongest forces in Irish life were, and are, religion and nationalism. If Cullen had had the full support of his bishops and priests, he might have emerged a clear-cut victor. He was not pro-British, as the Fenians charged. But at least one priest disobeyed him and was protected by John MacHale, the legendary Archbishop of Tuam.[17] Cullen would not let the remains of Terence Bellew MacManus, a Young Irelander who died in California after escaping from Australia, into any Dublin church when the American Fenians transported the body to Ireland for burial: he rightly interpreted the move as revolutionary propaganda. Kickham replied in the *Irish People* by telling the priests to stay out of politics. Yet Fenianism was not an anti-clerical movement; to call it anti-religious was false. The attacks on Fenianism weakened the political influence of the Catholic Church for a time, but peasant nationalism required the help of priests and revolutionaries, as the Land League and the 1918–21 struggle demonstrated.

The Fenians were Catholics, but Fenianism was not 'a Catholic movement'. It was not influenced by the Church in any way. It stood for the United Irishmen doctrine of the separation of Church and state, which worked well in America. It was not greatly influenced by the revolutionary movements of Europe, which were directed against despotic governments, while England was a liberal democratic state.

Fenian Government-in-exile

Fenianism was an Irish international conspiracy directed against the British government. Its plots were potentially dangerous, but it accomplished little because its leaders feuded among themselves. The American Fenians set up an Irish Senate and government-in-exile in New York, and maintained an army of Union army veterans, some of whom invaded Canada in June of 1866.[18] Despite elaborate plans for rebellion in Ireland, all that resulted were arrests, betrayals, executions. John Mitchel thought Fenianism failed because England was at peace in the late 1860s and the Irish were fighting alone. 'It is not that I stand for "civilized" warfare,' he said. 'The Irish have the clear right to strike at England anywhere or anyhow, in Canada, in Ireland, in London, by steel or gunpowder or firewood. But I hold that those who undertake any such warfare at present, whether civilized or uncivilized, must perish and perish in vain.'[19]

The Fenian conspiracy never really died. The IRB continued as a secret organization in Ireland until the early 1920s and was responsible for planning the 1916 rebellion. The Fenian Brotherhood in America split into factions, which came together as Clan-na-Gael, meaning 'Family of the Irish', with 'camps', or clubs, from coast to coast. In the 1880s Clan-na-Gael initiated a terrorist campaign in English cities as 'the lawful weapon of the weak against the strong', in the words of one Fenian leader.[20] Explosives were placed in the House of Commons, Scotland Yard, railway stations, and under London Bridge. O'Donovan Rossa, whose cause while in prison Marx had espoused,[21] preached terrorism when permitted to go into exile in America. His colleague, John Devoy, the best of the Fenian organizers, denounced such tactics, as did John O'Leary and the IRB in Ireland. (O'Leary said there were deeds a man must not do, even for his country.)

The courage on the gallows and in prison of rank and file Fenians won the admiration of Irish nationalists everywhere, even of those who disagreed with their methods. O'Leary, in his reminiscences, put it like this:

> . . . the heart of the country always goes out to the man who lives and dies an unrepentant rebel. The rebel can reckon upon nothing in life; he is sure to be calumniated, he is likely to be robbed, and may even be murdered, but let him once go out of life, and he is sure of a fine funeral.[22]

Gustave Cluseret, commander of the military forces of the Paris Commune, collaborated with Fenianism and was astonished that so radical a movement could take root in Ireland, 'hitherto a stranger to any sentiment except the faith and clerical rule'. The Fenian programme was 'first, complete independence of Ireland from English power; second, a free church and a free state; third, the republican form of government', he said.[23]

Fenianism impressed William Ewart Gladstone, the English Liberal Party leader, by its violent fanaticism. He diagnosed that three injustices gave Fenianism support in Ireland: the established Protestant Church, the land system, direct English rule. In 1869, he disestablished the Church of Ireland, and in 1870 sponsored an Irish land bill. These measures did not cure Irish discontent, but they were a beginning. In 1886, Gladstone introduced the first 'Home Rule for Ireland Bill' with the statement:

> The two questions of land and of Irish government are, in our view, closely and inseparably connected, for they are the two channels through which we hope to find access, and effectual access, to that question which is the most vital of all – namely the question of social order in Ireland.[24]

Fenianism should get much of the credit for the educational process that made English politicians aware that something was seriously wrong with the social and political system in Ireland. Fenianism was responsible also for raising the national consciousness of the peasantry to the point where it became clear that they would be satisfied with nothing less than a social revolution that would give them ownership of the land, and a political revolution that would permit them to govern themselves. In a study of Irish republican ideology this must be emphasized, for 'consciousness' – false or not – is a child of ideology.[25]

'The New Departure'

The ideology of Fenianism was uncompromising Irish nationalism. It spoke of its American-model Irish Republic as being 'virtually established'. It drew its membership in Ireland from the labouring poor, the younger sons of tenant farmers, shop assistants in market towns and cities, rural teachers.[26] A Fenian was recognized in his own community as a rebel against state and Church. Yet some Fenian leaders were quite conservative and did not want to get entangled in tenant struggles: the farmer was better off than the labourer and the mechanic, they argued. They sneered at the alliance of 'aristocratic shopkeepers, attorneys, parish priests, and others of the *haute monde*' that presumed to speak for the peasantry. [27]

Because of their own abortive effort at revolution, the Fenians were astonished by the support a movement for amnesty received in Ireland. Tens of thousands attended meetings and the agitation for the release of Fenian prisoners turned into an attack on landlordism and a demand for Home Rule. Marx, in London, took a keen interest in the amnesty agitation, and was quick to note the change. The English had all 'the material prerequisites' for the social revolution, he noted, in a confidential communication to the General Council of the First International, but they lacked 'revolutionary fervour'. 'The only point where one can hit official England really hard is *Ireland*,' he stressed, because 'Ireland is the *bulwark* of English landlordism'. If it fell in Ireland, it would fall in England. It was easier to strike it in Ireland for '*the economic struggle there is concentrated exclusively on landed property*, since this struggle is at the same time national, and since the people there are more revolutionary and exasperated than in England. Landlordism in Ireland is maintained solely by the *English army*'. Marx saw a 'social revolution' breaking out in Ireland, once 'the forced union' with England ended. In such a struggle, landlordism would lose not only 'a great source of wealth', but also its *greatest moral* force, i.e. that of *'representing the domination of England over Ireland. . .'*. Because 'any nation that oppresses another forges its own chains', Marx concluded that before the English working class could emancipate itself 'the enslavement of Ireland' must cease: '. . . to encourage the social revolution in England. . . a great blow must be struck in Ireland.'[28]

This is an extraordinarily shrewd assessment of Irish politics, except for one detail: 'the social revolution' of the land struggle was completed before 'the forced union' between England and Ireland was broken. Perhaps Marx thought the English government would not abandon its agents, the landlords; but Gladstone was prepared to do exactly that, by stages. However, it is noteworthy that in 1870 Marx could predict Ireland's social and national struggle of the 1880s.

The Fenian prisoners were released and their leaders were exiled to America and France. Among those who went to America was John Devoy, realist and revolutionary, who spent the rest of his long life – he lived till 1929 – plotting the overthrow of British rule in Ireland.

Devoy built Clan-na-Gael, or United Brotherhood,[29] into a powerful organization of the 'Irish nation in the United States' – to use the words of Sir William Harcourt, Gladstone's Home Secretary – 'to act in concert with the IRB in Ireland and Great Britain and assist it with money, war material and men'.[30] Devoy planned the rescue of Fenian prisoners in Australia, bought a whaling ship, the *Catalpa,* and hired a crew to whisk them to safety in America from the power of the British Empire and its navy. The plan succeeded.[31]

Devoy's strategy involved building a great movement of Irish exiles in America and, when England was involved in war, offering the IRB at home the opportunity to rise. In 1876 he interviewed the Russian ambassador in Washington, during a time of tension between the Czar and England over the crumbling Ottoman Empire, and asked his help. 'Gentlemen, we have no doubt of your sincerity,' the Russian told the Clan delegation, according to Devoy's memoirs, 'but you are really a small party; you don't represent Ireland'. Devoy had to agree that this was so.

In December 1877 two Clan leaders, Dr William Carroll and James J. O'Kelly (later a Parnellite member of parliament in London), presented a plan to the Spanish government for seizing Gibraltar. This, too, was rejected. The Clan spent $60,000 on John P. Holland's submarine experiments on the Passaic River in New Jersey. They abandoned the idea of destroying the British from under the seas, but the US and German navies adopted Holland's plan.

In the autumn on 1878 the unorthodox and resourceful Devoy fell back on Fintan Lalor's 1847-48 proposal for agrarian revolution. He called it the 'New Departure'. It was part of a four-year plan to give Ireland independence by 1882, the centenary of Grattan's parliament. Devoy said the Clan would back the Home Rule movement under Charles Stewart Parnell, a landlord and member of the Protestant Ascendancy, as part of a struggle for independence and peasant proprietorship. Michael Davitt,[32] Fenian founder of the Land League, supported the 'New Departure', but the conservative leadership of the IRB (Charles Kickham and John O'Leary) would not and they expelled the radical Fenians who joined the new movement. The IRB itself entered a long twilight period as a result. In the 'New Departure',[33] the Land League and the Irish Parliamentary Party combined to strike the 'great blow' against British power in Ireland that Marx had predicted. The success of the policy vindicated James Fintan Lalor's 1847–48 writings on how to undo the conquest.

All the founders of the Land League – Davitt, Matt Harris, Patrick Egan, Thomas Brennan – were Fenians. No constitutionalist had anything to do with it. Archbishop MacHale called the organizers 'strolling men'.[34] The money Devoy sent to pay for the first meetings came from O'Donovan Rossa's 'skirmishing fund' for terrorism in England. Devoy thought it could be put to better use financing an anti-landlord agitation.

Davitt said orthodox Fenianism, by refusing to deal with social issues, 'had nothing to offer to the mass of the Irish people except the experiences of penal servitude and the records of the abortive rising of 1867'.[35] Davitt himself who spent seven years in prison, had decided that the Irish made poor conspirators and in future that he would work openly for Irish independence.[36]

Parnell was willing to work with Fenians; and, as he stated in a controversial speech in Cincinnati in 1880, was willing to break the 'last link' with England.[37] No doubt Parnell was playing to the Clan-na-Gael gallery in America. He was quite well aware that, speaking ideologically, peasant Ireland cared little how it was governed, as long as it was well governed; republicanism as such had little appeal: perhaps because it antagonized the Church. In the period 1879 to 1891 these subtleties of self-government were not discussed. They became an issue after the 1916 Easter Rising.

Parnell as National Leader

The Land League conducted 'a kind of guerrilla social warfare' against landlordism, Davitt said.[38] Its most intense phase was from the summer of 1879 until the so-called 'Kilmainham Treaty', in May 1882, when Parnell and other leaders were released from prison. Coercion was suspended and Parnell promised to work for Gladstone's 1881 Land Act. In the bitter phase of the struggle, as evictions and peasant 'outrages'[39] mounted, the 'boycott' weapon was introduced by the Land League against tenants who bid for farms from which the occupants had been evicted. Davitt denounced all strong-arm tactics, but not 'boycotting', which took its name from its first victim, Captain Boycott, a land agent of Lord Erne, who became 'an object of scorn and contempt', because he lived 'on the fat of the land' while the natives tilled 'rocks, old walls, heath and brush-wood'. His real crime was that he refused to reduce rents by one quarter following a bad harvest. No labourer would work for him; no servant would cook for him; he could not save his crops; the tenants refused to pay him any rent. He had a guard of six policemen; Orange workers were imported from Ulster to save his harvest and English soldiers guarded them – 2000 troops in all, according to Davitt.

After six months Captain Boycott left for England with his family.[40] When the government seized the League's leaders, the Ladies Land League[41] – founded in America by Parnell's sister – took their place. Money poured in from America to aid the victims of the land war. Despite a caution from the Pope, 'to do nothing which is contrary to the obedience due to the legitimate authorities',[42] the outlawed Land League issued a 'No-Rent Manifesto' – a general strike against payment of rents – which proved ineffective, because the local leaders were in jail.

'This form of resistance cannot be suppressed,' said Engels, viewing the situation from England. 'Force is useless against it, and it will disappear only with the causes responsible for it.' On the other hand, he told the German Social Democratic leader, Eduard Bernstein, that a Fenian rebellion was out of the question because the 14,000 armed constabulary and 30,000 regular troops in Ireland, who could be easily reinforced, would suppress any Irish rising while England was at peace. 'Therefore all that is left to

Ireland is the constitutional way of gradually conquering one position after the other,' Engels continued. 'And here the mysterious background of a Fenian armed conspiracy can remain a very effective element.' [43]

That, of course, was Parnell's policy. Davitt did not agree with him. 'English rule in Ireland had never been so shaken and demoralized since 1798 as it was in 1881–82, nor had [Dublin] Castle rule ever been so fiercely and effectively assaulted in the century. The country was absolutely ungovernable. . .'[44]

First Home Rule Bill

The Land League was a movement of the Catholic peasantry; the Protestants of Ulster were not part of it. Occasionally Protestants were used, as in the Captain Boycott case, to harvest the landlord's crops. The Fenian founders of the Land League, and the Land League itself, had no role after 1882.[45] With a disciplined party behind him in the British Commons, Parnell concentrated on winning Home Rule. He seemed close to victory when Gladstone brought in the first Home Rule Bill in April 1886. 'Our ineffectual and spurious coercion is morally worn out,' the Liberal Party leader explained.

> I cannot conceal the conviction that the voice of Ireland, as a whole, is at this moment clearly and constitutionally spoken. I cannot say it is otherwise when five-sixths of its lawfully-chosen representatives are of one mind in this matter. There is a counter voice; and I wish to know what is the claim of those by whom that counter voice is spoken, and how much is the scope and allowance we can give them. Certainly, sir, I cannot allow it to be said that a Protestant minority in Ulster, or elsewhere, is to rule the question at large for Ireland. I am aware of no constitutional doctrine tolerable on which such a conclusion could be adopted or justified. But I think that the Protestant minority should have its wishes considered to the utmost practicable extent in any form which they may assume.[46]

The Prime Minister listed a series of safeguards for Protestant Ulster, but rejected any clause that would veto the demand of 'Ireland at large' for self-government, including partition. And he would not reserve certain matters, such as education, to provincial councils.[47]

The Tories and Protestant Ulster made common cause against Home Rule. They agreed it would be bad for Ulster, for Ireland, for the United Kingdom and for the empire. Questions of trade and industry were most important. Ulster linen dominated the markets of Britain and the United States. Belfast's shipyard built steamships and great liners. Compared with Ulster, Catholic Ireland was backward. Ulster's Protestant industrialists and wage-earners, landlords and tenants, united against Home Rule. 'Indeed, Ulster presents at this moment a great object-lesson to all those who desire to study the condition of Ireland,' wrote H.O. Arnold-Foster, in the *Political Science Quarterly* in 1889. 'Ulster must be seen to be comprehended. There is something in the outward and visible signs of wealth and prosperity and order in that province which is more impressive than any amount of comparative statistics.' He stated the case against Home Rule: 'Ireland never was a nation; it is even true to say that the Irish never possessed a nationality.'[48]

The Protestants of Ulster developed their own anti-nationalist ideology based on their rights as British subjects. They would fight rather than submit to Catholic rule, their leaders declared. The nationalists considered such talk bluff: once parliament decided to enact Home Rule, Protestant Ulster would obey the law. They had little idea of the gulf between them and the Unionists. Arnold-Foster interpreted accurately the ideology of the Unionists.

> Protestant Ulster is incomparably ahead of the rest of Ireland in strength, wealth, prosperity, respect for law and love of personal independence.... Rightly or wrongly the northern Protestants believe that to allow Ulster to be taxed and administered by a Dublin Parliament would be to deliver it over to ruin. They regard the Parnellites as men who, having failed in every honest trade, have earned and are earning a living from the doubtful trade of politics. They believe, moreover, that these men are rightly charged with being principal or accessory to the commission of gross felonies; they know their nominees to have been in trade and traffic with men whose whole life has been devoted to treasonable practices against the country to which they owe allegiance. They look at Limerick and Dublin on the one side, and they look at Belfast and Lurgan on the other; they compare life in Kerry and life in Antrim; and they say, naturally enough: we decline to become the prey of the men who have done these things and who have produced these results.[49]

Nationalist Ireland never fully understood this deep-rooted prejudice against its economic backwardness, peasant character, customs, culture, way of life, religion. Such attitudes were blamed on ignorance and on British efforts to keep the people divided, the more easily to rule them.[50] It was a matter of class as much as anything else. W.E.H. Lecky, the historian, was a Protestant who favoured Home Rule until the land war. The character of that struggle convinced him 'how radically and profoundly unfit Ireland was for self-government', in the words of a modern historian.[51] Whatever the reason, Tory Britain and Unionist Ireland, first delayed, then defeated Home Rule as Gladstone and Parnell had envisaged it in 1886.[52]

The De-Anglicization of Ireland

In the last decade of the nineteenth century some nationalists unintentionally erected more barriers with Protestant Ulster. Spoken Irish had survived as the vernacular of the peasantry along the Atlantic coast. In these poor areas of subsistence farming and fishing the Great Famine struck particularly hard, and the language suffered in the exodus that followed. Translations of the old Celtic stories in the 1880s, and especially Standish O'Grady's *History of Ireland: Heroic Period*, inspired the young. 'A nation's history is made for it by circumstances, and the irreversible progress of events,' O'Grady wrote, 'but their legends they make for themselves.'[53] Back from Fenian exile, John O'Leary introduced W.B. Yeats to the works of Thomas Davis. Yeats wrote *The Wanderings of Oisin*. Intellectuals began to interest themselves in the dying Irish language. Dr Douglas Hyde, a poet and scholar, delivered a lecture in Dublin in November 1892 on 'The Necessity for De-Anglicizing Ireland'. The son of a Protestant (Church of Ireland) rector, Hyde learned Irish as a boy in Connacht. He collected Gaelic folk songs and folk tales and translated them. A Unionist in politics himself, in his lecture he taunted the nationalists for discarding 'with a light heart the best claim which we have upon the world's recognition of us as a nationality' – the Irish language – and with it the bricks of nationality. New ones must be made. Unionists and nationalists should join in the work of restoring the native language to its proper place in Irish life. The founding of Maynooth seminary and the rise of O'Connell had 'made an end of the Gaelicism' of the Irish, he charged. And thus an ancient civilization died.

> Thomas Davis and his brilliant band of Young Irelanders came just at the dividing of the line, and tried to give to Ireland a new literature in English to replace the literature which was just being discarded. It succeeded and it did not succeed. It was a most brilliant effort, but the old bark had been too recently stripped off the Irish tree, and the trunk could not take as it might have done to a fresh one. It was a new departure, and at first produced a violent effect. Yet in the long run it failed to properly leaven our peasantry who might, perhaps, have been reached upon other lines.[54]

'Our once great national tongue' must be revived and the spiritual Irish nation saved, Hyde continued. 'In order to de-Anglicize ourselves we must at once arrest the decay of the language.' The peasantry who used Irish in their daily speech must be made to feel proud of it.

> We can, however, insist, and we *shall* insist if Home Rule be carried, that the Irish language, which so many foreign scholars of the first calibre find so worthy of study, shall be placed on a par with – or even above – Greek,

> Latin, and modern languages, in all examinations held under the Irish Government. We can also insist, and we *shall* insist, that in those baronies where the children speak Irish, Irish shall be taught, and that Irish-speaking schoolmasters, petty sessions clerks, and even magistrates be appointed in Irish-speaking districts. If all this were done, it should not be very difficult, with the aid of the foremost foreign scholars, to bring about a tone of thought which would make it disgraceful for an educated Irishman. . . . to be ignorant of his own language – would make it at least as disgraceful as for an educated Jew to be quite ignorant of Hebrew.[55]

From Hyde's lecture sprang the movement to save the Irish language, the Gaelic League, which shaped profoundly twentieth-century Irish nationalist ideology, particularly republicanism, although that was never Hyde's intention. The Gaelic League created a cultural and political revolution. Out of it grew *Sinn Fein* – an amalgam of Young Irelandism, Fenianism and Gaelicism. Its members learned Irish (or tried to), read Davis and Mitchel, and purchased the weekly, *The United Irishman*, edited by a young compositor named Arthur Griffith, who preached the economic theories of Friedrich List, 'the man who saved Germany from falling a prey to English economics, and whose brain conceived the great industrial and economic Germany of today'.[56]

The Sinn Fein Idea

Sinn Fein was not a physical-force movement, but the young people who imbibed its ideology were anti-English and anti-constitutional politics. Mainly of peasant background, but living and working in Dublin, they brought a fierce Fenian enthusiasm to their new politics. Sinn Fein, which means 'ourselves', embraced in somewhat narrow fashion all things Irish, from culture to commerce. Most of them graduated to Sinn Fein from the non-political Gaelic League, which became the transmission belt for a virile and aggressive Irish-Ireland ideology. Few of the thousands who attended Irish-language classes managed to master the tongue, but almost all made the transition from cultural to republican nationalism. Four of the seven signatories of the 1916 Rising's 'Proclamation of the Irish Republic' had 'been to school to the Gaelic League', as P.H. Pearse, their spokesman, phrased it.[57]

Sean O'Casey tells how he, a Dublin labourer, went to work each day with Father Eugene O'Growney's primer, *Simple Lessons in Irish,* in his pocket, awaiting the chance to take it out and learn a phrase of Gaelic.[58] The Frenchman, L. Paul-Dubois, writing in 1906, noticed

> how serious, deep and infectious is the enthusiasm of the crowds, young and old, clerks and artisans for the most part – with an 'intellectual' here and there – who are gathered together in an ill-lit hall. . . .Evidently here are people who have been transformed to the core of their being by this somewhat severe study, and by the importance of the role which they wish to play, and which in fact they do play.[59]

The man who put the label 'Irish-Ireland' on the kind of ideology this assortment of clubs and societies produced was D.P. Moran, editor of the weekly magazine, *The Leader*. Moran believed the political system Irish-Irelandism would build must be Catholic. Non-Catholics would have to subscribe to this Catholic concept or leave Ireland. This excluded all Protestants by definition. Not everyone accepted this view, of course. Protestants were active in the Gaelic League. Moran was a maverick who made fun of the Gaelic League and Sinn Fein, calling the latter 'the green Hungarian band', because of Griffith's admiration for Francis Deak, who won a free parliament, constitution and dual monarchy for his country; Griffith had a similar plan for Ireland.[60] But a certain sectarian, even a racialist tone distinguished early Sinn Fein ideology from predecessor nationalist movements.[61] The influence of Moran and Griffith, because of their journalism, was widespread in 'Irish-Ireland' circles. Some of Moran's word coinages – 'West Briton' for Irishmen who aped English ways and admired the English political system, is an instance – became popular in Dublin.[62]

Such narrow thinking led to blinkered vision. Gaelic and Irish became synonymous terms, which they were not; then Gaelic and Catholic became synonymous, which they were not. (The woman who gave Sinn Fein its name was a Protestant.) Irish history was interpreted in racialist (or ethnic) terms: Gaelic civilization versus the English conquest; the Celt against the Anglo-Saxon. Such views further alienated Ulster Protestants, colonial settlers from the early seventeenth century. What would be their role in the new Gaelic Ireland of Sinn Fein? Was there a place for them? Would the Gael be 'restored' to his ancient patrimony? There was no great discussion of these ideas, but 'Gael' versus 'Gall' was the backdrop to Sinn Fein ideology.

Hyde was not responsible for the narrowing of national ideology. He shunned politics and wanted cultural not political change. Some of the blame must go to Hyde's Gaelic League colleague, Eoin Mac Neill, an Ulster Catholic from the Glens of Antrim. For MacNeill, the Roman Empire (except its Christian phase), the Renaissance, the Reformation, the Enlightenment and the French Revolution were great evils. Many of his ideas can be traced to Herder; others to Davis. In 1909 he became Professor of Early Irish History at University College, Dublin. 'To MacNeill belongs the credit of having dragged Celtic Ireland practically single-handed from the antiquarian mists into the light of history,' one historian declares.[63] MacNeill saw Celtic civilization through a romantic haze. He was insufficiently critical, his theories and facts were often wrong, he thought the Irish nation derived from the blending of Christian and Gaelic cultures in the fifth and sixth centuries, he downgraded the thinking of Grattan and Tone in the development of Irish nationalism. Nationality he saw as distinct from nationalism, which he distrusted.

> Nationality is to be distinguished from Nationalism, which is a political doctrine, meaning localised Statism; it is a fact, not a theory; a nation is a species of genus government. Nationality is the type of civilization which a people has developed, which has become that people's tradition, and is distinctive of that people.[64]

This conflicts with republican ideology of the United Irish, Young Ireland, Fenian varieties, but can be adapted to the Gaelic traditionalism of the Jacobites. Republicanism has no connection with Gaelic Ireland's hierarchical and aristocratic society. There is much of MacNeillism in the writings of his disciple, Pearse, who grafted it to Irish republicanism; Pearse interpreted this republicanism as 'separatism', as indicated by his axiom 'not free merely, but Gaelic as well; not Gaelic merely, but free as well'.[65] This agrees with another MacNeill statement: 'For my own part, if Irish nationality were not to mean a distinctive Irish civilization, I would attach no very great value to Irish national independence.'[66] These ideas permeated the new Irish Free State; MacNeill was its first Minister for Education.

The Political Ideas of P.H. Pearse

'I have said again and again that when the Gaelic League was founded in 1893, the Irish Revolution began,' said Patrick H. Pearse three years before the 1916 insurrection. In the ideology of modern Irish republicanism – using that term to denote physical-force nationalism – Pearse is a most important figure, for three reasons: he represents the Gaelic ideal, he symbolized the 1916 Rising, his political writings were treated as Holy Writ in the first fifty years of the Irish state. A religious Catholic and most tolerant person, he has come under close scrutiny of late. Theologically, some of his ideas are considered unsound because he expressed his nationalism 'in terms of the Christian faith'.[67] He is condemned for his glorification of bloodshed and war. Writing of heroism in a noble cause, at Christmas 1915, he used extravagant terms to describe 'the homage of millions of lives given gladly for love of country'.[68] He hoped the war would bring the French back to the Catholic faith. (This may explain his curious silence on republicanism, which in Ireland stemmed from the French Revolution. He thought highly of Wolfe Tone – but as a *separatist*, in fact, *the* separatist of Irish politics.)

Pearse is a most unusual leader of a revolutionary movement. He was a conservative who wished, like MacNeill, to restore Gaelic Ireland. He never joined Sinn Fein, or any political party. Until 1911 – 12 he showed little interest in politics. During the Home Rule crisis of 1912 he spoke in Dublin with MacNeill, in Irish. 'The morning Home Rule passes,' Sir Edward Carson said, he would set up a government for 'the Protestant province of Ulster'.[69] Pearse, who was unknown outside the ranks of the Gaelic League – he was the editor of its bilingual weekly, *An Claidheamh Soluis* (The Sword of Light) – also made a pledge: if England reneged on Home Rule there would be 'red war in Ireland'. Since few understood him, no one paid him any heed. But Pearse was a man of his word in everything he said or wrote.

Before 1912 Pearse's chief interest, apart from Irish, was St Enda's, his school for boys in Dublin. All secondary education in Catholic Ireland was controlled by the Church. Pearse thought anglicization was the purpose of the Irish educational system. In education he was a pioneer. The teaching at St. Enda's was in Irish. 'My school should be an Irish school in a sense not known or dreamt of in Ireland since the Flight of the Earls' (O'Neill and O'Donnell in 1607), Pearse explained. He saw no contradiction between the pagan virtues of the Celtic hero Cuchulainn and the Christian virtues required of schoolboys in the Ireland of his time. For this Father Shaw takes him to task.[70] Pearse used metaphors from Christ's passion to explain Irish history. 'The people who wept in Gethsemane, who trod the sorrowful way, who died naked on a cross, who went down into hell, will rise again glorious and immortal, will sit on the right hand of God, and will come in the end to give judgment, a judge just and terrible.'[71] He turned Tone, Davis, Mitchel and Lalor into four 'evangelists' of Irish separatism. As Father Shaw notes, this was a remarkable performance inasmuch as Tone was a rationalist, a Jacobin whose doctrines were condemned by the Catholic Church, whose views 'were not, prima facie, likely to be accepted by any large number of his countrymen'.[72]

Pearse accomplished a synthesis between revolution and Catholicism in Ireland. A devout Catholic, he could not be attacked on religious grounds. He was sanctified after 1916. He was a mystic like Joseph Plunkett, another 1916 leader and poet. His colleagues included James Connolly, a Marxist, and Tom Clarke, a Clan-na-Gael dynamiter.[73]

Taking 1912 as Pearse's starting point in politics, it is plain from his editorials in a little Irish-language magazine he founded called *An Barr Buadh* (the Trumpet of Victory) that he held the concept that an elite group – perhaps seven 'just men' or a band of knights – would save Ireland from English betrayal. Pearse's concern was separate nationhood for Ireland, without which Gaelic civilization could not be rebuilt. Thus far he differed from MacNeill, who had no faith in statehood. It is as a Gaelic enthusiast seeking his ends by political means that one must view Pearse, a point overlooked by critics and admirers alike. His *Barr Buadh* writings make it clear that he was a *separatist*, not an ideological republican like Tone; his view of the United Irishmen, Young Ireland and the Fenians is a *separatist* view. Republicanism was unknown in Gaelic Ireland. Pearse's views were influenced by his rejection of the anti-clericalism, so much a part of continental republicanism, especially in France, Spain, Italy and Portugal, at the turn of the century. But he joined the IRB, took an oath, drafted the Proclamation and signed it – as did Connolly, the socialist revolutionary, who would have had little use for 'the bourgeois republic' it proclaimed. MacDonagh and Plunkett thought much as Pearse. All of them died for the Irish Republic and its revolutionary right to exist.

In his *Barr Buadh* articles, Pearse charged that the great majority of his generation had sold themselves to the foreigner, though unaware of it. This sweeping condemnation was based on a broad definition of selling oneself and included old pensioners. The majority who favoured Home Rule did not want freedom but peace.[74] It was necessary to have a group to defend the honour of the Irish people in the struggle that lay ahead and especially in the peace following it. Such a group would mobilize the people, if England conceded Home Rule, presumably to defend it. They would fight if Ireland was denied Home Rule. Pearse saw this small band coming from the high-minded Irish-Irelanders.[75] Home Rule was a first step to independence; Parnell had much the same concept. Pearse's definition of independence was Irish rule without foreign interference. 'Ní Síothcháin go Saoirse' (No Peace till Freedom),[76] he declared. It has become a republican slogan. Nationalist Ireland should arm for independence as Field Marshal Lord Roberts, the victor of the Boer War, had urged the English to arm and Kaiser Wilhelm II had urged the Germans to arm. Pearse did not make his proposal so that the Irish would fight, but to be able to defend themselves if attacked. If Home Rule were withheld, there would be 'red war' in Ireland, Pearse wrote. He advised the Irish to remain faithful to Irish-Ireland and to Christianity, and not to bother with Communism and other foreign ideas, which had made England and indeed most of Europe un-Christian. Irish priests and lay persons should stand shoulder to shoulder in defence of their interests until they had won their rights.[77]

Pearse's views sound almost medieval and strangely innocent. Four years later the Catholic mystic Pearse would stand shoulder to shoulder with the Marxist Connolly in defence of the Irish Republic they had proclaimed in arms. How Pearse reached that point has more to do with the anti-Home Rule campaign of the English Tory establishment than with his own development as a revolutionary thinker.

An Bárr Buadh died after eleven issues. Few knew of its existence. Pearse founded a political society Cumann na Saoirse (Liberty Club), to recruit the vanguard he spoke of in his articles, the Irish speakers who would defend the national honour. There were never more than a dozen club members but all turned out for the 1916 Rising, which was the work of a heroic band asserting Ireland's right to independence – in the name of the Irish people, but without their support.[78]

Founding of the Irish Volunteers – By the IRB

By 1913 it was clear that the English Establishment would resist Home Rule by all means including force. A retired army officer was recommended by Lord Roberts to head the Ulster Volunteers and 100 peers and 120 Tory members of parliament founded a 'British League for the Support of Ulster and the Union'. The *Times* (11 June, 1913) said the Conservative Party stood behind Carson, whose declaration 'Ulster will not accept Home Rule on any conditions whatsoever' was well known. 'Home Rule was impossible for Ireland if Belfast and the surrounding parts are against the scheme,' Carson added in explanation of his strategy to maintain the Union. Or, as Winston Churchill said: 'We are then at the position that the minority in Ireland claim the right for all time and in all circumstances to bar the path of progress for the whole of the rest of Ireland, and to bar it not merely by constitutional means but, if necessary, by the use of armed force.' He quoted Disraeli:

> I am not at all prepared to admit that there are two nations in Ireland. I look upon the Irish nation as one people. For the last forty years they have been a homogeneous people. If we come to an analysis of the elements of a nation. . . I am not sure that we shall be able to prove that the English people are so homogeneous as political philosophy now requires people to be. I treat the Irish nation as one.[79]

In October 1913 Churchill said:

> Think of the consequences to Ireland if Home Rule were defeated now by violence or by threats of violence. Ever since the Act of Union British political leaders without distinction of party, have endeavoured by every means in their power to divert the Irish national movement into constitutional channels. . . . To the chagrin of the revolutionary forces and factions in Ireland and America and to the joy of law-abiding Irishmen of every colony of the Empire and throughout the world, the cause of Home Rule has at last been carried, without violence or sedition, but by constitutional and Parliamentary action, to the threshold of complete achievement. And if we are now to be told that this whole process of constitutional remedy for the redress of grievances is to be nullified utterly by the pinch of violence, and that a minority in a single province is by audacity to bar the way for all time to the whole progress of the Irish nation and interpose a bully's veto more arbitrary than the veto of the Crown. . . then, I say, if such things could happen, constitutional and parliamentary action and patient law-abiding agitation for the redress of grievances would in every part of the British Empire, and indeed throughout the civilized world, be discredited and mocked, and those dark and furious methods of lawless violence which civilized society has always banned would receive a supreme and devastating vindication.[80]

Churchill's 'revolutionary forces and factions in Ireland and America' were the IRB and Clan-na-Gael. The first was very small and could hardly exist without support from America. The second was in decline and John Devoy was growing old. Young men like Bulmer Hobson, a Belfast Quaker, and Denis McCullough, a Belfast Catholic, were trying to take over the revolutionary organization from the old guard, but these internal squabbles hardly affected the national question. Hobson was given 'a very hostile reception' in Leitrim during an election contested by Sinn Fein, he told Joseph McGarrity on 4 October 1907. He was attacked from the altar by a priest as 'an enemy of the Catholic Church'. The priest 'advised the people not to go to any meeting I spoke at'. But another IRB organizer, a local man named Seán MacDermott, 'is doing great work'. (Seán MacDermott was one of the planners of the 1916 Rising.)

Clan-na-Gael, in a letter to officers and members on 2 October 1912, took credit for weakening the Anglo-American alliance, by campaigning against the Arbitration Treaties, and it helped the young men take over the IRB monthly organ, *Irish Freedom*. But it had little influence beyond that. In 1912 Seán MacDermott went to the Clan Convention in Atlantic City as IRB delegate. He reported that the IRB had about 2000 members in Ireland and Britain. The same year Tom Clarke, the old Clan dynamiter of the 1880s who had spent fifteen years in English prisons, told a friend in America (28 June): 'You will be pleased to know that things are better here than they have been in many years. Have no fear, the young fellows – the ablest in the country, are all right. . . .' On 8 December 1913 Clarke wrote to McGarrity: 'Joe, it is worth living in Ireland these times – there is an awakening – the slow, silent plodding and the open preaching is at last showing results – things are in full swing on the up side – and we are breathing air that compels one to fling up his head and stand more erect.'[81]

What made the national picture 'brighter than it has been in many a long year – certainly as far back as my memory goes', for Tom Clarke, was the founding of the Irish Volunteers in Dublin on 25 November 1913. The proposal came from the IRB. Eoin MacNeill wrote 'The North Began' in the Gaelic League weekly, praising the founding of the Ulster Volunteers and suggesting that nationalist Ireland do likewise. The Volunteers of 1782, he noted broadly, 'became the instrument of establishing self-government and Irish prosperity'.[82]

The first important convert made by the new IRB leadership was Pearse, who started writing for *Irish Freedom* in the spring of 1913. Clarke considered him ideal for their purposes: a good writer, orator, teacher, respectable public figure. Through Pearse they reached other young intellectuals – Joseph Plunkett, poet and son of Count Plunkett, and Thomas MacDonagh, a lecturer at the National University. The IRB chose Pearse as a member of the Provisional Committee that met under the chairmanship of Eoin MacNeill, in the autumn of 1913, to found the Irish Volunteers. At the end of the year Pearse joined the IRB and in the spring of 1914 met Devoy and McGarrity[83] in New York, where he lectured to raise money for St Enda's. Devoy seems to have dismissed him as a sentimentalist; but McGarrity, who was something of a sentimentalist himself under a rugged exterior, took to Pearse, who made strong speeches about Irish independence. Home Rule or no Home Rule, he said, the 'substantial business of achieving nationhood' remained, adding, 'and I do not know how nationhood is achieved except by armed men; I do not know how nationhood is guarded except by armed men'.[84]

The same theme of course runs through Pearse's writings from 1912, so it was not a case of playing up to the wild men of the Clan-na-Gael. Pearse believed what he said. He seems to have determined that the Irish Volunteers would act towards England as the Volunteers of 1782 acted 'to secure and maintain the rights and liberties common to the whole people of Ireland'.[85] Failing that, the 'just men' of Irish-Ireland he had appealed to in his *Barr Buadh* editorials would act at the proper time as the conscience of the nation. At any rate, McGarrity saw in Pearse a man who could be trusted to do his Fenian duty. Hobson, who had been in America at the same time, wrote to McGarrity on 18 May 1914 on his return:

> I saw Pearse who landed on Friday last. He was very pleased with his visit, as indeed he ought to be, and very grateful for the help you gave him. He told me of your plans re the Volunteer movement. I am strongly of the opinion that it is up to the people at home to help themselves. They can do it if they want to and they won't do it if they think that America will do it for them.

Hobson went on to talk of a new newspaper project, and he wanted McGarrity's help. Pearse had talked of buying guns, not of setting up a paper, which appealed more to McGarrity's spirit.

After June 1914 McGarrity's communications were with Pearse, not Hobson; and they concerned plans for a rising. On 1 June 1914 a letter from the headquarters of Clan-na-Gael to all officiers and members declared:

> The people of Ireland are returning rapidly to the old belief of physical force and a more virile and wholesome spirit has taken possession of the young men than has been apparent since the days of Fenianism. We have reason to believe that this revival of the old spirit is not prompted by any dangerous miscalculations as to the power of Ireland to fight the British Empire when it is at peace with the rest of the world and we are assured that no hot-headed projects of premature insurrection are harboured.

Pearse clearly had his mind made up to stage a rebellion at some point between the start of the war and its ending. He left no doubt about his intentions and those who say he deceived MacNeill in 1916 are being pedantic.[86] In May 1915 he wrote in the journal published by the Irish Volunteers:

> We want recruits because we are absolutely determined to take action the moment action becomes a duty. If a moment comes – as a moment seemed on the point of coming at least twice during the past eighteen months – when the Irish Volunteers will be justified to their consciences in taking definite military action, such action will be taken. We do not anticipate such a moment in the very near future; but we live at a time when it may come swiftly and terribly. What if Conscription be forced upon Ireland? What if a Unionist or

> a Coalition British Ministry repudiate the Home Rule Act? What if it be determined to dismember Ireland? What if it be determined to disarm Ireland? The future is big with these and other possibilities.[87]

In his final writings – *Ghosts* (Christmas 1915), *The Separatist Idea* (February 1916), *The Spiritual Nation* (February 1916), *The Sovereign People* (March 1916) – Pearse stated his credo of Irish nationalism, based on the teachings of 'the fathers of our national faith before and after Tone'.[88] Using 'nationality' in the MacNeill sense, he quoted a remark of the seventeenth-century Gaelic historian, Geoffrey Keating, to explain his meaning: 'He [Keating] spoke of Ireland as 'domhan beag innti féin', a little world in herself.'[89] Pearse proceeds to Tone, a man of the Enlightenment, who had no romantic notions about the lost Gaelic world; who, as Father Shaw rightly remarks, 'seems to have been completely insulated from Gaelic Ireland'.[90] Pearse is at pains to prove that Gaelic Ireland, from the landing of the Normans in 1169, to the defeat of O'Neill and O'Donnell at Kinsale in 1601, was separatist; he includes Patrick Sarsfield, commander of James II's Irish Catholic army in 1691. On what common ground did Hugh O'Neill, Sarsfield and Wolfe Tone stand? Pearse saw them as Irish nationalists; or at least as separatists. He was ambivalent about Tone and Emmet, the revolutionists, but welcomed them into his national pantheon as separatists. 'Both, however, were Nationalists first, and revolutionists only in so far as revolution was essential to the establishment of the nation.'[91] He was wrong. Tone and Emmet were revolutionists, not nationalists, in Pearse's understanding of the word.

How Pearse viewed Irish history and the ideological conclusions he drew from his readings of it are important because of his extraordinary influence on Irish republicanism, and on the Irish state. His biographer, Ruth Dudley Edwards, quotes Department of Education guide-lines on the teaching of modern Irish history.

> The continuity of the separatist idea from Tone to Pearse should be stressed. The events leading up to the Rising of 1916 and to the struggle that followed it will be so fresh in the minds of all teachers that there can be no difficulty in dealing with them vividly, or with the great language movement that was the inspiration of the leaders.[92]

Pearse's ideas were acceptable in the new nation-state to those who took pre-1921 Sinn Féin as their starting point, for he had expressed them in Gaelic and Catholic terms untainted by secularism. The four 'evangelists' – Tone, Davis, Mitchel and Lalor – were less acceptable without Pearse's endorsement.[93] Tone was remote, his writings unavailable. Davis was safe, except for his views on education and sectarianism, which were ignored. Mitchel's descriptive *Jail Journal* writing was good for anthologies. Lalor was forgotten.

Pearse, it must be said, was a hero to all except those who rejected 1916 on moral or political grounds, and they were not heard until Father Shaw wrote his essay. The violence in Northern Ireland caused others to question Pearse's premises. In an age when war is considered the worst of evils, Pearse's writing about 'the red wine of the battlefield' warming 'the old heart of the earth', whatever the reason for it, is unacceptable. But he had also written that war is terrible 'and this is the most terrible of wars', yet not more terrible than the evils which it would end. 'It is not more terrible than the enslavement of the Poles by Russia, than the enslavement of the Irish by England. . . . What if the war sets Poland and Ireland free? If the war does these things, will not the war have been worth while?' [94]

"The Sovereign People"

In the Dublin of his time Pearse was a respectable figure. He said so himself. 'Personally, I am in a position to protest my respectability. I do all the orthodox things.'[95] Barrister, writer, teacher, editor, leading member of the Gaelic League, Pearse had class and status, but not money: he was a near-bankrupt because of St Enda's. Class and status were almost as important as money in pre-1914 Dublin, according to both James Joyce and Sean O'Casey. After Pearse joined the IRB, which Bulmer Hobson says was 'a little secret movement meeting in back rooms' [96]before 1914, he found a high purpose. His oratory and writing were to the taste of Tom Clarke and Seán MacDermott, the new leaders of the IRB, and they made him their public spokesman. He was affected by the Dublin lock-out of 1913 and grew more liberal in his social outlook. In the article proclaiming his 'respectability', Pearse wrote: 'My wild oats were sown and reaped years ago. I am nothing so new-fangled as a socialist or a syndicalist. I am old-fashioned enough to be both a Catholic and a Nationalist.' That is an accurate estimate of his politics.

The 'masters of Dublin' were led by the Catholic nationalist and capitalist, William Martin Murphy. Before 1913 Pearse had blamed all of Ireland's ills on England. During the great strike, he was forced to examine the lives of the 'breadless men' and their families, who lived on 'black tea and dry bread' in one-room tenements.

There are tenement rooms in Dublin in which over a dozen persons live, eat and sleep. High rents are paid for these rooms, rents which in cities like Birmingham would command neat four-roomed cottages with gardens. The tenement houses of Dublin are so rotten that they periodically collapse upon their inhabitants, and if the inhabitants collect in the streets to discuss matters the police baton them to death.[97]

Pearse's last pamphlet, *The Sovereign People*, is both Catholic and socialist in tone, a contradiction in terms in the spring of 1916. Pearse's social awareness, stirred by the Dublin strike, the influence of James Connolly, and a reading of James Fintan Lalor as part of his attempt to synthesize the writings of the four 'evangelists' of Irish nationalism, led to *The Sovereign People*, which is a startingly radical document by one who until 1913 had wanted nothing more than the restoration of an idealized Gaelic state.

Reducing his social ideas to 'a few simple propositions', Pearse wrote: 'The end of freedom is human happiness. The end of national freedom is individual freedom; therefore individual happiness. National freedom implies national sovereignty. National sovereignty implies control of all the moral and material resources of the nation.' These ideas were embodied in the First Dáil's social programme of January 1919, only because Pearse had written them. Even so, there was some opposition by Michael Collins and the IRB, as we shall see.

Expanding on his propositions, Pearse wrote:

. . . national freedom involves control of the material things which are essential to the continued physical life and freedom of the nation. So that the nation's sovereignty extends not only to all the material possessions of the nation, the nation's soil and all its resources, all wealth and all wealth-producing processes within the nation. In other words, no private right to property is good as against the public right of the nation. But the nation is under a moral obligation so to exercise its public right as to secure strictly equal rights and liberties to every man and woman within the nation. . .[98]

These ideas are reflected in the proclamation of 'the Provisional Government of the Irish Republic to the People of Ireland', Easter Monday 1916:

The Republic guarantees religious and civil liberty, equal rights and equal opportunities to all its citizens, and declares its resolve to pursue the happiness and prosperity of the whole nation and of all its parts, cherishing all the children of the nation equally, and oblivious of the differences carefully fostered by an alien government, which have divided a minority from the majority in the past.

One may dismiss this as rhetoric, which in fact is what the new Irish State did; but the Proclamation has Pearse's style, he should get the credit for it, and he meant every word of it.

Connolly's Fenian Socialism

The decisive social influence on Pearse, and consequently on modern Irish republican radical ideology, was James Connolly, who spent a lifetime preaching socialism to the working class of Scotland, Ireland, England and the United States. The son of an Irish immigrant labourer, Connolly was born in Edinburgh in poverty and spent the forty-eight years of his life in the same condition. Some of his writings are original works of scholarship, particularly *Labour in Irish History*, which was not always read, or indeed available, outside left-wing and trade-union circles in Ireland. An organizer for the Wobblies (Industrial Workers of the World) and the Socialist Party in America, unlike most of his syndicalist colleagues, Connolly believed in political action. When he emigrated in 1904 Connolly joined Daniel De Leon's Socialist Labour Party; he clashed with that dogmatist over the roles of religion and trade unionism. Between 1896 and 1903, Connolly served his time in Dublin trying to build an Irish Socialist Republican Party.[99] In those years he developed his Irish-style socialism along the following lines:

> If you remove the English army tomorrow and hoist the green flag over Dublin Castle, unless you set about the organization of the Socialist Republic your efforts would be in vain. England would still rule you. She would rule you through her capitalists, through her landlords, through her financiers, through the whole array of commercial and individualist institutions she has planted in this country and watered with the tears of our mothers and the blood of our martyrs. . . . Nationalism without Socialism – without a reorganization of society on the basis of a broader and more developed form of that common property which underlay the social structure of Ancient Erin – is only national recreancy.[100]

Connolly contended that the Irish question was a social question; the struggle of the Irish against their English masters was in reality a struggle for the means of production in Ireland – land. Without such an understanding, Connolly claimed, Irish history was 'a hopeless chaos of sporadic outbreaks, treacheries, intrigues, massacres, murders, and purposeless warfare'.[101] The Anglo-Irish Ascendancy was England's garrison in Ireland; the Catholic middle class was bound by material self-interest to England; only the Irish poor – small tenant farmers, agricultural labourers, workers in towns and cities – resisted foreign rule and formed the rank and file of every rebel movement.

In nationalist Ireland clericalism would not permit socialists to obtain a hearing, Connolly learned. However, he persisted. When he returned to Ireland in 1910 he worked as a union organizer in Belfast. Connolly discovered that although in other lands Protestantism stood for political freedom and political radicalism, in Ireland it was synonymous with Toryism. Catholicism, which elsewhere stood for political backwardness and 'servile worship of aristocracy', in Ireland was 'almost synonymous with rebellious tendencies, zeal for democracy, and intense feeling of solidarity with all strivings upward of those who toil'. The reasons for such attitudes were understood by those who knew the history of Ireland, Connolly said. Better than any socialist or nationalist of his time, Connolly understood Belfast.[102]

Connolly stood well with other nationalists because of his theories on the national question, though they disliked and distrusted his socialism. Although friendly with Arthur Griffith, Connolly attacked him for admiring List, who measured prosperity 'by the volume of wealth produced in a country, instead of by the distribution of that wealth amongst the inhabitants'.[103] During the Home Rule crisis of 1912–14 Connolly maintained that the Liberals would betray Ireland and when partition was proposed in the spring of 1914 he declared

> . . .such a scheme should be resisted with armed force if necessary. (For it) would destroy the Labour movement by disrupting it. It would perpetuate in a form aggravated in evil the discords now prevalent, and help the Home Rule and Orange capitalists and clerics to keep their rallying cries before the public as the political watchwords of the day. In short, it would make division more intense and confusion of ideas and parties more confounded.[104]

Connolly attacked the leaders of the Irish Parliamentary Party, John Redmond and Joe Devlin, for agreeing to the exclusion of six of Ulster's nine counties from Home Rule for six years, calling it 'the betrayal of the national democracy of industrial Ulster'. He warned that the result would be 'a carnival of reaction both North and South', and continued: 'To it Labour should give the bitterest opposition, against it Labour in Ulster should fight even to the death, if necessary, as our fathers fought before us.'[105] Connolly was the first to see that 'temporary' partition – the six-year exclusion clause – was a hoax: a Tory election victory 'would only require the passage of a small Act of not more than three or four lines to make the exclusion perpetual'.[106]

When the First World War began in July 1914 Connolly was bitterly disappointed that the Second International did not oppose it. Socialists joined the armies of their respective states. The workers of Germany marched against the workers of England and France.

When Jim Larkin went to America in September 1914 Connolly took his place as head of the Irish Transport and General Workers Union, editor of the weekly *Irish Worker*, and commandant of the labour defence force, the Irish Citizen Army – founded during the 1913 strike.[107] Connolly, a soldier in his youth, trained the Citizen Army in street fighting. If the Germans landed, he said, the Irish would be justified in joining them, 'if by doing so we could rid this country once and for all from its connection with the Brigand Empire that drags us unwillingly into this war'. Connolly added:

> Should the working class of Europe, rather than slaughter each other for the benefit of kings and financiers, proceed tomorrow to erect barricades all over Europe, to break up bridges and destroy the transport service that war might be abolished, we should be perfectly justified in following such a glorious example and contributing our aid to the final dethronement of the vulture classes that rule and rob the world.[108]

The Labour movement should consider measures to prevent food leaving Ireland until the working class in the towns had enough to eat, Connolly wrote. That might mean more than a transport strike: 'It may mean armed battling in the streets to keep in this country the food for our people.' Whatever the crisis, the working class democracy should face it. 'Starting thus, Ireland may yet set the torch to a European conflagration that will not burn out until the last throne and the last capitalist bond and debenture will be shrivelled on the funeral pyre of the last war lord.'[109] Connolly left little doubt that, like the IRB, he would use the war to strike at British imperialism.

Connolly's writings grew more reckless after 1915. When the censor closed the *Irish Worker* by making it impossible for a commercial printer to produce it, Connolly installed a hand press at union headquarters under Citizen Army guards. His *Workers' Republic* stated the issues and its own purpose clearly. Connolly's notes on street-fighting, citing examples from Paris of 1848 and the Commune, and Moscow of 1905, are still used in works on guerrilla warfare.[110] When the body of O'Donovan Rossa was brought to Ireland from America for burial in Glasnevin in August 1915, Connolly wrote:

> We on our part affirm that we march behind the remains because we are prepared to fight for the same ideas. And we shall be all the more nerved for fight when we remember that the Banner of Fenianism was upheld by the stalwart hands of the Irish working class of the day, as the militant organization of the same class today is the only body that without reservation unhesitatingly announces its loyalty to the Republican principle of

national freedom for which the Fenians stood.[111]

High casualties among the Irish in Flanders distressed Connolly. He said the Ulster Nationalist leader, Joseph Devlin, was responsible for creating widows and orphans on the Falls Road – the nationalist section of Belfast – because he had supported the war, then stayed at home and drove around in a big motor car. He charged Devlin, Redmond and John Dillon with 'unparalleled national betrayal', because they had urged young Irishmen to join the British army. In contrast, 'we presented to the world the spectacle of the organized Irish working class standing steadfastly by the highest ideals of Freedom so that the Flag of Labour became once more the standard of National Liberty'.[112] Connolly called the Irish fighting in the Dardanelles 'poor slaves. . . who are asked to carry rifles, and add to the number of Irish corpses that manure the hills and ravines before the guns of the Turk'.[113] And again:

> Consider well what this (British) Empire is doing today, and then see if you can withhold your admiration.
>
> At the present moment this Empire has dominions spread all over the Seven Seas. Everywhere it holds down races and nationalities that it might use them as its slaves, that it might use their territories as sources of rent and interest for its aristocratic rulers, that it might prevent their development as self-supporting entities and compel them to remain dependent customers of English produce, that it might be able to strangle every race or nation that would enter the field as a competitor against British capital or assert its independence of the British capitalist.
>
> To do this it stifles the ancient culture of India, strangles in its birth the new born liberty of Egypt, smothers in the blood of ten thousand women and children the republics of South Africa, betrays into the hands of Russian despotism the trusting nations of Persia, connives at the partition of China, and plans the partition of Ireland.[114]

In the Autumn of 1915 Connolly published *The Re-Conquest of Ireland* – the title is from Fintan Lalor – with a two-fold thesis: that the conquest was capitalist and the re-conquest must be socialist. Written in Connolly's usual lucid, forceful style, *The Re-Conquest of Ireland* linked British policy in Ireland with British policy in India and in general to Belgian policy in the Congo: in other words it was imperialist. Organized labour should take the lead in winning national independence, as the tenant farmers and labourers of the Land League had defeated landlordism. The pamphlet is anarcho-syndicalist: in Connolly's ideal Ireland of the future

> A system of society in which the workshops, factories, docks, railways, shipyards, etc., shall be owned by the nation, but administered by the Industrial Unions of the respective industries organized as above seems best calculated to secure the highest form of industrial efficiency combined with the greatest amount of individual freedom from state despotism.

To win political power, Connolly continued, Irish democracy needed the support and the power of industrial unionism. Working class political power must come 'out of the Industrial battlefield as the expression of the organized force of Labour.' Explained Connolly:

> With Labour properly organized upon the Industrial and political field each extension of the principle of the public ownership brings us nearer to the re-conquest of Ireland by its people; it means the gradual resumption of the common ownership of all Ireland by all the Irish – the realization of Freedom.[115]

From November 1915, it was clear that Connolly planned to attack the British Empire with more than words, nor did he care who knew about it. He pointed out that the Irish Citizen Army's constitution pledged its members 'to work for an Irish Republic and the emancipation of Labour'. It was 'at the disposal of the forces of Irish nationality for the ends common to all.' He said plainly what he meant:

> An armed organization of the Irish working class is a phenomenon in Ireland. Hitherto the workers of Ireland have fought as parts of the armies led by their masters, never as members of an army officered, trained, and inspired by men of their own class. Now, with arms in their hands, they propose to steer their own course, to carve their own future.
>
> Neither Home Rule nor the lack of Home Rule will make them lay down their arms.
>
> However it may be for others, for us of the Citizen Army there is but one ideal – an Ireland ruled and owned by Irish men and women, sovereign and independent from the centre to the sea, and flying its own flag over all the oceans. . . .
>
> The Irish Citizen Army will only cooperate in a forward movement. The moment that forward movement ceases it reserves to itself the right to step out of the alignment and advance by itself if needs be, in an effort to plant the banner of Freedom one reach further towards its goal. . . .[116]

In December 1915 Connolly criticized the IRB for its plots and conspiracies that never amounted to anything. 'We do not call for public pronouncements from them, but every man is the guardian of his own conscience and responsible to that conscience if he shirks his duty to his country and its cause . . .', Connolly wrote. 'How can you make that choice wisely if you do not *know* what that leader's policy for the future is?'[117]

A week later he wondered 'how many of our people have been

sacrificed to suit the ambitions of the nice statesmen who, gorging themselves at Guildhall banquets, complacently order out sons of Irish mothers to a horrible death on the sands of Mesopotamia in a quarrel in which the poor of Ireland have not the remotest interest'.[118] Shortly before Christmas 1915 Connolly remarked that a nation, to be worthy of independence, must fight for it. 'No man can swim until he has entered the water and failed and been half drowned several times in the attempt to swim,' he wrote, adding:

> Ireland is not the Empire, the Empire is not Ireland. Anything in Ireland which depends on the Empire depends upon that which the fortunes of war *may* destroy at any moment, depends upon that which the progress of enlightenment *must* destroy in the near future. The people of India, of Egypt, cannot be for ever enslaved.
>
> Anything in Ireland which depends upon the internal resources of Ireland has a basis and a foundation which no disaster to the British Empire can destroy, which disasters to the British Empire may conceivably cause to flourish. . . .[119]

Connolly's verbal violence against the leaders of the IRB drew Pearse to comment that if the Citizen Army rose alone, it could do no more than 'riot for a few days'. Connolly suspected the British would round up all revolutionaries before anything could be done.[120] 'We believe in constitutional action in normal times,' he wrote. 'We believe in revolutionary action in exceptional times. These are exceptional times.'[121]

Connolly, the anarcho-syndicalist, believed in direct action. He would confront British imperialism in its own backyard. He would protest against Ireland's participation 'in this thrice-accursed war', because from that protest 'there will arise anew the spirit of Irish revolution'. Here are the ideological reasons why Connolly went out 'to be slaughtered' in 1916.[122] He had no doubt at all of the outcome, nor did he fully trust the IRB and Irish Volunteers, who were his allies. He told his followers – a mere 300 or so – to hold on to their guns when the fighting was over for they would need them. But he hated imperialism, he hated capitalism, he hated Britain, and he wanted an independent Ireland, even if it was non-socialist. Sean O'Casey wrote: 'The high creed of Irish nationalism became his daily rosary, while the higher creed of international humanity that had so long bubbled from his eloquent lips was silent forever, and Irish labour lost a leader.'[123]

As if to refute charges of pro-Germanism, Connolly hung a banner across the front of Liberty Hall (the union headquarters) with the inscription: 'We Serve Neither King Nor Kaiser But Ireland.' Nevertheless, he thought that Germany was the victim of British intrigue and he was for the Germans if not for the Kaiser, to judge by his 1914–15 writings.

Connolly forced the IRB leaders to draw him into their counsels following an editorial in the *Workers' Republic*, titled 'What is Our Programme?', in which he wrote that the Labour movement delighted in analysis and definition and could not live on illusions, for its feet must rest on the solid earth. Labour had a programme. It did not believe freedom would be realized without fighting for it.

> We believe that in times of peace we should work along the lines of peace to strengthen the nation, and we believe that whatever strengthens and elevates the working class strengthens the nation. But we also believe that in times of war we should act as in war. We despise, entirely despise and loathe, all the mouthings and mouthers about war who infest Ireland in time of peace, just as we despise and loathe all the cantings about caution and restraint to which the same people treat us in times of war.
>
> Mark well then our programme. While the war lasts and Ireland still is a subject nation we shall continue to urge her to fight for her freedom.
>
> We shall continue, in season and out of season, to teach that the 'far-flung battle line' of England is weakest at the point nearest its heart, that Ireland is in a position of tactical advantage, that a defeat of England in India, Egypt, the Balkans or Flanders would not be so dangerous to the British Empire as any conflict of armed forces in Ireland, that the time for Ireland's battle is NOW, the place for Ireland's battle is HERE. That a strong man may deal lusty blows with his fists against a host of surrounding foes, and conquer, but will succumb if a child sticks a pin in his heart.[124]

Connolly was invited by the IRB to join its Military Council — a revolutionary committee to plan the Easter Rising.[125] 'The seed' he had sown, to use his own metaphor, was ripe and would soon blossom. The rebellion was confined to Dublin because Eoin MacNeill countermanded Pearse's mobilization orders to the Irish Volunteers.[126] 'A few determined men who have made up their minds to die, may inflict immense loss upon the assailants in street warfare,' Connolly had written in the *Workers' Republic*, quoting Field Marshal Viscount Garnet Joseph Wolseley.[127] The losses were not great, but the determination to die was and it changed Irish history.

The Fenian dead had risen to strike a blow at England in time of war, as Tone had done and Mitchel had preached. Lord Salisbury, for the Tories, had said in 1889 that it would take 'blood' and 'conflict' and 'military force' to change the English will on Ireland: and here was 'blood' and 'conflict' and 'military force'. Irish constitutionalism had failed, the lesson read. The Parliamentary Party had collaborated with England's war and been spurned for it. The rebellion in Dublin was no more than a protest in arms by men – and women – who believed in the doctrine of physical force. Henceforth the gun would be the court of last resort in the case of Ireland versus England. Anyone who fired a shot at a British soldier in Ireland had the sanction of Pearse, Connolly and Irish history. It was, and is, the final argument for Irish republicans.

An underground conspiracy, the IRB, an Irish language revivalist, Patrick Pearse, and a socialist agitator, James Connolly, combined to produce the drama of the Easter Rising. Each was essential for the task. Unlike previous struggles, in 1916 *ideology* created the event. The people did not rebel. They did not agree with the rebels or their goals. The Irish farmers were more prosperous than at any time in their history, because of high prices for foodstuffs. Home Rule was on the statute books; Ireland was content. As Eoin MacNeill put it in February 1916, the 'basis for successful revolutionary action. . .deep and widespread popular discontent' did not exist.

The Rise of Post-1916 Sinn Féin

Nationalist Ireland opposed the Rising. Prisoners herded through the streets of Dublin to the docks, for internment in Britain, were hooted. Support for the Allied cause was strong in Ireland. Irishmen in the British Army were praised in the press for their valour. Only a small minority supported the Irish Volunteers; only a tiny minority of the Volunteers joined the rebellion.[128] When word of the Rising reached Cork, some separatists condemned it as 'a criminal mistake', believing it the work of Connolly and his Citizen Army who had no support and much hostility outside Dublin.[129]

It was true, as Father Shaw notes in his *Studies* essay and as Augustine Birrell, Britain's Chief Secretary of Ireland from 1907 to 1916, confirms, that the Irish were never loyal to Britain. Yet this does not explain the extraordinary change in ideology that occurred within a year of the Rising. The people, it seemed, swung from constitutional nationalism to republicanism in less than a year. What to Birrell was 'nothing more than a Dublin row',[130] had 'changed utterly', in Yeats's words. Ballads were sung and poems and plays written about the martyred – significant word – leaders who had become secular saints. During the Rising, Birrell told Prime Minister Asquith: 'The horrible thing proves how deep in Irish hearts lies this passion for insurrection.'[131] Birrell was a good judge of Ireland, but there must be more to the change than that.

British state documents tell us something of the change in national ideology. In a way, there was little change: in 1917–18 nationalist

Ireland transferred allegiance from the Irish Parliamentary Party to Sinn Fein. After 1918 most Catholic bishops and the great majority of priests supported Sinn Fein, whose political policies, as opposed to its means, differed little from those of the Parliamentary Party. Before 1916 only a few priests and probably no bishop would support Sinn Fein. Even in 1918 individual priests, considered 'extreme nationalists', were disciplined by their bishops. The most notable case was Father Michael O'Flanagan, a leading member of Sinn Fein.

The shift to the rebels did not occur immediately. The Rising, Birrell decided, was the work of a 'small combination of the old Physical Force Party, one or two Labour men like James Connolly, now in the Castle badly wounded, and idealistic youths sick of the *Freeman's Journal*, plus an *idle* crowd'[132]: an assessment not too wide of the mark, as we have seen. What followed, from 1917 to 1921, was that nationalist Ireland acted in concert, as under O'Connell and Parnell. Nationalist Ireland was not converted to republicanism. Most leaders of the 1917–21 movement were not republicans in ideology. Eamon de Valera, the new Sinn Fein chief, always denied he was 'a doctrinaire republican'. Many of his lieutenants of the period quickly discarded their oath of fealty to the Irish Republic in 1921. Because of that, the matter of oaths assumed much importance in the debates on the Treaty in 1921–22 and later. De Valera himself took an oath to the King in 1927 that he had sworn never to take.

The Ideology of Sinn Féin

Sinn Féin had no connection with the Rising, although Arthur Griffith was jailed because of it. However, British officials and the general public persisted in calling it 'the Sinn Féin Rebellion' because all extreme nationalists were thought to be members of that organisation. Sinn Féin began in 1905 as an amalgamation of anti-parliamentary nationalist groups, including the IRB's 'Dungannon Clubs'.[133] Griffith and Bulmer Hobson did not agree, although the former had belonged to the IRB at one time.[134] Apart from List's economics and Deak's politics, Griffith's Irish-Ireland stew relied on abstention from the British parliament to win independence. Before 1917 this remained a theory because Sinn Féin failed to win any seats in parliament.

Griffith latched on to List without realizing, apparently, that the German economist did not think his protectionist theories applied in a small country. Likewise with Deak, Griffith did not seem to know that Hungary, for all its dual monarchical forms and 'free institutions', was ruled by aristocrats who treated their peasants as shabbily as any Irish landlord.

Ireland must be self-reliant and self-sufficient, Sinn Féin proclaimed. It must build new industries and guard them with tariff walls; the people must buy Irish manufactures even if they cost more. The effect of such preaching on industrialized Belfast no one bothered to estimate. The problem with Sinn Féin was that it had a lot of half-baked ideas, which Griffith guarded jealously because he had developed them. But those who joined the movement did so because it was anti-British. It lost most of its original supporters and from 1909 was in decline. Eamonn Ceannt, the 1916 signatory, resigned because of Griffith's anti-labour attitude in 1913.

Griffith was a man of integrity, narrow and doctrinaire. He had many admirers because of the consistency of his politics, his own obvious sincerity, and his journalistic skill. These included James Connolly, and the respect was returned. James Joyce considered Griffith's *United Irishman* 'the only newspaper of any pretensions in Ireland' and thought Sinn Féin more effective than the Parliamentary Party.[135]

Throughout his political life Griffith stayed close to the ideas he expressed at the founding convention of Sinn Féin. His vision was of a middle class Ireland with its own industry, culture and political way of life.

> Let the Irish people get out of their heads the insane idea that the agricultural and the manufacturing industries are opposed. They are necessary to each other, and one cannot be injured without the other suffering hurt. We must further clear their minds of the pernicious idea that they are not entitled or called upon to give preferential aid to the manufacturing industries of their own country. Sir, if that idea were not met and combatted there would be an end to all hope of an Irish manufacturing arm. 'My object,' said List, 'is at all costs to save Germany from the destruction which the commercial policy of England designs for her.' Our object is, at all costs, to save Ireland. 'On the development of the German protective system,' List wrote, 'depends the existence, the independence, and the future of German nationality. Only in the soil of general prosperity does the national spirit strike its roots, produce fine blossoms and rich fruits – only from the unity of material interests does mental power arise and again from both of them national power.' The fruits of List's teaching is the Germany of today. It is part of the policy of the National Council (Sinn Féin) to bring about that unity of material interests which produces national strength. . . .[136]

The Provisional Committee of the Volunteers, in 1913, contained some members of Sinn Féin, but Griffith was sceptical of armed movements and conspiracies. When the First World War began Griffith urged Irish nationalists to follow a policy of neutrality by pursuing the interests of Ireland 'irrespective' of the interests of England or Germany or 'any foreign country'.[137] Mitchel's writings, if not his armed policies, influenced Griffith, and he was aware of the '48 leader's statement that 'in the event of a European war a strong national party could grasp the occasion' to strike for Irish freedom. He knew that the IRB would use the opportunity to plan a rebellion, but Griffith had little faith in its capability to do so. He edited a daily paper, *Éire-Ireland,* which charged that Irish regiments were being sacrificed at the front to save English regiments; the paper lasted for one month; British military confiscated the printing works.[138] But Griffith was never without a public voice for long and he issued a bi-weekly, *Scissors and Paste,* of clippings from English and American papers, to beat the censors.

> It is high treason (Griffith explained to his readers) for an Irishman to argue with the sword the right of his small nationality to equal political freedom with Belgium or Serbia or Hungary. It is destruction to the property of his printer now when he argues it with the pen. Hence while England is fighting the battle of the Small Nationalities, *Ireland* is reduced to *Scissors and Paste.*[139]

When it, too, disappeared Griffith issued a new weekly, *Nationality,* in June 1915. Printed in Belfast, *Nationality* managed to stay clear of the censor until the Easter Rising.

In 1916, Sinn Féin had one branch in Dublin. When the Rising became 'the Sinn Féin Rebellion',[140] the Parliamentary Party made the most of the label in order to show that nationalist Ireland had no connection with the madness. Redmond, as leader of the Party, called the Rising the work of Germany. 'My first feeling, of course, on hearing of this insane movement, was one of horror, discouragement, almost despair,' he said.

> I asked myself whether Ireland, as so often before in her tragic history, was to dash the cup of liberty from her lips; was the insanity of a small section of her people once again to turn all her marvellous victories of the last few years into irreparable defeat. . . on the very eve of her final recognition as a free nation.

He described the Rising as an 'attempted blow at Home Rule' . . . . 'Germany plotted it, Germany organized it, Germany paid for it.'[141] The Archbishop of Cashel thought Irish history proved that 'all revolutionary measures are doomed to failure'.[142] William Martin Murphy's nationalist *Irish Independent* conducted an editorial campaign against the badly-wounded Connolly, demanding his execution.[143]

After the surrender the British commander, General Sir John Maxwell, used priests to travel through rebel lines 'advising compliance with Pearce's [sic] instructions'.[144] On 3 May, the first day of executions, he declared: 'Now that the rebellion in Dublin and elsewhere has been crushed the COG-in-C [Maxwell] intends to arrest all dangerous Sinn Féiners, including those who have taken an active part in the movement although not in the present rebellion.'[145] Sinn Féin was singled out as the target of the military; in every parish police arrested known 'Sinn Féiners'. By September the Lord Lieutenant was assured by the competent authorities that 'the Sinn Féiners appear totally disorganized'; the executive of the Volunteers 'are either executed or imprisoned or have absconded'.[146] However, by 18 December 1916 the Commissioner of the Dublin Metropolitan Police, W.E. Johnstone, wanted displays of pictures of rebel leaders in shop windows and elsewhere banned. 'Unfortunately disaffection in this country could hardly be more widespread than it is,' he reported to the War Office.[147]

The 'disaffection' had taken place in a few months after the executions and wholesale arrests. Since everyone blamed Sinn Féin for the rebellion, Sinn Féin inherited the glory when it became a noble deed. At Christmas interned prisoners were released by the new Prime Minister, David Lloyd George. They were welcomed home as heroes and bonfires burned on the hills. By February 1917, Arthur Griffith was publishing *Nationality* again. By June sentenced prisoners were released. In by-election after by-election Sinn Féin candidates defeated the Parliamentary Party. The most notable victory was in East Clare, where the candidate Eamon de Valera, the only surviving commandant of the Rising, campaigned in Volunteer uniform. He won by a margin of more than two-to-one and became the spokesman of resurgent Sinn Féin.[148] Thus Sinn Féin became the beneficiary of the Easter Rising, although it had no part in it. Sinn Féin ideology dominated the national movement from 1917 to 1921. The Irish nation-state was its product. Griffith's ideology, not the ideology of Pearse and certainly not that of Connolly, dominated the state for its first forty years.

Sinn Féin took the leadership of nationalist Ireland from the Parliamentary Party, not because of its policy, or because the Irish people were converted to its doctrines, but because of English repression. As P.S. O'Hegarty explains:

> The German Plot, Partition, Conscription – everything combined to throw more and more elements in the country over to Sinn Féin. The Labour Party gave it a free hand; and finally, its bitterest opponent, the Irish Hierarchy, came over to it and practically gave it their blessing. No such unity and no such enthusiasm had been seen in Ireland since the early Parnell days.[149]

The 'German plot' refers to the arrest of leading members of Sinn Féin, in May 1918, when police captured an Irish ex-prisoner of war who had landed in the West of Ireland from a German submarine with instructions to contact the leadership of the movement; 'partition' – to the exclusion of six Ulster counties from Home Rule; 'conscription' – to the speedy passage through parliament of a draft for Ireland – although 180,000 Irishmen had volunteered for the forces. Connolly's heirs in the Labour Party were persuaded not to contest elections, but to support Sinn Féin, the national resistance to British rule. Finally, the Irish bishops supported Sinn Féin in denouncing conscription. All Irish nationalists signed a declaration at their church gates 'denying the right of the British government to enforce compulsory service in this country', pledging themselves 'solemnly to one another to resist Conscription by the most effective means at our disposal'.[159] All parties – parliamentary and Labour as well as Sinn Féin – supported a declaration, drafted by de Valera, that said:

> Taking our stand on Ireland's separate and distinct nationhood and affirming the principle of liberty that the governments of nations derive their just powers from the consent of the governed, we deny the right of the British Government or any external authority to impose compulsory military service in Ireland against the clearly expressed will of the Irish people. The passing of the Conscription Bill by the British House of Commons must be regarded as a declaration of war on the Irish nation. . . . The attempt to enforce it will be an unwarrantable aggression, which we call upon all Irishmen to resist by the most effective means at their disposal.[151]

Sinn Féin did not repudiate its past programme, but de Valera found a formula to bring it into line with the ideals of the 1916 Rising. 'Sinn Féin aims at securing the international recognition of Ireland as an independent Irish Republic,' the new constitution of the party declared. 'Having achieved that status the Irish people may by referendum freely choose their own form of government.' This was the forerunner of many such de Valera formulations: the bold statement to win the radicals, followed by the cautionary reservation to keep the moderates happy. One could make what one wished of the declaration. Sinn Féin would 'deny the right and oppose the will of the British Parliament or the British Crown or any other foreign government to legislate for Ireland; make use of any and every means available to render impotent the power of England to hold Ireland in subjection by military force or otherwise'.[152]

Sinn Féin and the bishops found common ground on the conscription issue. Most priests supported the movement. There was nothing socially radical about Sinn Féin. No man of property need fear it. A quotation from Connolly on an election poster was denounced by a priest as against Catholic teaching. Sinn Féin remained silent. It did not stand by Connolly.[153]

In December 1918 Sinn Féin swept the old Parliamentary Party out of Irish politics by winning seventy-three of the hundred and five Irish seats. The Unionists won twenty-six, the Irish Party six – a drop from eighty. No one could doubt any longer that a new day had dawned in Ireland. Nationalist Ireland had dismissed its old representatives for being ineffectual guardians of the national interest. However, in percentage of votes, Sinn Féin's victory was not quite as overwhelming as the seats gained would suggest.[154] Despite the Connolly heritage, it told Labour to wait, in the interests of 'national unity'. Labour obeyed and lost its place in the national struggle, except to declare strikes against the use of trains by British military. (An anti-conscription general strike on 23 April 1918, had been a more effective demonstration of nationalist solidarity than Sinn Féin's declarations.) No Labour representative attended the meeting of the first Dáil Éireann (National Assembly) in the Mansion House, Dublin on 21 January 1919. It was a Sinn Féin assembly, not a national one for that reason, a matter that drew no comment then or later. Labour in Belfast contested four seats and garnered 12,164 votes, which was not bad in the circumstances.

An Irish Parliament

Dáil Éireann described itself as the parliament of the Irish Republic 'proclaimed in Dublin on Easter Monday, 1916, by the Irish Republican Army acting on behalf of the Irish people'. A series of declarations demanded that the free nations of the world recognize Irish independence and that England withdraw its garrison from Ireland. A democratic programme, drafted by Irish trade union and Labour leaders, was thought too socialist and was heavily edited. But even in diluted form it has a radical ring:

> We declare in the words of the Irish Republican proclamation the right of the people of Ireland to the ownership of Ireland and to the unfettered con-

> trol of Irish destinies to be sovereign and indefeasible, and in the language of our first President, Pádraic Pearse, we declare that the nation's sovereignty extends not only to all men and women of the nation, but to all its material possessions; the nation's soil and all its resources, all the wealth and all the wealth-producing processes within the nation and with him we re-affirm that all rights to private property must be subordinated to the public right and welfare. . . .
>
> It shall be our duty to promote the development of the nation's resources, to increase the productivity of the soil, to exploit its mineral deposits, peat bogs, and fisheries, its waterways and harbours, in the interest and for the benefit of the Irish people.
>
> It shall be the duty of the Republic to adopt all measures necessary for the recreation and invigoration of our industries, and to ensure their being developed in the most beneficial and progressive co-operative and industrial lines. . . . It shall also devolve upon the National Government to seek co-operation of the Governments of other countries in determining a standard of Social and Industrial legislation with a view to a general and lasting improvement in the conditions under which the working classes live and labour.[155]

Twenty-seven Sinn Féin members attended the first parliament: thirty-four others were in prison, eight were on missions abroad. The chief spokesmen of the movement could not be present: Arthur Griffith and Eamon de Valera were in jail under the 'German plot'. Had they been present it is unlikely the socialist-influenced democratic programme would have appeared as a Dáil document. De Valera was a conservative, a 'pure nationalist'. Griffith, according to P.S. O'Hegarty, an admirer, was

> naturally a believer in evolutionary methods in politics rather than in revolutionary methods, and, in a free Ireland, would I think be found on the side of what the *Times* would call 'stability'. He is no great believer in the rights of man, and modern radical catch-cries leave him cold: his creed being rather the rights of nations and the duties of man, the rights of a nation being the right to freedom and the right to the allegiance and service of all its children, and the duties of man being to fear God and serve his nation.[156]

When both men got out of prison — de Valera escaped with the help of Michael Collins, hid out for a while, then sailed secretly for America — the democratic programme was buried and never exhumed, not even for the purposes of an occasional rhetorical flourish. The conclusion is inescapable that very conservative men controlled Sinn Féin, and consequently Dáil Éireann. They stripped republicanism of whatever social radicalism it contained. The writings of Connolly, if not Pearse, even the Proclamation itself, were muted in the interest of good relations with the Catholic Church, conservative farmers and businessmen. The premise of this most conservative revolt – that the independence struggle should take precedence over everything – went unchallenged except by Connolly's labour militants, who saw Sinn Féin as just another capitalist political party.[157]

A State of War

The first Dáil Éireann, in one of its declarations, said that 'the existing state of war between Ireland and England can never be ended until Ireland is definitely evacuated by the armed forces of England'.[158] Such language was not used during the 1918 election campaign: Sinn Féin merely said that if given a mandate it would take Ireland's case to the Peace Conference at Versailles. Later, Republicans maintained the Irish Republic received a mandate in 1918; the claim is difficult to sustain. Sinn Féin's mandate, at best, was to win international recognition for Irish independence.

After the meeting of the First Dáil, Sinn Féin took a subsidiary role to the Volunteers. The movement was revived in 1917 at the same time as Griffith's Sinn Féin. On the day the First Dáil met, a party of Volunteers ambushed two constables of the RIC (Royal Irish Constabulary) escorting a cart-load of explosives from a quarry, at Soloheadbeg in County Tipperary, shot them dead and seized the gelignite.[159] This was the start of a guerrilla war that continued to July 1921. It was a war of ambushes, raids on police and military barracks, assassinations and sabotage. No one sanctioned it, no one decided the tactics used, no one planned it. Local Volunteers needed arms and attacked the police to get them. The Volunteers, by order of the Dáil, were called the Irish Republican Army. Dublin Castle called them 'franctireurs', also an accurate term. It was the first of this century's wars of national liberation, although much milder, in retrospect, than its successors.

There were two key military engagements that seemed to be decisive, because they changed the mind of the British Prime Minister on the kind of conflict taking place in Ireland. We have the evidence for this in the Cabinet minutes, as recorded by Tom Jones, the Secretary. The first was the ambush at Kilmichael, West Cork, in November 1920, when an élite force of Auxiliaries (ex-officers of the First World War) was wiped out by an IRA column. The second was at Crossbarry, near Cork City, in April 1921, when the same IRA column, under the same commander, Tom Barry, defeated an encircling movement of British regular troops. The first convinced Lloyd George that more than the old Irish assassination tactics were at work. The second convinced him he must treat with

Sinn Féin or reconquer Ireland by force. He decided to talk.

If any organization stood behind the Volunteers it was the revived IRB, whose new leaders probably saw themselves performing the same role as Clarke and MacDermott. The most important of the new leaders was Michael Collins, who played a minor role in the Rising, was interned, and on release looked after ex-prisoners, thus drawing into his own hands the loose strands of what, for want of a better term, could be called 'Irish-Ireland'. In 1917, Michael Collins was twenty-seven years of age. He reorganized the IRB, then dominated its ruling inner circle. He had no formal education beyond primary school, had worked in the Post Office in London, was of small-farm background – a Ribbonman operating at national level. The Rising was a shock – too romantic, he told a friend. 'Connolly was a realist, Pearse the direct opposite. There was an air of earthy directness about Connolly. . . . I would have followed him through hell had such action been necessary. But I honestly doubt very much if I would have followed Pearse – not without some thought anyway.'[160]

Realists appealed to Collins. There would be no more glorious protests in arms, he decided. He built a cadre of realists around him, first in the IRB, then at Volunteer headquarters, where he took over Pearse's old post as Director of Organization before becoming Director of Intelligence, finally, in Dáil Éireann, as the underground government's very effective Minister for Finance. Collins was a doer. Essentially a well-informed opportunist with very few scruples, his entire ideology could be stated in five words: 'The Irish should govern themselves.'

Like Clarke and his colleagues, Collins's authority rested on the IRB tradition. He hand-picked the candidates for the 1918 election, although he never completely controlled Sinn Féin. He stage-managed the meeting of the First Dáil and ordered Seán T. O'Kelly, a veteran member of Sinn Féin and the IRB, to water down and rewrite the democratic programme. (He was in England during the opening ceremonies, planning de Valera's escape from prison.)

In the IRB, Collins combined in himself the roles of Clarke and MacDermott; they had recruited others to do the work; Collins did it all himself. The Chief of Staff of the Volunteers, Richard Mulcahy, was an IRB man, as were almost all the GHQ staff. But they were essentially Collins's men. Collins was the brain of nationalist resistance. When country guerrillas needed arms and advice they went to Collins. He built an effective intelligence system, infiltrated Dublin Castle and eliminated its agents. For a century and a quarter, Dublin Castle had subverted all Irish rebel movements. Collins subverted

Dublin Castle.[161]

In 1920 the IRB revised its constitution. The first object of the Organization (the usual name for the IRB) was 'to establish and maintain a free and independent Republican Government in Ireland'. But a Republic had been established and was in existence. The second object was to 'support every movement calculated to advance the cause of Irish National Independence – consistent with the preservation of its own integrity'. Presumably, disestablishment of the Irish Republic, in 1922, could be said, however paradoxically, 'to advance the cause of Irish National Independence'.[162] At any rate Collins put forward that argument, in one way or another, during the debate on the Treaty.

Clause 20 of the IRB Constitution reads:

> The Supreme Council of the Irish Republican Brotherhood is hereby declared in fact, as well as by right, the sole Government of the Irish Republic. Its enactments shall be the Laws of the Irish Republic until Ireland secures absolute National Independence, and a permanent Republican Government be established.

At that time, of course, there was a Government of the Irish Republic, responsible to a National Assembly, attempting to function. Clause 22 said: 'The President of the Irish Republican Brotherhood is in fact, as well as by right, President of the Irish Republic.' This clause was altered in September 1919, the 1920 Constitution notes, to read: 'The President of the IRB shall direct the working of the Irish Republican Brotherhood, subject to the control of the Supreme Council of the Executive thereof.'

Since Michael Collins was the President of the Supreme Council of the IRB, there was bound to be confusion as to who actually, and indeed legally, controlled the movment for national independence. And this, in fact, is what happened. The Irish split was not so much a matter of ideology as a series of hair-splitting legalisms about oaths to the King and to the Republic.

The Ideology of Struggle

Chief Secretary Hamar Greenwood, in a statement from Dublin Castle, on 14 November 1920, declared that the IRA

> in their murderous endeavour to smash the British Empire and weaken Anglo-American friendship, are bringing the South and West of Ireland to political anarchy and economic ruin. As a result of the stoppage of the railways there will follow the stoppage of the mails and the stoppage of the payment of old age and other pensions that now depend upon mail deliveries. . . . No government can allow railwaymen subsidized out of the

pocket of the taxpayers to refuse to carry police and soldiers.[163]

Public officials who gave their allegiance to Sinn Féin (or Dáil Éireann) were often summarily murdered by Crown forces. This was the policy of 'official reprisals'. Lloyd George explained the rationale in these words: 'If it is a war, they cannot complain if we apply some of the rules of war. In war, if men come in civilian clothes behind your lines, armed with murderous weapons, intending to use them whenever they can do so with impunity – in war they are summarily dealt with.'[164]

Each side had its own ideology of struggle – or terror. The government wanted to defeat the rebels and maintain the empire; the IRA wanted to make British government in Ireland impossible – and largely succeeded; Dáil Éireann had little control over the IRA – which was Collins's fault – but it wanted to establish Ireland's right to self-determination with public opinion in England, the United States and Western Europe: it achieved considerable success, but not recognition of the Irish Republic, which was its goal. The US Congress passed a resolution (see Appendix VII). The hunger-strike of Terence MacSwiney, Lord Mayor of Cork, and the execution of Kevin Barry, an eighteen-year-old medical student, won international sympathy for the Irish.

This was indeed an ideological battle. MacSwiney refused to eat food because English rule in Ireland was 'a thing of evil incarnate'. There could be no parley with it, 'any more than there can be truce with the powers of hell'. He could quote Catholic theologians in support of rebellion against tyranny. British occupation was founded upon usurpation and should be resisted, he wrote.[165] MacSwiney could only lose his battle by failing to die: in death he proved his case for liberty. 'Tyrannies may persecute, slay or banish those who defend it; the thing itself is indestructible. It does not need legions to protect it nor genius to proclaim it. . . .One man alone may vindicate it, and because that one man has never failed, it has never died.' MacSwiney's words were the most powerful ideological force on the side of Sinn Féin.

Kevin Barry, the boy soldier captured in arms after a Dublin ambush, was less of a mystic and more of a Tone-Connolly republican than MacSwiney. He wanted economic freedom for the Irish people, he said, and he admired Jim Larkin – which was unusual enough for a product of middle-class Dublin. He was the first to be executed after 1916, but certainly not the last, and songs about Kevin Barry continue to be sung around the world. He could have escaped the hangman by signing a simple statement. He refused. More than MacSwiney, perhaps, he symbolized the kind of men who made up the guerrilla army that had taken on an empire.[166]

The Belfast Boycott

The biggest ideological victory the British achieved in Ireland in 1919–21 was handed them *gratis* by Dáil Éireann and Arthur Griffith. This was the nationalist boycott of Belfast goods, a flagrantly sectarian decision. Republicans who objected were told it was a Dáil matter and not for general discussion. The reason for it was the attacks on Catholics in Belfast.[167] 'There is not a word to be said in favour of the Ulster boycott,' says P.S. O'Hegarty. 'It is an utterly shameful episode in the history of Sinn Féin.'[168]

It is probably true that the Belfast boycott reflected the mood of nationalist Ireland, a matter important to Sinn Féin. In the countryside, Sinn Féin was influenced by the big shopkeeper, the important farmer, the parish priest, the national teacher: the old Parliamentary Party had been influenced by the same forces. Even in the changed national circumstances these voices were reactionary. Sometimes the sons of small farmers, or even labourers, climbed to positions of leadership in the Volunteers and thus there was a form of social mobility prior to the establishment of the nation-state; which is as far as the 'revolution' went.[169]

Dáil Éireann was nominally responsible for the IRA, but in fact exercised little control over that body. The Republican government set up arbitration courts and issued edicts and the people obeyed them. They gave 'the Republic' their allegiance. (There were even death sentences for 'ordinary' capital crimes). Dáil Éireann's representatives went to America, England and France to explain the Irish case. The IRA operated largely as an autonomous body under the authority of Michael Collins and his GHQ staff. When its demands grew too heavy, Dáil Éireann intervened.[170]

The actions of the British government in Ireland were questioned in parliament and attacked in the liberal press. Sir Oswald Mosley, the future Fascist leader, left the government benches because the policy of 'official reprisals' was handing Sinn Féin 'propaganda against this country all over the world' and 'tore into shreds the elaborate growth of centuries, that sense of justice which separates men from the animal'.[171] *The Nation* of London commented: 'The world holds that murder as a system of government is worse than murder as a method of rebellion. . . for this reason if for no other, all who care for our honour and our future should press for negotiation.'[172]

Anti-British opinion was growing in America, even among the non-Irish. British methods, the American consul in Dublin told the Secretary of State in January 1921, 'have turned thousands of nationalists into Sinn Féiners and added hundreds to the 'active list' of the Irish Republican Army. To maintain order thousands of new troops have been brought into Ireland and the country is an armed camp'.[173] A committee of prominent Americans heard the testimony of Irish witnesses and issued a report condemning British methods.[174]

Le Temps of Paris sent a correspondent to Ireland who wrote that 'the ideal of independence which inspires the Irish seems to be first and foremost in their minds beyond all other considerations'. But they also believed English rule had ruined them economically. In less than eighty years the population had fallen from 8.2 million to 4.3 million, whereas that of Britain had more than doubled from 18.2 million to 40.8 million. England did not want a large Irish population because that would make Ireland strong. Irish goods were barred from the markets of the world by England, but English goods monopolized the Irish market. Irish industry faced unfair competition and Irish resources were undeveloped.[175]

Dublin Castle became concerned about a book, *De Iersche Kwestie,* written by a Dutch journalist, and asked the embassy at The Hague to talk to the editors and owner of the *Nieuwe Rotterdamsche Courant,* the paper the writer represented in London. The embassy did so and reported, 'I believe that this action is producing some effect, and that good results may be expected.'[176]

The British tried to link Sinn Féin with the Bolsheviks, but to no avail. The new regime in Russia was willing to recognize the Irish Republic but de Valera was cool to the idea: he wanted President Wilson to recognize the Irish Republic first, and failed.[177] He feared Sinn Féin would be considered radical if they had relations with Russia. (The Dáil's most radical move was to name Countess Markievicz, the former Constance Gore-Booth, to the Cabinet, the first woman in Europe to hold such a post; she had fought with the Citizen Army in 1916.)[178] No state, in fact, recognized the Irish Republic: perhaps because of British influence; or perhaps because none believed that Sinn Féin's underground government represented Ireland.

If the guerrilla war had started almost by accident, with companies of Volunteers seeking arms where they could, its continuation was in some measure an act of desperation. Ernie O'Malley, one of the IRA's field organizers and a brilliant guerrilla officer, wrote: 'Their [the British] campaign of terror was defeating itself. It had made conservatives liberals and had treated the luke-warm as extreme; it had affected the discipline of their army and police.'[179] Michael Collins told Carl Ackerman, correspondent in Dublin for a number of American papers, 'It is only a question of time until we shall have them cleared out. We have got them beaten today, virtually, so that the worst stages are past and we are now coming to the final. The people of this country are with us and they do not give a damn what the English do.' There would be no surrender or compromise and the Irish did not want their country divided.[180]

That was in April 1921. The Government of Ireland Act, dividing Ireland into Protestant-dominated and Catholic states, was put into effect the following month when elections were held for the two parliaments of divided Ireland. Sinn Féin faced no opposition in 'Southern Ireland'; the members became the Second Dáil. In Northern Ireland, the King opened the new parliament. The Nationalists refused to participate and violence continued.

Britain asked for a truce to start talks with Sinn Féin, as they insisted on terming Dáil Éireann; it came into effect on 11 July, 1921. The IRA was close to exhaustion, with few arms and no great resources beyond the backing of nationalist Ireland. Yet it had fought the British Empire to a standstill. It could do so, as P.S. O'Hegarty says, because 'the historic Irish Nation shook itself clear of the after effects of th eighteenth century and ousted the conception of an Ireland deriving its constitutional authority from English decrees'.[181] The people may not have realized it – certainly they would not have put it in such terms – yet that is what happened, undoubtedly.

On 6 December 1921 the Dáil Éireann delegates, including Griffith and Collins, but not de Valera, signed a Treaty with England which gave nationalist Ireland the international status of a nation-state, as a dominion of the British Empire. Dáil Éireann narrowly approved the Treaty, by sixty-four votes to fifty-seven. Sinn Féin, the only party in the Dáil, split into two factions. Treatyites and Anti-Treatyites, or Republicans as they called themselves later. The Irish Free State was born on 6 December 1922, while nationalist Ireland fought a civil war over the Treaty with England. The war was about definitions of freedom and the form of the state, but most people did not understand any of that.

The Role of the IRA

The IRA fought the guerrilla war of 1919–21 and was the midwife of the nation-state. By destroying British administration in nationalist Ireland the IRA in thirty months accomplished what the Parliamentary Party had failed to do in almost fifty years: it forced a settlement of the Irish question.

This lesson was learned while the long years of agitation and political preparation were ignored. The IRA, after August 1919, took an oath to 'support and defend the Irish Republic and the Government of the Irish Republic, which is Dáil Éireann, against all enemies, foreign and domestic'. But when the Dáil 'betrayed the Republic' by accepting the Treaty, the IRA, in the spring of 1922, withdrew its allegiance and fell back on its own convention for authority.

The post-Treaty IRA took the place of the IRB as the guardian of the Republic. Its ideology was shaped by the doctrine of armed force and the abstentionist political theory of Sinn Féin. Like the IRB, it was funded by the Clan-na-Gael.[182]

V
Republicans against the Nation State, 1922-1962

Ideology split the Irish national movement in 1922. The ostensible issue was the Anglo-Irish 'Articles of Agreement for a Treaty', signed on 6 December, 1921, and debated in Dáil Éireann from 14 December to 7 January, with a recess for Christmas. The Agreement did not mention the Dáil at all.

The ideology was this: acceptance of the Treaty meant abandonment of the Republic proclaimed in 1916 and constitutionally ratified by Dáil Éireann in January 1919. The British government never seriously considered recognizing the Republic;[1] and the Irish negotiators, in effect Arthur Griffith and Michael Collins, never seriously pressed the issue of the Republic. Even de Valera was ambivalent about it.

When Lloyd George met de Valera in July 1921 he went away with the impression that the President of the Irish Republic was willing to drop the Republic, recognize the King, and stay in the British Empire. But he would not accept partition.[2] De Valera's formula to get over the empire difficulty was 'external association'.[3] He was offered dominion status for the twenty-six counties – the settlement agreed to five months later – and on his return to Dublin de Valera told the Dáil, in August 1921, 'we are not Republican doctrinaires as such, but our goal is an independent Ireland'.[4] Two months later de Valera reorganized his Cabinet. He dropped two 'republican doctrinaires' – both aristocrats, interestingly enough[5] – and was left with two intransigent Fenians[6] to balance Griffith, who was not a republican, and Collins, a pragmatist. De Valera seemed to think he could convince the British to accept his 'external association' formula, which would allow him to describe the state, for purposes of domestic politics, as a republic: the position he reached sixteen years later with the 1937 'new constitution'. The men he had arguing the case for him in London, Griffith and Collins, did not believe in 'external association'. They were not even republicans. 'It was Cromwell who taught them republicanism,' Churchill said of the

Irish.[7]

Partition, the second issue, was the most important. Sinn Féin believed in the absolute unity of Ireland, though two speakers, during the debate on the Treaty, would accept partition as a temporary measure to penalize the Unionists, they claimed.[8] 'What he [de Valera] chiefly seemed to want was *Irish unity* – that we should not *impose* partition, that there should be an All-Ireland Parliament with real financial and other powers, while leaving to Ulster the autonomy she now enjoys so long as she wishes to retain it,' Tom Jones told the Tory leader, Bonar Law. [9] The British replied, 'no coercion of Ulster'.[10] Said Bonar Law:

> The real difficulty of the Irish business will prove now as always in the past, to be Ulster. I greatly fear that de Valera will find it impossible to treat Ulster as entirely outside his sphere and on the other hand I am sure that no settlement can be carried in England which imposes anything on the new Ulster Parliament which they do not freely accept. [11]

The Unity of Ireland

Bonar Law always made it clear that there could be no British pressure on Protestant Ulster to bring them 'in any way under the control of a Dublin parliament'.[12] De Valera told Lloyd George: 'We cannot admit the right of the British Government to mutilate our country, either in its own interest or at the call of any section of the population. We do not contemplate the use of force. If your Government stands aside we can effect a complete reconciliation.'[13] One difficulty for Lloyd George lay in that he had already partitioned Ireland when he decided to talk to Sinn Féin. No doubt the timing was deliberate. Sir James Craig, leader of the Ulster Unionists and head of the new government in Belfast, would not discuss the matter and he had the support of the Tories. There could be no Irish settlement without Tory support.

'The great difficulty with de Valera is the question of the unity of Ireland,' Lloyd George told C.P. Scott, editor of the *Manchester Guardian*, on 28 July, 1921. 'He insists on an All-Ireland Parliament.'[14] Griffith and Collins wanted a united Ireland too. The weakness of the Ulster case, from a British point of view, as Lloyd George and his colleagues soon realized, was that two of the six counties, under the Belfast parliament, Fermanagh and Tyrone, had nationalist (Catholic) majorities. They were being forced against their will – in other words *coerced*, as Collins stressed – to accept a government they both feared and hated. Lloyd George called Ulster 'a defile' on the road to an Irish settlement.[15] When Collins said, 'The present six counties implies coercion; South and East Down, South Armagh, Fermanagh and Tyrone, will not come in [to] Northern Ireland and it is not fair to ask them to come in', Lloyd George replied: 'This [partition] was a compromise, not our proposal, but a compromise to get out of a problem which wrecks every [Irish] Bill. In the main the Nationalists accepted it in 1914 and 1916. They had our credentials then and you have them now. Don't father this compromise on us.' [16]

As a compromise solution, partition suffered from the fatal defect that if self-determination for nationalist Ireland must mean coercing Protestant Ulster, leaving partition as the only way out of the situation, self-determination for the Protestants of Ulster must mean coercing the Catholics of Ulster to accept partition. With Catholics the majority in much of the six counties outside the Belfast area, how could the issue be resolved? It was not resolved; it was ignored.

By April of 1921 it appears that the outlines of an Irish settlement were in Lloyd George's mind but he had to move cautiously. In June the Belfast parliament opened and partition was a fact. In July Lloyd George offered de Valera dominion status for the twenty-six counties. The alternative to acceptance was full-scale war. Through Lord Beaverbrook, the press baron, Lloyd George sought to influence Conservative opinion in favour of an Irish settlement.[17] The weakness of partition lay in the counties of Fermanagh and Tyrone. How could he justify the inclusion of counties with nationalist majorities in Northern Ireland? If Sinn Féin made it an issue 'they will have manoeuvred us into a defile out of which we cannot extricate ourselves'. He was relieved when de Valera did not mention either Tyrone or Fermanagh at their initial meeting and Lloyd George concluded that the Sinn Féin leader was 'an unskillful negotiator but you cannot always count on his being maladroit'.[18]

Lloyd George's way out of the 'defile' presented by Tyrone and Fermanagh was a Boundary Commission, which was intended to trap the Sinn Féin negotiators.[19] The commission would resolve problems of population and political allegiance in Ulster. It was hinted that the commission would strip Northern Ireland of large tracts with nationalist majorities, leaving the area non-viable politically and economically. Collins disliked the scheme when Tom Jones presented it, but reluctantly accepted it; Griffith wanted a plebiscite rather than a commission. Later, he confirmed in a letter to Lloyd George – as a political favour to the latter – that if Ulster accepted the Boundary Commission she need not join the Free State. Instead of standing on national principles, the chief Sinn Féin negotiators were working out political deals with a master of politics and were out-manoeuvred as a result. Parnell would not have fallen into such a trap; and de Valera adroitly avoided it.

The Debate in the Dáil

Defending the Treaty in the Dáil, Collins claimed it 'will lead very rapidly to goodwill, and the entry of the North-East under the Irish Parliament'.[20] Sean Milroy, the Sinn Féin deputy for Fermanagh-Tyrone, used some of the London arguments to support the Treaty.

> The fact is that the provisions of the Treaty are not partition provisions, but they ensure eventual unity in Ireland. But, as a matter of fact, whether there were partition provisions or not, the economic position and the effects on the six counties' area is this, that sooner or later isolation from the rest of Ireland would have so much weight on the economic state of these six counties as to compel them to renew their association with the rest of Ireland. That trend of economic fact will be stimulated by the provisions of this Treaty, and the man who asserts that partition is perpetuated in that Treaty is a man who has not read or understands what are the provisions in the Treaty.[21]

These arguments were not strongly challenged by the anti-Treatyites. Dr Pat MacCartan, an IRB leader, who said he would vote for the Treaty because the underground government had abandoned the Republic by negotiating with the British in the first place, declared: 'You have sold the North in making this Treaty.'[22] When someone objected to 'sold' he amended it to 'betrayal'.[23] An IRA officer said England had established a new Pale in Ireland through partition and he accused the pro-Treatyites of abandoning the nationalists of Ulster.[24] The Sinn Féin deputy for the Ulster county of Monaghan – not one of the six counties – Seán MacEntee of Belfast, annoyed many Treatyites, perhaps for the way he put his points, when he protested against partition and the Boundary Commission clause of the Treaty, which he described as a means 'not to bring the six counties into Ireland, but to enable them to remain out of Ireland'.[25] He thought England would find it profitable to subsidize the North not to join the rest of Ireland. 'Mark my words, under this Treaty Ulster will become England's fortress in Ireland – a fortress as impregnable as Gibraltar, a fortress that shall dominate and control Ireland even as Gibraltar controls the Mediterranean.'[26] The pro-treatyite deputy, Ernest Blythe, the only Ulster Protestant in the Dáil, disagreed. 'I have no doubt under this business and under these arrangements, and the necessity they will feel for material reasons for union, combined with propaganda, these terms will lead in a comparatively short time to the union of that part of the country with the rest of Ireland.'[27]

The issue of the oath of allegiance to the Crown was more hotly argued. Under the Treaty the Irish Free State would enjoy the same dominion status as Canada, Australia, New Zealand and South Africa. The first three dominions had been settled by Englishmen, with the exception of Quebec, a conquered province. South Africa was a union of English colonies and Boer republics, the latter defeated in war. Such states would find little difficulty in swearing allegiance to the King of England as head of the British Commonwealth of Nations. Three years earlier all Sinn Féin deputies had sworn allegiance to the Irish Republic. Collins tried, but failed, to have an oath to the Irish Constitution rather than to the King; Lloyd George would have none of that, although he did moderate the terms of the oath. The oath presented little difficulty for Griffith, the dual monarchist; or indeed for Collins, who thought little about such matters. During the negotiations they sought to barter allegiance for Irish unity. 'The P.M. thinks they will accept the Crown, all else being arranged,' Jones recorded.[28] Lloyd George presented them with the choice, 'the empire' or 'war', in the final hours of the negotiations, and would not permit them to report back to Dublin: they must sign immediately or face war within three days. The anti-Treatyites charged that the document had been signed 'under duress'. One of the delegates, Robert Barton, discussing the pressure he faced that night, confirmed the charge.[29]

Upholding the Republic

The deputies who opposed the Treaty were called Republicans, although some had other reasons for their stand. Professor William Stockley, for instance, went to some trouble to explain that one form of government to him was much as another; yet he remained a 'Second Dáil Republican' to the end of his days. De Valera, who led the opposition to the Treaty, knew that he spoke for a minority in the country, whatever about the Dáil – and he soon learned that he represented a minority there, too. Most deputies did not defend the Republic they had sworn to uphold, offered the alternative of the Treaty.

The business interests were for the Treaty. The Unionists were for the Treaty. Those who feared that rejection of the Treaty must inevitably mean permanent partition and those who doubted that the Republic could maintain itself against England wanted the Treaty.[30] The Catholic Church was for the Treaty. Ulster Nationalists who took their political advice from the Church rather than from Sinn Féin were for the Treaty. (Sinn Féin was weak in the North.) A terrorist militia, the 'B' Specials, intimidated Nationalists.[31] Collins warned Lloyd George that he would have to coerce the Nationalists of Ulster to accept the Unionist parliament in Belfast, and Griffith had predicted: 'It will never function; 400,000 people when dragged in will not obey it.'[32] Churchill thought it might work through the Council of Ireland provision of the 1920 Government of Ireland Act, a kind of 'superparliament'. Griffith argued that the 'one-quarter of the population is equal to three-quarters of the population' in the Council of Ireland clause would ensure Nationalist rejection.[33]

But Griffith was a poor prophet on all counts. The Nationalists accepted the Belfast Unionist government because they had no choice; Sinn Féin was divided over the Treaty and the Nationalists had no support from the rest of Ireland. The Unionists rejected the Council of Ireland, for they wanted no link, however innocuous, with the Dublin parliament. They proceeded to turn the North into a Protestant-Unionist state by legislation and decree and to regulate it by means of the Special Powers Act of 1922. In a short time the North's Nationalists discovered they were second-class subjects of the Crown. The British government did nothing to protect them. The Treaty did not end partition. It made it possible.

De Valera's letter to McGarrity, of 21 December, 1921, lists the Catholic Church among the opponents of the Republic. 'Had the vote been taken on Thursday last when the Dáil adjourned [for Christmas], it was thought we might have got a majority of one or two against the treaty,' he wrote. 'But the press is hard at work throughout the country trying to get the local public bodies, County Councils, etc., to pass resolutions in favour of the treaty – and the Church is also hard at work.'[34] It was a mild criticism in the circumstances. The British had lobbied some bishops during the Treaty talks to get their support for a compromise settlement. The chief go-between was Alfred Cope, British Under-Secretary at Dublin Castle. In November 1921, when a break seemed imminent over allegiance to the Crown, Cope told Jones 'he was certain he could get the *Freeman* to oppose such a break and also some of the Church dignitaries'. Jones's account from his diary:

> He told me that Griffith, Collins and Barton were crossing to Ireland that night and that Griffith was returning to London on Friday night. There was therefore no time to lose if opinion in Dublin was to be influenced. Later the same evening, as he told me afterwards, he saw the Archbishop of Tuam in his bed in a Jeremyn Street Hotel and told him to return to Dublin the following morning and to get busy with Fogarty, the Sinn Fein Treasurer, and with Archbishop Byrne.[35]

It was a test of Cope's influence that he could get the Archbishop of Tuam, the metropolitan of the province of Connacht, to leave his bed in London, return to Ireland and pressure the Archbishop of Dublin, and also Dr Fogarty of Clare, a pro-Sinn Féin bishop, into pushing the British line on the negotiations regarding the future government of Ireland. The British could also summon to their aid the *Freeman's Journal*, the long-established voice of Irish constitutional nationalism. 'Things are humming on the other side,' Jones wrote happily in his diary, ten days before the Treaty was signed. 'The Bishops especially busy.'[36] With the Church against the Republic, its fate was sealed.

Even people who normally would be considered extreme republicans undermined the Republic, de Valera noted. (He had in mind the IRB.) De Valera believed that his 'Document Number Two' counter-proposal to the Treaty would almost certainly be accepted by Britain, but it would not have stopped partition. Document Number Two was 'external association'. There was no oath of allegiance to the King. It would maintain the Republic in domestic politics. The proposal lost in the Cabinet, then in the Dáil. De Valera might have won in the Dáil, he believed, but for the IRB. Michael Collins controlled the IRB. Collins saw the Treaty as a step to 'a free and independent Republican government of Ireland'. His IRB argument was that the Treaty gave Ireland 'freedom to achieve freedom'. A variant on this was that the Irish Free State would be 'a stepping stone' to the Republic.[37]

'The only hope was to try in private session to get the Dáil to turn down by a large majority the Treaty as signed, and to offer our counter-proposals to the British,' de Valera wrote to McGarrity. 'But MC [Michael Collins] had got the IRB machine working. The Dáil members of the IRB were told that acceptance of the Treaty would be the quickest way to the Republic, and a lot of other stuff which time only will explode.'[38]

De Valera's arguments against the Treaty were cogent, but his alternative — 'external association' — was hard to grasp. Griffith called it 'a quibble of words'.[39] During de Valera's American tour, 1919-20, he had offered England a guarantee similar to the Platt Amendment, which gave the US the right to intervene in Cuba's affairs. It had created a storm and a split with John Devoy, who was outraged. De Valera claimed he was victimized by his political enemies because of it; that he had meant something else entirely and did not intend to surrender Irish sovereignty to England. The Irish in America divided into pro-de Valera and anti-de Valera camps.[40]

It was a weakness of de Valera that, publicly at least, he was seen to be a theological hair-splitter; this might have been understandable in a lawyer, but de Valera was a professor, not a lawyer. During the Treaty debate he saw a distinction between ratifying the settlement and approving it; the former he thought inconsistent with the Republic.[41] Although he had faithfully upheld the unity of the country in talks with the British Prime Minister and within his own Cabinet,[42] he did not list partition as a major objection to the Treaty. De Valera made much of the instructions the delegates had received from the Cabinet; but he himself had refused to lead the delegation despite the appeals of his ministers.[43] He also questioned Collins and Griffith on the credentials they had presented to Lloyd George, who maintained all through the talks that he was negotiating with Sinn Féin, a nationalist political party, rather than with Dáil Éireann, the illegal national assembly of the Irish Republic. De Valera's persistence in this matter of credentials forced Collins to lie to the Dáil on the first day of the debate and Griffith supported the falsehood. This perturbed Lloyd George. No credentials had been presented to him and he had seen none.[44] 'Had they been formally presented we should have had to reject them,' said Jones of the incident. 'It looked as if Collins had lied for the sake of his country and for that course there was scriptural precedent,' was Lloyd George's comment. He stayed away from the House of Commons to avoid questions on the matter. 'I think to shuffle in order to help yourself out or to make any political capital would be disgraceful,' he told his Cabinet colleagues, 'but to shuffle in order to help a leader in another country who is fighting hard for peace is another matter and not, I think, discreditable'.[45]

Ideology of Independence

De Valera was later accused of equivocation on the question of republicanism; but as the symbol of the Republic he took a strong ideological stand during the Treaty debate. Although he did not believe in an 'isolated republic' he defended the Republic proclaimed in 1916 and established constitutionally by the Irish nation in 1919, he said.[46] He made much of the oath of allegiance to the King of England, and he was right, for all deputies had sworn an oath to uphold the Republic. 'To take an oath you don't mean to keep is dishonourable,' he announced sternly.[47] Yet some years later he, too, took an oath to the King which he called 'a mere formality'; he had to take it to enter the Free State parliament, for the Treaty demanded it.[48] Later he abolished the oath and scrapped the clauses he had found most objectionable in the Treaty. He was right when he said the Treaty would not 'end the centuries of conflict between the two nations of Great Britain and Ireland'.[49]

Griffith and Collins set the ideological tone of the Treaty case. 'We have brought back the flag,' said Griffith.

> We have brought back the evacuation of Ireland after 700 years by British troops and the formation of an Irish Army. We have brought back to Ireland her full rights and powers of fiscal control. We have brought back to Ireland equality with England, equality with all the nations which form that Commonwealth, and an equal voice in the direction of foreign affairs in peace and war.[50]

British troops would still be in Ireland – in the six Northern counties and in coastal enclaves. Irish control of its own finances would be limited to the budget; in the main Britain controlled the economic decisions of the Irish state until 1979, when the Republic joined the European Monetary System and the link with sterling was broken. The state won control of its foreign affairs 'in peace and war', as de Valera demonstrated in the Second World War when he maintained Irish neutrality and denied England the 'Treaty ports' she had handed over in the summer of 1938.

Griffith's main point was that Ireland could now rebuild 'the Gaelic civilization broken down at the battle of Kinsale'.[51] She could thus effect 'the greatest revolution that has ever been made in the history of the world – a revolution of seeing the two countries standing not apart as enemies, but standing together as equals and as friends'. It was unusual for Griffith to engage in such a flight of hyperbole, but the circumstances, he may have felt, demanded it.

Collins's personality entered into the debate: men voted for the Treaty because, if it was 'good enough for Mick Collins, it's good enough for me'. This led to a blistering attack on him by Cathal Brugha, Sinn Féin's uncompromising Minister for Defence – 'the honestest and finest soul in the world, but . . . a bit slow at seeing fine differences and rather stubborn', de Valera said of him.[52] Many were jealous of Collins: Brugha probably, Stack certainly, de Valera perhaps. De Valera feared Collins would make himself the leader of a Republican party by claiming the Treaty as a step to full independence – which was indeed his argument.[53]

Griffith called Collins 'the man who won the war'. But if the war had been won, Brugha threw back, why were they arguing about the Treaty? 'If my name is to go down in history I want it associated with the name of Michael Collins,' said Griffith. 'Michael Collins was the man who fought the Black-and-Tan terror for twelve months, until England was forced to offer terms.'[54] Collins himself said:

> I am the representative of an Irish stock . . . . Our grandfathers have suffered from war, and our fathers or some of our ancestors have died of famine. I don't want a lecture from anybody as to what my principles are to be now. I am just a representative of plain Irish stock whose principles have been burned into them, and we don't want any assurance to the people of this country that we are going to betray them. We are one of themselves. I can state for you a principle which everybody will understand, the principle of 'government by the consent of the governed'.[55]

One by one, men who followed Collins and were deputies of the Dáil – men in the top ranks of the IRB and the headquarters staff of the IRA – rose to proclaim their concept of an independent Irish state, more or less as Griffith and Collins had laid down.

> Alex McCabe:
>
> To me, recognition of Irish nationality and the securing of practically complete control of our army and natural resources which this Treaty brings us, are things that no Republican in his sober moments could or should refuse to accept.[56]

> Ernest Blythe:
>
> I believe the Irish people, when they voted for a Republican majority in this Dáil, and when they declared themselves for an Irish Republic, were not thinking of constitutional privileges very much, but were thinking of the complete freedom of Ireland. I think that is the ideal for which the Irish people have declared . . . but I believe the main thing that was in their minds was the securing of the complete independence of Ireland.[57]

> Richard Mulcahy:
>
> We have not been able to drive the enemy from anything but from a fairly good-sized police barracks. We have not that power . . . . On the other hand the Treaty leaves the Irish people that they will be in absolute possession of their country's resources, and, in my opinion, with full executive power and control over them.[58]

> Michael Hayes:
>
> Under this Treaty you can get the Irish language and get Irish ideals with freedom.[59]

> Kevin O'Higgins:
>
> It gives to Ireland complete control over her internal affairs. It removes all English control or interference within the shores of Ireland.[60]

> Pádraic Ó Máille:
>
> Well, what is good enough for Michael Collins is good enough for me because I believe it is the best for Ireland.[61]

Piaras Beaslai:

We can make our own constitution, control our own finances, have our own schools and colleges, our own country, our own flag, our own coinage and stamps, our own police, aye, and last but not least, our army . . . . Why, for what else have we been fighting but for that?[62] . . . The Irish people did not fight for a Republic. They fought for Ireland for the Irish.[63]

William Sears:

You talk about 1918! The man who would tell you he would stand by the Republic in 1918, what does he say today?[64]

Gearóid O'Sullivan:

That fight [of 750 years] I take to be a fight of the Gaelic state against the foreign sovereignty which was being forced upon it by England. That fight was not always a fight for an isolated Republic or an isolated monarchy. In fact one of the hardest fights in Irish history was made against that great Republican, Oliver Cromwell.[65]

Patrick Hogan:

The time-honored authentic demand of Ireland is for independence, and in comparison with that the form of independence . . . was no more than a secondary consideration . . . . For many hundreds of years Ireland has been struggling for existence, spiritual and material; for many hundreds of years the iron has entered her soul, and during those long years of struggle Ireland's statesmen had at no time an inclination to be meticulous about the form, and Ireland had never perhaps less inclination than at this moment.[66]

Desmond FitzGerald:

And I consider that in accepting [the Treaty] . . . that we are not in any way breaking any pledge or abandoning any principle by doing what we are doing. It seems to me that we have one thing to rest assured of, the one thing that was made clear by the last few years' history of this country, and that is, that the tradition of Irish independence and of Irish nationality was too strongly embedded in us to be overcome by British terror, or by the disastrous period which preceded 1916.[67]

Defending Republicanism

Opponents of the Treaty made the constitutional claim that ratification meant disestablishment of the Republic. The chief logician of this line of argument was Erskine Childers, son of an English father and Anglo-Irish mother, who belonged to the ruling élite of the British Empire. Childers was passionately devoted to the right of Ireland as a small nation to full independence. He had helped arm the pre-war Irish Volunteers. An authentic war hero, a specialist in military affairs, a fine writer, an authority on international relations, a skillful propagandist for Sinn Féin, he was secretary of the Irish delegation during the Treaty negotiations. The British, aware of his talents, successfully isolated him, which was not so difficult since Griffith disliked him. Griffith saw him as de Valera's man on the team. Childers fought the Treaty every step of the way: in London, in Dáil Éireann, in the field during the Civil War, finally before a firing squad. He told his fellow-deputies:

> I wish to recall this assembly to the immediate subject before us . . . the question whether Dáil Éireann, the national assembly of the people of Ireland, having declared its independence, shall approve of and ratify a Treaty relinquishing deliberately and abandoning that independence. I must say for my own part that I missed in the speeches both of the Minister for Foreign Affairs [Arthur Griffith] and the Minister for Finance [Michael Collins] some note, however distant, of regret for the effect in significance of the step they were taking, and had taken, in London, that is, they were asking this assembly, Dáil Éireann, to vote its own extinction in history . . . . The proposals on our side were honourable proposals. They stated in explicit terms that they demanded the preservation of the independence of our country, to exclude the King of England and British authority wholly from our country, and only when that was done, and Ireland was absolutely free in Irish affairs, to enter an association on free and honourable terms with Britain.[68]

Childers was wrong in his estimate of the Treaty's curbs on Irish constitutional development, though perhaps not wrong in the circumstances of December 1921. The occupation of Ireland's ports in time of war must mean, he believed, that England could make 'any use whatever . . . of this island whether for naval or military purposes'. If Britain had retained the 'Treaty ports', then this would have been true. With the recovery of the ports seventeen years after the Treaty, his proposition was nullified. The Treaty depended for its interpretation on a British Act of Parliament, Childers pointed out; consequently, he inferred, Irish sovereignty must stem from the same source, rather than from the people of Ireland. The Treaty, its advocates claimed, did permit the development of full Irish sovereignty within the area of the Irish Free State. But that happened only after years of conflict with British governments.

In time, de Valera scrapped all the restrictions on Irish sovereignty built into the Treaty except one, partition, which proved unamenable to any constitutional change.[69] Childers was right to stress that, as matters stood in December 1921, the Treaty, set in opposition to the 1919 Republic, theoretically meant the surrender by the Irish people of their 'right to freedom'. This interpretation led to a civil war among Sinn Féiners within six months of the Dáil's approval of the Treaty. Childers, the Republican political theorist, a victim of that struggle, was vilified before his execution not only by leading members of the Treatyite government – former comrades – but also by Winston

Churchill, who hated him for deep ideological reasons.[70]

Austin Stack, the Republican Minister for Home Affairs, rejected dominion status for an ancient land like Ireland: Canada, Australia and New Zealand had 'sprung from England' and were 'children of England'. Their peoples regarded England as their motherland.

> This country, on the other hand, has not been a child of England's nor never was. England came here as an invader, and for 750 years we have been resisting that conquest. Are we now after those 750 years to bend the knee and acknowledge that we received from England as a concession full, or half, or three-quarter Dominion powers? I say no.[71]

Professor William Stockley did not feel 'any particular interest in a Republic as such' and quoted Edmund Burke that such a form of government could be as capable of cruelty as the most absolute monarchy. But 'the dilemma in which Ireland is placed by this Treaty is the climax to the treatment of a weak nation by the strong and the bully.'[72]

All six women members of the Dáil opposed the Treaty. The most radical attack was by Countess Markievicz, who saw the Treaty as a betrayal of Connolly and the Republic proclaimed in 1916. She stood for Connolly's ideal of 'a Workers' Republic'. Interrupted by a shout of 'Soviet Republic', she declared that 'the interests of England are the interests of the capitalistic class'. She spoke of the 'stony road' to ultimate freedom: 'and I, for one, will stand on the road with Terence MacSwiney and Kevin Barry and the men of Easter Week'. She said Ireland's freedom was worth blood, she would willingly give her blood for it and she appealed 'to the men of the Dáil to stand true'.[73]

Mary MacSwiney claimed that in January 1919 the Irish people had 'cast off for ever their allegiance to any foreigner'; they would stand by that, but 'it is always a minority that saves the soul of a nation in its hour of need'. The Irish had waged 'a spiritual fight' of right against wrong 'and the things of the spirit have always prevailed'.[74] She declared herself a rebel against the new Free State, a pledge she kept, becoming in the late 1920s and 1930s the spokeswoman of the 'Second Dáil' and in time a most bitter enemy of de Valera. ('Second Dáil' Republicans insisted that the Republic had not been legally disestablished.) Apart from that, Miss MacSwiney's republicanism, in common with most of her Second Dáil colleagues, was of a conservative cast; when listing the leaders of the 1916 Rising, she ignored Connolly.[75]

Mary MacSwiney's colleagues in the 'Second Dáil' wilderness

of the 1920s and 1930s, Brian O'Higgins and Seán Ó Ceallaigh (J.J. O'Kelly, better known by his pen-name 'Sceilg'), put their case against the Treaty in similar terms. Both were conservatives and traditionalists. Both had been active in Irish-Ireland causes from the turn of the century. O'Higgins, an Irish Volunteer, took part in the 1916 Rising. Ó Ceallaigh, editor of the *Catholic Bulletin*, did much to raise the national consciousness after the Rising by the articles in his journal. Both identified their nationalism in stridently Catholic terms.[76] O'Higgins was Deputy Speaker of the Dáil, Ó Ceallaigh Minister for Education in the Republican government of 1921, but not a member of the Cabinet.

O'Higgins would not surrender now 'the one ideal and dream of my life – an independent Irish-Ireland, and so I mean to vote against the Treaty.'[77] Ó Ceallaigh called it 'a Treaty of surrender, subjection, servitude, slavery, and as such, I appeal to you not to be content with its retreat from ratification to approval, but to drive it from approval, to rejection and from rejection to the oblivion from which it should never have emerged'.[78] For the rest of his life, Sceilg delivered the same message to the small group that remained faithful to the 'Second Dáil'.[79]

Cathal Brugha, apart from his attack on Collins, rejected the Treaty on principle, with an appeal to history that sheds light on physical-force republicanism:

> There has been a body of opinion in this country . . . that has always repudiated English authority in this country. Each generation had that body of opinion in it, and whenever they found themselves strong enough they went out in insurrection against England and English authority here. The last one, as you know, was in 1916 when we established our Republic; it was ratified in January 1919, and we have carried on our functions with a *de jure* and *de facto* government since; and here, when we are in so strong a position and we so strong and England so weak and with so many enemies as she has now more than ever, we are asked to do such a thing as this. Why, if instead of being so strong, our last cartridge had been fired, our last shilling had been spent and our last man were lying on the ground and his enemies howling round him and their bayonets raised, ready to plunge them into his body, that man should say – true to the traditions handed down – if they said to him: 'Now, will you come into our Empire?' – he should say, and he would say: 'No, I will not.' This is the spirit that has lasted all through the centuries, and you people in favour of the Treaty know that the British government and the British Empire will have gone down before that spirit dies out in Ireland.[80]

Liam Mellows spoke for radical republicanism. There were few radicals in the Second Dáil when it needed a radical stand. There was no Labour deputy in the Dáil. Labour had presented the Irish case for independence at the international labour and socialist conference in Berne in February 1919.[81] The Second Dáil was composed of IRA Volunteers and members of Sinn Féin, lower middle class for the most part, with a sprinkling of farmers, shopkeepers, shop assistants, teachers, journalists, lawyers. Apart from Countess Markievicz,[82] there were no socialists among them. Mellows was 'a Fenian radical', not a socialist.[83] His speech against the Treaty made the case that the delegates had no right to surrender the Irish Republic of which they were the plenipotentiaries. They could not sign away the rights of Ireland.

> They had no power to agree to anything inconsistent with the existence of the Republic. Now either the Republic exists or it does not. If the Republic exists, why are we talking about stepping towards the Republic by means of this Treaty? I for one believed, and do believe, that the Republic exists, because it exists upon the only sure foundation upon which any government or republic can exist, that is, because the people gave a mandate for that Republic to be declared. We are hearing a great deal here about the will of the people, and the newspapers – that never even recognized the Republic when it was the will of the people – use that as a text for telling Republicans in Ireland what the will of the people is . . . . The people are being stampeded; in the people's minds there is only one alternative to this Treaty and that is terrible, immediate war . . . . That is not the will of the people, that is the fear of the people. The will of the people was when the people declared for a Republic. [84]

Séamus Robinson and Seán Moylan commanded IRA brigades in South Tipperary and North Cork. They were uninfluenced by the IRB-controlled GHQ staff, which took its politics from Collins. They opposed the Treaty. They spoke for the rank and file of the Volunteers in the South, where most of the fighting had taken place. Robinson had commanded the action at Soloheadbeg and had fought in 1916. He said he spoke for Liam Lynch, Officer Commanding the 1st Southern Division, Ernie O'Malley, Officer Commanding the 2nd Southern Division, Oscar Traynor, Officer Commanding the Dublin Brigade, Michael MacCormaic, Officer Commanding the 3rd Southern Division. 'If we had no political outlook we would not be soldiers at all,' he said when de Valera objected. He thought a charge of treason should be brought against Griffith and Collins. [85]

The Drift to Civil War

The Treaty arguments on Irish independence became standard republican ideology for fifty years, even when their proponents had abandoned them. Hence their importance to an understanding of modern Irish republican ideology. The arguments inevitably ended in civil war, for both sides had guns and they took up polar positions.

Yet, apart from Mellows, who saw the Republican position as anti-imperialist, the ideological lines were unclear at the time. De Valera's summary in his letter to McGarrity of the forces ranged against the Republic – Church, ex-landlords, business interests – indicates he could have clarified the issues on other than legalisms, but was too cautious and conservative to do so. It would have meant rallying the people of 'no property', as Mellows said when he looked back ruefully on events from a prison cell in the early autumn of 1922. To save the Republic meant falling back on the dispossessed; de Valera would not do that. Ratification of the Treaty, by election, was inevitable. De Valera told McGarrity privately, that he was tempted several times 'to take drastic action, as I would be entitled to legally, but then the army is divided and the people wouldn't stand for it, and nobody but the enemy would win if I took it'.[86] No Republican leader attempted to rally the people behind the Republic they had sworn to defend.

The British looked on the debate and subsequent events with some nervousness. Churchill, as Colonial Secretary, was responsible for Ireland. He said of the new (pro-Treaty) Dublin government:

> Their view is that the Irish Republic was set up by the Irish people . . . and that this Irish Republic can only be converted to an Irish Free State by the decision of the Irish people. That is not our view. We do not recognize the Irish Republic. We have never recognized it, and never will recognize it.

When an election was held, the Republic would be disestablished, the Treaty state would take over. 'These matters do not affect us in our procedure in any way,' continued Churchill.[87] Then he asked: 'But is it not a desirable thing that upon the authority of the Irish people recorded at an election, the Republican idea should be definitely, finally and completely put aside?'[88]

Collins seemed to think he could keep the Republic by some subterfuge that would free him from the strait-jacket of the Treaty. He looked for loopholes in the document, pressed his own programme of step-by-step republicanism – especially in the draft constitution for the Irish Free State, which the British rejected[89] – and countered Orange terror in Ulster by organizing border operations against the wishes and indeed without the knowledge of his own government. The 'B' Specials were 'a military force under the guise of a police force'.[90] The military adviser of the Unionist government in Belfast was Field Marshal Sir Henry Wilson, ex-Chief of the Imperial General Staff. When the attacks on Catholics in Belfast intensified, Collins exchanged arms with the anti-Treaty section of the IRA and police barracks in Tyrone and Derry were raided by forces loyal to him. A sceptical Churchill told the Commons: 'These raids were entirely planned and carried out by people resident in Tyrone and Derry with the desire – so it is alleged – to get some protection for themselves against the terror from which they are suffering.'[91] He said he was relaying information given him by the Provisional Government in Dublin.

Collins probably was aware from his intelligence sources that most of the killings in Belfast were not the work of irate Protestants, but of the police. This is still not widely known and officially has never been admitted. One of the most horrible acts of the time was the shooting of the MacMahon family, of which Churchill said: 'I think one would have to search all over Europe to find instances of equal atrocity, barbarity, cold-blooded, inhuman, cannibal vengeance – cannibal in all except the act of devouring the flesh of the victim – which will equal this particular event.'[92] These and other killings were the handiwork of a special reprisal unit of the Royal Irish Constabulary under District Inspector John W. Nixon, who was made a Member of the British Empire (MBE) for his services.[93] The anti-Catholic, anti-Nationalist terror continued through the spring and summer of 1922. Homes were burned, people were murdered, Catholics were driven from their jobs – particularly in the shipyards – thousands became refugees. The situation eased when civil war broke out in the South at the end of June 1922 with the attack on the Four Courts, the IRA headquarters. [94]

The IRB and the Republic

Between January 1922 and his death by ambush on 22 August, 1922, Michael Collins acted more as the leader of the IRB than as the leading minister of a constitutional government. The IRB carried the Treaty, de Valera said, by endorsing it. 'The Dáil members of the IRB were told that acceptance of the Treaty would be the quickest way to the Republic, and a lot of other stuff which time only will explode,' he told McGarrity.[95] The Supreme Council had decided that 'the present peace treaty between Ireland and Great Britain should be ratified'. Mary MacSwiney said the IRB was using all its energies 'to pull down the Irish Republic' and that 'a solid block of forty IRB men voted for that Treaty'.[96] One can say that had the IRB opposed the Treaty it would not have been carried in the Dáil, whatever about the country.

What then? And why? Collins had decided, it would seem, that the Treaty was as much as England would grant nationalist Ireland in

1921. After all, it was a great advance on the Home Rule Act that became law in 1914 – and was not implemented, essentially because the Unionists would not have it. Under 'the Government of Ireland Act, 1914'

> on and after the appointed day there shall be in Ireland an Irish Parliament consisting of His Majesty the King and two Houses, namely, the Irish Senate and the Irish House of Commons.
>
> Notwithstanding the establishment of the Irish Parliament or anything contained in the Act, the supreme power and authority of the Parliament of the United Kingdom shall remain unaffected and undiminished over all persons, matters and things in Ireland and every part thereof. . . .[97]

The Treaty granted the Irish sovereignty 'over all persons, matters and things in Ireland and every part thereof', Collins (and the IRB) could reason, except for partition, and he accepted Lloyd George's contention that the Boundary Commission would make that inoperable. The only oath that mattered to an IRB man was the one to 'the Organization', and Collins could well argue that in a matter of years he would make Ireland a republic in fact if not in name. His final goal remained: 'A free and independent Republican Government in Ireland.'[98]

Collins believed the Treaty would help him achieve that goal. Without the Treaty Ireland would be at England's mercy. These are sound arguments, if one is accustomed to working secretly and in subversive ways, in the manner of the IRB. They can be republican arguments; but they are not revolutionary arguments. Again, the lack of clarity on ideology reveals itself. What exactly were they fighting for between 1918 and 1921? (de Valera thought they could get 'external association', a compromise between the two, but apart from Childers no one knew what he meant.) Succeeding generations of Irish republicans have been stuck with these unanswered questions and the IRB has not been around to guide them: it died with Michael Collins at Béal na mBláth, in his native West Cork, while he was on an IRB mission it would seem, attempting to re-unite the warring factions of Irish republicanism.[99]

The British wanted the Treaty implemented, which was natural enough. They estimated that 70 per cent of the Southern electorate favoured it.[100] Then Collins signed an electoral pact with de Valera *not* to make the Treaty an issue in the June vote, and the British were aghast.

'The Irish leaders move in a narrow world,' Churchill explained to the Cabinet. 'They had been men of violence and conspiracy and had hardly emerged from that atmosphere. They had been discussing an agreed election between the two factions by which was meant that so many seats would be assigned to de Valera and so many to the Free State.' Churchill wrote Collins 'a strong letter pointing out that this would be a travesty of democratic principles'.[101] Collins answered that for him the de Valera pact was more important than the Treaty. The British decided the pact abrogated the Treaty and Collins was summoned to London.

'The more serious trouble is in the north-east – how to restrain the South and Ulster from flying at each other's throats and plunging into Civil War,' Jones told Lloyd George. 'I think the North (Henry Wilson and Co.) are forcing this in order to embroil us on their side against the South and get us back into the pre-Treaty position. This is incidentally playing de Valera's game. We undertook the military defence of Ulster and we ought to do it *with scrupulous justice between the two parties*.'[102]

Collins was belligerent. 'He talked on at a great rate in a picturesque way about going back to fight with his comrades . . . that we seemed to be bent on war, that we would do nothing to put Belfast right, and on and on at great length about the Ulster situation.'[103] He distrusted the British government, was 'obsessed' with the North.[104] Lloyd George said 'Collins was just a wild animal – a mustang.' The only leader the Irish had was Griffith.[105] Griffith, of course, was the only Irish leader of substance amenable to the Prime Minister's wishes. The Treaty had almost broken down; Lloyd George talked of seizing the Irish ports 'and that once we got embroiled we should inevitably be drawn into the interior'.[106]

Churchill told the House on 31 May that 'the cruel warfare between Catholics and Protestants which is being waged in the streets of Belfast' had made the position of the Provisional Government more difficult, 'exasperating the Catholic majority throughout Southern Ireland, and increasing the supporters of Mr. de Valera and the extremists who follow him'.[107] Collins listened to the debate from the gallery. Also participating, as a Unionist member for an Ulster constituency, was Field Marshal Sir Henry Wilson, considered by both sections of Sinn Féin as the chief source of anti-Nationalist terrorism in the North. Three weeks later Wilson was shot dead in London. Churchill blamed the Republicans under Rory O'Connor in the Four Courts for the assassination; but the order came from Collins, acting through the IRB. Few nationalists in Ireland mourned Wilson. He was identified in the public mind with the pogroms in Belfast, however unfairly.[108] However, his killing was the pretext that finally tumbled the two Sinn Féin factions into Civil War.[109] The electoral pact between Collins and de Valera was over anyway, because of a supposedly provocative speech by Collins in Cork on 14 June, 1922, the eve of the poll; the real reason was that Lloyd George would not have it because it was 'the Republic in disguise', he told C.P. Scott, editor of the *Manchester Guardian*.[110]

For Collins, the Wilson assassination backfired. He would have assumed that the deed would curb the killings in Belfast. But the British government directed its anger at Dublin, not at Craig, and the Four Courts had to be attacked or the Treaty would fall. If the Treaty collapsed, the British would stay in the South and there would be no Irish Free State – no nation-state, after all the blood that had been shed for it. Collins and Griffith were at one in wanting an Irish government, whatever its powers. Neither Griffith nor his ministerial colleagues knew anything of Collins's involvement in the Wilson assassination; the government issued a fierce denunciation of the 'anarchic deed'. Two men were executed for it and Collins tried to rescue them up to the end.[111]

The Ideology of Civil War

Collins borrowed two field guns from the British to shell the Four Courts, and that seemed to upset the Republicans. They maintained for a time that British officers dressed in Free State uniforms had carried out the shelling. Irishmen who had served in the British army manned the guns. There were few casualties in the Four Courts. Rory O'Connor saw the defence as a grand gesture against the Treaty – another Republican weakness – and surrendered. Liam Mellows wanted to fight on. Most of the garrison could have escaped with the help of their former comrades who were shooting at them, once the shelling stopped. It was a friendly beginning to a bitter Civil War. The garrison went to Mountjoy Prison, and on the way a few took off for the hills.[112]

O'Connor was the catalyst of the Civil War, but he had no idea how to stop the Treaty and get back to the Republic. Given Collins's position, the Treaty might well have been defeated by political means. But no political initiative emerged from the Republican side during the Civil War, except near the end when de Valera stepped in to find a basis for ending hostilities.

The British, or at least Churchill, appeared to think that the men in the Four Courts were Reds; he feared 'Dublin would fall into the hands of Rory O'Connor's troops and the Industrial Workers of the World', he told the Cabinet, unless the British army intervened![113] While the Four Courts was burning, Churchill was asked in the House of Commons about its great law library and irreplaceable records and documents. His reply succinctly stated one aspect of the ideology of the Civil War. 'When men are fighting, and fighting about matters so important as the foundations of their country, buildings and records will often suffer . . . . I will only say this – that a State without archives is better than archives without a State.' [114]

In its proclamation explaining the attack on the Four Courts the Provisional Government declared:

> You are faced with a conspiracy whose calculated end is to destroy the Treaty signed by your representatives and endorsed by yourselves. Under that Treaty the government and control of your own country and its resources have been surrendered back to you after centuries of usurpation. You are asked to reject this surrender and to engage in a hopeless and unnecessary war with Great Britain. The people in the Four Courts say they are fighting for a Republic. In reality they are fighting to bring the British back. [115]

The Four Courts garrison did not have the support of all Republicans. They did not accept the leadership of Eamon de Valera and only on the eve of the attack did they recognize the authority of the IRA Chief of Staff, Liam Lynch. They had been working with Collins on operations in the six counties and had no reason to think he would launch an all-out assault on them. They were watching the British army, still in Dublin, and the situation of the Nationalists in the North. Following the attack on the Four Courts, other Republican units came to the defence of 'the Republic'. There was no plan, no political or military leadership, and the IRA – a term now applied only to anti-Treaty Republicans – quickly lost its strongholds in Dublin and Munster and adopted guerrilla tactics, as in the campaign against Britain. But a people tired of conflict and talk of war gave the Republicans little support. Many believed the anti-Treatyites were merely trying to upset the election results. Others were puzzled by it all. Most saw no alternative to the Treaty's 'freedom to win freedom'. In the North, Nationalist resistance to partition collapsed in a wave of demoralization. [116]

Writing from Mountjoy Prison on 25 August to Austin Stack, Liam Mellows urged the co-ordination of Republican political and military forces to defeat the Treaty. He proposed a popular social programme to keep 'the great body of workers . . . on the side of independence'. His programme called for nationalization of industry, the banks, and the confiscation of large estates.

> In our efforts now to win back public support to the Republic we are forced to recognize – whether we like it or not – that the commercial interests so-called – money and the gombeen men – are on the side of the Treaty, because

> the Treaty means Imperialism and England. We are back to Tone – and it is just as well – relying on that great body 'the men of no property'. The 'stake in the country' people were never with the Republic. They are not with it now – and they will always be against it – until it wins.[117]

This is the only radical document to emerge from the Civil War and it was published by the Free State to link the Republicans to Communism. No leading Republican supported Mellows. His ideas were discussed among the prisoners in Mountjoy, including Peadar O'Donnell who a half-dozen years later came up with a similar programme for the IRA, resulting in Saor Éire (Free Ireland), which was banned by Church and state.

One may trace the IRA obsession with purely military means to the Civil War, itself a legacy from the attitude of Collins's GHQ staff to politics during the fight against the British, as Mellows notes. The Republicans had no politics, they sometimes liked to claim. This meant that their supporters relied on de Valera's politics. It is hard to argue with Professor Michael Hayes, pro-Treaty deputy and Speaker of the Dáil, who says: 'the civil war would have been no more than a riot only for Dev's political cloak over it.'[118]

De Valera's popular support stayed amazingly firm through the Civil War, as evidenced by the election of August 1923 when the reorganized Sinn Féin party won forty-four seats to the government's sixty-three. De Valera widened this base after breaking with 'the Republic' and forming Fianna Fáil in 1926, till February 1932 when he won power with seventy-two seats to the Treatyites fifty-seven. He held office till 1948, when a coalition of parties ousted him for three years. It is a remarkable political record and de Valera's personal leadership must get the credit for it, not republicanism. There was nothing radical about his leadership, but the Irish electorate was conservative by and large, and apart from the national issue de Valera did little to change Irish society.

De Valera's 'Acquiescence or Resistance'

De Valera's argument, stated in September 1922, while in hiding from his erstwhile colleagues of the Provisional Government, was this:

> If the Republicans stand aside and let the Treaty come into force, it means acquiescence in and abandonment of the national sovereignty and in the partition of the country – a surrender of the ideals for which the sacrifices of the past few years were deliberately made and the sufferings of these years consciously endured.
>
> If the Republicans do not stand aside, then they must resist, and resistance

means just this civil war and armed opposition to what is undoubtedly, as I have said, the decision of the majority of the people.[119]

Such resistance was futile, de Valera suggested. Republicans faced a state backed by England and an authoritarian Church. For many, the edicts of the Church were Holy Writ in 1922.[120] If Republicans could not defeat the Treaty militarily or politically, what were they to do? De Valera's answer was to revise the Treaty. This could be done, he suggested, by

ignoring England. Acting in Ireland as if there was no such person as the English King, no Governor-General, no Treaty, no oath of Allegiance. In fact acting as if Document 2 were the Treaty. Later we could act more independently still. Whilst the Free State was supposedly in existence would be the best time to secure the unity of the country . . . . If we can get a single state for the whole of the country, then the future is safe.[121]

De Valera's policy was not republican but it was the one he followed through the Civil War, which ended in May 1923 with a unilateral declaration of a cease-fire by the anti-Treatyites.[122] He followed it in the revived Sinn Féin of 1923-26, in Fianna Fáil, through his years as leader of the opposition in the Free State Dáil. From 1932 he implemented this policy, step by step till the new Constitution of 1937, which embodied all provisions of his programme save one – a united Ireland. He made the Irish Free State a republic, in all but name, while staying in the British Commonwealth: his 'external association' formula of 1921. The Executive Authority (External Relations) Act permitted the King to act for Éire in diplomatic matters so long as the state was associated with the Commonwealth. In fact, despite defeat in the Civil War, de Valera's programme triumphed in time.

Republicans Resist the State

The Republicans who fought the Civil War and were defeated continued to resist the Treaty and the state it brought into being. They would not acquiesce, they would not surrender national sovereignty, they would not accept partition; the consequence was years of futile armed opposition to 'the decision of the majority of the people', as de Valera foresaw.

These were the Republicans of the IRA, which was reorganized after the Civil War. The shadow Republican government that de Valera led through 1922-25 believed itself the sole legitimate authority in Ireland. On 14 November, 1925 an IRA convention withdrew allegiance from this 'Second Dáil' government, because 'it had utterly failed to perform the functions for which it was organized – the interest, protection and defence of the people and territory of the Republic of Ireland'. The IRA became separate from all Republican organizations, subject to its own elected Executive, 'the only existing government which had taken steps for the protection and defence of Ireland, refusing any semblance of allegiance to the British government':[123]

The Sinn Féin Ard Comhairle, meeting in Dublin on 13 January, 1926, summoned an Ard Fheis for 9 March to discuss 'whether with a view to massing the people of Ireland against the Oath of Allegiance . . . it could be promised officially on behalf of the organisation . . . that if the oath were removed the Republican members would sit with the other representatives of the people in the Free State assembly', which though non-sovereign controlled the lives of a large section of the Irish people. De Valera lost. He resigned as 'President of the Republic'[124] and two months later founded Fianna Fáil. The 'Second Dáil' continued to meet, however unreal its situation, and in 1929 it devised a new constitution for the shadow Republic.

The IRA, however, did try to base its ideology on reality. This led it, via Peadar O'Donnell's anti-land annuities campaign, to found Saor Éire in September 1931. Saor Éire described itself as 'an Organisation of Workers and Working Farmers', with three objectives:

1. To achieve an independent revolutionary leadership for the working class and working farmers towards the overthrow in Ireland of British Imperialism and its ally, Irish Capitalism.
2. To organize and consolidate the Republic of Ireland on the basis of the possession and administration by the workers and working farmers, of the land, instruments of production, distribution and exchange.
3. To restore and foster the Irish language, culture, and games.[125]

Item three excepted, these were radical socialist goals. They were based on the writings of James Connolly, which only labour supporters had bothered to read during the turmoil of the preceding decade.

It is possible that the increasingly reactionary policies of the Free State government and the ruling Cumann na nGaedheal party, its coercion laws and anti-Republican repression, pushed the IRA to the left. If the Free State depended upon England for support, the IRA would seek help from the Soviet Union. A mission to Moscow sought arms and received none. The IRA exchanged some intelligence data on England for a cash subsidy. IRA officers travelled to Russia for military training, which ended abruptly when British intelligence heard of it: Stalin was looking for British recognition and did not want his policy upset.[126]

Kevin O'Higgins, Vice President of the Executive Council of the Irish Free State and Minister of Justice, sought even closer ties with Britain than the Treaty demanded. The Collins-IRB line of a stepping-stone to the Republic was dropped. The Boundary Commission was botched by Eoin MacNeill. Nationalists had to contend with:

> Special police, the coercion which would be necessary to hold Tyrone and Fermanagh, 45,000 special constables in a statelet of six counties; abolition of proportional representation, changing of the Constitution in order to deprive Nationalists of their due place in parliament and local administration.[127]

But all was acceptable to President William T. Cosgrave and company so long as Article 5 of the Treaty was dropped. (Article 5 insisted that the Free State pay its share of the British national debt.) It was dropped – and the Boundary Commission was dropped with it.

Before his assassination, in July 1927, O'Higgins was planning to introduce Griffith's dual monarchy by having the King of England crowned King of Ireland, too. 'The details he discussed at length with various English representatives,' his biographer Terence de Vere White writes. 'The King was to come to Ireland and be crowned by both the Primates of the Catholic Church and the Church of Ireland [Anglican] in Dublin.'[128] For O'Higgins it was a way out of the partition dilemma: common loyalty to the Crown would reconcile nationalist and unionist. First, he thought it would take ten years to accomplish but he changed his estimate to five years. Republicanism had no tradition in Gaelic Ireland, O'Higgins argued: Tone brought the idea from France, the Fenians got it from America. The rebel proclamation in 1916 had given republicanism 'a mystical character' (as de Vere White phrases it) for many Irish nationalists. O'Higgins was the most imperial-minded of the Free State ministers. He discussed his monarchist plan with Lord Carson, the man who led Ulster against Home Rule, and with L.S. Amery, the Dominions Secretary. The plan died with O'Higgins.[129] The British found the idea 'unacceptable', and Sir James Craig opposed 'any form of union with the Free State', according to British Cabinet papers.

Republican Congress

With de Valera in power after 1932, the IRA faced a very difficult problem. He held the initiative on the national question and split the IRA. The Church had denounced Saor Éire as 'Communistic' and an IRA convention in April 1932 decided not to revive it. Peadar O'Donnell in the following years urged the IRA to adopt a programme he called 'Republican Congress' – meaning unity with all 'anti-imperialist forces'.[130] The demand for some such unity grew as the former government party, Cumann na nGaedheal, fashioned a corporative-state programme and organized a semi-Fascist League of Youth, nicknamed 'Blueshirts' because of their Mussolini-Hitler style uniforms.[131]

Before breaking decisively with the Republican Congress idea in March 1934, at an evenly-divided convention, the IRA issued its own socialist programme claiming national sovereignty extended to the nation's soil, its resources and all its 'wealth and wealth-producing processes'.[132] A fierce ideological argument broke out inside the IRA. The militarism of the Civil War was dropped while discussion raged on the future of 'the Republic'. The radicals wanted a socialist republic along Connolly lines;[133] the traditionalists insisted that 'the Republic' must be Gaelic in culture and Catholic in social outlook. The 'Second Dáil' Republicans, who controlled what was left of Sinn Féin, abhorred socialism. Mary MacSwiney, J.J. O'Kelly (Sceilg) and Brian O'Higgins, attacked the left republican programme of national ownership of the land as 'Communist' and 'inconsistent with Christian ethics',[134] while others cited the works of St Thomas Aquinas in defence of private property.

Peadar O'Donnell, the chief theoretician of the Republican left, claimed that declarations of policy about the ownership of land and industry were useless. 'It is the nature of the struggle that matters', he asserted. 'There were many fine statements at the opening of the First Dáil in January 1919 but in the end the ranches were protected and a form of landlordism preserved.'[135] O'Donnell took issue with de Valera calling himself a republican: Document No. 2 was not 'the Republic', he argued. De Valera's concern was Irish sovereignty, not the form of the state. The separatism of the United Irishmen embodied the old Gaelic monarchist tradition as well as the republicanism of Tone.[136]

The Republican Congress was an attempt to outflank de Valera on 'the Republic' by uniting all those without 'a stake in the country' into 'an organizing centre for anti-imperialist activities on the part of people, irrespective of their party or organizational affiliations', in the words of the Congress chief organizer, George Gilmore. Because of 'the failure of the Republican movement of 1918-23, and the stagnation of the years that followed', Gilmore believed that the republican population of Ireland was unorganized for the most part. 'But that population remains Republican,' he insisted, and could be 'rallied upon definitely anti-Imperialist activities.'[137] However, it was de Valera, not the IRA or Gilmore's Congress, who rallied the Irish people against British imperialism by removing the Crown from the domestic affairs of the Irish state and repudiating the land annuities and other financial shackles, actions which led to the 'economic war' with England.

Whether Gilmore's analysis was right or wrong, Congress failed to draw 'the Republican population of Ireland' into 'anti-Imperialist activities'. It drew the tirades of clerics and anti-Communists, helped tenants in Dublin, published a lively weekly paper, and in its last act organized an Irish section of the International Brigades to fight against Franco in the Spanish civil war, led by one of its founders, Frank Ryan.[138]

The IRA continued its difficult task of reconciling social radicalism with traditionalist physical-force methods of freeing Ireland, or as the *Governmental Programme* put it: 'Not only must they be the organized and armed vanguard but they must also supply leadership and guidance in directing the thoughts of the people along constructive revolutionary lines.'[139] The role was beyond the IRA's capacity. Its attempt to establish a political party in 1935 foundered on the question of recognizing the Free State. If it could not recognize the state, it must abstain from parliament. The electorate would not support a policy of abstention. Cumann na Poblachta, the IRA political party, flickered dimly in 1936 before it died. The IRA thought Sinn Féin a useless weapon politically, and hopelessly reactionary. Father Michael O'Flanagan, President of Sinn Féin in 1934-35, tried to change this image: a socialist, he wanted the party to deal with the problems of the day. He failed, and his Sinn Féin colleagues expelled him.[140]

The Bombing Campaign

Father O'Flanagan had said in his presidential address to Sinn Féin that

> the immediate task that lies before us is to clarify our minds on the essential principles of pure republicanism, to apply them with unswerving consistency in the daily activities of our organization, to show how their general application would solve all the pressing problems of the whole people of Ireland, and to work out in detail a plan of government, that will make the enlightened public opinion of Ireland the dominant and effective controlling influence, in all the secular affairs of the Irish people.[141]

No plan of government could prevail against the reality of a government accepted by the people of the twenty-six counties (Free State), headed by a man whose integrity, principles, courage and course of action the majority admired. This was the problem of Irish republicanism in the 1930s. The people were not concerned with how republican or unrepublican or even anti-republican de Valera was: he was attempting, as he himself put it, 'to get the Irish nation on the march again'; whereas the IRA, and for that matter Sinn Féin, lacked 'any ability to lead our people anywhere except back into the morass'.[142] De Valera also had a popular mandate to solve the national question. The IRA took its mandate from history, Sinn Féin from the far-off election of December 1918, de Valera from the last poll.

In such circumstances the only hope of the IRA was to outflank de Valera on the national question by tackling it head on, by armed action; but it had neither the resources nor the popular support required. In America the head of the Clan-na-Gael, Joseph McGarrity, recalled the dynamite campaign of 1881-85. Organized by the anti-Devoy 'Triangle' leadership of the Clan,[143] it had little to recommend it; the IRB opposed it. The Irish-American dynamiters put explosives in the House of Commons, under London Bridge and other symbols of empire. McGarrity knew one of the dynamiters well – Luke Dillon who spent fourteen years in a Canadian prison for trying to blow up the Welland Canal during the Boer War. McGarrity admired him greatly as a man of action. He decided a similar terrorist policy would suit the circumstances of the 1930s IRA. He wrote a memorandum referring in very general terms to his plan, urging the IRA to 'take the field' and 'end a nightmare of thirteen years'. The Clan-na-Gael would supply the funds. 'We will make the name of Ireland again a household word in America,' he promised. 'The countries of the world will follow our lead and again we have before us the fight of a nation to be free instead of the petty bickerings of two faction parliaments.' He proposed a bombing campaign in England.[144] The scheme was rejected by the Army Council of the IRA, but one leader, Seán Russell, supported it. Russell, in the movement since 1913, had worked under Collins in GHQ from 1919 to 1921. He agreed with McGarrity that what England feared most in Ireland was 'the fanatical deed'. In June 1936 de Valera banned the IRA. No organization that advocated the use of force would be permitted to exist in the state, he said.[145] The leader who had kept the warring factions in the IRA together through the years, Moss Twomey, was jailed. Russell went to America and reached an agreement with McGarrity. He was dismissed from the IRA. 'We are forced to say that we view with the deepest concern the friction existing with regard to your organization,' the Clan Executive informed the Army Council.[146]

Russell's supporters took control of the IRA at a convention in the spring of 1938. When Russell was named Chief of Staff, most of the old leaders left the organization, including Seán MacBride, its best political brain, and Tom Barry, the legendary guerrilla leader of 1919-21. (Barry objected to a bombing campaign on moral grounds.)

The rank and file supported the plan for a terror campaign in Britain. Sinn Féin and the 'Second Dáil' also supported Russell, who would have no truck with socialism. The 'Second Dáil' handed over its 'powers' to Russell, in December 1938, to keep in trust for the Irish people. There were only seven faithful members left.

In January 1939, after sending an ultimatum to England, the IRA bombing campaign opened and continued for about fourteen months. It was poorly prepared and not very effective. Great care was exercised to ensure no loss of civilian lives. A premature bomb in Coventry killed five persons, and two IRA volunteers, Peter Barnes and James McCormack, were hanged.

The Germans had their eye on the game. Russell told McGarrity on 3 March, 1939 that they had 'sent over a representative to get in touch with us. They are very interested in our performance.' The representative had a long talk with Russell and it was agreed to send a man to Germany. This was done. 'Our man made a good impression, with the result that they are coming here to meet us on the spot to get down to real business.'[147]

Not much came from the German connection. Russell was neither a Nazi nor a Fascist, but a simple patriot, who wanted Britain to withdraw from Ireland. Despite his early optimistic reports to McGarrity on the bombing (letter of 3 March, 1939), he must have been disappointed by the level of operations, for in April 1939, without notice to McGarrity, he sailed for America and never returned to Ireland. De Valera was expected to attend the World's Fair in New York and Russell may have decided to upstage him. He knew de Valera well and thought highly of his political leadership. It was de Valera's attitude to force that Russell disagreed with: he did not believe partition could be ended any other way. Of all the IRA leaders of the 1920s and 1930s, Russell was probably the most conservative, politically and socially.

Russell was arrested in Detroit in June 1939 because the King and Queen of England were across the river in Windsor, Ontario. Russell's arrest created a row in Congress, sparked by James McGrannery, then a Congressman, later President Truman's Attorney-General. Russell was released on bail, but could not leave the country. In April 1940 he slipped aboard a ship bound for Genoa. A representative of the German Foreign Office met him and took him to Berlin. He was given sabotage training, received by Foreign Minister Joachim von Ribbentrop, but refused to divulge his plans, if he had any. The Germans agreed to transport him to Ireland by U-boat. Travelling with Russell was Frank Ryan, the former IRA and Congress leader, captured by Franco's forces and imprisoned during the Civil War, who was turned over to the Germans in July 1940. The cramped space and lack of air on the submarine, combined with an ulcerated stomach, led to Russell's death one hundred miles west of Ireland. He was buried at sea and Ryan returned to Germany.[148]

There was no revolt in the North. But the IRA continued its activities despite repression.[149] De Valera jailed all IRA activists and executed some of them. Russell's successor, Stephen Hayes, was tried by his own GHQ as a spy but fled to the police. At the end of the war the IRA hardly existed.

German intelligence found it difficult to work with the IRA. They had dealt with Flemings, Bretons and Croatians, but the IRA did not fit into any of these patterns. One Nazi agent wrote after the war:

> In spite of the fine qualities of individual IRA men, as a body I considered them worthless. A leader once boasted to me that he had in a certain district – I was not really interested – 5000 sworn members. I answered him that I personally would be completely satisfied with 500 men who knew how to obey an order. I would march with them to Belfast and destroy the Harland and Wolff shipyards, and these men would have done more for Ireland than 5000 talking about the Second Dáil and Third Dáil and their legality.[150]

However, IRA volunteers were not storm-troopers, but in their own eyes guardians of an old tradition, an old ideology with its own peculiar way of looking at politics and the world.

What did Russell and the IRA hope to gain from a link-up with Nazi Germany, the enemy of small nations? Help to fight England. The ideology of physical-force nationalism is based on the motto that 'England's difficulty is Ireland's opportunity'. That indeed was Seán Russell's only policy.

Rise and Fall of Clann na Poblachta

The only Republican voices heard during the Second World War years belonged to Brian O'Higgins, the 'Second Dáil' traditionalist, the redoubtable Maud Gonne MacBride and her son, Seán MacBride, former IRA leader and a leading barrister who defended IRA prisoners and organized reprieve committees. Maud Gonne spoke on public platforms, defending prisoners' rights. O'Higgins published his *Wolfe Tone Annual*, which dealt with past struggles for freedom. (His *Wolfe Tone Weekly* was suppressed in 1939.) The 1944 *Annual* was banned because its 'whole tenor . . . was to the effect that no government had a right to exist here against the wishes of one or two individuals who wanted to use force to overthrow it.'[151] O'Higgins protested against this characterization, saying that he had called for 'a spiritual revolution in Ireland'.

O'Higgins identified Irish republicanism almost completely with Irish Catholicism. In the banned 1944 *Annual*, for instance, he wrote of the Irish during the penal period, 'their Catholic faith, and a national tradition extending back over a thousand years, kept their souls and minds out of reach of the enemy's hellish plan'. He added: 'That spiritual tradition has saved Irish Nationality from extinction and defeated all the schemes and plans of a powerful and unscrupulous enemy.'[152] For O'Higgins, as for Pearse, 'the spiritual thing' was 'the essential thing in Nationality . . .'.[153] He preached that 'If an English-speaking, soccer-playing, jazz-dancing Ireland were cut away politically and economically from England tomorrow, she would not be free.'[154]

Maud Gonne MacBride said of IRA volunteers imprisoned for the bombing campaign in Britain: 'The brave young men who have decided to carry war into England are getting the same terrible sentences when captured that Tom Clarke and his comrades got last century.'[155] She demanded political treatment for all Republican prisoners.

Republicans who disagreed with the bombing campaign met in 1943 to establish some kind of constitutional party that would give them the right to speak out; they had been connected with the IRA's Cumann na Poblachta of the mid-1930s. But not until July 1946 was such a party launched. It was called Clann na Poblachta and was led by Seán MacBride.[156] Clann abandoned parliamentary abstention, recognized the state, recruited new members from the disaffected, and quickly became a force in post-war Irish politics as a constitutional party working for a republic and the unity of Ireland. The founders declared:

> For many years a large section of Republican opinion has felt that Republicans should take an active part in the political life of the nation. It was felt that it would be possible to work for the achievement of Republican ideals by purely political means.
>
> It was felt that the cycle of repression and violence which have marked the history of the last quarter of a century could provide no solution and could only weaken the national effort.[157]

During the wartime 'emergency', the old Sinn Féin ideology which had helped create the state reached its apogee. Neutrality was maintained and the people fed, despite German bombs, destruction of shipping, British threats and notes from Washington. Nationalist Ireland stood firm behind de Valera. Any attempt to violate that neutrality would be met by force. Yet the state had no arms industry and was dependent upon Britain for equipment. The British wanted the 'Treaty ports' – Cobh, Berehaven, Lough Swilly – peacefully, not because Churchill had any moral scruples about seizing them but because Britain was totally dependent upon US supplies and Irish-Americans were an important constituency of the ruling Democratic Party. Although many individual Irish-Americans disagreed with Irish neutrality, it is safe to say that the memory of their old nationalist heritage would not permit them to tolerate a British invasion of Éire in 1940-41, which would have meant a severe crisis for Churchill's champion, President Franklin D. Roosevelt. The US might have moved in the spring of 1944, but Roosevelt had a fourth term in mind. In February 1942 he assured de Valera that the US had no intention of invading Éire, and the Irish leader, replying to the US note of 21 February, 1944, repeated his own longstanding pledge that 'our territory would never be permitted to be used as a base for attack upon Britain'.[158]

The Irish state stood the test of war because of the ideology on which it was built. The cost was high. Industries closed because of lack of raw materials. Most of the young emigrated to Britain – and at least 150,000 joined the British armed services. The rest supplied labour for Britain's war industry. Éire sent Britain food and co-operated with Whitehall on defence. Despite Unionist insistence conscription did not apply to Northern Ireland, although Churchill planted US bases and training camps there and its hedgerow country served as a model exercise ground for Normandy.

Was neutrality so much make-believe then? Not really. It was shaped by nationalist ideology and it gave full legitimacy to the Irish nation-state. For that reason it was very necessary and perhaps only a de Valera could have carried it through. But it isolated Ireland from the non-Axis world.

The post-war economy was stagnant. By 1948 the people were ready for change and the more radical policies of MacBride's Clann na Poblachta were an attractive alternative to de Valera's conservatism and autocratic style of leadership. Although wildly attacked as 'Communist' by Fianna Fáil, Clann na Poblachta won ten seats in the March 1948 election – six of them in Dublin – and held the balance of power in the Dáil, less than two years after its birth. A coalition of Clann, Labour, Farmers, Fine Gael and Independents ousted de Valera. MacBride became Minister for External Affairs and his lieutenant, Dr Noel Browne, Minister for Health in the new coalition. Browne began to implement his party's plan to eliminate TB, build hospitals and a health service. His 'mother and child' scheme was denounced by the bishops as 'socialist' and contrary to faith and morals 'because the right to provide for the health of children belongs to parents not the state'. Fearing a Church-state clash amid charges of anti-clericalism, the Clann surrendered to the bishops, fired Browne, and destroyed itself.[159] Saor Éire cast a long shadow. However, the founders of the Clann insist that the Browne affair was 'only a step in a determined effort' to wreck the party, which may reflect IRA conspiracy theories.[160] Browne's political career subsequently – he joined and was expelled from Fianna Fáil, founded the National Progressive Democrats and merged it in the Labour Party, left Labour and founded the Socialist Labour Party, disagreed with its policy on the North and became an ordinary member – suggests that he finds difficulty working with others. He remains a socialist.

Despite its numerical weakness as a component of the coalition – two ministers in a Cabinet of fourteen – the Clann influenced government policy in striking fashion. Its goal of making the state a republic, its opposition to NATO while Ireland was partitioned, its hope of turning British control of Northern Ireland into an international talking point if not an issue, were all realized. More important was its influence on economic policy, which stemmed from republican social radicalism of the 1930s. Fianna Fáil had sought to change Irish farming from cattle for the British market to tillage; it had some success. Fianna Fáil tried to break the British stranglehold on Irish trade by establishing light industries with state support in the form of bounties and tariffs. Success here was less marked. Unemployment and emigration remained high. The state could not match Britain's post-war social services and the contrast between North and South grew embarrassing: because of the British link the North enjoyed not only superior social services but better rates of pay, better education, more efficient farming, better housing, better roads.

MacBride maintained that 'the main fault in our economy is underdevelopment due to the export of our capital which in turn inevitably results in the export of our people'.[161] Clann programmes, started by the government, included large-scale afforestation, land reclamation, creation of an Industrial Development Authority to sponsor new industries, and a drive for new export markets to lessen dependency on Britain.[162] At the time less than one-fifth of the working population of about 1.25 million was engaged in industrial production, as against one-third in Denmark, for example.

Prodded by Clann, the coalition government repealed the External Relations Act of 1936 (de Valera's 'external association' with the British Commonwealth) and on Easter Monday 1949, thirty-three years after the 1916 Rising, the Irish Republic was formally inaugurated. The British government retaliated by providing, in the Government of Ireland Act, that Northern Ireland could not be detached from the United Kingdom without the consent of its legislature. Some saw this as an attempt at making partition permanent, given the population of the North and Unionist control of the electoral system. The North was also of 'strategic interest' to Britain, as the Cabinet papers of the time reveal.[163]

MacBride's justification for repealing the External Relations Act and declaring a republic was an orthodox statement of Irish republican ideology: 'The Crown and outworn forms that belong to British constitutional history are merely reminders of an unhappy past that we want to bury, that have no realities for us and only serve as irritants.'[164] MacBride was a doctrinaire republican, de Valera was not. MacBride would have the Republic first and then a united Ireland. De Valera reversed that order: the constitution of the state and its institutions made it a republic. What it was called was not important. (It seemed important enough at one time.) He hoped, quite unrealistically, his 'external association' formula would end partition. 'We are a democracy with the ultimate sovereign power resting with the people,' he declared.[165] No one could argue with that on the political level. Economically, the state was dependent, not independent. Still, it tended to isolate non-Fianna Fáil republicans, whether Sinn Féin, 'Second Dáil', or IRA. Clann na Poblachta broke through this isolation. It solved the political issue – except partition – and then talked about economic independence.

The Republic declared, MacBride tried to pressure Britain on the partition question and found his opportunity early in 1949 when the US government invited Dublin to sign the North Atlantic Treaty. MacBride, in reply, blamed Britain for partition.

> In these circumstances, any military alliance with . . . the State that is responsible for the unnatural division of Ireland, which occupies a portion of our country with its armed forces, and which supports undemocratic institutions in the north-eastern corner of Ireland, would be entirely repugnant and unacceptable to the Irish people. No Irish Government, whatever its political views, could participate with Britain in a military alliance while this situation continues, without running counter to the national sentiment of the Irish people.[166]

The US position was that partition was a matter for the Irish government, the British government and 'the northern counties', as Dean Acheson told MacBride in March of 1951. Talking to President Truman some days later, MacBride was informed that partition 'was an issue between two countries with which the United States was equally friendly'.[167] In January 1952 funds for Ireland under the Economic Co-operation Act were suspended under the Mutual Security Act of 1951.[168] Clearly the Irish question retained some of its old sting in US and international politics.

MacBride thought partition could be solved peacefully, although he also argued that the Irish people had the right to establish territorial unity 'by any means at their disposal, including the use of force,' adding, 'I certainly do not regard the use of force, or even suggestions as to the use of force, as desirable or realistic.' He considered Britain responsible for partition, which could not subsist without the imperial government's 'political, economic and military support'. If Britain withdrew her support a solution would be found based on 'the common interest of the Irish people'. No party in the Dáil dissented from this view and MacBride made it national policy to mobilize 'world opinion in such a manner as to ensure that Britain will understand clearly that the maintenance of partition constitutes a real inconvenience to her and is an actual hindrance to her own policies'. Among MacBride's domestic proposals was making Dáil Éireann truly the parliament of all Ireland, as in 1919-21, by opening its doors 'to the representatives from the occupied portion of Ireland'.[169]

Many Ulster Nationalists favoured MacBride's plans. However, his scheme 'of a Republican Confederation to co-ordinate and direct the anti-partition movement in the Six Counties', got nowhere because his party was in tatters as a result of the Browne affair. MacBride held a not uncommon republican view that the IRA had no function in the Republic. Some Northern IRA officers agreed with him. In 1950-51 these officers discussed the MacBride approach, their chief figure being Liam Kelly of Pomeroy, County Tyrone. The IRA barely existed in the Republic at the time, apart from a Dublin headquarters and some scattered units. However, the new development alarmed the IRA. Kelly's men planned a raid on a British base near Derry, failed to get GHQ sanction and Kelly was dismissed. The reason obviously was to wreck the MacBride plan.

Kelly agreed with MacBride that the 1937 Constitution claiming 'the national territory consists of the whole island of Ireland, its islands and the territorial seas', and the following article declaring that 'pending the re-integration of the national territory'[170] the laws of the Dublin parliament would extend only to the twenty-six counties, gave Northern Nationalist representatives the right to sit in the Dublin parliament, and thus help to bring about the re-integration of the national territory. By 1953 Kelly's following had grown in Tyrone; when he sought election to Stormont as an abstentionist Republican he succeeded, and almost immediately was jailed for making 'seditious statements'. His case won national attention. While in prison, in June 1954, Kelly was elected to the Irish Senate, with the help of Seán MacBride; released in August he was given a wild 'welcome home' by his constituents, amid clashes with police, the first open Nationalist demonstration against Unionist rule since before the Second World War.

Deciding that the only hope of 're-integrating the national territory' lay in a policy of force, Kelly established an open political movement, Fianna Uladh (Warriors of Ulster), with a secret military arm, Saor Uladh (Free Ulster). In November 1955 he attacked a police barracks at Roslea, County Fermanagh, the opening move in what he hoped would be an armed rebellion.[171] But the IRA refused to be drawn into his war, denounced Kelly for recognizing the 'partitionist 26-counties state', and made preparations for its own campaign. Kelly could not sustain his effort and it faded away.

IRA Guerrilla Campaign, 1956-1962

It is also part of the ideology of Irish republicanism that only the IRA has sufficient prestige to undertake armed action and win a measure of popular support. The IRA has a history of continuous resistance to British rule and British interference in Irish affairs since 1919, when Dan Breen and his comrades attacked the RIC at Soloheadbeg. This resistance has not always been very effective, but it exists, underground, plotting and arming, like the IRB before it. The IRA's constitution states its objects as:

> 1. To guard the honour and uphold the sovereignty and unity of the Republic of Ireland.
> 2. To establish and uphold a lawful Government in sole and absolute control of the Republic.
> 3. To secure and defend civil and religious liberty and equal rights and equal opportunities for all citizens.
> 4. To promote the revival of the Irish language as the everyday language of the people, and to promote the development of the best mental and physical characteristics of our race.

The means for achieving these goals are force of arms; organizing, training, and equipping the manhood of Ireland as an efficient military force; and assisting 'all organizations working for the same objects'.[172]

The supreme authority of the IRA is the annual convention, which elects an Executive; the Executive's sole function is to pick a Council, whose members are known only to the Executive. The Council appoints a Chief of Staff to execute, with a GHQ staff, IRA policy.

De Valera and the IRA sought support from the same strata of the population: small farmers, agricultural labourers, the working class in the towns. Because of his wartime repression of the IRA, de Valera lost electoral support in the poor small-farm areas of the West of Ireland, from Leitrim to Kerry, which have been traditionally republican.[173] The IRA has support among the Nationalist population of Belfast and in the Nationalist-majority counties of Tyrone, Fermanagh, the areas of South Down, South Armagh, South Derry and Derry City. When US troops landed in Northern Ireland in January 1942 de Valera protested against the action and the IRA 'Northern Command', in Belfast denounced it. In March the Northern Command ordered its activists to sabotage 'war industries and enemy military objectives', although lacking the power to enforce its edicts.

The post-war IRA leadership decided to concentrate on a new generation of activists, who knew nothing of the old factional feuds, and to avoid radical politics. They took over the moribund Sinn Féin and revived it, to give the IRA a legal base. But Sinn Féin was not just a front for the IRA. It was very conservative and careful of its 'national image'. The IRA took over an independent republican monthly paper, the *United Irishman*, to publicize its own and Sinn Féin's activities. The IRA would stay non-political, while Sinn Féin would seek popular support.[174] It would have no truck with MacBride's Clann na Poblachta – or with Kelly's Fianna Uladh. The IRA made only one concession to the 1949 Republic: it prohibited the use of force in the twenty-six counties.[175] Beginning on a small scale in Derry in June of 1951, the IRA tried to arm its units by raiding British military barracks. The most spectacular was Armagh in June 1954.[176] An IRA spokesman said the arms were 'for use against the British occupation forces still in Ireland and they will be used against them, please God, in due course'.[177] An attempt to raid Omagh military barracks four months later failed; eight volunteers from the South were captured and received sentences of twelve and ten years' imprisonment. But as usual with revolutionary movements in Ireland, failure led to success: the young men in the dock were part of a proud tradition. The felons were nominated for Northern Ireland constituencies in the May 1955 United Kingdom election, and two were elected in the Nationalist counties of Tyrone and Fermanagh.[178]

Sinn Féin polled 152,310 Nationalist votes. The significance of this vote has been variously argued, but the fact remains that the Nationalists of the North cast their ballots for IRA volunteers captured raiding a British military base in Northern Ireland. It sounded to many like the 1918 vote all over again, if on a reduced scale.

Five months after the May 1955 election the IRA raided a military camp in Wales and two captured volunteers received life sentences; the arms seized were recovered. Dissension grew within the ranks of the IRA, particularly in Dublin. The leadership was too conservative, had no intention of fighting, and good men were being sacrificed to build up Sinn Féin, it was charged.[179] The group was expelled and linked up with Kelly. With this reinforced strength, Saor Uladh demolished customs huts along the border in November 1956. The IRA Army Council, which had postponed a decision on a guerrilla campaign plan several times, was forced to take action or be outflanked by Kelly and the dissidents.[180] The campaign opened on the night of 11-12 December 1956 with attacks throughout Northern Ireland. A manifesto stated:

> This is the age-old struggle of the Irish people versus British aggression. This is the same cause for which generations of our people have suffered and died. In this grave hour, all Irish men and women, at home and abroad, must sink their differences, political or religious, and rally behind the banner of national liberation . . . .
>
> The whole of Ireland – its resources, wealth, culture, history and tradition – is the common inheritance of all our people regardless of religious belief. The division of this country by Britain, and its subjection to British political control in the North and to British economic domination in the South, must now be ended forever. It is up to this generation of Irish men and women to receive for all time our unity, independence, and freedom from foreign domination. The alternative, if the present situation continues, is extinction as a nation.
>
> The foe will use his considerable resources to divide us by fanning the fires of bigotry and sectarianism – twin enemies of Irish Republicanism. Let us be on our guard, a free Ireland cannot tolerate the one or the other . . . .[181]

The guerrilla plan, code-named 'Operation Harvest', hoped to reopen the Irish question by confronting Britain directly in the North. The question could not be reopened constitutionally because of the Ireland Act of 1949; since no movement existed to organize a campaign of civil disobedience and passive resistance in the North, the only other means was force. This was the IRA justification for its armed campaign. It also made the ideological claim, based on the physical-force tradition, that it had 'the sanction of history'.[182] If

Unionist force could veto Home Rule, then Nationalist force could veto partition. The tactical thinking behind 'Operation Harvest',[183] the IRA resistance plan, was that in the Nationalist-majority regions of Tyrone, Fermanagh, South Armagh, South Down, South Derry and Derry City, a Fintan Lalor-style rejection of Stormont's authority could be developed, backed by the judicious use of force built on Nationalist support. Belfast was excluded from the plan to avoid sectarian confrontation and repetition of 1920-22 style pogroms.

The weaknesses of the plan were: first, the arms raids had alerted the Stormont government which felt it could handle IRA activities by means of the Special Powers Act, the 'B' Specials and the RUC;[184] second, the IRA was poorly armed – some rifles, submachine-guns, a couple of Brens, hardly any ammunition and no explosives; third, the IRA had no money; fourth, its Northern organization was rudimentary, apart from small units in Belfast, Derry, Fermanagh and Armagh; fifth, it had only loose political ties with the local Nationalists, who gave the campaign covert but not open support, and the IRA had no political organization by which it could reach the people with its message. Sinn Féin had put down few roots in the Nationalist areas and the movement was banned anyway within days of the opening of the campaign, under the Special Powers Act. For these reasons the Northern resistance campaign became largely a matter of armed forays over the border from nearby Monaghan, Louth, Cavan, Leitrim and Donegal, although that was not the original plan. By harassing the guerrillas and their bases the forces of the Republic could contain the raids without much difficulty.

The coalition government fell in the spring of 1957 – on a Clann na Poblachta motion. De Valera returned to power with a massive majority, aided by Sinn Féin which ran a score of candidates on the premise that if given a majority it would enter the Dáil and form a government. Otherwise it would remain abstentionist. Since it could not win a majority with only twenty candidates it did very well to have four elected. The four could not take their seats because of abstention, and represented no threat to de Valera. The 1957 election did prove that a strong groundswell of sympathy existed for traditionalist republicanism. But the reality behind the vote was that de Valera had a mandate to jail without trial republicans who supported the IRA, or Sinn Féin, or even sold the *United Irishman*.[185] And he carried it out.

The 1955-57 explosion of national feeling ended in internment camps and prisons in Northern Ireland and the Republic. One explanation of why traditional republicanism failed so abysmally is that it had no political support and no organization to mobilize such support – like the IRA during the Civil War. Sinn Féin had only the flimsiest political roots in the North, its programme was unrealistic and at least thirty years out of date. The IRA lacked, in consequence, not only the military resources to implement 'Operation Harvest' but also the political resources, and when it tried to do something about this in underground conditions it clashed with the overground and strictly constitutional leadership of Sinn Féin. The material conditions for an 'Operation Harvest' campaign existed in the Nationalist North.[186] But, lacking the *means* to carry out its mission – and the *means* were political as much as military – while weakened by internal wrangling, defeat of the IRA was assured.

> Nevertheless, given the restrictions of orthodox theory, the personalities of the past, the paucity of political vision, and (on their own terms) the specific limited campaign envisioned, the Republican Movement was for the first time in a generation organized in relation to a specific plan of operation with logically divided responsibility – i.e. organized to undertake properly a limited but open-ended military campaign in the Six Counties.[187]

As Bowyer Bell observes, this should have been only one facet of republican policy 'instead of the whole plan of action'. However, the movement could not have capitalized on its success, he adds. The Dublin government, under de Valera, remained 'exceptionally stable' through it all. De Valera used the old arguments of the 1930s and 1940s against the IRA in entirely changed circumstances. It was possible to outflank him on the national question, but Sinn Féin failed to do it. It feared, as the analyst notes, 'contamination from the Political Game'.[188] Traditionalist thinking as well as traditionalist fears could not cope with the situation. Politically, de Valera had the field to himself.

When the campaign was abandoned in February 1962, the statement announcing the decision blamed 'the attitude of the general public whose minds have been deliberately distracted from the supreme issue facing the Irish people – the unity and freedom of Ireland'.[189] This was unfair to the 'general public' of the North and border counties who bore the financial and other burdens of the campaign. The IRA itself escaped any criticism in the final summing-up.

Ideologically, the campaign stressed the values of the United Irishmen, in all statements issued by the headquarters of 'the Resistance Movement', as the IRA termed its guerrilla organization in the field. Manifestos and proclamations contained the same republican, secular political message. While pointing out, correctly, that the majority in Northern Ireland supported the British constitution, Barritt and Carter add:

> The IRA was, however, careful to oppose religious bigotry, and to stand for the spirit of 1798, when Protestant Dissenters and Catholics stood side by side in rebellion. It was careful, too, not to provoke the civilian population; of 157 incidents involving fire-arms or explosives in the year following the [1956] manifesto, none was directed against the civil population.[190]

Ideological Motivation of the IRA

The IRA used minimum force and employed it only in Nationalist areas and against 'Crown forces'. For that reason the sectarian issue did not surface. Casualties were low. Among the IRA dead were Seán Sabhat (South) and Feargal O'Hanlon, whose names became nationally known because they were killed in action at Brookeborough, County Fermanagh, on New Year's Day 1957. This raises the question of ideological motivation.

Terence de Vere White, in his biography of Kevin O'Higgins, says, 'Revolutionists throw to the surface fierce and dangerous men as well as pure-souled idealists. There were men who shot down policemen and British soldiers but who were quite incapable of enunciating any political theory. They took to violence as a duck to water and revelled in a revolutionary period.'[191] He was writing of the original guerrilla struggle of 1919-21.

Professor Murphy says,

> Though regarded with hesitation by older IRA men, it was felt that a Northern campaign would attract maximum sympathy in the South, where years of anti-partition propaganda had conditioned public opinion to think of 'our six counties' as being 'occupied' by British troops. In this sense, a military campaign against Northern Ireland was the inevitable outcome of thirty years of public self-delusion about partition.[192]

F.X. Martin says men like Brian O'Higgins 'have directly influenced the political views of Irish youth between 1916 and 1972. The Pearse-O'Higgins view of Irish history may be inaccurate (simply because it is one-sided) but it has sent and is sending young men out to die more certainly than did the *Cathleen ní Houlihan* of Yeats.'[193] He goes on to cite Seán Sabhat and Feargal O'Hanlon to prove his case.

Here are three views, by representative IRA volunteers of the 1950s campaign, on why they fought. The first is by Eamon Timoney, a native of Derry.

> I considered the partition of Ireland to be the greatest political problem which Ireland possessed – it divided the country geographically, economically and

> socially and it provided Irish politicians of all parties, North and South, with material for speeches and excuses for either unwillingness or inability to solve emigration, unemployment, and a seeming national lethargy.
>
> Partition existed because Britain had imposed it, and according to the British 1949 Act it would end when a majority of the Northern Ireland parliament so wished. Inasmuch as the Stormont parliament had the power to determine how its legislators would be elected, and considering how Stormont had gerrymandered constituencies to ensure Unionist power, the British 1949 Act was a cynical 'cocking of the snoot' at the majority of the Irish people. . . . I joined the IRA not because I supported IRA traditional policy *vis-à-vis* the Twenty-Six Counties government, but because I believed in force to solve partition and the IRA was the only organization with such a policy. I felt that IRA tactics of the Forties had been disastrous, but that the IRA would have learned from past mistakes and would not alienate Twenty-Six Counties support in the future.
>
> I joined the IRA not merely to end British involvement in Irish affairs, but because I believed that a united Ireland would generate a new national consciousness, a dynamic idealism which would, if not solving, then proceed more rapidly to a solving of Ireland's economic and social problems.[194]

The second is by Manus Canning, also a native of Derry. He says 'the most persausive general factor' that made him join the IRA was that he grew up in the Bogside, a Catholic ghetto, in 'an intensely nationalist home with a very good library of Irish-Ireland books which I was encouraged to read'.[195]

The third, by Seán O'Hegarty, a native of Cork City, states:

> The philosophy that drew me into the ranks of Republicanism in the 1950s was the conviction that the majority of the Irish people wished for the unity and self-determination of the country, that such unity and self-determination were the essential conditions for the freedom and development of Ireland and that these could never be fully realized while Britain retained a presence in the country.

Republicanism failed 'to mature and develop as a political and social philosophy'. It could think only in military terms; its ideology of physical force was inflexible; it could not respond 'to the political realities of the Fifties'. A blinkered movement, it did not understand that 'while martyrdom might at times be a necessary condition of success, it is seldom, of itself, a sufficient condition for victory'.[196]

Any objective analysis of the IRA's 1950s campaign would surely arrive at much the same conclusions as these three men, who acted on their beliefs, made great sacrifices because of them and spent years in prison as a result. Nationalism is a powerful force, but an ideology that does not represent reality may well be admired but is never going to attract mass support. In the 1950s the IRA represented only the tradition of physical force and did not really reflect the interests of the Nationalist population of the North. The dead hand of history lay heavily upon it, destroying effectively any hope the IRA had of achieving its goal – the Irish Republic as defined by Wolfe Tone.[197]

VI
The Final Rebellion in the 1970s

From 1921, when it was established, until 1972, when it was abolished, the state of Northern Ireland was governed by the Unionist Party, an arrangement designed to last for ever. But between 1968 and 1972 the system collapsed. The Nationalists would not permit it to work. After the British government stepped in, in 1969, the Unionists lost the Ulster Special Constabulary ('B' Specials) and some of the Special Powers Act. The British army fought the Provisional IRA. Internment without trial was used against Nationalists only. A change had to be made and Edward Heath, the British Tory Prime Minister, prorogued the Stormont parliament,[1] which meant in effect that he abolished it by merely signing a decree.

If the bombs and bullets of the Provisional IRA helped bring down Stormont, a general strike of Protestant workers toppled its successor, the power-sharing Executive of Nationalists and Unionists, which had been carefully crafted by the British and Irish governments and leaders of the two communities in the North. The Nationalists were represented by the Social Democratic and Labour Party (SDLP). The Unionists were split three ways. Power-sharing was designed to bring peace to Northern Ireland. There was also provision for a Council of Ireland, to unify the island 'by planned and agreed steps'. It was the first to be discarded. The Protestants would not have it; the Dublin government surrendered it as a gesture towards peace. The Protestants, whose most vocal spokesman is the fundamentalist clergyman, the Reverend Ian Paisley, would not have power-sharing either. A general strike, enforced by the Protestant Ulster Defence Association, while the British army looked on, ended the experiment in May 1974. The North remained in political limbo, following a Constitutional Convention which failed to produce a settlement acceptable to all. Inter-party talks broke up in disagreement. Then on 7 January, 1980, the Thatcher government opened another constitutional conference and on 2 July 1980 issued a discussion document guaranteeing that Northern Ireland would remain part of the

United Kingdom while 'the majority' desires it, proposing an 80-member Assembly elected by proportional representation with an Executive responsible for agriculture, commerce, education and social services, and suggesting a form of power-sharing via Assembly committees.[2]

The UDA, with a base among the Protestant working class of Belfast, wants an independent Northern Ireland with constitutional features borrowed from the United States, such as a Chief Executive elected by direct vote, a Supreme Court and a Bill of Rights. A few Nationalists see negotiated independence as one way out of the tangle; most distrust it as a new form of Protestant domination. The theorists of an independent Northern Ireland agree that there must be a Unionist-Nationalist consensus for the scheme to work. The Unionists would sever their traditional link with the United Kingdom; the Nationalists would forsake their traditional goal of a united Ireland. Majority vote (Protestant) would rule, with specific guarantees for the Catholic minority; such as chairmanships of powerful parliamentary committees, as in the US Congress. American, British and perhaps EEC money would keep the state afloat in its early years. The partition of Ireland would be made permanent, although certain links would be maintained with the Republic and with Britain.[3]

It took only fifty years to demonstrate that Northern Ireland was not a viable state, politically or economically. A wholly Protestant Unionist state might have survived. But in that case why have a separate state at all, since the demand of the self-described 'loyalists' was to keep all Ireland part of the United Kingdom of Great Britain and Ireland? Nationalists, constitutionalist and physical force, wanted an Irish parliament with equal representation for Protestants and Catholics. What happened in the end was that Britain forced two Home Rule parliaments on Ireland: one in Belfast for the Protestants, one in Dublin for the Catholics. The fact that Belfast was subordinate to London and that Dublin in time established its full independence does not change the confessional character of the settlement.

The British government gave Stormont its head. Ulster Protestants were 'masters in our own house', as the conventional phrase had it. Craig said, after he became Lord Craigavon: 'All I boast is that we are a Protestant Parliament for a Protestant people.'[4] Translated, this meant Stormont was a colonial assembly for the settlers of British descent, with representation permitted the native Catholics who were of course a conquered race. A 'Croppy' was a rebel, vintage of 1798, but a popular Ulster Unionist war-cry applied to Catholics was 'Croppies lie down!' Government was conducted on sectarian lines, as was politics. To keep Northern Ireland a settler state by 'democratic means' – the only means permitted in the United Kingdom – there must be a permanent Protestant majority and in areas where that was not possible it must be manufactured electorally to ensure 'a Protestant state for a Protestant people'.

For Nationalists, the state had no legitimacy.[5] It had been imposed upon them by force and special laws, and a Protestant militia secured 'peace, order and good government' – the functions of the Northern parliament as laid down in the Government of Ireland Act of 1920 that created it. The Minister for Home Affairs decided, more or less, what Nationalists could do politically: when and where they could meet and march, the boundaries of their electoral districts and other matters like that.

The Cameron Commission, our most authoritative source for the state of civil liberties in Northern Ireland before September 1968, because its task was to report the cause of the civil rights disturbances, noted:

> The powers have on the whole been exercised with a view to suppressing the IRA and obtaining information about its plans and activities. For this reason these powers, especially those to enter and search, have borne most heavily upon the Roman Catholic part of the population.[6]

The Status of Catholics

The Cameron Commission reached a number of conclusions, all favourable to those who sought civil rights. It sustained charges that Catholics were discriminated against in housing, local voting and employment. It noted that there was no effective parliamentary opposition in Northern Ireland. It did not deal with partition, the heart of the problem, because that was not part of its brief. It commented on some grievances of Catholic Nationalists:

> Not only has the Government of Northern Ireland since it was established been a Unionist [and therefore Protestant] Government, but at the local level Councils have tended to reflect the particular religious majority in their areas, except that in certain areas, notably in certain of those in which disorders occurred, namely Dungannon, Armagh and in particular Londonderry, the arrangement of ward boundaries for local government purposes has produced in the local authority a permanent Unionist majority which bears little or no resemblance to the relative numerical strength of Unionists and non-Unionists in the area. As we show later, we have to record that there is very good reason to believe the allegation that these arrangements were deliberately made, and maintained, with the consequence that the Unionists used and have continued to use the electoral majority thus created to favour Protestant or Unionist supporters in making public appointments – particularly those

of senior officials – and in manipulating housing allocations for political and sectarian ends.[7]

The report noted the divisiveness of religion in Northern Ireland – the Catholic Church insisted upon segregated education – and 'the conflict of political loyalties'. Catholics were concentrated west of the River Bann and tended to be economically poorer than the Protestant population. Among Catholics there was 'a sense of resentment and frustration at the failure of representations for the remedy of social, economic and political grievances'. Protestants were suspicious and fearful of 'political and economic domination by a future Catholic majority' which created 'a dangerous, and politically explosive, sectarian tension'.[8] The inquiry found that

> the weight and extent of the evidence which was presented to us concerned with social and economic grievance or abuse of political power was such that we are compelled to conclude that they had substantial foundation in fact and were in a very real sense an immediate and operative cause of the demonstrations and consequent disorders after 5th October 1968.[9]

Membership of the ruling Unionist Party was not open to Catholics, Cameron pointed out, adding, that 'the Orange Order does in fact exercise influence within the Unionist party does not admit of any real doubt'.[10] Its summary of conclusions on the causes of disorder include discrimination in housing and jobs, manipulation of local government electoral boundaries, no official interest in Catholic complaints, resentment 'as to the existence of the Ulster Special Constabulary [the 'B' Specials] as a partisan and para-military force recruited exclusively from Protestants', and Protestant counter-fears, inflamed and provoked by Paisley's anti-civil rights organizations.[11] The pre-5 October 1968 civil rights protests – the Caledon squatting incident in the early summer, and the Dungannon march of August 24 – attracted police, public and media attention, but no notable support from the Nationalist population.[12] The Derry ban drew thousands of Nationalists to the streets; the police attacks were seen on television. The message was clear: in the Nationalist city of Derry a march for decent housing was a subversive act. This, not discrimination, caused the Nationalist explosion. Beginning in Derry, it spread to Belfast and other towns in the summer of 1969. It had been building for fifty years.[13]

A Segregated Society

Because of the sectarian nature of the state, Nationalists were permanently excluded from any share in power. But even in Derry, where two-thirds of the population were Catholics, that is to say Nationalists in politics, the Unionists so managed the system that they kept government of the city in their own hands.[14]

Segregated education also helped the Unionists, and kept the two communities apart from the cradle to the grave. The state schools were Protestant. The Catholics had their own schools, heavily subsidized by the state. The Catholic bishops insisted on this. One said: 'In these days particularly when anti-religious influences are growing in strength we feel we can protect the faith of the next generation only through our schools.'[15]

According to the Rose survey, 69 per cent of Catholics favour integrated education and 64 per cent of all adults do.[16] It has been claimed that Catholic schools keep the Nationalist tradition alive in Northern Ireland; but, as Rose also points out, factors outside the school are more influential on political outlook. In brief, as Rose noted before the latest conflict began, the arguments against force are 'not always simple in a land where the regime itself was founded in consequence of a popular civil war'.[17] (The statement should be read against Mannheim's comment that ideology is an incomplete picture of reality in which the viewer sees those aspects of a situation that suit him.[18] Nationalists in South Armagh, Tyrone, Fermanagh and Derry, for example, would rephrase Rose's statement to read, 'in a land where the regime itself was founded in consequence of a ruthless civil terror'. They would not consider their view propagandist, merely a picture of reality, however incomplete.) At university level education is integrated. More working-class Catholics than working-class Protestants go to college, it is suggested, because the latter are more apt to apprentice to a trade.[19] In Northern Ireland Catholics are the unskilled work force; today their bright children go to university. (The British educational system must get the credit for this.)

The influence of the Catholic clergy in Nationalist communities is strong. Priests dominate neighbourhood associations, are active in all kinds of causes including prisoners' rights.[20] Prisoners are mainly from the Catholic ghettos of Belfast and Derry. Rural parish clergy once dominated Nationalist politics; their influence continues behind the scenes. If no longer blatantly proclaimed by pastoral decree, or from the altar, no one should underestimate Church influence on Nationalist politics; no policy condemned by the bishops will prevail. Rose discovered, for example, that 62 per cent of Catholics, as against 30 per cent of Protestants, thought it 'very important for church members to obey priest or minister'; his survey also found that 41 per cent of Catholics, as against 38 per cent of Protestants, thought it 'very important for citizens to obey government'.[21]

For most Nationalists the 'government' was not Belfast or London, but Dublin. That is an ideological view. For practical purposes, of course, they deal with the authority on the ground. Leaders of the Social Democratic and Labour Party regularly confer with the Dublin government and raise funds in the Republic.[22] Unionists call that 'disloyal' because the Republic is 'a foreign country'. Nationalists travel on Irish passports, issued in Dublin. They do not recognize partition: Ireland is one country. Belfast excepted, they see themselves part of the majority in Ireland, rather than a minority in the North. For these reasons, Professor Rose discovered in 1968, almost on the eve of the turbulence, that 34 per cent of the Catholic population disapproved of the Constitution; that is to say of the state's right to exist. On the other hand, 10 per cent of Protestants disapproved of the Constitution.[23]

Other forces sustain nationalism in Northern Ireland: Irish language and culture, Irish games, and 'an Irish view of life' – another way of saying 'ideology'. A Tyrone nationalist and a Kerry nationalist share much the same ideology. Games are all important: the games of the GAA – Gaelic Athletic Association – football and hurling. Hurling is mentioned in tales of the Red Branch of Ulster.[24] On 1 November 1884 nationally-minded Irishmen founded the GAA and four of the seven were Fenians. The GAA and nationalism were linked henceforth. The hurling stick, a *caman* in Irish, was looked upon as a nationalist weapon by the British authorities. Two thousand men with hurling sticks marched behind Parnell's coffin. The GAA then is more than an athletic association: it is a declaration of national faith and it is strong in Nationalist Ulster.

Although Nationalism in rural Northern Ireland is conservative, in Belfast and Derry it has a strong socialist content. The Social Democratic and Labour Party, successor to the old Nationalist Party as the parliamentary representative of the Catholics, has as its goal 'to organize and maintain in Northern Ireland a socialist party', and proposes 'the public ownership and democratic control of such essential industries and services as the common good requires'.[25] There was always strong Connolly socialist sentiment among Catholic workers in Belfast. The founders of the Republican Labour Party broke with the Northern Ireland Labour Party in 1949 on partition. Various strands of republican labour politics represented the working-class Nationalists of Belfast, their ideology fashioned by economics and politics. They dismissed the old Nationalist Party as a collection of 'Green Tories'.

Because of the constitutional issue, Labour was weak and divided in Belfast. Out of a House of Commons (Stormont) of fifty-two members, Labour of all shades never managed to win more than a half-dozen seats. Labour was thought weak on the border question by the Protestant working-class, and the Unionists made the most of this suspicion. A book on Northern Ireland, published in 1955, has this sentence: 'The Protestant workman never quite forgets that since the Plantation the Roman Catholics have been the principal threat of undercutting in the labour market.'[26] During the Second World War an ultra-loyalist section broke with the Northern Ireland Labour Party to form the Commonwealth Labour Party. In 1949, the NILP's parliamentary representation was wiped out. The cause of the split and of the electoral debacle was the same: partition. This one issue so frightened the NILP that it would not support civil rights in 1968 and Paddy Devlin, its chairman, resigned.[27]

Catholic workers could not undercut Protestants in the skilled labour market, such as the shipyards, for they found it nearly impossible to get or hold such jobs.[28]

Although Belfast and its hinterland were industrialized in the nineteenth century, Northern Ireland is an agricultural society. Small family farms averaging thirty acres predominate. The industrial base – capital goods and textiles produced for export – is narrow. All raw materials are imported.[29] Partition eliminated the North's main Irish market.

As a result of the Second World War and the Cold War, Northern Ireland lost its capital goods markets in Eastern Europe and China. Shipbuilding declined: it had fallen during the inter-war years anyway, and was saved by the 1939-45 boom. Cotton replaced linen. The result, as in the pre-war years, was economic depression. In social services the North stayed step-by-step with Britain. It became a welfare state, whereas the Republic by comparison was backward. Ulster agriculture benefited from British subsidies. In an attempt to diversify its manufactures Northern Ireland adopted legislation providing plants and financial aid for firms starting new industries or expanding old ones.[30] Foreign companies were attracted to the area and Nationalists charged that most of the new industries were established east of the Bann, in the Belfast region of heavy Protestant concentration, while unemployment soared in the Catholic centres of Derry, Newry and Strabane. A 1980 report on human rights practices in the 154 member states of the United Nations by the US Department of State, for 1979, observes:

The Northern Ireland economy in recent years has suffered from lack of growth because of its dependence on declining industries. There have been strong allegations over the years of substantial variances between the economic status and privileges of the Protestant and Catholic communities in Northern Ireland. Despite British government efforts in recent years to redress this imbalance, the Protestant part of the Northern Ireland community continues to be more prosperous, to be on the average more highly skilled, and to control most of the economy. In spite of British efforts to attract investment, the unemployment rate in Northern Ireland is about double that of the United Kingdom as a whole, and this burden falls disproportionately on the Catholic population. In an effort to improve the lot of the Northern Ireland community, the British government has put large sums of money into Northern Ireland in comparison with the rest of the United Kingdom. The government's expectation is that an improved economic situation would have a favourable impact on the political problem. However, the long-term economic prospect is still uncertain.

The economic situation has an impact on the political, though perhaps not of the kind envisaged by the US Department of State. The Nationalist (Catholic) one-third of the population 'consisted chiefly of small farmers, shopkeepers, publicans and unskilled labourers, with some reinforcement from the professions, especially law and medicine'. Rural Nationalists are conservative and close to their priests, a strong reason for Protestant mistrust: they are sure a united Ireland would be dominated by the Catholic Church. The small minority of Ulster Protestants who support a united Ireland harp on this fear. The most notable is Surgeon John Robb, a Presbyterian, who advocates a federal Ireland.[31]

Catholic versus Protestant, Nationalist versus Unionist, on this matter of national identity, Richard Rose writes:

The crux of the difficulty is the strong association between Irishness and Catholicism: 72 per cent of those who call themselves Irish are also Catholics. Protestants reject political identification with the 'mere Irish'. This act of rejection does not, however, give Protestants a positive sense of community focused on political symbols; instead, they fall back upon their religion for symbols of identity. The absence of a secure political identity like that enjoyed by the indubitably Irish Catholics can be a source of personal anxiety. This interpretation is supported by the tendency of Protestants to feel more strongly than Catholics about their identity – whatever they choose – and for those who identify strongly to be more likely to hold Ultra views. The identification of the Ultras with Protestantism rather than nationality explains the success of the Rev. Ian Paisley politically. He voices fears arising from what ordinary people perceive as the common threat of clerical ecumenism and British negotiation with the Republic about the Border.

Because Catholics see discord in nationality terms whereas Protestants see it in religious terms, politics in Northern Ireland involves ideologically unrelated conflicts. Disaffected Catholics claim that the appropriate solution

> is nationalist – to abolish the Border to create a 32-counties Republic of Ireland. Protestants tend to see their regime as a bulwark of religious faith against Catholics within the six counties, against the mere Catholic Irish outside their Provincial pale, and against the forces of terror and darkness everywhere growing stronger in a threatening and increasingly ecumenical world. By their own standards, each side is right and uncompromisingly so.[32]

This analysis rings true. If it is true, there are three sides to the conflict and all are at cross-purposes. Catholics are nationalists, they want a united Irish state. Protestants are defending the Reformation. The British see themselves as peace-makers. Robb agrees that the first step to peace in Ireland is the creation of conditions for consensus between Protestants and Catholics in order to remove 'the impossible dilemma of dual loyalty'.[33] The question is political; it can have only a political solution. If Rose is right, Protestant loyalty to Britain is less of a barrier to a consensus than fear of Catholic domination.

Most Northern Nationalists want a constitutional solution. They support the SDLP. A small minority supports the Republican Clubs' candidates of the Official IRA. Catholics and Protestants are ambivalent on the use of violence. In Belfast many Catholics believe that without violence or the threat of it they would be driven out by the Ultra-Protestant organizations – Paisleyites, Ulster Volunteer Force, UDA – or whatever name is adopted. Many are likewise convinced that the British are responsible for partition, and thus for their plight, and will do nothing about it unless forced to act. The IRA for that reason is supported by many Nationalists, including some who publicly denounce it.[34] It is a maxim of Nationalist politics to vote for the moderates, but to feed and succour the IRA. There are three reasons for this attitude. First, a permanent minority finds it impossible to effect change constitutionally. Second, Northern Ireland was carved out of Ireland by the threat of violence (1912-14) and actual violence (1920-22), and Ireland will be reunited only by the same means. Third, the IRA is heir to the long tradition of resistance to foreign rule.

The Origins of the Civil Rights Movement

Brian Faulkner, the last Prime Minister of Northern Ireland, wrote of the 5 October 1968 Derry march:

> It is a job for historians to decide at what stage the IRA took over the Civil Rights Movement; but it is quite clear, and it seemed quite clear to me at the time, that irrespective of the ideals of those who started it off, subversive elements were quick to realize the opportunities for exploitation and to jump on the band wagon. As I said in a speech on the day that the

> Londonderry march was taking place, civil rights was 'a very convenient banner for a republican to hoist aloft'.[35]

The truth, however, was that the IRA did not just infiltrate and take over the civil rights movement in Northern Ireland: it began it. Its purposes were quite open and not sinister at all, resulting from a reappraisal of its own role following the failure of the 1950s armed resistance campaign.

The IRA in the 1950s campaign was forced to accept the fact that its own Nationalist supporters were more anti-Unionist than anti-British. As the political game was played in the North, the Unionists held all the cards. They had a British financial subsidy, British support when needed, and no British interference in their affairs. They ran a police state disguised as a democracy along somewhat the same lines as South Africa's *apartheid* society, although much milder in practice. (There was the difference, however, that the Northern Ireland state could do without its Catholic population, since their labour is not essential to the economy). Few paid much attention to the plight of the Nationalists.

The weakness of republicanism in the North, from the point of view of its origins and theory, was that it was a Catholic movement. There had been pockets of Presbyterian republicans with traditions going back to '98, but they would have nothing to do with the Catholic variety. In Belfast, in the 1940s, there was a company of Protestant republicans under John Graham, which grew out of the Ulster Union Club of Denis Ireland.[36] Although segregated in one company, their existence kept the IRA aware of the United Irishmen ideal at least. The tendency of the IRA to be a Catholic defence organization was always strong in Belfast because of the pogroms.

These circumstances caused a group of radical republicans, representing different periods of struggle, to establish a Wolfe Tone Society in 1963, the bicentenary of the birth of 'the father of Irish republicanism'. It contained Protestants, Catholics and one Jew – the artist, Harry Kernoff. The object was to create some kind of bridge to, at least, some Protestant intellectuals in the North through discussions, seminars, lectures. The society did not achieve a great deal, but it was a meeting place for republicans, socialists, Communists, Irish language revivalists, and it developed new ideas. It established sister societies in Belfast and Cork, held sparsely-attended forums on Ireland's future, and at one of these discussed 'the rights of man in Ireland', taking the phrase from the Presbyterian United Irishmen of the 1790s, called attention to the special laws against republicans in both Northern Ireland and the Republic – the Special Powers Act and the Offences Against the State Act – and noted that in fact to advocate Tone's Republic was a criminal act.[37]

The *Irish Democrat* of London, a pro-Communist monthly published for Irish immigrants in Britain, kept the British left informed about the lack of full civil rights for Catholics in Northern Ireland, and its editor, Desmond Greaves, wrote a pamphlet on the subject.[38] The *Democrat* was published by the Connolly Association, founded in 1939, which held meetings on the Irish Question in London, Manchester, Liverpool, Birmingham and other centres of Irish population, and looked after Irish political prisoners in England during the war years. Two post-war members of the Connolly Association, Dr Roy Johnston, a physicist, and Anthony Coughlan, a social scientist, returned to Dublin in the early 1960s and joined the Wolfe Tone Society shortly after it was formed. Civil rights in the North became a topic in Dublin among the intellectuals of the Wolfe Tone Society and Ciarán Mac an Ailí, a solicitor, suggested as a solution a campaign of civil disobedience. The question was, would the Nationalists respond?

For the first time since the 1930s a left-wing view of the Northern problem had a platform. Communism had little footing in Ireland and none at all outside Belfast and Dublin. Belfast's Communists were almost all of Protestant background and influential in trade unions. In the 1920s the Third International thought a revolutionary situation, favourable to Communism, would develop in Ireland. Jim Larkin founded a Communist Party, but it faded away and accomplished nothing. In 1933, another attempt was made to launch an Irish CP by Seán Murray, but it had to be done under cover and the members were subject to physical as well as polemical attacks from Catholic confraternities and others.[39] The CP found a platform in Republican Congress, 1934-36; but Congress had difficulty getting a hearing and was denounced as a Red front. (Congress and the CP sent about 150 volunteers to fight with the International Brigades in Spain. The last act of Congress was to issue a manifesto in 1940, in the names of Peadar O'Donnell and George Gilmore, warning Republicans against linking the movement to Nazi Germany.)[40]

After the German invasion of Russia in 1941, the Irish Communist Party quietly disbanded. A Northern Ireland Communist Party, closely allied with the British CP, continued to operate from Belfast. Anti-Communism, however, could always attract a following in Dublin. A Catholic group, called *Maria Duce* (later *Fide*), under Father Denis Fahey, issued anti-Communist tracts, including a widely distributed pamphlet, *The Tragedy of James Connolly*, which attacked the 1916 leader's socialism as anti-Christian. (Father Fahey also wrote anti-Semitic pamphlets on the lines that Bolshevism and capitalism were 'a Jewish conspiracy' and that the real rulers of Russia were the Jews.)

The reorganized IRA of the late 1940s went along with these fears, scared of any contact with Communism because of the Church and the Cold War, and issued an anti-Communist statement defending its own goals and warning against possible Red contamination. The *United Irishman* could not discuss Connolly's socialism; even simple economics was suspect because it inevitably led to the question: who should own the means of production in an independent Ireland? The Social and Democratic Programme of the First Dáil was considered too radical to be circulated and discussed.

When the IRA in the 1960s examined its own role in the North it found it had pockets of traditional republican supporters, mostly inactive, and little else. The Wolfe Tone Society's republican left, socialists and Communists discussed a campaign for civil rights, as carried out in the American South. Roy Johnston was asked to join the IRA 'to help along a politicization process that had already started', he said;[41] he was then told to approach left-wing trade unionists in Belfast and the Northern Ireland Communist Party on the proposed civil rights movement. They agreed to help, but the 'national issue' – the divisive factor in Northern politics – would have to be omitted from civil rights demands, as would purely socialist issues or for that matter all party political issues. The IRA hoped to reach some common ground with the Protestant working class of Belfast via the Communist Party. But many Northern republicans, especially in Belfast, would have nothing to do with the Communists or indeed demands for civil rights. They were 'physical-force men' pure and simple who would have no truck with 'constitutionalism', however disguised.

In August 1966 the Wolfe Tone Societies of Dublin, Belfast and Cork held a conference on civil rights in Maghera, County Derry, attended by some IRA leaders; and another in Belfast in November 1966. On 29 January, 1967 the Northern Ireland Civil Rights Association was launched as a broadly based movement. The IRA did not control it. Neither did the Communist Party. It included 'persons of known extreme republican views and activities as well as members of the Northern Ireland Liberal and Labour parties', the Cameron Commission reported. Betty Sinclair, a veteran Belfast Communist trade unionist of Protestant background, was first chairman (from February 1968 to February 1969). The commission said her influence was exercised 'in favour of peaceful demonstrations and against the pursuit of courses designed or likely to lead to violence'.[42] Others in the leadership were Dr Conn McCluskey and his wife, Patricia, of Dungannon, who for years had been publicizing cases of discrimination against Catholics in jobs and housing. NICRA was what it said it was – an organization for civil rights. For the first eighteen months of its life, few noticed it.

Indeed in the beginning NICRA caused more trouble for the IRA, cautiously groping its way toward a new policy, than for Stormont. Traditionalist republicans in Belfast and elsewhere in the North wanted no truck with reformers and/or Communists. NICRA made little progress in Belfast. Derry was more promising, as the 5 October, 1968 march demonstrated. NICRA then stated its demands boldly: universal franchise in local elections, electoral boundaries drawn by independent commissions, compulsory points system for housing, repeal of the Special Powers Act, disbandment of the 'B' Specials and withdrawal of the Public Order Bill which the Unionists were pressing through Stormont to halt civil rights demonstrations.

For anyone even slightly acquainted with the politics of Northern Ireland this seemed a utopian list of demands; yet a year or so after 5 October, 1968 most of them were granted. Reforms always came too late; they were given grudgingly and in response to growing violence, and were forced through a reluctant Stormont by the British government. The Nationalists hardly needed this lesson to convince them that only violence could win minimum concessions in Northern Ireland.

There was much talk of 'left-wing extremists', meaning not the IRA or the Communist Party, but students from Queen's University who called themselves People's Democracy – in response to a police order to state the name of the organization sponsoring a march in Belfast. Led by Michael Farrell, a lecturer, and Bernadette Devlin, a student, People's Democracy was generally branded 'Trotskyist' or 'Trotskyite'. Miss Devlin was unsure of her politics, other than that they were 'socialist': she wanted the Protestant and Catholic working class to unite and establish a Workers' Republic.[43] In the first days of January 1969 People's Democracy staged a march from Belfast to Derry, in imitation of Martin Luther King's Selma-to-Montgomery march. (The Northern Ireland marchers were much influenced by the struggle for civil rights in the United States and copied its tactics and songs; for example, 'We Shall Overcome' took the place of Fenian songs.)

At Burntollet Bridge, near Derry, the marchers were ambushed by Paisleyites and police. The Reverend Ian Paisley, founder and moderator of the Free Presbyterian Church, had been on the Northern

Ireland scene for a decade, denouncing Rome, Catholics, Fenians and Lundys.[44] (A Lundy was anyone who conciliated Catholics. The original Lundy, a governor of Derry, wanted to surrender the city to James II's Papist army.) Paisley's followers were organized in the Ulster Constitution Defence Committee and later the Ulster Protestant Volunteers. His military adviser, Major Ronald Bunting, was a retired British army officer. Paisley's men had killed two Catholics going home from work in Malvern Street, Belfast, one night in 1966, apparently mistaking them for two others they believed were guilty of some 'anti-Protestant' crime. Their trial suggested that the pogrom spirit of 1920-22 and 1935 still lived in Belfast.

The IRA Declares for Socialism

The IRA of the 1960s had no master plan to take over the North. In 1967-68 the movement was so insignificant that many people thought it had disbanded.[45] The circulation of the *United Irishman* stood at 14,000 – down from 144,000 in September 1958, when the guerrilla campaign still had some slight hope that it would expand and make the North an international issue, like Algeria or Cuba. This merely demonstrates an ideological maxim of Irish republicanism that action creates a movement, not preaching. But what kind of action? For the IRA leaders, civil rights was no more than a gesture at first. They felt the people did not understand the goals of republicanism. Why had the people not supported the guerrilla campaign? The people, in fact, had done all that had been asked of them. The campaign's weakness was political.

The IRA in the mid-1960s decided to win the confidence of the people on economic issues. But the IRA is not so much an organization as a tradition. The organization is built in action, as in 1917 to 1921, although a revolutionary nucleus can exist at other times, as with the IRB from 1900 to 1913. The 1960s IRA talked of resistance in stages: economic, political, armed. They read Connolly on socialism and Mellows on why the Republic lost the Civil War. They read the 1916 Proclamation for meaning rather than rhetoric, and the 1919 Social and Democratic Programme. In 1968 they openly declared for a Socialist Republic 'as envisaged by Connolly and in keeping with the sentiments of the Proclamation of 1916'.[46]

Their ideology set, the IRA next turned to the North and the civil rights campaign it had put in motion. It discovered that its creation, NICRA, had become a mass movement and could not be fully controlled. A heterogeneous collection of persons and groups and ideas and events sought to guide developments in the North. Ideologues often see political developments in static terms. They spend their lives talking revolution and when it appears fail to recognize it. Roy Johnston, who had become the IRA's expert on revolutionary theory as well as politics, explains:

> The lack of contact with the students allowed an immature ultra-leftist element to emerge, and even sometimes to appear to lead. The basic cause of the rapid escalation was, in my opinion, the heroic but ill-advised and provocative march on Derry through the Orange strongholds of Antrim in January 1969. Burntollet need not have happened. It achieved nothing except to inflame sectarian hatred.[47]

Much of this may be correct; there was no revolutionary situation in the North, unless one interprets the simmering hatred of the Nationalists for the Unionist system and state, which finally surfaced on 5 October, 1968, as revolutionary. The basic error in Johnston's analysis, however, is his failure to see that any civil rights agitation must provoke an Orange reaction. The US model could not be transferred to Northern Ireland. In America the majority agreed with the premise of civil rights: they thought it wrong that blacks should be second-class citizens. In the North of Ireland few Protestants thought Catholics suffered any discrimination. If a Catholic was denied a government job, it was because he was disloyal. If he was denied a house, it was because the local Unionists wanted to keep the political balance as it always was, with themselves in control. If there was higher unemployment in Catholic areas, it was because Catholics preferred drawing the dole to working. And so on. Catholics did not recognize the legality of the state and would not challenge its discrimination by legal means. Perhaps they would have lost. But Section 5, Sub-Section 1 of the Government of Ireland Act, 1920, the constitutional justification for the Northern Ireland state, prohibits laws that give 'a preference, privilege, or advantage, or impose any disability or disadvantage, on account of religious belief'.[48]

Once the campaign for civil rights took off, it was bound to develop its own momentum and inevitably would be transformed into a civil disobedience movement, as foreseen by Ciarán Mac an Ailí. Given the traditions and conditions of the North, could such a movement remain non-violent? The history of the North suggests 'no'. Johnston and others surmised, no doubt, that NICRA would grow gradually; and so it might have, or even died, but for William Craig's order banning the march of 5 October, 1968.

On this matter, as on much else, the IRA Chief of Staff, Cathal Goulding is straightforward. The IRA wanted to attract Protestants to its standard. The republicans should speak for 'the working classes, the small farmers, the dispossessed, the exploited', he said. It was in the Wolfe Tone tradition to rally 'the men of no property' under the republican banner. Civil rights might achieve such an assembly, although the history of such movements is that they are more middle class than working class. Goulding saw it this way:

> We were only beginning to learn the technique of political agitation and how to conduct a campaign for civil rights. We realized what Wolfe Tone had meant two hundred years before when he made his appeal to the men of no property in Ireland. These were the only people who would fight imperialism because these were the people who were being exploited by imperialism, politically, economically, and culturally.[49]

Unfortunately for the IRA, one man's ideal is another man's evil. When civil rights was made an issue between Protestants and Catholics by Paisley, the few Protestants in the movement withdrew. In Northern Ireland politics there is no room for ambiguity. One is with 'us' or with 'them'. Tone's slogans belong to the past. People's Democracy served Paisley's needs. The resulting Protestant backlash and the bombs set by Paisley's 'secret army'[50] – whether sympathetic to him or controlled by him hardly matters – drove Terence O'Neill from office, and Paisley and his military adviser, Major Bunting, were released from prison by O'Neill's successor, Major James Chichester-Clark, and welcomed home as heroes.

July-August 1969: the North in Flames

Chichester-Clark, like his cousin O'Neill, belonged to the landed gentry. He tried to defuse Paisleyism by agreeing that civil rights was a conspiracy of extreme socialists to establish a 'Workers' Republic' in Ireland. At an Orange Day rally, on 12 July, he warned 'the Irish-American lobby' and the US Congress that if the civil rights advocates succeeded they would create 'an Irish Cuba'. Said the Prime Minister: 'Let them find out how the great American companies established here would view the establishment of a workers' republic, one of whose first acts would be to expropriate foreign undertakings'.[51]

No one ever called Chichester-Clark a great or far-seeing statesman. The best James Callaghan could say was he 'is a very even-tempered man and rarely lets his emotions show'.[52] Chichester-Clark's speech annoyed conservative Catholics, who were looking for equal legal rights even as British subjects, not a Communist state. The situation by then had moved out of Stormont's control. Orange bands paraded through a Catholic housing estate in Belfast – named, ironically, 'Unity flats' – and Nationalists waved republican tricolours. A Catholic home was burnt, Catholic families fled from the Crumlin Road, a Protestant home was fire-bombed. 'But the bulk of the intimidation in July was practised on Catholics, and a good many families felt it necessary to move,' the Scarman Tribunal reports.[53]

For Catholics, Belfast was always the flash-point. An act of statesmanship, such as the summoning of a conference to discuss grievances and how to remedy them, might have saved the situation. There was no statesmanship in the Stormont government of 1969. Its main concern was its own survival. If British troops were mobilized to aid the civil power and restore order, would they be subject to Belfast or to London? James Callaghan, as Home Secretary, had no doubt about the proper answer to that question: to London of course. Would the Unionist Party, in such a grave crisis, be 'master in our own house?' Hardly: Stormont could lose its autonomy. It could even be abolished.

Aware of the trap he faced, Chichester-Clark played what Callaghan calls 'his strongest card'. He told the British that if they intervened 'we would be taking on an open-ended commitment'.[54] The blackmail here was that the Protestants wanted their own government and if Stormont was suspended or – and perish the thought – abolished, they would fight the British. Although Callaghan got the message, he insisted 'that the continuing use of British troops would make political intervention inevitable'. He did not want to use British troops, but 'a government which could not control the streets or the population was not a government in our understanding of the word.'[55]

Derry was in ferment through the summer of 1969, with minor riots rising and dying away. What finally started the fire was the Apprentice Boys march of 12 August. 'Before the procession, a few Apprentice Boys tossed coins from the City Walls towards small knots of people below,' says the official inquiry. 'It was a gesture of contempt which can only have inflamed the Bogside.'[56] This is an understatement. The Bogside is the Catholic ghetto of Derry. Someone flung a handful of nails across a metal crush barrier at the marchers. 'From this small beginning developed a riot which, enveloping the city for two days and nights, was not brought under control until the army entered William Street at 5 pm on 14 August,' states the official report.[57]

Barricades grew on the streets. Police armoured cars were fire bombed. Police reinforced by Paisleyites invaded the Bogside and were driven out with bottles and stones. A priest told the Scarman Tribunal he could only 'regard it as a community in revolt rather than just a street disturbance or riot'.[58] Businessmen manned the barricades with students, workers, unemployed, housewives, and the occasional 'itinerant anarchist'. Tricolours and 'Starry Ploughs' – the flag of Connolly's Citizen Army in the 1916 rebellion – rose behind the barricades. The police regrouped and tried to clear the barriers, using tear gas. By dawn 'the area had become enveloped in a pall of gas, covering the streets and penetrating the houses'.[59] The Tribunal is certain no defender carried or used firearms. The first shots were from a Sterling submachine-gun, standard police equipment. The police used guns to relieve a besieged barracks, it seems, but had no orders to fire. They tried to parley with community leaders and were told 'that marauding Paisleyites, openly supported by the police, had wrecked and burned premises in the Bogside, that a heavy blanket of tear gas had taken its toll of human suffering, that law and order had broken down, and that the Stormont government was incapable of governing'.[60] The Tribunal interpreted this as 'a call to arms', but it was no more than James Callaghan had told Chichester-Clark a week earlier.

The conference between the police and community leaders broke up because the latter wanted to listen to Prime Minister Jack Lynch of the Republic address 'the nation' on television and radio. Lynch said the Irish government could 'not stand idly by' in such a crisis. He would send troops, field hospitals and ambulances to the border. A 'small minority' in the Dublin government wanted to do more. This minority included the most senior ministers in Lynch's Cabinet: Neil Blaney, Charles Haughey, Kevin Boland, 'with support from [James] Gibbons and with [Michael] Moran not opposed but obsessed with the overriding need to guard against "subversives"'.[61] They may have wished to send Irish troops over the border to Derry to guard the Nationalists from the RUC. Irish troops could have occupied a number of other points in the North without clashing with the British army, it was believed. Instead, the Irish government decided to ask Britain to request that UN peace-keeping forces be sent to Northern Ireland because British troops were unacceptable to the Irish people.

On 14 August, British troops moved into Derry and a day later into Belfast. No one died in Derry. In Belfast, ten civilians were killed and 145 wounded. The Irish Foreign Minister then urgently asked the Security Council to send a force to Northern Ireland. He received a polite hearing. His speech was 'moderately phrased'. The Council adjourned, apparently by arrangement with the British,[62] and the Irish request was ignored.

A Nationalist Revolt

The Scarman Tribunal was critical of Lynch's speech and actions, but ideologically it was the least he could have done in the circumstances. His party, Fianna Fáil, was part of the republican tradition. It, too, had to satisfy its ideology by making a gesture to the beleagured Nationalists. Many believed that the events in Derry would end in a massacre of Catholics. It might have happened if 'B' Specials were ordered into the Bogside. The defenders had no guns. Next day the rebellion – for such it was – spread to Belfast, Coalisland, Dungannon, Dungiven, Armagh, Newry and Crossmaglen.[63]

In times of tension in Northern Ireland, Belfast is the focus of Catholic fears. Catholics form one-third of the city's population. They live in their own districts. Catholics isolated in Protestant areas live in fear of a massacre. Nationalist activity outside of Belfast may stir sectarian violence in the city. It happened in 1920-22.[64] It almost happened in 1969. No civil rights demonstrations were held in Belfast because of the risk of provoking sectarian violence.[65] A small group of young civil rights activists staged a protest march to a police station to denounce RUC actions in Derry. The crowd grew. Police sent out armoured cars and an antiquated grenade exploded under one of them. Shots were fired. These events occurred in Catholic districts and no Protestants were involved. In reprisal, Protestant groups started to burn out Catholic families on Divis Street. The police did not stop them.

'The major casualty of the night 14-15 August was the complete loss of confidence by the Belfast Catholic community in the police force as then constituted and the determination thereafter by subversive elements such as the IRA to exploit the opportunities for urban guerrilla warfare in Belfast,' reports the Scarman Tribunal.[66] The 'subversive elements' might reply that they were doing no more than defending their communities. The Scarman Tribunal heard independent evidence that Protestant groups opened fire first. They may have believed, as in December 1688, that 'a general insurrection of the Irish' was intended. In communal conflicts, rumour and deductions based on rumour do irreparable damage. Belfast Catholics were convinced that a Protestant-police plot existed to burn them out – or some of them believed it. Belfast Protestants were convinced the IRA was trying to overthrow the state, and the RUC was sure they were right. Believing one's own fantasies or illusions is also a function of ideology.

What was taking place, it is now possible to determine, was a spontaneous rebellion, without plan, or leadership, or organization.

Stormont had lost control of the Nationalist streets in Belfast and Derry and other towns of the North. It never regained that control. British troops restored British rule in fact, although when they entered Derry and Belfast to patrol the streets the Nationalists felt *they* had won a great victory. They welcomed the soldiers and offered them cups of tea as a gesture of hospitality; but they did not dismantle the barricades.

The Provisional IRA was born in the flames of Belfast as the Catholic Defenders, although it did not come into being officially for another four months. Those republicans who returned the fire of the police and the Protestant mobs were convinced it would all happen again and that next time there would be a massacre, unless the Nationalists had guns to defend themselves.[67]

The IRA Split

The Provisional IRA's account of these events states: 'But when the inevitable happened in Belfast's beleagured nationalist ghettos on 14 August 1969 the victims to their horror found themselves without protection from the one source they hitherto trusted – the Irish Republican Army.'[68] The men who later founded the Provisionals denounced the 'Communists' in the IRA for political decisions that downgraded military training and preparation, introduced politics, and abandoned traditional republicanism. The 'Communist advisers' were Roy Johnston and Anthony Coughlan, but the chief target of traditionalist wrath was Cathal Goulding, Chief of Staff since September 1962, when the IRA seemed finished, never to rise again, except to hold ideological commemorations in churchyards once a year on Easter Sunday.

In the movement most of his life, thirteen years in English and Irish prisons, Goulding, who was of working-class background, had become convinced that the IRA must concern itself with the needs of ordinary people if it ever hoped to achieve its goals. He had helped reorganize the IRA after the debacle of the 1940s and he faced much the same task and for the same reason in the 1960s. He held that military campaigns of the kind the movement had engaged in since the independence struggle of 1919-21 'were a failure because the people were not committed to, or involved in, the struggles'. People were activated not by abstract ideals of freedom, he believed, but by social realities. 'Wages, working conditions, standards of living, housing, personal freedom, voting rights, equality with other sections of the community in the exercising of all these basic rights.'[69]

Social consciousness was not new to republicanism, of course. It was an issue for each generation: Mellows's 'Notes from Mountjoy', Saor Éire, Republican Congress, the men in the Curragh internment camp in the 1940s, the guerrillas in border farmhouses in the 1950s campaign, the prisoners in Crumlin Road, Mountjoy, the Curragh – all had raised social questions and discussed them. What did the Republic mean to the people? How would it better their lives? Co-operativism was important in the declining West and republicans in the 1960s tried to help. But the civil rights movement caught fire too fast and burned too quickly for the IRA. And the North moved too rapidly from non-violence to violence for the 'new departure' to win support.

The traditional IRA answer to every situation was the gun. There were few guns in August 1969. Some traditionalists saw a plot by the Communists to win respectability and a political base via the republican movement. Proposals calling for a National Liberation Front – an anti-imperialist alliance of all left groups, including the Communist Party – strengthened these suspicions. Johnston, whose fertile brain drafted the NLF plan, conceded that the CP could never become a mass party in Ireland. But the IRA had the appeal to create a mass movement in an alliance of urban socialists and rural radicals. In this scheme, the CP leaders saw themselves as spokesmen of the urban workers, with the republicans building the rural base.[70] Hence the NLF – workers and peasants, if you will, struggling for Ireland's independence! There was little reality behind such notions in the Ireland of the 1960s.

The main complaint of the traditionalists was that the IRA had no guns to defend the Nationalists of Derry and Belfast. They blamed the influence 'of former members of the Communist Party of Great Britain who came back to Ireland with the intention of setting up an ultra-left front based on the Republican Movement, had diverted the movement to political and social agitiation to the almost total exclusion of the traditional military role.'[71] In Belfast, a stronghold of traditional republicanism, a *putsch* in September 1969 replaced the social radicals with veteran hardliners.[72] The new Belfast leadership next sent an ultimatum to GHQ: Goulding must go; Seán Garland, a hero of the 1950s campaign, could take his place; Johnston must be expelled; other GHQ staff, including Séamus Costello and Michael Ryan, would have to resign. Belfast was told such changes were matters for the Army Council and the General Army Convention. The Belfast Brigade then withdrew allegiance from GHQ in Dublin.

At the December 1969 convention, Goulding defended his actions of August. 'When the situation blew up in the six counties after

August 12th,' he said,

> we armed and equipped four active service units and sent them up to the Border areas. I ordered them to stand to, to use them as effectively as possible under the circumstances, but I also warned them not to take any action in the Border areas. The lull had set in at this time and as I knew that the areas behind the barricades were not armed sufficiently to defend themselves and if some action by us on the Border sparked off the UVF [Ulster Volunteer Force] and the 'B' Specials to resume their attacks on the people behind the barricades the people there would be slaughtered and the Republican Movement would be destroyed for ever. This I believe was what the South of Ireland government wanted. It would leave a clear field to them to unite with the right wingers in NICRA to complete the takeover bid they made some time ago.[73]

There was some justification for Goulding's fears. An attack on the border would have united all Protestants behind Stormont and provided evidence that the outbreaks in the North were part of an IRA plot. In such a situation the 'B' Specials might have been unleashed in the Bogside and Belfast. At the least they would have received *carte blanche* to terrorize the nationalist countryside of Tyrone, Fermanagh and Derry.[74] The IRA could not send guns to Belfast and Derry because it had few weapons. It may be, as charged by the Provisionals later, that GHQ was dilatory about sending guns because the leadership feared an outbreak of sectarian fighting in Belfast, which they could not control. In fact, one reason for the lack of decision-making at the top during those crucial August days may be that Goulding was out of the country, in London, talking to emissaries of the Haughey-Blaney bloc in the government about money and arms to defend the nationalists in the North.

The Arms Conspiracy

Dublin was concerned by reports of the growth of left-wing, particularly Communist, ideas in the civil rights movement which was under Marxist leadership of one kind or another. The government doubtless was also concerned by the influence of Johnston and Coughlan on the leaders of the IRA. Fianna Fáil, as 'the Republican Party' (the English form of its name, according to itself), was always conscious of its own national position *vis-à-vis* the traditionalist republicans who refused to recognize the legality of Dáil Éireann. Early in 1969 some members of Fianna Fáil approached IRA officers in Derry, offering them money and guns on condition that they set up a 'Northern Command' independent of 'the Communist-dominated leadership'. Since many in the Northern IRA were hostile to the socialist line, the tactic made sense. In this instance, however, the wrong man was approached.

When events in the North reached crisis point, in August 1969, the Dublin government delegated its border Cabinet members – Blaney of Donegal, Brennan of Donegal, Faulkner of Louth, with the Ministers for Finance (Haughey) and Defence (Gibbons) – to keep an eye on the situation and 'to do what was practicable to assist the nationalist community resist an all-out onslaught', should such take place, which was not unlikely. Most reports to the Cabinet on the North were made by Blaney. By delegating authority to a sub-committee, although it was not designated as such, the government could get on with its other work.

Funds were allotted for relief of distress in the North under Haughey's control. Public relations men were sent to Irish embassies to explain the situation internationally. Army intelligence officers were sent North to monitor events and prepare to help the besieged Nationalists should the need arise. The army general staff was asked by the Minister for Defence, on behalf of the government, about aid in the event of an attack on the nationalists and it replied somewhat negatively. In the words of one Cabinet Minister, the government insisted that 'if these people are being slaughtered we must provide help.' The general staff then said it could train men and keep supply lines open for provisions. In the event of what was called a 'doomsday situation', it was also directed to plan for intervention which it interpreted to mean to 'prepare and train the forces for incursions into Northern Ireland [and] make weapons and ammunition available . . . .'[75]

Following the August riots Citizen Defence Committees (or Catholic Defence Committees) sprouted in nationalist areas. In effect a Catholic militia grew up behind the barricades in 'Free Derry' and 'Free Belfast' funded by the Irish government and often advised by Irish army officers. A meeting was held of leading 'defenders', mostly traditional republicans, in Bailieborough, Co. Cavan, presided over by Captain James Kelly, an Irish army intelligence officer. All agreed their most pressing need was for arms to defend themselves. Kelly later flew to Vienna to arrange for the purchase of small arms with Irish government funds, to be shipped secretly to Dublin and cleared through customs with the help of Finance Minister Haughey. The arms, one account has it, were to be kept in the Republic until needed; another account suggests the Belfast (Provisional) IRA planned to seize them and take them North. At any rate Goulding's 'Red IRA' would get none of them.[76]

How much the Taoiseach, Jack Lynch, and his government knew

about all of this has been the subject of much controversy over the years. Lynch said he knew nothing until told on 20-21 April 1970 by the career head of the Department of Justice, Peter Berry, the effective controller of the Special Branch. It is also thought that the Special Branch was kept informed of all developments in the smuggling of arms by British intelligence. Kevin Boland, the most republican Minister in the Cabinet, agrees that the government as such had no official knowledge of the arms deals or that military intelligence officers were operating in the North. But he insists that all members of the government, including Lynch but excluding his deputy, Erskine Childers, knew of these matters. It was important, for Dublin's relations with London, that the imported weapons not be traceable to the Irish authorities. Hence the secrecy and alleged 'conspiracy'.

In this view, the arms were being imported 'unofficially' on behalf of the government and Berry and the Special Branch, informed by the British, found themselves having to deal with this situation. The whole affair became a public issue when the leader of the opposition, Liam Cosgrave, was informed anonymously. Haughey and Blaney were dismissed. Haughey was charged with conspiracy to import arms into the Republic. In the dock with him were Captain James Kelly, Albert Luykx, a Belgian living in Ireland and John Kelly, a Belfast IRA officer. All were found to be not guilty by a jury and acquitted in Ireland's most celebrated arms case, echoes of which continue to reverberate down the years.

Haughey's political career was in ruins. Later the rank and file of Fianna Fáil elected him party secretary, because of his 'republican stand' and in 1975 he was chief architect of its policy on Northern Ireland. When Fianna Fáil returned to office in 1978, Haughey returned to the front bench as Minister for Health. Then on 9 December 1979, after Lynch resigned as Prime Minister and party leader because of rank-and-file dissatisfaction with his policy of apparent cooperation with Britain on border security, Haughey succeeded him.[77]

In any democratic state the government would have fallen as a result of the arms case involving at least two ministers in the spring of 1970. It did not happen in Ireland because republican ideology justified them. As Kevin Boland noted, the Fianna Fáil party faced a crisis of conscience in 1969-70 over the North: this is what it had been established for – to give leadership to nationalist Ireland in a time of crisis – and it failed.

Boland resigned because of this failure, as he saw it. He knew nothing of the arms shipment. His position on that was also based on principle: the Prime Minister and his Minister for Defence were given a vote of confidence by Dáil Éireann when they were not entitled to it. In an extreme situation it would have been right to put arms in the hands of Ulster nationalists to defend themselves.

For Northern nationalists there was no crisis of conscience. They looked to the government in Dublin for protection. How that protection was provided was a matter for the government. The alternative was to rely on the British for protection, an intolerable situation for nationalists.

Some traditional republicans in the South were uneasy because Northern republicans walked in and out of government offices in Dublin. But Northern republicans are a pragmatic lot. They have rarely concerned themselves with such finer points of theory as the legitimacy of the Third Dáil (Free State), or why de Valera left Sinn Féin in 1926 to found Fianna Fáil. Such ideological hair-splitting was the basis of republicanism in the 1920s, 1930s, and 1940s. Republicans in the North dealt with a real situation: the British connection. As most of them saw it, the Republic was 'free Ireland'.

John Kelly, in the dock in Dublin beside an ex-minister, Charles Haughey – whose roots also were in the North – told of his role in the 1950s campaign and of the August 1969 outbreaks in Belfast. He had been in Crumlin Road prison (Belfast) for many years between these two events, had tried to escape and was caught, and also had time to think about the politics of his divided country. Of August 1969, he said:

> It seemed to us at the time that the Unionist government had decided that the people of the Falls and the Ardoyne areas of Belfast had to be taught a lesson – in the 'Croppies must be made to lie down' tradition. The so-called forces of law and order, the RUC and the 'B' Specials, supported by an armed loyalist mob, were let loose against these areas. They sprayed whole streets with bullets and poured heavy machine-gun fire into blocks of flats, and, meanwhile, the loyalist mob came surging through the streets and several hundred homes went up in flames . . . .

The Nationalist answer was the Citizens' Defence Committee, with John Kelly as chief organizer in Belfast and later throughout the North. He thought it reasonable that the Irish government should help them. He thought it unreasonable that they should be later arrested and put on trial for smuggling arms. 'There is no victory for anybody in these proceedings, my Lord,' Kelly told the court. 'There is only an echo of sadness from the graves of the dead generations.'[78]

When Eamon de Valera founded Fianna Fáil as a constitutional

Republican Party in 1926, he called on 'the dead generations' to witness his reasons, which were: 'To assert the right of the nation to its complete freedom. To oppose all claims of any foreign power to dictate to them or to interfere in any way in the government of Ireland. To repudiate any assent to the partition of Ireland and to bring partition to an end.'[79]

John Kelly and de Valera were talking the same language. They had the same goals, a united independent Ireland. They appealed to the same gods – 'the dead generations'. (Pearse in 1915, at the grave of O'Donovan Rossa, made the same appeal.) They shared the same ideology, although their view of political reality was different. When John Kelly spoke from the dock, de Valera was President of Ireland. The ideology Kelly summoned to his side in court had made that possible.

Because of its ideological origins, the Fianna Fáil government faced a dilemma in August 1969. Kevin Boland, the party's republican conscience in government, wanted the Republic to act decisively on the side of the Nationalists. He wrote later:

> My only interest in being in politics was as a Republican. It had become clear that the government was anything but Republican . . . and, with the situation in the Six Counties becoming more critical with every hour that passed, and the apparent non-existence of the IRA, I considered a rescue operation to be a matter of extreme urgency.[80]

Birth of the Provisionals

Boland influenced his friend, Charles Haughey, who hardly needed influencing because his own roots were in South Derry. Blaney was influenced by his own traditions and his Donegal constituency, next door to Derry. Taking these factors into account, 'the conspiracy' was not that remarkable. This 'Republican bloc' threatened Lynch's leadership of Fianna Fáil. The ministers, the most conservative members of the Cabinet, were capable of raising a 'Red scare' when it suited them; but their impulse on the North seems to have stemmed from ideological nationalism, and was not an attempt to destroy the growth of socialist ideas within the republican movement, although they would like to accomplish that, too.[81]

For sound reasons, detailed in Goulding's December 1969 convention statement, the Official IRA would dispute this analysis. The basis of the IRA split, as Goulding saw it, was the 'Communist issue'. The government of the Republic was prepared to help the Nationalists of the North with money and arms, and use the IRA as a conduit, provided it changed its socialist policies and got rid of its

'Reds'. Goulding told the army intelligence officer who conveyed these 'suggestions' that he would not discuss members of the movement, that policies were made by conventions, and that 'if they wanted to cooperate we were willing but that they would have to accept us as we were. . . .'[82] Since the Blaney-Haughey bloc could not get its way, the result was the birth of the Provisional IRA, born in the convention split of 1969. Supporting this contention further is Blaney's own claim that he was indeed the founding father of the Provisional IRA.

It is true that ideologically the Provisional IRA was a reaction to the so-called 'Communist programme' of the IRA leadership. The first to raise the matter publicly was Séamus (Jimmy) Steele. Others followed his lead. The polemics of the early Provisionals are full of anti-Communist pieties. Still, given Irish nationalist tradition, an armed movement would have grown out of the events of August 1969, whatever it was called. The name 'IRA' was important in the North. As has been noted in this study, the IRA is more a tradition than a movement. IRA officers in the North were the natural leaders of any armed force, like the IRB of 1913-14. Republicans in the South would send money and supplies, as indeed happened. Such a force did exist before the IRA split in December 1969. IRA volunteers from the 1940s period defended Catholic districts of Belfast in August 1969. Old comrades in Dublin, including primarily Jack McCabe, collected arms and ammunition. The Belfast *coup* of September 1969 helped this development and the Belfast Brigade of the IRA became the natural vanguard of the new movement. The Catholic Defence Committees supplied the recruits. The movement found a name after the December 1969 split when those who opposed Goulding's policies established a 'Provisional Army Council'.

How did those who stood behind the Nationalist barricades view their situation? Their ideology, of course, was nationalist, which gave them a particular view of the North's politics and Britain's role in it. A 'spirit of rebellion' undoubtedly existed from August to November 1969. Despite all the discussion inside the IRA in the previous years, the situation caught the leaders by surprise and their explanation of what had taken place revealed their confusion. Clear leadership was lacking and disillusionment set in behind the barricades. There were conservatives frightened of Communists; 'pure Catholics' who hated the Protestants who had dominated them for so long; there were radicals who hoped that this was the revolution. They differed on tactics: passive self-defence was the most popular; the militants wanted to take the fight to the 'enemy' – police, army, government.[83]

Two Ideologies – Two Republican Movements

The December 1969 IRA convention endorsed Goulding's leadership but contained a bloc of delegates uncompromisingly opposed to the abandonment of the abstention policy – which went back to 1922 – and to any further truck with the Communists in a 'National Liberation Front'. The strongest traditionalist centres – Belfast and Kerry – were not represented, having previously broken with the leadership. In these circumstances the 'minority', with some justification, could claim to be actually the 'majority' of all republicans. This was the reasoning behind the founding of the 'Provisional Army Council of the IRA'. It was 'provisional' until such time as a regularly assembled convention established an Executive and Army Council. A traditionalist must have legitimacy.

Nominal republicans were always the bane of the leadership. They did nothing but maintain their republican purity by refusing to recognize government institutions in theory, but not in practice of course. Such republicans were strong in Kerry: it was a legacy of the Civil War. Tony Meade, a 1950s guerrilla and mid-1960s editor of the *United Irishman*, saw the clash at first as a conflict between radical activists and these traditionalists:

> There is the division between those more revolutionary people who are not afraid to take public action on issues which concern the people and those who are, in effect, establishment people. These are quite happy with the general set-up in the country and their own areas and definitely unwilling to stand publicly against local injustices, fearing thereby to lose their present status of rather exclusive brethren who in all outward essentials accept the system but on the question of the legality of the State are dissenters.[84]

In the final analysis, Meade concluded, the loyalties of these people were not to the elected leadership of the republican movement but to the dead of the Civil War and the Republic of 1916-21. 'The only difficulty with this argument is that the people have refused to cooperate,' was Meade's unanswerable rejoinder. To a legitimatist, nothing is unanswerable. Ruairí Ó Brádaigh (Rory Brady), founding President of Provisional Sinn Fein, explained republican ideology in the old way:

> The 'Treaty' states, both North and South, subservient economically to Britain, suppressed the All-Ireland Dáil which was the embodiment of the Republic. For the Republican Movement then, a Republican today is one who rejects the Partition Statelets in Ireland and gives his allegiance to and seeks to restore the 32-County Republic of Easter Week.[85]

These are theological not political arguments, but ideology is as much theology as it is politics, which it sees through a distorted lens of its own creation. In practical everyday politics, the radicals were bound to have the better case, given a normal situation. But Ireland in 1969-70 was not 'a normal situation'. The Officials, as the Goulding radicals were called after the split, probably were happy to lose the traditionalists so that they could get along with the job of making Ireland socialist and independent. They were accused by the Provisionals of seeking to establish 'extreme socialism leading to dictatorship', endangering 'Irish and Christian values'. At Easter 1970 the Provisionals declared: 'Irish freedom will not be won by involvement with an international movement of extreme socialism.' Atheistic Communism is a good issue in Catholic Ireland, and the Provisionals' first Chief of Staff, Seán Mac Stiofáin (Stephenson), was something of an anti-Communist zealot, his memoirs suggest.[86]

The bedrock of Provisionalism was Belfast. The simple issue was 'defence of the people', according to Joe Cahill, a veteran IRA officer and later Belfast commander. 'We receive our support from the Nationalist people and it is our job to defend them.' Many Provisional leaders, including Rúairí Ó Brádaigh, held the same view. Before August 1969 the Nationalists would have been satisfied with reforms; afterwards they wanted Stormont disbanded. This view was expressed by one of the most influential IRA leaders in the North, Joseph B. O'Hagan of Lurgan. The fight had to be won, he said. 'Winning' meant moving from defensive to offensive warfare against the British presence in Northern Ireland.[87]

Goulding held another view: 'There can be no Ireland in Wolfe Tone's sense without the Protestant working class. They must be reached. We believe we are on the right road. The 1919 Dáil Éireann Democratic Programme was buried and ignored and now we are going to the root of the Irish question.'[88] Through the decade of turmoil in the North the Officials have pursued this unambiguous non-sectarian policy, but have failed to reach the Protestant working class, or influence them. The Republican Congress founder, George Gilmore, himself of Ulster Protestant stock, admired their dedication, but remarked: 'There's an iron curtain between Nationalists and Unionists. Only Labour would hope to do the job they [the Official IRA] are trying to do and Labour has fallen down.'[89]

Symbolically, the first Provisional action was the defence of a Catholic church, St Matthew's, in Ballymacarret, East Belfast, under Billy McKee, the IRA commander, which a Protestant mob tried to raze in late June 1970. McKee was wounded, one of his men was killed. Four Protestants died. Was this a sectarian battle? 'No,' replied a Provisional leader. 'There was no planned attack on the Protestants.'[90]

There is a 'religious dimension': Catholics are on one side, Protestants on the other. Religion distinguishes the combatants. Religion maintained Protestant ascendancy; Protestant ascendancy means Unionist ascendancy – loyalty to Britain. Those who oppose this are rebels. When a Tory government came to power in Britain, the Unionist authorities, over the weekend 3-5 July 1970, curfewed the Falls Road while British troops searched Nationalist homes for arms. The Official IRA defended the Falls. Troops killed four civilians, in their own streets by their own houses. They had broken no law. They died because they lived in a Nationalist area. A *Sunday Times* team of reporters wrote:

> Illegal confinement, summary search and exposure to unprecedented amounts of CS gas outraged large sections of the Falls Road population. Their conviction that the 'invasion' had been politically motivated was confirmed, as they saw it, when the army drove two beaming Unionist ministers, Captains William Long and John Brooke, on a tour round the subjugated Falls.[91]

That summer the Provisionals mounted a bombing campaign. Their demands were: a British declaration of intent to leave Ireland, abolition of Stormont, amnesty for prisoners. Having objectives one can win, and then appearing to win them, is bound to give an insurgent movement the impression of invincibility. No Irish republican could disagree with the 'conditions' set by the Provisionals. However, the Officials managed to support the unsupportable – Stormont, on the grounds that the Protestants saw it as their institution; hence an Irish institution. This policy was drafted by Anthony Coughlan; his thesis was that a call for the abolition of Stormont would lead to a redrawing of the border and permanent partition. Republicans should demand a reformed Stormont, not abolition. No Irish nationalist, let alone a republican, could accept such a thesis. The guarantee against Protestant ascendancy, for example, must be a Bill of Rights passed by the British parliament. When such bills were introduced in London they were defeated. Coughlan argued that the existence of Stormont 'would guarantee their [Protestant] right of secession from the United Kingdom . . .'.[92] On this logic Protestant Ulster could secede from an all-Ireland state. No republican would concede such a right.

By contrast, the Provisional stand was simple and direct: 'In the struggle for civil rights the abolition of Stormont would, as an interim measure, be a step forward. It would make much easier the achievement of full rights and would bring us into direct confrontation with Westminster. English imperialism, both in its old and new forms, has been the root cause of Ireland's ills.'[93] When the British government prorogued Stormont in March 1972, the Provisionals could claim the victory.

The British action was probably designed to wipe the slate clean of the bombings, the killings, the August 1971 internment, and the 'psychological torture' – which led to condemnation of Britain by the European Commission on Human Rights – culminating in the killing of thirteen civil rights marchers in Derry on 30 January, 1972 by British paratroopers.[94] Suspension of Stormont enabled Britain to seek a new settlement, unencumbered by failed experiments. The result was the Sunningdale Agreement: a power-sharing Executive representative of Catholics and Protestants,[95] which was toppled by the Protestant strike of May 1974.[96]

The Provisionals continued bombing and shooting, except for periods of truce with the British army, when sectarian killings, explosions in pubs and cafés and 'tit-for-tat' murders, filled the void. Much of this was the work of Protestant paramilitary – Ulster Defence Association, Ulster Volunteer Force, Red Hand Commandos – and vigilante groups who responded to Provisional violence by shooting Catholics and bombing their pubs and cafés in Belfast. Some sectarian killings were done in the name of Wolfe Tone. The La Mon restaurant atrocity and the South Armagh minibus massacre were carried out by republicans. In the latter incident a Catholic worker was permitted to live while his Protestant mates were shot to death. That was surely making a sectarian point.[97]

In this three-sided war – sometimes four and five-sided when republican factions began to shoot one another – the Provisionals were fighting the forces of the Crown and in the process killing any agents of the Crown that came into their line of fire: soldiers, police, reservists in the Ulster Defence Regiment, prison warders (female as well as male), judges, and sundry alleged informers, including a South Armagh postman, whose integrity was vouched for by the Primate of All-Ireland, Dr Tomás Ó Fiaich, who came from the same village. They bombed shops, bars, hotels – killing fourteen persons with a petroleum-type explosive on one occasion, though not intentionally; they apologized for it, which was no comfort for the dead or their relatives. Industries were blasted in a phase of 'economic warfare' and businessmen were killed – but that ceased quickly.

The pattern of operations was to have no pattern: to strike when not expected. These tactics were effective, judged strictly as tactics.

It was urban guerrilla warfare, ruthless in character, though not as ruthless as that of the FLN in Algiers, which General Massu subdued. The car bombs were the worst: cars could be stolen easily, taken to a target, abandoned; a fast coded call to the security forces; the rest was up to the military and/or police. If they got the message right, no one was hurt. Often there was confusion, an explosion, and horribly mangled bodies for the evening news. In the village of Claudy the one public telephone was out of order and a half-dozen people died.[98]

There were some restraints: Nationalist public opinion would tolerate certain kinds of operations, not others. The car bombing had to stop. If one accepts the Provisionals' premise that they are fighting a war, that their instruments of violence are not always controllable, that to be militarily significant they must carry out certain operations, with insufficient safety precautions, it must be conceded that they have not been totally irresponsible in their conduct or choice of target. If one rejects their premise, or their right to wage war, the argument changes: there is no justification for anything they do. This is the view of successive governments of the Irish Republic and of all parties, with some reservations. Dr Conor Cruise O'Brien, the severest critic of Irish republican ideology in our time, blames the 'Irish vision of England' for the Provisional IRA:

> The possessed, by possessed I mean the IRA, derive, from the intensity of the vision which grips them an abundant sense of justification. Since England is synonomous with guilt and oppression, any blow against England, however terrible it may seem, is a blow for righteousness and liberty.[99]

What if the vision be right? Did not England repress the Irish by armed force and turn their country into a colony? Does it not still retain the right to decide the political future of the Irish? Or some of them? Does she not repress the Irish still?[100] Right or wrong, how can the state deal with this 'vision'? By brainwashing those Irish who hold such a vision? The 'vision' in the end is the ideology of the IRA. How does one correct another's ideology, if one considers it wrong? How does one determine the truth or falsity of an ideology, other than to say, with Marx, that all ideology is 'false consciousness'?

The 'vision' of England's wrong-doing may fuel the actions of the IRA, but it is the fact of England's presence that leads to the violence. The ideology of the IRA is violent: it holds that England will not yield to any argument bút force. To employ force in politics is to engage in the Clausewitzian definition of politics – 'that war is nothing but a continuation of political intercourse with an admixture of other means'.[101] Clausewitz was talking about states, but that hardly invalidates his definition. The IRA in any event sees itself as the legal successor of the 'Second Dáil', and as such the government of the Irish Republic. In the conditions of Northern Ireland it will argue that force alone can change the political balance there. Force is power. Politics is about power. Without power there is no way of reopening the Irish question. England indeed will not even discuss the matter unless forced to talk. In May 1974 the British government refused to use troops to defend the power-sharing Executive, its own creation, against the Ulster Workers' Council and the Ulster Defence Association. In July 1980 it offered a settlement that gave Nationalists less than they had received at Sunningdale six and a half years before. What prevails in the end is power.

The logic of the British position is that because Ulster's Protestants have been able to block a settlement of the Irish question in 1914, 1921, 1925 and 1974, they will do so again. 'The first assumption to be made is that any political progress will be followed by a flare-up of violence'[102] by the Protestant population. The Provisional IRA could claim that their force is merely shifting slightly the balance of power in favour of the Nationalists, who, after all, are a majority in Ireland and want a united country.

The early tactics of the Provisionals seemed modelled on those of Colonel George Grivas, the rightist leader of EOKA in Cyprus, rather than on the Irish guerrillas of 1919-21, who served as models for many resistance movements. This is 'punitive warfare' to intimidate the enemy.[103] Collins was a master of it. Grivas struck at the British, sometimes the Turks, and near the end Communists, to convey political messages. Presumably the Provisionals are conveying some political message, which the British, the Unionists and others understand. If they do not, the exercise is wasted. This is terrorism, undoubtedly. On the other hand, as has been said quite often, 'One man's terrorist is another man's freedom fighter.'

Accepting the premise of the Provisionals, one may criticize this type of campaign, as it has been criticized by, among others, the late Cardinal Conway of Armagh, and the Official Republicans, on the grounds that it cannot achieve a united independent Ireland, so long as almost one million Protestants oppose the 'vision'. Even if the British are forced to withdraw, will that unite Ireland? Some Provisionals hint at an Algerian solution: the *colons* simply packed up and returned to France. Northern Ireland is very different. An unsigned article in *An Phoblacht*, the Provisional weekly, published in Dublin, said:

> Broadly, the Irish struggle is paralleled by Algeria's fight for freedom, one which also was hampered by a colonial enclave, one which, also, in its latter stages, was marked by the same collusion between fascist gangs and the French imperial armed forces, involving horror massacres similar to the recent cross-Border outrages . . . .[104]

Few in Ireland, Catholic or Protestant, Nationalist or Unionist, would accept the Algerian parallel, and certainly not the Algerian solution. Ulster's Protestants have been in north-east Ireland for nearly 400 years; their colony is older than the first English colonies in North America. The plantation of Ulster began at the same time as the Jamestown colony. Scots had been migrating peacefully to Ulster since the last quarter of the sixteenth century. They have tilled Ulster's land and built Ulster's industry. They have a right to be there.

Political Positions of Provisionals and Officials

The Provisionals see themselves as the armed vanguard of the Nationalist population, the defenders of that population, which is Catholic, and to this extent their role is somewhat analogous to the Defenders of the 1790s.[105] The Officials, on the other hand, do genuinely preach the secular doctrines of the United Irishmen, as interpreted by Connolly, but their base, too, is in the Nationalist community. Brian Faulkner, as Prime Minister, sought to divorce the Provisionals from the Nationalist population by saying their goal was to attack the British army, not redress the grievances of Catholics. Faulkner was a far shrewder politician than his predecessor. 'The wholesale rioting of 1969 had produced an atmosphere of community distrust in which the IRA could thrive, posing as the last line of defence for the Catholic community,' he wrote.[106] The Provisionals outwitted him by keeping their war a popular struggle – and in the Catholic ghettos it was a popular struggle.

The weakness of the Provisionals is political and its struggle can't be won by military means alone. They have adopted fully the IRA tradition of the superiority of the military over the political; contradicting Mao's axiom, the IRA gun controls the Sinn Féin party. The reasoning in the IRA goes back to Rory O'Connor, who occupied the Four Courts in 1922 and repudiated all political authority because Dáil Éireann had betrayed the Republic by endorsing the Treaty. The Civil War was fought by military means, without political leadership, and failed disastrously. The 1920s and 1930s saw constant debate, reopened in the 1950s, inside the IRA, on the primacy of 'action' over 'politics'. The call for 'action' created the Provisionals in 1969.

But war, as Clausewitz noted, is a trinity: political objectives, military operations, popular passions. The first and last are in the realm of political ideas. They can be dealt with only by political means. Even military operations are not autonomous: they must have an overall political purpose. A purely military revolutionary movement makes no sense. Hence Mao's dictum: 'The gun must never command the party.'

The Provisionals have no political organization worthy of the name in the North. Sinn Féin is banned. It has little influence over the decisions of the IRA anyway. Sinn Féin in the Republic is ineffective, despite, or because of, the republican tradition. Although the Provisionals have two astute political minds in Rúairí Ó Brádaigh and Dáithí Ó Conaill, their most daring ideas have failed to take concrete shape. Dáil Uladh, a parliament of Ulster's nine counties, was one. The 'Federal Ireland' idea was another. The Provisionals keep losing allies: first, Paddy Kennedy, Republican Labour member of Stormont; then Frank McManus, Unity MP for Fermanagh-South Tyrone at Westminster.[107] They formed a 'Resistance Council' with Michael Farrell of People's Democracy, but that alliance also fell apart.

Sinn Féin's 'Éire Nua' programme had little appeal for Nationalists; now it seems it has little appeal for the Provisional IRA. The idea of Dáil Uladh, as part of a federal Ireland, was modelled partly on the Swiss cantons. Professor Alfred O'Rahilly of Cork drafted a federal constitution in 1922 to get away from the British system: it was rejected by Treatyites and anti-Treatyites.[108] Federal structures do not develop in this way. De Valera saw a federal solution to partition, but with the North's parliament continuing under Dublin rather than London. Before they could hand over three Ulster counties to Dáil Uladh, the Provisionals would have to win power in Dublin first. As they outlined their plan,[109] the people of Donegal, Monaghan and Cavan had no say in the arrangement, and no choice in the matter, it seems.[110]

'The Structure of the New Ireland' contains a Charter of Rights, based on the UN's Universal Declaration on Human Rights, and a 'Programme for Social and Economic Development' that talks vaguely about 'co-operative enterprises in production, distribution and exchange'. Although the Provisional IRA says it will establish a 'democratic socialist republic' in Ireland, this is unmentioned in 'the Structure of the New Ireland', which declares:

> In the drafting of this programme our aim has been to outline a social system

which could strike a balance between Western individualistic capitalism, with its poor and hungry amid plenty, on the right, and Eastern Soviet State capitalism (or any of its variations) with its denial of freedom and human rights, on the left.[111]

The young Provisionals of Belfast are more radical than the founders of the movement. *An Phoblacht* of Dublin has amalgamated with *Republican News* of Belfast and the tone of the weekly is defiantly leftist.[112] The radicals, apparently, want to scrap the federal Ireland programme of *Éire Nua* and replace with with a unitary socialist republic. Ideas like these so shocked the traditional Republicans in the late 1960s that they cleansed the movement by creating it anew, as it were. The Provisional radicals of the 1980s denounce the Officials, the radicals of the 1960s, as reformists who have abandoned the revolution as well as the national struggle. 'The old warhorses have been put out to grass,' is how a founding figure of the Provisionals put it sadly. He was talking about himself and some of his colleagues.[113]

The Official IRA has gone through a number of transitions in the decade since the split. For one thing, the emphasis is on the party, not on the IRA. It is widely believed that 'the Official IRA' has been disbanded and its members – those who did not join the breakaway Irish Republican Socialist Party of Séamus Costello in 1974 – were absorbed into Sinn Féin, which has added the descriptive 'the Workers' Party' to its title. (There was a move to drop the name 'Sinn Féin'.) These changes suggest the ideological development of the Officials (to use the shorthand term) from a physical-force organization to a socialist party that emphasizes economic rather than national issues.

On the other hand, the old leadership of the 1960s is still running things: Tomás MacGiolla, President of Sinn Féin since 1962; Seán Garland, GHQ officer since 1953, now General Secretary of the Workers' Party; Michael Ryan, Quartermaster General in the 1960s, now press officer of the party; Goulding remains in the background – but he remains. The IRA has not been disbanded, although its role is confined to the North, where the movement is organized in Republican Clubs and the stress is on politics.

These changes did not occur easily. When at the end of 1974 the Officials expelled one of their most powerful personalities, Séamus Costello, another ex-guerrilla of the 1950s campaign, he formed his own party, teamed up politically with Bernadette Devlin (Mrs McAliskey) to end 'imperialistic rule in Ireland, establish a 32-County Democratic Socialist Republic, with the working class in control of the means of production, distribution and exchange'.

He charged that the Officials had betrayed this objective 'by declaring a cease-fire during a period of escalating British aggression'.[114] The war of words became a war of bullets, a phenomenon of 1970s republican ideological differences; most of the killing was in Belfast. Among the dead was Liam MacMillan, Official IRA commander in Belfast. Seán Garland was badly wounded in an attempt on his life in Dublin. Costello himself was killed by a shotgun blast while reading a paper in his car: there is some mystery as to the political connections of the killer and his motives.

Politically the Officials had trouble equating ends and means. They solved the problem that plagued the IRA down the years, that of political control of the gun. But having adopted a socialist approach to the problem of the North, how were they to proceed? They must reach the working class. The Catholic working class? The Protestant working class? Both?

Interpreted broadly, socialism means control of state power by the working class. The struggle 'to control the means of production, distribution and exchange' cannot be done by proxy. In the North, the Protestant working class potentially is a powerful force. The Catholic working class is weak. The Protestants form the skilled, the Catholics the unskilled members of that class which is divided along religious or, this study would suggest, colonial-heritage lines. Among Protestant workers the Orange Order is a more influential institution than trade unions which, contrary to popular belief, are relatively weak. Most trade unionists belong to British-based unions. 'Indeed, trade unionism in Northern Ireland grew up as part of the trade union movement in Great Britain and in the main is organically connected with it.'[115] After the turmoil of a decade only 400 Catholics worked in the shipyards in a labour force of 7,000. They were apprentices.

Catholics are the poor, the unemployed. This is the economic reality. It is hard to find common ground for a Catholic-Protestant working-class struggle. Is class more important than caste? The economic question also involves Protestant, or colonial, privilege. The British army supports Protestant ascendancy because it supports the *status quo*, two British social scientists have observed.[116] It is one of the reasons the national question is a living issue in the back streets of Derry and Belfast, as well as in Churchill's 'muddy byways of Fermanagh and Tyrone'. The social and national questions go together, Connolly said. *How* is unclear. The Officials have fared no better than anyone else in their answers, which are often confused, reflecting the confusion on the Northern problem in the minds of so many who seek to resolve it.

In their efforts to unite Protestant and Catholic workers – they seem to have abandoned the small farmers, North and South – the Officials have come to some surprising conclusions on the national question, given their tradition and history. They blame the Irish Catholic middle class, not British rule, for Ireland's failure to industrialize. They see the 'Irish bourgeoisie' as their enemy, not 'British imperialism'.[117] They reject 'terror and violence as means to achieve state power'. They favour devolved government in the North – 'a democratic assembly [elected] by proportional representation' and 'a Bill of Rights for all'.[118] They have alienated their former allies, the small Irish Communist Party, by describing themselves as 'the vanguard of the working class' in Ireland. They have been accused of betraying the national question by adopting the 'two nations' (Protestant and Catholic) theory, that all true republicans consider heretical. (They deny it). Finally, they support industrialization via multinationals, according to *The Irish Industrial Revolution*, a matter disputed strongly by the president of Sinn Féin, the Workers' Party, Tomás Mac Giolla: 'We want the state sector to industrialize the country. We fear the influence and power of the multinationals to make Ireland follow US policies and to control the country's natural resources.' The Officials reject the two-nations' theory and also that there are two communities in the North. They see a British economic withdrawal underway; British economic power is being replaced by US investment and US economic power. As realization of this sinks in a change will come in Protestant attitudes. Paisley today speaks for these 'ordinary Protestants'. The Unionist monolith has broken up into different groups and parties and 'that's a hopeful sign'. The party believes in a secular, socialist Republic.[119]

Priests and Patriots

Dr Garret FitzGerald, leader of Fine Gael, the chief opposition party in the Republic, once suggested that the Provisionals had the support of the priests in the North against the Marxist Officials; that accounted for their success in 1969-70. Father Desmond Wilson, a Belfast priest, said in January 1972 that violence was justified in the North because the nationalist people had no recourse to courts or politics. 'I believe personally that no one in Ireland today has a right to condemn violence unless he is prepared at the same time to give us a reasonable alternative.'[120] The Provisionals, he told a Seminar at the national Catholic seminary, Maynooth, were driven to adopt a policy of force for lack of a better philosophy. Priests did not approve of some of their actions, such as bombing and shooting innocent people in cold blood, but their campaign was directed at the state, not Protestants.[121] The identification of priests (the Church) and patriots (the Provisionals) probably settled the ideological issue among most Northern Nationalists.

What makes a Provisional? This answer may be typical:

> I have most of my life been brought up in a Republican tradition. . . . . However, I grew up in a situation of such degradation and unemployment and humiliation that the life our people lived was just no life at all. I said to myself that when I grow up and get married I will want for my children something better than this.[122]

IRA leaders in the North, like the rank and file are of working-class or small-farmer background. Few come from the middle class, fewer are intellectuals.[123] Seamus Twomey, whose explanation is given above, was commander of the Belfast Brigade in the early 1970s during the period of heaviest fighting, and later became Chief of Staff of the Provisional IRA. He is in his late fifties and has spent many years in prison, a normal enough condition for a Belfast republican. (After the interview he went back to prison again, this time in the Republic).

'Our first prime and main objective is the unification of our country,' Twomey says. 'This means getting the British out of the occupied part of the country. After that the whole system in North and South would have to be changed.'

Twomey's politics are traditionalist and unsophisticated, as befits a man who grew up in Nationalist Belfast of the 1930s and spent much of the 1940s interned. He describes himself as 'a socialist . . . but at the same time a right-winger.' Still, 'some of my greatest comrades in the movement would have very left-wing tendencies'. But there was no division in the ranks because of this, he averred.[124] His basic ideology, one could assume is that all social and economic problems will be resolved when Ireland is united and free. Protestants see that as Catholic domination; as an ideology it undoubtedly has a strong Catholic content. It seeks to be loyal to Tone's ideas. But would Tone recognize it as Republicanism?

Twomey's successor, Gerry Adams, came to political maturity in the 1970s and his political ideas reflect the natural radicalization of an armed struggle conducted among the Catholic ghetto poor of Belfast and Derry. Consciously or not, he seems much closer to Connolly's 1913 analysis than other voices: 'And out of this struggle the Catholic has, perforce, learned toleration. He has learned that his struggle is, and has been, the struggle of all the lowly and dispossessed, and he has grown broadminded with the broadmindedness of the slave in revolt against slavery.'[125]

There are two ways to reach the Protestant workers, Adams says: the first is to convert the loyalists who are sustained by British force – the way adopted by the Officials; the second is to follow Connolly: to get rid of Britain, 'the prop that sustains loyalism'. Then you are in a situation where you can develop radical policies in an all-Ireland democracy. One must fight on two fronts, the national and the social.[126] So far, this view seems confined to Belfast, among the fighters, and may be a tendency rather than a coherently developed political philosophy. Time will tell. What is demonstrably true, however, as Brigadier Frank Kitson observes, is that guerilla struggles 'are fought in the last resort, in the minds of the people.'[127] What counts is the ideology and that has more to do with politics than with policies, however well drafted.

VII
Conclusions and Solutions

Since 1800 four attempts have been made to settle the Irish question. The first was the Act of Union, which bound Ireland to Great Britain under the British parliament and failed. The second was Home Rule, which the British parliament finally accepted in 1914, but never implemented because of the opposition of the Ulster Unionists; it ended in the partition of Ireland. The third was the Anglo-Irish Treaty of 1921, which created the Irish Free State and left the Northern Nationalists trapped under Protestant ascendancy. The fourth was the Sunningdale Agreement of 1973, which tried 'power-sharing', based on a consensus of Protestants and Catholics; it collapsed after five months.[1] A fifth 'settlement' is being attempted as this is written. Few believe it will succeed. If a settlement by consent fails, there must be an imposed settlement. What is the problem? In the view of the US Department of State it is this:

> In Northern Ireland, the British government is dealing with two sharply divided traditions, each with its own myths and stereotypes stemming from centuries of intermittent hostility and compounded by systematic campaigns of distortion and propaganda on both sides.[2]

Any settlement must take account of the ideologies of the two traditions and reconcile them, in so far as it can. The first is Irish nationalism, *viz.*, that Ireland is one country and should be an independent state; the second is the Protestant political doctrine (which may or may not be classified as 'Protestant nationalism'), 'to stand by one another in defending for ourselves and our children our cherished position of equal citizenship in the United Kingdom, and using all means which may be found necessary to defeat the present conspiracy to set up a Home Rule parliament in Ireland'.[3] That was written in 1912. It remains the basic political belief of the overwhelming majority of Ulster Protestants.

The Republic of Ireland In the 1980s

Unionists always saw the Irish struggle in religious terms, a conflict created, they believed, by the desire of Irish Catholics to disrupt the United Kingdom and the British Empire in order to establish their own parliament. In this view, the Catholics were the secessionists. The Unionists defended the 1801 Act of Union, saving six counties in Ulster from the designs of Irish nationalism. To consider Protestant Ulster a separate nation in an Ireland of two nations is to misunderstand Unionist intransigence. Ulster Protestants do not want to be a nation; they want to remain British.[4] But as Professor George O'Brien noted: 'A sentiment so deeply felt, so tenacious and so enduring, is not to be ignored. Irish nationalism is a fact that has to be reckoned with in any political dealings with Ireland.'[5] Its links with Catholicism are strong because it was a movement of the peasantry. Republican (physical-force) nationalism was a movement of the lower orders in the towns and of the emigrants in Britain and North America. Irish nationalism created a peasant movement, middle-class led, that won Catholic emancipation (1829), defeated landlordism (1880s) and established a nation-state (1921).

These victories were achieved under strong leaders: Daniel O'Connell, Charles Stewart Parnell and Eamon de Valera. All had more ambitious political goals. In O'Connell's case, it was repeal of the Union. In Parnell's case, Home Rule for all Ireland. In de Valera's case, a sovereign state for all Ireland. Each took Irish nationalism one step nearer its ultimate goal. Each would have been satisfied with a parliament for all Ireland. Each died in the knowledge that he had failed. There is no nationalist leader in Ireland today who approaches the personal authority of these men, or the feelings of near-idolatry they excited in their followers. They are examples of Max Weber's charismatic leaders, men who derived their authority from the masses through 'personal devotion and personal confidence'.[6] Each spoke for the Irish nation. They stood above parliament and Crown and, on occasion, even Church. O'Connell could denounce the popular violence of the anti-tithe movement and retain his authority. Parnell could condemn the Invincibles for the Phoenix Park assassinations in a time of coercion and, in effect, disband the Land League. De Valera could shoot and jail members of the IRA. It is one of the weaknesses of contemporary Irish nationalism that no similar authority exists to state its demands.

The Republic of Ireland is the creation of Irish nationalism and an example of how an ideology can change the status of a country from colony to nation-state. In this respect Ireland has been a headline for the so-called Third World. A movement of peasants and urban workers, led by a small Catholic middle-class of shopkeepers, lawyers, physicians, journalists – much like the leaders of constitutional nationalism in Northern Ireland today – was held together, not by a vague national sentiment but by a sense of economic oppression in Parnell's day, and by national oppression in 1917–21. Curiously, the economic prosperity of 1917–21 strengthened political nationalism. 'Militant nationalism,' Eric Strauss has remarked, 'became the ideology of the politically alert lower middle and working class, and radiated back into the villages where the new gospel was eagerly absorbed by the small tenants and landless men.'[7] The form of self-government was not the important issue: before 1916 nationalists would have been satisfied with Home Rule. They accepted the Treaty; de Valera's authority alone gave validity to the Republicans opposed to it. In the Civil War, de Valera lost some of that authority and from 1922 to 1926 was in the political wilderness. But by 1932 he had won the confidence of the Irish Free State electorate, despite the divisions of the Civil War. He never really lost it again, although he was denied office in 1948 and 1954 when all other parties combined against him.[8] One consequence of the Treaty was that, because of partition, the Irish Free State was a Catholic state. Had the Ulster Unionists taken their place in Ireland, as Ireland – rather than in the North as an outpost of British rule – this would not have occurred. Both Ulster Unionism and Irish nationalism shared the values of British constitutional democracy, if little else; with two parliaments and a Council of Ireland they might have created a more peaceful and prosperous country than today's Ireland.

Socially-radical republicanism had no influence during the 'War of Independence' (1919–21), although the tradition was there from Tone through Lalor, Davitt and Connolly. But these were individuals; they did not transmit their ideas to a movement. (This writer once asked Maire Comerford, a veteran of the independence struggle, why Irish socialism died with Connolly. 'Connolly was an engine without a train,' was her explanation.)[9] Because Catholic social thinking of a fairly reactionary kind dominated the new nation-state, all radicalism was considered the advance guard of Communism. Socially-radical republicanism might have received a hearing in de Valera's shadow in the 1930s had it gone about building a movement differently: what resulted was a split IRA, an ineffective Republican Congress – considered no more than a Communist front – and the slide backwards to pure republican militarism from 1938 to the 1960s. Clann na Poblachta raised the possibility of such a socially-radical party for a time; it destroyed itself by its inept handling of the Dr Browne 'mother and child' scheme. Had Clann challenged clerical interference in politics, instead of apparently condoning it, it would have gone down, but like Parnell – with its banner flying.

The victory of Sinn Féin in 1917–21 was political; it had no social dimension. The declarations of the First Dáil were window-dressing to appease Labour. Despite persistent Sinn Féin preaching about industrialization, the Free State did a minimum to nourish native industries. The new rulers prided themselves on their conservatism and their constitutional advances.[10] De Valera developed these and by 1939 he could confidently proclaim neutrality in the Second World War. The economic price was high and the small industrial gains of the 1930s were almost wiped out. Dublin and Belfast moved farther apart.

The First World War gave Irish farmers the highest income they had ever enjoyed. This prosperity ran from 1914 to 1920; the Irish state's birth coincided with an economic downturn. The condition of rural labourers was particularly bad. The state remained a British economic dependency: England was its agricultural market; England supplied it with consumer goods. Livestock was the cash crop and the source of capital accumulation – only the accumulation was in London. The most notable economic achievements of the 1920s were the Shannon hydro-electric scheme and a sugar beet factory in Carlow. The rural poor and the landless solved their problems by emigration: 25,000 to 30,000 left annually in a population of less than 3.5 million. There were no welfare services – the poor were left to charity and pauperism; and there was little change in the terrible conditions in Dublin's slums.

De Valera's assumption of office in 1932 coincided with the world depression. Cattle exports fell and were subsidized because prices fell too. Although industrial production rose 40 per cent between 1931 and 1936, protectionism created its own problems. After the Second World War the economy expanded again, then in the 1950s grew sluggish once more. Emigration rose and real national income stagnated.[11] In brief, independence had profited Ireland very little.

The real change in the Republic's economy coincided with de Valera's retirement from active politics in 1959 and the first five-year programme of economic expansion, 1958–63. Sinn Féin protectionism was abandoned and foreign investment invited, with generous tax concessions and factory space for firms willing to produce for export.[12] The multinational corporations saw the

Republic as a base to enter the EEC and picked up the invitation. In January 1973 the Republic joined the EEC, with Britain, and is now proclaimed as 'the most profitable base for US industry in Europe,' where 'the average rate of return on capital employed by US corporations in 1975 and 1976 was 29.5 per cent – almost 250 per cent the European average and better by far than any other European country.'[13] The Republic's economic growth is the highest in Europe.

The industrial drive, spearheaded by the multinationals, combined with the benefits farmers are gaining from the European Economic Community under the Common Agricultural Policy (CAP) which de Gaulle negotiated in 1965 to protect France's farmers,[14] has changed the face of Ireland. The dynamism of the Irish economy has drawn praise from Roy Jenkins, former British Chancellor of the Exchequer, the top official in Brussels, who says that many member-states might envy the pace of the Irish, who are now it seems, for the first time in their history, 'riding high.'[15] Ireland's undeveloped West draws heavily from the EEC's regional development funds, designed to raise living standards in backward areas.[16]

> During its first two years of membership of the European Community, Ireland received a total in grants and subsidies from the Community of approximately £114 million. In addition, it received more than £36 million in low interest loans from the European Investment Bank and the European Coal and Steel Community. The bulk of the money came from the Guarantee Section of FEOGA (the Farm Fund) to support Intervention, but grants and subsidies were also approved from the Guidance Section (almost £4 million), from the European Social Fund (approximately £7.5 million) and for various regional studies, all of which went towards helping combat some of Ireland's regional problems.[17]

The result is that today fewer people work in agriculture than in industry in the Republic; late marriages – once a problem of the countryside – are disappearing; emigration has ceased, except for the 'brain drain', and most of the population is under twenty-five years of age. Ireland, a developing nation, is transforming itself from a Third World to a First World state.[18] To achieve this, the Republic of Ireland has followed the capitalist road. It has given the multinational companies a base to sell their products in the European Community as Irish products, which doubtless they are, having been produced by Irish labour.

For the Republic, membership in the Common Market has been all gains – except for high food prices in the towns. Economic dependence on Britain is over. Britain's cheap food policy kept

Ireland poor. The EEC's agricultural protection policy is making Ireland rich; or at least it is making Ireland's farmers rich, which is no longer the same thing.

It would seem that the Irish nation-state has achieved its political and economic goals, although many express doubts about industrialization through the use of multinational industries that are capital-intensive rather than labour-intensive. Unemployment in the Republic is alarmingly high. Some multinational corporations close down and go elsewhere when recession threatens. These industries 'import most of their raw materials and have few backward or forward linkages with domestic industries'. Their contribution 'to employment has been relatively small'. Since profits can be repatriated they make little contribution to the balance of payments. Because of the absence of 'linkages with the rest of the economy' they may actually hinder development. Using multinationals in this way 'implies a failure to build on the country's natural advantages in activities like food processing and mineral processing, which would secure a greater regional diffusion of the benefits of industrial development. Greater linkages would help to develop a larger pool of native entrepreneurs.'[19]

One argument against membership of the EEC is that the Republic must surrender to Brussels some of its hard-won sovereignty. At present the important economic decisions are made in Brussels, not in Dublin, and at some point it is inevitable that the political decisions will be made there too. The EEC is attempting by means of functional unity to develop political unity and has reached the stage of having a parliament, although a virtually powerless one. This will change. As Hans Morgenthau noted:

> Once all the functional organizations have been established as going concerns, sovereignty will have been transferred in fact to a common European government by gradual steps, without the individual nations really being aware of it.[20]

If nationalist ideology is less important in the Republic of Ireland today the reason may be that it has fulfilled its function and is needed no more. Certainly it is not needed in the Sinn Féin sense of the term. The nation-state exists and has taken its place beside West Germany, France, Holland, Belgium, Italy, Luxembourg, Denmark and Great Britain in the European community, by virtue of its long struggle for national sovereignty. Culturally, there is little difference between England and Ireland today. The Gaelic revival is dead. The small-farmer class, the repository of the nationalist tradition, is dying. There may be a law of national development operating here: when the economy 'takes off', nationalism declines. Nationalism created the conditions for industrial development through its offspring, the nation-state. Industrialization means modernization and the end of the peasantry. The Republic is a modern state with a growing economy and a standard of living on a level with Britain. For its middle class, life is much as in other Western states. Censorship has disappeared. Contraceptives are being legalized despite Church displeasure. Western bourgeois values of the post-Christian era are beginning to prevail.

In such an era, it may be argued, it is anachronistic to think that religious, communal or national differences will be more powerful than the integrative forces based on economic and political co-operation existing in Europe. Here then is one possible solution to the Irish question: some form of unity within the EEC.

Religion and Nationalism

There are two forces one should not underestimate in Irish politics: the Catholic Church and the ideology of nationalism. It may be that the Republic would prefer not to tackle the thorny question of Northern Ireland, but it is a problem that will not go away.

The Fianna Fáil party wants 'to secure, by peaceful means, the unity and independence of Ireland as a democratic republic'. Fianna Fáil is the fount of traditional nationalism, populism and undoctrinaire republicanism. De Valera is its founding father. It is the largest party in the state. Fianna Fáil rejects force, but urges Britain to encourage unity 'by agreement' and 'to implement an ordered withdrawal from her involvement in the Six Counties of Northern Ireland'. As an interim step, Fianna Fáil would accept devolved government in the North, with political institutions to assure civil rights and security. Constitutional and legal problems would be resolved with Northern representatives on the basis of 'goodwill and understanding'; an all-Ireland court, with appropriate machinery, would uphold fundamental rights and 'ensure the maintenance of peace and security'. The wording is deliberately vague, except for the clause that says Britain should guarantee 'appropriate financial support for a specified period to enable the transition to take place smoothly in stable and economic conditions'.[21]

Fine Gael, the main opposition in the Republic, began as the Treatyite party and has always been close to Britain. Under Prime Minister Liam Cosgrave it was willing to permit the North to remain within the United Kingdom indefinitely, and to scrap Articles 2 and

3 of the Republic's Constitution which claim all Ireland as the national territory. Eliminating these clauses would involve a referendum which Cosgrave was afraid he would not win.[22] In the general election of 1977, Cosgrave and his coalition government were soundly defeated and his attitude and that of his ministers to the Northern problem may have had much to do with the defeat. Conor Cruise O'Brien, the Labour Minister for Posts and Telegraphs, considered the chief appeaser of intransigent Unionism, lost his seat, as did the Fine Gael Minister for Justice, Patrick Cooney, responsible for harsh measures against the Provisional IRA. Despite the new prosperity of the EEC – and the problems that went with it – these results indicated that the old nationalist ideology was not yet dead.

Following the election debacle, Cosgrave quit as party leader and was succeeded by Dr Garret FitzGerald, who, in February 1979, issued a detailed proposal on a limited confederation of North and South within the EEC. The confederal authority would be responsible for security, foreign affairs and some financial matters. London, Washington and Brussels would give financial assistance until the new system found its feet. FitzGerald, an economist, made the important point that the North would be better served today linking itself to 'the dynamic economy of the Republic rather than the, relatively speaking, declining British economy'.

The forty-four-page document spoke of 'a new relationship ... between North and South' resulting from such a system, but Unionists remain suspicious. The Fine Gael plan, nevertheless, has received more attention from Belfast and London than any other similar statement by a political group in the South.[23]

On 21 May 1980, the new Taoiseach, Charles Haughey, held talks with Mrs Thatcher, the British Prime Minister, on Northern Ireland ostensibly, but in fact to establish some kind of relationship between the heads of government. Mrs Thatcher made it clear before the two met that the constitutional position of the North was an internal British matter. Nothing changed with the talks.

The Irish-American Dimension

Whatever settlement is arrived at on Northern Ireland must be accepted by most Unionists, most Nationalists, and guaranteed by the Irish, British and US governments. The Protestant Ulster Defence dimension' is assuming importance. The Protestant Ulster Defence Association, which seeks an independent Northern Ireland, wants the United States to guarantee the security of the new state *vis-à-vis* the Irish Republic.[24]

Irish-American politicians have become increasingly involved in the problem, not only because of their background and the sentiments of their constituents, but because of Irish-America's traditional role in the struggle for an independent Ireland. The Provisional IRA initially won the backing of many Irish-Americans because it was a Catholic defence force, was anti-Communist, and was fighting for 'Irish unity and independence' – in effect for 'the old cause'. Both London and Dublin were alarmed by the extent of IRA aid, in funds and guns, and appeals were made to Irish-American leaders to denounce violence. The support body of the Provisional IRA in America, Irish Northern Aid, established the Irish National Caucus as an umbrella group to lobby legislators on behalf of a united Ireland. Its chief Capitol Hill supporter, Congressman Mario Biaggi, a conservative Democrat from the Bronx, set up the Ad Hoc Committee on Irish Affairs, which sought to interest Congress in the Irish problem. The Irish National Caucus, under Rev. Seán McManus, a Co. Fermanagh priest in Washington, gradually severed the guiding reins of Irish Northern Aid and went its own way, supported by conservative Irish-Americans who did not wish to be associated with gun-running or explosions and generally following the line of Father Denis Faul's Association for Legal Justice in Northern Ireland.

On 17 March 1977, Senator Kennedy, Speaker Tip O'Neill, Governor Hugh Carey and Senator D.P. Moynihan, issued a statement condemning IRA violence and calling on Irish-Americans to give no money or encouragement to terrorism. The statement was repeated a year later. In 1979 the statement switched emphasis: instead of blaming the Provisionals and Irish-American money for the violence in Northern Ireland, it blamed Britain's lack of interest in a settlement. A settlement, they believed, must involve some form of a united Ireland. 'We're dissatisfied with the lack of progress by the British government,' said Governor Carey. In 1980 the four, supported by other Irish-American politicians, urged Britain to declare for a united Ireland.[25]

The man most responsible for interesting Irish-American politicians in pressing for a Northern Ireland settlement is John Hume, leader of the Social Democratic and Labour Party, founded in August 1970 'to promote the cause of Irish unity based on the consent of the majority of people in Northern Ireland.'[26] The SDLP is the constitutional voice of the Nationalist community. The Sunningdale Agreement on 'power-sharing' satisfied the leaders of the SDLP and 94 per cent of the Nationalist community, according to opinion polls.

Hume's approach remains non-violent, but he is also aware that Unionist intransigence will continue while the hardliners believe Britain will support them. Speaker Tip O'Neill went to England and Ireland in April 1979 during the British general election; in a Dublin speech he said Northern Ireland was being treated as a 'political football' by Conservatives and Socialists.[27] This caused a storm in Britain, which was aggravated by Governor Carey: he suggested Rhodesia-style sanctions by the U.S. Congress against Britain unless an attempt was made to settle the Northern Ireland problem. The Conservatives won and in December 1979 Prime Minister Margaret Thatcher called a constitutional conference in Northern Ireland which, although it came to nothing, was an effort to meet Irish-American criticism. Meanwhile Britain continues to insist that Northern Ireland is an 'internal problem', which is the official U.S. view also.[28]

Ending Violence

Violence involves three parties: the Provisional IRA and its sometime allies of the Irish Republican Socialist Party; the Ulster Defence Association and other Protestant paramilitary groups; the British security forces. The violence of the Provisionals is directed against the British to secure a statement of intent to withdraw from Northern Ireland; it sometimes carries out reprisals for the killing of Catholics. The UDA had not participated in violence for a number of years before the assassination of Lord Mountbatten in August 1979, it claimed, but reserves its right to change its mind on this. In fact it uses fronts and other Protestant paramilitary groups for its sanguinary operations. Overt British army violence is aimed at restoring 'law and order' by defeating terrorism, meaning the Provisional IRA.

The Provisional IRA is a Belfast phenomenon. It would not exist without Belfast. It could not carry on its war without Belfast. Its tactical decisions are made in Belfast. The armed movement in the rest of the North looks to Belfast for leadership. Support may come from the Republic in the form of arms and propaganda, but Belfast is the heart of the struggle. Brian Faulkner understood this when he told Prime Minister Edward Heath that 'the core of the problem [was] the 200,000 Catholics in Belfast'.[29] To use Mao's well-known analogy, the Catholics are the sea in which the Provo fish swim. Such a situation has not existed in previous Irish rebellions, not even in the Dublin of 1919–21. Faulkner was the first to analyze the change. The old tactics of terrorizing the Catholics could not work in the 1970s; the Provisionals could continue to operate while that support was maintained.

At the same Cabinet meeting, Lord Home, former Prime Minister and Heath's Foreign Secretary, asked Faulkner what effect removing troops from Catholic areas would have. 'And I said it would mean surrendering the people of those areas into the control of the IRA.' When Reginald Maudling said 'time was running against us', Faulkner quoted General Harry Tuzo, commander of British forces in the North, 'that the IRA in Belfast would be under control by the end of March. . .'.[30] Military men have a habit of making exaggerated statements in counter-insurgency situations. Through the 1970s British Ministers of State, relying on the estimates of military advisers, would periodically announce the imminent defeat of the Provisional IRA. If some way could have been found to remove the 200,000 Catholics from Belfast, no doubt 'the security problem' would have been solved.

An example of the military mind at work is Richard Clutterbuck's *Protest and the Urban Guerrilla.*[31] Dr Clutterbuck retired from the British army in November 1972 with the rank of Major-General, having served in four major insurgencies: Palestine, Trieste, Malaya and Singapore. He took up a lectureship in 'International Politics, Political Violence and Revolution' at the University of Exeter. His book is mainly about Northern Ireland and he is well briefed on the subject – by the military. He notes that in early 1972 'the IRA organization was beginning to collapse'.[32] He makes the common error of confusing IRA organizational strength with organizational support: if support for the IRA is strong, then the IRA is strong. He speaks of the low intelligence of IRA commanders;[33] but if their intelligence was so inferior, what is one to say of the intelligence of those who could not defeat them after a decade of trying?

Finally, he insists that Derry's 'Bloody Sunday', 30 January, 1972, in which thirteen civil rights marchers were killed, was 'a gun battle'.[34] The shooting was one-sided, non-military witnesses agreed. Father Edward Daly saw civilians with arms, but they did not use them and they were not marchers. None of the victims had a weapon, a matter Dr Clutterbuck omits to mention. 'This leads to a much deeper moral question,' says Dr Clutterbuck.

> Over half of those killed were under twenty. Six were only seventeen. Whether or not these six were members of the 'Derry Young Hooligans', the existence of such a force was not in question. . . .They placed their lives in the hands of the soldiers and capitalized on their restraints and discipline. . . .[35]

(Who must answer the moral question?) Witnesses agree with Sam

Dash's report which says army vehicles raced ahead of the civilians to cut them off in order to arrest them.

> But, the crowd of civilians started to run as soon as the vehicles were sighted. Some of the civilians ran up to Rossville Street in the direction of Free Derry Corner and others ran across the vacant lot in the direction of Rossville Flats. The testimony is clear, at this point, that the civilians were running not because they were fearful of being shot, but because they wanted to avoid being involved in the arrest operation, with its expected attendant use of rubber bullets and tear gas. According to most of the civilian eyewitnesses, within seconds after the vehicles came to a halt and the paratroopers jumped out, the shooting of live rounds by the paratroopers began. About thirty minutes later, it was all over, leaving twenty-six known civilians struck by army bullets, thirteen of whom died, and the other thirteen were wounded. No paratrooper was killed or wounded.[36]

Why not, if there was a gun battle? '. . .but the IRA shot badly and the soldiers shot well, used cover well and covered each other well,' explains Dr Clutterbuck.[37]

The Derry killings united nationalist Ireland. A demonstration in Dublin ended in the burning of the British Embassy. John Hume saw a united Ireland as the only answer. Conor Cruise O'Brien told the Home Secretary, Reginald Maudling, that his government should set a date for withdrawal, a course O'Brien had opposed.[38] Bernadette Devlin scratched Maudling's face in the House of Commons. Workers closed factories in the Republic and British aircraft were blacked at Irish airports. The *Financial Times* said 'a Pandora's Box of nationalism' had been opened up by the Derry shootings. There were protests in America. Cardinal Cooke of New York celebrated Mass at St Patrick's Cathedral for the victims. The *Times* of London said 'public opinion was shaken'.[39] The British government suspended Stormont a few weeks after 'Bloody Sunday'.

Less than six months later the Provisionals almost reversed the national mood. In Belfast, on 21 July, following the breakdown of a truce, their bombs killed nine persons, including two soldiers, and wounded 130 civilians.[40] The Provisionals insisted that three warnings were given for each bomb placed. Ten days later troops swept into 'Free Belfast' and 'Free Derry', the so-called 'no-go areas' cleared of security forces in August 1969. On the same day three car bombs exploded without warning in the village of Claudy and six people died. 'We seemed at last to be set on the road back to political dialogue, with the IRA effectively isolated,' commented Brian Faulkner.[41]

Britain's best counter-insurgency expert, Brigadier Frank Kitson, served as army commander in Belfast for part of 1971–72, and his observations, not intended particularly for Northern Ireland, suggest that there is no military solution for the kind of political problem that exists there.

> . . .the main characteristic which distinguishes campaigns of insurgency from other forms of war are primarily concerned with the struggle for men's minds, since only by succeeding in such a struggle with a large enough number of people can the rule of law be undermined and constitutional institutions overthrown.[42]

The 'struggle for men's minds' has to do with ideology, for it involves a people's view of politics. In Northern Ireland, minds are set and unlikely to change. The ideology is settled. When the political reality changes the ideology will change, not before. After all, ideology reflects and distorts reality.

Insurgency for Kitson is 'armed propaganda', which it is when rightly conducted. The Nationalist minority in the North can veto solutions; it cannot impose a solution. The Provisionals are well armed and highly motivated, according to the British intelligence estimate of their capabilities, and they can keep going for years. 'Any peace will be superficial and brittle', states the estimate. 'A new campaign may well erupt in the years ahead.'[43] Nevertheless, the Provisionals cannot achieve victory, if victory means a thirty-two county Irish Republic, federal or unitary. A minority will not prevail over a determined majority.

Like the IRA, the Ulster Defence Association can veto a solution, as it vetoed Sunningdale, but is unlikely to achieve an independent Northern Ireland. The UDA claims to speak for the Protestant working class of Belfast, and perhaps it does. It has no political organization. For its solution to work, most nationalists would have to accept it. At present, most reject it.[44] Could an independent Northern Ireland survive? Not at present, but if it was acceptable to both communities, London and Washington would help financially. There are poorer 'independent' states in the world than Northern Ireland. An independent Northern Ireland would remain in the British Commonwealth, its sponsors say.

The idea of an independent Northern Ireland may be a passing fad, like the Women's Peace Movement.[45] Or it may have a political reality based on the experiences of Protestant working-class Belfast. As for Nationalist acceptance of the scheme, most would probably agree with Ben Caraher's view:

> Neither side recognises Northern Ireland as a legitimate political unit, i.e.,

one within which a majority decision is accepted by all. Nationalists regard the area as one designed to make them a permanent minority. Loyalists, by their insistence on majority rule, appear to regard the area as a legitimate unit but, in fact, they do not. If demographic change produced a new majority in favour of union with the Republic, Loyalists would not accept this decision. They would simply demand that the Border be redrawn.

To be blunt, there is no prospect of such a political unit developing the cohesion and stability which would be required to enable it to survive as an independent State. It would inevitably fall apart, to be followed by repartition. An independent Ulster makes sense only as a Loyalist-dominated state.[46]

Paisley's ideology is Protestant evangelicalism. In 1971 he hinted that he could accept a united Ireland, provided the constitution were stripped of its Catholic clauses. He backed away quickly when Faulkner taunted him on it. Later he favoured 'direct rule' by Britain; then changed his mind. Later again he wanted Stormont restored. Paisley's biggest political achievement was to drive the land-owning gentry out of Unionist politics. He, too, retains a veto on a settlement: if he does not like it he can kill it. Paisley remains the most popular Protestant politician in the North of Ireland. His support for a settlement is essential to its acceptance by the Protestant community. A proposal emanating from the Protestant community, but without popular support, is associated with Surgeon John Robb, who has contributed some original ideas to the Irish question and how to solve it. Robb favours autonomy for Northern Ireland within a federal Ireland.

Autonomy – Ourselves with others rather than ourselves alone. I believe that the new federal Ireland out of which such a confederation could grow will start when the men of the North sicken of their dependence under a dynasty of direct rulers and seek to create the new way forward on the anvil of our own first negotiated independence.[47]

The Republic should forego all claim to the North so that the people there may debate in convention, 'freely, without duress or uncertainty, their future as it related to the island of Ireland'.[48] A federal Ireland, he points out, cannot be a Catholic Ireland, even in the form of its laws, because a Catholic Ireland and a united Ireland are incompatible.

The Official Unionist Party insists on the restoration of Stormont, which it calls 'the simple majority rule in Ulster'. What is Ulster? Ben Caraher's definition is concise and accurate: 'The largest area which could be safely guaranteed a Protestant majority in 1920.'[49] The Nationalists will not accept that formula. The minimum they will accept is power-sharing, although the form this will take is open to bargaining, and there must be some kind of 'Irish dimension' as a step to eventual unity 'by consent'.

Wolfe Tone's Ireland

The logical and sensible solution to the Irish question is Theobald Wolfe Tone's 1790s theory of a secular republic. Anything less must create a religious minority, or minorities, because of political Protestantism in the North that insists on monopolizing power and keeping Catholics underfoot and of Catholic bishops in the South who seek to enforce Catholic morality on everyone. Ulster Catholics will not accept the first and Ulster Protestants will not accept the second. Two forces stood guard against Tone's secular republic: the British government and the Catholic Church. The result was two confessional states in Ireland and a partitioned island.

Has Tone's formula any relevance today? Probably not: the material conditions which led to the rise of the United Irishmen in the era of the Industrial Revolution have changed completely. No economic interest now sees a united independent Ireland as relevant to its own prosperity. The rising business class in the Republic looks on the North as a drag on its own growth. The Protestant working class of Belfast is far too frightened of the political power of the Roman Catholic Church to accept a united Ireland. The Catholic bishops still demand the right to speak for 'the majority' on 'moral issues'; this means insisting on Catholic social teaching as the guide-rules for 'a Catholic state'. Bishop Jeremiah Newman, of Limerick, a modern, enlightened prelate, insists that Ireland must live by Catholic dogma. But Protestants cannot accept such a state; indeed will not accept such a state. Bishop Newman will not accept a secular state.

> One of the most annoying, frustrating and indeed dangerous features of contemporary Irish life is the way in which a self-opinionated and self-appointed minority is striving to force its view on a passive Irish public, on a people who wish for nothing better than to continue to live decent Irish and Christian lives such as they have known and to be afforded the socio-legal framework that will support them in doing so. Certainly the people whom I have met since I returned to Limerick – whether rich or poor – have, generally speaking, no hankering after a secular or internationalist Ireland of a kind that would progressively forget the things of fatherland and of God.[50]

In this age, nationalism is closely associated with militant religion, as in the Islamic revolution in Iran. Irish nationalism in the North of Ireland demonstrably is Catholic and priest-influenced. Bishop Newman's 'fatherland' is not Tone's Republic. The bishop may be closer to modern militant Irish nationalism in his ideological views than modern militant Irish nationalism is to Wolfe Tone's ideology. Tone was a secular internationalist of the kind the bishop deplores. By following the traditionalist path, the Irish people, Bishop Newman says, 'will be contributing to the buttressing of Western society in its present weakest dimension – the ideological'.[51]

This traditional nationalism is a strong force. Its links with religion were forged in a time of oppression, but it is not the political arm of the Catholic Church. Because of the nature of Northern Ireland society, priests and people are close, a defensive mechanism that would change in a 'normal' state, as it is changing in the Republic of Ireland. However, when traditional nationalism becomes the ideology of a state, as Bishop Newman demands, then it is a threat to Protestantism and is rightly seen as such. This is what the Protestant of the North rejects, not the secular ideology of the United Irishmen. (Nationalism is of course a secular religion.)

It is true that traditional nationalism in Ireland has never been anti-Protestant in a religious sense, or in the sense, for example, that evangelical Protestantism, of the Paisleyite variety, is steeped in anti-Catholicism. To this Reformationist zeal is added the fervour of the colonist, albeit one with deep roots in Ulster, who must guard the frontier against the savage native – who also happens to be a Papist.

This may be dismissed as exaggeration. But consider Ian Paisley, a representative type – representative in the sense that he is the one constant in the ever-changing *dramatis personae* of Northern Ireland politics over a twenty-year span – whose popularity as the voice of Ulster Protestantism is growing not declining. The Ulster colony was less than forty years old when the Irish rebellion of 1641 broke out. Paisley's description of that event is part of the mythology of Protestant colonialism:

> In 1641 the Roman Catholic Church decided to exterminate the Protestants in Ulster, and there took place one of the most barbarous and bloody massacres in Irish history. It was led by the priests of the Roman Catholic Church and the rivers of Ulster ran red with Protestant blood. In the town of Portadown, the River Bann was so choked with Protestant bodies that the Roman Catholics could walk dry-shod across the river.[52]

Paisley is no historian. This matter has been dealt with by W.E.H. Lecky in the first volume of his five-volume *History of Ireland in the Eighteenth Century*, using contemporary sources. Lecky, a professor at Trinity College, Dublin, an Irish Protestant and a Unionist member of parliament, after noting various statements on the numbers killed, varying from 50,000 to 300,000, adds:

> It may be boldly asserted that this statement of a sudden surprise, immediately followed by a general and well-organized massacre, is utterly and absolutely untrue. As is almost always the case in a great popular rising, there were, in the first outbreak of the rebellion, some murders, but they were very few; and there was at this time nothing whatever of the nature of a massacre.[53]

The rebellion broke out in the counties colonized a generation before; the settlers were driven from their homes, 'and their expulsion was soon accompanied by horrible barbarities'.[54] Only the English settlers were harmed; the Scots were at first left alone. The English settlers died 'from cold, and want, and hardship'.[55]

Paisley was questioned by the Scarman Tribunal on the propriety of repeating such stories, 328 years later, in a time of communal strife. Judge Scarman wondered if 1969 was a suitable time 'to remind Northern Irishmen, and others, about 1641'? He suggested that where there are two communities who see themselves threatened at a time of tension, 'is it not up to the leaders of each to exercise restraint?' That was what he was doing, Paisley said, in effect:

> It was better for the people to have attended a meeting of mine to hear straight speaking and then to leave and go home than have this pent up energy in their minds knowing that nobody was voicing the things that they felt should be voiced at that particular time, and I believe that I was a safety valve for this community.'[56]

If Paisley were merely a dangerous demagogue, matters would be bad enough. But he speaks for a bedrock of Protestant opinion, among the poor. He is a member of the British parliament and of the European parliament. Two members of his Democratic Unionist Party also sit in the British House of Commons for Northern Ireland constituencies.

Paisley mixes religion and politics in a sixteenth-century way and it is often impossible to tell which is which. The pass must be guarded against Papists. 'John Knox said that he feared one Mass in Scotland more than a regiment of the enemy,' Paisley told Queen Elizabeth.

> Your subjects fear the result of the proposed welcome of this idolatrous Mass-mongering representative of the Papal Antichrist and look to you to fulfill for them the words of the prophecy of Isaiah concerning the Church in Chapter 49, Verse 23 – 'And kings shall be thy nursing fathers, and their queens thy nursing mothers.[57]

These fundamentalist beliefs, couched in Biblical language and directed at Catholic enemies, are rooted in the ideology of Protestant working-class Belfast (and to a lesser extent other towns of the North) with its numerous churches, chapels, mission halls. Paisley voices their feelings that the Northern conflict is essentially religious, a direct attack on their values. These values cover a variety of matters, including loyalty to the Crown and 'the Protestant succession', the British way of life, the Puritan work ethic, the virtues of the Reformation, the vices of Rome. Defence of 'the Constitution' is defence of Protestantism. On the positive side, Paisley voices some of their social woes. His movement, however, despite his chameleon-like political changes and populist oratory, is essentially reactionary and backward.

The Protestant paramiliatry groups do not follow Paisley's leadership, but they admire him and would like to win his support for an independent Ulster. It is possible he may one day follow that path, although unlikely. He has never been consistent politically and is unpredictable. Strangely, Paisley is both feared and liked by Catholics: he is very much the plain Ulsterman in contrast to the land-owning gentry class who ruled the North in the past and were indistinguishable from the English aristocracy. Paisley says he is not against Catholics as such: his enemy is the Pope of Rome. The gulf between Paisley and the Catholic community is not unbridgeable, but he is unlikely to stray far from Reformation politics. Like the Reverend George Walker, who inspired and led the defenders of Londonderry after Governor Lundy wanted to surrender, Paisley will continue to carry the banner 'in defence of the interest of K. *William* and Q. *Mary*, and the *Protestant Religion*, against the enemies of both'.[58]

That of course is ideology. We have learned, however, that ideology, too, must take note of political reality. It may be forced to come to terms with political reality. In the North of Ireland the reality is that Britain can no longer play its old role. Once that is removed the political balance changes. The other reality has been pointed out by John Robb. He sees the critical confrontation between the two communities occurring when the North's population reaches 'the fifty-fifty flashpoint.'[59] Already 50 per cent of the under-fifteen population is Catholic. The concept of the democratic right of the majority to rule is fine while one is part of the majority. What is to be done when this is no longer true? Redraw the border? And keep redrawing it until Protestant Ulster is truly a laager? Or expel the Catholics? (This last it seems is no longer an option, and neither perhaps is the redrawing of boundaries.)

Peace in the North, and that means peace in Ireland, must involve some form of agreement between the Provisional IRA and the UDA on what will happen on the day after the British withdraw. An attempt to reach such an understanding occurred in 1975–6 when the Provisionals and the Ulster Unionist Council Co-Ordinating Committee held a series of meetings and agreed that Seán MacBride and Desmond Boal, a longtime associate of Ian Paisley, should continue the discussions as 'technical advisers'. According to Mr MacBride, 'we both said yes, on condition that we were acceptable to both sides, and we were acceptable to both sides.'[60] The initiative collapsed when the Dublin government learned of it and denounced it. MacBride's view was that violence would end only 'when both sides agree to stop shooting and to discuss a long-term solution', which is why he participated in the talks.[61] One matter both sides agreed on was a British withdrawal.[62] The abortive talks may have been one of the missed opportunities in the 1970s.

In *Labour in Irish History*, James Connolly praised the role of the 'Prentice Boys' of Derry 'in determining the attitude of that city towards the contending English Kings' in 1689.[63] George Gilmore, an Irish Republican who stems from the same Ulster Protestant tradition, argues: 'When the 'Prentice Boys slammed the gates in the face of the King of England they set in motion a stream of events that led their great grandchildren to found the independence movement (the United Irishmen) in 1791. They repudiated the divine right of hereditary monarchy and supported the King of their own choice who, they fondly hoped, would give them the liberties they sought.'[64] Both Connolly and Gilmore saw the actions of the 'Prentice Boys' in class terms; hence it is not out of the question that in the closing years of the twentieth century the descendants of the 'Prentice Boys' could make a social and political contract, 'of their own choice', with their fellow-Irish, precisely because their economic interests are not now bound up with England.

Outsiders are more hopeful about reconciliation between the traditions or ideologies in Ireland. An American Jesuit sees 'a new sensitivity towards the beliefs and traditions of others' in pronouncements by Irish Catholic bishops. 'Political leaders in both North and South talk of respecting the identity of different traditions or communities.'[65] The English Catholic review, *The Tablet*, says, 'The improbability today in Ireland is a massive reconciliation of North and South, but reconciliation may be nearer than we think. . . .'[66]

British intelligence, in considering 'the likely developments in the political life of the Province' over the next five years, suggested a number of possible scenarios. These included continued direct rule, devolved government, independence, and the emergence of 'a new party based on socialist policies transcending sectarian barriers. It thought this last unlikeliest of all because 'similar attempts since 1922 have always ended in failure'. The estimate adds: 'In Ireland the appeal of sectarian and nationalistic sentiment has always been stronger than that of left wing ideology. The continuing polarisation of the population on sectarian lines only emphasises the improbability of such an initiative.' [67]

This is quite true. Class politics never took root in the North, which makes Belfast different from other industrial cities in the United Kingdom. Protestant workers agree with their masters on the constitutional issue and vote Unionist by and large. Even socialists split on 'the Constitution', as we have seen. Some Protestant trade union leaders have followed Connolly's socialism, but the industrial rank and file in Belfast reject the class struggle. As always the argument is that 'the Constitution' – meaning the British connection – takes precedence over all other issues.

Britain no longer has an economic stake in the North: it costs the British Exchequer more than £1,000 million a year. Britain may still have a strategic interest in Ireland, as the 1949 Cabinet memorandum on the consequences of 'Eire's ceasing to be a member of the Commonwealth' suggests.

> Now that Eire will shortly cease to owe any allegiance to the Crown, it has become a matter of first-class strategic importance to this country that the North should continue to form part of His Majesty's dominions. So far as can be foreseen, it will never be to Great Britain's advantage that Northern Ireland should form part of a territory outside His Majesty's jurisdiction. Indeed, it seems unlikely that Great Britain would ever be able to agree to this even if the people of Northern Ireland desired it. There should therefore be no political difficulty, as circumstances now are, in giving a binding assurance that Northern Ireland shall never be excluded from the United Kingdom without her full and free consent. And, from the point of view of satisfying public opinion, not only in Northern Ireland but in this country also, there is positive political advantage in doing everything possible at this stage to strengthen the position of the North. [68]

Britain does have a political stake in the North because of her guarantee to the Protestants of Ulster that Northern Ireland shall remain part of the United Kingdom for as long as they desire it. The guarantee itself puts Britain in the position of having to use force against Irish nationalism, as has happened every decade since the Northern Ireland state was established. Because the guarantee is backed by force, many Nationalists maintain it can be changed only by force. Thus force is used against it, however hopeless may seem the odds. But, more important, the existence of the guarantee means that Ulster Protestants will not deal with the realities of political life in Ireland; their intransigence means that they must always prevail because they have Britain behind them. And it has provided the basis, as John Hume observed, 'of injustice, discrimination and repressive law, a situation in which the minority community [the one-third Catholics] have been the persistent losers and victims'.[69]

Jack Bennett, a Belfast Protestant republican and socialist, holds that the partition of Ireland and the creation of the Northern state denied Ireland the right of self-determination and democracy, and the solution is a British withdrawal from Irish affairs so that 'one sovereign government for all Ireland' will be established. In such an Ireland, he believes, Ulster Protestants would have the political and economic power to get 'the constitution they wanted and the freedoms they claim', in a balance of power arrangement that would keep any group from winning ascendancy.[69] This solution is similar to James Madison's prescription for maintaining representative government despite conflicting interests.[70]

The British guarantee is a veto over Ireland's right to nationhood. It constitutes interference in the affairs of one country by another. As such it is an international issue, no matter what Britain says about its being an 'internal problem'. No 'solution' based on *pax Britannica* can succeed.[71]

'Time works in Ireland's favour,' a Soviet television documentary on the island recently noted.[72] The Soviet Union has followed Ireland's troubles with sympathetic interest, but outwardly has not intervened. In the early 1970s the Soviet authorities offered more concrete aid to the Official IRA, then engaged in 'defensive operations' against the Crown. Quite suddenly the Russians changed their minds.[73] In May 1972 the Officials declared a unilateral ceasefire and the question of aiding 'the forces of Irish liberation' did not arise again. Soviet support for an anti-British guerrilla movement in Ireland would threaten the balance of power in the North Atlantic and might have led to a speedier resolution of the 'Irish question'. It might also have led to a major international crisis.

The ideology of Irish nationalism will continue to ripple the political waters until its conception of nationhood is achieved: when all in Ireland can live as citizens under their own government in their own state. To be true to its vision it must support equally the rights of Protestants to full citizenship as well as those of Catholics. There is in Ireland what Montesquieu called a 'general spirit' which all share, or at least have inherited: a history, a culture, a way of life, and – once the religious barriers are removed – a sense of how a society should be governed based on the common good. The state in Ireland must be secular, else it will dissolve in civil strife. Religion must be a matter of conscience, not of citizenship.

The nation-state is built by ideology, but its end is commerce, to 'fumble in a greasy till', as Yeats said. Once that is done, the vision – the ideology – fades away and the poet can ask:

> Was it for this the wild geese spread
> The grey wing upon every tide;
> For this that all that blood was shed,
> For this Edward Fitzgerald died,
> And Robert Emmet and Wolfe Tone,
> All that delirium of the brave?
> Romantic Ireland's dead and gone,
> It's with O'Leary in the grave.[74]

Notes

The research for this book was largely done in the USA – thus bibliographical references in the footnotes do not, occasionally, include European editions. To facilitate the reader the publisher has, where possible, included information on European editions in the Select Bibliography.

CHAPTER I

1. W.E.H. Lecky, *A History of Ireland in the Eighteenth Century* (London: 1913), iii, 24–5.
2. *The Shorter Oxford English Dictionary* (Oxford: 1965) gives the currency of the word as 1844 while the usage is associated with Ireland. A nationalist is 'One who advocates the claims of Ireland to be an independent nation **1846.**'
3. Hans Morgenthau, *Politics Among Nations* (New York: 1973), 5th ed., p. 160.
4. *Ibid.*
5. *Irish Historical Documents, 1172-1922*, ed. Edmund Curtis and R.B. McDowell, (London & New York: 1968), 'The Bull Laudabiliter', pp. 17-18. Adrian IV's successor, Alexander III, denounced the Irish as 'barbarous' and 'uncivilized' and ordered them to obey Henry under threat of excommunication.

   > If then you should carry your project into effect [the Bull *Laudabiliter* continues], let it be your care to instruct that people in good ways of life, and so act, both in person and by agents whom you shall have found in faith, in word, and in deed fitted for the task, that the Church there may be adorned, that the Christian religion may take root and grow, and that all things appertaining to the honour of God and the salvation of souls may be so ordered that you may deserve at God's hands the fullness of an everlasting reward, and may obtain on earth a name renowned throughout the ages.

   The Bull was granted to Henry through the diplomatic efforts of John of Salisbury; Adrian IV was an Englishman. It bears the marks of 'imperialist ideology', a moral mask to justify a policy of expansion and conquest.
6. See J.A. Watt, *The Church and the Two Nations in Medieval Ireland* (Cambridge: 1970), Chapters 1 and 2. It is also true, as W.L. Warren points out in *'The Interpretation of Twelfth-Century Irish History', Historical Studies VII,* ed. J.C. Beckett, (London: 1969), that many practices of the Irish Church, especially the marriage laws and easy divorce, must have horrified Rome and led to the charge that the Irish were 'ignorant and barbarous peoples'.
7. Marc Bloch, *Feudal Society* (London & Chicago: 1961), i, 188–9. The Normans established fiefs, counties, knight-service, manorial ownership of land, sheriffs, betagh tenure, stone castles.
8. See *Annals of Ulster*, 4 vols. vol i, AD 431–1056, trans. and notes by William Hennessy (Dublin: 1887); vol. ii, 1057–1378 (Dublin: 1893),

vol. iii, 1379–1541 (Dublin: 1895); vol. iv, introduction and index, ed., trans. and notes by B. MacCarthy (Dublin: 1901). *Ancient Laws of Ireland, Brehon Law Tracts,* vol. iv (Dublin: 1879). *Ancient Laws of Ireland, Uraicect Becc* and *Certain Other Selected Brehon Law Tracts,* vol. v (Dublin: 1901). *Uraicect Becc* means small primer. Text is in Irish with English on facing pages. Introduction states: 'The Celtic Irish never formed town communities, or were subject to any vigorous central authority; it was utterly impossible, therefore, that they could attain the ideas of law, which are evolved by the needs of a more compiex civilization; the peculiarities of the Brehon [code] is that professional lawyers of great acuteness and considered technical education developed in numerous written works the logical results of a purely archaic customary law.' (xiv, vol. v). These are available in the Public Record Office, London. Modern works include Kenneth Nicholls, *Gaelic and Gaelicized Ireland in the Middle Ages* (Dublin: 1972); James Lydon, *Ireland in the Later Middle Ages* (Dublin: 1973); J.F. Lydon, *The Lordship of Ireland in the Middle Ages* (Dublin & Toronto: 1972); John Watt, *The Church in Medieval Ireland* (Dublin: 1972).

9. The colonists, 'forsaking the English language, fashion, mode of riding, laws, and usages, live and govern themselves according to the manners, fashion and language of the Irish enemies, and also have made divers marriages and alliances between themselves and the Irish enemies aforesaid. . .'. These have sometimes been called the first *apartheid* laws, to keep the 'races' separate and pure (*Irish Historical Documents*, pp. 52–9).
10. *Ibid.*, 'The Remonstrance of the Irish princes to Pope John XXII, 1317.'
11. Sir Roger Casement, *The Crime Against Europe* (Philadelphia: 1915), p. 16. Casement was an Irishman, knighted for his humanitarian work exposing the exploitation of the natives in the Belgian Congo and the rubber plantations of the Putumayo, South America. He believed that a free Ireland, because of its geographical location, must end England's role as balancer in Europe.
12. Cited by Dr Ronan Fanning, 'The United States and Irish Participation in NATO: the Debate of 1950', paper read in Dublin, 18 April, 1978.
13. In May 1882, during the Land War, the British Chief Secretary of Ireland, Lord Frederick Cavendish, was stabbed to death with his Under-Secretary, T.H. Burke, on the day he took office, in the Phoenix Park, Dublin. Wilson was former Chief of the Imperial General Staff and military adviser to the new Belfast government. Airey Neave was Tory Party spokesman on Northern Ireland. Lord Mountbatten was a member of the Royal Family and a war hero.
14. Winston Churchill, *The World Crisis*, vol. v, 'The Aftermath' (London: 1929), p. 278.
15. *The New Cambridge Modern History*, iii, 524–5, says:

> A new interest in American colonisation for its own sake first appeared among Englishmen who had gained relevant experience in Ireland. Ireland was on the way to America. Many of the west-countrymen who attempted American settlements – Gilbert, Grenville, Raleigh – had been prominent in the settlement of Ireland and thought naturally of applying their experience in more promising surroundings, among less intractible people.

Gilbert received the first charter for the founding of a British colony in

1578. 'It might have gone hard with the Indians had he succeeded in founding a colony. In Ireland he always behaved with ferocious severity towards a conquered people.' Grenville and Raleigh, in 1585 and 1587, set up colonies in Roanoke, Virginia. Both colonies failed and Raleigh's colonists disappeared without trace.

16. Edmund Spenser, *A View of the Present State of Ireland* and *A Brief Note on Ireland.*
17. Pádraig O Snodaigh, *Hidden Ulster* (Dublin: 1973), notes that many Scottish Presbyterians who came to Ulster in the seventeenth century were Gaelic-speaking. 'At least it is certain that the Gaelic-speaking element among them was a very large one'. (pp. 4–5). Nevertheless, the gulf between settler and native did develop along national lines.
18. William Petty, *Treatise of Ireland* (1687). Petty estimated there were 1.3 million people in Ireland. He would 'bring a Million of them into England and leave the other 300 Thousand for Herdsmen and Dairy-Women behind and to quit all other trades in Ireland but that of Cattle only. . .'. Petty wrote the valuable *Political Anatomy of Ireland* (1687). The Soviet economist, A. Anikin, says of him: 'He occupies a place of honour among the great scholars of his time. This English nobleman was, as Marx put it, the father of political economy and in a sense the inventor of statistics'. (*A Science in Its Youth* [Moscow: 1975], p. 54). He also established a land-owning dynasty in Ireland. He was not a nobleman but the son of a clothier. Charles II knighted him.
19. Eric Williams, *Capitalism and Slavery* (London: 1964). The Cromwellian era marks a change in the form of colonialism. It gave England commercial predominance in the world. Christopher Hill, in *God's Englishman: Oliver Cromwell and the English Revolution* (London: 1972), lists among 'the removal of the obstacles to the development of English capitalism', the conquest of Jamaica, the exploitation of Ireland, the building of the navy and the Navigation Acts.
20. Karl S. Bottigheimer, *English Money and Irish Land: the Adventurers in the Cromwellian Settlement of Ireland* (Oxford: 1971).
21. *Irish Historical Documents,* 'Hugh O'Neill's War Aims', pp. 119–20. Sir Robert Cecil wrote the word 'Ewtopia' across the Earl of Tyrone's demands.
22. *Ibid.,* 'The Catholics' Demands, 1644', p. 152.
23. *Ibid.*, 'The Irish Parliament of James II, the Declaratory Act', pp. 169–71.
24. *Ibid.*, pp. 171–2.
25. Friedrich Engels, 'The Preparatory Material for the History of Ireland', *Marx/Engels: Ireland and the Irish Question* (Moscow: 1971), pp. 210–11.
26. *Ibid.*, p. 83, letter to Marx following tour of Ireland in 1856. Marx himself in an article for the New York *Tribune* (11 July, 1853) had much the same in mind when he wrote: 'England has subverted the conditions of Irish society. At first it confiscated the land, then it suppressed the industry. . . and lastly, it broke the active energy by armed force.'
27. Eric Strauss, *Irish Nationalism and British Democracy* (New York: 1951), p. 11. L.M. Cullen, *An Economic History of Ireland* (New York: 1972), thinks 'absentee rents probably accounted for about one-fourth to one-sixth of the total rent roll' (p. 45). Contemporaries were alarmed by the export of money.

28. Lecky, *op.cit.*, i, 174.
29. Marx, 'Outline of a Report on the Irish Question', December 1867, *Marx/Engels, Ireland* p. 132; Engels, Preface, English ed., *The Condition of the Working Class in England* (1892); *Marx/Engels, Ireland* p. 311.
30. Lecky, *History of Ireland*, i, 179–80.
31. The 'Sixth of George the First'.
32. The third Drapier Letter, quoted in John Middleton Murry, *Jonathan Swift* (New York: 1955), p. 366. William Wood, an English ironmaster, was given a patent, in July 1722, to coin money for Ireland. He obtained it by paying £10,000 to the Duchess of Kendal, George I's mistress. Wood's halfpence became an issue, because of Swift, between the Anglo-Irish colony and England. The uproar forced the English government to change its policy and end the coinage. Swift's question, 'is not their parliament as fair a representation of the people as that of England?' was perhaps doubly ironic: neither was representative of the people, but the Irish House of Commons did not even presume to represent the majority, the Catholics.
33. *Ibid.*, pp. 370–1.
34. Theobald Wolfe Tone, *Autobiography of Theobald Wolfe Tone* ed. R. Barry O'Brien (Dublin: 1893), i, 26. Tone, A Dublin Protestant barrister, founded the United Irishmen in 1791.
35. *Swift Selected Prose*, ed. John Hayward, (London: 1934), p. 436.
36. Sir Jonah Barrington, *The Rise and Fall of the Irish Nation* (Dublin: 1833), p. 24. Barrington explains the economics behind the politics.

> England, notwithstanding she had in some instances suspended, and in others prohibited, the exportation of Irish manufactures inundated the Irish markets with every species of her own; and with a view effectually to destroy all power of competition in Ireland, the great capitalists of England determined, even at any loss to undersell the Irish in their own markets – a loss, however, which they thought would be eventually and amply repaid by the monopoly which must necessarily succeed the utter destruction of the Irish manufacturers.
>
> This system it was impossible for the Irish manufacturer to resist or counteract; his capital was too small to bear the losses of competition; resistance would have been vain; he had therefore no alternative but to change his trade, or submit, and famish.

He decided to oppose the English system by refusing to import or buy English products. 'The manufacturing bodies, the corporate towns, the small retailers, the general merchants, at once universally adopted this vigorous determination. . . till they should acquire a restoration of their political rights' (pp. 27–8).

37. *Ireland from Grattan's Parliament to the Great Famine*, ed. James Carty, (Dublin: 1957), pp. 63–9.
38. The popular name for the Irish parliament from 1782 till 1800. Grattan did not control this parliament and was no more than the leader of the opposition; nor did it rule Ireland, which was the function of the English government. But it did pass legislation to support Irish trade and industry.
39. Quoted by Lecky, *History of Ireland*, i, 146.
40. *Ibid.*, pp. 145–52.
41. Quoted in *The Philosophy of Edmund Burke: a Selection from his Speeches and Writings*, ed. Louis I. Bredvold and Ralph G. Ross, (Ann Arbor: 1960), 'Tract on the Popery Laws', pp. 20–6. Burke was born in Dublin of Catholic parents, probably in January 1729; his father, a lawyer,

conformed to the Established Church about eight years before Burke was born. His mother remained a Catholic. He himself married a Catholic and supported Catholic emancipation.

42. Daniel Corkery, *The Hidden Ireland: a Study of Gaelic Munster in the Eighteenth Century* (Dublin: 1941), p. 185. The translation of O'Rahilly's poem is by Robert Dwyer Joyce. The book is a valuable guide to Gaelic literature of the penal period, although Corkery's view of Irish social life in the Munster of the eighteenth century is largely rejected today.
43. *Ibid.*, p. 288.
44. Hans Kohn, *The Idea of Nationalism*, (New York: 1946) p. 14.
45. See Maureen Wall, 'The Decline of the Irish Language' and Tomas O hAilin, 'Irish Revival Movements', *A View of the Irish Language, ed.* Brian O Cuiv (Dublin: 1969), pp. 81–90 and 91–100.
46. Hans Kohn, *The Idea of Nationalism* (New York: 1946), p. 15.
47. Tone, *Autobiography*, i, 40–1.
48. *Ibid.*, p. 47.
49. See Chapter II.
50. *The Declaration, Resolutions, and Constitution, of the Societies of United Irishmen.*
51. Letter to Thomas Russell, quoted by Frank MacDermot, *Theobald Wolfe Tone* (Tralee: 1968), p. 62.
52. Tone, *Autobiography*, i, 41.
53. *Ibid.*, p. 47.
54. *Original Prospectus of the United Irishmen.*
55. McNally was a scoundrel who betrayed his clients but his reports are candid and hardly self-serving (See Lecky, *History of Ireland*, iii, 381–2).
56. See Lecky, *History of Ireland*, i, 272–3.

> In Ireland, except in a few remote districts in the south and west, law was recognized by the Catholic community as a real, powerful, omnipresent agent, immoral, irreligious and maleficent. All their higher and nobler life lay beyond its pale. Illegal combination was consecrated when it was essential to the performance of a religious duty. Illegal violence was the natural protection against immoral laws.

The government depended on the clergy to keep the peasantry quiet. The clergy did not do so because they liked the government, merely because they opposed violence.

57. Lecky, *History of Ireland*, iii, 381.
58. *The Declaration, Resolutions, and Constitution of the Societies of United Irishmen.*
59. *Ibid.*
60. Hans Morgenthau, *The Decline of Democratic Politics* (Chicago: 1962), p. 181.
61. Quoted *ibid.*, p. 62. See also, Georges Lefebvre, *The French Revolution from its Origins to 1793* (London: 1962), pp. 274–5.
62. Morgenthau, *Democratic Politics*, p. 189. For the new world market see Richard J. Barnet and Ronald E. Muller, *Global Reach: the Power of the Multinational Corporations* (New York: 1974), pp. 72–104.
63. Morgenthau, *Democratic Politics*, p. 193.
64. Barnet and Muller, *Global Reach*, p. 193, which also notes that this situation is changing and poor countries are developing strategies 'that cut into the power of global corporations'.

65. Karl Mannheim, *Ideology and Utopia* (New York: 1936), pp. 49–50. See also George Lichtheim, *The Concept of Ideology and Other Essays* (New York: 1967).
66. Mannheim, *Ideology and Utopia*, p. 51.
67. Karl Marx, *The German Ideology* (London: 1970), p. 47.
68. *Ibid.*, p. 53.
69. *Ibid.*, p. 66.
70. Mannheim, *Ideology and Utopia*, p. 87.
71. 'Particular ideology' is an important concept that will not be dealt with in any detail in this study. However, the following example may help explain it. The Irish nationalist demand for independence is seen by Ulster Protestants as a mask to hide a Catholic takeover of all Ireland. This view was expressed by Sam Smyth, a founder of the Ulster Defence Association, to the author at a forum on Northern Ireland at the University of Massachusetts, Amherst, 1 September, 1975. Smyth said he could subscribe to the politics of the United Irishmen, but 'In Northern Ireland today there are no United Irishmen. There are only Catholics and Protestants.' (See Sean Cronin, *Tones Republic* [Dublin: 1975], p. 4). Smyth was assassinated six months later, apparently by the Provisional IRA. Machiavelli's remark is cited by Mannheim. During the Renaissance 'there arose a new adage calling attention to a common observation of the time – namely that the thought of the palace is one thing, and that of the public square is another' (Mannheim, *Ideology and Utopia*, pp. 55–6).
72. See Emmet Larkin, *The Roman Catholic Church in Ireland and the Fall of Parnell* (Chapel Hill, NC: 1979), p. 174.
73. Marx, 16 December 1867, *Marx/Engels, Ireland*, p. 142.
74. *Irish Historical Documents*, pp. 287–92.
75. T.W. Freeman, *Pre-Famine Ireland* (Manchester: 1957), pp. 140–1.
76. F.S.L. Lyons, *Ireland Since the Famine*, pp. 104–11. Also J.H. Whyte, *The Tenant League and Irish Politics in the Eighteen-Fifties* (Dublin: 1963).
77. Crane Brinton, *The Anatomy of Revolution*, (New York: 1965), pp. 132–7.
78. See Peadar O'Donnell, *There Will Be Another Day* (Dublin: 1963). O'Donnell, a left-wing Republican, started a campaign to withhold land annuities – monies paid the English government which had bought out the landlords under the land acts. O'Donnell's argument was that the land belonged to the Irish people. De Valera made non-payment part of his policy and, despite defeat in the 1922–23 Civil War, took office in March 1932. De Valera's view of the land is inscribed in the 1937 Constitution which he drafted: 'That there may be established on the land in economic security as many families as in the circumstances shall be practicable.' (Article 45,2,v.).
79. See Sean Cronin, 'Nation Building and the Irish Language Revival Movement', *Eire–Ireland* (Spring 1978).
80. For Corkery see *What's This About the Gaelic League?* (Dublin: 1941) iii; Eoin McKiernan, *The Will of a Nation* (St. Paul: 1963), pp. 8–9. His argument is that if the Irish nation wants the Irish language to survive it will survive; if it wants it to die, it will die. Also O Cadhain's *Irish Above Politics* (Dublin: 1964). The disappearance of the Gaeltacht was an economic matter: see Peadar O'Donnell, *The Role of the Industrial Worker in the Problems of the West* (Dublin: 1965). All are pamphlets.

81. F.S.L. Lyons, *Charles Stewart Parnell* (London: 1977), p. 144.
82. *Report on Manufactures, 1791,* puts the case for bounties and tariffs in a developing economy. The point is that all developing economies must protect their own products against the industrialized states, initially at any rate. Protective tariffs were a staple of US policy in the nineteenth century.
83. See William G. Shade, 'Strains of Modernization' and Sean O'Donnell, 'The Multinationals Justified?', *Eire–Ireland* (Spring 1979); also *Manufacturing in Ireland* (Dublin: 1962) by the Irish Industrial Development Authority.
84. NATO recognizes borders, including the partition of Ireland.
85. Publication was forbidden during the war. Said the censor of Lalor's writings: 'The work may be a classic; but it certainly is a piece of rank treason' (Lord Decies, chief censor, papers in Dublin Castle files at British Public Record Office, Kew, London). Second book cited is T.P. O'Mahony, *The Politics of Dishonour: Ireland 1916–1977* (Dublin: 1977).
86. *From Max Weber, Essays in Sociology* ed. H.H. Gerth and C. Wright Mills, (New York: 1958), 'The Social Psychology of the World Religions', p. 280. Al Cohan, *The Irish Political Elite* (Dublin: 1972) has some cogent points to make about the new Irish ruling class. 'The anti-Free State party of the Civil War and after has, in a sense, recognised the existence of the North *de facto* as a separate entity and, while supporting reunification, is realistic about its possibilities' (p. 6).
87. Samuel P. Huntington, *Political Order in Changing Societies* (New Haven: 1968), p. 55.
88. Under the Wyndham Act of 1903 the British government bought out Ireland's landlords and the tenants became owners of their farms by paying 'land annuities' to Britain.
89. See Damien F. Hannan, *Displacement and Development: Class, Kinship and Social Change in Irish Rural Communities* (Dublin: 1979); also Patricia O'Hara and Carmel Kelleher, *Adjustment Problems of Low Income Farmer* (Dublin: 1978).
90. See Kurt Jacobsen, 'Changing Utterly? Irish Development and the Problem of Dependence,' *Studies* (Dublin: Winter 1978). On Puerto Rico, see *New York Times,* 15 October, 1975, 'Puerto Rico Seeks Way Out As Economic Woes Mount.'
91. Among the Gaelic families who held on to their lands were the O'Briens of Clare and the MacMurrough Kavanaghs of Carlow. Although their Gaelic sense of family remained strong, they conformed in religion and politics to England. The 'Old English' families – some had been in Ireland since the twelfth century – were often Catholic or had conformed quite late, like the Dunsanys, for reasons of inheritance.
92. Paul Blanshard, *The Irish and Catholic Power* (New York: 1953), pp. 160–2.
93. F.S.L. Lyons, *Charles Stewart Parnell* (London: 1977).
94. *Ibid.* Archbishop William Walsh told Cardinal Manning in 1888 that the Irish 'were still struggling for their religion and their land and that the permanency of the one depended to no little extent on the possession of the latter'. But this is hardly an anti-Protestant tirade or call for a crusade. Two years later Cardinal Manning wrote to Archbishop Walsh urging that Parnell be replaced by a committee and that the bishops

and priests use the crisis to regain 'the lead and direction' of the Irish nationalist movement which they had lost ten years earlier (Lyons, *Parnell*, p. 484).

For an account of episcopal intrigue against nationalism during the Parnell divorce crisis see Larkin, *The Roman Catholic Church in Ireland and the Fall of Parnell.* The author's comment is appropriate: 'The part played by the Bishops and their clergy in this destruction of Parnellism was more than central – it was decisive' (p. 263). Archbishop Walsh of Dublin and Archbishop Croke of Cashel, the most nationalist of the hierarchy, used the divorce crisis to reimpose waning Church control of politics in Ireland. Cardinal Manning indeed wanted to subvert the nationalist movement using his influence with Gladstone, Rome and Walsh to accomplish his ends.

95. Denis Gwynn, *Daniel O'Connell* (Cork: 1947), p. 115. The Vatican, in 1814, granted the British government a veto over the appointment of Irish bishops. It was withdrawn when Irish Catholics almost unanimously objected. Similarly, when Pope Leo XIII issued a decree in April 1888 condemning the Plan of Campaign against landlordism, the Irish bishops refused to enforce it, because it would jeoparize 'both his [the Pope's] and their own authority in Ireland' (Larkin, *Catholic Church and Parnell*, p. 4).
96. See Larkin, *Catholic Church and Parnell*, final chapter 'Catholic Power'.
97. Rev. C.N. Stack, 'Unity and the Church of Ireland', *The Bell* (Dublin: January 1951). Childers opposed the Anglo-Irish Treaty, was captured in November 1922 during the Civil War, and executed. See Andrew Boyle, *The Riddle of Erskine Childers* (London: 1977).
98. *Ibid.*
99. Statement by Archbishop O Fiaich in October 1978 after appointment to the See of Armagh, which has thirty-five parishes in Northern Ireland and twenty-three in the Republic. He became a Cardinal in July 1979.
100. Quoted in J. Chartres Molony, *Ireland* (London: 1936), pp. 154–5.
101. Hans Morgenthau, *The Restoration of American Politics* (Chicago: 1958), p. 240.
102. See Andrew Boyd, *Holy War in Belfast* (Tralee: 1969). On the religious interpretation of the conflict, see Denis P. Barritt and Charles E. Carter, *The Northern Ireland Problem* (London: 1962), and Rosemary Harris, *Prejudice and Tolerance in Ulster: a Study of Neighbours and 'Strangers' in a Border Community* (Manchester: 1972).
103. Michael Hechter, *Internal Colonialism: the Celtic Fringe in British National Development, 1536–1966,* (Berkeley, Cal.: 1975), pp. 267–8.
104. See Richard Rose, *Governing Without Consensus* (London: 1971); David W. Miller, *Queen's Rebels: Ulster Loyalism in Historical Perspective* (Dublin: 1978), intro., pp. 1–6, and *Northern Ireland: a Role for the United States?* (Washington: 1979), Congressional Report for the House Committee of the Judiciary, interviews with leaders of Protestant paramilitary organizations, pp. 47–74. See also 'Interpretations of the Northern Ireland Conflict', by John Whyte of Queen's University, Belfast, a paper prepared for a workshop on multi-cultural societies, in Louvain, in April 1976, and for the Ford Foundation.
105. Patrick Buckland, *Irish Unionism: Two: Ulster Unionism and the Origins*

of Northern Ireland 1886–1922 (Dublin: 1973), intro., pp. xv–xxxvi; pp. 9–10.

106. In *Forward*, a Scottish socialist weekly, 3 May, 1913. Collected in *Socialism and Nationalism*, ed. Desmond Ryan, (Dublin: 1948), pp. 71–2.
107. *Ibid.*, 2 August, 1913, 'North-East Ulster', *Socialism and Nationalism*, p. 104.
108. For a description of 12 July, 'Orange Day', see Douglas Gageby, 'Northern Ireland', *Conor Cruise O'Brien Introduces Ireland*, ed. Owen Dudley Edwards (London: 1969), pp. 179–88.
109. The Belfast Chamber of Commerce told Prime Minister Gladstone in 1893: 'Since the union, we have been wedded to the empire and made progress second to none. . .'
110. Some surveys, such as M.W. Heslinga, *The Irish Border as a Cultural Divide* (Assen: 1962), and Richard Rose, *Governing Without Consensus* (London: 1971), have found that Northern Irish Catholics and Protestants share certain views and characteristics so there may be a question about the cultural division. However, the communities, as communities, do not share political and religious values. Their ideologies are in conflict: colonial versus anti-colonial, or nationalist. Rose attacks any economic interpretation of the problem, but ideology, of course, has to do with each side's perception of 'reality' – and Marx, Weber and Mannheim agree this has to do with the economic base.
111. *Toward Freedom: the Autobiography of Jawharlal Nehru* (Boston: 1963), p. 44.
112. Joseph Devlin, the Irish parliamentary party leader, persuaded an Ulster Nationalist Convention, on 23 June, 1916, to accept David Lloyd George's proposal to exclude the counties of Tyrone, Fermanagh, Armagh, Down, Londonderry and Antrim (the present Northern Ireland) from the Home Rule for Ireland Act as a temporary measure to satisfy the objections of the Unionists and the Tories. However, delegates from the nationalist-majority counties of Fermanagh and Tyrone and Derry City voted against the plan. See R.B. McDowell, *The Irish Convention, 1917–18* (London: 1970), pp. 51–4.

CHAPTER 2

1. *A Letter to the Whole People of Ireland* by M.B. Drapier (fourth Letter, 1724).
2. John Locke, 'An Essay Concerning the True Original, Extent and End of Government', para. 239, *Social Contract* (Oxford: 1947); also Chapter VIII, 'Of the Beginning of Political Societies.' Peaceful means of redress must first be tried, Locke makes clear ('Second Treatise', para. 203) and abuses should be resisted from the start to avert revolution (*ibid.*, para. 220).
3. Edmund Burke, 'A Letter to Sir H. Langrish', 1792, *The Works of Burke*, ed. F.W. Raffety, (London: 1928), v, 184-6.
4. The English Cabinet called it 'a solecism in politics to make the constitution of a colony the same as that of the mother country'. Quoted by Patrick O'Farrell, *Ireland's English Question* (New York: 1971), p. 59.
5. See *Freedom the Wolfe Tone Way* (Tralee: 1973), ed. Sean Cronin and Richard Roche, an anthology of Tone's writings. He signed *Reviews*,

'An Independent Irish Whig'.

6. Ibid., p. 89. *Enquiry* was signed 'Hibernicus'.
7. *Life of Wolfe Tone*, edited by his son, William Theobald Wolfe Tone, 2 vols, (Washington: 1826), i, 77. See also pp. 38–9, on the debate in Dublin caused by Burke's book and Paine's reply. *Reflections on the Revolution in France* appeared in November 1790, *The Rights of Man* in February 1791.
8. *Ibid.*
9. *The Declaration, Resolutions, and Constitution, of the Societies of United Irishmen.*
10. Tone, *Life*, i, 50-1.
11. Thomas H.D. Mahoney, *Edmund Burke and Ireland* (Cambridge: 1960), p. 172.
12. 'An Argument on Behalf of the Catholics of Ireland' is carried in full in *Freedom the Wolfe Tone Way, op. cit.*, pp. 101–24. The 'modifications' Tone suggested were: the franchise for those with freeholds of ten pounds a year, and striking off 'that wretched tribe of forty shilling freeholders, whom we see driven to the octennial market, by their landlords'.
13. *Ibid.*, p. 123.
14. *Ibid.*, p. 124.
15. Tone, *Life*, i, 86–7. 25 October, 1791.
16. Cronin and Roche (eds), *Freedom the Wolfe Tone Way*, p. 116.
17. See Rosamond Jacob, *The Rise of the United Irishmen* (London: 1937).
18. Edmund Burke, *Reflections on the Revolution in France* ed. Conor Cruise O'Brien (London: 1968), p. 188.
19. William Drennan, *A Letter to his Excellency Earl Fitzwilliam, Lord Lieutenant, &c. of Ireland* (Dublin: 1795), p. 41.
20. John Locke, 'An Essay Concerning the True Original, Extent and End of Civil Government', para. 96.
21. Tone to Russell, 25 October, 1795, *Freedom the Wolfe Tone Way*, pp. 161–2.
22. For contemporary view of Belfast, see R.R. Madden, *Antrim and Down in '98* (Dublin: n.d.), pp. 159–60.
23. Tone, *Life*, i, 79–80. The reference to England 'engaged in a foreign war' would suggest the United Irishmen, from the start, saw little hope of peaceful reform. On the matter of Irish debt, see Adam Smith, *The Wealth of Nations*, i, Chapter x, Part 2, and his insistence that Ireland and the American colonies were liable because Britain secured the liberty and property of the Protestants in Ireland and the colonists in North America.
24. *Ibid.*
25. *Ibid.*, pp. 85–6.
26. *Ibid.*
27. *Ibid.*, pp. 87–8. The Digges mentioned here was Thomas Digges from Baltimore, Md., a writer and adventurer, who had played some role in the American Revolution and was in consequence a hero in Belfast. However, he lost his reputation among the United Irish later on when he was caught shoplifting. See Frank MacDermot, *Theobald Wolfe Tone*, p. 45.
28. R.R. Madden, *Antrim and Down in '98*, 'Autobiographical Memoir of James Hope', pp. 86–154. Madden describes Hope as 'a poor mechanic,

self-taught and self-ennobled', at all times 'adverse to bloodshed'. He was an organizer for the United Irishmen, fought in '98, and with Robert Emmet in 1803. See short study by Sean Cronin, *Jemmy Hope: Man of the People* (Dublin: 1964).

29. Thomas Pakenham *The Year of Liberty* (London: 1972), p. 249.
30. Madden, *Antrim and Down*, p. 104. Hope says the Peep O'Day Boys and the Defenders 'lamented their past indiscretions' and 'resolved to avoid the causes which led to them'. Ulster for a short time seemed 'one united family'. Hope went to Dublin 'to disseminate our views among the working classes'.
31. Tone, *Autobiography*, i, 104.
32. *Ibid.*, p. 105.
33. *Ibid.*
34. *The Correspondence of Edmund Burke*, ed. P.J. Marshall and John A. Woods (Cambridge: 1968) vii, 374.
35. *Ibid.*, p. 378.
36. Lecky, *History of Ireland*, iii, 388. The report refers to the underground United Irishmen in 1795.
37. See Pakenham, *Year of Liberty*, pp. 184–6. Charles Dickson, *The Wexford Rising in 1798* (Tralee: 1955), thinks the Wexford Catholic rebels 'were inspired more by the spirit of the Defenders than of the United Irishmen' (p. 150), yet their pronouncements belie that. Theory and practice, of course, are not necessarily the same; yet Dickson points out that by the third week of the insurrection the United Irish oath was being administered. All accounts agree the United Irish organization hardly existed in Wexford when the rebellion began but its doctrines were abroad. The main grievances in Wexford were the tithes and the penal laws, Dickson says. These indeed were the main grievances of the Catholics in the 1790s. See also Padraig O Snodaigh, *'98 and Carlow* (Carlow: 1979). Of the Leinster rebels, he thinks those in Meath were Defenders not United Irishmen.
38. In 1780 a committee of the electors of Westminster under Charles James Fox urged similar reforms. See P.A. Brown, *The French Revolution in English History* (London: 1918), pp. 28–9. For similar radical demands see Carl B. Cone, *The English Jacobins* (New York: 1968). The Arthur O'Connor of the United Irishmen was an uncle of the Chartist leader, Feargus O'Connor. Joseph Lee ('Grattan's Parliament', *The Irish Parliamentary Tradition* [Dublin: 1973], p. 155) thinks the United Irishmen may have 'balked at the secret ballot, fearful of landlords losing their entire influence over their tenantry'.
39. In 1787 the English Dissenters opposed lifting restrictions on Catholics.
40. Drennan, *Letter to Fitzwilliam*, p. 50.
41. 'Letter to Thomas Burgh', 1 January, 1780, quoted *Burke's Politics, Selected Writings and Speeches of Edmund Burke on Reform, Revolution, and War* (New York: 1949), eds. Ross J.S. Hoffman and Paul Levack, pp. 120–1.
42. 'A Letter to Sir H. Langrishe', 1792, *Works of Burke*, v, 184–6. Burke was forced out of his Bristol constituency because of his support of Irish free trade and Catholic emancipation. 'America was to be conquered in order that Ireland should not trade thither,' he told the merchants of

Bristol *(Burke's Politics,* p. 127). Of the penal laws he said: 'Ireland, after almost a century of persecution, is at this hour full of penalties and full of Papists. . .' (*ibid.,* p. 158). In the same tract against the penal laws he called them 'a depravation of society' (*ibid.,* p. 161). The laws were a 'horrible and impious system of servitude' (*ibid.*, p. 169) and by depriving people of a means of livelihood and of education were 'the worst species of tyranny that the insolence and perverseness of mankind ever dared to exercise' (*ibid.*, pp. 169–70). 'It is injustice, and not a mistaken conscience, that has been the principle of persecution — at least as far as it has fallen under my observation,' he concluded (*ibid.*, p. 174).

43. The Catholic Relief Act of 1793 followed French offer to aid all oppressed peoples. Passed in the Irish parliament, it gave Catholics parliamentary and municipal franchise, the right to sit on grand juries, become magistrates, hold army and navy commissions, get university degrees, but excluded them from parliament and state offices. These were withheld until the 1829 Catholic Emancipation Act.
44. Undated letter written, probably, in January 1793, before Catholic Relief Act. See Edmund Burke, *Selected Writings and Speeches*, ed. Peter J. Shanlis, (Gloucester, Mass.: 1968), pp. 270–1.
45. See *Burke's Politics*, pp. 123–5. Burke's view was that Catholicism in Ireland should maintain its 'old course, because it is the old course, and because it has been the successful course'. The first President of Maynooth was Burke's friend, Dr Thomas Hussey, later Bishop of Waterford. Today, Maynooth is a constituent college of the National University of Ireland, and a seminary. Burke would like the Catholic Church to share established status with the Anglican in Ireland, as in Canada: 'Religion, to have any force on men's understandings, indeed to exist at all, must be supposed paramount to laws. . . . Religion, therefore, is not believed because the laws have established it, but it is established because the leading part of the community have previously believed it to be true. . .' (*ibid.*, p. 159).
46. The Catholic Convention met in Tailors' Hall, Back Lane, which was also used by the United Irishmen and the Grand Lodge of the Freemasons, on 3 December, 1792, and on behalf of the Catholic peers, prelates and delegates 'addressed a petition to the King'. (Tone, *Life*, i, 189).
47. *Ibid.*, p. 176.
48. Raffety, *Works of Burke*, v, pp. 195–6.
49. *Ibid.*, p. 199.
50. *Ibid.*, p. 202.
51. *Ibid.*, p. 203.
52. *Ibid.* Burke understood that the Ascendancy ruled Ireland through the Lord Lieutenant, or Viceroy, who represented the Crown and whose views were followed by the British Cabinet.
53. Marshall and Woods (eds), *Correspondence of Edmund Burke*, vii, 508, Moylan to Burke, dated 20 December, 1793. The plea for 'our clerical education' was met when Maynooth seminary was set up in April 1795 (see fn. 45).
54. *Ibid.*, ii, 509–11, to Douglas, 30 December, 1793.
55. *Correspondence of Edmund Burke and William Windham*, ed. J.P. Gibson, (Cambridge: 1910), p. 122 fn. Windham, a Whig, was Secretary of War in Pitt's coalition.

56. Letter dated 26 February, 1795.
57. 15 May 1795, quoted Mahoney, *Burke and Ireland*, p. 265.
58. Quoted by Lecky, *History of Ireland*, iii, 51–2.
59. *Ibid.*, p. 49.
60. Tone, *Life*, i, 214.
61. See Cronin and Roche (eds), *Freedom the Wolfe Tone Way*, pp. 154–5.
62. Drennan, *Letter to Fitzwilliam*, p. 28.
63. See Pakenham, *Year of Liberty*, p. 256.
64. Raffety (ed.), 'Conduct of the Minority', *Works of Burke*, v, 324.
65. Wolfe Tone's brother, Matthew, was an officer with the French forces. He wrote, 'the people throw themselves on their knees as we pass along and extend their arms for our success'. When Humbert surrendered to Lord Cornwallis at Ballinamuck, Matthew Tone and two Irish officers with the French were hanged by the English.
66. *Tone Papers*, Trinity College, Dublin. For full text, previously unpublished, see Appendix I in this volume.
67. *Freedom the Wolfe Tone Way*, pp. 195–200.
68. *Ibid.*
69. 'Letters on a Regicide Peace', *Works of Burke*, vi, 234. Hoche had pacified the *Vendée*, but by conciliation rather than ruthlessness.
70. See MacDermot, *Tone*, pp. 201–2. The author quotes the diary of Daniel O'Connell, the nineteenth-century Catholic leader, then a law student in Dublin, who doubted that the Irish were ready for liberty at that time.
71. See Mahoney, *Burke and Ireland*, pp. 306–8. Burke died shortly after writing this, to an unknown correspondent, on 9 July 1797, less than a year before all his predictions were verified in the bloodbath of 1798.
72. Tone returned to Ireland on a French warship, which was captured by an English naval force off the North Irish coast on 10 October, 1798. Condemned to death, he was found dying of a knife wound on the eve of the execution, an apparent suicide. He lived one week.
73. The successful French landing at Killala and defeat of a superior English force at Castlebar, 'and the desertion of the militia regiments, tended to impress the gentry with an idea that England alone could protect the country', Sir Jonah Barrington wrote in *Rise and Fall of the Irish Nation.* The Catholic bishops supported Union because they had decided that an Irish parliament, controlled by the Ascendancy, would not grant emancipation.
74. First diary entry, 1 March, the second, 8 April 1798.
75. When Russell, Tone's friend, returned from the Continent to reorganize the United Irishmen in Ulster and prepare for Robert Emmet's 1803 rebellion, he discovered that Northern Protestants had little interest in his ideas. He was arrested and hanged. For a different reason, perhaps, that other United Irishman, James Napper Tandy, failed to spark rebellion when he landed in Donegal in September 1798. He distributed a few proclamations and sailed back to France via the Orkneys and Norway, arriving in Hamburg, which was blockaded by the British who demanded that he be handed over to them for trial. Despite French threats, he was handed over and stood trial for his life in April 1801 and was sentenced to death.

    Tom Paine, in a letter to Robert Livingston, US Minister in Paris, recalled an incident of the American Revolution, when both of them prevailed on Washington to suspend a sentence of death on a British officer named Asgill, and urged some like pressure on Lord Cornwallis to have Tandy freed and returned to France. 'Cornwallis, you know, was in America while the affair of Asgill was pending, and I cannot see any impropriety. . . in your writing a note to remind Cornwallis of the circumstance and to hint to him your wish that he would be as friendly to Tandy as you had been to Asgill', wrote Paine. Tandy was freed and banished, and died in France. (See Sean Cronin, 'In Behalf of an Honest Man', *Irish Times*, 25 June 1979, dealing with discovery of Paine's letter among Livingston's papers in New York.)

76. For an understanding of the role of politics and religion see Andrew Boyd, *Holy War in Belfast.*
77. The phrase is Burke's. For constitutional developments in Northern Ireland, see J.C. Beckett *et al., The Ulster Debate* (London: 1972).
78. For Anglo-Irish Treaty, see Frank Pakenham, *Peace by Ordeal* (London: 1935).
79. The one tenuous link connecting Eire (Ireland) to the British Crown, the External Relations Act, was repealed and the state became a Republic in April 1949, confirming the actual constitutional position under de Valera's 1937 Constitution. See also *Bunreacht na hEireann – Constitution of Ireland* (Dublin: 1964).
80. See paper read by Irish Consul-General in New York, Gearoid O Clerigh, to Irish Teachers' Association of New York conference, at St Francis College, Brooklyn, on 11 November 1978.
81. See Earl of Longford and Thomas P. O'Neill, *Eamon de Valera* (Boston: 1971). For background on drafting of 1937 Constitution see pp. 294–300. The political atmosphere in the Ireland of the 1930s must be taken into account: the chief opposition to de Valera was toying with the corporate state philosophy and was ultra-conservative. De Valera himself, though broadly tolerant in such matters, held firmly to 'Catholic principles'.
82. See J.H. Whyte, *Church and State in Modern Ireland, 1923–1970* (Dublin: 1971). The most notorious example of Church interference in legislation is the 'Mother and Child Health Scheme' of 1950, which Whyte discusses in chapters five to nine and in the appendices. See also, Paul Blanshard, *The Irish and Catholic Power* (Boston: 1953), for this and other examples of clerical influence. Blanshard's thesis is no longer as valid as it was in the 1950s, but clerical power is still substantial.

CHAPTER 3

1. Gustave de Beaumont, *L'Irlande* (Paris: 1863), ii, 25.
2. Alexis de Tocqueville, *Journeys to England and Ireland*, ed. J.P. Mayer, (New York: 1968), p. 123.
3. The phrase was used by O'Connell in 1833 when the Whigs passed special coercion laws for Ireland. In March 1835, under the 'Lichfield House compact', O'Connell joined forces with the Whigs to keep the Melbourne administration in office, from April 1835 to August 1841, 'one of the

most decisive events in British political history between 1832 and 1847', according to Angus Macintyre, *The Liberator: Daniel O'Connell and the Irish Party 1830–1847* (New York: 1965), p. 144. For full account see pp. 139–66.

4. See Nicholas Mansergh, *The Irish Question, 1840–1921* (London: 1975), pp. 95–102.
5. In 1760 James Macpherson published, in Edinburgh, 'Fragments of Ancient Poetry Collected in the Highlands of Scotland', allegedly translations from Gaelic. In 1765 he published 'The Works of Ossian', which were read in translation by Johann Gottfried Herder, Goethe, Johann Paul Richter, Friedrich Klopstock, Felix Mandelssohn, Diderot, Napoleon, among others, who were carried away in their enthusiasm. Herder decided the stories and songs of a people were their archives; from this source he developed romantic nationalism. (See Isaiah Berlin's extended essay on Herder, *Vico and Herder*, [New York: 1977], pp. 171–2, 178.) A Gaelic poet, Michael Comyn, who died in 1760, wrote 'Oisin in the Land of Youth', before Macpherson's 'translations', a poem well known in O'Connell's native Iveragh, Co. Kerry, where tales of Oisin were plentiful, a matter he remarked on at the height of the controversy. A translation of Comyn's work inspired W.B. Yeats's early poetry and interest in the Celtic literary tradition and by this circuitous route Oisin influenced modern Irish nationalism. To say that romantic nationalism is based on a fraud would overstate the case: Macpherson took the Ossianic tales of the Gaelic *Fianna* and wove them into mediocre verse. The 'Homer of the North' – Oisin – inspired Herder, not Macpherson, as he later inspired Yeats's long narrative poem, *The Wanderings of Oisin* (1889).
6. The 'tribute' sometimes reached £13,000 a year, a massive sum in those days. (See Denis Gwynn, *Daniel O'Connell* [Cork: 1947], pp. 191–3). On O'Connell and French Revolution, see Gwynn, *ibid.*, pp. 37–9. On O'Connell as a landlord, see hostile articles in *The Times* 18 November, 1845, and 24 May, 1847, and the reply of his son, 20 December, 1845.
7. Gwynn, op. cit., p. 83.
8. O'Connell was sixty-five when he began the agitation with the words, 'I will terminate it only in death or Repeal' (*ibid*, p. 219). He urged his lieutenants to 'act cautiously' and win clerical approval for the campaign. He promised 1843 would be 'Repeal Year' and organized mass meetings with attendances of one hundred thousand and upwards, and always proclaimed his loyalty to the Queen.
9. *Thomas Davis, the Thinker and Teacher*, ed. Arthur Griffith (Dublin: 1914), pp. 8–9.
10. *Ibid.*, p. 9.
11. *Ibid.*, p. 12.
12. *Ibid.*
13. *Ibid.*, p. 13.
14. Charles Gavan Duffy *Young Ireland 1840–45* (London: 1896), i, 31.
15. *Ibid.*, p. 50.
16. Brian Boru defeated the Danes at Clontarf in 1014; Patrick Sarsfield led James II's Irish army at the Boyne, Limerick and to exile in France. Fitzgerald was a United Irishman.
17. Gavan Duffy, *Young Ireland*, i, 47.

18. Thomas Davis, *The Patriot Parliament of 1689,* ed. C. Gavan Duffy (London: 1893).
19. Yeats on Ferguson and Davis quoted by Colin Meir, *The Ballads and Songs of W.B. Yeats,* (New York: 1974), p.6. Ferguson, born in Belfast, educated at Trinity, knighted 1878, published *Lays of the Western Gael* in 1865. See also, *Autobiography of William Butler Yeats* (New York: 1965), particularly pp. 349–50, and *William Butler Yeats: Memoirs,* ed. Denis Donoghue (New York: 1972), pp. 65, 211–12. Davis's ballads are collected in *The Spirit of the Nation* (Dublin: 1845), which ran to more than fifty editions.
20. State system of elementary education under denominational control established in 1831.
21. See Padraic Fallon, 'The Poetry of Thomas Davis', *Thomas Davis and Young Ireland,* ed. M.J. McManus (Government Publications, Dublin 1945), p. 26.
22. Mitchel developed Davis's vague ideas on an armed movement, like the Volunteers of 1782, and Lalor filled out his theories on land ownership, based on Sismondi's thinking.
23. The Gaelic League was founded in 1893, Sinn Fein in 1905.
24. See *Irish Times,* 18 August 1975, lecture by Professor John A. Murphy at Derrynane Folk School, on O'Connell and the Irish language. When O'Connell made the remark, in 1833, Catholic Ireland west of a line from Derry to Cork was Irish-speaking.
25. *Davis, Thinker and Teacher,* pp. 83–4.
26. William Smith O'Brien, a member of an ancient Gaelic family descended from King Brian Boru, was a Protestant landlord and Whig member of parliament who joined the Repeal Association and became the political leader of Young Ireland. When Peel brought in a bill to set up colleges in Ireland's provincial centres to provide the middle-class with university education, Davis supported the scheme and O'Connell opposed it. The debate between O'Connell's Repealers and Young Ireland turned on confessional as against secular politics. For an account of the controversy, see Gavan Duffy, *Young Ireland,* ii, 165–90; Gwynn, *O'Connell* pp. 242–3.
27. O'Connell in 1843 followed much the same strategy for Repeal as he had adopted in the 1820s for Catholic emancipation: mass agitation by way of mass meetings. These last were extended and called monster meetings. They were to educate and give the people a sense of discipline and solidarity and frighten the Peel government. They were supported by the local clergy and the *Nation.* Of the forty meetings held only one was in Ulster – in a Catholic centre. When the Clontarf (Dublin) meeting was banned O'Connell complied with the order to avoid bloodshed; he said. He was found guilty of conspiracy and sentenced to a year in prison, but his conviction was reversed by the House of Lords.
28. The circulation of the *Nation,* according to Duffy (Young Ireland, ii, Appendix) was 10,730 for the quarter ending 31 December 1843, a respectable figure for an intellectual review. It cost sixpence a copy. Nine thousand copies were sold to agents and subscribers; the balance went to Repeal rooms, where the paper was read aloud to groups.
29. Gavan Duffy, *Young Ireland,* ii, 176–7. Belfast's Queen's College was

for Presbyterians, Galway and Cork for Catholics. There were no denominational tests and the bishops divided on the issue. But Archbishop John MacHale of Tuam opposed the principle of mixed Catholic-Protestant education, and O'Connell supported him. Mixed education was a principle of Young Ireland, of course. At the same time, Sir Robert Peel, in a separate bill, increased Maynooth's annual grant from £9,000 to £26,000.

30. *Thomas Davis and Young Ireland*, ed. M.J. McManus (Government Publications, Dublin: 1945).
31. Daniel Corkery, 'Davis and the National Language', *Thomas Davis and Young Ireland*, 'Davis would seem to be satisfied that the *life* of the country should be carried on in English, and the *dreaming* in Irish' (p. 21).
32. *Davis, Thinker and Teacher*, p. 2. Said Gustave de Beaumont: 'A bad aristocracy is the cause of all the woes of Ireland; and the evil of that aristocracy is in its being English and Protestant.'
33. *Ibid.*, p. 199.
34. Griffith speech to founding convention of Sinn Fein, 28 November 1905 (*United Irishman* 9 December 1905). On Sismondi's influence, see Edward Sheehy, 'Davis's Social Doctrines', *Thomas Davis and Young Ireland*, pp. 28–31.
35. *Davis, Thinker and Teacher*, p. 163. If the people were given the opportunity to become small proprietors, wrote Davis, 'there is much, perhaps every hope of retaining or regaining our homestead habits, and such a population need fear no enemy'.
36. *Ibid.*, p. 115. Davis adds: 'May Ireland be a nation! May she win independence by a free concession of her rights! for this too was the wish of his heart, though fate compelled him to forego it, and seek freedom with an armed hand.' No more than O'Connell, Davis did not fully face up to the alternative if England denied 'a free concession' of Ireland's rights – which was the case through the centuries.
37. *Ibid.*, p. 180.
38. 'Ribbonism', meaning the doctrines of the Ribbonmen, successor agrarian organization to the Defenders. Davis urged 'open combination', instead of 'secret conspiracy'. He was horrified by the assassination of landlords and their agents. He had no understanding of peasant life, or its realities. Sir George Cornewall Lewis, *On Local Disturbances in Ireland and on the Irish Church Question* (London: 1836), an authority on agrarianism who was consulted by various British governments, contended that outrages arose from the conditions of Irish land ownership, and that the agrarian societies were 'a vast trade union for the protection of the Irish peasantry'. They set the labourer's wages and the smallholder's rent. 'It is in fact the mould into which Irish society is cast; the expression of the wants and feelings of the great mass of the community,' Lewis declared.
39. *Davis, Thinker and Teacher*, p. 194. Davis believed landlordism had produced in Ireland 'a feudalism closely resembling in its evils that of France under the old regime' (*ibid.*, 195). The origin of this landlordism was confiscation, its continuation depended on British power, he said. Even here there is something of Lalor's later theory on repealing 'the Conquest'.

40. Gavan Duffy, *Young Ireland,* i, 138–40.
41. *Ibid.*
42. *Ibid.*
43. See Ruth Dudley Edwards, *Patrick Pearse: the Triumph of Failure* (London: 1977).
44. P.H. Pearse, *Political Writings and Speeches* (Dublin: 1952), pp. 299–329.
45. *Ibid.*, p. 303.
46. Thomas Jones, *Whitehall Diary* iii, 103–4.
47. *Dail Eireann. Official Report: Debate on the Treaty Between Great Britain and Ireland. Signed in London on the 6th December, 1921* (Dublin: 1922), p. 23.
48. *Davis, Thinker and Teacher,* p. 2.
49. *Ibid.*, p. 128.
50. See *The Memoirs of Desmond FitzGerald* (London: 1969), pp. 140–1. He was Minister for External Affairs of the Irish Free State in the 1920s and something of a monarchist himself, like his colleague, Kevin O'Higgins, who wanted to crown George V 'King of Ireland' in the Phoenix Park, as his biographer, Terence de Vere White, avers. Pearse and Joseph Plunkett, two signatories of the Proclamation of the Irish Republic, talked of crowning the German, Prince Joachim, King of Ireland, FitzGerald claims. Ernest Blythe, another member of the first Free State government, recalled hearing a similar proposal by Thomas MacDonagh, also a signatory of the Proclamation, and Plunkett in January 1916. (See *Irish Times,* 7 April and 15 April, 1966.) One Volunteer leader, Michael O'Rahilly from Kerry, assumed the Gaelic clan title, 'The O'Rahilly', although under Brehon law it was not a hereditary right. He died in the Rising, which he had opposed, and, as a Yeats poem makes clear, justified by his deeds his claim to call himself 'The O'Rahilly'.
51. Quoted by Donald Davie, 'The Young Yeats', in *The Shaping of Modern Ireland,* ed. Conor Cruise O'Brien, (London: 1960), p. 141.
52. Quoted by Mansergh, *The Irish Question,* p. 273.
53. *Autobiography of W.B. Yeats,* p. 349.
54. Gavan Duffy, *Young Ireland,* i, 87.
55. *Ibid.*, ii, 191.
56. Lalor's letter was dated 11 January 1847, and consisted of a fierce diatribe against O'Connell. 'As to the pledge of abstaining from the use of any but moral force,' he wrote, 'I am quite willing to take such pledge if, and provided, the English government agree to take it also. . . .' Lalor's main point was that the land question was more important than Repeal and would mobilize the peasantry behind a struggle for national independence. (See *James Fintan Lalor: Collected Writings,* ed. with biographical essay, L. Fogarty [Dublin: 1918] – a work banned by the British censor.)
57. John Mitchel, *The Last Conquest of Ireland – Perhaps* (London: 1876), p. 242.
58. John Mitchel, *Jail Journal* (Dublin: 1913), p. 78.
59. James Connolly, *Labour in Irish History* (Dublin: 1944), p. 182.
60. Article by Mitchel from Irish-American journal, *Shamrock,* on death of his colleague Thomas Francis Meagher, in *Thomas Davis and Young Ireland,* p. 93. See his introduction, *An Apology for the British Government in Ireland* (Dublin: 1905).

61. *Marx/Engels, Ireland*, p. 335, letter to Eduard Bernstein, 26 June 1882: 'Without war or the threat of war from without, an Irish rebellion has not the slightest chance.'
62. Pearse, *Political Writings*, p. 254.
63. Connolly, *Labour in Irish History*, p. 181.
64. See Sean Cronin, 'John Mitchel's Call to Protestant Ulster', *Capuchin Annual* (Dublin: 1976), pp. 81–92.
65. Dated 30 March 1847, *Lalor*, pp. xxii–xxiv. D'Arcy McGee was secretary of the Irish Confederation. He went into exile, first in America, then in Canada, after 1848 rebellion, changed his politics, and became federal Minister of Agriculture in Ottawa, and an architect of Canadian Confederation. He was assassinated by Fenians because of his fierce denunciations of his erstwhile colleagues.
66. D'Arcy McGee, 'A New Nation', *James Fintan Lalor*, ed. L. Fogarty, (Dublin: 1918), p. 22.
67. *Devon Commission Report* (Dublin: 1845), p. 1116.
68. See Cecil Woodham-Smith, *The Great Hunger* (London: 1962).
69. See Tomas O Neill, *Fiontan O Leathlobhair* (Dublin: 1962), pp. 23–29, 130–1. In the letter to Peel, Lalor said Ireland needed to improve the condition of its people's lives, but this could not be done until the Repeal movement was 'speedily and safely suppressed' and offered to supply information to that end.
70. Lalor, 'Letter to John Mitchel', *Lalor*, pp. 44–5.
71. John Stuart Mill, *Principles of Political Economy* (London: 1911), pp. 200–1. Mill blamed the 'system of land tenancy' for the Famine.
72. Fenian leaders.
73. Devoy, an exiled Fenian, linked the revolutionary movement with the land struggle.
74. *Irish Felon*, 8 July 1848.
75. Michael Doheny, *The Felon's Track* (New York: 1867), p. 95.
76. *Ibid.* Doheny says three thousand joined Smith O'Brien's rebellion and camped near the village of Mullinahone (p. 97).
77. See Denis Gwynn, *Young Ireland and 1848* (Cork: 1948). O'Brien, Meagher and two others were tried for high treason and condemned to death. In July 1849 they were reprieved and deported to Australia.
78. *The Times*, 2 August 1848.
79. *Ibid.*
80. *Ibid.*
81. *The Times*, 5 August 1848.
82. Cullen told the future Cardinal Newman: 'I trust you will make every exertion to keep the University free from all Young Irelandism, of which the spirit is so evident in the *Nation*!' Newman, an Englishman and a Tory, did not care for Young Ireland either, but some of his best professors were the men Cullen had in mind, and besides he was a tolerant man. (See Peadar Mac Suibhne, *Paul Cullen and His Contemporaries*, [Naas: 1961], i, 381.) A particular target of Cullen's anger among the Young Ireland leaders was Charles Gavan Duffy, editor of the *Nation* and the most conservative of the group. Cullen drove him out of Ireland in the mid-1850s. He went to Australia, entered politics, became Premier of New South Wales, was knighted by Queen Victoria and re-

turned to Ireland in the 1890s.

83. *The Pastoral Letters and Other Writings of Cardinal Cullen, Archbishop of Dublin,* (Dublin: 1882), ed. Right Rev. Patrick Moran, DD.

84. *Accounts and Papers – Ireland* (vol. xlix), session 1 February to 1 August 1849. The parliamentary papers state that 118 persons were arrested. Clarendon's report is dated 26 January 1849.

85. *The Times*, 16 August 1848.

86. See Sean Cronin, *The Revolutionaries* (Dublin: 1971), pp. 75–6, for an account of this little-known rebellion, surely the briefest in Irish history. *The Times* said on his death: 'Mr. Lalor was undoubtedly one of the (if not the) ablest as well as most dangerous of these men who perverted abilities of a very high order to the worst of purposes.'

CHAPTER 4

1. The movment was called the IRB, for Irish Revolutionary (or Republican) Brotherhood, in Ireland, the Fenian Brotherhood in America; hence the name 'Fenians'. John Devoy, the Fenian leader, wrote in *Recollections of an Irish Rebel* (New York: 1929), Chapter 2: 'The Fenian movement was started, not in Ireland, but in New York in 1855 (sic) . . . James Fintan Lalor might be said to be the real father of Fenianism as well as of the Land League.' Two men who had been with Smith O'Brien in the 1848 rebellion, James Stephens and John O'Mahony, formally launched the new revolutionary organization, in March 1858, in Dublin and New York. Stephens took charge of the Irish body, O'Mahony of the American. O'Mahony, a Gaelic scholar, came up with the name 'Fenian Brotherhood'. The movement in Ireland was secret, the movement in America open, basing 'our right of action upon our privileges as *American citizens* and keeping within the laws of these states', as O'Mahony explained to Charles Kickham in October 1863. Thus, from the start, the attitudes of the Fenians in America and in Ireland were at odds: the American Irish spurned secret methods, the Irish espoused them. Much of what the Fenians in America said and did was printed in the newspapers. When they landed in Ireland they took few precautions against capture.
2. See William D'Arcy, *The Fenian Movement in the United States, 1858–1886* (Washington: 1947); Brian Jenkins, *Fenians and Anglo-American Relations During Reconstruction* (Ithaca, N.Y.: 1969); Leon O Broin, *Fenian Fever: An Anglo-American Dilemma* (London: 1971); Joseph Denieffe, *A Personal Narrative of the Irish Revolutionary Brotherhood* (New York: 1906); John O'Leary, *Recollections of Fenians and Fenianism,* (London: 1896), *Fenians and Fenianism*, ed. Maurice Harmon (Washington: 1970).
3. *Marx/Engels, Ireland,* p. 148, Marx to Engels, 30 November, 1867.
4. *Ibid.*, pp. 143–4, 2 November, 1867. Lord *Abicorn's* correct name was Abercorn, Lord Lieutenant of Ireland, 1866–68, 1874–76.
5. *Ibid.*, pp. 280–1, 29 November, 1869. Kugelmann, a German physician, was a member of the First International.

6. *Ibid.*, p. 142, lecture in London, 16 December, 1867. The letters of Marx and Engels on Ireland were published in one volume in Moscow in 1971, with an introduction by Professor L.I. Golman. See also Norman B. Davis, *Nationalism and Socialism: Marxist and Labour Theories of Nationalism to 1917* (New York: 1967), and Seán Cronin, *Marx and the Irish Question* (Dublin: 1977), a paper delivered to a seminar of the Graduate Faculty of Political and Social Science of the New School for Social Research, under Professor Saul K. Padover, in May 1976.
7. John Stuart Mill, *Principles of Political Economy*, 1911 edition, pp. 199–200.
8. See Strauss, *Irish Nationalism and British Democracy*, on the Encumbered Estates Act of 1849, which in thirty years sold one-quarter of the land of Ireland to a new class of proprietor, usually Irish land agents, lawyers and large shopkeepers, which if anything made the lot of the tenant harsher. 'Of 32,610 landed proprietors, just over one-half (18,100) held a mere 474,000 acres or 2.3 per cent, a further quarter (8,010) held 1,956,000 acres (9.7 per cent), and the remaining 6,500 landowners held 17,720,000 acres (88 per cent) with estates averaging as much as 2,726 acres each. This handful of landlords dominated the Irish policy of the British Government'. (pp. 136–7).
9. Quoted by E.R. Norman, *The Catholic Church and Ireland in the Age of Rebellion* (London: 1965), pp. 144–5.
10. Cullen had secret information on the Fenian leaders: James Stephens was a socialist for a time, but he did not impose his view on the movement; John O'Leary, editor of the Fenian weekly, *Irish People*, was an agnostic; Thomas Clarke Luby was a Protestant. Cullen considered such men unfit leaders of Irish Catholics. The manager of the *Irish People*, Jeremiah O'Donovan Rossa, like Kickham, was an orthodox Catholic.
11. *Two Letters of the Most Reverend Dr. Cullen to the Catholic Clergy of Dublin on the Cholera, and Other Natural Scourges and on Orangeism and Fenianism* (Dublin: 1865), pp. 17–18.
12. Quoted by Mac Suibhne, *Cullen and His Contemporaries*, i, 299–300.
13. Two Letters, pp. 14–15.
14. Mac Suibhne, *Cullen and His Contemporaries*, pp. 397–405.
15. *Ibid.*
16. Norman, *Catholic Church and Ireland*, p. 145.
17. *Ibid.*, Chapter 3 'The Church and Fenianism'. MacHale was no revolutionary, but he distrusted both Cullen and the British government. Later he opposed the Land League. Cullen's own view seemed to be that the only proper authority in Ireland was the Catholic Church; England maintained the ascendancy of 'a small Orange faction' and Fenianism sought to alienate the Irish from their religion. *(Letter Read in all Churches in Dublin, January 27, 1868.)* The priest was Fr. Patrick Lavelle.
18. A force of 750 men seized Fort Erie and defeated a mixed Canadian-English militia unit at Ridgway, retreated to Buffalo and were arrested by US authorities. (See *Correspondence Respecting the Recent Fenian Aggression Upon Canada*, presented to both Houses of Parliament, Feburary 1867.)
19. Quoted Desmond Ryan, *The Fenian Chief* (Dublin: 1967), p. 244.
20. Captain John McCafferty in *The Irishman*, 8 March 1884, from Paris.

See *Devoy's Post Bag*, eds. Desmond Ryan and William O'Brien (Dublin: 1953), ii, 213 fn. On the campaign itself, see K.R.M. Short, *The Dynamite War: Irish-American Bombers in Victorian Britain*. Non-Clan followers of O'Donovan Rossa started the 'war' in 1881 and were known as 'skirmishers' – men who would 'keep up without intermission a guerrilla war' against England, as the *Irish World* (4 December, 1875), edited by Patrick Ford, envisaged it. (*ibid.* p. 35). Tom Clarke, the 1916 leader, was one of Clan-na-Gaels dynamiters – he emigrated a few years before the campaign – and received a life sentence for his part, serving almost sixteen years. (See T.J. Clarke, *Glimpses of an Irish Felon's Prison Life,* [Dublin: 1922].)

21. See Jememiah O'Donovan Rossa, *My Years in English Jails* (New York: 1874). Rossa was sentenced to life imprisonment in 1865, amnestied in 1870 and exiled to America. Marx and his daughter, Jenny, wrote articles telling of Rossa's treatment in prison.
22. O'Leary, *Recollections,* i, 152.
23. Quoted in Ryan, *Fenian Chief,* pp. 241–2. One section of the Fenians offered Cluseret command of their military forces.
24. *Irish Historical Documents,* 'William Ewart Gladstone on Home Rule, House of Commons, 8 April 1886', p. 287.
25. Marx, in *The German Ideology,* defined ideology as 'false consciousness'. But he also noted that 'consciousness can never be anything else than conscious existence, and the existence of men is their actual life-process' (p. 47). One could say that in Ireland the peasants were conscious of the struggle for the means of life and their nationalist tradition could easily relate them to the ideology of republicanism, i.e. independence and separation from England, as a long-term goal.
26. See O'Leary, *Recollections,* ii, 238.
27. See Strauss, *Irish Nationalism,* p. 149.
28. *Marx/Engels, Ireland,* pp. 161–2, 'Confidential Communication' to the General Council of the First International, written by Marx about 28 March, 1870.
29. The Clan was founded in New York in June 1867. In its internal correspondence it called itself the United Brotherhood, using the letters VC as a code: they immediately follow UB.
30. Clan Constitution of 1877.
31. See Seán Ó Luing, *Fremantle Mission* (Tralee: 1965). The year was 1877.
32. Michael Davitt's parents were evicted from their Mayo holding when Davitt was a boy. He grew up in industrial Lancashire. See Frank Sheehy-Skeffington, *Michael Davitt: Revolutionary Agitator and Labour Leader* (London: 1967).
33. The two points of the 'New Departure' were, self-government for Ireland and the creation of a peasant proprietorship – the Alpha and Omega of Irish nationalist ideology. On the IRB, see Leon O Broin, *Revolutionary Underground,* Chapter 1. The IRB's 1873 Constitution said a rebellion must be supported by the majority of the people of Ireland. The function of the organization was to wait for the 'majority' to reveal itself.
34. The first meeting of the Land League was held at Irishtown, County Mayo, to protest threatened evictions by the executor of an estate, a Catholic priest, Canon Geoffrey Burke. MacHale took the side of his priest and denounced Davitt and company. (See Davitt's *The Fall of Feudalism in*

Ireland [New York: 1904], 'The Irishtown Meeting'.)

35. *Ibid.*, pp. 117–18.
36. *Ibid.* 'Conspiracy and sporadic insurrection had failed. Other and more effective, if less heroic, plans were imperatively required if the Irish cause was not to die of an atrophy begotten of a dreamy do-nothingism, on the one hand, and a spiritless unaggressive constitutionalism on the other.'
37. Parnell was reported as follows: 'When we have undermined English misgovernment, we have paved the way for Ireland to take her place among the nations of the earth. And let us not forget that this is the ultimate goal at which all we Irishmen aim. None of us, whether we are in America or in Ireland, or wherever we may be, will be satisfied until we have destroyed the last link which binds Ireland to England.' For the controversy surrounding this speech, see Lyons, *Parnell*, pp. 111–12, and Emmet Larkin, *The Roman Catholic Church and the Creation of the Modern Irish State, 1878–1886* (Dublin: 1975), pp. 33–4.
38. Davitt, *Fall of Feudalism*, p. 321.
39. 'In Ireland the plundering and even extermination of the tenant farmer and his family by the landlord is called the property right, whereas the desperate farmer's revolt against his ruthless executioner is called an agrarian outrage.' (Jenny Marx, article for French Republican paper, *Marseillaise*, date-lined London, 2 April, 1870.)
40. *Connaught Telegraph*, 25 September, 1880, and pamphlet *Lord Erne and His Lough Mask Tenantry: Correspondence in reference to the agency of Captain Boycott* (Dublin: 1880); Davitt, *Fall of Feudalism*, pp. 276–7.
41. First Irish feminist movement and extremely effective.
42. Larkin, *Roman Catholic Church*, p. 72.
43. *Marx/Engels, Ireland* pp. 333–7, 16 June, 1882.
44. Davitt, *Fall of Feudalism*, pp. 355–64, for Davitt's reaction to Kilmainham Treaty, that put an end to the 'social insurrection'.
45. The ex-Fenians included Patrick Egan, treasurer of the League, and Thomas Brennan, an organizer, who fled to America following the assassination of Lord Frederick Cavendish, the new Chief Secretary, and Under-Secretary Burke, in the Phoenix Park, Dublin, after the 'Kilmainham Treaty', in May 1882. There was a connection, however tenuous, between men like Egan, Brennan, among others, and the Invincibles, the secret group responsible for the Phoenix Park assassinations. (See P.J.P. Tynan, *The Irish National Invincibles* [London: 1977]).
46. *Irish Historical Documents*, p. 287.
47. The Bill lost in the Commons by thirty votes, having split the Liberal Party.
48. H.O. Arnold-Foster, 'An English View of Irish Secession', *Political Science Quarterly*, vol. iv (Columbia University N.Y.: 1889).
49. *Ibid.*
50. For more on Ulster Protestant attitudes, see Patrick Buckland, *Ulster Unionism and the Origins of Northern Ireland 1886 to 1922* (Dublin: 1973): Geoffrey Bell, *The Protestants of Ulster* (London: 1976) and David W. Miller, *Queen's Rebels* (Dublin: 1978).
51. Patrick Buckland, *Irish Unionism*, vol. i: *The Anglo-Irish and the New Ireland 1885 to 1922* (Dublin: 1972), p. 7. Lecky represented Dublin

University (Trinity College), as a Unionist, in the British House of Commons.

52. Gladstone's Bill called for a popularly elected, representative lower house, and a partly-elected, partly-appointed upper house. It would mark the beginning of democratic government in Ireland. The Tories and Unionists saw it as the first step in the dismemberment of the empire.
53. Standish O'Grady, 'The Bardic History of Ireland', *One Thousand Years of Irish Prose*, ed. Vivian Mercier and David H. Greene (New York: 1952), pp. 14–15. O'Grady wrote: 'Other literatures have floated far away from that to which they owe their genesis. They resemble the full course of a stream which has had its source far away. The stream of the Irish bardic literature still lingers in the mountains which gave it birth. It is near the well-head.' (pp. 24–5).
54. *Ibid.*, pp. 78–89.
55. Douglas Hyde, *Thousand Years of Irish Prose*, 'The Necessity for De-Anglicizing Ireland'. There were other language movements before the Gaelic League, among the emigrants in America as well as in Ireland. But what made the movement initiated by Hyde's lecture different was that it became the ideology of modern Irish nationalism. This is best stated in words written by an Irish emigrant in Patrick Ford's *Irish World* (New York) in 1872. 'The Irish language should be cultivated in order to maintain Irish ideas and Irish nationality in their integrity,' wrote Michael J. Logan. (*Go Meiricea Siar*, [Dublin: 1979], ed. Stiofáin Ó hAnnracháin, p. 20.)
56. Quoted by R.M. Henry, *The Evolution of Sinn Féin* (Dublin: 1919), p. 75.
57. P.H. Pearse, *From a Hermitage* (Dublin: 1915). Because of the Gaelic League, Pearse wrote, 'Our country wears to us a new aspect, and yet she is her most ancient self.'
58. Sean O'Casey, *Pictures in the Hallway* (New York: 1942), p. 244.
59. L. Paul-Dubois, *Contemporary Ireland* (Dublin: 1908), p. 410.
60. Griffith preached that Irish members of parliament should meet in Dublin and legislate for Ireland as the representatives of the nation. He held that the old Irish parliament had been illegally disbanded by the Act of Union and that only 'the King, Lords and Commons of Ireland', like Hungary, an independent kingdom, could legislate for Ireland.
61. Thomas Davis, unfairly, has been blamed for this by Alf MacLochlainn ('Thomas Davis and Irish Racialism', *Irish Times*, 20 November, 1973) and Maurice R. O'Connell ('Thomas Davis: a Destructive Conciliator', *Irish Times*, 6 August, 1974) because of his romantic nationalism.
62. On Moran see Brian Inglis, 'Moran of the *Leader* and Ryan of the *Irish Peasant*', *The Shaping of Modern Ireland* pp. 108–123. (W.P. Ryan was a member of the Gaelic League. He clashed with Cardinal Logue and wrote *The Pope's Green Island* [London: 1912], telling his experiences.)
63. See F.J. Byrne, 'MacNeill the Historian', *The Scholar Revolutionary: Eoin MacNeill 1867–1945*, ed. F.X. Martin and F.J. Byrne (New York: 1973), p. 17.
64. Quoted *ibid.*, p. 24.
65. Oration delivered by P.H. Pearse at the grave of the Fenian, Jeremiah O'Donovan Rossa, Glasnevin cemetary, Dublin, 1 August, 1915.

66. Brian Farrell, 'MacNeill in Politics', *Scholar Revolutionary*, p. 188.
67. See Rev. Francis Shaw, S.J., 'The Canon of Irish History – a Challenge', the Irish Jesuit quarterly, *Studies* (Summer 1972). Fr. Shaw attacks Pearse's 'Messianic nationalism' and the notion that the Irish in 1916 were 'a generation in need of redemption by the shedding of blood'.
68. Pearse 'Peace of the Gael', *Political Writings and Speeches* (Dublin: 1952), pp. 213–18. Sean O'Casey satirized one of Pearse's 'blood passages' in his play on the 1916 insurrection, *The Plough and the Stars.*
69. Carson, a Dublin lawyer, was the leader of Ulster Unionism's crusade against Home Rule.
70. 'When we were starting St. Enda's I [Pearse] said to my boys: "We must re-create and perpetuate in Ireland the knightly tradition of Cuchulainn. . . better a short life with honour than long life with dishonour . . . . I care not though I were to live but one day and one night, if only my fame and my deeds live after me" ' (Patrick Pearse *The Murder Machine,* pp. 38–9). He also held up the early Celtic saint, Colmcille, as a model. Colmcille's declaration, 'If I die it shall be from the excess of the love I bear the Gael', appealed to Pearse.
71. Pearse, *The Sovereign People,* p. 345. Both passages are quoted by Father Shaw.
72. Fr. Shaw, 'The Canon of Irish History – a Challenge', *Studies*. There are a number of biographies of Pearse, the ablest and most detailed being Ruth Dudley Edwards, *Patrick Pearse: the Triumph of Failure* (London: 1977).
73. The seven signatories of the Proclamation of the Irish Republic in 1916 were: Thomas J. Clarke, Sean MacDermott, P.H. Pearse, James Connolly, Eamonn Ceannt, Joseph Plunkett and Thomas MacDonagh.
74. *An Barr Buadh*, 16 March, 1912.
75. *Ibid.*, 23 March, 1912, 'An nDíolfar Éire?' (Will Ireland be Sold?)
76. *Ibid.*, 6 April, 1912. His concluding paragraph warned the parliamentary leaders, John Redmond, John Dillon and Joseph Devlin, that they had no authority from the Irish people to guarantee peace to England until independence was granted.
77. *Ibid.*, 13 April, 1912, 'Do'n Ghnó Atá Rómhainn' (To the Deed that's Before us). A few days earlier (9 April) Bonar Law, leader of the Tory Party, said in Larne: ' . . . if this Home Rule Bill should by any chance be forced through . . . Heaven help the Government that tries to enforce it.' On the same day Sir Edward Carson said in Belfast: ' . . . if necessary they would treat the government with force.' (From daily newspaper reports).
78. Pearse's ideas are in his scattered writings – essays, plays, short stories. His *Political Writings and Speeches* (Dublin: 1922) has many of them. Also *Scribhínní Phádraig Mhic Phiarais* (Dublin: 1924) contains much of his writing in Irish, a language he mastered and helped to modernize through his short stories and plays. His views on education were very advanced: 'A school was less a place than a little group of persons, a master and his disciples.' (See *The Educational Writings of P.H. Pearse* [Cork: 1980], ed. Seamas O Buachalla.
79. *Winston S. Churchill: his Complete Speeches 1897–1963*, ed. Robert Rhodes James (London: 1974), vol. ii, 1908–1913, 'Government of Ireland Bill, January 1, 1913', House of Commons, pp. 2053–9.

80. *Ibid.*, 'Home Rule for Ireland', 8 October, 1913, Dundee, Scotland, pp. 2152–3.

81. The Hobson, MacDermott and Clarke letters are in the files of Joseph McGarrity. The point is that Churchill was right: the IRB was isolated and of no consequence in 1907 and not even Griffith's Sinn Féin wanted any part of it. When Hobson and MacDermott, influenced by the veteran Clarke, moved into the leadership around 1912, the IRB used the Ulster crisis to build a coalition with other national elements and founded the Irish Volunteers in response to Carson's Ulster Volunteers. The IRB stayed in the background but it moved men it could rely on, like Pearse, into key positions. Clarke and MacDermott broke with Hobson, because they felt he compromised the IRB position in the Volunteers by virtually handing the organization over to John Redmond and the Parliamentary Party in the summer of 1914 (see Hobson's letter to McGarrity, 14 July, 1914, appendix IV in this volume.) Clarke and MacDermott then single-mindedly moved toward rebellion with the aid of Devoy and the Clan, which supplied the money and the German arms. As treasurer and secretary of the three-member IRB Executive, Clarke and MacDermott controlled that organization. The third member, the President of the Supreme Council of the IRB, Denis McCullough, was told as little as possible, presumably because he was a friend of Hobson. Hobson opposed the Easter Rising. (See Bulmer Hobson, *Ireland: Yesterday and Tomorrow* [Tralee: 1968], for account of IRB in early years of century. It was sustained by Clan subsidy of £1000 a year – $5000). Hobson in letter to author, 17 June, 1969, wrote:

> At the meeting of the Supreme Council in August 1914 Clarke and MacDermott pressed for a resolution deciding to have an insurrection before the war ended. The Council was by no means unanimous and the terms proposed seemed quite vague and they appointed Clarke and MacDermott as a committee to go into the matter and report to a subsequent meeting of the Supreme Council. It was very indefinite. Clarke and MacDermott had power to co-opt others to act with them. They never reported back. The Council hardly ever met after that and was not kept informed of the doings of this sub-committee. . . . In effect the Military Committee created a secret organization within the IRB and only the members belonging to this group were allowed to know what was in preparation.

82. *An Claidheamh Soluis*, 1 November, 1913. On 8 November 1913 Pearse wrote 'The Coming Revolution' for the same journal. The founding meeting of the Volunteers was held at the Rotunda, Dublin, on 25 November, 1913, with about 4000 in attendance. Within six months the Volunteers had 75,000 members but no arms. Most controlling positions were held by the IRB and the Parliamentary Party saw the new movement as a threat.

83. McGarrity was the most important Clan leader after Devoy. He was born in Tyrone and emigrated to Philadelphia in 1893 at the age of sixteen. He made several fortunes and devoted the money to the Clan, the IRB, the Irish Volunteers, Sinn Féin, the IRA – to any organization that would *fight* for Irish independence. He supported Hobson, Clarke and MacDermott in their bid for the leadership of the IRB and financed the early issues of *Irish Freedom*, which they sponsored. He broke with Devoy in 1920 when the old Fenian clashed with de Valera; broke with de Valera and

supported the IRA in the 1930s; and finally master-minded and funded the IRA bombing campaign in England, 1939–40. (See Seán Cronin, *The McGarrity Papers* (Tralee: 1972).)

84. 'Oration on Robert Emmet,' delivered at the Brooklyn Academy of Music, 2 March, 1914. See Pearse, *Political Writings*, pp. 64–75.
85. Object of the Irish Volunteers. See *The Irish Volunteers, 1913–1915*, ed. F.X. Martin (Dublin: 1963). As Pearse noted in an ironic piece (January 1914), the Provisional Committee of the Volunteers 'includes United Irish Leaguers, Hibernians, Sinn Féiners, Gaelic Leaguers, and even a few who call themselves simply Separatists. . .'. (*Political Writings*, pp. 201–2).
86. See F.X. Martin, 'The Evolution of a Myth – The Easter Rising, Dublin 1916', *Nationalism: the Nature and Evolution of an Idea*, ed. Eugene Kamenka (New York: 1976). MacNeill was Chief of Staff of the Volunteers. Clarke and MacDermott, however, had established a Military Committee to plan a rebellion, using the Irish Volunteers. Hobson said they lacked IRB authority to do so. The Military Committee ignored MacNeill and his staff, including his adviser Hobson, and worked through staff officers who, like Pearse and MacDonagh, were members of the IRB.
87. Pearse, 'Why We Want Recruits', *Political Writings*, pp. 122–3. Pearse was the chief ideologist and political officer of the Irish Volunteers and his writings must be judged from that standpoint. The stress on arms and bloodshed he considered essential, it is only fair to assume, if the Volunteers were to be more than stage soldiers. See in this connection Seán Cronin, 'A Man Called Pearse: "Armed Action – Politics by Violent Means" ', *Irish Independent*, 13 November, 1979.
88. Pearse, 'Ghosts', *Political Writings*, p. 227.
89. *Ibid.*, p. 228.
90. Fr. Shaw, 'The Canon of Irish History – a Challenge', *Studies* (Summer 1972), p. 127. As Fr. Shaw suggests, Wolfe Tone was anti-Catholic for rationalist reasons – because of the 'superstitions' of its adherents and his contempt for 'priest-craft'.
91. Pearse, 'The Separatist Idea', *Political Writings*, p. 291.
92. Dudley Edwards, *Pearse*, p. 341.
93. The Republicans who rejected the Irish Free State did so in part because it did not live up to their conception of the ideals of Pearse. A Republican monument over Tone's grave at Bodenstown, County Kildare, carries a quotation from Pearse about Tone!
94. Pearse, 'Peace and the Gael', *Political Writings*, pp. 216–17, Pearse's play *The Singer* is almost pacifist and was produced around the same time. MacDara, the hero, says, 'I will take no pike. I will go into battle with bare hands'.
95. *Ibid.*, p. 176, October 1913.
96. Quoted by Dudley Edwards, *Pearse*, p. 212.
97. Pearse, *Political Writings*, p. 178.
98. *Ibid.*, p. 336. Despite his high regard for Connolly, Pearse remained an enemy of class warfare. He maintained that 'all surplus wealth shall go to the national treasury. . . . rather than be accumulated by private persons'.
99. See C. Desmond Greaves, *The Life and Times of James Connolly* (London: 1961); Samuel Levenson, *James Connolly* (London: 1973); Desmond

Ryan, *James Connolly* (London: 1924); Roger Faligot, *James Connolly* (Paris: 1978); Carl and Ann Reeve, *James Connolly and the United States* (Dublin and New York: 1979); Seán Cronin, *Young Connolly* (Dublin: 1978); Manus O'Riordan, *James Connolly in America* (Dublin: 1971).

100. Quoted by Cronin, *Young Connolly*, pp. 35–6.
101. *Ibid.*, pp. 101–2. Also: 'The Irish question is a social question, the whole age-long fight of the Irish people against their oppressors resolves itself, in the last analysis, into a fight for the mastery of the means of life, the sources of production in Ireland' (Arthur Mitchell, *Labour in Irish History*, [Dublin: 1974] pp. 167–8).
102. James Connolly, *Socialism and Nationalism* (Dublin: 1948), pp. 91–2. Conor Cruise O'Brien, *States of Ireland* (London: 1972) takes Connolly to task for his unrealistic attitude to Protestant Unionism. Far from being unrealistic, Connolly was the first to analyse the settler-colonial base of their politics. Professor John Whyte of Queen's University, Belfast, in a paper for the Ford Foundation, 'Interpretations of the Northern Ireland Conflict', (1976) uncritically accepts O'Brien's version of Connolly's views.
103. *Ibid.*, p. 87, 'Sinn Féin, Socialism and the Nation', *Irish Nation* (Dublin), 23 January, 1909.
104. *Ibid.*, p. 109. 'The First Hint of Partition', *Forward*, 21 March, 1914.
105. *Ibid.*, p. 111, *Irish Worker* (Dublin), 14 March, 1914.
106. *Gaelic American* (New York), 25 April, 1914. Connolly concluded his letter: 'Let it be heard and understood that Labor in Ireland stands for the unity of Ireland – an Ireland united in the name of progress, and who shall separate us?'
107. See Emmet Larkin, *James Larkin: Irish Labour Leader, 1876–1947* (London: 1965). Larkin founded the Irish Transport and General Workers' Union, in 1909, as part of the syndicalist 'One Big Union' concept. After the failure of the 1913 strike, he was despondent and went to America. The Citizen Army declared that 'the ownership of Ireland moral and material is vested of right in the people of Ireland'. (See Seán O'Casey, *Story of the Irish Citizen Army* [Dublin: 1919].)
108. 'Our Duty in this Crisis', *Irish Worker*, 8 August, 1914.
109. *Ibid.*
110. *Workers' Republic*, 24 and 31 June, 1915. 'The Irish Citizen Army and the Irish Volunteers are open for all those who wish to qualify for the exercise of those qualities' in street-fighting, Connolly concluded his 24 July piece. He urged 'active defence' of strongpoints, which, with the genius of the commander, the skill of his subordinates and the courage of the partisans, could defeat an enemy who feared to destroy private property. Connolly learned in 1916 that the enemy did not fear to destroy private property, at least not in Dublin.
111. *Ibid.*, 31 July, 1915. The funeral was organized by the IRB. At first, Connolly was reluctant to co-operate, knowing the Irish bent for commemorating the dead and that the funeral would amount to no more than a ceremonial occasion. 'When are you fellows going to stop blethering about dead Fenians?' he asked. 'Why don't you get a few live ones for a change?' He relented, on being assured by Tom Clarke that the funeral should be taken seriously. (Samuel Levenson, *James Connolly* [London: 1973], p. 274).

112. *Ibid.*, 28 August, 1915.
113. *Ibid.*, 25 September, 1915.
114. *Ibid.*, 9 October, 1915.
115. James Connolly, *Labour in Ireland* (Dublin: 1944), pp. 328–9. Connolly's anarcho-syndicalism is usually ignored by Communists, who want him in *their* pantheon, as his uncompromising Marxism is ignored by Irish Republicans who want him in *their* pantheon. A.D. Kolpakov, of Moscow State University, in an introduction to a Russian edition of *Labour in Ireland*, in January 1970, cited his 'anarcho-syndicalist mistakes' while praising his Marxist analysis of Irish society. Kolpakov wrote: 'Attracted by the ideas of "industrial democracy", of workers' power, which had arisen as a result of struggle in the industrial sphere, he advances the syndicalist slogan of "One Big Union", underestimates the role of the political party of the working class as the leader of the nation-wide struggle. However, having a keen sense of political realism and the ability to analyze a situation as it was taking shape, Connolly gradually freed himself of his errors.' Brian O'Higgins, a traditionalist Irish Republican who remained with Sinn Féin after Eamon de Valera left the intransigents in 1926, always insisted that Connolly died an Irish Catholic Republican, having abandoned Marxist socialism by making his peace with the Church, on 11 May, 1916, the eve of his execution.
116. *Worker's Republic*, 6 November, 1915.
117. *Ibid.*, 4 December, 1915.
118. *Ibid.*, 11 December, 1915.
119. *Ibid.*, 18 December, 1915.
120. See Seán Cronin, 'Connolly's Leap in the Dark', *Capuchin Annual* (Dublin), 1977.
121. *Workers' Republic*, 4 December, 1915.
122. Banned issue of *Irish Worker*, 19 December, 1914. Editorial published as leaflet called *Irish Work*. Connolly told his lieutenant, William O'Brien, on the day of the Rising: 'We are going out to be slaughtered.'
123. O'Casey, *Story of the Irish Citizen Army*.
124. *Workers' Republic*, 22 January, 1916.
125. The members of the Military Council were: Pearse, Tom Clarke, Seán MacDermott, Joseph Plunkett, Eamonn Ceannt and Connolly. Thomas MacDonagh was co-opted in April 1916. He commanded the Dublin Volunteers.
126. Pearse was Director of Organization of the Irish Volunteers.
127. *Workers' Republic*, 27 November, 1915.
128. There are numerous books on the Rising, the most detailed is Desmond Ryan's *The Rising* (Dublin: 1969), the most dramatic Thomas Coffey's *Agony at Easter* (New York: 1969). About 1000 Volunteers participated in the Rising. (See Appendix VI, 'Memorandum by Joseph McGarrity on 1916 Rising.') The Citizen Army mobilized 219 members. At the time there were 150,000 Irish on service with the British army. Total casualties were 450 killed and 2614 wounded. There were sixteen executions, including Sir Roger Casement hanged for treason. MacNeill's opinion is quoted by Lyons, *Ireland Since the Famine*, p. 358.
129. See *Devoy's Post Bag*, ii, 492, Mary MacSwiney to her brother Peter in New York.

130. Quoted F.X. Martin, *Nationalism* article, from *Things Past Redress* (London: 1937).
131. Quoted León Ó Broin, *Dublin Castle and the 1916 Rising* (New York: 1971), p. 114.
132. *Ibid. Freeman's Journal* was the organ of the Parliamentary Party.
133. For details of the founding convention of Sinn Féin see the *United Irishman*, 9 December, 1905. The first Dungannon Club was founded in Belfast by Bulmer Hobson. The historic convention of Protestant Volunteers, that demanded Ireland's legislative independence of England, met in Dungannon in 1782. Hence the name. The few clubs that were formed disappeared into Sinn Féin.
134. See Cronin, *McGarrity Papers*, Chapter 1. This is a matter of some mystery. Griffith's *United Irishman* was financed by the IRB. He himself was a member, but did not attend meetings after the early 1900s.
135. *Selected Letters: Joyce*, ed. Richard Ellmann (New York: 1975), p. 102. In the letter to his brother Stanislaus, in November 1906, he added: 'Of course I see that its success would be to substitute Irish for English capital but no-one, I suppose, denies that capitalism is a stage of progress. The Irish proletariat has yet to be created. A feudal peasantry exists, scraping the soil but this would with a national revival or with a definite preponderance of England surely disappear. . . . Griffith is afraid of the priests – and he has every reason to be so. But, possibly, they are also a little afraid of him too. After all, he is holding out some secular liberty to the people and the Church doesn't approve of that'. (p. 125). W.B. Yeats contributed to the *United Irishman* in its early days – it was founded in 1899 – but after Griffith's savage attack on Synge's *Playboy of the Western World* and the riots that followed, they became enemies.
136. *United Irishman*, 9 December, 1905.
137. Roger Casement, who had worked for the British consular service, held that the only hope for Irish independence lay in an alliance with Germany against England and then in the declaration of a sovereign state under international guarantees.
138. See Henry, *Evolution of Sinn Féin*, p. 178. The daily ran in November 1914.
139. *Ibid.*, p. 187.
140. Title of *Irish Times* handbook on the Rising, an invaluable source for details of the fighting. Griffith would have nothing to do with rebellion, as Bulmer Hobson points out in letter to author (17 June, 1969). 'The (Supreme Council) meeting held on September 9, 1914, was summoned by Clarke and MacDermott in an effort to commit Griffith and some others to their projected rising. In this it was not successful and the attempt was not repeated.'
141. Quoted in Seán Cronin, *Our Own Red Blood* (Dublin: 1966), pp. 63–4. See also F.S.L. Lyons, *John Dillon* (London: 1968), Chapter 13.
142. Cronin, *Our Own Red Blood*, p. 64.
143. For campaign against Connolly see Seán Cronin, 'Connolly's Leap in the Dark', *Capuchin Annual 1977*. Murphy, as Ireland's leading capitalist, and Connolly, as Ireland's leading socialist, were deadly enemies since the 1913 strike. British documents attest to the success of the anti-Connolly campaign: Maxwell confirmed death sentences on Connolly

and MacDermott on 9 May, which meant execution on 10 May. However, Prime Minister Asquith suggested halting the executions, and Maxwell complied. Following editorials in *Independent,* the two were executed on 12 May. Murphy saw both 1913 and 1916 as 'syndicalist plots', hence the anti-Connolly vendetta.

144. Public Record Office (PRO), London, War Office files on Ireland, dated 30 April, 1916.
145. *Ibid.*
146. *Ibid.*, 6 September, 1916. Report from HQ, Irish Command, in response to 'absolutely reliable' information that Sinn Féin was plotting a new rebellion and in touch with Berlin. Army Intelligence denied it. Actually the plotters were members of the Revolutionary Directorate, Clan-na-Gael. See Cronin, *McGarrity Papers,* pp. 64–5.
147. PRO (London) files, 18 December 1916.
148. See Longford and O'Neill, *De Valera*, Chapters 5 and 6. De Valera probably owed his life to his American birth: he was born in New York of a Spanish father and Irish mother, but had lived in Ireland from the age of three.
149. P.S. O'Hegarty *The Victory of Sinn Féin* (Dublin: 1924), pp. 29–30.
150. See Dorothy Macardle, *The Republic of Ireland* (Dublin: 1951), p. 250.
151. *Ibid.*, p. 250–1.
152. Henry, *Evolution of Sinn Féin*, p. 241.
153. *Ibid.*, p. 276.
154. See appendix VIII, an analysis of the voting in the 1918 election by Eamon Timoney by provinces and counties. In Ulster, the Nationalist Parliamentary Party won 73,451 votes to Sinn Féin's 109,835, the Unionist's 263,193, Labour's 12,164, and Independent's 9,833.
155. *Dáil Éireann Minutes of Proceedings of the First Parliament of the Republic of Ireland, 1919–1921:* Official Record (Dublin: 1921), pp. 16–23. See original Labour Party draft in appendix IX.
156. P.S. O'Hegarty, *The Illumination of Sinn Féin* (Dublin: 1919), pp. 30–1.
157. On 7 April, 1919, for instance, the British army proclaimed the city of Limerick 'a special military area', which meant that those entering the city had to have military permits. Limerick's United Trades and Labour Council declared a general strike as the city's answer to martial law. 'Shops, warehouses and factories are closed,' the *Irish Independent* of 15 April, 1919, reported. 'No work is being done and no business transacted.' A strike committee ran the city and was known popularly as 'the Limerick Soviet'. *The Times* of London said: 'They regulate the opening of the shops, and even direct the sales. They are also endeavouring to decide prices, though not with very much success' (22 April, 1919). The strike ended on 30 April, 1919, after intervention by the local bishop split the workers. (See Jim Kemmy, 'The Limerick Soviet' *Limerick Socialist,* April 1972 to February 1973.)
158. *Dáil Éireann Minutes . . . 1919–1921*, 'Message to the Free Nations of the World.'
159. For account of this action see Desmond Ryan, *Sean Treacy and the Third Tipperary Brigade, IRA* (Tralee: 1945).
160. Biographies of Collins include Margery Forester, *Michael Collins: the Lost Leader* (London: 1971), Rex Taylor, *Michael Collins* (London:

1961), both objective accounts. Piaras Beaslai, *Michael Collins and the Making of a New Ireland* (London: 1926), and Frank O'Connor, *The Big Fellow* (Dublin: 1965), are partisan.

161. Many pre-1916 IRB members withdrew on the grounds that a secret organization was no longer necessary because the Irish people were now united behind Sinn Féin, among them Cathal Brugha, Minister of Defence, Collin's nominal superior. De Valera urged other IRB men to follow his example.
162. *Irish Republican Brotherhood, Constitution as Revised to Date 1920:* By order of Supreme Council. The revised constitution provided for a Military Council. There was no such provision before 1916, and some – notably Dr Patrick McCartan, a member of the pre-1916 Supreme Council (which was never apprised fully of the plans of the Military Council) – charged that the 1916 Rising was itself an illegal act under the constitution of the IRB, and Bulmer Hobson agreed with them. As Bulmer Hobson points out (see fn. 82, Chapter IV above) the Military Council was really a sub-committee of the Supreme Council and had no IRB authority to decide on a rebellion which 'the majority of the Irish people' did not favour. Others insist the Supreme Council had given authority to the Military Council to plan and carry out a rising.
163. PRO, London, Dublin Castle documents.
164. *The Times*, 10 November, 1920.
165. Terence MacSwiney, *Principles of Freedom* (Dublin: 1936), pp. 185–95. (A collection of essays, written for various national publications.)
166. Seán Cronin, *Kevin Barry* (Cork: 1965).
167. PRO (London) Dublin Castle files note that from 20 August, 1920 to 30 August twenty people were killed and 279 injured following Protestant attacks on Catholics because of IRA activities. The boycott, however, began much earlier, in Tuam, County Galway, and was made a Dáil decree, after the August outbreaks, at Griffith's urging.
168. O'Hegarty, *Victory of Sinn Féin*, p. 53.
169. David Fitzpatrick, *Politics and Irish Life, 1913–21* (Dublin: 1977).
170. PRO (London) Castle files, captured document *re* Ballinamore 'arms fund'. Someone complained of being taxed twice, by the Dáil and the local IRA.
171. Robert Skidelsky, *Oswald Mosley* (New York: 1975), p. 101.
172. D.G. Boyce, *Englishmen and Irish Troubles* (Cambridge, Mass.: 1972), p. 101, from *Nation* of 19 February, 1921.
173. Quoted in Charles Callan Tansill, *America and the Fight for Irish Freedom* (New York: 1957) p. 408.
174. *Evidence on Conditions in Ireland* (Washington: 1921). Much of the report was the work of Dr William Maloney, who worked with Joseph McGarrity.
175. PRO, London, published 24 April, 1921.
176. *Ibid.*
177. Cronin, *McGarrity Papers*, Appendix VII; McCartan article in *The Kerryman*, Christmas 1938.
178. The Gore-Booths were Anglo-Irish landlords in Sligo. Yeats wrote many poems about Constance and her sister Eva. See Jacqueline Van Voris, *Constance Markievicz* (Amherst, Mass.: 1967). She was married to a

Polish count. She remained loyal to the Republic, the poor of Dublin who elected her, and to Connolly socialism. She died in poverty in Dublin in 1927. She had neither influence nor power in the Dáil Cabinet, but her name counted for much among Irish republicans.

179. Ernie O'Malley, *On Another Man's Wound* (London: 1936), p. 320.
180. *Boston Evening Transcript*, 2 April, 1921. The interview is in the PRO Castle files in London. Collins seemed in fine form. He sympathized with General Sir Nevil Macready, the British GOC-in-Ireland, whom he said was cut off in his headquarters. Collins himself was badly wanted and had a price of his head.
181. O'Hegarty, *Illumination of Sinn Féin*, p. 55. Works on the military phase of the struggle include: Charles Townshend, *The British Campaign in Ireland, 1919–21* (Oxford: 1975); Edgar Holt, *Protest in Arms* (London: 1960); Tom Barry, *Guerrilla Days in Ireland* (Dublin: 1949); Dan Breen, *My Fight for Irish Freedom* (Tralee: 1964). The Richard Mulcahy and Ernie O'Malley Papers are in University College, Dublin; Collins's Papers are in the National Library of Ireland.
182. By the McGarrity wing: the Clan split in 1920 when de Valera broke with Devoy. (See Cronin, *McGarrity Papers*, Chapters 9 and 10.)

CHAPTER 5

1. See Thomas Jones, *Whitehall Diary*, Vol. 111, *Ireland 1918-1925*, ed. Keith Middlemas (London: 1971), p. 104.
2. *Ibid.*, pp. 90–1, Jones to Bonar Law, the Conservative Party leader, 22 July, 1921.
3. It meant association with the empire but not membership. It was developed by Erskine Childers from an idea of de Valera's and was used by Nehru nearly thirty years later when an independent India remained in the Commonwealth.
4. *Dáil Éireann. Official Report: Debate on the Treaty between Great Britain and Ireland Signed in London on the 6th December, 1921* (Dublin: 1922), p. 336. quoted by Arthur Griffith, 7 January, 1922.
5. Countess Markievicz and Count Plunkett retained portfolios outside the Cabinet, without influence on policy. This must have been deliberate.
6. Cathal Brugha, Minister for Defence, and Austin Stack, Minister for Home Affairs.
7. Jones, *Diary*, p. 144, at Cabinet meeting.
8. *Dáil Report*, p. 275 – one was Eoin O'Duffy, leader of the semi-Fascist Blue Shirt movement in the 1930s, the other was Alex McCabe (pp. 218–23), who saw the North as an economic and cultural threat to a new Gaelic state. Both supported the Treaty; both belonged to the IRB.
9. Jones, *Diary*, p. 90.
10. *Ibid.* By 'Ulster' they meant 'Protestant Ulster'.
11. *Ibid.* 30 July, 1921. Bonar Law's views were important, as the leader of the Conservative Party in the coalition. He had put the Tories firmly

behind Sir Edward Carson and the Ulster Unionists against Home Rule in 1912-14, in effect vetoing the measure.

12. *Ibid.*, p. 92.
13. *Ibid.*, p. 94–5. Letter dated 10 August, 1921. During the Treaty debates Michael Collins said de Valera's pledge not to use force against Ulster made Sinn Féin impotent in the situation.
14. *The Political Diaries of C.P. Scott 1911-1928* (London: 1970), p. 395. Alfred Cope, Under-Secretary at Dublin Castle, wrote to Tom Jones (Secretary of the Cabinet) that partition, not the issue of the Republic, was the real obstacle to a settlement (Jones, *Diary*, p. 99), while a friend of Lloyd George, a Noncomformist minister, who met de Valera in Dublin in July 1921, told the Prime Minister: 'A united Ireland was the central thought in the Sinn Féin movement and the implications of the invitation [to a conference] as phrased seemed to be that negotiations should commence as from the basis of the present partition as an accomplished fact, (*ibid.*, p. 87).
15. Jones, *Diary*, p. 110. At Cabinet meeting, 7 September, 1921. He feared that if the government gave in to Sinn Féin it would have 'an effect in India and throughout Europe'.
16. *Ibid.*, p. 135. The areas listed by Collins had nationalist (Catholic) majorities. Arthur Griffith submitted figures to the British negotiators on the religious (and hence political) breakdown of Ulster's population. In the entire province of Ulster (nine counties) there were 890,000 Protestants as against 700,000 Catholics; but in the six Ulster counties, making up the new state of Northern Ireland, there were 820,570 Protestants to 429,161 Catholics.
17. See Lord Beaverbrook, *Politics and the Press* (London: 1925), Chapter V, 'The Irish Settlement'. Beaverbrook was a Conservative and a friend of Churchill and Lord Birkenhead, members of the British Cabinet negotiating with Sinn Féin. He was also a friend of the Irish maverick nationalist parliamentarian, Tim Healy, who was an unofficial adviser to the Irish delegates and later Governor General of the Irish Free State. Beaverbrook told Churchill (Jones, *Diary*, p. 147) that 'one of his men was in very close touch with Collins'.
18. Jones, *Diary*, p. 110. 'I do not know who will die for Tyrone and Fermanagh', the Prime Minister told his Cabinet dramatically on 7 September, 1921. 'The fight will be for Irish nationality, partly for Irish Catholic nationality.' The British case was weak on these two nationalist counties. 'He would rather break—if there was to be a break—now, on allegiance and Empire.' He won all his points—partition (including Fermanagh and Tyrone), allegiance and empire on 5 December, when the 'articles of agreement' for an Anglo-Irish Treaty were signed in London.
19. *Ibid.*, p. 156. When Collins said this would sacrifice Irish unity, Jones agreed; 'but what was the alternative?' And he spelled it out: 'Chaos, Crown Colony Government, Civil War.' Jones said the Boundary Commission was his own idea and that he would try to get Lloyd George to accept it. This was a lie; it was Lloyd George's idea, as the diary reveals. Collins was convinced that the 'Boundary Commission would make a political impossibility out of the Northern government', as George Dangerfield notes in *The Damnable Question* (Boston: 1976), p. 339. The Boundary Commission, to decide the border between the two Irelands, was 'a

tactical manoeuvre' by Lloyd George, as Griffith told de Valera; it met in 1925 and did nothing to determine the wishes of the inhabitants, but ganged up two-to-one against the Free State representative, Eoin MacNeill, who resigned, precipitating a government crisis which was settled at a meeting in London with Prime Minister Stanley Baldwin and Sir James Craig. The tripartite pact, on 3 December, 1925, confirmed the existing frontier (see Donal O'Sullivan, *The Irish Free State and its Senate* [London: 1940], pp. 175–88).

20. *Dáil Report*, p. 35, 20 December, 1921.
21. *Ibid.*, p. 73. Milroy reflected the views of Griffith and Collins. He had been with them in London advising on Ulster.
22. *Ibid.*, p. 74.
23. *Ibid.*
24. Seán Moylan of North Cork. His statement proved correct when the Boundary Commission was abandoned in 1925 and the border remained unchanged, with Tyrone and Fermanagh and the other nationalist areas remaining in Northern Ireland.
25. *Dáil Report*, p. 155.
26. *Ibid.*, p. 157. MacEntee was in de Valera's governments from 1932 to the late 1950s.
27. *Ibid.*, p. 194. Blythe became Vice-President of the Executive Council of the Irish Free State. He suggested coercion should be used against Northern Ireland in this debate, a view he later disavowed. At the close of his public career he opposed all moves to end partition except by consent of the Unionists.
28. Jones, *Diary*, p. 144. Jones adds cryptically, paraphrasing the Prime Minister presumably: 'You want to be the Jews of the world.'
29. 'The issue before us,' Barton said, 'was whether we should stand behind our proposals for external association, face war and maintain the Republic, or whether we should accept inclusion in the British Empire and take peace' (*Dáil Report*, p. 49).
30. See de Valera estimate of Republic's opponents in Cronin, *McGarrity Papers*, p. 105.
31. They numbered 42,000, were armed and funded by England. See Jones, *Diary*, pp. 194–5.
32. *Ibid.*, p. 136.
33. *Ibid.*, p. 137. 'You take a quarter and give it a parliament; and then you take a Council and give the quarter the same power as three-quarters,' Griffith said.
34. Cronin, *McGarrity Papers*, p. 109. De Valera added: 'The British will know that if they put the treaty to the country over our heads the country will ratify it, and will pay very little heed to our counter-proposals.' The Catholic Hierarchy was unanimously in favour of the Treaty.
35. Jones, *Diary*, p. 174.
36. *Ibid.*, p. 176.
37. See Cronin, *McGarrity Papers*, p. 112, and Chapter 12 'The IRB and the Treaty'.
38. *Ibid.*, p. 108.
39. *Dáil Report*, p. 21.
40. For details of the Cuban argument see Cronin, *McGarrity Papers*, pp. 76–7.

41. 'There could be no question of ratification of this Treaty. . . We can pass approval or disapproval' (*Dáil Report*, p. 53). At another point he said: 'The specific question that is here before us is the question as to whether we should or should not ratify the Treaty' (*ibid.*, p. 99).
42. At the Cabinet meeting in Dublin on 3 December, 1921, when discussing the Treaty draft, de Valera said he could not sign 'any document which would give north-east Ulster power to vote itself out of the Irish state'.
43. In the 21 December, 1921 letter to McGarrity, de Valera gave three reasons for this: he was the symbol of the Republic and wanted to avoid appearing to compromise it; he wanted to stay at home 'as a reserve' and in order to rally a united nation against Lloyd George; if the British accepted external association he wanted to use his influence with those Republicans who might see it as a compromise. (Cronin, *McGarrity Papers*, p. 110.)
44. Collins told the Dáil: 'The original credentials were presented and they read. . . ' (*Dáil Report*, p. 11), although a little later he amended this to say: 'I do not wish to create a wrong impression. I did not say accepted, I said presented' (*ibid.*, p. 13). When Austin Stack stated interrogatively 'they were not presented'—meaning the credentials—Griffith replied: 'I believe Mr. Lloyd George saw the document. They were not presented or accepted' (*ibid.*, p. 14). He was trying to pull Collins out of a hole, by lying, for he knew that Lloyd George had not seen the documents. The anti-Treatyites accepted the assurances. In fact the Dáil was deliberately misled on an issue crucial to its acceptance of the Treaty: did the delegates represent Dáil Éireann, the Republic, Sinn Féin, or just themselves? If they did not represent the Dáil, why was the Dáil debating the Treaty?
45. Jones, *Diary*, pp. 188–9.
46. *Dáil Report*, p. 274. De Valera announced his future policy after the Dáil ratified (or approved) the Treaty by sixty-four votes to fifty-seven. 'I will go down in that creed [republicanism] to my grave,' he said, after declaring that 'to know what the Irish people wanted I had only to examine my own heart. . .'.
47. *Ibid.*, p. 92.
48. In August 1927. For antagonistic view, see Donal O'Sullivan, *The Irish Free State and Its Senate* (London: 1940), pp. 214–18.
49. *Dáil Report*, p. 24.
50. *Ibid.*, p. 21.
51. *Ibid.*, p. 23.
52. Cronin, *McGarrity Papers*, p. 110, Letter to McGarrity, 21 December, 1921.
53. *Ibid.*
54. *Dáil Report*, p. 335.
55. *Ibid.*, p. 35.
56. *Ibid.*, p. 214.
57. *Ibid.*, p. 192.
58. *Ibid.*, p. 143.
59. *Ibid.*, p. 132.
60. *Ibid.*, p. 45.
61. *Ibid.*, p. 141.
62. *Ibid.*, p. 177.
63. *Ibid.*

64. *Ibid.*, p. 254.
65. *Ibid.*, p. 297.
66. *Ibid.*, p. 61.
67. *Ibid.*, p. 235.
68. *Ibid.*, pp. 36–7.
69. For a study of Irish foreign policy and constitutional development see Patrick Keatinge, *A Place Among the Nations* (Dublin: 1978).
70. *Dáil Report*, p. 39. Childers was executed by a firing squad in November 1922 for possession of a revolver, a present from Michael Collins. Winston Churchill at his capture called him 'that mischief-making murderous renegade. . . actuated by a deadly and malignant hatred for the land of his birth' (*Speeches*, iv, 3377).
71. *Dáil Report*, p. 27.
72. *Ibid.*, p. 90.
73. *Ibid.*, pp. 180–6. Mary MacSwiney also said that if the Dáil accepted the Treaty Ireland would abandon the anti-imperialist struggle, leaving India and Egypt to battle the British Empire alone.
74. *Ibid.*, pp. 108–27. She delivered the longest speech of the debate–Arthur Griffith complained that it ran for two hours and forty minutes. She rambled a good deal, cited history and the dead for precedent.
75. See in particular *Dáil Report*, p. 112.
76. In his *Soldier's Story of Easter Week* (Dublin: 1966), O'Higgins saw the Rising as 'a spiritual victory' (p. 93).
77. *Dáil Report*, p. 192.
78. *Ibid.*, pp. 136–9.
79. Ó Ceallaigh was Ceann Comhairle (Speaker) of the shadow 'Second Dáil' in the late 1920s and through the 1930s to December 1938, when the 'faithful deputies' transferred their 'authority' to the Army Council of the IRA to be held in trust for the nation. He was the only prominent Irish Republican to support Franco in the Spanish Civil War.
80. *Dáil Report*, p. 330.
81. See *Ireland at Berne* (Dublin: 1919) for labour presentation of the Irish case.
82. Countess Markievicz accepted Connolly's programme, led the Citizen Army at the College of Surgeons rebel garrison in 1916, and represented a Dublin working-class district in the Dáil.
83. See C. Desmond Greaves, *Liam Mellows and the Irish Revolution* (London: 1971) and Peadar O'Donnell, *There Will Be Another Day* (Dublin: 1963).
84. *Dáil Report*, p. 231.
85. *Ibid.*, pp. 288–92. Ernie O'Malley wrote: 'I had no longer any faith in Collins or Mulcahy. They would use the army [IRA] for their own purposes and slowly our men would either be absorbed or would have to return to their farms, businesses or universities.' (*The Singing Flame* [Dublin: 1978], p. 49).
86. See Cronin, *McGarrity Papers*, p. 109.
87. Churchill, *Speeches*, iii, 3193. Commons, 16 February, 1922.
88. *Ibid.*, p. 3194. When the Treaty was ratified by the Dáil, de Valera resigned as President, and was defeated for re-election by sixty votes to fifty-eight. Arthur Griffith formed a new 'Republican government'. Michael Collins became chairman of the 'Provisional Government' that took over from the

British administration under the Treaty. This left a most confusing situation, with several 'governments' in the country, including the Unionist one in Belfast, and the British, and none with much authority except among its own partisans.

89. Collins told Tom Jones the constitution would be 'damned democratic' (Jones, *Diary*, p. 199), but when the British vetoed it, he toned it down considerably to meet the requirements of the Treaty. It remained a 'damned democratic' document, however, compared with de Valera's Constitution of 1937.
90. Jones, *Diary*, p. 195. Britain paid for this sectarian police force.
91. Churchill, *Speeches*, iii, 3275–6, 22 March, 1922.
92. *Ibid.*, p. 3288.
93. Confidential document from the Ministry of Defence, Dublin, dated 20 February, 1924, circulated to 'each member of the Executive Council' of the Irish Free State, marked 'secret and confidential', a copy of which is in the author's possession. It is an intelligence document and notes that after the MacMahon murders, and after Collins and Sir James Craig (the Unionist Premier) had signed a pact in April 1922, Nixon's squad with a number of 'B' Specials, 'rushed into Arnon Street with an armoured Lancia, riddled the Nationalist houses, beating and kicking women and children, and murdered seven persons. Some were shot, others had their brains dashed out with the sledge hammer; one who was in bed with a baby one year old, was battered to death, and the baby was shot beside him.' (The killings were in reprisal for the shooting of a policeman). At the end of 1922, when the Royal Irish Constabulary became the Royal Ulster Constabulary in the North, Nixon was asked to resign. He was permitted to remain in the force, however, perhaps because he knew too much, and was recommended for the MBE, the document states. It names other members of the 'reprisal unit' responsible for murders in Belfast.
94. One section of the anti-Treaty IRA under Rory O'Connor occupied the Four Courts in April 1922 and rejected all constitutional authority except its own elected Executive. The anti-Treaty IRA had held a general convention of 26 March, 1922, attended by some 200 delegates who reaffirmed allegiance to 'the Republic', elected an Executive of sixteen by ballot, which then chose an Army Council of five. Liam Lynch was named Chief of Staff, with Liam Mellows, Quartermaster-General, Rory O'Connor, Director of Engineering, James O'Donovan, Director of Chemicals, Seán Russell, Director of Munitions, Ernie O'Malley, Director of Organization. (O'Malley, *The Singing Flame*, p. 64).
95. Cronin, *McGarrity Papers*, p. 108.
96. *Ibid.*, p. 112. Letter to her brother Peter in New York, in January 1922.
97. *Government of Ireland Act, 1914* (4 & 5 Geo. 5, ch. 90).
98. Cronin, *McGarrity Papers*, p. 112, Supreme Council statement on the Treaty.
99. The anti-Treaty IRA Chief of Staff, Liam Lynch, was in the South. He was a member of the IRB and was not arrested by Free State forces, who in fact let him travel from Dublin to the South after the Civil War began. Collins sent verbal messages to the Republican side, through various means, and it was understood that his trip South was to make peace. His death remains something of a mystery. His small convoy ran into a Republican road block rather than ambush at Béal na mBláth, and they had no plan to kill Collins.

In fact they were withdrawing when the brief flurry of shots occurred and were not aware that Collins was dead, although it was known he was travelling with the convoy: there was great respect for Collins in Cork, especially among his Republican opponents. Since it is not even certain that a Republican bullet killed him—there was no autopsy—the question remains: who killed him? (On 24 June 1978 the author interviewed the commander of the Republican force, Commandant Tom Kelleher, at Béal na mBláth.)

100. Jones, *Diary*, pp. 200–1. Lionel Curtis letter to Jones stated that his sources indicated 'that an overwhelming majority of the people favour the Treaty'.
101. See Margery Forester, *Michael Collins: the Lost Leader* (London: 1971), p. 304; Jones, *Diary*, p. 201. In Ireland it was assumed that Collins, not Griffith or de Valera, would head the new government.
102. Jones, *Diary*, p. 202. Emphasis in the original.
103. *Ibid.*, p. 203.
104. *Ibid.*, p. 204.
105. *Ibid.*, p. 206.
106. *Ibid.*, p. 208.
107. Churchill, *Speeches*, iv, 3221–2. Churchill also told the House that Republican forces had seized Belleek and Pettigo, villages on the border. He sent British troops to recover Belleek, which was in Fermanagh, and Lloyd George, who thought there was 'a strain of lunacy' in his Colonial Secretary, ironically celebrated 'the bloodless battle' with a champagne party. (See Jones, *Diary*, pp. 211–12.) In fact these IRA forces consisted of Treatyites and anti-Treatyites and Collins at this point was holding unity talks with the anti-government IRA leaders in Dublin.
108. See de Valera statement, Dorothy Macardle, *The Irish Republic* (Dublin: 1951), p. 737. 'I do not know who they were who shot Sir Henry Wilson, or why they shot him. . . . I know that life has been made a hell for the nationalist minority in Belfast and its neighbourhood for the past couple of years. . . . I do not approve but I must not pretend to misunderstand.'
109. On 26 June Churchill delivered an ultimatum to Dublin from the House of Commons, having previously ordered General Macready, British commander in Dublin, to shell the Four Courts. Macready diplomatically delayed implementing the order, sensing that was what the IRA in the Four Courts wanted. Churchill said 'that this sort of thing must come to an end. . . . If it does not come to an end . . . if it is not brought to an end . . . then it is my duty to say . . . that we shall regard the Treaty as having been formally violated . . .' (*Speeches*, iv, 3337). The Dublin government had its own reason for bringing affairs to a head: a high ranking officer of its army was kidnapped by the IRA and held in the Four Courts—in reprisal for the arrest of one of the garrison's officers. Since the government, headed by Arthur Griffith, had won fifty-eight seats in the June election, against thirty-five for the Republicans, seventeen for Labour, and eighteen others, all aligned against the anti-Treatyites, it was quite sure of its political position and acted accordingly.
110. Quoted by Forester, *Collins*, p. 308.
111. *Ibid.*, pp. 318–19. The two were Reginald Dunne and Joseph O'Sullivan, a crippled war veteran. See Rex Taylor, *Assassination* (London: 1961).

112. Interview with Peadar O'Donnell, member of the IRA Executive in 1922 and one of the Four Courts garrison (Dublin, 27 June, 1979). He believes that if Mellows had acted, while free, on the ideas embodied in his 'Notes from Mountjoy' (while a prisoner), the Civil War would have had a different ending.
113. Jones, *Diary*, p. 213. Where Churchill got this information is a mystery: so far as is known there were no Wobblies in the Four Courts.
114. Churchill, *Speeches*, iv, 3342.
115. Quoted *ibid.*, p. 3339. Ernest Blythe, in a four-part review of Eoin Neeson's *The Civil War in Ireland* (Cork: 1966), traced the origin of the conflict to Dáil Éireann's 'completely unattainable objective' of an Irish Republic in January 1919. (*Irish Times*, 12, 13, 14 and 15 July 1966).
116. See Macardle, *Irish Republic*, pp. 440–3.
117. See Mellow's 'Notes from Mountjoy' in Seán Cronin, *The Revolutionaries* (Dublin: 1971), pp. 185–91.
118. See Calton Younger, *Ireland's Civil War* (London: 1968), p. 464.
119. Cronin, *McGarrity Papers*, p. 124, letter to McGarrity dated 10 September 1922.
120. The Irish bishops in April 1922 condemned the anti-Treaty IRA. A joint pastoral on 10 October, 1922, denounced 'the armed campaign now being carried on against the government set up by the nation'. Republicans were declared excommunicated. During the guerrilla campaign against England only the Bishop of Cork took similar action, in December 1920, declaring all who participated in ambushes excommunicated.
121. Cronin, *McGarrity Papers*, p. 126, letter to McGarrity, 10 September, 1922.
122. Liam Lynch was killed in the Knockmealdown mountains on 10 April, 1923, and Frank Aiken succeeded him as Chief of Staff. On 24 May, 1923, Aiken issued a cease-fire order to the IRA. Arms were dumped for another day. Aiken's own 'not very deep analysis' (his words) of the defeat: 'the fact that it was a defensive war, and that we always thought the enemy would not go so far . . .'. He wrote of the need for offensive weapons in 'the future', adding 'if we have to fight another war with the Staters, it will have to be short and sweet, and our units will need to be trained in taking the offensive in large bodies.' Lack of civilian organization was 'chiefly responsible for our present position . . .' (*Éire*, 11 August, 1923). The Free State found and published the letter as proof that the IRA had used the cease-fire as a tactic. De Valera issued a statement on 3 August, 1923 rejecting the Free State construction:

> General Aiken's belief was, and is, that only on the foundation of the recognition of our country as a sovereign Independent State can a clean, ordered, or prosperous Gaelic nation be built. . . . If any peaceful method were available, no man would be more opposed than he to any resort to arms, but he, like the rest of us, is unable to blind himself to the fact that every peaceful avenue is being systematically cut off by our opponents, and by England [*Ibid.*].

In 1926, through Fianna Fáil, de Valera felt he had found his 'peaceful avenue', whereas the IRA continued to prepare another 'resort to arms'.

123. Letter from the Clan-na-Gael Executive to the Chief of Staff of the IRA, 1 October, 1929, based on documents received after the 1925 General Army Convention. Also Clan letter to members, 16 April, 1926. In fact

the Army Council, not the IRA Executive, exercised supreme authority, subject only to the annual convention.

124. De Valera statement, *Irish Independent*, 15 January, 1926. De Valera was succeeded as 'President of the Irish Republic' by Art O'Connor, Minister of Agriculture in the Republican Government of 1921, who shortly afterwards resigned and was not replaced. (See Cronin, *McGarrity Papers*, pp. 146–8).

125. *Saor Éire, Constitution and Rules*, adopted by First National Congress, Dublin, 26 and 27 September, 1931.

126. Interview with George Gilmore, member of the IRA Army Council in late 1920s and early 1930s, Dublin, June 1978.

127. Jones, *Diary*, p. 126. The year was 1925 and the British Tory government was headed by Stanley Baldwin. The Boundary Commission began its work in November 1924 with three members: Justice Feetham of South Africa, chairman; Eoin MacNeill for the Irish Free State; J.R. Fisher, British nominee for Northern Ireland. The commission's report was expected to be very favourable to the Free State. The details, leaked to the Tory *Morning Post* of London, in effect maintained the *status quo*, and Nationalists saw it as a betrayal. MacNeill resigned. Cosgrave felt that if de Valera's forty-eight deputies entered the Dáil, which they had boycotted since the Civil War, he might be defeated. They failed to do so, there was no boundary report, and Article 5 was removed. (Cosgrave said, according to British Cabinet minutes–*Irish Times*, 23 January, 1968–that the Boundary Commission report should be quietly 'burned and buried'.)

128. Terence de Vere White, *Kevin O'Higgins* (Tralee: 1966), pp. 216–17. For account of O'Higgins's discussion of monarchy with Leopold Amery, Dominion Affairs Secretary, see memo in Cabinet Papers, 'Proposed Creation of a Kingdom of Ireland', 13 December, 1926, an account of talks with O'Higgins at end of Imperial Conference, 23 November, 1926, and 10 December, 1926. He wanted 'a Dual Monarchy, such as that which existed between Austria and Hungary before the war'. Amery was sceptical of the plan which impaired 'the unity of a single Crown' and Foreign Minister Austen Chamberlain said this was 'not a proposal which we can countenance'. (See David Harkness, 'The Kingdom of Ireland', in series on British Cabinet Papers for 1926, *Irish Times*, 24 January, 1968.)

129. O'Higgins was shot to death 10 July, 1927. The motives, organization or identities of the assassins have not been established. T.P. Coogan, *The IRA* (London: 1970), p. 55, says the killers were two IRA volunteers 'acting unofficially', but cites no sources. On coercion measures generally in the new state, see J. Bowyer Bell, *A Time of Terror* (New York: 1978), Chapter 10. For details of Free State 'Republican' opposition to O'Higgins's policies, by those who followed Collins's line that the Treaty was a 'stepping stone' to independence, see Léon Ó Broin, *Revolutionary Underground*, Chapter 12. Also *The Truth About the Army Crisis* (Dublin: 1924), by army officers, led by Liam Tobin, an aide of Collins, who felt that remnants of the IRB controlled army appointments. The Minister of Defence, General Richard Mulcahy, was forced to resign on O'Higgins's insistence.

130. See George Gilmore, *The Irish Republican Congress* (New York: 1935).

131. See Maurice Manning, *The Blueshirts* (Dublin: 1970).

132. *Constitution and Governmental Programme for the Republic of Ireland*

(Dublin: 1934). The pamphlet includes the constitution of Óglaigh na hÉireann (Volunteers of Ireland), the IRA.

133. Connolly's aim was a syndicalist Workers' Republic. At its founding in September 1934, Republican Congress split almost evenly between those who demanded a Workers' Republic and the O'Donnell-Gilmore-Frank Ryan forces, who with the aid of the small Communist Party pressed the united front slogan, 'On to the Republic'. Congress also had the support of left-wing trade unionists and the hostility of many bishops and priests, but it did not draw a Church ban like its predecessor, Saor Éire. The minority, under former IRA leader Michael Price, supported by trade unionists and Connolly's son Roddy and daughter Nora, withdrew from the Congress when its resolution for a Workers' Republic on Connolly lines was defeated by ninety-nine votes to eighty-four. (See *Irish Workers' Voice*, 6 October, 1934.)

134. *An Phoblacht*, 31 January, 1931. See also *An Phoblacht*, 10 October, 1931. Moss Twomey, IRA Chief of Staff, delivered his answer to charges of Communism in the IRA, in *An Phoblacht* (*The Republic*, the IRA weekly) of 16 May, 1931, as follows: 'If it is Communism to undo the Conquest, the effects of which have wrecked the nation, to destroy landlordism in its many forms and restore their heritage to the dispossessed; to enable those who produce wealth to obtain the fullest advantage of the wealth; to break the stranglehold of the imperial banking system on Irish industry; to end robbery and exploitation by a privileged minority, then Tone, Emmet, Mitchel, Lalor, Connolly, Pearse and Mellows were Communists, and the Irish Republican Army is a Communist organization.'

135. *Ibid.*, 7 February, 1931. O'Donnell initiated anti-land annuities campaign and de Valera adopted it. See O'Donnell's *There Will Be Another Day.* Issue was settled in Anglo-Irish trade agreement in 1938.

136. Michael McInerney, *Peadar O'Donnell: Irish Social Rebel* (Dublin: 1974), p. 94. For a study of O'Donnell, the writer, see Grattan Freyer, *Peadar O'Donnell* (Lewisburg, Pa.: 1977).

137. Gilmore, *Republican Congress* (US edn), p. 5. See also the same author's *Republican Congress* (Dublin: 1968), a history of the movement.

138. Peader O'Donnell, *Salud! An Irishman in Spain* (London: 1937), pp. 239–56; also Michael O'Riordan, *Connolly Column* (Dublin: 1979).

139. *Constitution and Governmental Programme of the Republic of Ireland*, p. 5.

140. See *The Strength of Sinn Féin*, presidential address by the Rev. Michael O'Flanagan at the annual Ard Fheis of Sinn Féin, 14 October 1934 (Dublin: 1934). O'Flanagan was disciplined by the Church for his politics. Sinn Féin expelled him for taking a state job—on the Placenames Commission—and for speaking over the state radio. Vice President of Sinn Féin in 1917-21, he was an important national figure. He was the only priest in Ireland to support the Spanish Republic against General Franco. Sinn Féin was the political party of the 'Second Dáil'.

141. *Ibid.*, p. 11.

142. Cronin, *McGarrity Papers*, p. 157, de Valera to McGarrity, 31 January, 1934, after latter had asked him to make a pact with the IRA against England (see Appendix XII). For relations of British and Irish governments in the 1930s based on British Cabinet Papers, see series of articles by

Dr David Harkness in *Irish Times*, January 1968.

143. The leader of 'the Triangle' was Alexander Sullivan, an Irish-American politician and enemy of Devoy. He was also President of the National League of America.
144. Cronin, *McGarrity Papers*, pp. 160–174. Luke Dillon, born in Leeds, England, of Irish parents, grew up in America and never visited Ireland.
145. *Irish Press*, 24 June, 1936.
146. *Ibid.*, 8 October, 1937.
147. McGarrity Files. 'We feel happy that our efforts, which were made possible by yours, helped to provide a rallying centre for our Irish Nationalists in the States,' Russell wrote. The man sent to Germany was Jim O'Donovan, Russell's colleague on GHQ in 1919-21 as Director of Chemicals. A direct man, at a GHQ meeting after the Treaty was signed and ratified he called Collins to his face 'a traitor' who 'should have been courtmartialled for treason' (O'Malley, *The Singing Flame*, p. 53). Since it was a fundamental plank of de Valera's foreign policy that Ireland would not allow itself to be used as a base for an attack on Britain, the IRA's links with Germany alarmed him and were monitored closely. When war broke out in September 1939 the Irish government declared its neutrality and known members of the IRA were interned. The order was found unconstitutional and they were released. The constitution was amended and the government took emergency powers to jail Republicans. Hundreds were interned in the Curragh military camp. Others were tried by Military Tribunal, six were executed and three died on hunger strike.

    For an account of the bombing campaign in England, see Letitia Fairfield, *The Trial of Peter Barnes and Others: the IRA Coventry Explosion of 1939* (London: 1953). Joseph Collins, who served ten years in English prisons for his part in the campaign, has left an unpublished memoir (in possession of the author) which tells his jail experiences. 'A very difficult case, and a confirmed rebel, both here and in Ireland,' the Catholic chaplain noted in Collins's file after he was sentenced in August 1939. Three years later he noted, 'His dispositions are unchanged.' These remarks say much about the ideological outlook of the IRA volunteer in the 1940s.
148. Ryan died in Germany in June 1944. The German Foreign Office and Abwehr II thought Ryan, a well-known Irish revolutionary figure, would be useful at a certain stage of the war, for instance if the Allies decided to seize the 'Treaty ports'. The occasion did not arise. Ryan wanted to get to Ireland by any means. He thought the Germans would provide the means. See Sean Cronin, *Frank Ryan: the Search for an Irish Republic* (Dublin: 1980).
149. *Republican News*, a cyclostyled underground little paper turned out in Belfast, reported in May 1943 that on Saturday, 24 April, the IRA took over the Broadway Cinema on the Falls Road and held an Easter commemoration. The 1916 Proclamation was read by Séamus Steele, the Easter statement of the Army Council by Hugh McAteer, both of whom had escaped from prison and were being hunted by the police. The IRA statement said in part, 'the methods of Pearse and Connolly are our methods, their spirit is our inspiration, and their Proclamation of the Republic remains for us the fundamental declaration of the right and authority of our nation to resort to arms in defence of its inalienable right to sovereign

independence'. This was the most open action of the IRA in the North in the war years and the ideological message was the traditional one of physical force. The editor of *Republican News* was John Graham, a Belfast Protestant. For details of those years see J. Bowyer Bell, *The Secret Army: The IRA 1916-1979* (Dublin & New York: 1980), Chapter XI, pp. 214–36; also Tim Pat Coogan, *The IRA* (New York: 1970).

150. Hermann Goertz, 'Mission to Ireland, V', written while awaiting deportation to Germany in 1946. Goertz, an Abwehr II agent, committed suicide. His articles appeared in the *Irish Times*. Arrested by Irish security forces in November 1941, Goertz spent the war years in prison. For IRA relations with wartime Germany see Carolle J. Carter, *The Shamrock and the Swastika* (Palo Alto, Cal.: 1977), the wartime booktab, *Is Ireland Next?* (New York: 1942), a grab-bag of opinions reflecting the mood of the time. Also Bowyer Bell, *The Secret Army*, and T.P. Coogan, *The IRA*.
151. *Wolfe Tone Annual 1945*. Statement by Frank Aiken, de Valera's Minister in charge of censorship.
152. *Ibid.*, p. 4.
153. *Ibid.*, p. 10.
154. *Ibid.*, p. 146.
155. Nancy Cordozo, *Lucky Eyes and a High Heart: the Life of Maud Gonne* (New York: 1978), p. 398.
156. MacBride found the 1937 Constitution acceptable, he said, 'No King, no Oath, no appeal to Privy Council.' (Interview Dublin, 29 June, 1978.) This is quite true. As the chief political tactician of the IRA in the 1930s and its Chief of Staff after Moss Twomey's arrest in May 1936, MacBride distrusted Russell's action plan and left the IRA in June 1938 after it was adopted. Most of the old leadership of the movement left at the same time.
157. Clann na Poblachta statement, 6 July, 1946.
158. See Appendix XV for US note and de Valera's reply. The assurance on Britain was given in the Dáil on 29 May 1935. Until Pearl Harbour Irish neutrality was defended in the US by a committee for which Paul O'Dwyer was the spokesman. Irish neutrality came under fierce and sustained press attack in the US after Pearl Harbour. David Gray, US Minister in Dublin, was a pernicious influence in this issue. In May 1944 de Valera went to the country on his policy and gained seventeen seats. See T. Ryle Dwyer, *Irish Neutrality and the USA, 1939-47* (Dublin: 1977); Carter, *Shamrock and the Swastika; Ireland in the War Years and After , eds.* Kevin B. Nowlan and T. Desmond Williams (South Bend, Ind.: 1970); and Joseph Carroll, *Ireland in the War Years, 1939-1945* (New York: 1975).
159. See J.H. Whyte, *Church and State in Modern Ireland* (Dublin: 1971), pp. 196–272 and appendices.
160. On the Clann view of Dr Browne case, see 'Statement from Members of the Standing Committee', 16 April, 1951; Minutes of National Executive Meeting, 31 March–1April, 1951; Minutes of conversation MacBride-Browne, 9 November, 1950; MacBride statement at Ard Fheis (national convention) of Clann na Poblachta, 1 July, 1951. (These documents in possession of the author, but published in daily newspapers at the time.)
161. Statement at 1951 Ard Fheis on economic goals. The Irish state continued in a position of colonial dependency to Britain until entry to Common Market. For Irish economy see *Ireland: Some Problems of a Developing*

Economy, ed. A.A. Tait and J.A. Bristow (New York: 1972), Kieran A. Kennedy and Brendan B. Dowling, *Economic Growth in Ireland: the Experience since 1947* (Dublin & New York: 1975) and Patrick O'Malley, *Irish Industry Structure and Performance* (New York: 1972).

162. For Clann's economic policy there are the various party documents but also Ireland's application for funds under the European Recovery Programme, which was taken from party policy by MacBride as Minister for External Affairs. (*The European Recovery Programme: Ireland's Long-Term Programme, 1948-53*, presented to both houses of Oireachtas by the Minister of External Affairs–[Stationery Office, Dublin: 1948].) This was, in effect, a five-year plan with productivity targets. Ireland in 1946-47 had 'almost the lowest number of power units including tractors, horses and other work animals of any OEEC country', MacBride commented in the foreword to the document. There was one tractor for every thousand acres in Ireland compared with eight per thousand in Britain. MacBride was as much involved in economic planning as in foreign affairs.
163. British Cabinet Papers for 1948 and 1949 at PRO, London, dealing with the Irish state's formal withdrawal from Commonwealth. The 'strategic interest' document is a memorandum from the Cabinet Secretary to Prime Minister Clement Attlee.
164. *Dáil Debates*, 20 July, 1948.
165. Longford and O'Neill, *De Valera*, p. 429.
166. *Ireland's Position in Relation to the North Atlantic Treaty* (Dublin: 1950), p. 5. Irish reply dated 8 February, 1949.
167. See 'The United States and Irish Participation in NATO: the Debate of 1950', paper by Dr Ronan Fanning, read to the National Committee for the Study of International Affairs of the Royal Irish Academy, 18 April, 1978. Quotation from State Department's 'Memorandum of Conversation' of White House meeting on 23 March, 1951.
168. *Ibid.*, p. 17. Under ECA, the Irish Republic received a loan of about $128 million, a grant of about $18 million and technical assistance of about $1.25 million; the de Valera government refused to agree to the Mutual Security Act stipulation which would mean 'altering its established foreign policy'. On 12 September 1950, the Secretary of Defence, Louis Johnson, resigned after asking the National Security Council to make a report on Irish participation in NATO and the subsequent analysis noted Ireland's important strategic location.
169. July 1951 Ard Fheis statement on partition.
170. Bunreacht na hÉireann (Constitution of Ireland), Article 2.
171. Interview with Liam Kelly, New York, 19 April, 1979. After the Roslea raid Kelly moved to the border town of Monaghan in the Republic. His grandfather, Billy Kelly, was a Fenian and close friend of Tom Clarke, the 1916 leader; his father was a member of the IRB and the IRA. Kelly belonged to the tradition of physical force, but, like MacBride, he also saw the need for a strong political base.
172. *Constitution of Óglaigh na hÉireann* (Dublin: 1932), Articles 3 and 4.
173. See E. Rumpf and A.C. Hepburn, *Nationalism and Socialism in Twentieth Century Ireland* (Liverpool: 1977), p. 138.
174. In 1951 Patrick MacLogan, former abstentionist Republican member of parliament for South Armagh and chairman of Cumann na Poblachta in

1935-36, became President of Sinn Féin. He was one of the three architects of the reorganized republican movement, the others being Anthony Magan and Tomás MacCurtáin. A new Sinn Féin programme was adopted, clubs were established and elections contested. (See *Sinn Féin Social and Economic Programme.*)

175. Issued by IRA as 'General Army Order No. 9'.
176. The Commando-style operation was organized by four men: Seán Garland, Charles Murphy, Eamon Boyce, Leo McCormack—who was in jail when it took place. It put the IRA back in business and won the endorsement of most Ulster Nationalists. See Bell, *Secret Army*, pp. 258—61.
177. *United Irishman*, July 1954. No Nationalist raised on tales of 1916-23 would seriously dispute this statement at a time when books were published and newspaper articles written by veterans of the old struggle telling of the derring-do of the War of Independence. Politicians fulminated against partition. The thinking in Dublin and Cork and Limerick was that the IRA —which acted quite openly—was the resurrected pre-1916 Irish Volunteers. Summer camps were held after the raid on Armagh, the captured rifles were used for training and a film was made of the new volunteers preparing for the battle ahead, and sent to old republican sympathisers in America.
178. Thomas Mitchell for the constituency of Mid-Ulster, embracing parts of Derry and much of Tyrone, and Philip Clarke, for the constituency of Fermanagh-South Tyrone in the British Commons. Being felons, both men were deprived of their seats. Mitchell was re-elected with an increased majority; in the third by-election a constitutional nationalist split the Nationalist vote and a Unionist won the seat. The three elections enabled Sinn Féin to build an organization in the North, something it lacked before.
179. Bell, *Secret Army*, pp. 277—80.
180. A plan prepared in the early 1950s existed for certain contingencies, such as an attack on the Nationalist population in the North, and envisaged sabotage and civil disobedience. There were no local forces to put such a plan into operation and it is not an alternative to 'Operation Harvest', the 1956 guerrilla campaign plan.
181. Quoted by Denis P. Barritt and Charles F. Carter, *The Northern Ireland Problem: a Study in Group Relations* (London: 1972), pp. 130—1.
182. See *British Troops Must Go* (Dublin: 1961) for detailed exposition of this view, particularly pp. 14—15. Other documents explaining ideology of the campaign are *They Kept Faith* (1957); *Resistance* (1957); *An Appeal to Unionists* (1958). *Notes on Guerrilla Warfare* (1956) indicates the reasoning that led to 'Operation Harvest'.
183. One version of this was read in a Dublin court on 17 January, 1957—there were several drafts—and next day's *Irish Press*, *Irish Independent*, and *Irish Times*, carried it. The author, then IRA Director of Operations, was on trial. With 'Harvest' was an 'appreciation of the situation' which listed Dungannon army barracks as a target. It was demolished by explosives the following day. (See *Manchester Guardian*, 21 January, 1957.)
184. Using these powers, 'B' Specials and RUC could harass and arrest Nationalists; RUC's 'reserve' motorized units could deal with IRA raids.
185. Internment in the Republic lasted from July 1957 to March 1959, when it was ended because the European Commission on Human Rights had a case

under investigation. The Irish government's defence, which was accepted, was that an emergency existed threatening the life of the nation. In fact the volunteers were under orders (General Order Number 9) not to use force in the territory of the Republic. There was no 'emergency'.

186. See Paul Johnson, 'Ireland and Its Troubles', *New Statesman*, 27 September, 1958.
187. J. Bowyer Bell, 'An Interim Analysis of the Irish Republican Movement', confidential document, April 1967, p. 9.
188. *Ibid.*, p. 10.
189. *United Irishman*, March 1962.
190. Barritt and Carter, *The Northern Ireland Problem*, p. 131. See also 'An Appeal to Unionists', issued in February 1958 and published in the March 1958 *United Irishman*.
191. De Vere White, *Kevin O'Higgins*, p. 169. Mr de Vere White goes on to say that this is the material of Nazism, Fascism, Mosleyism, and in Ireland the IRA is 'an outlet for their anti-social impulses'.
192. John A. Murphy, 'The New IRA', *Secret Societies in Ireland*, ed. T. Desmond Williams (Dublin: 1973), pp. 161–2.
193. F.X. Martin, 'The Evolution of a Myth—the Easter Rising, Dublin, 1916', *Nationalism: the Nature and Evolution of an Idea*, p. 68.
194. Eamon Timoney, New York, 17 February, 1979. Timoney commanded the Derry City IRA. Arrested 30 March 1957, he spent the next half-dozen years in Crumlin Road Prison, Belfast.
195. Manus Canning, New York, 3 April, 1979. Canning was arrested in Essex, England in 1953 with a van-load of arms and was sentenced to eight years' imprisonment.
196. Séan O'Hegarty, Ottawa, 17 October, 1978 (See Appendix XVII). One of the Omagh Barracks raiders, in October 1954, O'Hegarty was captured and sentenced to ten years in Belfast Prison.
197. As noted earlier such a state would differ greatly from the existing Irish Republic. Longford and O'Neill, *De Valera*, (p. 444), write that some of the IRA met the then leader of the opposition in 1956 'and asked him to assist in their attacks or at least connive at them'. De Valera 'impressed upon them his belief . . . that partition could not be solved by force of arms. Their movement, he said, was bound to fail . . . . Events proved him right beyond question.' No source is given for this strange story which, on the face of it, is incredible to anyone who knows anything about IRA thinking in 1956. It may prove the appeal of physical-force nationalist ideology: the funerals for Sabhat and O'Hanlon drew many followers of Fianna Fáil in January 1957. Nationalism defeated the coalition in the election of March 1957. De Valera and Fianna Fail, not Sinn Féin and the IRA, reaped the benefits, however.

CHAPTER 6

1. The Northern Ireland parliament held its sessions at Stormont Castle outside Belfast where government offices also were housed. A statue of Sir Edward Carson, the organizer of Ulster Unionism against Home Rule, stands in front of it. When he unveiled it in 1934, Carson said: 'James Craig and I were the biggest rebels that ever stood. We were rebels to those who were rebels against the King.' (St John Ervine, *Craigavon*, p. 526.) Stormont was a monument to successful rebellion against the imperial parliament by a Protestant minority claiming to speak for Ulster, a province whose population was almost half Catholic and Nationalist.
2. *A Working Paper for a Conference*, published *Irish Times*, 21 November 1979, and *The Government of Northern Ireland: Proposals for Further Discussion*, published *Irish Times*, 3 July 1980. To test the public's view of the United Kingdom link, 'border polls' will be held at intervals, the latter paper declares. The guarantee to Unionists remains, but 'it is in the interest of both communities to recognise and develop the links that exist between Northern Ireland and the Republic of Ireland.' (That's the Irish dimension!) In regard to power sharing, the paper offers several possibilities, though the term is not mentioned. Nationalists might become members of the Executive or of committees that would 'scrutinize the actions of the Executive and offer advice to the administration and with stated powers.' The British government hopes for a managerial rather than a political Executive. Another suggestion for power sharing is 'a weighted majority in the Assembly' appointing Executive members, which would oblige the Chief Executive 'to obtain some support from minority representatives.' A likelier way of providing Nationalists with a share of power is via a Council of the Assembly, made up of committee chairmen and their deputies, its powers deliberately left imprecise, but which could include authority to delay, refer back or disapprove of legislation and public expenditure.
3. See *Irish Times*, 19 February, 1979, 'O'Dwyer Plays Host to Top Loyalists', article by Seán Cronin, report on US mission of UDA leaders. The policy has won support from some Irish-Americans, including Paul O'Dwyer. Governor Hugh Carey of New York (*Daily News*, April 22, 1979), accepts some parts of the plan—perhaps, like O'Dwyer, as a way out of the impasse.
4. Quoted Mark Tierney, *Modern Ireland* (Dublin: 1978), p. 230. Craig, a broker and distiller, became a baronet in 1918, and Lord Craigavon in 1927, rewards for his rebellion against the British government during the Home Rule crisis.
5. For fuller discussion of this see Richard Rose, *Governing Without Consensus: an Irish Perspective* (Boston: 1971).
6. *Disturbances in Northern Ireland: Report of the (Cameron) Commission* (Belfast: 1969), p. 13. The inquiry was headed by Lord Cameron, a Scottish judge, with a Catholic and Protestant on the commission from Queen's University. The commission found the civil rights movement drew 'support from a wide measure of moderate opinion on many sides and to that extent is a novel phenomenon' in Northern Ireland. The Report was critical of some elements in the Civil Rights Association, particularly People's Democracy, the left-wing students' group based in Queen's University, Belfast, in the late 1960s.
7. *Ibid.*, pp. 13–14.

8. *Ibid.*, p. 14.
9. *Ibid.*, p. 55. 5 October, 1968 is a key date in the recent history of Northern Ireland. A meeting scheduled by the Derry Housing Action committee, a small and uninfluential left-wing group, which the Cameron Commission said normally would not have attracted more than a couple of hundred supporters, if that, was banned under the Public Order Act by Home Affairs Minister, William Craig, who, at the same time, permitted an Orange organization, the Apprentice Boys, to stage a provocative procession. The nationalists of Derry defied the ban and clashed with the police. Rioting continued for two days.
10. *Ibid.*, p. 66.
11. *Ibid.*, p. 92.
12. Two new houses in Caledon, County Tyrone, were occupied by Catholic squatters without homes. The local council gave one house to a Protestant nineteen-year-old unmarried secretary; this led to the Dungannon march.
13. The present writer's theory, not the view of the Cameron Commission.
14. See Frank Gallagher, *The Indivisible Island: the Story of the Partition of Ireland* (London: 1957), pp. 225–65. Although this is a frankly partisan work stating the case against partition, the facts assembled on the gerry-mandering of local electoral boundaries in Northern Ireland to produce artificial Unionist majorities in Nationalist areas have not been challenged. The case of Derry, the second city of Northern Ireland, is particularly appropriate for such a discussion since the majority of its people did not want to be part of Northern Ireland at all.
15. Bishop of Down and Connor (Belfast), Dr Philbin quoted in Rose, *Governing Without Consensus*, p. 335.
16. *Ibid.*, p. 336. The state, as in Britain, provides more than 70 per cent funding for Catholic schools.
17. *Ibid.*, p. 340.
18. Mannheim, *Ideology and Utopia*, p. 36.
19. Miriam Daly, lecturer in economic history, Queen's University, Belfast, 'Women in Northern Ireland', paper read at Fordham University, New York, under auspices of Irish American Cultural Institute, 10 April, 1979, and subsequent interview. Mrs Daly was herself a victim of political violence: she was shot dead in her home on 26 June 1980.
20. Rev. Raymond Helmick, an American Jesuit, deals with this in English Jesuit magazine, *The Month*, August 1977. He says this clerical power is the type of 'Rome rule' that Protestants fear most, not the influence of the Catholic Church on Irish national politics.
21. Rose, *Governing Without Consensus*, p. 346, Table XI.3.
22. Ian McAllister, *The Northern Ireland Social Democratic and Labour Party* (London: 1977), p. 54.
23. Rose, *Governing Without Consensus*, p. 189, Table V.3.
24. The 'Ulster Cycle' includes the Tâin and the stories of Cuchulainn, Deirdre, Conor Mac Nessa, Ferdia, Naoise, *et al.*
25. See McAllister, *Social Democratic and Labour Party*, pp. 39–40. The party was founded in August 1970 from the civil rights activists elected to Stormont in the February 1969 election. The old Nationalist party had been weak in organization and strong in abstention from parliament. The SDLP reversed both. There is less clerical control in the SDLP. From 1973

the SDLP, strongly influenced by John Hume, deputy leader, and after Gerry Fitt's resignation, leader of the party, put its faith in power-sharing as the solution to the Northern Ireland problem.

26. John Sayers, 'The Political Parties and the Social Background', *Ulster Under Home Rule* (London: 1955), ed. Thomas Wilson, p. 72. The mutual suspicions, fears, hatreds go far back in Ulster and Protestant preachers could tell their flocks, as the Reverend George Walker noted in his diary during the siege of Derry, 1689, 'instances of Providence given them since they first came into that place, and of what consideration it was to the Protestant Religion at this time; and that they need not doubt, but that God would at last deliver them from the Difficulties they were under' (*A True Account of the Siege of London-Derry*, 2nd edn. [London: 1887], p. 62).
27. A founder of the SDLP and minister in the power-sharing Executive, Devlin broke with his party colleagues to support the UDA's independence plan.
28. In 1920-22 Catholics were expelled from the shipyards. About ten thousand workers, mostly Catholics but including Protestant radicals, lost their jobs in this way. By 1933 only two thousand in all worked in the yards.
29. For economy of Northern Ireland see K.S. Isles and Norman Cuthbert, *An Economic Survey of Northern Ireland* (Belfast: 1957); also Lyons, *Ireland Since the Famine*, pp. 718–47. Dr Lyons notes: 'By 1937 about sixty-three per cent of the whole population lived either in Belfast or in towns and villages within a thirty mile radius of the city' (p. 695).
30. For aid to industry see Isles and Cuthbert, *Economic Survey*, Chapter XIX; Lyons *Ireland Since the Famine*, pp. 735–6. A number of Industries Development Acts were passed 1945-53, Capital Grants to Industry Acts, 1954-62, Aid to Industry Acts, 1961-64 and Industrial Advice and Enterprise Acts in 1964 and 1967. The result of this legislation, the Unionist government claimed, was fifty-five thousand new jobs created by the one hundred and sixty or so new firms.
31. See *Country Reports on Human Rights Practices for 1979* by the Department of State, 4 February, 1980, Washington, DC, pp. 695-6. Nationalist occupations cited in Lyons, *Ireland Since the Famine*, p. 714. On John Robb's views see *Irish Times*, 26 January, 1979. Robb is the author of *New Ireland–Sell Out or Opportunity* (Belfast: 1972). The pamphlet urges Northern Ireland Protestants and Catholics to seek a federal Ireland as the only solution of the problem.
32. Rose, *Governing Without Consensus*, pp. 216–7.
33. *Irish Times*, 26 January, 1979.
34. In 1956-7, a Nationalist county councillor in County Fermanagh privately welcomed the IRA guerrillas and helped them; publicly he denounced armed force. Bernadette Devlin, *The Price of My Soul* (New York: 1969), pp. 36–7, tells of sirens going off in the night warning of the IRA attacks during the 1950s campaign, shortly after her father died; and of a place nearby called the Black Bog, which was used as a sanctuary by the guerrillas: '. . . though the authorities put searchlights on it by night and sent helicopters over it by day, the Black Bog never gave up an IRA man'. One night, during an alarm, Bernadette stood with her mother looking out at

the beam of the searchlights on the Black Bog. 'At least they'll never get your father now,' her mother said. Comments the author: 'And even if we didn't quite know what she meant, we could guess.' That passage tells a great deal about the attitude of Northern Nationalists to the IRA.

35. Brian Faulkner, *Memoirs of a Stateman* (London: 1978), p. 47. Lord Faulkner was Prime Minister 1971-72 and headed the 'power-sharing' Executive in 1973-74. He was killed in 1977 in a fall off a horse. He was Minister for Home Affairs during the 1950s campaign, and in his memoirs claims that 'the vital factor in stamping out terrorism . . . was the introduction of internment by the government in Dublin parallel with its introduction in Northern Ireland and prompt cooperation between the Gardaí [police in the Republic] and the RUC [Royal Ulster Constabulary]' (*ibid.*, p. 24). Faulkner was responsible for introducing internment in 1971, but circumstances had changed, and an aroused Nationalist population resented this method of dealing with grievances. The net result of the policy was to strengthen the Provisional IRA, which then was conducting an urban guerrilla campaign against British troops.
36. Denis Ireland was a Protestant nationalist and biographer of Wolfe Tone. In the 1950s campaign there was only one active Protestant Volunteer in the North. The IRA, in effect, had become an all-Catholic body. In the 1960s, Dr Roy Johnston, son of an Ulster Protestant Home Ruler (a professor of economics at TCD), joined the movement. Ivan Cooper, a Protestant, was a leading figure in the SDLP for a time, then faded from the scene. John Turnly, a wealthy North Antrim Protestant, joined the SDLP in the early 1970s, was identified with the 'Republican Wing' of the party, and in November 1977 was a founder of the Irish Independence Party. He was assassinated by unknown gunmen on 5 June 1980.
37. Seán Cronin, *The Rights of Man in Ireland* (Dublin: 1969), updated and revised version of lecture delivered in Castleblayney, County Monaghan, November 1964. Among the founders of the Wolfe Tone Society were: Lorcan Leonard, Uinseann Mac Eoin, Cathal Goulding, Harry White, Liam Burke, Jack Bennett, Risteárd de Róiste, Seán Cronin, Éamonn Mac Thomáis, Tomás Mac Giolla.
38. Desmond Greaves, *The Irish Question and the British People* (Ripley, Derby: 1963). As well, the *Tribune*, or Bevanite wing of Labour, always maintained an interest in Ireland and in the early 1950s published a pamphlet by Geoffrey Bing, *John Bull's Other Ireland*, about the undemocratic nature of the Northern Ireland state.
39. *The Catholic Mind*, May 1933, defended 'the young Catholics of Dublin who were responsible for the destruction of Connolly Hall [Dublin] but we blame the government for allowing matters to reach a head'. Connolly Hall was the headquarters of the Workers' Revolutionary Groups, a pre-CP organization. Because police guarded the gutted building it objected to 'a Catholic country offering protection to the hirelings of Russia who would destroy every vestige of our faith and defile the altars we worship at'. The 'Workers College' was also attacked: it taught 'the materialistic philosophy of the German Jew Karl Marx and his companion Engels'. For Irish CP, see *Communist Party of Ireland Outline History* (Dublin: n.d.).

   Jim Gralton, a Leitrim man who emigrated to the US before the First World War and became an American citizen, was deported from Ireland in

1933 for preaching Communism. He founded Irish Workers Clubs in New York and out of these grew the Transport Workers Union of America founded by Mike Quill, Austin Hogan and Gerald O'Reilly, Irish immigrants. Seán Murray visited the Irish Workers Clubs, in 1933, and wrote a pamphlet, published by the clubs, *Ireland's Road to Communism*. Murray, from Antrim, came out of the IRA.

40. The manifesto is titled 'Invasion. If the British Come? If the Germans Land? If Both Come—What Then? A Republican Answer?' It said: 'The IRA are anti-De Valera for good reasons and bad reasons, but they would not conspire to down De Valera to build up a puppet state for Germany. . . .'
41. *United Irishman*, January-February 1951, denounced 'atheistic communism . . . an ideology repugnant to the overwhelming majority of [Irish] people'.
42. *Disturbances in Northern Ireland*, p. 77. Miss Sinclair was elected chairman in February 1968 and held the post until February 1969, when she was succeeded by Frank Gogarty, Belfast. See also Vincent E. Feeney, 'The Civil Rights Movement in Northern Ireland', *Éire-Ireland*, (Summer 1974). The Cameron Report said of the IRA connection that it took 'a close interest' in NICRA from the start, provided stewards at demonstrations, maintained discipline and checked 'any disposition to indiscipline or disorder' (p. 78). This is a fair statement of the IRA's role: it started the movement, then let it walk by itself.
43. See Devlin, *The Price of My Soul*; Eamon McCann, *War and an Irish Town* (London: 1974); Farrell, *Northern Ireland*, pp. 249–52.
44. See Patrick Marrinan, *Paisley* (Tralee: 1973). The Cameron Report blames Paisley for the disorders in Armagh and Burntollet and for 'inflaming passions'. Otherwise the demonstrations might have been calm, the Report declares.
45. *This Week*, 31 July, 1970, interview with Cathal Goulding. 'By 1967 the movement had become dormant. It wasn't active in any political sense or even in any revolutionary sense . . . . Units of the IRA and the Cumainn [clubs] of Sinn Féin had become almost non-existent.'
46. *Ibid.*, IRA resolution at 1968 convention, quoted by Goulding, who felt that by its passage 'we had got away from the clap-trap and the clichés that we had allowed ourselves to be caught in over the years . . . that when we had got the British army out of Ireland, the people . . . could make up their own minds, and simply take what was rightly theirs'. 'It was essential,' he added, 'for those who were fighting for freedom to know exactly what freedom meant . . . not to have to wait for a priest or a landlord to tell them when to begin or when to stop fighting.'
47. *Hibernia*, 31 March, 1972. This was written after Johnston broke with the Official IRA early in 1972, following the shooting of Senator John Barnhill, a Unionist. Johnston believed the Officials were following the Provisionals in an armed campaign and he could not agree with that. NICRA was still the hope in the North, he felt. (*Irish Times*, 18 January, 1972.) He went back to the Communist Party and was subsequently expelled as a 'Eurocommunist'. He has since analysed the thinking of the Officials, the Provisionals and the Irish CP as 'Stalinist', which he defines as rigid, orthodox, regimented, intolerant and aggressively seeking 'to dominate potential allies' (*Hibernia*, 24 January, 1980).
48. See *Government of Ireland Act, 1920* (10 & 11 Geo. 5, Ch. 67), p. 6.

49. *This Week*, 7 August, 1970.
50. *Violence and Civil Disturbances in Northern Ireland in 1969, Report of the Tribunal of Inquiry*, headed by Justice Scarman (Belfast: 1972), concluded that 'all the five explosions were the work of Protestant extremists. Their purpose was to strengthen the campaign to topple then Prime Minister, Captain O'Neill, from power and to secure the release from gaol of Dr. Paisley and Major Bunting'. One of the culprits confessed and received twelve years after agreeing to turn state's evidence against five others. The five were found not guilty by a jury.
51. Quoted Marrinan, *Paisley*, pp. 183–4. Actually there was no strong lobby for civil rights among the US Irish, most of whom were as suspicious as Chichester-Clark of the young civil rights radicals, which Bernadette Devlin discovered when she toured America in 1969.
52. James Callaghan, *A House Divided* (London: 1973), p. 26.
53. *Violence and Civil Disturbances*, p. 31.
54. Callaghan, *House Divided*, p. 27.
55. *Ibid.* The successful defence of Derry against the Catholics is one of the great events in the ideology of Ulster Protestantism. Expecting 'a general Insurrection of the *Irish* intended on the 9th of December [1688], and considering that *Derry* as well as other places was to be presently possessed by the *Irish*', the Apprentice Boys of the town, on 8th December, 'run in all hast to the Main-Guard, snatcht up the Keys, and immediately shut up all the Four Gates, and the Magazine'. (*Walker's Diary*, pp. 15–16). If the Apprentice Boys are heroes, Colonel Lundy, the Governor, who would have surrendered the city, is the great traitor of Protestant Ulster.
56. *Violence and Civil Disturbances*, p. 68.
57. *Ibid.*, p. 69.
58. *Ibid.*, p. 74.
59. *Ibid.*, p. 76.
60. *Ibid.*
61. Kevin Boland, *Up Dev!* (Dublin: 1978), pp. 11–12. Boland was Minister for Social Services, Blaney Minister for Agriculture, Haughey Minister for Finance, Gibbons Minister for Defence, O Morain Minister for Justice.
62. Callaghan, *House Divided*, pp. 52–3.
63. *Violence and Civil Disturbances in Northern Ireland in 1969, Report . . .* (Scarman) covers all incidents thoroughly. Matters looked somewhat differently behind the barricades. For other views see Eamonn McCann, *War and an Irish Town*, pp. 58–71, and *Ulster* (London: 1972) by the *Sunday Times* (London) 'Insight Team'.
64. See *Weekly Irish Bulletin*, 12 June, 1922, issued by Dáil Éireann Publicity Department for details of sectarian killings (425), woundings (1,764), driven from homes (22,560), driven from jobs (8,586), from 21 July 1920, to 12 June, 1922.
65. *Violence and Civil Disturbances* (Scarman Report), p. 119.
66. *Ibid.*, p. 135. On the events in Belfast, see also *Sunday Times* Insight, *Ulster*, pp. 126–7.
67. Interview with Liam Burke, one of the defenders, in Dublin, 16 June, 1973. Burke was a leading IRA officer in the 1940s.
68. *Freedom Struggle by the Provisional IRA* (Drogheda: 1973). This illegal document carries no publisher's name. The printer was fined for issuing it

under the Irish Republic's Offences Against the State Act. The booklet contains an appendix with the Provisional IRA's 'Structure of the New Ireland': a federal parliament and four provincial assemblies—thus giving Ulster Protestants the appearance of having their own legislature.

69. Cathal Goulding, statement to General Army Convention of the IRA, 4 December, 1969.
70. Interview with Roy Johnston, Dublin, 23 August, 1970, on NLF. The CP view of proper division of responsibilities is from confidential source in a position to know, although it is possible the deduction is an estimate.
71. *Freedom Struggle by the Provisional IRA*, p. 10. Those referred to were Johnston and Coughlan.
72. The Belfast *coup* of 22 September 1969 was led by the veteran IRA man Billy McKee, supported by the 1940s leaders Hugh McAteer and Séamus (Jimmy) Steele. Steele, a pious and strict man, was dismissed from the IRA after years of service, for denouncing 'the Reds' at a commemoration funeral for Peter Barnes and James McCormick, the two IRA men hanged in England in February 1940. The denunciation on such an occasion was a warning to the leadership that it was on the wrong road; or it was an act of insubordination—depending on how one looked at it. GHQ decided to look at it as insubordination and made many enemies by dismissing a man who had spent seventeen years of his life in prison for republican activities and was a living legend in Belfast.
73. Goulding statement to convention, December 1969. The active service units were along the Donegal, Leitrim, Derry, Monaghan, Louth border. Supplies and communications were poor. Goulding issued a statement to strengthen Chichester-Clarke against Harold Wilson, he said. (Interview, 27 September 1969).
74. Goulding was right tactically. Escalation of the conflict along the border would be playing the 'Orange card' in the circumstances of August 1969.
75. For information on the government's decisions on the North, I am indebted to the then Fianna Fáil minister, Kevin Boland: interview in Washington, 22 April, 1980. See also *Irish Times*, 30 July 1980. Further information on the conspiracy and the directive to the Army is in *Magill*, May, June, July of 1980.
76. See James Kelly, *Orders for the Captain* (Dublin: 1971). He offered Goulding 'unlimited supplies', according to the latter. This was confirmed by Jack McCabe, later Quartermaster General of the Provisional IRA, who said Kelly worked with the chairmen of the Derry and Belfast Citizens' Defence Committees.
77. For an account of the trial see Tom Mac Intyre, *Through the Bridewell Gate* (London: 1971). For the official republican view see *Fianna Fáil and the IRA*, which was issued anonymously in 1970.
78. MacIntyre, *Bridewell Gate*, pp. 123–31.
79. *The Story of Fianna Fáil—First Phase* (Dublin: 1966), a party publication issued on the fortieth anniversary of its founding.
80. Boland, *Up Dev!*, p. 13. Boland wanted to resign, but de Valera, then out of active politics as nominal head of state, prevailed on him to remain in the Cabinet to avoid a government crisis. See the same author's *We Won't Stand (Idly) By* (Dublin: 1972), in which he propounds his republican ideology and belief in a united Ireland. After reading these books, and

bearing in mind the fact that Boland wrecked his political career, only the most prejudiced could doubt his sincerity.

81. Jack McCabe's view. A leftist politically, McCabe insisted that the national issue should take precedence over all else in the summer and autumn of 1969. Ruairí Ó Brádaigh, a leading IRA officer and first President of Provisional Sinn Féin, would agree in part with Goulding that the 'Communist issue' was one of the causes of the split.

> Their split with the IRA was not the result of Blaney intrigue, but of rank and file exasperation with IRA executives for unpreparedness last summer [1969] and for unrealistic policies such as alliance with Communist Party. He has no use for Blaney or for men like Séamus Brady. Opposes sectarianism . . . . Admits his rank-and-file are not so ecumenical . . .' (Cruise O'Brien, *States of Ireland*. p. 229).

82. Goulding statement to convention, December 1969.
83. This summary has grown out of several conversations with people who stood behind the barricades and with republicans who stood with them, or visited them. Jack McCabe perhaps stated a common republican opinion when he explained his own estimate: the people behind the barricades should be given the means to defend themselves; and if the opportunity came there should be a fight for 'the Republic'. He had a lot of faith in people, hardly any at all in leaders, and in that was fairly typical of the IRA volunteer. He feared that by November 1969 'a great opportunity had been lost and disillusionment had set in' (Interview, 6 September, 1970). Cathal Goulding, on the other hand, criticized the Defence Committees because they ostracised republicans loyal to GHQ and were influenced by small businessmen who wanted the barricades dismantled. (Interview, 27 September 1969).
84. *The Kerryman*, 17 January, 1970, 'What is a Republican?'.
85. *Irish Independent*, 9 December, 1970, 'What is Irish Republicanism?' See also Ruairí Ó Brádaigh, *Our People Our Future* (Dublin: 1973). John Joe McGirl, a veteran republican from Leitrim and former Sinn Féin TD (1957-61), expressed a typical traditionalist view at the Sinn Féin Ard Fheis, February 1970, which split, when he said he could not abandon abstention because 'men have died opposing Leinster House, men have been killed for refusing to enter that assembly'. McGirl's sincerity is not in doubt: he broke with his closest friend, Cathal Goulding on this issue (interview, Dublin, 31 May, 1971). For eighteen months after the split he sought a reconciliation, but insisted that the 'Officials' must resume the abstentionist policy.
86. Mac Stiofáin, *Revolutionary in Ireland* (Edinburgh: 1975). Born and raised in London, Mac Stiofáin became a convert to Catholicism and learned Irish in prison through Manus Canning, the Derry republican, and his own efforts. He thought the Communists insufficiently revolutionary he writes (p. 52), but later says he opposed Goulding's 'extreme socialism'. See also, Maria McGuire, *To Take Arms* (London: 1973), a defector's views.
87. Discussions in Dublin, 9 May, 1971. Same view was expressed by Dáithí Ó Conaill (David O'Connell) in Glencolumbcille, 31 August, 1970; 'Defence of the people is the first task of the Provisional IRA.' John Joe McGirl, Ballinamore, 1 September, 1970 said: 'IRA failure to defend the people

in August 1969 led to the split.' Ruairí O Brádaigh suggested same thing to C.C. O'Brien (*States of Ireland*, p. 229).
88. Dublin, 14 May, 1971.
89. Interview, Dublin, 5 May, 1971.
90. Dáithí Ó Conaill, Glencolumbcille, 31 August, 1970. Ruairí Ó Brádaigh discussed St Matthew's with C.C. O'Brien. 'In the St Matthew's fighting the defence was improvised by some of the Defence Committee, and by "some of our people". On both sides, deaths of fighters will be presented as civilian casualties: a question of compensation' (*States of Ireland*, p. 229).
91. *Sunday Times* Insight, *Ulster*, pp. 219–20. Also see Seán Óg Ó Fearghail, *Law (?) and Orders: the Story of the Belfast Curfew* (Belfast: 1970).
92. Anthony Coughlan, *The Northern Crisis: Which Way Forward?* (Dublin: 1969), p. 15.
93. *Freedom Struggle by the Provisional IRA*, p. 12.
94. See *Report of the Tribunal Appointed to Inquire into the Events on Sunday, 30th January 1972 . . . in Londonderry on that Day* (London: 1972) by Lord Widgery, and Sam Dash's reply, *Justice Denied: a Challenge to Lord Widgery's Report on 'Bloody Sunday'* International League for the Rights of Man in association with the National Council for Civil Liberties (London & New York: 1972). On internment see *Northern Ireland—the Mailed Fist: a Record of Army and Police Brutality from August 9-November 9, 1971* (Portglenone, County Antrim: 1972) by Campaign for Social Justice in N.I. and Association for Legal Justice, and *British Government Violations of Human Rights in NI* (Belfast: 1974) issued by NICRA.
95. See *Northern Ireland Constitutional Proposals, Presented to Parliament by the Secretary of State for Northern Ireland . . . March 1973* (London: 1973); Faulkner, *Memoirs*, Chapters 14–21; Paul F. Power, 'The Sunningdale Strategy and the Northern Ireland Majority Consent Doctrine in Anglo-Irish Relations', *Éire-Ireland* XII:I. See also NICRA comment, *Proposals for Peace, Democracy and Community Reconciliation* (Belfast: 1973).
96. For socialist and nationalist interpretation of why this 'settlement' collapsed see Jack Bennett, *Northern Ireland: Fourteen Days of Fascist Terror* (London: 1974). Bennett, a Belfast journalist, saw the 'lock-out' at first hand.
97. See Martin Dillon and Denis Lehane, *Political Murder in Northern Ireland* (London: 1973). Also *Irish Times*, 21 February, 1979, on 'the Shankill Butchers'. And Seán Cronin's *Tone's Republic: the Case Against Sectarianism* (Dublin: 1975), pp. 8–11. The Church of Ireland Primate and Archbishop of Armagh, Most Rev. John Armstrong, said in June of 1980 that in South Armagh and Co. Fermanagh 54 Protestants had been killed and he feared a pattern of sectarian intimidation. The Presbyterian Church shared the fear. (*Irish Times*, 19 June, 1980).
98. MacStiofáin, *Revolutionary in Ireland*, pp. 299–300, denies categorically Provisional responsibility for the Claudy bombing. David McKittrick in *Irish Times* (28 December, 1979), in review of a decade of killings wrote:

> The three Scottish soldiers; the bombing of McGurk's Bar; the Loyalist torture killings; the Provisional IRA bombs at Donegall Street, Oxford Street, Claudy;

> the bombs in Birmingham, Dublin and Monaghan; the Whitecross massacre, the Shankill butchers; the Miami Showband; the Maguire children; Lord Mountbatten; the eighteen soldiers; Bloody Friday, Bloody Sunday. And scores of others.

The list omits one of the worst horrors, at the La Mon hotel, in February 1978, when a dozen persons were fire-bombed to death in a mix-up over a phoned warning.

99. *Irish Times*, 18 January, 1978, report of Ewart-Biggs Memorial lecture delivered at Trinity College, Dublin, the previous night. Christopher Ewart-Biggs, UK ambassador to Ireland, was assassinated, presumably by the Provisional IRA, who said he was engaged in intelligence work. Dr O'Brien agrees that Ireland is an ex-colony, but at the same time 'there is no other people which . . . has played so large a part in colonizing other lands . . .'.

    Irish people do not see the bombing of civilians, intentional or not, as a heroic deed. A civilian is not a combatant. There is a moral law and it must not be flouted. The 1916 Proclamation specifically warned against dishonouring the cause by 'cowardice, inhumanity, or rapine'. This would seem to be the view of most Irish people.

    There is the question of what has come to be called 'terrorism': violence used against institutions of the 'enemy'. One must define both terms, 'terrorism' and the 'enemy'. If the 'terrorist' is the native attempting to drive out the foreign invader—the 'enemy'—he may use irregular forces, guerrilla bands, to strike at his troops, or he may use explosives to destroy his installations, or even assassination to eliminate his officials and agents. But no one is ever justified in using violence against innocent civilians, for any end. (On the uses of sectarian terrorism, see Liam de Paor, 'The Physical Force Men', *Irish Times*, 10 December, 1974). See also, Paul Wilkinson's *Political Terrorism* (London: 1974) and *Terrorism and the Liberal State* (New York: 1977).
100. The examples include continuing reports of torture and ill-treatment of prisoners—the latest is the Bennett Report, March 1979—the use of the counter-insurgency force, Special Air Service Regiment, particularly in South Armagh, an area almost one hundred per cent Nationalist. See also, Rona Fields, *A Society on the Run: a Psychology of Northern Ireland* (London: 1973); Frs. Denis Faul, Brian J. Brady, Raymond Murray, *A British Army Murder* (Cavan: 1974); Frs. Faul and Murray, *British Army and Special Branch RUC Brutalities* (Cavan: 1974); K. Boyle, T. Hadden, P. Hillyard, *Law and State: the Case of Northern Ireland* (London: 1975); David R. Lowry, 'Terrorism and Human Rights, Counter-insurgency and Necessity at Common Law', *Notre Dame Lawyer*, vol. 53, 1 (October 1977). See too, summary of human rights violations in Northern Ireland for the 1970s, in US State Department's *Country Reports on Human Rights Practices for 1979* (February 1980), under 'United Kingdom', pp. 690–8. Also, Tim Pat Coogan, *On the Blanket: the H-Block Story* (Dublin: 1980).
101. Karl von Clausewitz, *War, Politics and Power*—Selections from *On War* and *I Believe and Profess* (Chicago: 1962), transl. and ed. Colonel Edward M. Collins, USAF, p. 255.
102. John Midgley, 'The Poisoned Shamrock', *New York Times*, 2 May, 1979.
103. See Thomas C. Schelling, *Arms and Influence* (New Haven: 1973), pp. 170–81. Grivas, however, had a strategic plan: the campaign was to consist of actions designed to draw international attention to the Cyprus

problem. It would then become a question of international diplomacy. The French discovered in Algeria that although militarily successful, the newly-independent countries were against France at the UN and even her own allies would not vote for her. See also, Roger Trinquier, *Modern Warfare: French View of Counterinsurgency* (New York: 1964).

104. *An Phoblacht*, 15 August, 1975, 'No "Civil War" in the North.' One of the writers for *An Phoblacht* at that time, not the author of this article, was Desmond Fennell, a Catholic journalist, who saw two national groups in the North–Irish and British–the Catholics being the Irish group, the Protestants the 'British'. Tone's republicanism did not sit well with Fennell. He wrote a regular column, using the *nom de plume* 'Freeman', and his thinking was quite influential in developing a strong Catholic nationalism among Provisionals and their supporters. A neo-Stalinist group, the British and Irish Communist Organization, held the view that Ireland consists of two nations; Ulster Protestants being the British nation in Ireland beset by an 'imperialist' Irish Catholic nation. Clearly, ideology, unless related to reality in some form, can be very distorting.

105. However, the Provisionals also see themselves essentially as Irish republicans seeking to achieve Irish unity and independence and the British army's intelligence estimate, 'Northern Ireland: Future Terrorist Trends' (November 1978) tacitly agrees (See Appendix XVIII). 'The Provisional Movement is committed to the traditional aim of Irish nationalism, that is the removal of the British presence from Ireland . . . [believing] that this can only be achieved by violence.'

106. Faulkner, *Memoirs*, pp. 112–13.

107. McManus went on to form the Irish Independence Party which sought to stake out a more nationalist position than the SDLP, in November 1977 with Fergus McAteer, son of the veteran nationalist parliamentary leader, Eddie McAteer, and John Turnly, a North Antrim Protestant.

108. Roy Johnston, in a letter to *Hibernia*, 24 January 1980, said he and Sean O Bradaigh drafted the federal scheme adopted by the Provisionals in the mid-1960s.

109. See *Freedom Struggle by the Provisional IRA* (Drogheda: 1973), Appendix, pp. 94–8. It was proposed in June 1972 and seeks 'to establish a new society in Ireland–*Éire Nua*'.

110. The federal structure was an idea developed by the Wolfe Tone Society 'think tank' in the mid-1960s. The founders of Provisional Sinn Féin took it out of the drawer, brushed it off and issued it as their own. See also, Roy Johnston's letter in *Hibernia*, 24 January, 1980.

111. *Freedom Struggle by the Provisional IRA*, p. 98.

112. The amalgamation took place in January 1979.

113. Confidential talk in Dublin, 28 June, 1979, with leading Provisional, who remains a spokesman. 'The leadership is in the hands of the men who did the fighting in 1971', he said. 'Their ideas are close to Frank Ryan' (a founder of Republican Congress in 1934). The leadership is much more efficient militarily than its predecessors.

114. See *Framed Through the Special Criminal Court* (IRSP, Dublin: 1979). The 29 May, 1972 Officials' ceasefire was in response to a public outcry in Derry over the shooting of a local youth on leave from the British army. The Officials said they were ending armed action because of 'the

growing danger of sectarian conflict'.

Costello called his group the Irish Republican Socialist Party. It had an armed wing in the North, the Irish National Liberation Army, which claimed responsibility for the assassination of Airey Neave, Conservative spokesman on Northern Ireland. Mrs McAliskey withdrew from the party when it became clear, following armed confrontations with the Officials in Belfast, that it had a military arm, which Costello had denied.

115. Isles and Cuthbert, *An Economic Survey of Northern Ireland*, p. 212. See tables pages 211 and 571 comparing organized labour with UK.
116. R.S. Weiner and John Bayley, 'British Troops and Ulster's Political Leaders', *New Society* (London), 20 August, 1970. The Provisional IRA is 'essentially a working class organisation based in the ghetto areas of the cities and in the poorer rural areas', according to British army intelligence secret report 'Northern Ireland: Future Terrorist Trends' (see Appendix XVIII).
117. Eamonn Smullen, *Irish Industrial Revolution* (Dublin: 1977), pp. 7–9. The views may be those of the author, rather than party policy. He writes, 'Apart from American monopoly capital, the greatest benefactors [*sic*] of the IDA's programme was the Irish working class.' (p. 50). He says popular movements in Ireland are 'more interested in the division between North and South, opposing this party's efforts to prevent the eruption of sterile nationalism and sectarian violence' than in building a working-class movement. (p. 51). In *Teoiric*, the theoretical Journal of *SFWP*, Spring 1980, he states: 'We have two states in Ireland and our task is to win majority support in both states. In its efforts to carry out this task the Party is recognising to an ever increasing degree that we cannot remain prisoners of the past.'
118. *Irish Times*, 13 April, 1979.
119. Interview, Washington, 23 April, 1980. Despite its strong anti-sectarian stand the Workers' Party has not succeeded in building a united front with any section of the Protestant working class. It rejects the UDA concept of an independent Ulster. The party is organized in the North as 'the Republican Clubs'.
120. Radio Telefís Éireann (Dublin), 4 January 1972.
121. *Irish Press*, 5 January, 1972. Priests prominently concerned with the struggle are Denis Faul, Brian Brady, Raymond Murray.
122. *The Crane Bag*, vol. i, no. 2. (Dublin: 1977).
123. For background of IRA prisoners in Crumlin Road Prison, Belfast, during 1950s campaign, see Appendix XVI, compiled by Eamon Timoney. 'The Provisional IRA is essentially a working-class organization based in the ghetto areas of the cities and in the poorer rural areas', the earlier cited British intelligence estimate of the movement noted. ('Northern Ireland: Future Terrorist Trends', p. 4 – see Appendix XVIII).
124. Twomey interview, *Crane Bag*, vol. i, no. 2.
125. James Connolly, 'Catholicism, Protestantism and Politics', *Forward*, 3 May, 1913.
126. *Hibernia*, 25 October, 1979. At the 1980 Ard Fheis of Provisional Sinn Féin, in mid-January, strong leftist motions were passed denying the right of private ownership of large factories and large farms. (*Hibernia*, 24 January, 1980).

127. Frank Kitson, *Low Intensity Operations: Subversion, Insurgency & Peace-keeping* (London: 1971), p. 78.

CHAPTER 7

1. *Northern Ireland Constitution Act 1973* (Elizabeth II, Ch. 36). *The Government of Ireland Act* (1920) provided for a Council of Ireland, but the Belfast government would have nothing to do with it. This was the so-called 'Irish dimension' of the Sunningdale Agreement. At a minimum it involved co-operation between Dublin and Belfast, but could be developed to full unity. For Faulkner's view, see *Memoirs*, pp. 206–8. Faulkner calls the Ulster Defence Association-organized strike that brought down his power-sharing Executive in May 1974, 'an attempted *putsch*' (*Memoirs*, p. 262). The British did nothing. For his reaction to the strike, see *Memoirs*, pp. 260–77. He finds the statement of Glenn Barr, a leader of the strike movement: 'We are in a position to set up a provisional government', only a slight exaggeration. Its success owed more to the intimidation tactics of the UDA than to the co-operation of Protestant workers (*ibid.*, p. 261). The unions opposed the strike. The Provisionals gave it their benevolent neutrality, because if 'power-sharing' succeeded their campaign must end. However, most Nationalists supported the experiment and many Protestants were willing to try it.
2. The fifth attempted settlement began on 7 January 1980 with the opening of a constitutional conference in Belfast to discuss political structures for Northern Ireland. The State Department view is from *Country Reports on Human Rights Practices for 1979*, p. 606. The US officially entered the Northern Ireland problem with a statement by President Carter, in August 1977, promising financial help when peace was established. Speaker Tip O'Neill, Governor Hugh Carey of New York, Senators Edward Kennedy and D.P. Moynihan, have been actively involved in the Irish question for years.
3. John Magee, *Northern Ireland: Crisis and Conflict*, (Boston: 1974), p. 50, 'Ulster's Solemn League and Covenant', 28 September, 1912.
4. The 'two-nations' theory is put forward by persons of Irish nationalist background, not by Ulster Protestants who have a shared feeling of religious solidarity *vis-à-vis* Irish nationalism, but who have never claimed to be a separate nation. See also Paul F. Power, 'The Sunningdale Strategy and the Northern Majority-Consent Doctrine', *Éire-Ireland*, XII.I.
5. George O'Brien, *The Four Green Fields* (Dublin: 1936), p. 28.
6. *From Max Weber: Essays in Sociology*, ed. H.H. Gerth and C. Wright Mills (New York: 1958), 'Politics as a Vocation', p. 79. The essay, 'Structures of Power' (pp. 159–79), which deals with the theory of the nation, has several references to Irish nationalism, including that 'in spite of a common language, the Irish have no common national sentiment with the British' (p. 178). Weber says 'radical "nationalists" are often of foreign descent' (p. 173), which has been true in Ireland.

7. Strauss, *Irish Nationalism and British Democracy*, p. 280.
8. See Cornelius O'Leary, *Irish Elections 1918–1977: Parties, Voters and Proportional Representation* (Dublin: 1979): see particularly pp. 38–45.
9. Dublin, 23 June, 1979. She added: 'Connolly was dropped like a stone by de Valera, the Republicans and the Irish Labour Party'.
10. See D.W. Harkness, *The Restless Dominion* (New York: 1970).
11. See Cullen, *Economic History of Ireland*, Chapter 7.
12. The Irish Industrial Authority claims that the Republic of Ireland provides the highest rate of return on investment in the world. Exporters are permitted on hundred per cent tax relief on export earnings, which will continue to 1990, courtesy of the EEC. See John G. Gardner, *Republic of Ireland: Common Market Gateway* (Washington: 1973) and James R. Gallagher, *Republic Of Ireland Taxation* (Washington: 1974), both reprints from *The Tax Executive*, copyright Tax Executives Institute Inc., of Washington, DC. Also, Kieran A. Kennedy and Brendan R. Dowling, *Economic Growth in Ireland* (Dublin: 1975), particularly Part V, 'Conclusions and Implications', Chapters 16, 17 and 18. There are capital grants, training grants, loans and cheap factories, no taxes on exports, no restrictions on repatriating assets. The EEC insists on a ten per cent corporation tax from January 1981. Of the 656 firms that settled in Ireland from 1960 to 1978, 215 were American, and 176 British. (See Stewart Dalby, 'Mr. Haughey's Biggest Problem', *New Statesman*, 25 January, 1980).
13. Ireland, *Official News of Industrial Development in the Republic of Ireland*, No. 1, 1978.
14. See John Newhouse, *Collision in Brussels: the Common Market Crisis of 30 June 1965* (New York: 1967).
15. *Irish Times* editorial 'The CAP Factor', 25 January, 1979.
16. *A New Regional Policy for Europe* (Bruxelles: n.d.), *Regional Industrial Plans, 1973–1974* (Dublin: 1972); *Regional Policy in Ireland: a Review* (Dublin: 1974).
17. *A New Regional Policy for Europe*, p. 14. See also Patrick N. O'Farrell, *Regional Industrial Development Trends in Ireland, 1960–1973* (Dublin: 1975).
18. Meaning by 'Third World', developing countries and by 'First World', developed (industrialized) countries. The Communist bloc makes up the 'Second World'.
19. Kennedy and Dowling, *Economic Growth in Ireland*, pp. 286–7. For the political economy of multinational corporations, see Robert Gilpin, *US Power and the Multinational Corporation: the Political Economy of Foreign Direct Investment* (New York: 1975), and *The Multinational Corporation and Social Change*, ed. David E. Apter and Louis Wolf Goodman (New York: 1976).
20. Morgenthau, *Politics Among Nations*, p. 510. Morgenthau remarks: 'If they (the countries of the EEC) succeed, they will have overcome the obsolescent separatism of the nation state' (p. 511). However, since requests for aid must come through individual governments there is also a tendency in the EEC to strengthen national loyalties (pp. 512–13).
21. Fianna Fáil statement of policy on North was issued 29 October, 1975. One of its chief drafters was Charles J. Haughey, who was working his

way back to the party front bench after the arms trial. The party leader, Jack Lynch, was not enthusiastic about the plan and when he returned to power in 1977 did little about it. When Haughey took over the leadership of Fianna Fáil and became Taoiseach in December 1979, he said government policy on the North would be based on the 1975 statement. Before Lynch resigned, he had been attacked by Deputy Síle de Valera for departing from Fianna Fáil party doctrine on the North, although her views were sheltered in somewhat Aesopian language. Obviously most of Fianna Fáil's rank and file agreed with her.

22. Faulkner, *Memoirs*, p. 247.

23. *Ireland: Our Future Together* (Dublin: 1979). The author is Dr Garret FitzGerald, who also wrote *Towards a New Ireland* (Dublin: 1973). The son of an Ulster Presbyterian mother and Southern Catholic father, he is caught up in the problem personally and politically. His earliest work is an appraisal of the prospects of unity. The policy documents grew out of it. See also his lecture on the theme, *Irish Times*, 26 February, 1979. But ideologically he is talking of a Catholic state adjusting itself to the needs of a large Protestant minority, rather than to the requirements of a secular state in which religion would play no public role. This, too, is the attitude of Fianna Fáil.

24. The leader of the UDA is Andy Tyrie, its political adviser is Glenn Barr. They travelled with a delegation to the United States in the spring of 1979, lobbying for an independent Northern Ireland. They told Congressman Hamilton Fish (R-NY) and Congressman Joshua Eilberg (D-Pa.) in August 1978 of their hopes for a US guarantee. The Congressmen were acting as a sub-committee of the House Judiciary Committee holding hearings on the denial of visas to speakers of Provisional Sinn Féin and the Provisional IRA. (Committee report, June 1979). The UDA body calls itself the New Ulster Political Research Group. It has also met with a Fianna Fáil study group on the North, set up by Jack Lynch, and with Mr Haughey. The Fianna Fáil group seemed favourable to the UDA views. 'We cannot sulk on the sidelines', said James Leonard, Fianna Fáil TD for the border counties of Cavan and Monaghan. 'To think that full unity can be achieved in one simple step is to ignore centuries of our own history.' (*Irish Times*, 16 May 1980). See also *Northern Ireland: a Role for the United States* (Washington: December 1978) report to the House Committee on the Judiciary by two of its members on fact-finding trip to Northern Ireland, the Irish Republic and England, August/September 1978. Chapter 5, pp. 67–74, is on the UDA. The appendices include the Diplock Report of 1972, the Gardiner Report of 1975, Amnesty International Report of 1978, the Bennett Report of 1979, among other important documents. It concludes that the US government should 'reassess its present position on Northern Ireland and seek to assist in a political solution, such as it has done in the Middle East' (p. 221).

25. See 'Irish-American Leaders Switch, Chide U.K.', *New York Times*, 8 April, 1979. On aid, see Dennis J. Clark, *Irish Blood: Northern Ireland and the American Conscience* (Port Washington, N.Y.: 1977). See 'US Call for Britain to aid Irish Unity', *Irish Times*, 15 March, 1980. 'It is time for bolder vision in the name and cause of peace', the statement declared, urging Britain to join with the Irish government 'in working

to achieve peace and reconciliation.'

26. McAllister, *The Northern Ireland Social Democratic and Labour Party*, p. 168.
27. *Irish Times*, 20 April, 1979. O'Neill: 'While it is not for an American to say to the parties involved – this is the solution, or this is the path to be chosen, I have been deeply concerned by the lack of political progress in Northern Ireland over the last few years. . . together with all sides in Ireland we insist that Britain bears a heavy responsibility for the failures of recent years on the political front. We have been concerned that the problem has been treated as a political football in London or has otherwise been given a low priority. . . we do insist on an early, realistic and early initiative on the part of the incoming British government, so as to get negotiations moving quickly.'
28. *New York Times*, 8 April, 1979, 'Irish-American leaders'.
29. Faulkner, *Memoirs*, p. 143.
30. *Ibid.*
31. New York: 1973. A number of such studies have appeared with Ulster as the theme, subsidised by right-wing 'think tanks' in Britain and America. A later example is *Conflict Studies – Ulster: a Decade of Violence* (No. 108, London: June 1979). One of its conclusions: 'The way forward will be achieved by a police force of adequate size, properly trained and equipped . . .' (p. 24.) These are silly solutions.
32. Clutterbuck, *Protest*, p. 111. What is true is that at the end of 1971, Provisional IRA supplies in Belfast were at such a low level that the QMG was manufacturing explosives himself because of the shortage, with little regard for personal safety, when he was killed. (The Provisionals' QMG was Jack McCabe.) Thus intelligence was correct, the analysis wrong.
33. *Ibid.*, p. 112.
34. *Ibid.*, p. 118. See Chapter 10, 'Bloody Sunday,' pp. 118–31.
35. *Ibid.*, p. 127.
36. Dash, *Justice Denied*, pp. 42–3.
37. Clutterbuck, *Protest*, p. 127.
38. O'Brien, *States of Ireland*, p. 283.
39. Quoted by Faulkner, *Memoirs*, p. 140.
40. The British government offered the Provisionals a truce in June 1972; on 7 July, six Provisional leaders were flown to London to meet Whitelaw. The purpose of the exercise is not clear. For MacStiofáin's account, see *Revolutionary in Ireland*, pp. 278–89.
41. Faulkner, *Memoirs*, p. 172.
42. Frank Kitson, *Bunch of Five* (London: 1977), p. 282. On attitudes of the British military in Northern Ireland see *The Times*, 7 June, 1973, 'Stretching a Soldier's Patience'; *Times*, 15 August, 1977, 'Unnoticed Anniversary Marks Army's Eighth Year in Ulster'; *Financial Times*, 21 September, 1979, 'The Military Becomes Impatient'; and *Irish Times*, 24 January, 1980, 'Former North GOC calls for Victory Policy', reporting lecture by Lt. Gen. Sir Timothy Creasy who said 'given the national will and the efficient use of all our resources – military, police and civil – that are at the disposal of the modern state, terrorism can be defeated'.
43. British Defence Intelligence Staff report, dated 2 November, 1978. 'Northern

Ireland: Future Terrorist Trends', (see Appendix XVIII). See also, *Conflict Studies Ulster: a Decade of Violence* (no. 108, June 1979). A US sociologist, Martha Cranshaw, in a report for the State Department on 'Irish Terrorism', concluded that political violence would continue even if both communities accepted power sharing. (See *Irish Times*, 4 December, 1979) Without popular support, the Provisional IRA could not operate and power sharing would undermine that base. In 1974 the Provisionals considered power sharing a major threat to their campaign (Interview with David O' Connell, July 1974).

44. See 'UDA Unveils Proposals for Independent North', *Irish Times*, 30 March 1979, also *Irish Times*, 12 January, 1977, 'Independent North Rejected as Solution'.
45. See Richard Deutsch, *Mairead Corrigan and Betty Williams* (New York: 1977), translated from the French by Jack Bernard. The Peace Movement grew out of the killing of three children on 10 August, 1976, in Belfast, when a car, with a dead man at the wheel, crashed out of control after British soldiers shot the driver, a member of the Provisional IRA; but Catholic opinion turned for a time against the Provisionals' campaign of violence. The Peace Movement petered out after drawing world headlines when Protestants and Catholics marched for peace. The founders, Mairead Corrigan – aunt of the three children – and Betty Williams, shared a Nobel prize for peace. The movement which began in tragedy ended in tragedy when Mrs Anne Maguire, mother of the three children, took her own life in January 1980. Betty Williams resigned from the movement, which drew little public support after 1977. (See *Sunday Times*, 27 January, 1980, 'Peace People Are Crushed by the Nobel Prize'; *New York Times*, 24 January, 1980, 'Why Belfast Is Mourning'; *Hibernia* 31 January, 1980, 'Peace People: It's Time to Call It A Day.')
46. *Irish Times*, 12 January, 1977. Paddy Devlin, a founder of the SDLP, left the party because of his support for an independent Northern Ireland. Paddy Duffy, a leading member of the SDLP, also supports it. However, the SDLP as a party, and particularly John Hume as its Leader, will have nothing to do with the proposal.
47. *Irish Times*, 19 January, 1978. Sinn Féin means 'ourselves', sometimes translated as 'ourselves alone'. Robb was addressing a Fianna Fáil national youth conference.
48. *Ibid.*, 26 January, 1979. Robb's federalism eventually envisaged Wales, Ireland, Scotland and England (WISE) in one federation (*Irish Times*, 21 May, 1980), which he believed would lead to 'a lasting accommodation between Ireland and Britain.'
49. *Ibid.*, 12 January, 1977.
50. Jeremiah Newman, *The State of Ireland* (Dublin: 1977), pp. 125–6. Bishop McNamara of Kerry is another who insists that everyone must accept his theological views on contraception and divorce (*Irish Times*, 13 May, 1980). Opposing these restrictions on liberty in the name of Wolfe Tone's pluralism is the *Irish Times*, once the organ of the Unionist landlord class.
51. *Ibid.*, p. 126. The bishop's words follow a statement on political violence in Ireland, and of the need for 'a lasting settlement in our country'. He adds: 'Thank God, the signs are that this concern and understanding are

beginning to have effect and that we may hope that a new Ireland in which sectarian and political strife will be finally buried and in which all Irishmen will live together in justice and peace is about to emerge' (p. 125). How can such an Ireland emerge unless sectarianism is ended? Surely the bishop's values, no matter how laudable, will be unacceptable to those who reject his dogma.

In January 1980 Bishop Newman took issue on moral grounds with the Republic's Family Planning Act of July 1979, which legalized the supply of contraceptives in pharmacies through medical prescriptions. For Dr Newman, contraception is 'always immoral' and nurses, physicians, pharmacists and their assistants who have anything to do with it are morally in the wrong. Politicians and civil servants, 'whose business it is to frame these regulations (and) who have passed this legislation' are likewise morally accountable. The moral standards of 'the majority of the people of this country' should be upheld by the state. (*Irish Times*, 24 January, 1980, carries the bishop's address to nurses in full.) Here, again, Bishop Newman wants the moral code of the majority religion enforced by the state.

52. Quoted, in Marrinan, *Paisley*, pp. 193–4.
53. Lecky, *History of Ireland*, i, p. 47.
54. *Ibid.*, p. 49.
55. *Ibid.*, p. 50.
56. Marrinan, *Paisley*, p. 195.
57. *Protestant Telegraph*, 31 May, 1969, quoted by Charles Carlton, *Bigotry and Blood* (Chicago: 1977), p. 88, public letters to Queen Elizabeth.
58. Walker, *A True Account of the Siege of London-Derry* (London: 1887) p. 31.
59. John Robb, 'New North: New Nation', *The Tablet*, 24 March, 1979.
60. *The Crane Bag*, vol. 2, No. 1 & 2, 1978, 'Interview with Sean MacBride'. Also author's conversation with Mr MacBride, 8 August 1980.
61. *Ibid.*
62. Conversation, 8 August 1980.
63. p. 40.
64. George Gilmore's lecture on Republican Congress at Magee College, Derry, Summer 1980; copy in author's possession.
65. *America* (New York), 17 March, 1979.
66. *The Tablet*, editorial, 24 March, 1979.
67. 'Northern Ireland: Future Terrorist Trends', British army intelligence document, para II (see Appendix XVIII).
68. PRO, CAB 129/32 part I, ff 24–32, CP[49] 4. Ireland Report of Working Party, signed by Norman Brook, secretary to the Cabinet of Prime Minister Clement Attlee.
69. Introduction to Cronin and Roche (eds), *Freedom the Wolfe Tone Way*.
70. *The Federalist*, No. 10 (Hallowell: 1857), pp. 42–8.
71. John Hume, 'The Irish Question: A British Problem', *Foreign Affairs*, Winter 1979–80, explains the 'guarantee' thus: '. . .that Northern Ireland shall remain a part of the United Kingdom so long as a majority of the electorate so desire.' One may argue that the 'British guarantee' makes Northern Ireland an international issue, for it is blatant interference by the United Kingdom government in the affairs of a neighbouring country.

Senator Edward Kennedy apparently sees it in this light. In May 1979 and subsequently he suggested that as a first step to a settlement of the Northern Ireland problem the British government should withdraw the 'guarantee'.

Although Unionists dispute this view (for an example, see *New York Times,* 26 April, 1980, 'Britain, Ireland and Ulster', by Dennis Kennedy) the fact remains that Britain, in 1921, refused to coerce the one-fifth of the population of Ireland, who opposed a separate Irish state, but had no qualms about coercing the one-third of the population in Tyrone, Fermanagh, Derry, Armagh, Down and Antrim, who opposed partition. The final arbiter, it can hardly be denied, was force. 'British guarantee' means that force will be applied by Britain in Irish politics when and as required.

When Protestants objected to the term 'Constitutional Conference' the word 'constitutional' was dropped after the talks opened, in January 1980, to discover some formula for devolved government acceptable to both communities proving of course that the 'guarantee' is still in place.

72. Broadcast on Irish television, 3 August, 1980.
73. Confidential source.
74. 'September 1913', The Collected Poems of W.B. Yeats (New York: 1968), pp. 106–7.

Appendices

APPENDIX 1A

Proclamation prepared for French landing at Bantry Bay, under General Hoche, December 1796. (In Wolfe Tone Papers, Trinity College, Dublin).

PROCLAMATION BY GENERAL LAZARE HOCHE TO THE IRISH NATION *T.C.D., MS 2050, f.38*

To the Irish Nation

Liberty Equality

People of Ireland,

You have, at different periods, made known to the world, your abhorence for the slavery to which ambitious England has reduced your Country, & Notwithstanding your natural bravery, your endeavours to shake off the yoke, remain still unsuccessful, having constantly been thwarted by the dexterous perfidy of the english ministery which using all methods of corruption, caused a division at each time among your chiefs, & by means of their disunion, has kept you in bondage to this hour.

Now that the glorious & for ever memorable revolution of France, has rekindled that sacred fire of the love of liberty, which tiranny strove in vain, to extinguish in your hearts: your national secret & revolutionary committee thought it his duty to profit of the moment when the arms of france, every where triumphant, were allowed to succour Ireland & restore the Irish to their former independence.

In hopes of help then, said central committee applied to the Executive Power of the French Republick, & gave the most positive assurances of the dispositions wherein the Majority of the Irish were to become once more, a free people; intimating at the same time the sundry measures taken allready in private & some time since, for the success, and that nothing remained wanting, but the arrival of a french army with arms & ammunition; that on their landing, all the patriots able to serve, would croud to the french colours & soon contrive the total expulsion of the English & their followers out of the Irish territory.

The feeling exposure of your situation presented by your committee, your ardent wishes for relief together with a petition for assistance in the name of all Ireland, having raised in the bosom of all the French Republicans, these sentiments of generosity & benevolence which they bestow with pleasure on all people under oppression; the Executive power determined to fly to your aid, & in such manner as must answer your most sanguine expectations.

To this purpose I am now landed on the Irish shore at the head of a formidable army of Republicans, wont to conquer under their chiefs.

We present ourselves as sincere Friends to all who will embrace the cause of liberty, & we thirst after nothing but breaking your fetters and chastizing your tyrants.

This is no longer the miserable strife between the house of Hanover & that of the Stuards, the one to remain, the other to become again your Despot. No. -True Republicans fight only to vindicate the Rights of Equality & detest even the name of a Master.

Confiding that you share with us all, such noble sentiments, we offer you our hearts & our arms, to restore you to your national dignity: through an unbiassed choice you will make, of whatever form of government you think will secure the duration of your future independence.

The unlimited freedom every individual will enjoy of speaking his mind on persons & things, will inlighten your publick deliverations, will prevent errors, & the undisturbed order wherein I will assist you to maintain them, will guard you against the exuberance of enthusiasm, often more dangerous than the attempts of malice.

The example of other nations, the experience acquired by their various essays, every thing, gives you the expectation of an happiness, which your friends Purchased at a high Price, & that their generosity offers you, at the cheap cost of taking one single step, with the boldness & dignity suitable tho the will & pleassure of four millions of individuals.

There is not, to besure, one thinking, man in Ireland, who does not feel the advantages of your geographical position, of your population, the fecundity of your soil, the activity strength and courage of the inhabitants, the number, the goodness & propitious situation of your sea ports.

His indignation therefore must be raised to the utmost, when he casts an eye on the shocking misery of most of his countrymen, & reflects that all these gifts of nature, are thrown away on them, if placed as they are near the english government, they do not contrive proper means, to confine its systematical tyranny, within the natural limits of old cruel England.

In deed it is from that invading spirit, that England successively attained, the power of benumming all the resources of Ireland, both physical & moral.

English policy took care at all times, to keep up a diffidence & animosity between the different religious sects, the fanaticism whereof the court of London knew artfully how to stir up & direct, to prevent the junction of your forces, against your common enemy.

From your discords, arose the facility England found, to treat you like perfect slaves, by excluding you from all places whether civil, military, or ecclesiastick; under pretence of the roman rites adopted by the three quarters of the Irish; the other quarter being presbyterians, are by the English, equally anathematized as dissenters.

With this single scheme, every thing became in a short lapse of time, the prey of an handful of protestant foreigners, all low creatures devoted to english machination & plunder.

These supporters of despotism, by dint of spoliations & injustice towards your fore fathers & yourselves, are now become the allmost sole possessors of land properties in Ireland; the income whereof, passing to England, leaves you to starve; & for fear you should ever rise from this state of indigency, through some commercial industry, the English act of navigation, in striping you of the clear gains, took care also to prevent your ever attaining to either force or wealth at sea.

Your sham representation in parliament being totally null, as to your national interest, leaves you bereft of the most distant hopes for redress to your grievances.

The laws against purchasing land properties, measures taken to hinder roman catholiks from, even holding farms on long leases (which have in need of late met with temporary lenities) these cruel regulations have reduced the most part of the country people, to turn journeymen & servants to the usurpers, on the very spot that belonged to their ancestors.

Both by the publick school settlements, & your want of means, you are debarred from all possibility of giving your children any education, & the english government carried tyranny to the pitch, of proscribing your own native language.

Let me end this sorrowfull description by reminding you of the multitude of Irish, descended from the most ancient families in this formerly flourishing country, exhibiting at this moment to publick view, in the streets of proud London, the picture of the lowest degradation, where they are reduced for bread, to take to the vilest occupations & stand butts to the bitter & contemptuous derision of an insolent english Mob.

In opposition to all this misery, consider what blessings must attend you, if you have the spirit to cause for yourselves, a form of independent government, calculated to your highest advantage, & knowing no bounds to it's Power, but what is merely impossible, or denied by the sovereign Will of the People; where a fraternal toleration of all religious worships, will put an end to these animosities wherewith the perfideous Policy of england, made the roman catholiks & presbyterians, turn about, tools to her ambition.

Consider again in this new order of things, what increasement of strength you will reap, for the common wellfare, from an hearty & undissembled union; how much you will thereby be enabled to resist with success, all such as would dare attempt to disturb your peace, by opposing them, with all the resources arising to you, from a population abounding with men of genius & courage, from a soil productive of all the necessaries of life & an industrious activity wisely directed towards the numerous facilities you have for exportations, & beneficial returns; and thereto, the stopp of emigration to north America & other parts, whereby you have been considerably weakened this while past, & from whence numbers will come back, to enjoy the peace & plenty of their native home.

The abolition of all privileges & distinctions, will procure you a national representation, justly proportionnel to the number represented, offering each individual, the prospect of seeing his talents & his virtue honourably recompensed, by the free choice of his countrymen.

Finally, you have an independent national Constitution, calculated to the utmost of your prosperity, & supported by the friendship of the french Republick, steady to her allies, terrible to her foes, & determined to overthrow all opponents to her liberty & yours.

People of Ireland – such & manifold are the results of liberty, & I offer them to you, in the name of the generous Republick of France. To this purpose, I am

There shall be exact lists kept of the names & surnames of all that will come, with the dates of their arrival, & notes will be taken of their behaviour, that in the sharing of the enemy's spoils, strict justice be done to every man's seal in the cause of his country.

The militia & others shall likewise, be admitted to share; with one reference to the date of their junction.

In the like manner will be used, all Irish sailors & persons, whether pressed, or enlisted on board the english navy; & if they bring any english prize into your harbours, or those of France, the full value shall be paid them, on proper averment.

But if notwithstanding these encouragements & contrary to my expectations, any Irish man whould prove so ill natured to his mother country as to sacrifice her glory & wellfare so some private & selfish considerations, & take part with the common foe, I here equally declare, that wherever the Republicans can come at him, the monster shall be used, not as prisoner of war, like the english troops, but with out mercy, as a rebel & a traitor, & that his lands & chattels shall be confiscated.

We will invite all legal & publick powers, to confiscate the properties belonging to emigrated or run away persons, as also to such, who under an insidious neutrality, would offer to remain unconcerned in the danger of their country, promising themselves the advantage of declaring for the strongest side, after the conflict; and as such cowardice would be of the most contemptible kind, to be further punished, by the transportation of the culprit.

Until the circumstances admit the assembling of provisional representatives for the establishment of a regular national administration; I hereby invite all patriots of knowledge & experience, to acquaint me with every reflection, observations, or means that localities will warrant, & would be conducive to a speedy organization of the revolutionary powers.
vested with full powers to realize every one of the aforesaid promises.

The first use I will make of these powers, shall be for your tranquillity: in consequence I here solemnly declare, that the army I have the honour of commanding, will, during it's whole stay in Ireland, live in good order & military discipline, and that any offender against the liberty & security of persons or their properties, against the reverence & freedom due to all religious Worships, or against the dignity & authority of the magistrates legally nominated, by the good People of Ireland, shall be sentenced to death, in the four and twenty hours after his committment, whatever his rank or quality may be.

Having thus secured every one against all idle fears, I shall expect to find on your part, all the zeal & the facilities to pursue my further operations; I entertain no doubt of seeing all sincere friends to the wellfare of Ireland, croud to our coulours, where they will be provided with necessaries, for such as are able to carry arms: they will, in so doing, enforce our means to expell quickly our common enemy, & from their speed in joining the army, will chiefly depend, the more or less of blood shed, of which I shall allways be desirous to spare the loss.

People of Ireland,

I have here now made known to you, the intention of the French Nation, in your behalf, I have thereto made bold to add my own personal sentiments, with the freehearted candour of a Soldier, whose sole ambition is to answer the purpose I am sent for; let me then tell you, that you are come to the Pass, where all Europe's attention is fixed on your future, behaviour, which will decide, whether your really deserve to become a free nation. Let every Irish man rise spontaneously throughout the Island; my brave brother soldiers and I, will be your central mark to rally on; date not look the enemy in the face, and victory is sure, complete & allmost without a blow.

Such as you perceive the benign rays shooting from the sun, dissipate the fetid & pestilential vapeurs arising from a sink, & give death to the myriad of reptiles living on corruption: such also will the beams of burning patriotism strike tyranny to the heart, & anihilate all its satellites, when once in the presence of a numberous body of brave men, they hear the unanimous outcry of —

Liberty and Equality for ever.

Given at the head quarters of the French army the

The general commander in chief of the French army,

L. Hoche

APPENDIX 1B

Extract from Theobald Wolfe Tone's *An address to the people of Ireland on the present important crisis, 1796*

At length, the time is arrived when a friend to the liberty and independence of Ireland may venture to speak the truth, and examine into the situation and interest of his country, without fear of being stopped short by that most unanswerable of all arguments, an information in the Court of King's Bench, at the suit of his majesty's Attorney General.

It is long since every honest Irishman has mourned in secret over the misery and degradation of his native land, without daring to murmur a syllable in the way of complaint. Not even our groans were free! Six hundred years of oppression and slavery have passed in melancholy succession over our fathers' heads and our own, during which period we have been visited by every evil which tyranny could devise, and cruelty execute; we have been scattered, like chaff, over the land, and our name has been forgotten among the nations; we have been massacred and plundered, insulted and despised; we have been reduced to that lowest state of human degradation, that we almost ceased to respect ourselves; we have doubted whether the opinion of our oppressors was not just, and whether we were not, in fact, framed for that submission, to which we have been bent by the pressure of so many centuries of hard, unremitting, unrelenting tyranny.

But if the judgments of Providence be slow they are certain. The villain must not hope to walk in credit to his grave, nor the tyrant to insult forever with impunity the misery he has caused. The pride and arrogance of England have at length called down upon her head the tardy and lingering justice which her manifold crimes have so long provoked; the sufferings of Ireland, prostrate and humbled as she has been, even to the dust, seem to have awakened the attention of him who rules the destiny of nations; in his goodness and compassion he has at length regarded us, and placed in our hands the means, if we have the courage to be free.

Without being too much of an enthusiastic visionary, I think I may say I see a new order of things commencing in Europe. The stupendous Revolution which has taken place in France; the unparalleled succession of events which have, in defiance of the united efforts of all the despots of Europe, established that mighty Republic in the broad and firm basis of equal rights, liberties and laws; the abasement, contrary to all human probability, of her enemies every one of whom has, in his turn, been forced to yield to her ascendant genius, with the exception thus far, of Austria, and especially of England, whose fall has only been delayed to make her degradation more terrible, and the triumph of her victorious rival the more complete; all this I say, has satisfied my mind, that the ancient system of tyranny must fall. In many nations it is already extinct, in others, it has received its death wound, and though it may for some time train a feeble and lingering existence, its duration is ascertained, and its days already numbered. I do not look upon the French Revolution as a question subject to the ordinary calculation of politics; *it is a thing which is to be*; and, as all human experience has verified that the new doctrine ever finally subverts the old; as the Mosaic Law subverted idolatry: as Christianity subverted the Jewish dispensation; as the Reformation subverted Popery; so, I am firmly convinced, the doctrine of Republicanism will finally subvert that of Monarchy, and establish a system of just and rational liberty, on the ruins of the thrones of the despots of Europe.

But whether this opinion be well or ill founded, the question I mean to examine will not be affected by the result. Fortunately, or unfortunately, for Ireland, her cause is independent of the theory. The object for her immediate consideration is not whether she shall adopt this or that form of government, but whether she shall be independent under any. She has too many solid, substantial, heavy, existing grievances, to require much ingenuity, or subtle argument to convince her of her interest and her duty, and the question on which we must take an instant determination, will, if I mistake not, be decided as soon as it is stated.

The alternative which is now submitted to your choice, with regard to England, is one word *Union* or *Separation*! You must determine, and that instantly, between slavery and independence; there is no third way. I will not insult you by doubting what will be your decision. I anticipate your immediate and unanimous declaration, which establishes forever liberty to yourselves, and independence to your country.

To a magnanimous people it is unnecessary to prove, that it is *base*, to an enlightened people it is unnecessary to prove, that it is *ruinous*, to exist in dependence on the will of a foreign power, and that power an ambitious rival. To you this is not matter of mere speculating. You feel it in your Government, in your laws, in your manners, in your principles, in your education; with all the great moral and physical advantages of which you are possessed, you are unnoticed and unknown as a nation in Europe; your bodies and your minds are bent down by the incumbent pressure of your tyrant; she, to maintain whose avarice and ambition you are daily forced to spill your best blood, in whose cause you fight without glory and without profit, where victory but rivets your chains the faster, and where defeat adds to slavery, mortification, and disgrace. In vain are you placed in the most advantageous position for unlimited commerce; in vain are you blessed with a fruitful soil, and every requisite for trade and manufactures, with inexhaustible mines, with navigable rivers, and with the noblest harbours in Europe. All these advantages are blasted by the contagious presence of your imperious rival, before whose influence your strength is withered, your resources crushed, and the rising spirit of emulation strangled in the birth. It is England who debauches and degrades your gentry; it is England who starves your manufacturers, to drive them into her fleets and armies; it is England who keeps your wretched peasantry half-fed, half-clothed, miserable and despised, defrauded of their just rights as human beings, and reduced, if the innate spirit of your country did not support them, as it were, by miracle, below the level of the beasts of the field; it is England who buys your legislators to betray you, and pays you with the money levied on yourselves; it is England who foments and perpetuates, as far as in her lies, the spirit of religious dissension among you, and that labours to keep asunder Irishman from Irishman, because, that, in your cordial union among yourselves, she sees clearly the downfall of her usurpation, and the establishment of your liberties; it is England who supports and nourishes that rotten, aristocratic faction among you, which, though not the tenth part of your population, has arrogated to itself five-sixths of the property, and the whole of the patronage and power of your nation; a faction, which, to maintain itself by the power of England, is ready to sacrifice, and does daily sacrifice your dearest rights to her insatiable lust of gold and power.

Life of Wolfe Tone, edited by his son, William Theobald Wolfe Tone, Washington, 1826. Vol. ii, pp 273–276

APPENDIX II

Leaflet of the National Council of Sinn Fein, undated, but probably 1903–5. (In McGarrity Papers, National Library of Ireland).

Irishmen!

IT is absurd to talk against British Tyranny in Ireland when you join, or let your sons, brothers, or friends join the British Navy and the British Army.

If there were no British Navy and British Army there would be no British Government here to oppress you.

If there were a weak British Navy and British Army, the British Government would not be able to maintain the infamous **Union** under which your Industries have been ruined, your soil given over to the bullocks, your population cut down one-half, and your taxation increased fivefold.

There would be a weak British Navy and Army if the Irish did not enlist.

The Irish are the real fighting element in England's armed forces. Without the Irish England would have been beaten by Napoleon a hundred years ago and by the Boers yesterday.

Don't continue to help England to be strong enough to oppress Ireland.

O'Connell said he committed a crime who gave strength to the enemy. The Irishman who enlists in England's armed forces gives strength to the foreigners who rule the country.

Keep out of the British Navy, Army, and the Royal Irish Constabulary. Advise your friends to do so and pass this around.

Published by the National Council of Sinn Féin.

APPENDIX III

The Dungannon Club in Belfast was controlled by the IRB.
(Leaflet from McGarrity Papers, National Library of Ireland).

WEST BELFAST BRANCH

OF THE

NATIONAL COUNCIL.

The WEST BELFAST BRANCH of the NATIONAL COUNCIL has been formed by amalgamating the Dungannon Club with the membership of the late West Belfast Branch, and has opened its Winter Session for 1907-8.

It is starting an active campaign to further the SINN FEIN Movement in Belfast and district. Every Irish Nationalist, willing to work for a Self-Reliant Irish Ireland, is cordially invited to join its ranks.

The SINN FEIN Movement aims at creating an Ireland that will trust in itself instead of trusting in the English Parliament, that will build up its own National life, Politically, Industrially, and Educationally, relying on the Irish People and on no other. It aims at rallying the whole Irish people to assert the Independence of their Country, and to make Ireland a great Nation Intellectually and Commercially.

Its methods are simple and effective. Politically, it proposes to withdraw the Irish Representatives from Westminster, and restore the Political centre of Ireland to Ireland, where it should always have been. Sending representatives to the English Parliament, as provided by the Act of Union, admits the validity of that Act, and is an admission on our part of the right of England to rule our country. By withdrawing them we cease to recognise the right of England, and by a widespread passive resistance movement we can make English Government in Ireland impossible.

Industrially, by a rigorous boycott of all English Manufactures and products, and by adopting a voluntary protection in favour of Irish Manufactures, and by always giving them preference we can make Ireland prosperous.

Intellectually, by doing all in our power to improve the education of our members and the Irish people, along lines similar to those employed by the Gaelic League in their classes, and local and provincial colleges, and by helping on the work of the Gaelic League.

The results of this policy will be a vigorous and healthy National life, and the crowning result will be the winning of the National Independence of Ireland.

In this work every Irishman is invited to join us. Catholic and Protestant are working together, and we wish to bring them closer together. Further information about the Movement or the Branch can be had from the Secretaries.

The next Meeting of the Branch will be held on ....

at .... Meeting starts at .... p.m.

APPENDIX IV

Letter from Bulmer Hobson, IRB organizer of the Howth gun-running in July 1914, to Joseph McGarrity of the Clan-na-Gael on John Redmond's demand for control of the Irish Volunteers, which Hobson supported, thus splitting him from Tom Clarke and Seán MacDermott. 'R.C.' is Roger Casement. 'Old Man' is John Devòy, 'G.A.' is Gaelic American. (In McGarrity Papers, National Library of Ireland).

1 College Street, Dublin
14th July 1914

My dear Joe

I intended writing you this good while about the situation here but have had so much work & worry that I never got it done. I hardly know where to start. So many things both good and bad have happened here. However, I suppose you will have seen R.C. and he will have explained our situation over here. If you have not, don't fail to see him. Have a long talk with him, and I need not tell you that he is a good man to have as regards the Provisional Committee and Redmond. When he forced the situation we had no alternative but to accept his terms or else break the Volunteer movement. We could not have fought him for half of the Committee would have seceded and only the separatists would have been left on it. Redmond would have collared nine members of the Volunteer movement and that would have been an end of it as a real volunteer force. The only thing we could do was to yield him a Phyrric victory and stay on and try to keep things right from the inside. He has not gained control and I don't think he will. He could not if our friends acted with intelligence and unity, though both these commodities are rather scarce with some of them.

I had a letter from the old man in which he blames us for your difficulties in America. I don't quite see how we are to blame. If we had not accepted his demand he would have done the same thing, with exactly the same results. Some of my friends here have made it impossible for me to continue as editor of Freedom and now the old man has cut me off the G.A. In consequence my entire income has been wiped out. I do not see how I can continue to give time to the movement. To have opinions is too expensive a luxury even in our own movement. The Volunteers are doing splendidly and could be made a real force and I should have liked to have taken a hand in bringing that about. But I am too tired and disgusted just now to do more than try to find a way out of my difficulties. Unless I can start a paper I will leave Ireland.

I have not had a letter from O'Keefe since I left Phila. and nothing has resulted from our scheme of a syndicated letter from the Papers. I suppose that like the rest of my plans has broken up too. I am afraid this is turning into a very melancholy letter but the folly of some of our people starting to quarrel now when we could pull things through by standing together is heart-breaking.

I do not anticipate that Redmond's action here will affect the movement very much, though of course it is very damaging in America. Several of his nominees are deadly enemies and will never work together, while all the best men on the Committee are sound on essential questions. The deciding factor will be rifles. If we get them all will be well and if we cannot it doesn't much matter who is in control. I think we shall get them and that things will be right. However, you have probably heard all the news from R.C. and I hope that your work will not be so seriously impeded as it seems to be at present. We recognize your difficulties here and are grateful for the splendid help you have already given us. Is there any chance now of your coming across next month? I hope so. Remember me to Mrs. MacGarrity and Mrs. Hynes. Perhaps you would ask O'Keefe to write and let me know if any business can be done. With best wishes.

Your friend
Bulmer

APPENDIX V

Proclamation of the Irish Republic Easter Monday, 1916

POBLACHT NA H EIREANN.

THE PROVISIONAL GOVERNMENT
OF THE
IRISH REPUBLIC
TO THE PEOPLE OF IRELAND.

IRISHMEN AND IRISHWOMEN: In the name of God and of the dead generations from which she receives her old tradition of nationhood, Ireland, through us, summons her children to her flag and strikes for her freedom.

Having organised and trained her manhood through her secret revolutionary organisation, the Irish Republican Brotherhood, and through her open military organisations, the Irish Volunteers and the Irish Citizen Army, having patiently perfected her discipline, having resolutely waited for the right moment to reveal itself, she now seizes that moment, and, supported by her exiled children in America and by gallant allies in Europe, but relying in the first on her own strength, she strikes in full confidence of victory.

We declare the right of the people of Ireland to the ownership of Ireland, and to the unfettered control of Irish destinies, to be sovereign and indefeasible. The long usurpation of that right by a foreign people and government has not extinguished the right, nor can it ever be extinguished except by the destruction of the Irish people. In every generation the Irish people have asserted their right to national freedom and sovereignty; six times during the past three hundred years they have asserted it in arms. Standing on that fundamental right and again asserting it in arms in the face of the world, we hereby proclaim the Irish Republic as a Sovereign Independent State, and we pledge our lives and the lives of our comrades-in-arms to the cause of its freedom, of its welfare, and of its exaltation among the nations.

The Irish Republic is entitled to, and hereby claims, the allegiance of every Irishman and Irishwoman. The Republic guarantees religious and civil liberty equal rights and equal opportunities to all its citizens, and declares its resolve to pursue the happiness and prosperity of the whole nation and of all its parts, cherishing all the children of the nation equally, and oblivious of the differences carefully fostered by an alien government, which have divided a minority from the majority in the past.

Until our arms have brought the opportune moment for the establishment of a permanent National Government, representative of the whole people of Ireland and elected by the suffrages of all her men and women, the Provisional Government, hereby constituted, will administer the civil and military affairs of the Republic in trust for the people.

We place the cause of the Irish Republic under the protection of the Most High God, Whose blessing we invoke upon our arms, and we pray that no one who serves that cause will dishonour it by cowardice, inhumanity, or rapine. In this supreme hour the Irish nation must, by its valour and discipline and by the readiness of its children to sacrifice themselves for the common good, prove itself worthyof the august destiny to which it is called.

Signed on Behalf of the Provisional Government,

THOMAS J. CLARKE.
SEAN Mac DIARMADA. THOMAS MacDONAGH.
P. H. PEARSE. EAMONN CEANNT.
JAMES CONNOLLY. JOSEPH PLUNKETT.

APPENDIX VI

Memorandum by Joseph McGarrity on 1916 Rising.

(Joseph McGarrity, the Clan-na-Gael leader, was closely involved in the arrangements for a rebellion in Ireland in 1916. This memorandum, drafted some time after the Rising, was among his papers.)

James Smith, who made a trip to Ireland as special messenger from the Clan-na-Gael, lived at 2419 South Mole Street, Philadelphia; was born in Tyrone, Ireland. He had a brother killed in the world war on the English side, and had been a member of the Board of Erin Hibernians. This connection and letters from his mother in Ireland made it possible for him to get a passport and make the trip, when it was very hard to get a man who could get a passport and at the same time be willing and trustworthy to go. He brought the last instructions to Tom Clarke before the Easter Rising. Following instructions he called on Tom Clarke at his shop and residence on Great Britain Street, Dublin. On entering he asked for a cigar. Tom Clarke appeared suspicious of him, or perhaps he was suspicious of a man who entered Tom's shop about the same time and was undoubtedly watching Smith, who was a stranger in town. Tom gave Smith the cigar, and looking towards the door (that is, the store door) and keeping his eye on Smith and the party that followed Smith into the store, he told his little girl to give the gentleman his change, and backed into the door leading to the residence part of the house. He did not come out again until Smith left, if he came at all; he was evidently fearful of a trap and took no chances.

Smith left the Clarke shop and proceeded to take the next train north to Tyrone, where he sought and found Doctor Patrick McCartan, and through another party, delivered the message, which reached Tom Clarke the following day. See Smith's own narrative and Doctor McCartan's also.

Miss Plunkett (Count Plunkett's daughter) followed Smith with the message and some funds. We did not know when Smith volunteered to make the trip that Miss Plunkett was available. Smith did his service to Ireland well. He acted wisely and discreetly and deserves the gratitude of his countrymen. His narrative gives dates, etc.

February 12th 1916:
Received the following message from Patrick H. Pearse. 'Send rifles to Limerick, between Good Friday and Easter Sunday; may have to strike before then, but in any case cannot delay longer. Men would be imprisoned. Answer.'

Note: there was considerable delay in getting the answer ready as the German representatives in America had to be interviewed several times and they, in turn, had to code cable their government: When we finally got from the Germans a statement of what they proposed to do, the following message was sent, to Pearse and Clarke.

March 9th 1916:
'Will send 20,000 rifles, 10 machine guns, small boats, to place near Tralee, between 23rd and 25th April.'

The R.D. [Revolutionary Directorate] met on March 10th at 23 East 94th

Street, New York. [Diarmuid] Lynch, who was in America, was returning to Ireland and we sent by him £2300 pounds to the Volunteers.

Saturday night, April 22nd 1916 at 11.30 p.m. I received from D.F.C. [Judge Daniel F. Cohalan], New York, the following message (remember, this would be about five o'clock in Ireland Easter Sunday morning); the message from Valencia, Ireland, and relayed to me by telephone, was as follows: 'Tom successfully operated on today. [signed] O'Sullivan.'

This [code] was arranged beforehand.

Note: I answered 'Thank God,' and burning with excitement and anxiety, I left my home alone, 5412 Springfield Avenue, Phila., and walked east a mile or so and prayed for the success of my countrymen against their centuries old foe. I watched the skyline in the direction of Ireland and imagined I should really see some sign of the battle that I believed was then raging in many parts of Ireland. I was bound to secrecy and could not talk of the matter until the newspapers finally got the story, which I think happened in the following way: Jeremiah A. O'Leary of New York had called some of the New York newspapers and asked the editors why they were suppressing the news of a rebellion now going on in Ireland, and after persistent calling the editors began to seek for the story. The fighting was on two or three days before the newspapers in America were in a position to give it to the world. The rest is history.

May 2nd 1916:

I was in New York and heard of the brutal execution of the Irish leaders Clarke, Pearse, McDermott, etc.

APPENDIX VII

65TH CONGRESS, 1st SESSION. } H. J. RES. 88.

IN THE HOUSE OF REPRESENTATIVES.

MAY 14, 1917.

Mr. MASON introduced the following joint resolution; which was referred to the Committee on Foreign Affairs and ordered to be printed.

JOINT RESOLUTION

To declare the liberation of Ireland one of the purposes of the present war.

Resolved by the Senate and House of Representatives of the United States of America in Congress assembled, That Ireland, a distinct and historic nation, anciently possessed of freedom, in the opinion of Congress and of the American people, of right ought to be free and independent; and be it further

Resolved, That as the Irish nation has contributed a very numerous and valuable element to the American Nation, and as the United States is committed by American traditions and by recent utterances of the President to the principle of freedom for small nations, the liberation of Ireland from all foreign domination is hereby declared one of the objects for which the United States fights in this present war; and all money hereafter voted by Congress for the prosecution of this war, and all loans hereafter authorized to be made to any nation now at war shall be voted and authorized with the condition that the liberation of Ireland is one of the purposes of the war; and be it further

Resolved, That the liberation of Ireland means the complete separation of the island of that name, together with such small islands as are now administered as part of it, from all involuntary and subordinate political connection with any other nation and the complete freedom of the adult inhabitants to decide by full and fair vote upon their form of government, and the complete freedom of such government as they may erect to determine its relations with other nations and to exercise all the functions of an independent nation, and the recognition of Ireland as a free nation, in accordance with this definition, shall be a part of the peace terms secured by the representatives of the United States in negotiations with any and all of the belligerent nations; and be it further

Resolved, That if the people of Ireland shall request the assistance and advice of the United States in the establishment of their future government the President, the Vice President, and the Speaker of the House of Representatives shall appoint a commission of five American citizens to proceed to Ireland and render such assistance and advice up to, but not beyond, the time when the people of Ireland shall adopt

99160—17

a constitution; but the United States shall not attempt to mold the course of the Irish nation and shall assume no responsibility for the new government to be erected in Ireland; and be it further

Resolved, That upon the adoption of a constitution by the people of Ireland, if said constitution shall erect a republican government, the Secretary of the Treasury is hereby authorized to purchase bonds of the Irish government so established, provided said bonds bear interest at not less than three per centum, to the amount of $100,000,000, and to reimburse the Treasury by the sale of United States bonds to an equal amount and bearing an even interest.

APPENDIX VIII

The 1918 election in which Sinn Fein won 73 of the 105 Irish seats. (Eamon Timoney: Belfast Prison Study).

General Election 1918: Analysis of Voting

TABLE 1: *Votes Cast (excluding University Seats)*

	Sinn Fein	*Other*	*Total*	*% S.F.*	*Electorate*	*S.F. vote % of Electorate*
Ulster	109 835	358 641	468 476	23·45	656 445	16·73
Munster	87 609	39 650	127 259	68·84	178 579	49·06
Leinster	193 346	114 913	308 259	62·72	442 205	43·72
Connacht	104 409	30 626	135 035	77·32	216 686	48·18
Total:	495 199	543 830	1 039 029	47·66	1 493 915	35.15

TABLE 2: *General Election 1918: Analysis of Voting – Ulster*

Constituency		*Sinn Fein*	*Other than SF Vote*				*Total*
			Nat.	*Unionist*	*Lab.*	*Ind.*	*Other*
Antrim	–East	861		15 206			15 206
	–Mid	2 791		10 711			10 711
	–North	2 673		9 621			9 621
	–South	2 318		13 270			13 270
Armagh	–Mid	5 688		8 431			8 431
	–North	2 860		10 239			10 239
	–South	79	4 345				4 345
Belfast	–Cromac	997		11 459	2 508		13 967
	–Duncairn	271	2 449	11 637			14 086
	–Falls	3 245	8 488				8 488
	–Ormeau	338		7 460		4 833	12 293
	–Pottinger	393		8 574	2 513	659	11 746
	–St. Annes	1 341		9 155		1 752	10 907
	–Shankill	534		11 840	3 674		15 514
	–Victoria	395		9 309	3 469		12 778
	–Woodvale	1 247		12 232			12 232
Donegal	–East	40	7 596	4 797			12 393
	–North	7 003	3 075				3 075
	–South	5 787	4 752				4 752
	–West	6 712	4 116				4 116
Down	–East	3 876	4 312	6 007			10 319
	–Mid	707		10 639			10 639
	–South	33	8 756	5 573		436	14 765
	–West	1 725		10 559			10 559
	–North	–		9 200		2 153	11 353
Fermanagh	–North	6 236		6 768			6 768
	–South	6 673	132	4 524			4 656
Londonderry	–City	7 335	120	7 020			7 140
	–North	3 951		10 530			10 530
	–South	3 425	3 981	8 942			12 923
Monaghan	–North	6 842	2 709	4 497			7 206
	–South	7 524	4 413				4 413
Tyrone	–North East	56	11 605	6 681			18 286
	–North West 8	10 442		7 696			7 696
	–South	5 437	2 602	10 616			13 218
		109 835	73 451	263 193	12 164	9 833	358 641
Queens University, Belfast–		118		1 487			1 487
Cavan–	East SF unopposed						
–	West SF unopposed						

APPENDIX IX

The original Democratic Programme for Dáil Éireann which was revised on orders of the IRB. (The William O'Brien Papers, National Library of Ireland).

THOMAS JOHNSON'S DRAFT ON DEMOCRATIC PROGRAMME AS SUBMITTED AT THEIR REQUEST TO THE SINN FEIN LEADERS, JANUARY, 1919

Repeating the words of the Proclamation of the Provisional Government of the Irish Republic:— 'We declare the right of the people of Ireland to the ownership of Ireland and to the unfettered control of Irish destinies to be indefeasible.'

And further, in the language of its first President, Patrick H. Pearse, we declare 'that the Nation's sovereignty extends not only to all men and women of the Nation but to all the material possessions of the Nation, the Nation's soil, and all its resources, all wealth and wealth-producing processes within the Nation. In other words, no private right to property is good as against the public right of the Nation'. ('The Sovereign People', 31st March, 1916.)

We further declare that as the Nation in the exercise of its sovereignty may entrust its soil and its resources, its wealth and wealth-producing processes, to the care and charge of any of its citizens, to use and exploit for the Nation's enrichment on such terms and subject to such conditions as may be deterninded by the whole people, so the Nation must ever retain the right and power to resume possession of such soil or wealth whenever the trust is abused or the trustee fails to give faithful service.

In the same manner as we affirm that the duty of every man and woman is to give allegiance and service to the commonwealth, so we declare it as the duty of the Nation to ensure that every citizen shall have the opportunity for spending his or her strength and faculties in the labour of wealth-production or the service of the people. In return for willing service, we in the name of the Republic, declare the right of every citizen to an adequate share of the produce of the Nation's labour. The Irish Republic shall always count wealth and property by the measure of health and happiness of its citizens. It shall, therefore, be the first duty of the Government of the Republic to make provision for the physical, mental and spiritual well-being of the children to ensure that no child shall suffer hunger or cold from lack of food, clothing or shelter, that all shall be provided with ample means and facilities requisite for the education and training of free citizens of a free Nation.

A condition precedent to such education is to encourage, by every reasonable means, the most capable and sympathetic men and women to devote their talents to the education of the young.

To promote the development of its resources, to increase the productivity of its soil, to exploit its mineral deposits, peat bogs and fisheries, its waterways and harbours — in the interests and for the benefit of the Irish people — the Nation, exercising its rights of sovereignty, shall deem it to be a duty to organise and direct into fruitful contact the labour of men with the land and raw materials and machinery of industry. Wherever the land, the mineral deposits and other forms of productive wealth are wrongfully used, or with-held from use to the detriment of the Republic, there the Nation shall resume possession without compensation.

In the sphere of over-seas commerce, the Republican Government to safeguard the economic interests of the Nation shall itself undertake the organisation of the import and export of merchandise so as to prevent the shipment from Ireland of food and other necessaries until the wants of the Irish people are fully satisfied and the future provided for, and to obviate the waste of life and labour which competitive commerce involves and the risk of destroying Irish productive undertakings.

It shall be the purpose of the Government to encourage the organisation of the people/citizens into Trade Unions and Co-operative Societies with a view to the control and administration of the industries by the workers engaged in these industries.

It shall also devolve upon the National Government to seek the co-operation of the Governments of other countries in determining a standard of social and industrial legislation with a view to a general improvement in the conditions under which the working classes live and labour.

Finally, the Republic will aim at the elimination of the class in Society which lives upon the wealth produced by the workers of the Nation but gives no useful social service in return, and in the process of accomplishment will bring Freedom to all who have hitherto been caught in the toils of economic servitude.

APPENDIX X

Letter from Executive of 'Second Dáil' to John J. Hearn, of the American Friends of the Irish Republic, December 1927. (John J. Hearn Papers, in possession of Máire Comerford).

DÁIL ÉIREANN
Government of the Republic of Ireland

Oifig an Uachtaráin

Baile Átha Cliath
13ad Mí na Nodhlag 1927

John Hearn Esq.,
Westfield
Mass. U.S.A.

Dear Mr Hearn

At a meeting of Dáil Éireann on the 10th inst. certain changes were made and decisions arrived at of which it is necessary to acquaint you immediately.

(1) President O'Connor who has been studying law has been called to the Bar and intends to practise. In the circumstances, he felt it necessary to tender his resignation as President of the Republic, and the Dáil though deeply

regretting the necessity, felt bound to accept the resignation.

(2) It was decided to elect an Executive of five members pending a decision on the question of the Presidency, and we enclose for your information a copy of the resolution passed.

(3) It was decided to issue a Manifesto to the subscribers of the Republican Loan in the U.S. with reference to the Dáil Bonds.

We enclose a copy of this Manifesto and we shall send by the next mail copies to the following:— The Monitor, Irish World, Irish Republic, Chicago, Advocate, New York, Leader, San Francisco.

We would ask you to wire us immediately on receipt of this communication, and we shall then communicate the Manifesto to the Press here, and to the American Associated Press.

The Cabinet desires you to carry on as usual, and hopes to send you the communication you desire before Christmas.

We send the greetings of the Government of the Republic

Sinne G.N. Count Plunkett
Máire nic Shuibhne
Daithi R. Ceannt
Brian Ó hUiginn
Cathal Ó Murchadha

APPENDIX XI

This letter from the Chairman of the Clan-na-Gael in America to the Army Council of IRA, 1 October 1929, tells something of the difficulties of Irish Republican ideology in the 1920s. (McGarrity Papers, National Library of Ireland).

October 1st, 1929

To
Army Council I.R.A.

A Chairde:

The Executive of the Clan na Gael received your communication No. 99 which accompanied a document addressed to the Hon. Ramsay MacDonald, 10 Downing Street, London and signed by Seán Ua Ceallaigh as President of the Executive Council, An Dáil. Your request made in the communication No. 99 that our Executive give publicity to and circulate the document addressed to the Rt. Hon Ramsay MacDonald among public men and Government officials was most carefully considered at a meeting held here on Sept. 16th, 1929, and it was unanimously decided inadvisable for our Executive or our organization to give publicity to or circulate the document referred to for many reasons, some of which I will enumerate:—

1. In view of the fact that the Irish Republican Army in November 1925 — or thereabouts — withdrew from the recognized Irish Republican Government because of the fact that in the belief of the I.R.A. the Government had utterly

failed to perform the functions for which it was organized for the interest, protection and defence of the people and territory of the Republic of Ireland. Having withdrawn from the said Government and thereby assuming the duties of Governmental protection and defence functions in which the aforesaid Government failed, it is our belief that the I.R.A. Council or Army Executive assumed the role of Government of the territory of Ireland, and your official notice at the time sent to this organization of the Clan-na-Gael led us to believe that you were to look to the Army Executive as the only existing Government which had taken steps for the protection and defence of Ireland refusing any semblance of allegiance to the British Government. On this declaration by the Army Officials at that time and in the belief that the Army were the one force in Ireland most worthy of our allegiance and most entitled to our support the Clan-na-Gael formally decided to give allegiance and support to the I.R.A., not only as the Army of Ireland, but as the Provisional Government of the country and withdrew all support and allegiance to any other organization or force claiming or representing themselves as the Government of the Republic of Ireland.

2. We feel that it would do an injury to the organization of the Clan-na-Gael if we should circularise a petition addressed to Rt Hon Ramsay McDonald which in essence asks England to give the people of Ireland the right or chance to express their own free will without any threat of war from England. Some of the members of the Executive seem to read into the correspondence passing between the Army Council and the Executive Council of 'Dáil Éireann' as recognizing the 'Dáil Éireann' as a Governmental entity. For the benefit of those who have some doubts on the subject your Executive might give us a clear understanding as to the status of the said Dáil Éireann in the eyes of the Army Council? As the question is likely to arise here it is well to have a clear understanding.

Regards
Fraternally Yours

APPENDIX XII

Letter from President de Valera to Joseph McGarrity, on differences with the IRA. (McGarrity Papers, National Library of Ireland).

Saorstát Éireann

Roinn an Uachtarain
department of the president

Baile Átha Cliath
Dublin

Strictly personal
and confidential

January 31st, 1934

My dear Joe:

I refrained from replying to your letter of October 2nd. The fact is that to reply to it would require a book, that is, if I wished the reply to be convincing. You suggested that you might possibly be coming here. I hoped you would, so that I might give the "talking to" which as I re-read your letter I would give the world for an opportunity of doing. I do not think I ever got a letter which required such patience to read through. There was a pain in every line of it.

Bob Brennan is going over, and I am giving him instructions to take up the points in this letter of October 2nd with you and to give you the answers. I do not want the risk of an intimate letter, such as I would have to write myself, falling into hostile hands.

You talk about coming to an understanding with the I.R.A. You talk of the influence I would have both here and abroad. You talk as if we were fools and didn't realise all this. My God! Do you not know that ever since 1921 the main purpose in everything I have done has been to try to secure a basis for national unity. How can you imagine for one moment that I don't realise what division in the Republican ranks means at a time like this. But is this need and desire for unity to be used as a means of trying to blackmail us into adopting a policy which we know could only lead our people to disaster. It has taken us ten long years of patient effort to get the Irish nation on the march again after a devastating Civil War. Are we to abandon all this in order to satisfy a group who have not given the slightest evidence of any ability to lead our people anywhere except back into the morass.

We desire unity, but desires will get us nowhere unless we can get some accepted basis for determining what the national policy shall be and where leadership shall lie. What is the use of talking any more with people who are too stupid or too pigheaded to see this. A nation in its struggle can no more be successful than an army can without a plan of campaign and an accepted leadership to see it through. The Cease Fire proposals put forward by us at the end of the Civil War and accepted by all the Republican forces at the time was the only basis that those of us who had been through the whole fight since 1913 could discover. The oath was the barrier which made this basis impossible until we removed it. I do not believe the wit of man will discover any other basis. No one has attempted to suggest any substitute. If this country is not to be a

Mexico or a Cuba, a basis must be found, or else the party that has got the confidence of the majority here will have to secure order by force. There is no alternative. We have undertaken a responsibility to the people at present living, to the future, and to the dead. We will not allow any group or any individuals to prevent us from carrying it out. Those who are barring our path now are doing exactly what Cohalan & Co. did in 1919 to 1921.

With all good wishes
Sincerely Yours
Eamon de Valera

APPENDIX XIII

Minutes of IRA Army Council Meeting, December 4, 1938, on bombing campaign in England. (Copy of original minutes in author's possession).

At a meeting of the Army Council on Dec. 4, 1938, Chief of Staff and Chairman of Army Council reported on meeting with some members of Second Dáil regarding transference of powers. Brian O'Higgins was favourable. So was Mary MacSwiney. The surviving members of the Second Dáil had met the previous night. Present were Count Plunkett, Brian O'Higgins, J.J. O'Kelly (Sceilg), Mary MacSwiney and Cathal O Murchadha. Tom Maguire and Prof. Stockley were absent; the latter was ill. The Second Dáil was anxious to know how its members could collaborate with the Council in the proposed campaign. They wanted to know whether the signing of an independent proclamation or an addendum to the Army proclamation or a formal transfer of their powers would be best. They rejected the first two approaches in favour of the last.

They did not consider any guarantees necessary in the event they transferred their powers other than that the Council would assume their trust as they had kept it. They sought an answer from the Army Council by 7 o'clock, when their session was to be resumed, as to which of the above courses the Army preferred.

A discussion developed on the Proclamation. The Chief of Staff said he has asked Mr. X to write a few paragraphs to clarify issues raised by three members at previous meetings. When these were read an argument followed on the meaning of the words. One member (code name Joyce) said the words were purely and simply a condemnation of Communism, without giving any positive direction as to what the Army policy was or would be when the Republic came into existence, and that the 'Governmental Programme' of the Army should be reiterated in the Proclamation. 'F' (Russell) said that various points in the Governmental Programme were wrong and that it should not be discussed at all. He and another member (code: Harris) maintained that the Army's work was to put the English out of Ireland and that if and when the Third Republican Dáil came into existence, by the free vote of the Irish people, every Irish citizen would be bound to give it allegiance.

Two members (code names Joyce and Allen) protested against this. They said it was the duty of the Army to bring into existence the Republic visualised in the Proclamation of 1916. Joyce said he considered political freedom without economic freedom useless; that if he thought the outlook of the Army Council on that matter was reflected to any large extent in the Army he would not remain in it.

A short paragraph written by Allen was then submitted to the meeting. It was decided to insert this paragraph embodying the principle 'of equal educational and economic opportunities' in the proclamation.

Joyce strongly criticized the preparations for the British campaign which, he said, might start at any moment without even the knowledge of the Army Council. To mention only one feature of the campaign: he did not believe the state of the Army in Britain was adequate. He was in favour of prosecuting the British campaign but he needed to satisfy himself as a member of the Army Council that all possible preparations had been made for it; if other members of the Army Council were prepared to go ahead with it in the absence of such knowledge he was not.

'F' put the case for activities in Britain on the basis that the I.R.A. should do all in its power now without too much previous consideration of the factor of ultimate success.

Allen said the Army Council did not know what was going on. He was prepared to go on with the campaign, he said, even though it was against his better judgment.

Forde (code name) said that organizational work and preparations in Ireland should not be eclipsed by the British campaign.

Harris said it was a mistake to think that the struggle was to be fought out in England. What was required was action to command respect.

Joyce proposed the following resolution: 'That the Army Council decision of May 21, 1938, be rescinded for the moment, and that a military committee be appointed to examine and report to the Army Council on preparations for the British campaign from the point of view of organization, operations, supplies, personnel and finance.'

During the discussion some speakers referred to the Army Council decision concerning a barracks attack. The Chief of Staff said he had consulted the O/C Belfast on this and that they concluded it could not be done.

Allen amended the Joyce resolution as follows: 'That operations be not launched in Britain until the Army Council received a report from staff, as to preparations for British campaign.' (The remainder of the resolution was the same as Joyce's.) Joyce withdrew his resolution and the amendment was put to the meeting as a resolution. There was some discussion then as to whether it was in order to put it as a resolution to the meeting and on a vote three (Joyce, Allen and Forde) were for and four (Busher, Brennan – code names – 'F' and Harris) were against. Harris did not want the resolution if defeated put on the minutes, but no decision was taken on that.

Joyce withdrew the resolution and intimated his intention to resign from the Council. (Earlier he had queried deaths of Kelly, McCafferty and J.J. Reynolds in border explosion after report had been made on raising funds for dependents on a local basis. He had asked for a sworn inquiry into the deaths. 'F' suggested the machinery of investigation be cut to a minimum, despite Joyce's insistence that a report of the inquiry be submitted to the Army Council. Joyce also protested that no GHQ representative had been at Reynolds's funeral and that it was the Chief of Staff's function to go there. The Chief of Staff said he was absent 'due to an urgent matter on the border'.)

When the Council resumed on Dec. 8, Busher, Brennan, Harris, 'F' and O'Leary (code name) were present. Forde was noted absent. O'Leary was proposed as secretary. The question of Joyce's resignation came up: 'He reiterated his reasons for resigning'. Joyce's resignation was accepted, four voting for it. The meeting unanimously agreed to accept Dáil powers.

APPENDIX XIV

Ultimatum from the IRA to the Rt. Hon. Viscount Halifax, G.C.B., in 1939 before the bombing campaign in England. (Original draft in McGarrity Papers, National Library of Ireland).

IRISH REPUBLICAN ARMY

General Headquarters,
Dublin
Jany 12th, 1939.

to:
His Excellency
The Rt. Hon. Viscount Halifax, G.C.B.

Your Excellency.

I have the honour to inform you that the Government of the Irish Republic, having as its first duty towards its people the establishment and maintenance of peace and order here, demand the withdrawal of all British armed forces stationed in Ireland.

These forces are an active incitement to turmoil and civil strife, not alone in being a symbol of hostile occupation, but in their effect and potentialities as an invading army.

It is secondly the duty of the Government to establish relations of friendship between the Irish and all other peoples and to achieve this we must insist upon the withdrawal of British troops from our country and a declaration from your Government renouncing all claim to interfere in its domestic policy or external affairs.

The Irish people have no cause of hostility to any European nation, even those nations whose natural development may bring them into conflict with British interests, and we are desirous of making it clear that we shall in no event take part in a war of aggression against any people or permit the nation to be regarded as having any community or identity of interest with Britain that would make us liable to attack by British enemies.

The occupation of our territory by troops of another nation and the persistent subvention here of activities directly against the expressed national will and in the interests of a foreign power, prevent the expansion and development of our institution in consonance with our social needs and purposes, and must cease.

Neither the Government of the Irish Republic nor the Irish People are actuated by any feelings of hostility to the people of Britain. Rather would we welcome a better understanding but this can be brought about only on the basis that each of the two peoples is absolutely free to pursue its own course unhampered by the other. We shall regret if this fundamental condition is ignored and we are compelled to intervene actively in the military or commercial life of your country as your Government are now intervening in ours.

The Government of the Irish Republic believe that a period of four days is sufficient notice for your Government to signify its intentions in the matter of the military evacuation and for the issue of your Declaration of Abdication in respect of our country. Our Government reserve the right of appropriate action without further notice if upon the expiration of this period of grace, these conditions remain unfulfilled.

ON BEHALF OF THE GOVERNMENT AND ARMY COUNCIL OF ÓGLAIGH NA h-ÉIREANN (Irish Republican Army)

(Signed) Patrick Fleming

Secretary

APPENDIX XV

Eire's neutrality gave rise to the fear on the part of the United States that important Allied military information was seeping through Ireland to Axis channels. On March 10, 1944, the State Department revealed a request to the Irish government concerning the removal of Axis deplomatic and consular agents from Ireland. The texts of the United States' appeal and of Eamon de Valera's refusal follow (Current History, *May 1944).*

UNITED STATES' REQUEST

Your Excellency will recall that in your speech at Cork, delivered on the fourteenth of December, 1941, you expressed sentiments of special friendship for the American people on the occasion of their entry into the present war and closed by saying: "The policy of the state remains unchanged. We can only be a friendly neutral." As you will also recall, extracts of this speech were transmitted to the President by your Minister in Washington.

The President, while conveying his appreciation for this expression of friendship, stated his confidence that the Irish government and the Irish people, whose freedom is at stake no less than ours, would know how to meet their responsibilities in this situation.

It has become increasingly apparent that despite the declared desire of the Irish government that its neutrality should not operate in favor of either of the belligerents, it has in fact operated and continues to operate in favor of the Axis powers and against the United Nations on whom your security and the maintenance of your national economy depend. One of the gravest and most inequitable results of this situation is the opportunity for highly organized espionage which the geographical position of Ireland affords the Axis and denies the United Nations.

Situated as you are in close proximity to Britain, divided only by an intangible boundary from Northern Ireland, where are situated important American bases, with continuous traffic to and from both countries, Axis agents enjoy almost unrestricted opportunity for bringing military information of vital importance from Great Britain and Northern Ireland into Ireland and from there transmitting it by various routes and methods to Germany. No opportunity corresponding to this is open to the United Nations, for the Axis has no military dispositions which may be observed from Ireland.

We do not question the good faith of the Irish government in its efforts to suppress Axis espionage. Whether or to what extent it has succeeded in preventing acts of espionage against American shipping and American forces in Great Britain and Northern Ireland is, of course, impossible to determine with certainty. Nevertheless it is a fact that German and Japanese diplomatic and consular representatives still continue to reside in Dublin and enjoy the special privileges and immunities customarily accorded to such officials. That Axis representatives in neutral countries use these special privileges and immunities as a cloak for espionage activities against the United Nations has been demonstrated over and over again.

It would be naïve to assume that Axis agencies have not exploited conditions to the full in Ireland as they have in other countries. It is our understanding that the German Legation in Dublin, until recently at least, has had in its possession a radio sending set.

This is evidence of the intention of the German government to use this means of communication. Supporting evidence is furnished by the two parachutists equipped with radio sending sets recently dropped on your territory by German planes.

As you know from common report, United Nations military operations are in preparation in both Britain and Northern Ireland. It is vital that information from which may be deduced their nature and direction should not reach the enemy. Not only the success of the operations but the lives of thousands of United Nations' soldiers are at stake.

We request therefore that the Irish government take appropriate steps for the recall of German and Japanese representatives in Ireland. We should be lacking in candor if we did not state our hope that this action will take the form of severance of all diplomatic relations between Ireland and these countries. You will, of course, readily understand the compelling reasons why we ask as an absolute minimum the removal of these Axis representatives whose presence in Ireland must inevitably be regarded as constituting a danger to the lives of American soldiers and to the success of Allied military operations.

It is hardly necessary to point out that time is of extreme importance and that we trust your Excellency will favor us with your reply at your early convenience.

DE VALERA'S REPLY

The note of the American government was handed to me by the American Minister on February 21. I informed him at once that the request it contained was one with which it was impossible for the Irish government to comply. The Irish government have since given the matter careful consideration and I now confirm the reply which I then gave verbally.

The Irish government have also received the assurance of the American government, conveyed to the Irish Minister at Washington and later confirmed by the American Minister here in an interview with me on February 29, to the effect that the American government did not contemplate proceeding to military or other measures because of the reply which had been given.

The American Minister quoted in particular the President's personal message to me of February 26, 1942, that 'there is not now nor was there then the slightest thought or intention of invading the territory of Ireland or of threatening the security of the Irish' and added that this attitude was unchanged.

The Irish government wish to express their appreciation of this assurance. They were indeed surprised that so grave a note as that of February 21 should have been addressed to them. The terms of the note seemed to them all together out of harmony with the facts and with the traditional relations of friendship between the Irish and American peoples.

They doubted that such a note could have been presented had the American government been fully aware of the uniform friendly character of Irish neutrality in relation to the United States and of the measures which had been taken by the Irish government, within the limits of their power, to safeguard American interests.

They felt, moreover, that the American government should have realized that the removal of representatives of a foreign state on the demand of the government to which they are accredited is universally recognized as the first step towards war, and that the Irish government could not entertain the American proposal without a complete betrayal of their democratic trust. Irish neutrality represents the united will of the people and Parliament. It is the logical consequence of Irish history and of the forced partition of national territory.

Already before American entry into the war, the policy of the Irish government toward Britain, America's ally, had been directed toward carrying out the intentions indicated in a statement of policy made by me in the Dail Eireann on May 29, 1935, namely that 'our territory would never be permitted to be used as a base for attack upon Britain.'

That policy has during the war been faithfully pursued. From the beginning, by the establishment of strong observation and defense forces, by a wide and rigorous censorship of press and communications, by an extensive anti-espionage organization and by every other means within our power, we have endeavored to prevent the leakage through Ireland of any information which might in any way endanger British lives or the safety of Great Britain.

Since the United States entered the war the same spirit of scrupulous regard for American interests has been shown. American officials have had an opportunity of seeing the measures which have been taken – they have indeed made favorable comments on their effectiveness – and it is satisfactory to observe that in the note itself not a single instance of neglect is alleged and no proof of injury to American interests is adduced. Should American lives be lost it will not be through any indifference or neglect of its duty on the part of this State.

As was known to the American officials, it is true that the German Minister had a wireless transmitter, but he had been for a long time debarred from using it and it has been in the custody of the Irish government for some months. As regards the two parachutists dropped in Ireland last December, they were apprehended within a few hours. Two other agents dropped here since the war began met with a similar fate. The fifth, who arrived during the first year of the war, remained at large until December 3, 1941, but the police were aware of his presence here almost from the first moment of landing, and successful activities on his part were rendered impossible.

The total number of persons, inclusive of these parachutists, suspected of intentions to engage in espionage, and now held in Irish prisons, is ten foreign and two Irish nationals. These are the facts, and it is doubtful if any other country can show such a record of care and successful vigilance.

The British government have informed the Irish government that they welcome the initiative of the American government in sending the note and that they attached the utmost importance to it. The Irish government do not wish to comment on this, except to remark that it is perhaps not known to the American government that the feelings of the Irish people toward Britain have, during the war undergone a considerable change, precisely because Britain has not attempted to violate our neutrality.

The Irish government feels sure that the American government would agree that it would be regrettable if any incident now should alter that happy result.

The Irish government are therefore safeguarding, and will continue to safeguard, the interests of the United States, but they must in all circumstances protect the neutrality of the Irish state and the democratic way of life of the Irish people. Their attitude will continue to be determined not by fear of any measures which could be employed against them, but by goodwill and the fundamental friendship existing between the two peoples.

APPENDIX XVI

List of occupations of IRA prisoners in Belfast Prison, 1956–60. Compiled by Eamon Timoney, one of the prisoners.

*Year Imprisoned**	*Name*	*Address*	*Age*	*Occupation***
1953	J. Campbell	Newry	30	Shoe-maker
1954	L. McCormick	Dublin	36	Labourer
	E. Boyce	”	28	Bus conductor
	T. Mitchell	”	23	Brick-layer
	P. Kearney	”	28	Bus conductor
	J. McCabe	”	34	Labourer

	P. Clarke	”	21	Civil Servant
	L. Mulcahy	Cork	28	Baker
	S. O'Callaghan	”	21	Audit clerk
	S. O'Hegarty	”	21	P.O. linesman
	H. Brady	Lurgan	21	Poultry packer
	K. O'Rourke	Banbridge	30	Brick-layer
1956	T. Cooney	Cork	21	P.O. clerk
	J. Linehan	”	20	Labourer
	W. Gough	”	20	Driver
	S. Houston	Keady	23	Electrician
	J. Smith	Bessbrook	18	Draughtsman
	J. Kelly	Belfast	20	Marine engineer
	D. Lewsley	Lurgan	20	Baker
	J. Madden	Cork	20	Brick-layer
	P. Monaghan	Co. Tyrone	21	Farmer
1957	P. Constantine	Dublin	28	Carpenter
	P. Duffy	Dundalk	41	Factory machinist
	S. Hand	”	34	Driver
	P. Shaw	”	20	Factory machinist
	G. Loy	Newry	20	Factory machinist
	A. Loy	Newry	25	Plumber
	T. Kearns	”	20	Van salesman
	P. Doyle	Dublin	27	Chemist's assistant
	P. Hodgins	”	21	Woodworker
	P. McStravick	Lurgan	24	Labourer
	D. O'Hagan	Belfast	23	Free-lance journalist
	P. McGrogan	”	24	Central heating engineer
	T. Ferron	”	20	Grocer's assistant
	J. Corbett	”	21	Labourer
	E. Timoney	Derry	29	Railway clerk
	P. O'Kane	Co. Derry	32	Farmer
	P. Fox	Derry	23	Driver
	M. Monaghan	Derry	20	Mechanic
	L. McGowan	”	19	Factory machinist
	P. Gillespie	Co. Derry	26	Farmer
	C. Mellon	Sion Mills	23	Publican
	D. Donnelly	Omagh	18	Student
	S. McHugh	Beragh	27	Carpenter
	J. Devlin	Co. Tyrone	25	Farmer
	P. Devlin	”	20	Labourer
	F. McCabe	”	17	Barman
	A. McCarroll	”	18	Brick-layer
	F. Cullen	”	18	Labourer
	H. D'Arcy	”	18	Farmer
	J. D'Arcy	”	19	Farmer
	T. McCool	Derry	29	Labourer
	L. McKinney	”	20	Shirt-cutter

	K. Mallon	Coalisland	24	Labourer
	F. Talbot	”	22	Factory machinist
	E. Mulholland	Lurgan	18	Poultry packer
1957	E. Murphy	Dublin	22	Baker
	J. Robinson	Coalisland	24	Fisherman
	J. O'Donnell	”	24	Labourer
	B. O'Neill	”	31	Driver
	J. Herron	”	34	Farmer
	P. O'Neill	”	24	Farmer
	S. O'Neill	”	23	Farmer
	T. O'Malley	Belfast	51	Labourer
	P. Collins	”	40	Labourer
1958	S. McRory	Ballymena	26	Printer
	H. McRory	”	22	Printer
	J. McKernan	”	22	Plumber
	B. Loughran	”	29	Van salesman
	S. Loughran	”	23	Gardener
	T. O'Kane	Belfast	27	Labourer
	K. Carson	Enniskillen	22	Civil Servant
	E. Goodwin	”	17	Joiner
	F. Goodwin	”	19	Electrician
	H. Martin	Co. Fermanagh	24	Carpenter
	P. Traynor	Co. Monaghan	25	Farmer
	D. Foley	Tralee	18	Clerk
	A. Meade	Limerick	20	Clerk
	W. Reilly	Armagh	19	Labourer
	J. Owens	Co. Fermanagh	22	Carpenter
1959	F. Lanney	Co. Monaghan	33	Clerk
	F. McArdle	Newry	21	Seaman
	P. Loy	”	18	Factory machinist
	J. Healy	”	18	Grocer's assistant
1960	S. Garland	Dublin	24	Labourer
	G. Haughian	Lurgan	21	Poultry packer
	L. Flanagan	Co. Derry	22	Labourer
	D. O'Connell	Cork	22	Carpenter
	J. O'Hagan	Lurgan	36	Businessman
	T. Cosgrove	Belfast	18	Carpenter
	R. Murray	”	18	Sheet metal worker
	D. McPhillips	Lurgan	24	Labourer
	D. Egan	Galway	24	Grocer's assistant
	M. Daly	Co. Armagh	26	Farmer
	O. Carraher	”	25	Farmer

* Serving sentences in excess of three years.

** The actual trade engaged in is given despite the fact that many listed as tradesmen were in the course of serving apprenticeships.

General Observations on the value of this list and the analyses
This list – plus the information gleaned from an examination of press reports on border arrests during the 1956–62 period – would prove conclusively the falsity of the assertion made by the Twenty-six Counties Attorney-General, at the European Human Rights Court (Lawless Case), that the incidents in the Six Counties were, in the main, caused *(a)* by people whose homes were in the Twenty-Six Counties and *(b)* by people operating from bases within the Twenty-Six Counties.[1]
The list reveals that in the post-12 December 1956 period, of twenty-nine full-time Republicans on active service captured in the Six Counties, sixteen were from the Twenty-Six Counties and thirteen from the Six Counties. Unless a man was known to be suspected by the RUC, and consequently liable to internment, he remained at home and continued in normal employment.

1. Lawless case was entered by Sean MacBride November 1957, accepted as admissable August 1958. For account see *'Lawless' Case*, publication of the European Court of Human Rights, Strasbourg, 1961.

APPENDIX XVII

Seán O'Hegarty of Cork was a prisoner in Belfast Prison from 1954 to 1962. The following are his comments on IRA ideology. (Prepared at request of Seán Cronin, Ms in his possession).

I

The philosophy that drew me into the ranks of Republicanism in the 1950s rested on the conviction that the majority of the Irish people wished for the unity and self-determination of the country, that such unity and self-determination were the essential conditions for the freedom and development of Ireland and that these could never be fully realised while Britain retained a presence in the country.

Britain thwarted Irish aspirations in two ways. Her physical support of the regime in the Six Counties was a denial of the legitimate and absolute right of the Irish to national sovereignty. This, coupled with her neo-colonial influence throughout the rest of the country, prevented the growth of an Irish nation with its roots in its own history and culture – an Irish Ireland.

I was forced to the conclusion that physical force offered the only avenue by which this situation might be changed. Britain was certainly not willing to withdraw voluntarily from Ireland or further the creation of a united Ireland. Further, it was clear from its record that the Dublin government would do nothing to undermine the hegemony of Britain in Ireland. Indeed, the years since 1921 saw continued and close cooperation between Dublin and Westminster, uninterrupted British dominance of the economy and the rapid decline of what remained of the Irish cultural heritage. One might very well paraphrase Trotsky and declare that the revolution had been betrayed by the so-called revolutionaries of the post 1916 period.

This view of the situation in Ireland of the early fifties found its natural expression in the Republican doctrine of 'Break the connection with England'. The acceptance of Republicanism and physical force reflected, on my part, a sense of Irish history and nationhood (a sense of that 'shared experience' that Mill spoke of), an awareness of the continuing injustice of Britain's denial of legitimate Irish aspirations and, on a more emotional and idealistic level, the desire, noted by Pearse, to emulate the great men who had gone before. This last element in my outlook can be attributed to the schooling of the Christian Brothers who went to great lengths to instill in their students a fairly thorough knowledge and appreciation of Irish history and culture.

In my opinion, the Republican Movement would fulfill a dual function. The Army would provide a military challenge to the British in the Six Counties. In addition, because of a more refined political and social consciousness, Republicans would furnish the leadership necessary to raise the level of awareness of the people to the need for creating a truly Irish nation state founded on the best in its own past. Unless this latter objective could be achieved, territorial unity would have only limited meaning for me. According to this interpretation, Republican doctrine was essentially an expression of political and cultural nationalism. The viability of the nation, internally and internationally, hinged on control by the Irish of a State building on traditional Irish values and traditions. Anybody who contested this view would be denying the deepest aspirations of the Irish people and, in doing so, would have to be treated as a rebel. Needless to say, the Unionist majority in the Six Counties immediately fell into this category.

The reasoning that led me to join the Army reflects fairly accurately, I think, the factors that motivated most Republicans of the time. Further, I believe that the principal elements of Republican philosophy continue to hold true today. Thus, British withdrawal from Ireland is essential to the realisation of Irish political aspirations. Again, I do not believe that this withdrawal can be effected without the use of force, or at the very least, the real and persistent threat of force.

II

While these fundamental tenets of Republican thought remain valid, it is clear, in retrospect, that the interpretation and application of Republicanism to changing political conditions suffered from some serious shortcomings, in the past. The most serious of these was, perhaps, the fact that the traditional teachings of Republicanism, passed on from generation to generation, were simplistic and specific to a particular era. Ireland has never received from Republicanism what it most needed, namely, a coherent, constantly developing social and political philosophy. We have never been blessed with those who could flesh out the basic premises of Republicanism to provide a rationale for consistent political as well as military action, through time. Such a process is one of continual reinterpretation and refinement of received doctrine in the light of constantly changing social and political reality.

This failure of Republicanism to mature and develop as a political and social philosophy had serious consequences. It resulted in the neglect of political action as one means of promoting Irish unity, and an exclusive concentration on physical force. This neglect, in turn, prevented Republicans from assuming a position of leadership in social life from which the people could be organised and their political consciousness aroused. Since Republicans were wandering in a political wilderness, isolated from the daily life and concerns of the nation, they were unable to challenge or offer a viable alternative to the existing regimes in Ireland. This, in turn, weakened the appeal and credibility of the Movement as a whole. Republicans were caught in a vicious circle: because they lacked a contemporary social and political philosophy, they were unable to think or act outside the military sphere and this, in turn, destroyed the possibility of welding the people together on a broad front of integrated military and political action. Consequently, Republicans have at all times been committed to rebellion rather than revolution. Its one vital element was physical force, and this inflexible ideology had to be applied in isolation, unsupported by organised political sentiment in the country at large.

Republicans were thus placed in an untenable position, unable to manoeuvre ideologically or politically. A rigid philosophy made them incapable of observing and understanding political change, with the result that they were unable to respond to the political realities of the fifties.

One of the foremost of these was that Britain, at that time, could not be described as 'the source of all our ills' except in a historic sense. Indeed, major problems such as economic dependence, excessive emigration and cultural malaise resulted far more from the moral cowardice and stupidity of the so-called Irish government than from British imperialism. In the North, Britain was not pursuing an active policy of traditional colonialism. On the contrary, it could be argued that the North reaped considerable benefits from the British welfare state. Finally, little if any emphasis was placed on the fact that the majority of the population of the Six Counties wished to remain under the Crown. The fact that this sentiment might be transformed into formidable armed opposition against a united Ireland, or that it could provide the single most significant stumbling block to national unity, was completely overlooked by the Movement. The opinions and attitudes of the northern Unionist never once prompted Republicans to examine the need to redefine church-state relations, accept constitutional change or conceive of modernisation in such vital areas as education and family law.

None of these facts were worthy of recognition or discussion among Republicans bound by the simplistic concept of an Empire as hellishly evil in Ireland of the twentieth century as she had been at the time of Elizabeth or Cromwell. As in the past, there could be no compromise nor any thought among Republicans on the different policies and methods that might be applied, in conjunction with physical force, towards the objective of Irish unity. As one commentator noted, it never occurred to Republicans that, instead of trying to expel Britain to the end of uniting Irishmen, they ought attempt to unite Irishmen with a view to expelling Britain. Unfortunately, Republican ideology recognised only one path to freedom.

While the British presence in Ireland was at least reflected in the existence of the I.R.A. and the preparations for a campaign, the power and existence of the Dublin government hardly warranted attention. Republican ideology could not easily grapple with such a concept. It should not exist. It arose from a treasonable treaty signed by renegades who sold their heritage for a mess of pottage. As a result, the practical significance of the Irish state was assumed away in a welter of moral posturings and sterile distinctions between *de jure* and *de facto* authority. Republicans had obviously never heard of Lenin's dictum that there is no morality in these matters, only expediency. Consequently, it never seemed to occur to anybody that a firm foothold and strong organisation in southern politics could be strategically and tactically vital to the success of a prolonged campaign in the North. As always, the Movement was blinkered. It could not see that military and political action were not antithetical but complementary factors in the same game. It could not understand that, while martyrdom might at times be a necessary condition of success, it is seldom, of itself, a sufficient condition for victory.

These thoughts sum up, for me, the substance and spirit of the Republican Movement of the fifties. Its few strengths, many weaknesses and crippling mistakes were not, of course, characteristic of that period alone: the weaknesses and flaws in an immature ideology made themselves felt time after time. And who can say that the weaknesses and flaws did not exact a heavy toll? The Movement certainly got its complement of martyrs but, like the body counts in Vietnam, they did not indicate success or victory. The hard political realities won the day. The Army was ill prepared to undertake a prolonged struggle against a determined enemy on his own ground. In the absence of any real political opposition, the Dublin government was able to fulfil its role of aiding and abetting that enemy and, finally, the people in general made it clear that they no longer considered martyrdom a sufficient condition to win their overwhelming support.

It is always easy, of course, to evaluate a situation after the event. The fact is that everybody connected with the Movement at the time was responsible for its shortcomings. I myself am not interested in the sterile exercise of allocating blame. I am far more interested in the assessment of the Movement's past, in the hope that the mistakes and shortcomings might be eliminated, for the future.

APPENDIX XVIII

British army intelligence document on the likely trends in the tactics and weaponry of Irish Republican terrorists up to the end of 1983, dated 2 November 1978, leaked to the press in May 1979. (Copy of document in author's possession; sent by private source).

SECRET

QMG Secretariat
MOD Form 102 :s25/II82

D/DINI/2003
3/135

NORTHERN IRELAND: FUTURE TERRORIST TRENDS

INTRODUCTION

1. Throughout the present Northern Ireland campaign there have been many changes in both the tempo and nature of terrorist activity. A variety of causes, political, operational and logistical have precipitated these fluctuations which frequently have also been forced upon the terrorists by Security Force action. But beneath the changes a definable process of evolution has been taking place.

2. The paper[1] which examined the Future Organisation of Military Intelligence in Northern Ireland saw the need for a study to identify future trends in terrorist tactics and weaponry for the guidance of combat development and operational requirements staffs.

3. In its study of the Threat the same paper assessed that the Provisional leadership is deeply committed to a long campaign of attrition. The Provisional IRA (PIRA) has the dedication and the sinews of war to raise violence intermittently to at least the level of early 1978, certainly for the foreseeable future. Even if 'peace' is restored, the motivation for politically inspired violence will remain. Arms will be readily available and there will be many who are able and willing to use them. Any peace will be superficial and brittle. A new campaign may well erupt in the years ahead.

4. In 1977 PIRA adopted the classic terrorist cellular organisation in response to their difficulties. But at other times their tactics and weaponry have changed for reasons that cannot be forecast, such as the influence, often transitory, of individual leaders and the professional ability of key terrorists. Also an isolated incident, such as 'Bloody Sunday', can radically alter support for violence. Thus forecasting has often to be based on speculation rather than hard intelligence. Nevertheless there are trends in terrorist weaponry and tactics which can be identified. We need to project these as best we can if we are not to fall behind in devising counter measures.

1. D/DINI/2002/K dated 28 Feb 78.

SECRET

5. In the paper we have focussed on the Republican threat which is harder and more sophisticated than that posed by Loyalist paramilitaries. It follows that we do not consider the implications of a resurgence of serious inter-sectarian strife.

AIM

6. The aim of the paper is to examine the likely trends in the tactics and weaponry of Irish Republican terrorists up to the end of 1983.

SCOPE

7. We consider first the aspirations of the Republican terrorists with a brief examination of the political changes which might affect their campaign. We next examine their resources and the main constraints under which they operate. We then, after discussing the terrorists' organisation, seek to determine the strategy they are likely to adopt and consequently the targets they may select. Terrorist weaponry and tactics are then examined with a view to assessing the likely developments during the next 5 years.

8. We have imposed the following limitations on the paper:

a. Irish terrorism in Great Britain is outside its scope.

b. Its technical content does not go beyond that needed to formulate the broad parameters of equipment which may lie within the terrorists' grasp.

c. It stops short of examining possible countermeasures demanded by the developing trends.

TERRORIST ASPIRATIONS AND LINKS

THE PROVISIONAL IRA

9. The Provisional Movement is committed to the traditional aim of Irish nationalism, that is the removal of the British presence from Ireland. The PIRA leadership is dedicated to the belief that this can only be achieved through violence. It follows that the Provisionals will strive to continue the struggle in some form or other while the British remain in the Province. Meanwhile their immediate aims are to achieve:

a. A declaration of intent by the British to withdraw from Northern Ireland.

b. An amnesty for all 'political' prisoners, including the release of all PIRA prisoners in gaol on the mainland.

c. The recognition of the right of the Irish people to decide their own destiny, free from British interference.

THE OFFICIAL IRA

10. The traditional aims of the Official IRA (OIRA) are similar to those of the Provisionals. But the Officials are Marxist whereas the Provisionals are motivated by an inward looking Celtic nationalism. The Officials' political stance appeals more to middle class and intellectual groups than that of the Provisionals. OIRA has preserved a cease fire since 1972 and has striven, with a modicum of success, to expand its influence through legitimate political activity under the names 'Sinn Fein The Workers Party' and 'The Republican Clubs'. It devotes much

SECRET

effort to maintaining links with left wing subversive organisations in Europe. Although there is no sign that OIRA will alter its stance during the next 5 years, it is nevertheless ready to re-enter the campaign.

EFFECTS OF POSSIBLE POLITICAL CHANGE

11. In considering the will of the Republican terrorists and their supporters to continue the present struggle we need to examine the likely developments in the political life of the Province. The following are perhaps possible scenarios:

a. The present form of government may continue. We would then expect there to be a general atmosphere of political calm, though politicians would be frustrated. Government policy would be principally one of containment and the underlying problems would remain unsolved.

b. The current system of direct rule may be modified by introducing another elected upper tier of local government.

c. The Government may achieve its aim of restoring devolved government in the near future, although this seems unlikely.

d. The concept of independence might take firmer root. But the 2 communities interpret the objective differently.

e. A new party based on socialist policies transcending sectarian barriers may emerge. But similar attempts since 1922 have always ended in failure. In Ireland the appeal of sectarian and nationalistic sentiment has always been stronger than that of left wing ideology. The continuing polarisation of the population on sectarian lines only emphasises the improbability of such an initiative.

12. Only the first alternative, continued direct rule, offers any real prospect of political calm and hence waning support for the terrorists during the next 5 years. Under any other scenario Republican fears of a Protestant ascendancy being re-established would enable PIRA to pose as the defenders of the minority interest. Even if the present system of government is maintained the current muted support for the forces of law and order will remain delicately balanced and susceptible to any controversial government decision or Security Force action. We see no prospect in the next 5 years of any political change which would remove PIRA's raison d'etre.

FUTURE TERRORIST GROUPINGS

13. We expect the Provisionals to remain the dominant terrorist organisation throughout the next 5 years. PIRA may well gain further support from the Irish Republican Socialist Party (IRSP), the splinter group from OIRA, which has recently been trying to improve its operational capacity. If the Provisionals and Officials combined to form an active alliance not only would they pose a far more powerful threat but they would also probably attract more tangible support from international terrorist groups. However there are fundamental political differences between the 2 movements and bitter animosity between individuals and family groups. Rivalry is sharp and they are unlikely ever to settle their differences. The prospect of the Provisionals substantially increasing their strength through alliances with other groups in Ireland is thus remote.

14. The Provisionals have some elusive links with overseas terrorist movements, notably the PLO, and possibly other European groups, which are built up on a mutual interest in weapons and in violence for its own sake. These contacts provide a potentially rich source of weapons and of an exchange of ideas on terrorist techniques. However there are no signs that PIRA has either the in-

SECRET

tention or the ability deliberately to foster them.

TERRORIST RESOURCES

MANPOWER

15. The Provisionals cannot attract the large numbers of active terrorists they had in 1972/73. But they no longer need them. PIRA's organisation is now such that a small number of activists can maintain a disproportionate level of violence. There is a substantial pool of young Fianna aspirants, nurtured in a climate of violence, eagerly seeking promotion to full gun-carrying terrorist status and there is a steady release from the prisons of embittered and dedicated terrorists[2]. Thus, though PIRA may be hard hit by Security Force attrition from time to time, they will probably continue to have the manpower they need to sustain violence during the next 5 years.

16. *Calibre of Terrorist*

a. *Leadership*. PIRA is essentially a working class organisation based in the ghetto areas of the cities and in the poorer rural areas. Thus if members of the middle class and graduates become more deeply involved they have to forfeit their life style. Many are also deterred by the Provisionals' muddled political thinking. Nevertheless there is a strata of intelligent, astute and experienced terrorists who provide the backbone of the organisation. Although there are only a few of these high grade terrorists there is always the possibility that a new charismatic leader may emerge who would transform PIRA yet again.

b. *Technical Expertise*. PIRA has an adequate supply of members who are skilled in the production of explosive devices. They have the tools and equipment and they have the use of small workshops and laboratories.

c. *Rank and File Terrorists*. Our evidence of the calibre of rank and file terrorists does not support the view that they are merely mindless hooligans drawn from the unemployed and unemployable. PIRA now trains and uses its members with some care. The Active Service Units (ASUs) are for the most part manned by terrorists tempered by up to ten years of operational experience.

d. *Trend in Calibre*. The mature terrorists, including for instance the leading bomb makers, are usually sufficiently cunning to avoid arrest. They are continually learning from mistakes and developing their expertise. We can therefore expect to see increased professionalism and the greater exploitation of modern technology for terrorist purposes.

17. *Popular Support*. Republican terrorists can no longer bring crowds of active sympathisers onto the streets at will as a screen for gunmen. Indeed there is seldom much support even for traditional protest marches. But by reorganising on cellular lines PIRA has become less dependent on public support than in the past and is less vulnerable to penetration by informers. The hardening segregation of the communities also operates to the terrorists' advantage. Although the Provisionals have lost much of the spontaneous backing they enjoyed early in the campaign, there is no sign of any equivalent upsurge of support for the Security Forces. There are still areas within the Province, both rural and urban, where the terrorists can base themselves with little risk of betrayal

2. Statistics of Prison Releases at Annex A.

SECRET

and can count on active support in emergency. The fear of a possible return to Protestant repression will underpin this kind of support for the Provisionals for many years to come. Loyalist action could quickly awaken it to a much more volatile level.

FINANCE

18. PIRA is probably now more dependent on a steady source of income than it was when mass popular support provided a momentum of its own. Activists expect regular pay and are not content with low quality weapons. But we cannot accurately judge the extent to which they line their own pockets. However, recently a much firmer discipline has been exercised and we expect this to continue. Although we have but fragmentary knowledge of income and expenditure we can draw some deductions on PIRA's financial state.

19. *Income.*

a. *Commercial Activity.* Incompetence and dishonesty have been hallmarks of the Provisionals' commercial undertakings. The Eire Nua Cooperatives, which started in 1974/75, have been unprofitable and drinking clubs have been little better. None of PIRA's numerous commercial ventures seem to bring in much income with the possible exception of the "Black Taxis". But Police activity is now inhibiting the use of the latter.

b. *Theft.* Armed robbery within Ireland is almost certainly the greatest source of income for PIRA. In the North since 1971 thefts have been running at some £500,000 per year. In the South up to 1976 the annual loss was about £700,000 but in 1977 it was over £900,000 and the figure for 1978 was already close to £1M by mid-June. The proceeds of the theft of readily marketable goods also sometimes go to the Provisionals. We estimate that income from theft is running at at least £550,000 per year and that occasional spectacular raids will provide additional infusions of ready cash.

c. *Racketeering.* The main continuing forms of racketeering are protection payments from shops and businesses, and fraud involving dole money and 'lost' pension books. We estimate that the annual income through this is about £250,000. Unless PIRA step up extortion and terrorism we would expect this figure to decline over the next 5 years in the face of RUC countermeasures.

d. *Remittances from Overseas.* The Provisionals have had some success in obtaining funds from overseas groupings of people of Irish descent. The Irish Northern Aid Committee (INAC) in the USA, with a subsidiary in Canada, is the largest source. It currently declares support (for prisoners aid) at a rate of £55,000 per year. Actual remittances are probably at least 25% higher. Some aid is also received from Australia and New Zealand. We doubt whether PIRA receives financial aid from Libya or any other overseas government. We assess that the total income from overseas is about £120,000 annually.

e. *Green Cross.* Green Cross is the name given to aid for Republican prisoners and their families. Much of the money from overseas is raised on this pretext. Collections for it in Great Britain, the Republic and Roman Catholic areas in the Province probably amount to some £30,000 annually.

20. *Expenditure*

a. *Pay.* The largest item of expenditure is probably pay for terrorists and for those who work full or part time for Provisional Sinn Fein (PSF). A report of June 1978 indicates that normal terrorist pay is now £20 per week (as a

SECRET

supplement to the dole). We estimate that some 250 people would draw this and perhaps 60 would get £40 per week (£7,500 per week, £400,000 per year).
b. *Other Costs.* Apart from arms expenditure the Provisionals have to bear the cost of their prison welfare work including payment to prisoners' dependants, travel and transport costs and propaganda expenses especially the Republican newspapers whose sale does not cover their cost.
21. *Tentative Balance Sheet.* Despite our scanty knowledge we suggest the following balance sheet for PIRA:

a.	*Income*	
	Theft in Ireland	£550,000
	Racketeering	£250,000
	Overseas Contributions	£120,000
	Green Cross UK and Eire	£30,000
		£950,000
b.	*Expenditure*	
	Pay (@ £7,500 per week)	£400,000
	Travel and Transport Costs (@ £1,000 per week)	£50,000
	Newspapers and Propaganda	£150,000
	Prisoners, dependents welfare	£180,000
		£780,000
c.	Available for arms, ammunition and explosive	£170,000

22. *Future Finance and Capacity for Arms Purchase.* In the years ahead the Provisionals will probably have difficulty in maintaining some of their sources of income. We do not expect them to be able to make good any deficit from overseas. They may well therefore have to rely increasingly on armed robbery. However, if they are forced to make economies the Provisionals would only cut back on arms expenditure as a last resort. Indeed we believe that the purchase of arms will continue at roughly its present level[3]. Acquisition, possibly even through gift, of a few costly prestige weapons such as surface to air missiles cannot be ruled out.

EXTERNAL SUPPORT FOR TERRORISM OTHER THAN FINANCE

THE REPUBLIC

23. Republican sentiment and the IRA tradition emanates from the South. Although the Fianna Fail Government are resolutely opposed to the use of force, its long term aims are, as Mr Lynch himself admits, similar to those of the Provisionals. Any successor to Lynch in the ruling party will probably follow at least as Republican a line of policy. Fine Gael, though traditionally less Republican, is also now committed to a roughly similar line. We have no reason to suspect that PIRA obtains active support from government sources, or that it

3. Guide of Cost of Weapons is at Annex B.

SECRET

will do so in the future, but the judiciary has often been lenient and the Gardai, although cooperating with the RUC more than in the past, is still rather less than wholehearted in its pursuit of terrorists.

24. The headquarters of the Provisionals is in the Republic. The South also provides a safe mounting base for cross border operations and secure training areas. PIRA's logistic support flows through the Republic where arms and ammunition are received from overseas. Improvised weapons, bombs and explosives are manufactured there. Terrorists can live there without fear of extradition for crimes committed in the North. In short, the Republic provides many of the facilities of the classic safe haven so essential to any successful terrorist movement. And it will probably continue to do so for the foreseeable future.

UNITED STATES AND CANADA

25. Supporters of Republicanism in Ireland have exploited the fact that the Irish/American vote is important to United States politicians. Although by no means all expatriate Irish are sympathetic to the Provisionals, powerful lobbies have been built up to give political encouragement to Republicans in Northern Ireland and to criticise British policy. Propaganda is eagerly exploited to gather support for the Provisionals in both the USA and Canada. Since 1972 the United States has become PIRA's main weapons source, either through purchases or through thefts. Despite several successful prosecutions arms are still reaching the Province; we do not know whether in a steady trickle of small consignments or whether in bulk, but suspect the former. We believe that the Provisionals will be able to maintain political, financial and material support from North America at about the current level.

SOVIET BLOC

26. Although the Official IRA adheres to orthodox Marxism there are no indications of any substantial link between the Soviet Union and either wing of the IRA. Nor do we anticipate any links developing in the next 5 years. However we expect arms of Soviet origin to continue to arrive in the Province through various proxy sources.

THE MIDDLE EAST

27. The Middle East terrorist organisations, notably the PLO have such a wealth of arms available that they could easily supply PIRA without detriment to their own capability and without necessarily obtaining the support of their sponser governments, such as Syria and Libya. The 'Claudia' shipment of March 1973, involving some 5 tons of arms of largely Soviet origin, did not implicate the Soviet authorities. Further proof of Middle East involvement was given when the 'Towerstream' (ex-Cyprus) consignment was intercepted in Antwerp in November 1977. The weapons, though mainly old, were serviceable and of types still very much in demand by terrorist groups. They included RPG7 antitank rockets, mortars and military explosive. The Middle East is a potentially valuable source of weapons in the years ahead.

FUTURE EXTERNAL SUPPORT

28. For future political support and encouragement the Provisionals will continue to look mainly to the United States. There are signs that they are also working up support from people of Irish extraction in Australia and New Zealand. PIRA will probably also try to extend their links to subversive groups in Europe

and the Middle East. But the Provisionals fear that close association with other political ideologies would tarnish the essential Irishness of their movement. They will therefore probably refuse any material support which comes with political strings attached. To sum up, a shortage of arms has never inhibited PIRA and is unlikely to do so in the future.

THE TERRORIST ORGANISATION [4]

DUBLIN LEADERSHIP

29. The heart of PIRA lies in Dublin and is based on the Provisional Army Council (PAC), the decision making body responsible for general policy, and "GHQ" responsible for the more detailed staff functions such as finance, arms supply and training. The PSF is controlled by the Ard Comhairle (Party Executive). A number of individuals are members of two, or even all 3, of these organisations, and the inter-relationship between the groups probably varies from time to time. The PSF seem firmly subordinated to PIRA though political considerations could in future demand a higher priority. We know little of the detailed working of the hierarchy in Dublin. In particular we have scant knowledge of how the logistic system works, nor do we know the extent to which the older, apparently retired, Republican leaders influence the movement. Since members of the senior leadership can seldom, if ever, be tied to actual terrorist crime they will probably continue to enjoy a free hand. But if sterner measures by the Irish Government forced the leadership underground the latter would probably adapt to the new situation and continue the struggle.

INTERMEDIATE AND LOWER LEVEL OF COMMAND

30. There has been considerable turbulence among the leadership at the lower levels through the campaign. Relationships between the various groups have altered with the changing personalities. The Northern Command concept has probably been accepted and, although the leadership is still fluid, the chain of command is effective. However, the prime architect of the new cellular system based on Active Service Units (ASUs), there was a partial reversion towards the traditional brigade organisation. Indeed this lack of leadership continuity seems endemic to the Provisionals and is exacerbated by Security Force attrition.

SYSTEMS OF COMMUNICATION

31. One of the weaknesses of the Provisionals' organisation is its communications. The leadership has always tried to exercise tight control both over policy and over the allocation of weapons and funds. Thus detailed instructions frequently have to be passed through several links both within the Republic and in the Province. The cell system probably exacerbates the problem. Certainly response times seem slow. We suspect that the terrorists fear to pass explicit information on the telephone. The main system of communication is therefore probably by courier, though meetings of leaders are held both North and South of the border and some members of the leadership travel widely themselves. Sinn Fein Centres provide convenient meeting places. At the tactical level

4. PIRA Organisation Chart is at Annex C.

SECRET

there is some use of short range radios. Indeed the Provisionals' communications will probably remain vulnerable to interdiction by the Security Forces for many years yet.

FUTURE DEVELOPMENTS

32. We believe that the terrorist organisation will continue to depend for policy and material on the South. The Dublin leadership will continue to exercise overall control even if it has to operate more covertly. Northern Command will be retained; but the middle level of command will remain fluid. The expertise of the ASUs will grow and they will continue to be PIRA's prime offensive arm. At the lowest levels there will remain a lunatic fringe of young hooligans who will only occasionally be involved in terrorism but who will keep old sectarian fears alive. They will inhibit the return of public confidence.

TERRORIST STRATEGY AND TARGETTING

BACKGROUND

33. From the start of the present campaign to about the end of 1973 much of the terrorist violence was indiscriminate. Large blast bombs were often detonated in shopping areas causing heavy civilian casualties. There were frequent 'convoy' shootings and sectarian attacks. But recently there has been a marked trend towards attacks against Security Force targets and away from action which, by alienating public opinion, both within the Catholic community and outside the Province, is politically damaging. It is also arguable that PIRA still sees itself as an 'Army' and clings to the remnants of what they believe to be a military code of ethics. This constraint is often blurred and its force will probably continue to decline but there have, for example, been few attacks on the families of either soldiers or RUC.

34. PIRA strategy is based on the premise that a campaign of attrition with its attendant costs in both lives and money, will eventually persuade HMG to withdraw from Northern Ireland. The Provisionals probably aspire to raising the tempo of their operations to such a level that the normal processes of administration and government break down. But having failed to achieve this in the earlier part of the campaign, they probably realise that they now have little hope of success. Indeed, they may accept that to raise the level of their activity beyond a certain point would evoke such intense response from the Security Forces that their organisation would suffer disproportionately to the success achieved. Irish terrorists have usually been careful to preserve their personal safety, and the strength of the organisation during the next 5 years is likely to remain such that the leadership will wish to avoid action that could put large numbers of its men at risk. A further influencing factor is that the PIRA leadership appreciate that their campaign will be won or lost in Belfast. Although operations elsewhere are important, and in the Border area easier to achieve, success in Belfast is critical.

PROPAGANDA

35. Propaganda has an important bearing on PIRA strategy. The leadership is becoming increasingly sensitive of the need to avoid alienating support not only in the Roman Catholic areas of the Province but also in the Republic and among those of Irish extraction overseas. The Provisionals continue to justify their

SECRET

activities by claiming that they are merely reacting to the Security Forces and that violence is the only response to the repression of the Catholic community in Northern Ireland. In the interests of publicity PIRA may well stage a few spectacular attacks to indicate that their normal lower posture stems from restraint rather than weakness. On the other hand, we cannot exclude the possibility that PIRA, like terrorists in West Germany and Italy, might reject the fruitless quest for popularity and accept that they can achieve more if unfettered by pursuit of a favourable public image. The balance of probability however is that propaganda will continue to influence strategy and the selection of targets.

ATTACKS ON PEOPLE

36. *General*. Members of the Security Forces are likely to continue to be the main targets for terrorists attack. But PIRA have never yet sustained their attacks for long on any one branch, eg the Army, UDR, RUC, RUC Reserve and Prison Officers. However, as they become more sophisticated and as they become more perceptive, PIRA may try to implement a more systematic campaign of assassination. Other potential assassination targets are:

a. *Men of Influence*. PIRA have not mounted sustained attacks on the men of influence such as politicians, top government officials, members of the judiciary, and senior members of the RUC and the Army. But the Provisionals may decide to target them in the future in imitation of terrorism in West Germany, Italy and Spain.

b. *Collectors of Intelligence*. The terrorists are already aware of their own vulnerability to Security Force intelligence operators and will increasingly seek to eliminate those involved.

c. *Businessmen*. Attacks on businessmen are politically damaging and are thus unlikely.

d. *Internal*. The disciplining of those who have committed crimes, either against their own terrorist organisations or who act as common criminals, and those involved in inter-factional feuds will probably continue.

37. *Kidnap*. Kidnapping for both financial and political bargaining has been favoured by many other terrorist organisations. But it forms no part of traditional IRA tactics. Both the Niedermeyer and Herrema incidents, the only pre-planned kidnaps in this campaign, were carried out by maverick groups without the authority or subsequent support of the leadership. Those involved lacked the skill to carry the kidnap through to the bargaining stage. In Ireland prominent personalities are generally well guarded and PIRA may appreciate that neither HMG nor the Government of the Republic would readily submit to this kind of coercion. Kidnap however provides excellent publicity and might be attempted by PIRA under special conditions such as an attempt to gain concessions. Opportunity kidnap of Security Forces may continue but in general the risk is low.

38. *Security Force Installations*. Security Force bases and installations such as permanent check points and radio re-broadcast stations provide prestige targets for the terrorist. He will undoubtedly wish to improve his capability to attack them.

39. *Commercial property*. Attacks on commercial property present PIRA with a predicament. On the one hand they may alienate public opinion yet on the

SECRET

other they inflict high cost damage and they expose the inadequacy of the Security Forces. This dilemma was highlighted by the Provisionals' ban on commercial bombing imposed after the La Mon attack in February 1978. A ban which was lifted as the public's memory of the incident started to fade.

40. *Public Utilities and Government Offices.* During the current campaign there have been few attacks against public utilities. However, sustained and systematic attack, particularly on the electricity supply system, could be very damaging and would tie down large numbers of the Security Forces. While the terrorists remain short of commercial explosive their ability to attack steel and reinforced concrete targets is limited. But this could be offset by a detailed knowledge of the layout of public utilities which would then reduce the amount of explosive needed. Also PIRA have probably refrained from sustained attacks on such targets because of the political damage that would result from imposing indiscriminate hardship on members of both sections of the community. But the Provisionals may overcome this inhibition in the future. Meanwhile they will continue to seek forms of attack, such as the bombing of administrative offices, that will embarrass the authorities without causing disruption to the consumer. Government offices will probably also be selected for attack.

41. *Transport.* Trains and railway lines have been attacked fairly frequently during the campaign and large numbers of buses have been burned. Attacks of this sort are difficult to counter and involve little risk to life. They will probably continue. Air traffic constitutes a prestige target. The Provisionals would probably not wish to shoot down a civil aircraft but the same restraint does not apply to a military aircraft. And PIRA might well wish to disrupt travel arrangements at Aldergrove where even relatively unspectacular activity could result in intimidation of travellers and pilots with all the attendant publicity.

HIJACKING

42. The hijacking of vehicles for the immediate use of terrorists continues to be an almost daily occurrence in Northern Ireland. Small aircraft have been hijacked 3 times, twice to drop primitive bombs and once to provide a means of escape for prisoners. Hijacking with a view to taking hostages has not been attempted nor have there been attacks of the kind mounted by the South Moluccan extremists in Holland to hold hostages in a train, school or office block. The Provisionals probably rate the chance of a successful outcome to any hostage-taking operation as low and therefore not worth either the risk or the adverse publicity. We expect the existing pattern of hijack activity to continue.

LIKELY TRENDS IN STRATEGY AND TARGETTING

43. Although PIRA is likely to follow an erratic path in the years ahead we expect to see a continuation of the general trend towards more precise targetting and greater expertise. Propaganda considerations will probably still influence targetting. But a change in leadership might radically alter this. We expect PIRA to attempt to acquire the skills and weaponry needed to refine their attacks on:

a. Members of the Security Forces.
b. Security Force bases and installations.
c. Public utilities, communications, government offices and transport.
d. Any other targets specifically linked with British rule in Northern Ireland.

SECRET

TACTICS AND TYPES OF ATTACK

MAIN CHARACTERISTICS OF PIRA TACTICS

44. The principle that the terrorist must have a safe method of escape is the dominant feature in PIRA tactics. PIRA very seldom plan operations that involve high risk and if in doubt they abort the mission. Shooting attacks are mainly conducted on the "shoot and scoot" principle. Indeed there is a discernible pattern in PIRA tactics. Successful techniques are frequently repeated and the same targets are often attacked several times. We must therefore be prepared for PIRA to use any technique which has proved successful in the past, regardless of how long ago.

FACTORS AFFECTING WEAPONRY[5]

45. Developments in weaponry for a terrorist organisation usually follow a somewhat random pattern. The terrorist can only be partially successful in acquiring equipment to suit his needs. He will often have to accept any weapon he can get and bend his tactics to exploit it as best he can. Thus, apart from finance, changes in the terrorist armoury will depend on:

a. The need to meet specific operational requirements.

b. Evolutionary improvement of existing home made devices. This is dependent on the skill and initiative of those working for the terrorist organisation.

c. The need to find an alternative weapon, or system of attack, if the Security Forces produce a satisfactory countermeasure or succeed in cutting off the supply of either the weapon itself or a critical component. (For instance the adoption of improved forms of home-made explosive following our success in cutting off commercial explosive supplies). Such changes, though born of weakness, can lead to the adoption of improved systems or weapons.

d. The more or less chance availability of weapons through theft or from supplies that other terrorist organisations are prepared to make available.

e. Availability of weapons on the open market.

f. The desire for prestige weapons for propaganda and publicity purposes even though in practical military terms they may be of little use.

g. The limitations imposed by his meagre resources, the difficulties of maintaining a complex weapon and little access to spare parts. The terrorist therefore looks for simple cost-effective systems.

46. Additionally the terrorist will always seek to acquire weapons which are simple and easy to conceal.

FIREARMS, MORTAR AND ROCKET ATTACK

47. *Handguns.* PIRA hold a variety of handguns divided fairly evently between revolvers and pistols. The handgun is chiefly used for close quarter assassination and punishment shootings. As far as we know PIRA have not used silencers. The efficiency of the standard modern handgun is adequate for terrorist needs. In the early years of the campaign handguns were often used from the cover of a crowd. But the terrorist is unlikely to regain the kind of mass support needed for this tactic. We would not expect him to give higher priority to the acquisition of new handguns than he does today.

5. Estimate of Current PIRA Arms Holdings – Annex D.

SECRET

48. *Rifle, SMG and Machine Gun.*

a. A wide variety of small arms is available to terrorists in Northern Ireland, many of which, being old or somewhat unsuitable, are kept in reserve or for use by less experienced men who may lose them. For small arms attacks the terrorists' main needs are:

(1) A highly portable, easily concealed combat weapon mainly for use at ranges up to 150 metres. The 53.5 mm (.223 in) Armalite satisfies this requirement and to a large extent obviates the need for a SMG. There is no shortage of these weapons and a steady trickle of new ones reach the Province. PIRA also have a few Soviet AK47 assault rifles (AK47), another very successful short range weapon. But machine pistols effective at up to 200 metres are even more attractive weapons. The Israeli Uzi, the Czech Scorpion and the Polish M63 are useful examples which PIRA could probably obtain with little difficulty.

(2) A sniping rifle providing a good chance of a first round kill at ranges of up to about 300 metres. Light weight and ease of concealment and semi-automatic action are again desirable. The M742 Remington Woodmaster (.3006 in) meets these requirements and the weapon is plentiful in Ireland. There are many other common hunting rifles commercially available which have a similar performance.

(3) A heavier rifle for long range engagements which also fires an armour piercing round. The World War II .30/.3006 Garand, of which the Provisionals have an adequate stock, meets this need.

b. *The Machine Gun.* This is a prestige weapon but its size and weight make it difficult to remove or hide after an incident. Maintenance and spare parts present problems and for good performance the firer needs professional training. The weapon is likely to prove unreliable in terrorist hands. Its use, particularly in urban areas, involves considerable risk to the local population. While it is potentially an effective weapon in a rural ambush and for covering an escape across the border, we believe that its acquisition will not produce any important changes in terrorist tactics or capability.

c. *Sights.* Until recently PIRA's shooting attacks have been inaccurate. Zeroing of weapons has been poor. But simple telescopic sights have been fairly frequently used. Marksmanship has now improved probably due to better training. Improved sights may be acquired since they and image intensification equipment can now be obtained in many countries. A system for illuminating the point of impact on a target using a helium/neon visible laser is commercially available in Switzerland and could be improvised by PIRA from equipment readily found in technical college laboratories. There is thus much scope for improving the performance of snipers. As PIRA become more tightly grouped and more professional in their approach we would expect to see developments along these lines.

49. *Mortars.*

a. The mortar provides the terrorist with the safest and most effective method of attack on hard targets such as Security Force bases and vital areas such as Aldergrove Airport. The Provisionals have developed a succession of effective improvised mortars culminating, so far, with the Mk 9. This is simple to make and fires a bomb weighing some 40 lbs containing 15–20 lbs of explosive.

SECRET

It has been used twice at ranges of 100 and 165 metres but has been tested by RARDE to ranges in excess of 300 metres without failure.

b. *Future Use.* The Provisionals may have been deterred from using mortars by lack of success (in 71 attacks between 1973 and January 1978 no member of the Security Forces has been killed). But intelligence indicates that PIRA have not abandoned their use altogether, new types may even be under development. We would expect to see more attacks with the Mk 9 against those targets that can be safely approached and more use of light weight mortars such as the Mk 6 which has a range of 1200 metres. PIRA may well acquire commercial mortars which would enable them to attack from ranges of some 3000 metres. For instance, commercial mortars were found in the consignment discovered in Antwerp in November 1977 and they can be obtained with comparative ease on the open (arms) market.

50. *Anti-Armour*

a. *Rifle.* The .30/.3006 Garand armour piercing round has been largely ineffective against armoured vehicles used in Northern Ireland since the up-armouring of the Saracen and Humber. The 8.62mm armour piercing round for the Kalishnikov has a lower performance than the Garand round. Indeed there seems little scope for PIRA to improve on the Garand in the small arms field.

b. *RPG.* RPG-2 and the earlier marks of RPG-7 although obsolescent in most armies are effective anti-armour weapons. Large stocks of them exist in many parts of the world. So far PIRA's inadequate training has resulted in the mishandling of the RPG-7, but this could change. The RPG-7 range of 500 metres against static targets also makes it a useful weapon against buildings such as Security Force bases and prison walls. If Irish terrorists are successful in tightening their links with more sophisticated groups they could well obtain the RPG-7 in useful quantities. The Antwerp arms haul of November 1977 contained 36 of these rockets and 7 launchers.

c. *The Bombard.* Between September 1974 and May 1976 PIRA made 3 attacks using a stand-off anti-tank bombard launched from a steel tube buried in a hedge and containing a conical warhead filled with 6lb of commercial explosive. Tests by HVLE showed this weapon to be effective against the rear doors of the Saracen and large areas of the Humber. Up-armouring has since reduced the risk but the Provisionals have not used the bombard subsequently. There remains a possibility that the Provisionals will return to this form of attack.

d. *Wire-guided Weapons.* There is no role for wire-guided anti-tank weapons in Northern Ireland against vehicles. In view of their cost we doubt if PIRA would obtain them for use against buildings.

51. *Anti-Aircraft.* PIRA's attacks on aircraft have been few and ineffective: Small arms fire and the RPG-7 have been the main methods. The M60 machine gun is a potentially useful weapon against helicopters given a suitable mounting or specially constructed fire position. We believe that it has been used in this role but so far without effect. We know the PIRA has long wished to obtain hand-held anti-aircraft missiles. The black market price for the SA-7 in 1976 was £7,000, seemingly within the Provisionals' grasp. Very little training is needed for successful use of SA-7. Once the sensor is locked on a target, an audible signal is given and the firer has only to release the missile. It is a very attractive weapon for the terrorist. As the earlier types of missiles are super-

SECRET

seded in the Middle East and other armouries there is the possibility that some SA-7s may reach PIRA's hands.

52. *Grenades.* The IRA have produced some 30 kinds of improvised grenade and in late 1977 2 types of Russian military grenades were used. Commercial grenades also formed part of the Claudia shipment. Grenades have never been particularly effective in Northern Ireland and we have no reason to think they will become an important part of Irish terrorist weaponry in the next 5 years.

53. *Likely Trends.* The Provisionals may well acquire machine pistols but the Armalite and the Remington Woodmaster are suitable weapons for close quarter and sniping use. We expect the main development in the next 5 years to be better sights including possibly a laser sighting aid and night vision aids. Weapon handling and tactics used particularly in rural attacks will probably improve. The Provisionals may attempt to step up their use of mortars. They may re-adopt the Mk 6 or a similar weapon for ranges up to 1200 metres and the Mk 9 for ranges under 300 metres. Similarly PIRA will probably continue to attempt to obtain commercial mortars. The RPG-7 may well reappear for attacks on armoured vehicles and possibly on Security Force bases or prisons. Although in general we expect the Provisionals to concentrate on simple weaponry, some anti-aircraft missiles may be in their hands before the end of the period.

EXPLOSIVE ATTACKS ON PERSONNEL AND VEHICLES

54. *Desired Weapon Characteristics.* The terrorist will wish to have explosive devices satisfying the following criteria:

a. The explosive should be stable in storage, in transit and, when placed, impervious to weather conditions.

b. The bomb should be initiated so that it will secure a kill on the target but not against an unintended victim.

c. It should be quick and simple to lay and conceal. There should be a minimum demand on the skill of the terrorist involved in placing or initiating it.

d. The components should be cheap, readily available, and if possible not such as to call suspicion on the owner. As far as possible they should be undetectable to search instruments.

55. *Methods of Initiation.*

a. *Victim Operated.* PIRA have shown much ingenuity in devising victim operated or booby trap devices. Discriminate attack has been achieved by exploiting some unique or habitual activity carried out by the target or by luring the target into a suitable place for attack. The Security Forces can be attacked by these methods in situations where civilians are unlikely to be endangered. The techniques are too many to list and there is no discernible trend. But as electronic intruder alarms become even more common and readily available, new techniques are open to the terrorist. Items of electronic equipment operated by the Army such as search devices could themselves be exploited as triggers for devices.

b. *Land Line.* Land line provides a reliable method of initiation but problems of concealment render it impracticable in many situations. The firer must normally remain at fairly close range and is therefore vulnerable.

c. *Radio Control.* Radio controlled bombs were first seen in 1972 but there

6. Summary of Conclusions on Weapons – Annex E.

SECRET

has only been a gradual increase in their use. The McGregor 27 MWs radio sold for control of model aircraft and boats has normally been used. The main refinement has been the use of pulse coding of the firing message. Further refinements readily open to the terrorists are changes of frequency band, including perhaps the use of medium wave. Short range line of sight radio is adequate when the radio operator is himself watching the device. If he were further away using a more powerful radio he would need an observer. The use of this extra man, who must be in communication with the firer, adds to the complexity of the firing procedure with consequent opportunity for error. Thus there may be little incentive to obtain a more high powered set with a view to remote firing. The devices used so far bear the stamp of being made by one man or under the supervision of one man. But only comparatively simple skills are needed. We would not expect PIRA to have great difficulty in expanding production and we expect this to happen. If and when the terrorist believes that we can defeat the McGregor he will probably turn to other types of radio. Indeed he may do so at any time merely to enhance his capability.

EXPLOSIVE ATTACKS ON PROPERTY

56. *Desired Weapon Characterisation.* Many of the characteristics of the anti-personnel and anti-vehicle bomb are needed for bombs directed against property. Additionally the terrorist needs a device that can be quickly or covertly placed and a system of initiation, usually time delay, that will enable him to escape and, in some types of attack, ensure that the explosion takes place at a suitable moment. The terrorist has found that fire damage is generally most cost-effective than blast damage particularly against commercial property. The most easily concealed incendiary weapon is the cassette incendiary. However to be effective it must be placed amongst readily combustible material in a place where the resultant fire will not be quickly discovered. Thus, although useful against shops, it is inappropriate for attack on PIRA's higher priority targets. The cased blast incendiary is suitable for use against a wider range of targets. But at present, starved of commercial explosive, the terrorist lacks an effective method of cutting steel. For attack on public utilities he will wish to develop a way of doing this by means of a quickly emplaced charge.

57. *Tactics of Emplacement.* The main trend in emplacement is towards easing the job of the terrorist who places the device. The cased blast incendiary can be hung on the security grille of a door or window. The more traditional technique which is still in use is to take bombs into buildings either concealed in bags or by forced entry often using firearms. Although little used in recent years, large bombs in cars provided an effective blast weapon and can be delivered either by the terrorist himself or by coercing an innocent driver to deliver it. This is known as the "proxy bomb" technique and normally involves the taking of a hostage. The question of remote delivery of weapons has been considered earlier in the paper. Availability of long delay timers makes it feasible for bombs to be emplaced at a target before suspicion arises, even during the construction phase of a building or at a site to be visited by a VIP. Such bombs were used at the time of HM the Queen's visit to the Province in August 1977. It is a method that may well be used in the future and since such a bomb could be so deeply concealed as to be virtually undetectable, could possibly be used in conjunction with political demands as an alternative to taking a hostage.

SECRET

59. *Methods of Initiation.* Some of the methods of initiation used for personnel or vehicle targets can be used against property. Terrorists have used chemical delays, many types of clock, the "Parkway Timer" (sold as a reminder for expiry of a parking meter) and more recently the electronic delay timer. The latter can be built from readily purchaseable items by anyone able to follow a circuit diagram of a relatively simple kind. Such systems are very accurate and can produce delays of weeks, or, with a power source of long duration, even years. We would expect to see more use of these long delay timers particularly with a view to causing explosions at sensitive moments such as the time of a VIP visit.

FUTURE TRENDS IN THE USE OF EXPLOSIVE

59. Ingredients for the manufacture of home made explosive are simple, plentiful and untraceable. Other bomb-making components will also remain readily available. But the Provisionals have been slow to exploit the effective techniques for explosive attack that we know to be within their knowledge and competence. We believe that, possibly aided by external contacts, their performance will improve. In particular we would expect to see developments on the lines of:

a. More use of radio controlled devices.

b. More use of small blast and blast incendiary weapons that are quick and easy to emplace.

c. The development of effective methods of cutting steel.

d. More use of long delay electronic timers.

CHEMICAL AND BIOLOGICAL ATTACK

60. Since 1970 there have been several low grade reports that terrorists have intended to sabotage water supplies using chemicals. Suitable pollutants could easily be obtained but PIRA would have difficulty in making any such attack selective. Indiscriminate sabotage of this sort would be against their interests.

61. Contamination of food supplies to Security Forces from civil contractors by either chemical or biological means would be possible. The contractor would of course be readily identified and there are practical difficulties in making such an attack sufficiently effective to be worthwhile.

62. The Provisionals have used bottles of ammonia and acid as a form of chemical grenade but with little effect. They could also use large containers of chemicals to assist in some complex operation such as gaining entry to a defended location or in a prison escape. Again there are practical difficulties and there are probably few situations in which there would be any strong incentive to use such a technique.

NUCLEAR ATTACK

63. It is beyond the capability of Irish terrorists to obtain a nuclear weapon of fission or fusion type or even components of such a weapon. Nor do we expect them to establish links during the next 5 years with any organisation which could help them to obtain such a device. Anyway they would not stage an incident in any part of Ireland which might produce nuclear pollution. Thus we believe that the contingency planning covering nuclear incidents elsewhere in the United Kingdom will embrace the small risk from Irish terrorists.

SECRET

CONCLUSION

64. The Provisionals' campaign of violence is likely to continue while the British remain in Northern Ireland. During the next 5 years we see little prospect of change in the inter-relationship between the various terrorist groups in Ireland but we expect PIRA may become gradually more influenced by overseas terrorist groups. We see little prospect of of political development of a kind which would seriously undermine the Provisionals' position. (Paragraphs 9–14).

65. PIRA will probably continue to recruit the men it needs. They will still be able to attract enough people with leadership talent, good education and manual skills to continue to enhance their all round professionalism. The movement will retain popular support sufficient to maintain secure bases in the traditional Republican areas. (Paragraphs 15–17).

66. We believe there is little chance of the Provisionals receiving increased financial aid from overseas. They may have difficulty in maintaining some of their other sources of income and they will probably have to rely increasingly on armed robbery. The purchase of arms will continue to command a priority call on funds. But they will probably be unable to afford extravagant weapons, although we cannot exclude the possibility that they make a few prestige purchases such as the RPG-7 and SA-7. (Paragraphs 18–22).

67. We believe that the Republic will continue to act as a haven for terrorists and that they will continue to receive arms through Eire, particularly from the USA and through contacts with overseas terrorists groups. We believe however that there is little risk of any foreign government giving active support to PIRA. (Paragraphs 23–28).

68. We expect the Provisionals' organisation to retain its current higher command structure in the Republic, its "Northern Command" and its increasingly professional ASUs. The middle level of leadership is likely to remain unstable and the link between the top leadership in Dublin and the active terrorist groups on the ground may weaken. (Paragraphs 29–32).

69. The Provisional campaign over the next 5 years will probably be one of attrition rather than of intense activity, though the tempo of operations will fluctuate as in the past. (Paragraphs 33–34).

70. Propaganda considerations will frequently dictate PIRA strategy both in avoiding action that would alienate public opinion and in mounting spectacular attacks that would capture the Press headlines. (Paragraph 35).

71. We foresee a continued trend towards greater professionalism and selectivity in targetting. We believe that PIRA will concentrate its attacks on members of the Security Forces and their bases and at the infrastructure of Government including the public utilities. (Paragraphs 36–43).

72. The desire to save their own skins dominates PIRA tactics. Nevertheless there are traceable patterns of terrorist activity including a tendency to resort to methods that have been successful in the past. The Provisionals are probably content with their current armoury but they may attempt to acquire machine pistols. We expect to see improved sniper techniques using advanced weapon sights. PIRA will continue to use improvised mortars at infrequent intervals and may also endeavour to obtain standard military mortars. There will be a strong incentive to acquire anti-tank and even anti-aircraft rockets. (Paragrraphs 44–52).

SECRET

73. The well tried methods of attack using improvised explosive devices will continue. The variety of victim operated devices may increase by the use of commercial intruder alarm systems. We would also expect to see more emphasis on radio controlled devices, improvised explosive methods for cutting steel and long delay electronic timers. (Paragraphs 55–60).

74. We believe that Irish terrorists are unlikely to use chemical, biological or nuclear methods of attack during the next 5 years. (Paragraphs 60–63).

RECOMMENDATIONS

75. We recommend that the findings of this paper be used as the basis for further study aimed at:

a. Developing concepts of operations that will enable us to keep ahead of the terrorist.

b. Identifying any hitherto unforeseen gaps in our current equipment holdings and equipment devlopment programme.

c. Identifying areas in which further analysis both of terrorist techniques and of the degree of success of our own countermeasures could usefully be undertaken.

76. We further recommend that this paper should be reviewed and updated annually to provide continuing guidance to interested departments.

2 November 1978
J M G

Sources

Primary sources are used throughout. Chapter I (Introduction: the Roots of Irish Nationalism) relies heavily on: *Irish Historical Documents, 1172–1922* (ed. Edmund Curtis and R.B. McDowell); the four-volume translation of the *Annals of Ulster;* and the six volumes of the *Ancient Laws of Ireland*, produced by the Brehon Law Commission between 1865 and 1901, as well as on the Gaelic poetry and chronicles of the period, Swift's *Drapier's Letters* and Grattan's speeches.

Chapter II (The United Irishmen and Secular Nationalism) is based for its argument on the writings of Theobald Wolfe Tone, 'the father of Irish Republicanism', and the Irish correspondence of Edmund Burke, the revolutionary movement's most notable ideological antagonist and a man who may have had more effect than Tone on the development of Irish nationalism.

Chapter III (The Romantic Nationalism of Young Ireland) uses the writings of Thomas Davis, Charles Gavan Duffy, John Mitchel and James Fintan Lalor; the contemporary journals, *The Nation, The United Irishman* and *The Irish Felon;* the correspondence of William Smith O'Brien; official reports and parliamentary papers.

Chapter IV (The Struggle for an Irish Nation-State) is built upon the correspondence of Karl Marx (and Engels, who often wrote these pieces) in the *New York Daily Tribune* on conditions in Ireland and English reaction to them, and the documents and memoirs of Fenianism and Fenians; reports of the Land League period; Michael Davitt's *The Fall of Feudalism in Ireland;* Gaelic League, Sinn Féin, IRB and Socialist Republican papers in the William O'Brien Collection at the National Library; material on the 1916 Rising, the subsequent resistance to British rule and the Treaty negotiations in 1921. For this last Tom Jones, secretary of the British Cabinet, is an invaluable guide; hence the heavy use of his edited papers, *Whitehall Diary*, vol. iii.

For Chapters V (Republicans Against the Nation-State), VI (The Final Rebellion: Northern Ireland in the 1970s) and VII (Some Conclusions and Solutions), I have used: much unpublished material from the papers of Joseph McGarrity, the Irish-American Clan-na-Gael leader; the letters of Sean Russell (called 'McGarrity Files' here) and papers of John J. Hearn, Westfield, Mass., a leading figure in the American Association for the Recognition of the Irish Republic; IRA files of the 1930s, 1940s, 1950s and 1960s; and numerous personal interviews.

For the last two chapters I have also used the reports of British government commissions on the troubles in Northern Ireland.

1. *Interviews*

A more correct word may be 'conversations'. The persons listed below played important roles in republican activism from 1916 to the present day. Their opinions were sought on matters familiar to them and which, in almost all cases, they knew of at first hand. The names of the individuals involved are recognizable to those familiar with Irish revolutionary activities.

Tom Barry, IRA guerrilla commander 1920–23, Chief of Staff 1937.

Neil Blaney, Fianna Fáil Minister 1950s to 1970.

Kevin Boland, Fianna Fáil Minister 1950s to 1970.

Séamus Brady, journalist.

Liam Burke, Belfast republican leader in 1940s, imprisoned, founder Wolfe Tone Society 1963.

Joseph Cahill, Belfast Provisional IRA commander 1970–71, sentenced to death in 1940s.

Manus Canning, Derry IRA in 1950s, prisoner in England 1953–59.

Joseph Collins, West Cork IRA in 1920s and 1930s, prisoner in England 1939–49.

Máire Comerford, First Dail secretary 1919–21. Republican activist 1919–24 and later.

Seamus Costello, IRA guerrilla organizer in 1950s, leading figure 1963–74, founder IRSP.

Miriam Daly, lecturer in economic history at Queen's University, Belfast, ex-chairman IRSP.

Seán Garland, IRA organizer from 1953, guerrilla commander in 1950s, imprisoned in South and North, Official IRA after split, General Secretary Sinn Féin the Workers' Party.

Cathal Goulding, IRA activist in 1940s, reorganized movement after the war, prisoner in England 1953–60, Chief of Staff from 1962.

George Gilmore, IRA officer 1916–34, founder Republican Congress in 1934.

Charles Harkins, Republican and socialist activist in 1930s.

Roy Johnston, theoretician of republican involvement in civil rights movement.

Tom Kelliher, Cork IRA officer, at Crossbarry and Béal na mBláth ambushes, 1921 and 1922.

John Kelly, Belfast IRA, jailed 1957 to early 1960s, chairman Belfast Citizens' Defence Committee, tried with Charles Haughey and Captain James Kelly for arms smuggling.

Liam Kelly, Co. Tyrone IRA, imprisoned in 1940s, founder of Fianna Uladh and Saor Uladh, Irish Senator in 1950s, led guerrilla movement in North in 1950s.

Con Lehane, IRA in 1930s, lawyer, founder Clann na Poblachta, party leader in Dáil Éireann.

Seán MacBride, aide to Michael Collins in 1921, in Four Courts garrison 1922, GHQ officer of IRA in 1920s and 1930s, Chief of Staff 1936–37, resigned 1938, founder Clann na Poblachta, Minister for External Affairs 1948–51, founder Amnesty International, UN Commissioner for Namibia in 1970s, Nobel and Lenin peace prizes.

Jack McCabe, IRA in 1930s, prisoner in England 1939–49, Provisional IRA leader 1969–71.

Tomas Mac Giolla, IRA in 1950s, President Sinn Féin 1962–70, Official Sinn Féin after 1970.

John Joe McGirl, IRA in 1940s. Sinn Féin TD 1957, Provisional Sinn Féin, interned in Belfast.

Malachy McGurran, IRA guerrilla column in 1950s, Chairman Northern Republican Clubs in late 1960s and 1970s.

Tony Meade, IRA in 1950s, in Belfast prison in 1950s and 1960s, editor *United Irishman* in 1960s.

Ruairí Ó Bradaigh, President Provisional Sinn Féin, TD for Longford-Westmeath 1957–61, IRA leader.

Dáithi (David) O'Connell, IRA guerrilla organizer in 1950s, prisoner in Belfast in 1950s and early 1960s, Provisional IRA leader, on negotiating team in London, July 1972.

Peadar O'Donnell, IRA Executive, in Four Courts garrison 1922, editor *An Phoblacht* in 1920s, chief theoretician of left-wing in IRA, founder Saor Éire and Republican Congress, editor of literary magazine, *The Bell,* in 1940s, novelist.

Seamus (James) O'Donovan, IRA GHQ officer 1919–21, on Seán Russell's staff in 1938–9.

Paul O'Dwyer, Co. Mayo-born New York lawyer and Democratic Party reform wing leader, defender of Irish national rights, headed American League for Undivided Ireland.

J.B. O'Hagan, Lurgan, imprisoned in 1940s, IRA guerrilla leader in 1950s, Provisional IRA.

Seán O'Hegarty, Cork IRA, captured after Omagh raid in 1954, prisoner in Belfast to 1962.

Gerald O'Reilly, IRA Civil War to late 1920s, Clan-na-Gael in New York, Republican Congress, organizer Transport Workers' Union of America.

Michael Ryan, IRA in 1950s campaign, Official IRA in 1970s.

Myles Shevlin, republican lawyer, supported Provisional IRA.

Sam Smith, founder of UDA.

Eamon Timoney, Derry IRA, in 1950s campaign, guerrilla organizer, in Belfast jail. Supplied analysis of key 1918 election won by Sinn Féin (see Appendix III).

Moss Twomey, IRA officer in North Cork in War of Independence and Civil War, Chief of Staff 1926–36, jailed by de Valera 1936–38 and again in 1940, wide knowledge of IRA history.

Sighle Bean Uí Dhonnchadha (née Sheila Humphreys), Cumann na mBan (IRA auxiliary) leader in Civil War and through 1920s, often jailed, signed 'Athlone Manifesto' for Congress in 1934.

Harry White, Belfast IRA, sentenced to death in South in late 1940s, Wolfe Tone Society founder, worked with Jack McCabe in mobilizing aid for North republicans in August 1969.

Bulmer Hobson, IRB leader – correspondence.

2. *Unpublished Material*

Joseph Collins's story of his IRA and prison experiences. Statements on why they joined the IRA by Eamon Timoney, Manus Canning and Sean O'Hegarty. Memoranda and letters from McGarrity Papers in National Library of Ireland; the Seamus O'Donovan Papers in National Library of Ireland; the Hearn and Helena Molony Papers in custody of Maire Comerford; Gerald O'Reilly Papers in New York; some letters of Stephen Hayes – the IRA Chief of Staff (1939–41) charged by his associates with betraying the movement to the de Valera government – also in possession of Maire Comerford. 'An Interim Analysis of the Irish Republican

Movement', April 1967, by Dr. J. Bowyer Bell. The Hoche proclamation of December 1796 in the Wolfe Tone Papers at Trinity College, Dublin. 'General Election 1918: Analysis of Voting' (see Appendix VIII) was drafted by Eamon Timoney while a political prisoner in Belfast Prison in the late 1950s and early 1960s and performs two functions: it is a valuable insight into a key election test as far as voting patterns are concerned and it is also an insight into the mind of an IRA activist then working under the University of London's external study project. Scattered IRA files yielded important documents from many campaigns. Parts of the British army intelligence document 'Northern Ireland: Future Terrorist Trends', 2 November 1978 were leaked to the press, May 1979 (see Appendix XVIII). Free State secret document, 'District Inspector John W. Nixon, MBE', throws important light on some murderous events.

3. *General Histories*

Beckett, J.C., *The Making of Modern Ireland, 1603–1923* (London: 1966).
Curtis, Edmund, *A History of Ireland* (Oxford: 1961).
Dangerfield, George, *The Damnable Question* (Boston: 1976, London: 1977).
Lyons, F.S.L., *Ireland Since the Famine* (London & New York: 1971).
McCaffrey, Lawrence J., *The Irish Question, 1800–1922* (Lexington, Ky.,: 1968).
Macdonagh, Oliver, *Ireland* (Englewood Cliffs, N.J.: 1968).
Moody, T.W., and Martin, F.X. (eds), *The Course of Irish History* (Cork: 1967).

4. *Official Publications*

Government of Ireland Act, 1914, (4 & 5 Geo. 5. Ch. 90).
Government of Ireland Act, 1920.
Articles of Agreement for a Treaty Between Great Britain and Ireland, December 6, 1921.
The Unity of Ireland, partition debated in Seanad Eireann (the Irish Senate), speech by Eamon de Valera, head of government, from Seanad Eireann official records, January 26, 1939, and February 7, 1939 (Dublin: 1939).
Bunreacht na hEireann (Constitution of Ireland), Dublin: 1937.
Commission on the Restoration of the Irish Language: Summary, in English, of the Final Report, Dublin: 1963. also *The Restoration of the Irish Language: Government White Paper,* Dublin: 1965.
Constitution of the Irish Free State, Dublin: 1922.
Dail Eireann. Minutes of Proceedings of the First Parliament of the Republic of Ireland, 1919–21: Official Record, Dublin: 1921.
Dail Eireann. Official Report: Debate on the Treaty Between Great Britain and Ireland Signed in London on the 6th December, 1921, Dublin: 1922.
Dail Eireann. Official Report for the Periods 16–26 August 1921 and 28 February to 8 June 1922, Dublin: 1922.
Disturbances in Northern Ireland: Report of the (Cameron) Commission, Belfast: 1969. Also, *A Commentary by the Government of Northern Ireland to Accompany the Cameron Report,* Belfast: 1969.
Northern Ireland Constitutional Proposals, Presented to Parliament by the Secretary of State for Northern Ireland by Command of Her Majesty March 1973, London: 1973.
Offences Against the State Act, 1939, Dublin: 1939. Also, *Offences Against the State (Amendment) Act, 1940,* Dublin: 1940.
Report of the Tribunal Appointed to Inquire into the Events on Sunday, 30th January 1972, Which led to loss of Life in connection with the procession

in Londonderry on that Day by the Rt. Hon. Lord Widgery, OBE, TD, London: 1972.

Report of the Advisory Committee on Police in Northern Ireland, Belfast: 1969.

Report of the Joint Working Party on the Economy of Northern Ireland, Belfast: 1969.

Report of the Royal Commission on the Rebellion in Ireland, London: 1916.

Report of Working Party, Ireland, British Cabinet Memoranda, 1949, considering what consequential action may have to be taken by the United Kingdom Government as a result of Eire's ceasing to be a member of the Commonwealth; and modifications to working party's proposals, submitted by Prime Minister (CAB 129/32 part I ff 24–32 CP [49] 4 Ireland, and CAB 129/32 part I ff 37–39 CP [49] 5.) London: Public Record Office, Kew, Richmond.

5. *Non-Government Documents/Publications*

Amnesty International *Report of an Enquiry into Allegations of Ill-Treatment in Northern Ireland*, London: 1972.

Bloch *Report of the Independent Public Inquiry into Abuse and Torture of Irish Prisoners*, at Liberty Hall, Dublin, 19–21 May, 1978, chaired by Judge E. Bloch of France.

Critchley (Julian) Report for Bow Group of the Conservative Party, *Ireland: a New Partition*, London: 1972. Also, American Committee for Ulster Justice, *Critique of the Critchley Plan* by Paul O'Dwyer, New York: 1972.

Samuel Dash's *Justice Denied: a Challenge to Lord Widgery's Report on 'Bloody Sunday*, New York: 1972 (The Defence and Education Fund of the International League for the Rights of Man in association with the National Council of Civil Liberties).

Irish Republican Brotherhood, *Constitution as Revised to date, 1920.*

Irish Republican Army, 'Constitution of Oglaigh na hEireann,' March 1932; 'Constitution and Governmental Programme for the Irish Republic', 1934; 'Notes on Guerrilla Warfare', 1956; Chief of Staff's 'Report to General Army Convention', December 1969; *Recommendations on the National Liberation Front, on the Structure of the Movement, on the Relationship of Sinn Féin to the Other Branch of the Movement* (IRA), *on Electoral Policy*, Dublin: 1969; Commission Document No. 2 on 'The Six Counties', and Commission Document No. 3 on 'The Twenty-Six Counties', as amended, January 5, 1969. (These recommendatons and commission reports combined with events in the North, created a split in the Republican Movement.)

Provisional Sinn Féin, *Where Sinn Féin Stands*, Dublin: 1970, gives the opposition's traditionalist viewpoint and details moves that led to split.

Provisional Sinn Féin, *Social and Economic Programme*, Dublin: 1970.

John Hume, leader of SDLP, 'The Irish Question: a British Problem', in *Foreign Affairs*, Winter 1979–80.

Edward M. Kennedy, statement to US House of Representatives Committee on Foreign Affairs, Sub-Committee on Europe, February 28, 1972, *Hearings on Northern Ireland.*

Jack Lynch, Prime Minister of Republic of Ireland, 'The Anglo-Irish Problem', in *Foreign Affairs*, pp. 601–17, July 1972.

Senator George S. McGovern, report to the Committee on Foreign Relations, US Senate, August 1977, *Ireland in 1977.*

NICRA, *Proposals for Peace, Democracy and Community Reconciliation,* Belfast: March 1973.

Report of a Commission of Inquiry appointed to examine the purpose and effect of the Civil Authorities (Special Powers) Acts (Northern Ireland) 1922 & 1933, British National Council of Civil Liberties, London: 1936.

6. *Newspapers and Periodicals*

An Claidheamh Soluis, Gaelic League bi-lingual organ in first decade of century.

An t-Oglach, IRA official organ for internal circulation.

Glor Uladh, 1955–56, organ of Saor Uladh.

Irish Felon, 1848, John Martin publisher, Fintan Lalor editorial writer.

Irish Freedom, IRB monthly organ, 1910–14, Bulmer Hobson editor.

Irish Tribune, 1848, Kevin Izod O'Doherty editor.

Irish Worker, pre-First World War, Jim Larkin and James Connolly editors, organ of Transport Workers Union.

Nation, Young Ireland organ, Gavan Duffy editor, Thomas Davis, chief writer.

Nationality, 1915–17, Arthur Griffith editor.

Northman, 1936, Republican paper circulating in Six Counties.

Poblacht na hÉireann (Republic of Ireland), 1922, Liam Mellows and Erskine Childers editors.

An Phoblacht, maintained erratic existence in 1920s and 1930s, with Peadar O'Donnell, Frank Ryan, Sean MacBride, Donal O'Donoghue and Tadhg Lynch, as successive editors.

An Phoblacht, organ of Provisional IRA/Sinn Féin, from February 1970.

Republican News, Belfast, organ of Provisional IRA, merged with *An Phoblacht* in 1979.

Resistance, occasional publication in 1950s campaign for Northern IRA.

The United Irishman, 1848, John Mitchel editor.

The United Irishman, 1899–1905, Arthur Griffith editor.

The United Irishman, since 1948, monthly organ Sinn Féin/IRA – Officials since 1970 split; ceased publication May of 1980.

The Republic, Belfast, Bulmer Hobson editor, 1905.

Weekly Irish Bulletin, 1919–21. Erskine Childers, Robert Brennan, Frank Gallagher and Desmond FitzGerald editors.

Workers' Republic, 1898–1903, James Connolly editor, organ of Irish Socialist Republican Party.

Workers' Republic, 1915–16, James Connolly editor, successor to *Irish Worker* as the voice of the Irish Transport and General Workers Union in Dublin.

Liberty (Dublin).

Irish Socialist, organ of the Irish Communist Party.

Other newspapers and journals include: *The Times* (London), *Irish Times* (Dublin), *Irish Independent* and *Irish Press* (both Dublin), *Belfast Telegraph, Belfast Newsletter, Cork Examiner, Derry Journal, The Kerryman* (Tralee), *Hibernia* (Dublin), *Guardian* (formerly *Manchester Guardian), New Statesman and Nation, The Leader* (Dublin), *Inniu* (Dublin), *Comhar* (Dublin), *Capuchin Annual* (Dublin). Also, *New York Times, New York Daily News, Washington Post, Eire-Ireland* (St. Paul), *America, Nation, Gaelic American, Irish World, Irish Echo, Irish Advocate, Irish People, Commonweal, New Republic, Economist*

(London), *Time, Newsweek, World View, Observer* (London), *Sunday Times* (London), *Sunday Telegraph, Newark Evening News.*

Select Bibliography

Chapter I: Introductory Survey

Bagwell, Richard, *Ireland Under the Tudors* 3 vols, (London: 1885–90).
— *Ireland Under the Stuarts* 3 vols, (London: 1909–16).
Bernard, T.C., *Cromwellian Ireland: English Government and Reform in Ireland, 1649–60* (Oxford: 1975).
Blacam, Aodh de, *Gaelic Literature Surveyed* (Dublin: n.d.) Subjective look at Gaelic poetry and prose through Middle Ages and penal times.
Bottigheimer, K.S., *English Money and Irish Land* (Oxford: 1971).
Bloch, Marc, *Feudal Society*, vol. i, *The Growth of Ties of Dependence*, (London & Chicago: 1961).
Breathnach, Michael (ed), *Fion na Filidheachta* (Dublin: n.d.) Collected poems from Gaelic Ireland.
Brinton, Crane, *The Anatomy of Revolution* (New York: 1968).
Burke, W.P., *Irish Priests in the Penal Times, 1660–1760* (Shannon, Ireland: 1969).
Carew, Sir George, *Pacata Hibernia*, vols 1 and 2, Standish O'Grady (London: 1886).
Coonan, Thomas L., *The Irish Catholic Confederacy and the Puritan Revolution* (New York: 1954).
Corkery, Daniel, *The Hidden Ireland: a Study of Gaelic Munster in the Eighteenth Century* (Dublin: 1941).
Cullen, L.M., *An Economic History of Ireland Since 1660* (London & New York: 1972).
Curtis, Edmund, and McDowell, R.B., *Irish Historical Documents 1172–1922* (London: 1968).
Curtis, Edmund, *A History of Medieval Ireland* (London: 1938).
Dunlop, R.T., *Ireland Under the Commonwealth* (Manchester: 1913).
Edwards, R. Dudley, *Church and State in Tudor Ireland* (Dublin: 1935).
Farrell, Brian (ed), *The Irish Parliamentary Tradition* (Dublin: 1973).
Flower, Robin, *The Irish Tradition* (Oxford: 1947).
Green, Alice Stopford, *The Making of Ireland and Its Undoing, 1200–1600* (London: 1909).
— *History of the Irish State to 1100* (London: 1925).
Haberman, Jurgen, *Theory and Practice* (Boston: 1971).
Harris, Nigel, *Beliefs in Society* (London: 1971).
Henry, Francoise, *Irish Art in the Early Christian Period* (Dublin: 1954, Cornell UP, Ithaca, NY: 1965).

Hechter, Michael, *Internal Colonialism: the Celtic Fringe in British National Development, 1536–1966* (Berkeley, Cal.: 1975, London: 1978).
Hill, Christopher, *The Century of Revolution, 1603–1714* (London: 1961).
— *God's Englishman: Oliver Cromwell and the English Revolution* (London & New York: 1970).
Kinsella, Thomas, *The Tain* (Oxford: 1970). Translation of the pre-Christian Ulster epic.
Knorr, Klaus E., *British Colonial Theories, 1570–1850* (Toronto: 1944, London: 1963).
Kohn, Hans, *The Idea of Nationalism* (New York: 1946).
Lacey, Robert, *Robert, Earl of Essex* (London & New York: 1971).
— *Sir Walter Raleigh* (New York: 1973).
Lehane, Brendan, *The Quest of Three Abbots* (New York: 1968), (London: 1969).
Lichtheim, George, *The Concept of Ideology and Other Essays* (New York: 1967).
Locke, John, *A Letter Concerning Toleration* (Indianapolis: 1965).
Lydon, J.F., *The Lordship of Ireland in the Middle Ages* (Dublin & Toronto: 1972).
MacCurtain, Margaret, *Tudor and Stuart Ireland* (Dublin: 1972).
MacLysaght, Edward, *Irish Life in the Seventeenth Century: after Cromwell* (Cork: 1950).
MacNeill, Eoin, *Celtic Ireland* (Dublin: 1921).
Mannheim, Karl, *Ideology and Utopia: an Introduction to the Sociology of Knowledge* (New York: 1955; London: 1960).
Marx, Karl, *The German Ideology* (London: 1970).
Molyneux, William, *The Case of Ireland Stated*, reprinted from the first edition of 1698 with an introduction by J.C. Simms (Dublin: 1977).
Moody, T.W., *The Londonderry Plantation, 1609–41: the City of London and the Plantation in Ulster* (Belfast: 1939).
Morgenthau, Hans, *Politics Among Nations* 5th edn, (New York: 1973).
— *Politics in the Twentieth Century*, vol. iii, *The Restoration of American Politics* (Chicago: 1958, London: 1962).
Nicholls, Kenneth, *Gaelic and Gaelicised Ireland in the Middle Ages* (Dublin: 1972).
O'Connor, Frank, *A Short History of Irish Literature* (New York: 1967).
Orpen, G.H., *Ireland Under the Normans* (Oxford: 1911).
Sir Charles Petrie, *The Great Tyrconnel: A Chapter in Anglo-Irish Relations* (Cork: 1972).
Petty, William, *The Political Anatomy of Ireland* (Dublin: 1691). Reprint, Shannon, 1970.
Simms, J.G., *The Williamite Confiscation in Ireland, 1690–1703* (London: 1956). (London: 1956).
— *Jacobite Ireland, 1685–91* (London & Toronto: 1969).
Spenser, Edmund, *A View of the Present State of Ireland*, ed. W.L. Renwick (Oxford: 1970).
Story, George, *An Impartial History of the Affairs of Ireland During the Last Two Years . . . Written by an Eye-Witness to the Most Remarkable Passages* (London: 1691).
— *A Continuation of the Impartial History of the Wars of Ireland* (London: 1693). Story was a chaplain in the Williamite army.
Strauss, Eric, *Irish Nationalism and British Democracy* (London & New

York: 1951).
Swift, Jonathan, *Selected Prose Works of Jonathan Swift,* ed. John Hayward (London: 1934). Includes extracts from *Irish Tracts: A Proposal for the Universal Use of Irish Manufacture* (1720); *A Letter to the Shop-Keepers, Tradesmen, Farmers and Common-People of Ireland Concerning the Brass Half-Pence Coined by One William Wood...* (1724); *A Full and True Account of the Solemn Procession to the Gallows at the Execution of William Wood Esquire and Hard-Ware Man* (1724); *An Answer to . . . A Memorial . . .* (1728); *A Modest Proposal for Preventing the Children of poor People in Ireland, from Being a Burden to their Parents or Country; and for making them beneficial to the Public* (1729).
Walker, George, *A True Account of the Siege of London-Derry* (London: 1887).
Watt, John, *The Church in Medieval Ireland* (Dublin: 1972).
Weber, Max, *The Protestant Ethic and the Spirit of Capitalism* (New York: 1958, London: 1967).
Williams, Eric, *Capitalism and Slavery* (New York: 1966).

Chapter II: The United Irishmen and Secular Nationalism

Barrington, Sir Jonah, *Rise and Fall of the Irish Nation* (Dublin: 1833).
Bolton, G.C. *The Passing of the Irish Act of Union* (Oxford: 1966).
Brown, P.A., *The French Revolution in English History* (London 1918).
Burke, Edmund, *Reflections on the Revolution in France* ed. C.C. O'Brien (London: 1968).
Byrne, Miles, *Memoirs* (Dublin: 1906).
Cone, Carl B., *The English Jacobins* (New York: 1968).
Cronin, Seán, *Jemmy Hope: a Man of the People* (Dublin 1964).
Cronin, Seán, and Roche, Richard (eds), *Freedom the Wolfe Tone Way* (Tralee: 1973). Anthology of Tone's writings, including his more obscure pamphlets.
Dickson, Charles, *The Life of Michael Dwyer* (Dublin: 1944).
— *The Wexford Rising in 1798 – its Causes and its Course* (Tralee: 1955).
— *Revolt in the North: Antrim and Down in 1798* (Dublin: 1960).
Drennan, William, *A Letter to His Excellency Earl Fitzwilliam, Lord Lieutenant* (Dublin: 1795). *The Drennan Letters . . . 1776–1819* ed. D.A. Chart (Belfast 1931).
Grattan, Henry, *Speeches of the Rt. Hon. Henry Grattan* 4 vols, (London: 1844).
Hobson, Bulmer (ed), *The Letters of Wolfe Tone* (Dublin: n.d.).
Ireland, Denis, *Patriot Adventurer, Extracts from the Memoirs and Journals of Theobald Wolfe Tone* (London: 1936).
Jacob, Rosamond, *The Rise of the United Irishmen, 1791–94* (London: 1937).
Landreth, Helen, *The Pursuit of Robert Emmet* (New York: 1948, Dublin: 1949).
Lecky, W.E.H., *History of Ireland in the Eighteenth Century,* 5 vols, (London: 1913).
Lefebre, Georges, *The French Revolution,* transl. Elizabeth M. Evanson (New York: 1962, London: 1969).
— *The Directory,* transl. Robert Baldick (New York: 1964, London: 1965).
— *The Thermidorians,* transl. Robert Baldick (London: 1965, New York: 1966).
Locke, John, *The Second Treatise of Government* (Indianapolis: 1952).

Madden, R.R., *The United Irishmen: their Lives and Times*, 4 vols, (London: 1842–46).
— *Antrim and Down in '98* (Dublin: n.d.).
— *Life and Times of Robert Emmet* (Dublin: n.d.).
McCabe, Leo, *Wolfe Tone and the United Irishmen* (London: 1937).
MacDermot, Frank, *Theobald Wolfe Tone* (Tralee: 1968).
Mahoney, T.H.D., *Edmund Burke and Ireland (London:* 1960).
McDowell, R.B., *Irish Public Opinion, 1750–1800* (London: 1944).
McNeill, Mary, *The Life and Times of Mary Ann McCracken (1770–1866): a Belfast Panorama* (Dublin: 1960).
McNeven, William James, *Pieces of Irish History* (New York: 1807).
Marshall, P.J., and Woods, F.A., *The Correspondence of Edmund Burke* (Cambridge: 1968).
Maxwell, Constantia, *Dublin Under the Georges, 1714–1830* (London: 1937).
Mitchel, John, *The History of Ireland – A Continuation of the History of the Abbe MacGeoghegan* (Glasgow & London: n.d.).
O Broin, Leon, *The Unfortunate Mr. Robert Emmet* (Dublin: 1958).
O'Brien, George, *The Economic History of Ireland in the 18th Century* (Dublin: 1918).
O'Connor, Arthur, *State of Ireland* (London: 1802).
Paine, Thomas, *Rights of Man* in *Basic Writings of Thomas Paine* (New York: 1942).
Pakenham, Thomas, *The Year of Liberty: the Bloody Story of the Great Irish Rebellion of 1798* (London: 1969, New York: 1972).
Smith, Adam, *Wealth of Nations*, 2 vols, (New York: 1910).
Life of Wolfe Tone, edited by his son, William Theobald Wolfe Tone, 2 vols, (Washington: 1826).
Tone, Theobald Wolfe, *Autobiography of Theobald Wolfe Tone*, ed & intro. by R.Barry O'Brien, 2 vols, (Dublin: 1893).
Toynbee, Arnold, *The Industrial Revolution* (London: 1884, Boston: 1956).

Chapter III: The Romantic Nationalism of Young Ireland

Atkinson, Norman, *Irish Education: a History of Educational Institutions* (Dublin: 1969).
Barrow, G.C., *The Emergence of the Irish Banking System, 1820–45* (Dublin: 1975).
Beaumont, Gustave de, *L'Irlande* (Paris: 1863).
Berlin, Isaiah, *Vico and Herder: two Studies in the History of Ideas* (New York: 1977).
Connolly, James, *Labour in Irish History* (Dublin: 1910).
Davis, Thomas, *National and Historical Ballads, Songs and Poems* (Dublin: 1845).
— *Essays and Poems* (Dublin: 1945).
Doheny, Michael, *The Felon's Track* (London & New York: 1867).
Donnelly, James S. Jr., *The Land and the People of Nineteenth-Century Cork* (London: 1975).
Duffy, Charles Gavan, *Young Ireland 1840–45* 2 vols, (London: 1896).
Fogarty, L., *Father John Kenyon: a Patriot Priest of '48* (Dublin: n.d.).
— *James Fintan Lalor: Patriot and Political Essayist, 1807–49* (Dublin: 1918).
Freeman, T.W., *Pre-Famine Ireland* (Manchester: 1957).

Gibson, Florence, *The Attitudes of the New York Irish Toward State and National Affairs, 1848–1892* (New York: 1951).
Griffith, Arthur (ed), *Thomas Davis, the Thinker and Teacher* (Dublin: 1914).
Gwynn, Denis, *Young Ireland and 1848* (Cork: 1947).
— *Daniel O'Connell* (Cork: 1947).
— *Thomas Francis Meagher* (Dublin: 1961).
Hobsbawm, E.J., *The Age of Revolution, 1789–1848* (New York: 1964, London: 1965).
Kane, Robert, *The Industrial Resources of Ireland* (Dublin: 1844).
Inglis, Brian, *The Freedom of the Press in Ireland, 1784–1841* (London: 1954).
Macintyre, Angus, *The Liberator: Daniel O'Connell and the Irish Party, 1830–1847* (London & New York: 1965).
Mansergh, Nicholas, *The Irish Question, 1840–1921* (London: 1969).
Marcus, Steven, *Engels, Manchester and the Working Class* (New York: 1974).
Mitchel, John *An Apology for British Government in Ireland* (Dublin: 1905).
— *Jail Journal* (Dublin: 1913).
— *The Last Conquest of Ireland – Perhaps* (London, Manchester & Glasgow: n.d.).
Marx, Karl, and Engels, Frederick, *The Revolution of 1848–49* (New York: 1972). Articles from the *Neue Rheinische Zeitung.*
Nowlan, Kevin B., *Charles Gavan Duffy and the Repeal Movement* (Dublin: 1963).
— *The Politics of Repeal, 1841–50* (London: 1965).
O Neill, Tomas, *Fiontan O Leathlobhair* (Dublin: 1962).
O Tuathaigh, Gearoid, *Ireland Before the Famine, 1798–1848* (Dublin: 1972).
Renan, Ernest, *The Poetry of the Celtic Races, and Other Studies* (London: 1896).
Smith, Cecil Woodham, *The Great Hunger: Ireland 1845–49* (London: 1962).
Tocqueville, Alexis de, *Journeys to England and Ireland* ed. J.P. Mayer, (London: 1958, New York: 1968).
Ward, J.T., *Chartism* (London: 1973).
Whitridge, Arnold, *Men in Crisis: the Revolutions of 1848* (New York: 1949).
Williams, T. Desmond, and Edwards, R. Dudley, *The Great Famine* (Dublin: 1956).

Chapter IV: The Struggle for an Irish Nation-State

Barry, Tom, *Guerrilla Days in Ireland* (Tralee: 1962).
Beach, Thomas M., *Twenty-Five Years in the Secret Service* (London: 1893).
Beaslai, Piaras, *Michael Collins and the Making of a New Ireland,* 2 vols, (Dublin: 1926).
Beaverbrook, Lord, *Politicians and the Press* (London: 1925).
— *The Decline and Fall of Lloyd George* (London: 1963).
Bennett, Richard, *The Black and Tans* (London: 1959).
Bourke, Marcus, *John O'Leary: a Study in Irish Separatism* (Tralee: 1967).
— *The O'Rahilly* (Tralee: 1967).
Boyce, D.G., *Englishmen and Irish Troubles: British Public Opinion and the Making of Irish Policy, 1918–22* (Cambridge, Mass.,: 1972).
Boyd, Andrew, *Holy War in Belfast* (Tralee: 1969).
Buckland, Patrick, *Irish Unionism* 2 vols, (Dublin: 1972–3).

Brennan, Robert, *Allegiance* (Dublin: 1950).
Brown, Malcolm, *The Politics of Irish Literature: from Thomas Davis to W.B. Yeats* (London & Seattle: 1972).
Cashman, D.B., *The Life of Michael Davitt and the Secret History of the Land League* (London: n.d.).
Christie, Ian R. (ed), *Essays in Modern History Selected from the Transactions of the Royal Historical Society on the Occasion of its Centenary* (London: 1968).
Churchill, Winston S., *The World Crisis*, vol v, *The Aftermath: a Sequel to the World Crisis* (London: 1929, New York: 1941).
— *His Complete Speeches 1897–1963*, ed. Robert Rhodes James, 8 vols, (London: 1974).
Clarke, Thomas, *Glimpses of an Irish Felon's Prison Life* (Dublin: 1922).
Clarkson, J.D., *Labor and Nationalism in Ireland* (New York: 1925).
Coffey, Thomas M., *Agony at Easter: the 1916 Irish Uprising* (New York: 1969).
Collins, Michael, *The Path to Freedom* (Cork: 1968).
Colum, Padraic, *Arthur Griffith* (Dublin: 1959).
Comerford, Maire, *The First Dail* (Dublin: 1969).
Connolly, James, *Labour, Nationality and Religion* (Dublin: 1910).
— *Reconquest of Ireland* (Dublin: 1915).
— *Socialism and Nationalism* intro. notes Desmond Ryan, (Dublin: 1948).
— *Labour and Easter Week* intro. William O'Brien, (Dublin: 1949).
— *The Workers' Republic* intro. William McMullen, (Dublin: 1951).
Crawford, R. Lindsay, and Braithwaite, R., *Orangeism: its History and Progress* (Dublin: 1904).
Cronin, Sean, *Kevin Barry* (Cork: 1965).
— *Our Own Red Blood* (Dublin: 1966).
— *The Revolutionaries* (Dublin: 1971).
— *The McGarrity Papers* (Tralee: 1972).
— *Young Connolly* (Dublin: 1978).
Cullen, Paul Cardinal, *The Pastoral Letters and Other Writings of Cardinal Cullen, Archbishop of Dublin*, ed. Bishop Patrick Moran, 3 vols, (Dublin: 1882).
D'Arcy, Rev. William OFM Conv., *The Fenian Movement in the United States, 1858–1886* (Washington: 1947).
Davis, Norman B., *Nationalism and Socialism: Marxist and Labor Theories of Nationalism to 1917* (New York: 1967).
Davis, Richard, *Arthur Griffith and Non-Violent Sinn Fein* (Dublin: 1974).
Davitt, Michael, *The Fall of Feudalism in Ireland* (London & New York: 1904).
Denieffe, Joseph, *A Personal Narrative of the Irish Revolutionary Brotherhood* (New York: 1906).
Devoy, John, *Recollections of an Irish Rebel* (New York: 1929, Shannon: 1969).
Post Bag ed. William O'Brien and Desmond Ryan, 2 vols, (Dublin: 1948–53 & 1979).
Edwards, Owen Dudley, and Pyle, Fergus, *1916: the Easter Rising* (London: 1968).
Edwards, Ruth Dudley, *Patrick Pearse the Triumph of Failure* (London: 1977).
Ellmann, Richard, *Selected Joyce Letters* (London & New York: 1975).
Ervine, St John, *Craigavon* (London: 1949).
Farrell, Brian, *The Founding of Dail Eireann – Parliament and Nation-Building* (Dublin: 1971).
Fitzpatrick, David, *Politics and Irish Life: Provincial Experience of War and Revolution* (Dublin: 1977).

Forester, Margery, *Michael Collins – the Lost Leader* (London: 1971).
Fox, R.M., *James Connolly, the Forerunner* (Tralee: 1946).
Gaughan, J. Anthony, *Austin Stack: Portrait of a Separatist* (Dublin: 1977).
Glynn, Anthony, *High Upon the Gallows Tree: the Story of the Manchester Fenian Rescue of 1867 and of Allen, Larkin and O'Brien* (Tralee: 1967).
Greaves, C. Desmond, *Life and Times of James Connolly* (London: 1961).
— *Liam Mellows and the Irish Revolution* (London: 1971).
Griffith, Arthur, *The Resurrection of Hungary* (Dublin: 1904).
Gwynn, Denis, *The Life and Death of Roger Casement* (London: 1931).
— *The Life of John Redmond* (London: 1932).
Handlin, Oscar, *Boston's Immigrants: a Study in Acculturation* (Cambridge, Mass.: 1959).
Harmon, Maurice (ed), *Fenians and Fenianism* (Dublin: 1968 & Seattle: 1970).
Henry, R.M. *The Evolution of Sinn Féin* (Dublin: 1920).
Hobson, Bulmer, *The Creed of the Republic* (Belfast: 1907).
— *Ireland: Yesterday and Tomorrow* (Tralee: 1968).
Holt, Edgar, *Protest in Arms: the Irish Troubles, 1916–23* (London: 1960).
Hone, Joseph, *W.B. Yeats*(London: 1943).
Hurst, Michael, *Parnell and Irish Nationalism* (London: 1968).
Hyde, H. Montgomery, *Carson* (London: 1953).
Inglis, Brian, *Roger Casement* (London: 1973).
Jenkins, Brian, *Fenians and Anglo-American Relations During Reconstruction* (London: 1969).
Jones, Thomas, *Whitehall Diary:* vol. iii, *Ireland 1918–1925*, ed. Keith Middlemas, (London: 1971).
Larkin, Emmet, *James Larkin: Irish Labour Leader, 1876–1947* (London: 1965).
— *The Roman Catholic Church and the Creation of the Modern Irish State, 1878–1886* (Dublin: 1975).
Lee, Joseph, *The Modernization of Irish Society, 1848–1918* (Dublin: 1973).
Lynch, Diarmuid, *The IRB and the 1916 Rising*, ed. Florence O'Donoghue, (Cork: 1957).
Lyons, F.S.L., *John Dillon* (London: 1968).
— *Charles Stewart Parnell* (London: 1977).
Lysaght, D.R. O'Connor, *The Republic of Ireland* (Cork: 1970).
Mac an Bheatha, Proinsias, *Tart na Córa*, Séamas O Conghaille a Shad agus a Shaothar (Dublin: n.d.).
Macardle, Dorothy, *The Irish Republic* (Dublin: 1951).
Martin, F.X. (ed), *The Irish Volunteers, 1913–1915* (Dublin: 1963).
— *Leaders and Men of the Easter Rising* (London & New York: 1967).
Martin, F.X., and Byrne, F.J., (eds), *The Scholar Revolutionary: Eoin MacNeill, 1867–1945*, and *The Making of the New Ireland* (Shannon & New York: 1973).
Marx, Karl, and Engels, Frederick, *Ireland and the Irish Question*, ed. L.I. Golman, (Moscow: 1971).
McCartan, Patrick, *With De Valera in America* (Dublin: 1932).
McCay, Hedley, *Pádraic Pearse: a New Biography* (Cork: 1966).
McDowell, R.B., *Alice Stopford Greene: a Passionate Historian* (Dublin: 1967).
— *The Irish Convention 1917–18* (London: 1970).
MacGiolla Choille, Brendan (ed), *Intelligence Notes, 1913–16* (Dublin: 1966).
McHugh, Roger, *Dublin 1916* (London & New York: 1966).
MacSwiney, Terence, *Principles of Freedom*, 3rd ed., (Dublin: 1936).

Miller, David, *Church, State and Nation in Ireland, 1898–1921* (Dublin: 1973).
— *Queen's Rebels* (Dublin: 1978).
Moody, T.W., *The Fenian Movement* (Cork: 1968).
Norman, E.R., *The Catholic Church and Ireland in the Age of Rebellion, 1859–1873* (London: 1965).
Nowlan, Kevin B. (ed), *The Making of 1916: Studies in the History of the Rising* (London: 1969).
O'Brien, Conor Cruise, *Parnell and His Party, 1880–90* (Oxford: 1957).
— (ed), *The Shaping of Modern Ireland* (London: 1960).
O Broin, Leon, *The Chief Secretary Augustine Birrell in Ireland* (London: 1969).
— *Dublin Castle and the Easter Rising* (Dublin: 1966, New York: 1971).
— *Fenian Fever: an Anglo-American Dilemma* (London: 1971).
— *Revolutionary Underground : the Story of the Irish Republican Brotherhood, 1858–1924* (Dublin: 1976).
O'Casey, Sean, (*as P. O Cathasaigh*), *The Story of the Irish Citizen Army* (Dublin: 1919).
— *Pictures in the Hallway* (London & New York: 1942).
— *Drums Under the Windows* (London: 1945, New York: 1947).
O'Connor, Frank, *Michael Collins and the Irish Revolution* (Dublin: 1965).
O'Connor, T.P., *Memoirs of an Old Parliamentarian*, 2 vols, (London & New York: 1929).
O'Donnell, Frank H., *A History of the Irish Parliamentary Party*, 2 vols, (London: 1910).
O'Donovan, Jeremiah (Rossa), *My Years in English Jails*, ed. Sean Ua Cearnaigh, (Tralee: 1967).
O'Faolain, Sean, *Constance Markievicz or the Average Revolutionary* (London: 1934).
— *Vive Moi! An Autobiography* (Boston: 1963, London: 1965)
O'Farrell, Patrick, *Ireland's English Question* (London: 1971).
— *England and Ireland Since 1800* (Oxford: 1975).
O'Hegarty, P.S., *Sinn Féin: an Illumination* (Dublin: 1919).
— *Ulster: a Brief Statement of Fact* (Dublin: 1919).
— *The Victory of Sinn Féin* (Dublin: 1924).
O'Leary, John, *Recollections of Fenians and Fenianism*, 2 vols, (London: 1896).
O Luing, Sean, *Art O Griofa* (Dublin: 1953). Biography in Irish of Arthur Griffith.
— *Freemantle Mission: the Dramatic Story of a Daring Fenian Rescue* (Tralee: 1965).
O'Malley, Ernie, *On Another Man's Wound* (London: 1936).
O Snodaigh, Padraig, *Comhghuaillithe na Reabhlóide 1913–16* (Dublin: 1966).
Pakenham, Frank (Lord Longford), *Peace by Ordeal* (London: 1935). The Treaty negotiations.
— and O'Neill, T.P., *Eamon de Valera* (London: 1970, Boston: 1971).
Paul-Dubois, L., *Contemporary Ireland* (Dublin: 1908).
Ryan, A.P., *Mutiny at the Curragh* (London: 1956).
Ryan, Desmond, *The Phoenix Flame* (London: 1937).
— *Sean Treacy and the Third Tipperary Brigade IRA* (Tralee: 1945).
— *The Fenian Chief: a Biography of James Stephens* (Dublin: 1967).
— *The Rising* (Dublin: 1969).
Ryan, Mark F., *Fenian Memories* (Dublin: 1946).

Ryan, W.P., *The Pope's Green Island* (London: 1912).
Schrier, Arnold, *Ireland and the American Emigration, 1850–1900* (New York: 1958).
Scott, C.P., *The Political Diaries of C.P. Scott, 1911–1928* (London: 1970).
Shaw, G. Bernard, *How to Settle the Irish Question* (Dublin & London: 1917).
— *The Matter with Ireland*, ed. Dan H. Laurence and David H. Greene, (London & New York: 1962).
Sheehy-Skeffington, Frank, *Michael Davitt: Revolutionary Agitator and Labour Leader* (London: 1967).
Short, K.R.M., *The Dynamite War: Irish-American Bombers in Victorian Britain* (Dublin: 1979).
Skidelsky, Robert, *Oswald Mosley* (London & New York: 1975).
Stephens, James, *The Insurrection in Dublin* (London: 1978).
Stewart, A.T.Q., *The Ulster Crisis* (London: 1967).
Tansill, Charles Callan, *America and the Fight for Irish Freedom* (New York: 1957).
Taylor, Rex, *Michael Collins* (London: 1958).
Thompson, William Irwin, *The Imagination of an Insurrection, Dublin Easter 1916: a Study of an Ideological Movement* (Oxford & New York: 1967).
Thornley, David A., *Isaac Butt and Home Rule* (London: 1964).
Townshend, Charles, *The British Campaign in Ireland 1919–21: the Development of Political and Military Policies* (Oxford: 1975).
Tynan, P.J.P., *The Irish National Invincibles* (London: 1894).
Van Voris, Jacqueline, *Constance Markievicz: in the Cause of Ireland* (Amherst: 1967).
Ward, Alan J., *Ireland and Anglo-American Relations, 1899–1921* (London: 1969).
Williams, G. Desmond, (ed), *The Irish Struggle, 1916–26* (London: 1966).
— *Secret Societies in Ireland* (Dublin: 1973).
Wilson, Thomas (ed), *Ulster Under Home Rule* (Oxford: 1955).
Wright, Arnold, *Disturbed Dublin: the Story of the Great Strike of 1913–14* (London: 1914).

Chapter V: Republicans Against the Nation-State

Ayearst, Morley, *The Republic of Ireland: Its Government and Politics* (New York: 1970, London: 1971).
Barker, A.J., *Bloody Ulster* (London: 1973).
Bell, J. Bowyer, *The Secret Army: the IRA, 1916–1979* (Dublin & Boston: 1980).
Boyle, Andrew, *The Riddle of Erskine Childers* (London: 1977).
Blanshard, Paul, *The Irish and Catholic Power* (Boston: 1953, London: 1954).
Bretherton, C.H., *The Real Ireland* (London: 1925).
Bromage, Mary C., *De Valera and the March of a Nation* (London: 1956).
Carter, Carrolle J., *The Shamrock and the Swastika* (Palo Alto: 1977).
Carroll, Joseph T., *Ireland in the War Years, 1939–45* (Newton Abbot: 1974, New York: 1975).
Carson, William A., *Ulster and the Irish Republic* (Belfast: 1956). Has an

introduction by David A. Gray, US minister to Dublin during the Second World War.
Collins, Joseph: Manuscript of his IRA and prison experiences (copy in possession of Seán Cronin).
Coogan, Tim Pat, *Ireland Since the Rising* (London: 1966).
— *The IRA* (London: 1970).
Cordoza, Nancy, *Lucky Eyes and a High Heart: the life of Maud Gonne* (New York: 1978).
Cox, Tom, *Damned Englishman* (New York: 1975) a bibliography of Erskine Childers.
Cronin, Sean, *They Kept Faith* (Dublin: 1957).
— *Resistance: the Story of the Struggle in British-Occupied Ireland* (Dublin: 1957).
— *Ireland Since the Treaty* (Dublin: 1971).
Dwyer, T. Ryle, *Irish Neutrality and the USA, 1939–47* (Dublin: 1977).
Fairfield, Letitia, *The Trial of Peter Barnes and Others: the IRA Coventry Explosion of 1939* (London: 1953).
Freyer, Grattan, *Peadar O'Donnell* (Lewisburg, Pa.: 1973).
Gilmore, George, *Labour and the Republican Movement* (Dublin: 1966).
— *Republican Congress* (Dublin: 1969).
Gwynn, Denis, *The History of Partition, 1912–1925* (Dublin: 1950).
— *The Irish Free State 1922–7* (London: 1928).
Hand, Geoffrey (intro), *Report of the Irish Boundary Commission* (Shannon: 1969).
Harkness, D.W., *The Restless Dominion* (London: 1969, New York: 1970).
Kelly, J.M., *Fundamental Rights in the Irish Law and Constitution* (Dublin: 1967, New York: 1968).
Kohn, Leo, *The Constitution of the Irish Free State* (London: 1932).
Macardle, Dorothy, *Tragedies of Kerry* (Dublin: 1924).
McInerney, Michael, *Peadar O'Donnell: Irish Social Rebel* (Dublin: 1974).
MacManus, Francis (ed), *The Years of the Great Test, 1926–1939* (Cork: 1967).
Mansergh, Nicholas, *The Irish Free State: its Government and Politics* (London: 1934).
Manning, Maurice, *The Blueshirts* (Dublin: 1970).
— *Irish Political Parties: an Introduction* (Dublin: 1972).
Murphy, John A., *Ireland in the Twentieth Century* (Dublin: 1975).
Neeson, Eoin, *The Civil War in Ireland, 1922–23* (Cork: 1967).
O'Donnell, Peadar, *The Gates Flew Open* (London: 1932).
— *Salud! An Irishman in Spain* (London: 1937).
— *There Will be Another Day* (Dublin: 1963).
O'Flaherty, Liam, *The Life of Tim Healy* (London: 1927).
O'Higgins, Brian, *Tony D'Arcy and Sean MacNeela: the Story of Their Martyrdom* (Dublin: 1940).
— *Wolfe Tone Annual* (Dublin: 1945).
— *Wolfe Tone Annual* (Dublin: 1955).
— *Wolfe Tone Annual* (Dublin: 1961).
O'Malley, Ernie, *The Singing Flame* (Dublin: 1978).
O'Sullivan, Donal, *The Irish Free State and Its Senate* (London: 1940).
Rumpf, E., and Hepburn, A.C., *Nationalism and Socialism in Twentieth-Century Ireland* (Liverpool: 1977).

Sheehy, Michael, *Is Ireland Dying?: Culture and the Church in Modern Ireland* (London & New York: 1968).
Tobin, Liam, *The Truth About the Army Crisis* (Dublin: 1924).
White, Terence de Vere, *A Fretful Midge* (London: 1957).
— *Kevin O'Higgins* (Tralee: 1966).
Whyte, J.H., *Church and State in Modern Ireland* (Dublin: 1971).
Younger, Calton, *Ireland's Civil War* (London: 1968).

Chapter VI: The Final Rebellion: Northern Ireland in the 1970s

Barrit, Denis P., and Carter, Charles F., *The Northern Ireland Problem: a Study in Group Relations* (Oxford: 1972).
Bennett, Jack, *Northern Ireland: Fourteen Days of Fascist Terror* (Ripley, Derby: 1974).
Boland Kevin, *"We Won't Stand (Idly) By,"* (Dublin: 1973).
— *Up Dev!* (Dublin: 1978).
Boyd, Andrew, *Brian Faulkner and the Crisis of Ulster Unionism* (Tralee: 1972).
Boyle, T., Hadden, T. and Hillyard, P., *Law and State: the Case of Northern Ireland* (London & Amherst: 1975).
Brady, Seamus, *Arms and the Men: Ireland in Turmoil* (Wicklow: 1971).
Budge, Ian and O'Leary, Cornelius, *Belfast: Approach to Crisis* (London & New York: 1973).
Busteed, M.A., *Northern Ireland* (London: 1974).
Callaghan, James, *A House Divided: the Dilemma of Northern Ireland* (London: 1973).
Clark, Wallace, *Guns in Ulster* (Belfast: 1967).
Coogan, Tim Pat, *On the Blanket, The H-Block Story* (Dublin: 1980).
Cronin, Sean, *The Rights of Man in Ireland* (Dublin: 1969). Updating and revision of paper originally delivered in November 1964.
Crozier, Brian and Moss, Robert, *The Ulster Debate* (London: 1972). Report of Institute for the Study of Conflict.
Dash, Samuel, *Justice Denied: a Challenge to Lord Widgery's Report on 'Bloody Sunday'* (London & New York: 1972).
De Paor, Liam, *Divided Ulster* (London: 1970).
Devlin, Bernadette, *The Price of My Soul* (London & New York: 1969).
Dillon, Martin and Lehane, Denis, *Political Murder in Northern Ireland* (London: 1973).
Edwards, Owen Dudley, *The Sins of Our Fathers: Roots of Conflict in N.I.* (Dublin: 1970).
Farrell, Michael, *Northern Ireland, the Orange State* (London: 1976).
Faul, Denis, Brady, Brian and Murray, R., *British Army and Special Branch RUC Brutalities* (Cavan: 1972).
— *The Hooded Men: British Torture in Ireland* (Dungannon: 1974).
— *The Flames of Long Kesh* (Dungannon: 1974).
Faulkner, Brian, *Memoirs of a Statesman*, ed. John Houston (London: 1978).
Fields, Rona M., *A Society on the Run: a Psychology of Northern Ireland* (London: 1973).
Gallagher, Frank, *The Indivisible Island: the Story of Partition* (London: 1957).

Gray, Tony, *The Orange Order* (London: 1972).
Greaves, C. Desmond, *The Irish Question and the British People: a plea for a new approach* (Ripley, Derby: 1963).
Harbison, John F., *The Ulster Unionist Party, 1882–1973* (Belfast: 1973).
Hastings, Max, *Ulster 1969: the Fight for Civil Rights in Northern Ireland* (London: 1970).
Hezlet, Sir Arthur, *The 'B' Specials: a History of the Ulster Special Constabulary* (London: 1972).
Isles, K.S., and Cuthbert, N., *An Economic Survey of Northern Ireland* (Belfast: 1957).
Kelly, Henry, *How Stormont Fell* (Dublin: 1972).
Kiely, Benedict, *Counties of Contention: a Study of the Origins and Implications of the Partition of Ireland* (Cork: 1945).
Lawrence, R.J., *The Government of Northern Ireland: Public Finance and Public Services, 1921–1964* (London: 1965).
McAllister, Ian, *The Northern Ireland Social Democratic and Labour Party: Political Opposition in a Divided Society* (London: 1977).
McCann, Eamonn, *War and an Irish Town* (London: 1974).
Magee, John, *Northern Ireland: Crisis and Conflict* (London & Boston: 1974).
MacGuffin, John, *Internment* (Tralee: 1973).
— *The Guineapigs* (London: 1974). Description of torture techniques – sensory deprivation – used in Northern Ireland.
MacStiofain, Sean, *Revolutionary in Ireland* (Edinburgh: 1975).
Marrinan, Patrick, *Paisley: Man of Wrath* (Tralee: 1973).
Moody, T.W., *The Ulster Question, 1603–1973* (Cork: 1974).
Moody, T.W., and Beckett, J.C., *Ulster Since 1800: a Political and Economic Survey* (London: 1954).
O'Brien, Conor Cruise, *States of Ireland* (London: 1972).
O Fearghail, Sean Og, *Law (?) and Orders: the Story of the Belfast Curfew* (Dundalk: 1970).
O'Neill, Lord Terence, *The Autobiography of Terence O'Neill, Prime Minister of Northern Ireland, 1963–1969* (London: 1972).
O Snodaigh, Padraig, *Hidden Ulster: the Other Hidden Ireland* (Dublin: 1973).
O Tuathail, Seamus, *They Came in the Morning, Internment, Monday August 9, 1971.* (Dublin: 1971).
Paisley, Ian, *Northern Ireland–What is the Real Situation?* (Greenville, SC: 1970).
— *United Ireland – Never!* (Belfast: 1972).
Probert, Belinda, *Beyond Orange and Green: the Political Economy of the Northern Ireland Crisis* (Dublin & London: 1978).
Riddell, Patrick, *Fires Over Ulster* (London: 1970).
Robb, John, *New Ireland: Sell-Out or Opportunity* (Belfast: 1972).
Rose, Richard, *Governing Without Consensus* (London & Boston: 1971).
— *Northern Ireland: Time of Choice* (London & Washington: 1976).
Shearman, Hugh, *Not an Inch: a Study of Northern Ireland and Lord Craigavon* (London: 1943).
Sunday Times (Insight Team), *Ulster* (London: 1972).
Sweetman, Rosita, *On Our Knees – Ireland 1972* (London: 1972).
Target, T.W., *Unholy Smoke* (London: 1969).
US Congress Committee on Foreign Affairs, *Northern Ireland Hearings before the Subcommittee on Europe* (Washington: 1972).

Wallace, Martin, *Drums and Guns: Revolution in Ulster* (London: 1970).
— *Northern Ireland: Fifty Years of Self-Government* (Newton Abbot: 1971).
Walsh, Dick, *Géarchéim in Éirinn* (Dublin: 1970).
Winchester, Simon, *In Holy Terror* (London: 1974).

Chapter VII: Conclusions and Solutions

Acton, Lord, *Essays on Church and State* (London: 1952, New York: 1968).
Arthur, Paul, *The People's Democracy* (Belfast: 1974).
Barker, Sir Ernest, *Social Contract – Locke, Hume, Rousseau* (London: 1947).
Bell, Geoffrey, *The Protestants of Ulster* (London: 1976).
Bennett, Jack, *The Northern Conflict and British Power* (Dublin: 1973).
Berlin, Isaiah, *Four Essays on Liberty* (London: 1969).
Biggs-Davidson, John, *Catholics and the Union* (Belfast: 1972). Introduction by G.B. Newe, the only Catholic to serve, however briefly, in a Stormont Cabinet. The author is an English Catholic Conservative member of parliament.
Boyd, Andrew, *The Two Irelands* (London: 1968).
Carlton, Charles, *Bigotry and Blood: Documents on the Ulster Troubles* (Chicago: 1977).
Carr, E.H., *Nationalism* (Oxford: 1939). A report by a Study Group of members of the Royal Institute of International Affairs.
Chubb, Basil, *A Source Book of Irish Government* (Dublin: 1964).
Clark, Dennis J., *Irish Blood: Northern Ireland and the American Conscience* (Port Washington, N.Y.: 1977).
Clutterbuck, Richard, *Protest and the Urban Guerrilla* (London & New York: 1973).
Deutsch, Richard, *Mairead Corrigan and Betty Williams* (New York: 1977).
Edmunds, Sean, *The Gun, the Law and the Irish People* (Tralee: 1971).
Elliott, William Y., and McDonald, Neil A., *Western Political Heritage* (New York: 1950).
— *Sketches of the New Ireland* (Galway: 1973).
FitzGerald, Garret, *Planning in Ireland* (Dublin: 1968).
— *Towards a New Ireland* (Dublin: 1973).
— *Ireland: Our Future Together* (Dublin: 1979). Fine Gael Party policy document.
Frank, Andre Gunder, *Lumpenbourgeoisie: Lumpendevelopment* (New York: 1972). On Latin America.
Fraser, Morris, *Children in Conflict* (London: 1973, New York: 1977).
Gilpin, Robert, *US Power and the Multinational Corporation: the Political Economy of Foreign Direct Investment* (New York: 1975).
Hobbes, Thomas, *Man and Citizen*, ed. Bernard Gert, (Garden City, N.Y.: 1972).
Hull, Roger H., *The Irish Triangle: Conflict in Northern Ireland* (Princeton: 1976).
Kamenka, Eugene (ed), *Nationalism: the Nature and Evolution of an Idea* (New York: 1976).
Kennedy, Kieran A., and Dowling, B.R., *Economic Growth in Ireland Since 1947* (Dublin: 1975).
Kennedy, Kieran A., and Bruton, R., *The Irish Economy* (Brussels: 1975).
Kitson, Frank, *Low Intensity Operations: Subversion, Insurgency and Peace-*

Keeping (London: 1971).
— *Bunch of Five* (London: 1977).
Link, Werner, and Feld, Werner J., *The New Nationalism: Implications for Transatlantic Relations* (New York: 1979).
MacIver, R.M., *Group Relations and Group Antagonisms* (New York: 1951).
McKiernan, Eoin, *The Will of a Nation* (St. Paul: 1963).
McManus, Frank, *Peace Plan for Ireland* (Washington: 1976). Expanded version of *Ulster – the Future*, published in 1972.
Mitchison, Rosalind (ed.) *The Roots of Nationalism: Studies in Northern Europe* (Edinburgh: 1980) Papers of a conference at the University of Wales, September 1975.
Manhattan, Avro, *Religious Terror in Ireland* (London: n.d.).
Moss, Robert, *Urban Guerrillas* (London: 1972).
Morgenthau, Hans, *Politics in the Twentieth Century:* vol. i, *The Decline of Politics;* vol. ii, *The Impasse of American Foreign Policy;* vol. iii, *The Restoration of American Politics* (London & Chicago: 1962).
Newhouse, John, *Collision in Brussels: the Common Market Crisis of 30 June 1965* (London & New York: 1967).
Newman, Jeremiah, *The State of Ireland* (Dublin: 1977).
Northern Ireland, Central Office of Information, Reference Pamphlet 135.
Ó Brádaigh, Ruairí, *Our People Our Future* (Dublin: 1973).
O'Brien, George, *The Four Green Fields* (Dublin: 1936).
O'Farrell, Patrick, *Regional Industrial Development Trends in Ireland 1960–1973* (Dublin: 1975).
O'Leary, Cornelius, *Irish Elections 1918–1977: Parties, Voters and Proportional Representation* (Dublin: 1979).
O'Malley, Patrick, *Irish Industry: Structure and Performance* (Dublin: 1971).
O'Sullivan, P. Michael, *Patriot Graves: Resistance in Ireland* (Chicago: 1972).
Penniman, Howard R. (ed), *Ireland at the Polls* (Washington: 1978).
Pinson, Koppel S., *Nationalism in the Western World* (Washington: 1959).
Rousseau, Jean-Jacques, *The First and Second Discourses,* ed. Roger D. Masters, (New York: 1964).
Shafer, Boyd F., *Nationalism: Myth and Reality* (New York: 1955).
Snyder, Louis L. (ed), *The Dynamics of Nationalism: Readings in its Meaning and Development* (Princeton, NJ: 1964).
— *Varieties of Nationalism: a Comparative Study* (Hinsdale, Ill: 1976).
Stewart, A.T.Q., *The Narrow Ground: Aspects of Ulster, 1609–1669* (London: 1977).
Tait, A.A. and Bristow, J.A., *Ireland: Some Problems of a Developing Economy* (Dublin: 1972).
Tierney, Mark, *Modern Ireland* (Dublin: 1978). Revised edition.
Vaizey, John, *Economic Sovereignty and Regional Policy* (Dublin: 1975).
Weber, Max, *From Max Weber, Essays in Sociology,* eds. H.H. Gerth and C. Wright Mills, (London: 1948, new ed. 1970; New York: 1958).
Whitaker, T.K., *Second Programme for Economic Expansion* (Dublin: 1964).
— *Third Programme for Economic and Social Development* (Dublin: 1969).
Whitaker, Urban G. (ed), *Nationalism and International Progress* (San Francisco: 1960).
— *N.I. Economic Development* Irish Congress of Trade Unions: (1962).
Five Long Years, film broadcast on 12 August 1974 on 'This Week' programme

of the British Independent Television Authority.
Journal of International Affairs, Vol. 27, No. 2, 1973; 'Civil War in Ireland : a Tragedy in Endless Acts?', and 'One People or Two? – the Origins of Partition and the Prospects for Unification in Ireland' by Thomas E. Hachey.

Glossary

Act of Union, 1800; abolished Irish parliament and put Ireland under British parliament as part of United Kingdom. Took effect on 1 January 1801.

Anglo-Irish Treaty, 1921; established the Irish Free State and gave 'Northern Ireland' the right to secede from rest of Ireland. Resulted in civil war, 1922–3.

Tom Barry, IRA guerrilla leader 1920–21; victor of Kilmichael and Crossbarry key engagements.

Boundary Commission, established under Treaty to determine boundaries between Northern Ireland and Free State. Large nationalist areas in North expected transfer to Free State but commission broke up in disagreement; issued no report; seen as betrayal of Northern nationalists.

'B' Specials, Protestant militia in Northern Ireland.

Neil Blaney, Irish minister who reported to Cabinet on Northern Ireland, 1969–1970; dismissed in arms crisis.

Ernest Blythe, Vice President Irish Free State, 1927–32.

Harry Boland, IRB organizer and envoy in America; killed in civil war, 1922.

Kevin Boland, nephew of above; resigned from Irish government in 1970 arms smuggling crisis but not involved in case.

Dan Breen, IRA guerrilla, fought at Soloheadbeg – first engagement of 1919–21 war.

Noel Browne, Minister of Health in first coalition, 1948. Bishops opposed his 'Mother and Child' free health plan and government fell.

Cathal Brugha, Sinn Féin Minister for Defence, 1919–21; killed in civil war, 1922.

James Callaghan, British Home Secretary in 1969 and later Prime Minister.

Roger Casement, Ulster Protestant in British consular service; exposed colonial exploitation of Belgian Congo and of Indians in Putumayo; knighted as a result. Declared for Irish independence in 1914; went to Germany for aid; returned to Ireland by submarine in 1916; was arrested; tried for high treason and hanged.

Catholic Emancipation, 1829; civil rights for Catholics.

James Chichester-Clark, Prime Minister of Northern Ireland, 1969.

Erskine Childers, Anglo-Irish; ran guns to Howth for Irish Volunteers in July 1914; British war hero in 1914–18; took side of Sinn Féin 1919–21; opposed Treaty, executed in civil war, 1922.

Clan-na-Gael, Irish-American revolutionary organization, founded 1867.

Clann na Poblachta, radical republican party founded 1946.

Thomas J. Clarke, spent fifteen years in English prisons as Clan-na-Gael dynamiter; IRB leader of 1916 rebellion.

Michael Collins, IRB organizer; chief military figure of IRA, 1919–21; signed Treaty; killed in civil war, 1922.
James Connolly, socialist leader of the 1916 Rising.
W.T. Cosgrave, head of Free State government, 1922–32.
Lord Craigavon (Sir James Craig), first Prime Minister of Northern Ireland 1921–41.
Cumann na Poblachta, IRA political party 1935–6.
Dail Eireann, national assembly of Ireland; illegal 1919–21.
Thomas Davis, founder of *Nation* and Young Ireland in 1842.
Michael Davitt, Fenian and founder of the Land League in 1879.
Eamon de Valera, President of Sinn Féin and of Irish Republic (1919–21); founder of Fianna Fáil (1927). In office 1932–48; 1951–4; 1957–9.
Bernadette Devlin, student radical; member British parliament for mid-Ulster, 1969.
Joseph Devlin, Belfast Irish Parliamentary Party leader.
John Devoy, Clan-na-Gael leader. Author of 'New Departure'.
Charles Gavan Duffy, editor of *Nation*.
Robert Emmet, led 1803 insurrection; hanged. Popular hero.
T.A. Emmet, brother of above; United Irishmen leader; exiled to America and became Attorney General of New York.
Fianna Fail, political party founded by de Valera in 1926 when he broke with Sinn Féin; Ireland's largest political party; populist.
Brian Faulkner, last Prime Minister of Stormont; headed power-sharing Executive in 1974.
Fenian Brotherhood, the American branch of the Fenian movement; term was generally applied to Irish movement as well.
Fine Gael, name of pro-Treaty Cumann na nGaedheal party of 1922–32. Chief opposition in Republic; sometimes in power as leading party of coalition.
First Dail, Sinn Féin deputies who were elected in December 1918 and met in Dublin in January 1919 as Dail Eireann (National Assembly of Ireland).
Lord Edward Fitzgerald, United Irishmen leader; killed 1798: Romantic hero.
Garret FitzGerald, leader of Fine Gael; ex-Foreign Minister; economist; author of two books on Northern Ireland and plan for a settlement.
Gaelic League, founded 1893 by Douglas Hyde and Eoin MacNeill.
George Gilmore, IRA leader in 1930s; founder Republican Congress 1934.
Cathal Goulding, Official IRA leader.
Henry Grattan, leader of 'Patriot' party in Irish parliament at time of American Revolution; with aid of Protestant Volunteers won its independence of English parliament.
Arthur Griffith, founder of Sinn Féin, 1905; chief Irish delegate in Treaty talks; head of government, January-August 1922.
Charles J. Haughey, Fianna Fáil Minister in 1960s and 1970s; charged in arms conspiracy; elected Prime Minister in December 1979.
Bulmer Hobson, chief of the young men who reinvigorated the moribund IRB from 1905 till 1912 when they took over from the 'old guard'. Founder and chief organizer of the Irish Volunteers; broke with Clarke and MacDermott over Redmond's demands on the movement in 1914 and opposed the 1916 Rising.
General Lazare Hoche, commander of French expedition to Bantry Bay, 1796.
John Hume, leader of SDLP in Northern Ireland.

IRA (Irish Republican Army), name of Irish Volunteers from 1919 and applied to those who opposed the Treaty in arms.

IRB (Irish Republican or Revolutionary Brotherhood), 1867–1924.

Liam Kelly, Northern Ireland republican leader; founder of Fianna Uladh (a party) and Saor Uladh (an armed force).

Charles J. Kickham, Fenian leader; novelist.

James Fintan Lalor, 1848 revolutionary; theorist of resistance to landlordism.

Land League, founded by Fenians in 1879; organization of tenant farmers which defeated landlordism.

Jack Lynch, Fianna Fail Prime Minister in 1960s and 1970s.

Countess Markievicz, radical republican; Minister of Labour 1919–21.

Hugh MacAteer, IRA leader 1940s.

Sean MacBride, IRA leader in 1930s; founder of Clann na Poblachta; Minister for External Affairs 1948-51; founder Amnesty International; holds Nobel and Lenin peace prizes.

Sean MacDermott, IRB leader 1910–16.

Joseph McGarrity, Clan-na-Gael leader 1903–1940.

Thomas D'Arcy McGee, Young Ireland leader; Canadian politician; assassinated by Fenians.

Thomas Francis Meagher, 1848 leader; commanded Irish Brigade on Union side in Civil War; Governor of Montana territory.

Liam Mellows, radical republican leader; executed without trial in civil war, 1922.

John Mitchel, editor *United Irishman*; 1848 leader; transported to Australia.

Richard Mulcahy, Collins's deputy; commander of Free State forces in civil war.

'New Departure', policy proposed by John Devoy in 1878 for alliance between revolutionaries and constitutional nationalists in land and Home Rule agitations.

NICRA, Northern Irish Civil Rights Association, body responsible for civil rights demonstrations in 1968–69.

Conor Cruise O'Brien, Irish writer; historian; politician and polemicist against the IRA.

William Smith O'Brien, landlord Repealer; led 1848 rebellion.

Daniel O'Connell, Irish nationalist leader from 1810 to 1847.

Rory O'Connor, IRA leader 1922; occupied Four Courts, Dublin; executed in civil war.

Peadar O'Donnell, IRA leader; founder Republican Congress 1934; novelist.

Kevin O'Higgins, Vice President Irish Free State from 1922 to assassination in 1927.

John O'Leary, Fenian leader; editor *Irish People*; friend of Yeats.

John O'Mahoney, founder of the Fenian Brotherhood in New York, 1858.

Ernie O'Malley, IRA guerrilla organizer, 1920–21.

Hugh O'Neill, Earl of Tyrone; led rebellion against Queen Elizabeth, 1595–1601.

Owen Roe O'Neill, nephew of above; officer of Spanish army, led Gaelic Ireland in 1640s.

Terence O'Neill, Prime Minister of Northern Ireland, 1963–69.

Orange Order, organization of Protestants founded in 1795 after 'Battle of the Diamond' in Co. Armagh between Protestant and Catholic tenants and labourers over land tenure and rents.

Ian Paisley, Northern Ireland Protestant leader; founder of Democratic Unionist Party.

Charles Stewart Parnell, leader of Home Rule movement in 1880s.

P.H. Pearse, Gaelic League editor; writer; a founder of Irish Volunteers; joined IRB; led 1916 Rising.

People's Democracy, student group in civil rights movement led by Bernadette Devlin and Michael Farrell.

Provisional IRA, formed 1969 as result of split with Marxist line of Official IRA.

John Redmond, leader of Irish Parliamentary Party, 1900–1918.

Sean Russell, IRA leader 1930s, planned bombing campaign in Britain; died on board German submarine returning to Ireland, August 1940.

Thomas Russell, United Irishmen founder; executed 1803.

Frank Ryan, IRA leader and founder of Republican Congress, 1934; led contingent to fight in Spain for Spanish Republic; died in Germany, 1944.

Patrick Sarsfield, commander of Irish forces of James II against William of Orange.

SDLP (Social Democratic and Labour Party), constitutionalist nationalist party in Northern Ireland.

Second Dail, 1921–22, claimed to represent all Ireland in name of Irish Republic. A number of Republican deputies insisted it was never legally disestablished by Irish people, that it was the only legal parliament of Ireland, and handed over its 'powers' to IRA in 1938. Provisional IRA revived this claim and 'authority' in 1970.

Sinn Féin, founded 1905 on policy of abstention from British Parliament; abstained from Dublin and Belfast parliaments after 1922.

Stormont, a castle outside Belfast, seat of Northern Ireland parliament and government.

Sunningdale, Agreement in December 1973 for 'power-sharing' between Protestants and Catholics in Northern Ireland.

Theobald Wolfe Tone, father of Irish republicanism and theorist of its ideology; sought aid of French revolutionaries to free Ireland.

Wolfe Tone Society, founded in Dublin in 1963 by left republicans and socialists; a 'think tank' for the republican movement.

Unionists, governing Protestant party in Northern Ireland; before 1921 applied to all who favoured Ireland's union with Great Britain in United Kingdom.

United Irishmen, radical republicans of 1790s; founded by Wolfe Tone and Presbyterian merchants of Belfast in October 1791, 'on the principles of civil, political and religious liberty'.

Index